FROMMER'S
SCANDINAVIA ON $35 A DAY

by Darwin Porter

1985-86 Edition

Published by Frommer/Pasmantier Publishers
A Division of Simon & Schuster, Inc.
1230 Avenue of the Americas
New York, NY 10020

ISBN 0-671-52437-2

Manufactured in the United States of America

*Although every effort was made to ensure the accuracy
of price information appearing in this book,
it should be kept in mind that prices
can and do fluctuate in the course of time.*

CONTENTS

MAPS

The author gratefully acknowledges the enormous editorial contributions of Margaret Foresman and Danforth Prince, both of New York City.

A WORD ABOUT PRICES: The author of this book has spent laborious hours of research trying to ensure the accuracy of prices appearing in this guide. As we go to press, I believe we have obtained the most reliable data possible. However, in an uncertain world, where often the owners themselves don't know what tariffs they will charge the following year, I cannot offer guarantees for the prices quoted. In the lifetime of this edition—particularly in its second year (1986)—the wise traveler will add *at least* 20% to the prices quoted.

A DISCLAIMER: Although every effort was made to ensure the accuracy of the prices and travel information appearing in this book, it should be kept in mind that prices do fluctuate in the course of time, and that information does change under the impact of the varied and volatile factors that affect the travel industry. Readers should also note that the establishments described under Readers' Selections or Suggestions have not in many cases been inspected by the author and that the opinions expressed there are those of the individual reader(s) only. They do not in any way represent the opinions of the publisher or author of this guide.

SCANDINAVIA ON $35 A DAY

The Reason Why

THIS BOOK IS DESIGNED chiefly for budget-conscious voyagers who for too long—and maybe for the wrong reasons—have been reluctant to strike out for the northernmost fringe of Europe to answer some vital questions: Are the Swedes really that blond and that beautiful? Do Trolls lurk behind the waterfalls of Norway? Can the Danes cook as well as they say they can? Would a genuine Finnish sauna—plus a beating with birch branches—give a person a new lease on life? Do Arctic bananas grow in Iceland?

Why this reluctance on the part of some to go and find the answers on their own? Perhaps returning travelers have been too effective in spreading the word via the closed-circuit grapevine that prices in these far-northern countries are paralyzing.

SCANDINAVIAN COSTS—LEGEND AND FACT: Some of the fat-tab stories spread over coffee tables would surely—and often do—send economy-minded vacationers into convulsions. Here are some typical retorts to suggestions that it's possible to live inexpensively in Scandinavia: "At this market in Turku (Finland), I saw salmon priced at $18 a pound!" "I was charged $3.50 for coffee in a restaurant in Stockholm." "For this anemic little grapefruit in Norway, we had to pay $3.25."

These stories are too often true, and will persist as long as there are foolish spenders. But it is misleading to draw conclusions that such prices are typical of Scandinavia. When salmon is as expensive as flamingo tongues (as it was during one recent severe shortage in Finland), only the most die-hard devotees buy it. Everybody else, tourist and Finn alike, switches to other treats of the sea.

A trail-blazer such as Leif Ericsson isn't needed to discover restaurants that charge $3.50 for coffee. Without a proper guide, it is easy to get trapped in places where individual tabs rival the national budget of Nepal. But the rarefied prices of these deluxe citadels are no more representative of the average Scandinavian restaurant than the haute cuisine of Lutèce is typical of the restaurants of New York City.

As for the anemic little grapefruit, who comes to Scandinavia dreaming of a bowl of citrus? After most visitors have feasted at a Norwegian cold-table breakfast—where they are likely to be served the works, ranging from herring balls to goat's-milk cheese—all thoughts of grapefruit sections and blossoms of orange trees fade away with last night's aquavit hangover.

What is the truth about Scandinavian prices? When this guide was inaugurated, they were among the highest in Europe, far exceeding the cost of living in such Southern European cities as Madrid, Lisbon, even Rome. However, in the wake of currency devaluations, a strong U.S. dollar, and low inflation, Scandinavian prices are now more in line with those of the southern tier of Europe. A visit to Scandinavia for a traveler of moderate means is, as of this writing, more possible than it's been in 15 to 20 years. Even so, the first-time visitor still must know how to avoid pitfalls and keep costs trimmed. In this guide, many of the ground rules for low-cost living will be spelled out.

Country by Country

How do prices in the specific Scandinavian countries stand in relation to each other? Here's a quick rundown:

The land of milk and cheese, **Denmark** was one of the cheapest countries in Western Europe, for those who were neither cigarette smokestacks nor alcoholics (both of these items have always been saddled with excessive taxes). After a dangerous inflationary spiral in the late '70s and '80s, Denmark is currently much more affordable—and filled with bargains.

In **Copenhagen,** Denmark's capital city, tabs are still steep, but the visitor is getting more value for the dollar than was possible in a decade. Nevertheless, to help defray the expense of operating a welfare state, certain costs have remained high. At present, a painful 22% *Moms* (pronounced "mumps" and just about as hard to take) tax is added to all items sold and services rendered—and that means hotel rooms and restaurant meals. Your only compensation is that when you're paying the tax, you're keeping some elderly person from having to mortgage Tara to pay for needed medical care.

My most serious suggestion for 1985–1986 is that you cut short your stay in the Danish capital and spend more time in the countryside. On both the "Little Mermaid" island of Funen and on Jutland, the "Big Bessie" of Denmark, the krone-wise visitor will encounter especially good value, particularly if he or she stays out of the cities, except for routine visits. Family-style meals and down-on-the-farm type rooms are available at this country's half-timbered *kros* (inns).

Denmark gives good value for the dollar, especially in the restaurants serving bountiful meals and in the shops with excellent buys. Its big-city, first-class hotels offer less value per krone and will receive scant, if any, attention in this guide. Today's budget visitor, more than ever, will have to count kroner—but he or she can still emerge with a rewarding and moderately priced holiday.

Norway, the most northerly country of Scandinavia, is also one of the richest, owing in part to its oil reserves in the North Sea. It also has its *Moms,* or "Value Added Tax," currently 16%.

The budget traveler has to proceed with caution in Norway, although it is still possible to have a low-cost holiday in this magnificent country. To begin with, one of the most compelling reasons to visit Norway—to see its glorious scenery—need not cost anything once your transportation there has been paid.

Knowing that their reputation for high costs has deterred visitors, the industrious Norwegians have come up with many cost-cutting travel deals. These include bargain rail passes, low-cost "vacation menus" available at dozens of restaurants, and various packages of hotel discounts, one of which this past summer offered a standard price for a double room, regardless of how many children a family had. These special discounts change from year to year, and visitors contemplating a visit to Norway should get up-to-date information about discount packages from a travel agent or from a branch office of the Norwegian Tourist Association.

Dramatically situated, **Oslo** and the old Hanseatic port of **Bergen** (Norway's second city and the gateway to Europe for increasing numbers of North Americans) are the most expensive centers, but even they contain moderately priced pensions (boarding houses) and cafeterias serving good and reasonably priced dishes. The true bargains of Norway, however, are found not in its big

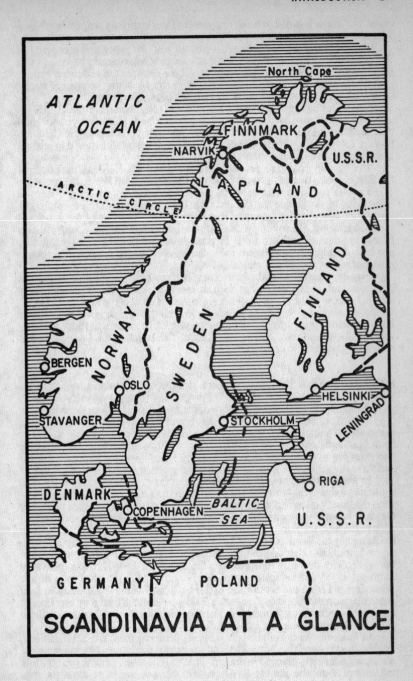

SCANDINAVIA AT A GLANCE

cities, but in the less-discovered rural oases of this curiously shaped fjord-and-lake country.

As any green-eyed Scandinavian can tell you, the peace and prosperity of Sweden makes for more money for the Swedes. Consequently, a visit to this welfare state can—*but need not*—be costly. Like Denmark, Sweden has experienced low inflation and devaluations of its currency. With the present strong dollar, it is cheaper to visit Sweden than it has been in a decade.

Regal but modern **Stockholm** remains the most expensive target in Sweden, but it has many bargains which will be described. However, you will find that the living is easier and kinder to thin wallets once you venture into the countryside. Literally thousands of basic moderate-bracket facilities nestle in settings that range from lakeside retreats to seaside resorts.

In **Finland** prices in recent decades have been high. **Helsinki,** the queen of the Baltic, is also one of the most expensive destinations in Western Europe.

I prefer to play a beat-the-devil game in Finland, by outlining dozens of cost-saving ways of living and dining there. For example, in its three leading cities, student dormitories (many of them comparable to leading "second-class" hotels in Europe, often with private baths) are transformed into young-at-heart hotels in summer; private families provide shelter for the most financially pinched of budgeteers; and many meet-the-Finn–type restaurants dish up bountiful, but reasonably priced meals.

Finally, **Iceland,** a land of extremes, is a costly destination. Inflation has been rampant, but the dollar has been strong. Restaurants are never really very cheap, because of the high cost of having to import most of the foodstuff. Tourist menus in many establishments do bring some relief. Summer hotels and private homes which accept paying guests are reasonable alternatives to the regular all-year hotels, where costs can be prohibitive. I've outlined the lowest possible means of staying there comfortably.

SOME REASONS WHY: Often, as you travel through certain European countries, such as Italy, you are left with the distinct impression that you've come to pay homage to the grandeur and glory of the past. Not so in Scandinavia.

Denmark, Norway, Sweden, Finland, and Iceland are as old as the runic stones of the Viking kings, but they are also as avant-garde as the blond beauty in the radiantly colored Marimekko dress twirling her hair at a disco. These countries are as traditional as a Grieg concert, but have steadfastly fought for and virtually achieved social equality and the emancipation of women.

In **scenery** and **sights,** Scandinavia is in the vanguard of world tourism. The sunlit midsummer nights at the top of Europe; the fjords and waterfalls of Norway; the silvery lakes and majestic forests of Finland; nomadic Lapps with their reindeer herds; trips north of the Arctic Circle; the glaciers, volcanoes, and lava cliffs of Iceland; the fairytale hamlets of Denmark; fun-loving capital cities such as Copenhagen; Sweden's Göta Canal and her ancient moated castles; glacier-capped mountains shaped like the faces of gigantic trolls in Norway; the ruins of the walled city of Visby in the Baltic; the balsa raft *Kon-Tiki;* the excavated ninth-century Viking ships in Oslo; the Bergen wharf; the 1628 man-of-war *Wasa* dredged from the Stockholm harbor; sisu and sauna in Finland; an Iron Age village on the island of Zealand; a 2000-year-old petrified man on Jutland; dozens of open-air museums and Tivoli-esque amusement parks—all these make for unique sightseeing elements.

In **folklore,** the Scandinavian countries preserve their age-old traditions, despite their progressive hop, skip, and jump into the future. Norwegian girls, on occasion, are still married in dragon-dip stave churches, and the country folk tell visitors about the giant trolls who live in the mountains, or about the mischievous gnome-like *nisser,* even the deceivingly beautiful *huldre* (carefully tucked away in those bikinis is a cow's tail).

Scandinavia has preserved its heritage in its widely acclaimed open-air **museums,** collections of old farmsteads and cottages, town houses and merchants shops on the the outskirts of all five capitals, and in many towns and villages as well. The five-star attractions are outside Copenhagen (Frilands-Museet), in Århus on the island of Jutland (a personal favorite); both in Turku and on the island of Seurassaari, near Helsinki; on Bygdoy outside Oslo (Norsk Folke-museum), and in Stockholm (Skansen). In addition, Norway boasts the Sandvig Collections and the Open-Air Museum, both at the May Hill in Lillehammer.

At many of these open-air museums, such as the one in Oslo, folklore evenings are staged. Many of the oldest dance forms in Scandinavia, some going back to the Middle Ages, have been preserved. Such late 16th-century steps as the *springar* or *gangar* are danced by colorfully costumed performers in peasant dress. In the tradition-rich province of Dalarna, Sweden, the residents dance around the maypole to usher in midsummer.

In **architecture,** Norway had its stave churches, Sweden its elegant and stately châteaux, Denmark its thatched-roof cottages, Finland its stately fortresses—but all the countries have leaped into the 21st century with dazzlingly progressive architecture that heralds the world of tomorrow today.

In its **urban life,** Scandinavia thrives. City or town life is still pleasant in these five countries; you can walk in the parks at night, enjoy clean streets, and find a moderately priced place at which to dance. But don't limit your tour just to the capitals. The people are even friendlier in the small cities, towns, and villages. Trondheim in Norway offers more nightlife than Oslo. Both Århus and Aalborg in Denmark are medium-size cities, with large appetites for dancing and drinking. Gothenburg, likewise, is a friendlier town than Stockholm. Uppsala, Sweden, a university town, also offers many advantages over its larger neighbor, Stockholm.

In **design,** particularly in home furnishings and accessories—such as porcelain, glass, enamelware, textiles—the Scandinavian countries are pace-setters. Utilitarianism has been blended harmoniously with aesthetic qualities. The works of the glassblower, the silversmith, the cabinetmaker, the weaver, among others, are on display in the leading design centers in all the cosmopolitan centers. Shopping or just looking remains one of the major activities in these countries. Often it's easy to arrange visits to the leading workshops, where it's possible to meet both the designers and crafts people.

In **food** and **drink,** Scandinavian countries have added a unique banquet to the world's table—everything from smörgåsbord to smørrebrød, from whipped-cream-topped cloudberries to Danish bleu cheese and pastry, from reindeer steak to aquavit. Lots of exotic surprises are in store for the visitor with an experimental palate. Ever had black pudding made with cow's blood? Beer bread? Frikadeller with lingonberries? Pickled elk's meat? Moose stew?

In the **arts,** Scandinavian men and women have staked out a claim to greatness. Such playwrights as Sweden's August Strindberg *(Miss Julie)* and Norway's Henrik Ibsen *(Peer Gynt* and *Hedda Gabler)* have won worldwide reputations. Their plays are produced today in Sweden and Norway as frequently as the English warm up Shakespeare.

The visitors who want to combine looking at scenic beauty with searching for art treasures (or for the former homes or workshops of artists) will find the pickings rich in Scandinavia.

In Bergen, one may visit the former summer home of Edvard Grieg, the composer. And the symphonies of Sibelius draw a never-ending stream to Finland.

Oslo has been called the city of Edvard Munch, its love-and-death painter; also of Gustaf Vigeland, its controversial sculptor ("Was he a genius or a madman?").

Sweden enters the art scene with her favorite sons, Carl Milles, whose dramatically expressive sculptured works are displayed in what used to be his own gardens in a suburb outside Stockholm, and painter Anders Zorn, whose home in Mora in the province of Dalarna may also be viewed by the public.

Copenhagen has an entire museum devoted to that restrained classicist, Bertel Thorvaldsen, the best known of Danish sculptors.

In **literature,** Sweden's Selma Lagerlöf *(The Wonderful Adventures of Nils)* helped the feminist cause when she became the first woman to win the Nobel Prize for letters. Her home, Mårbacka, in her beloved Värmland, may be visited, along with Rottneros Park, the *Ekeby* of her novels. But the most famous literary pilgrimage in all of Scandinavia is to the home town of that *Ugly Duckling,* Hans Christian Andersen, on the island of Funen in Denmark.

The best reason for visiting Scandinavia has been saved for the last—that is, the chance to meet its handsome, alert, and energetic **people.**

Getting to know these wonderful people, to whom English is a second language, being invited to their homes, learning the basic and subtle differences between a Dane and a Norwegian, a Finn, an Icelander, and a Swede are the highlights of any trip to Scandinavia.

Friendly is a word too often used—and sometimes misused—when applied to a body of people. The Scandinavians, however, live up to the essence of the word.

There are other and more specific reasons, of course, for visiting these five countries, but these remain to be explored and discovered in the pages ahead. Let's continue, for the moment, with some general comments about travel abroad.

A CREDO OF TRAVEL: Millions of North Americans have now passed the stage where one takes a single, go-for-broke trip to the Old World. Air transportation has opened up the possibility of more frequent travel to Europe, and extended that pleasure to a type of low-income or middle-income person who never expected to be able to see where grandmother came from, be it Jutland, Dalarna, or Värmland.

Consequently, today's new-breed travelers want to keep costs at a minimum while experiencing the genuine charm of the countries they visit. Those fleeting, in-and-out, blurred visits to cathedrals and museums may be a thing of the past. Increasing numbers of North Americans are seeking a personal contact with Europeans, hoping to live alongside them and share their life. Such a goal—that of obtaining a greater in-depth experience of the best of Europe—is one of the purposes of this book.

To illustrate one side of the travel picture, let's take a glance at a popular little village in Sweden, in a part of the country noted for its folklore, handicrafts, and native dress. An expensive hilltop retreat attracts the better heeled visitor who spends time walking around the corridors inspecting inflation-priced merchandise behind glass—and fellow tourists. Both items are dull. Later, he or she will dance to a band imported from Spain. If a visitor to Sweden has but one night to spend in a regional province, maybe—just maybe—it would be a good idea to have some experience, however perfunctory, with the country that one has paid a lot of money to come and inspect.

In dramatic contrast is the experience of a group of German and Danish tourists, who were staying at a budget-priced log-cabin homestead in a forest setting beside a silvery lake. The group was gathered around a raised hearth, listening to the colorful owner of the establishment dramatize the folklore and history of the old-world province. The light in the room filled with antiques was flickering on the red-cheeked faces of a family who would later present a songfest. That which at one time had been natural and typical—gathering together around an open fire after dinner—for all the visitors was an original and exceptionally charming experience, an easy and peaceful way to absorb the cultural heritage of Sweden.

But this book is concerned not only with the spiritual meaning of value, but with its monetary meaning as well. The hotels and restaurants I recommend were judged primarily on the basis of whether they offered a substantial return —either a good, comfortable room or an abundant, well-prepared meal—for the prices charged.

Exploring Scandinavia on $35 a day is a dollars-and-sense reality, spelled out in facts and figures in the chapters ahead.

$35 A DAY-WHAT IT MEANS: The $35 a day of the title covers the *basic costs of living* in any one of the Scandinavian countries. That is, the price of a room and three meals a day.

Of course, transportation—the biggest expense—is extra, as are tips and the cost of sightseeing, laundry, alcohol, tobacco, entertainment, and shopping. However, in keeping with the goal to inform, all of these extra expenses are discussed in the chapters ahead, as well as the best methods of keeping these added costs trimmed to the bone.

Here is how the basic expenses break down: $18 per person for a room (based on double occupancy), $3 for breakfast, $6 for lunch, and $8 for dinner.

For this amount of money, the hotels and pensions recommended will offer basic necessities, but never private baths—at least hardly ever. In every case, a reasonable standard of cleanliness and comfort has been insisted upon. A restaurant in this budget classification may lack red velour draperies, relying instead on a stripped-down, pine-tabled Nordic modern, but I insist that the food be prepared in a clean kitchen and served presentably.

Remember, then, that the $35 a day per person will never buy luxury or even first-class accommodations, but it will provide value—enough to prove that Scandinavia has many bargains.

At the end of the regular listings of hotels and restaurants will appear a "splurge" section intended for those readers who want more comfort, more plumbing, more elaborately prepared food in restaurants—in other words, a few more frills. Roughly speaking, splurges are for those willing to spend some $15 or more beyond the budget allotment of the title.

Scandinavians welcome and invite the young and adventurous to tour within their borders in the summer months. And these countries probably are better equipped and organized to greet them than any of the other lands of Europe. Hundreds of streamlined accommodations, such as low-cost hostels and dormitories, exist throughout all five nations. Many of these room-and-board facilities for students or for the young of all ages are outlined in this book.

SCANDINAVIA OFF-SEASON: Once an American couple touring Sweden in August entered a room draped in red velvet, bedecked with crystal, stained glass, and potted palms—all turn-of-the-century style, a perfect blending of Queen Victoria's taste with that of Lillian Russell. The dining room was closed. They asked why. The manager said it wouldn't be open until September—when "the season" begins. That was their first realization that "the season" in Scandinavia doesn't always mean the tourist-heavy months of July and August. In fact, many of the major establishments close early on the summer afternoons, when the Scandinavians head for their huts in the wilderness.

Several factors have to be considered when you decide on the proper time to visit these five countries. Obviously, most travelers are limited by vacation schedules. But if any free choice is involved, you'll want to bear in mind the following:

First, Scandinavia's hotel accommodations are overflowing during the peak summer visiting months, when all five countries play host to their greatest hordes of visitors, both foreign and domestic (the Scandinavians are their own best tourists). Although new hotels are being built, they still do not fill the need. There is little incentive to build resort hotels in lands that have such a short season.

But the season need not be short.

It has been repeated often enough to become a cliché, but off-season does offer, usually, reduced hotel rates except in such cities as Stockholm, where hotel tariffs are often lowered in July and August. Even if not granted reduced rates, a visitor at least has a better chance to snare an accommodation in the off-season. This can make for less frenetic fretting—both in an attempt to find a room and in getting to look at the *Wasa* without being trampled underfoot. As we will see in the next chapter, the off-season reduced rates offered by airline companies make for a further powerful incentive.

May and June are the personal favorites of thousands of visitors, including Swedes, who cross over to Norway and vice versa. The skies over Scandinavia are so bright that the visitor needs to wear sunglasses around the clock. Spring is ushered in with the Walpurgis Night festivities (triumph of life over death) in both Sweden and Finland. Tivoli Gardens open in May in Copenhagen. Flowers, the Norwegian passion, begin to blossom along the fjords.

All the pageantry of the folklore festivals—bonfires, maypole dancing, student shenanigans—comes alive during these two months. The festivities reach their peak with the midsummer celebrations in June. In addition, tourists have a chance to attend a number of dance, drama, and music festivals, such as the Sibelius Festival in Helsinki.

Stockholm, however, doesn't begin its major cultural festival—opera, theater, ballet, concerts—until September. From fall until May, the music, drama, and dance season lasts in all five capitals—everything from the Royal Danish Ballet to the Royal Opera of Stockholm. It may turn cold outside, but the joint's jumping inside through the long Scandinavian winter.

For those interested in arts and crafts, the big month to visit is October, when Helsinki, Copenhagen, Oslo, and the three Swedish cities of Stockholm, Gothenburg, and Malmö join hands fraternally in the Scandinavian Design Cavalcade, featuring exhibits and displays combined with intriguing tours of workshops. This is also the time of the big exhibitions and trade fairs.

Norway, in particular, is making a strong bid for winter sports enthusiasts. Winter in Scandinavia is the time of the big championship meets. February through April are the major skiing months. The centers of Geilo and Lillehammer (north of Oslo) are the leading winter resorts in Norway, but fast-rising Voss in Western Norway has broken into the sweepstakes, too.

Norway doesn't have as exciting an après-ski life as centers in the middle of Europe enjoy, but what it does offer is sometimes more intriguing. Barn dances, sleigh rides, and such events as an "evening with the trolls" make one quickly forget about the more jaded international centers.

In all five countries, Yuletide is a festive occasion. In many parts of the countries, such as in Lillehammer, Norway, there are singing and dancing, sleigh rides, torch parades, hot wine punch—an old-fashioned Nordic Christmas, ideal for those who have a nostalgia for the Yules of yesteryear.

EURAILPASS: Many in-the-know travelers to Europe have for years been taking advantage of one of its greatest travel bargains the Eurailpass, which permits unlimited *first-class* rail travel in any country in Western Europe, except the British Isles but good in Ireland. Passes are purchased for periods as short as 15 days or as long as three months, and are strictly nontransferable. The pass is sold only outside of Europe and North Africa and only to residents of countries outside those areas. Vacationers may purchase a 15-day Eurailpass for $260; otherwise, a 21-day pass costs $330; a one-month pass, $410; two months, $560, or three months, $680. Children under 4 may travel free, and children under 12 pay only half-fare.

But if you're under 26 you are eligible for the best of all—the **Eurail Youth-pass.** This godsend costs $290 for one month, $370 for two months, and allows unlimited *second-class* rail travel in 14 countries (the same countries which are included in the standard Eurailpass).

Senior citizens traveling on the railroads of Scandinavia also get a break. **Inter-Rail Senior** is a one-month pass available to men or women 65 years of age and over. This pass permits the purchase of rail tickets in Europe with a 50% reduction on all the state railway lines of the country where the pass was issued and free unlimited use of the entire railway network of the other 17 countries that are members of Inter-Rail Senior. For other discounts available to senior citizens, refer to the listings in the various "preview" chapters.

The advantages of the Eurailpass are indeed tempting. No tickets, no supplements—simply show the pass to the ticket collector, then settle back to enjoy European scenery. Seat reservations, however, are required on some trains.

Obviously, the one- or two-month vacationer gets the biggest economic advantages. It's ideal for such extensive trips. A pass-holder might like to visit such faraway sights as Lisbon, Madrid, or Rome after a tour of Scandinavia.

Travelers on the 15-day, 21-day, or one-month excursion have to estimate the approximate rail distance they expect to cover before determining if such a pass is economically advantageous. To obtain full advantage of the ticket for 15 days to one month, a traveler would have to spend a great deal of time on the train.

In addition, holders of a Eurailpass are entitled to considerable reductions on certain steamships and bus tours. You'll get a 15% savings on boats which navigate between Aalborg and Oslo, Frederikshavn or Copenhagen and Oslo. There are many free boat crossings between Sweden and Denmark. Write Eurailpass for details.

Travel agents in all towns and railway agents in such major cities as New York, Montréal, Los Angeles, or Chicago sell the tickets. The pass is also available at the office of CIT Travel Service, the French National Railroads, the German Federal Railroads, and the Swiss Federal Railways.

SCANDINAVIAN RAIL PASS: In addition to the Eurailpass, the state railroads of Denmark, Finland, Norway, and Sweden have come up with an economical Scandinavian Rail Pass. The pass entitles you to unlimited rail travel in first and second class for 21 days. The pass cannot be purchased in North America but can be bought in any Scandinavian rail station. The cost is $155 for a second-class or $235 for a first-class ticket. Children under the age of 12 pay half-price. The pass is also valid on the ferry crossings between Denmark and southern Sweden—Helsingør–Helsingborg and Copenhagen–Malmø. On the other crossings the pass entitles you to a discount of 50%. Between Sweden and Finland, the discount applies on the Stockholm–Helsinki or Turku route, between Norway and Denmark on the Kristiansand–Hirtshals route, and between Sweden and Denmark on the Gothenburg–Frederikshavn route.

For further information, get in touch with the **Scandinavian National Tourist Offices,** 655 Third Ave., New York, NY 10017 (tel. 1/212/949/2333).

PEOPLE-TO-PEOPLE: **Friends Overseas** is an American-Scandinavian people-to-people program which has been operating since 1971. It places American visitors to Sweden, Denmark, and Norway in touch with Scandinavians who have expressed a keen interest in meeting Yanks of similar interests and backgrounds. Americans, as a result, are not only introduced to Scandinavians, but they also meet their friends and families, and get to know their cities and lives more intimately. Several names and addresses are provided each American applying, and letters must be written before visitors depart from the United States. For further information, write to Friends Overseas, 68-04 Dartmouth St., Forest Hills, NY 11375. Send a *long,* self-addressed envelope, and please include information as to your occupation or occupational goals, plus specifics on your travel plans (with spouse, friend, or alone).

It's important to give the approximate dates you expect to be in Norway, Sweden, and Denmark, rather than just the season or month. You should also include your profession or what you're specializing in at a university. The project is run by Larry Eisner, who has been a guidance counselor in the East Northport Junior High School on Long Island for more than 20 years. Friends Overseas is an outgrowth of his many visits to Scandinavia.

THE ORGANIZATION OF THIS BOOK: Here now is how *Scandinavia on $35 a Day* plans to survey the budget scene in these parts.

We'll explore each country separately, beginning with Denmark in Chapter I. Denmark will be followed by Norway in Chapter V, then Sweden in Chapter X, Finland in Chapter XVII, and finally Iceland in Chapter XX. An introductory section will precede the detailed discussion of each country.

The preview section will be backed up in each case by data on how to reach a country, plus how to settle into each of the capital cities of Scandinavia (Copenhagen, Oslo, Stockholm, Helsinki, and Reykjavík). The top budget hotels and restaurants will first be spotlighted. Then these chapters will deal with major sightseeing attractions, shopping, nightlife, the pick of the most interesting one-day excursions.

After each capital has been explored, we'll delve into the countryside of each of the five countries, discovering their most charming scenery, hamlets, fishing villages, offshore islands, and then their other leading cities, such as Bergen and Gothenburg. The cream of the hotels and restaurants in this book's price range will be previewed, along with the major sights.

THE FUTURE OF THIS BOOK: On a recent trip to Lappeenranta, Finland, I encountered a North American schoolteacher who shops "in bargain basements all year so I can spend my summer traveling." She was bubbling over with her "finds," wonderful little restaurants and hotels. I informed her of our unique method of sharing discoveries with other budget travelers, the "Readers' Selections" sections of this book.

Here's how it works: When a reader goes to Scandinavia, he or she may discover a hotel, restaurant, or sightseeing attraction not described in this book. Those finds may run the gamut from a Lapp family that takes in paying guests in northern Sweden to an isolated old half-timbered inn off the beaten tourist trail in Denmark.

Because of the quicksilver nature of hotel and restaurant policies, comments on any of the recommended establishments are also appreciated—a good method of ensuring that readers will receive friendly service at the hotels and restaurants listed. Because a hotel is recommended in this edition is no guarantee that it has "squatter's rights" to space in any subsequent editions if its service and quality deteriorate.

Scandinavia on $35 a Day hopes to be a living book, a two-way link between its readers and its author. Please send comments, discoveries, or criticisms to Darwin Porter, c/o Frommer/Pasmantier Publishers, 1230 Avenue of the Americas, New York, NY 10020.

The $25-a-Day Travel Club—How To Save Money On All Your Travels

In this book we'll be looking at how to get your money's worth in Scandinavia, but there is a "device" for saving money and determining value on *all* your trips. It's the popular, international $25-a-Day Travel Club, now in its 22nd successful year of operation. The Club was formed at the urging of numerous readers of the $$$-a-Day and Dollarwise Guides, who felt that such an organization could provide continuing travel information and a sense of community to value-minded travelers in all parts of the world. And so it does!

In keeping with the budget concept, the annual membership fee is low and is immediately exceeded by the value of your benefits. Upon receipt of $15 (U.S. residents), or $18 U.S. by check drawn on a U.S. bank or via international postal money order in U.S. funds (Canadian, Mexican, and other foreign residents) to cover one year's membership, we well send all new members the following items.

(1) *Any two* of the following books

Please designate in your letter which two you wish to receive:

Europe on $25 a Day
Australia on $25 a Day
England and Scotland on $25 a Day
Greece on $25 a Day
Hawaii on $35 a Day
Ireland on $25 a Day
India on $15 & $25 a Day
Israel on $30 & $35 a Day
Mexico on $20 a Day
New York on $35 a Day
New Zealand on $20 & $25 a Day
Scandinavia on $35 a Day
South America on $25 a Day
Spain and Morocco (plus the Canary Is.) on $35 a Day
Washington, D.C. on $35 a Day

Dollarwise Guide to Austria and Hungary
Dollarwise Guide to Canada
Dollarwise Guide to the Caribbean (including Bermuda and the Bahamas)
Dollarwise Guide to Egypt
Dollarwise Guide to England and Scotland
Dollarwise Guide to France
Dollarwise Guide to Germany
Dollarwise Guide to Italy
Dollarwise Guide to Portugal (plus Madeira and the Azores)
Dollarwise Guide to Switzerland
Dollarwise Guide to California and Las Vegas
Dollarwise Guide to Florida
Dollarwise Guide to New England
Dollarwise Guide to the Northwest
Dollarwise Guide to the Southeast and New Orleans
Dollarwise Guide to the Southwest

(Dollarwise Guides discuss accommodations and facilities in all price ranges, with emphasis on the medium-priced.)

Dollarwise Guide to Cruises
(This complete guide covers all the basics of cruising—ports of call, costs, fly-cruise package bargains, cabin selection booking, embarkation and debarkation and describes in detail over 60 or so ships cruising in Alaska, the Caribbean, Mexico, Hawaii, Panama, Canada, and the United States.)

How to Beat the High Cost of Travel
(This practical guide details how to save money on absolutely all travel items—accommodations, transportation, dining, sightseeing, shopping, taxes, and more. Includes special budget information for seniors, students, singles, and families.)

The New York Urban Athlete
(The ultimate guide to all the sports facilties in New York City for jocks and novices.)

Museums in New York
(A complete guide to all the museums, historic houses, gardens, zoos, and more in the five boroughs. Illustrated with over 200 photographs.)

The Fast 'n' Easy Phrase Book
(The four most useful languages—French, German, Spanish, and Italian—all in one convenient, easy-to-use phrase guide.)

Where to Stay USA
(By the Council on International Educational Exchange, this extraordinary guide is the first to list accommodations in all 50 states that cost anywhere from $3 to 25 per night.)

A Guide for the Disabled Traveler
(A guide to the best destinations for wheelchair travelers and other disabled vacationers in Europe, the United States, and Canada by an experienced wheelchair traveler. Includes detailed information about accommodations, restaurants, sights, transportation, and their accessibility.)

Marilyn Wood's Wonderful Weekends
(This very selective guide covers the best mini-vacation destinations within a 175-mile radius of New York City. It describes special country inns and other accommodations, restaurants, picnic spots, sights, and activities—all the information needed for a two- or three-day stay.)

Bed & Breakfast—North America
(This guide contains a directory of over 150 organizations that offer bed & breakfast referrals and reservations throughout North America. The scenic attractions, businesses, and major schools and universities near the homes of each are also listed.)

(2) A one-year subscription to *The Wonderful World of Budget Travel*

This quarterly eight-page tabloid newspaper keeps you up to date on fast-breaking developments in low-cost travel in all parts of the world bringing you the latest money-saving information—the kind of information you'd have to pay $25 a year to obtain elsewhere. This consumer-conscious publication also features columns of special interest to readers: **The Traveler's Directory** (members all over the world who are willing to provide hospitality to other members as they pass through their home cities); **Share-a-Trip** (offers and requests from members for travel companions who can share costs and help avoid the burdensome single supplement); and **Readers Ask . . . Readers Reply** (travel questions from members to which other members reply with authentic firsthand information).

(3) A copy of *Arthur Frommer's Guide to New York*

This is a pocket-size guide to hotels, restaurants, nightspots, and sightseeing attractions in all price ranges throughout the New York area.

(4) Your personal membership card

Membership entitles you to purchase through the Club all Arthur Frommer publications for a third to a half off their regular retail prices during the term of your membership.

So why not join this hardy band of international budgeteers and participate in its exchange of travel information and hospitality? Simply send your name and address, together with your annual membership fee of $15 (U.S. residents) or $18 U.S. (Canadian, Mexican, and other foreign residents), by check drawn on a U.S. bank or via international postal money order in U.S. funds to: $25-A-Day Travel Club, Inc., Frommer/Pasmantier Publishers, 1230 Avenue of the Americas, New York, NY 10020. And please remember to specify which *two* of the books in section (1) above you wish to receive in your initial package of member's benefits. Or, if you prefer, use the last page of this book, simply checking off the two books you select and enclosing $15 or $18 in U.S. currency.

During the term of your membership, no books will be mailed to you unless you specifically request them. There are "no strings attached" to your membership.

A PREVIEW OF DENMARK

IF SOMETHING IS ROTTEN in the state of Denmark, I don't know what.

The sun seems to come up in the morning just to shine on these friendly people—everybody from bicycle-riding grandmothers to soot-blackened chimney sweeps.

Except for Danish-governed Greenland and the Faroe Islands, the glory of the Danish Empire has long receded—but no one seems to be lamenting that. The Danes are engrossed in the 24-hour-a-day job of living, and that seems far more satisfying to them than sailing over to conquer England.

Every time you ask a Danish man what he's like, he begins by telling you he's really a very funny fellow—"not like the Swedes at all." Then you're fed a sampling of Danish humor, in the manner of Victor Borge. You're left not really knowing what a Dane is like, except to say that it's hard to find the Hamlet syndrome in the Danish mentality.

The Danes may live in a small package, but, like Mighty Mouse, they've got a powerful punch—and they come on with a big welcome (Americans, Canadians, and their old friends, the British, are particularly welcome—and in English, too). Denmark should be an important stopover even for those doing the most superficial whirlwind tour of Europe.

This country of islands is not a land of roly-poly butter-and-egg people, although it does boast a quarter of a million farmers (and eight million pigs). With almost no other raw materials (except its clever and handsome people), Denmark is a heavily industrialized nation, known for its products and arts and crafts.

The late British novelist Evelyn Waugh *(Brideshead Revisited)* called the Danes "the most exhilarating people of Europe." Few Danes would dispute this. And neither would I.

1. Flying to Denmark

Several airlines, especially SAS, fly into Denmark. In the previous edition of this guide, I flew SAS to Scandinavia (see below). But for my most recent trip, I chose a carrier based in Minneapolis—the end point of what might have been the most massive Danish migration in history to the New World.

Northwest Orient airlines began in 1926 when it won a contract for the mail route between Minneapolis/St. Paul and Chicago. By 1928, the company had expanded its routes to include passenger service over the Dakotas, Canada, and Montana. By 1947, service to both the East and West Coasts of the United States was firmly established, as well as breakthrough routings to the Far East. Today, the airline serves 70 cities in 16 countries, with destinations ranging from Fargo, North Dakota, to Shanghai and Dublin.

Although Northwest Orient flies from more destinations in the United States to more of the Far East than any other airline, its routes to Scandinavia are among its most popular. Selected from a fleet of full-size 747s, its planes whisk across the Atlantic from Minneapolis/St. Paul and New York's JFK airport once a week in either direction in winter and once a day during the peak of summer.

A wide range of fare options is available, from a low-season mid-week APEX ticket (where eastbound travel begins on a weekday any time between September 15 and May 15) and a glamorous and exceptionally comfortable executive-class splurge. Most passengers, however, seem to inquire about APEX (Advance Purchase Excursions) before moving on to the more expensive alternatives. It's easy to qualify: You're obligated to reserve a seat and pay for it at least 21 days prior to departure, and you must wait for between 10 days and three months before using the return half of your ticket. The return section of the ticket can be used on a weekend or during shoulder or high season without influencing the fare. At press time, a low-season midweek APEX ticket cost $730 round trip, although fares, of course, as at any airline, change as often as the delicacies at a Danish buffet table.

An even cheaper round-trip fare exists for travelers whose schedule permits the uncertainty of not knowing when they'll leave until 20 or fewer days before departure. Northwest (whose terminology differs from that at many other airlines) calls it an excursion fare and prices it at $628 (New York–Copenhagen) during low season, with no restrictions as to midweek or weekend travel. Reservations for this fare will not be accepted until 20 days prior to departure. Payment must accompany the reservation, which may not be changed or cancelled without a penalty fee of $100. Shoulder-season and peak-season rates are best discussed with a travel agent or a Northwest ticket agent after you have a clear idea of your travel dates and itinerary.

Although Northwest doesn't have first-class seating on its transatlantic routings the way it does on its Far Eastern trips, the closest thing a passenger can have to totally relaxed comfort is executive-class seating (a barely discernible downgrading from first class) which at this writing was priced at a maximum high-season fare of $703 each way. Of course, rates will change, but a Northwest ticketing agent, whose number is available from your local telephone directory, will be happy to discuss all rates and options with you when you're ready to implement your plans.

If things don't work out for you to fly Northwest Orient, then you might consider **SAS**, the Scandinavian Airlines System, which is made up of the flying expertise of three countries: Denmark, Sweden, and Norway. Naturally, in addition to its other worldwide routes, SAS flies from the U.S. to its home capitals, Copenhagen, Stockholm, and Oslo.

When the airline companies of Norway, Sweden, and Denmark (Finland and Iceland have their own national carriers) got together to form SAS after World War II, English was agreed on as the official language of the company.

The airline has five gateways from North America: transatlantic flights originate from New York, Chicago, Los Angeles, Seattle, and Anchorage, Alaska.

2. Getting Around

Denmark is easy to explore. It's not only small, but its transportation facilities are excellent. In this section, I will explore the various means of transport, ranging from bicycles to ferryboats.

AIR FLIGHTS (DOMESTIC): For those in a hurry, SAS operates daily service between Copenhagen and points on the mainland of Jutland. For example, it takes about 40 minutes to fly from Copenhagen to Aalborg, Denmark's third-largest city, in North Jutland. This is a temptation to many readers, especially since the fare to certain points in Denmark can be included in a transatlantic ticket at no extra charge, providing the extra cities are specified when the ticket is written. On many of its domestic flights, SAS grants family discounts—that is, full fare for one adult, half-fare for the other members, a true bargain.

BICYCLES: Denmark is one of the few countries that can be conveniently toured by bicycle. Youth hostels are generally enough to each other to make a bicycling trip possible (about 12 miles apart). For those whose bodies aren't so young but whose hearts and spirits are, bicycles with auxiliary motors can also be rented. You can rent a bicycle in almost all Danish towns with help from the local tourist offices.

Dantourist bureaus in Svendborg, Viborg, and Silkeborg offer a group of six to ten "ready-made" holiday excursions by bicycle. Prices depend on whether you stay at youth hostels or at low-cost inns or hotels. All age groups are accepted (the oldest participant so far has been 78). You have a variety of tours to choose from, and they last from three to nine days. Many of them offer you the choice of full or half board. Write to the **Danish National Tourist Office,** 655 3rd Ave., New York, NY 10017 (tel. 1/212/582-2802), for information.

Another program enables you to rent bicycles at train stations in North Zealand cheaply, and you may drop the bike at another station. For information on the **Go-by-Train, Rent-a-Bike** route, get in touch with the Tourist Information Office or the train station.

BOATS FROM COPENHAGEN: Copenhagen is a major port, offering boat trips to a variety of others. There are, for instance, several vessels to Malmö, Sweden (large ferry, hydrofoil, or the giant hovercraft). There are regular departures to Malmö, and the trip takes about 1½ hours.

You may prefer the so-called Flying Boat or hydrofoil. The trip to Malmö takes only 40 minutes. *Flyvebadene* departs every half hour from 6:15 a.m. until 12:30 a.m. The fare is 54 kroner (4.86) one way.

One can also get a boat to Oslo. There are regular boats from Copenhagen to Landskrona, Sweden, and from Dragør (Amager) to Limhamn, Sweden, as well as a regular boat to Swinoujscie, Poland.

READER'S MONEY-SAVING TIP: "I took the hydrofoil-steamer round trip from Copenhagen to Malmö and made a good discovery. On the boat, food, beverages, and beer are duty-free, and one can purchase cigarettes and snacks to take ashore for a long sightseeing day. Then back on a boat, and time to enjoy sandwiches and Elephant beer (excellent brew and only for export), and to acquire snacks and cigarettes to take along. The attendants are informative about Customs regulations concerning quantities of tobacco. But the savings are fantastic over ordinary heavily taxed Danish and Swedish goods" (J. R. Murphy, Phoenix, Ariz.).

BUSES IN THE COUNTRY: Denmark is serviced by an efficient, speedy network of buses and motorcoaches. Unless you rent a private car, the bus is sometimes your only link to certain villages. In rural Denmark, buses connect with railway terminals, so by using one or both means of transport you can see most of the country inexpensively.

The country offers round-trip tickets on its buses at one-way prices for those over 65. These reductions are not available, however, on Saturday and Sunday and over the Christmas and Easter holidays. All trips must be more than 20 miles in distance for this reduction to be granted.

CAR RENTALS: Every form of transportation has its own unique advantages, and justifiable arguments can be maintained in Denmark for everything from renting a bicycle to a river barge. Most travelers, however, will prefer the freedom that only a car can give, especially since that out-of-the-way inn or the castle you really want to see might be difficult to reach by sometimes tedious public transport. One of the best car-rental concerns in the country is **Budget Rent-a-Car,** which maintains offices in Copenhagen, Esbjerg, and Lyngby. A full array of well-maintained cars is offered on contracts that are usually cheaper by the week. If your trip is to take you through the rest of Scandinavia, you can rent a car in Copenhagen and drop it off in either Stockholm or Oslo for no additional charge (dropoffs in Helsinki are not permitted). Dropoffs in Vienna or Paris, on the other hand, require an additional payment of $200.

Most budget-oriented travelers will be interested in the cheapest car available, which is a peppy Fiat 55 or an Opel Corsa. Theoretically built for up to four passengers, one of these rents for $99 per week with unlimited mileage. Several conditions apply to this model and to all others listed below. They include a seven-day minimum rental, a reservation made at least three business days in advance, and the stipulation that all drivers have been in possession of their English-language license for at least a full year prior to the date of rental. (Drivers holding a license in a language other than English must accompany it with an international driver's license, available in the U.S. from AAA offices.) Drivers must be between the ages of 18 and 75. Be warned that a 22% government tax is imposed as an additional fee on any rental you negotiate. Payment can be made either in cash or travelers checks, which, if made at pickup time, will guarantee the $99 per week rental. Payment can also be made with a major credit card at dropoff time, although if a customer elects to use this method, the rate will be quoted in Danish kroner and adjusted to whatever dollar amount is in effect at the time.

A variety of cars other than the two mentioned above are available on weekly rentals with unlimited mileage. The same conditions apply as stated above. Manual-transmission Ford Escorts rent for $109 per week, while manual-transmission Ford Sierras, VW Golfs, and Honda Civics go for $135 per week. Each car in the latter category is designed for between four and five passengers, plus a conventional amount of luggage.

Be warned that the addition of an automatic transmission can hike your rental-car bill considerably. A Ford Sierra with automatic transmission, with the same restrictions, costs $180 per week with unlimited mileage.

A Word About Insurance

Budget Rent-a-Car builds an amount of insurance into its rates which experience has taught is adequate for most drivers and most accidents. If you are unlucky enough to have a mishap, however, you should know that unless you have purchased additional insurance (I always do), you'll be responsible for the first 1500 kroner ($135) of damage on small-and medium-size cars. You can waive all responsibility by accepting a policy offered by Budget. If you accept it, the counter attendant will have you sign a collision damage waiver, which will add 40 kroner ($3.60) per day or 240 kroner ($25.10) per week to your rental bill. It's usually worth it. You can also sign up for additional personal accident insurance for an extra 12 kroner ($1.08) per day.

For toll-free reservations throughout the United States, call 1/800/527-0700. In Canada, consult your local directory.

Avis, which I have used in previous years, is also well recommended and well represented in Denmark, with an excellent fleet of cars. There is a kiosk at Kastrup Airport which you'll see as you clear Customs (tel. 51-22-99), and an office at 1 Kampmannsgade (tel. 15-22-99).

Hertz also rents Fords and other fine cars in Denmark. Their largest car is usually a Swedish Volvo and their smallest a Ford Fiesta. For reservations, call 12-77-00 in Copenhagen. Their office is right opposite the Tivoli Gardens in the Royal Hotel building. Hertz often grants special low weekend rates, and the staff, with a little Danish humor, says that if you take the car for a week or more, they'll give you a "confidential rate."

FERRIES: Ferries connect much of Denmark, providing a vital link between such major points as Funen and Zealand. During the summer, it's important to book space, particularly if private cars are being transported. However, if a ferry is too jam-packed, do as the Danes do: stop somewhere and have a pilsner. Bookings on any of the state-owned services can be made at the Central Railway Station in Copenhagen (or at any of the local offices scattered throughout the country). Bookings are not necessary for short crossings. Tickets are purchased on board on short runs, and there is frequent service.

HITCHHIKING: It's generally safe and fairly easy, and, of course, a neat appearance helps a lot. Hitchhiking is fairly common in this friendly little country, and the Danes seem to genuinely like North Americans.

RAILWAY: All the major tourist centers are within easy reach of Copenhagen; each is hooked up either by efficient and speedy intercity rail service, top-notch and low cost. "Lyntog" express trains are as fast as summer lightning.

On Danish railways, children between the ages of 4 and 12 ride for half price (under 4, free). Senior citizens who are 65 or over get an off-season break. After mid-August and before mid-June, they get a round-trip ticket for the price of a one-way fare for trips exceeding 20 miles. The tickets are good except around Christmas and Easter.

For substantial reductions, inquire at the Central Railway Station (tel. 14-17-01) in Copenhagen about a monthly ticket, allowing unlimited rail travel in Denmark. A passport-type photograph is needed, and the cost is 1340 kroner ($120.60) in second class, 1695 kroner ($152.55) in first class. A family of at least three (providing one of the members is under 21) gets a 20% reduction by asking for mini-group tickets, but the distance must exceed 20 miles. Incidentally, just four persons (who don't have to be related) can travel together in Denmark, getting a 20% reduction on return tickets valid for two months.

3. Transportation in Copenhagen

Copenhagen is a paradise for those who don't mind wearing down their shoe leather. It's a walking city, since it's neat and compact—and many of the major sightseeing attractions lie within a short distance of each other (e.g., Tivoli, Carlsberg Glyptothek, National Museum, Christiansborg Palace, Thorvaldsen's Museum, the Armory).

Copenhagen has an intricate network of transportation that relies primarily on buses, as well as on inexpensive and efficient taxi service. Oddly, it would appear that Copenhageners use none of these modes of transportation, relying instead on their trusty bicycles (rentals easily available to tourists).

Copenhagen offers tourists tickets for unlimited travel on buses and trains. Incidentally, Eurail and Nordturistickets are accepted on the local trains in Copenhagen.

The Copenhagen Card

This personal discount card makes it easy to be a tourist in Copenhagen and North Zealand. It includes free and unlimited travel by bus and rail throughout the metropolitan area, including North Zealand, and 50% discount on crossing to and from Sweden, as well as free admission to many sights, attractions, and museums. The card is available for one, two, or three days and costs 75 kroner ($6.75), 125 kroner ($11.25), and 165 kroner ($14.85), respectively. Children under 12 are given a 50% discount. For further information, get in touch with the Danish Tourist Board in Copenhagen or New York City or the Copenhagen Tourist Association, 7A Nørregade (tel. 13-70-07).

AIRPORT: You'll arrive at **Kastrup Airport** outside Copenhagen. In keeping with the credo of this economy-oriented guide, cut costs right away by avoiding expensive taxis and taking one of the frequent coaches into the city terminal. A taxi to the center will likely run about 100 kroner ($9).

The coach fare is only 19 kroner ($1.71), and it's even cheaper to hop aboard local bus 32, which departs from the international arrival terminal about every 15 or 20 minutes. The bus will transport you to the Town Hall Square in downtown Copenhagen for only 7 kroner (63¢). Not only that, but the same ticket will give you the privilege of transferring to another city bus route, providing you do so within one hour after you purchased your initial ticket at the airport.

BICYCLING IN COPENHAGEN: Many visitors become cycling enthusiasts in Copenhagen. The riding craze is catching, affecting everyone from visiting firemen to homegrown grandmothers. Plenty of bicycles are available. To rent one, try **Københavns Cyklebors,** 157 Gothersgade (tel. 14-07-17). Rates are 35 kroner ($3.15) per day or 130 kroner ($11.70) per week. A 150-krone ($13.50) deposit is required. Open from 9 a.m. to noon and 1 to 5:30 p.m. weekdays, the shop closes at 1 p.m. on Saturday and is closed all day Sunday. You may telephone from the train station for a bike to rent.

BUSES: In Copenhagen, the network of buses is the least expensive method of getting around. Most buses depart from Town Hall Square, and the fleet is generally excellently maintained. Most North Americans plop down 7 kroner (63¢) for the standard ticket, not realizing that this entitles them to free transfers on all bus lines within 1 hour. For longer journeys a ticket can cost as much as 32 kroner ($2.88). You can save almost 25% on the fares by purchasing a set of 9 ticket coupons for 60 kroner ($5.40). Buses do not run from 12:30 to 5 a.m.

CITY TOURS: Either by boat or motorcoach, a number of sightseeing tours are offered in Copenhagen, ranging from mere get-acquainted jaunts to in-depth, serious looks at socialism. The inexpensive motorcoach tours depart from the Lur horn-blowers statue at the City Hall Square, and low-cost boat trips leave either from Gammel Strand (the fish market) or Nyhavn (the seamen's quarter).

For orientation, try the 1½-hour City Tour (2½ hours with visit to brewery), which departs daily at 10 and noon from May 15 to September 15. It costs 110 kroner ($9.90). This tour covers the major scenic highlights, including the Little Mermaid, Rosenborg Castle, and Amalienborg Palace, but you'll need a closer look later. On workdays, tours visit either the Carlsberg or Tuborg breweries.

I heartily endorse the City and Harbor Tour which leaves from May 1 to September 15 daily at 9:30 a.m., 1 p.m., and 3 p.m., a 2½-hour trip by launch and coach, departing from Town Hall Square. The cost is 150 kroner ($13.50) per person. The boat trip in the harbor goes through many canals, and you'll see the Little Mermaid and the Old Fish Market.

Another enticing excursion is the highly informative Industrial Art Tour, a behind-the-scenes preview of applied art as practiced in Copenhagen. This 2½-hour tour leaves at 1 p.m. from May 1 to September 15, costing 150 kroner ($13.50), and it's worth every øre. The workshops vary, but they generally include one of the major silversmiths (young women stamping spoons; gold-saving techinques such as straining the water after the workers wash up; craftspeople executing such designs as ruby-eyed butterflies). Then the tour visits one of the big porcelain factories, where visitors trace the steps the Little Mermaid figure goes through—in and out of ovens—before she finally sits, highly polished, on a shelf.

Shakespeare buffs will be interested in an afternoon Hamlet Tour, which leaves at 1:30 p.m. May 1 to September 30 daily and costs 200 kroner ($18) per person for a 5-hour trip to Hillerød, Frederiksborg Castle, and Elsinore.

Another popular trip is the Hans Christian Andersen Tour to Odense, leaving on Sunday from May 15 to September 15 at 8:30 a.m. for an 11-hour journey to Roskilde, Egeskov Castle, and the house and museum of the storyteller in Odense. The tour costs 375 kroner ($33.75) per person, not including lunch. It is necessary to make a reservation in advance for this trip.

S-TRAINS: This hookup of electric trains connects heartland Copenhagen with the expanding suburbs. A single ticket is 7 kroner (63¢). These tickets have the same conditions as those on the buses, already mentioned, and you can transfer from a bus line to an S-train using the same ticket. Eurailpass holders can generally ride free.

TAXIS: In Copenhagen, taxis offer excellent service—often with bilingual drivers. No fare hikes are charged at night. Watch for the **"FRI"** sign or green light. **TAXA,** the biggest company, operates the largest fleet of automobiles (tel. 35-35-35, a number nobody can forget). Be sure the taxis are metered. Tips are *included* in the meter price: 12 kroner ($1.08) at the drop of the flag and 6 kroner (54¢) to 7 kroner (63¢) per kilometer thereafter. The average ride within the city limits costs 20 kroner ($1.80) to 60 kroner ($5.40).

4. The ABCs of Life

The experience for the first-time visitor of plunging into Denmark can be confusing. However, armed with some "facts of life" about how to cope can ease your adjustment not only into Copenhagen, the capital, but into this fascinating country as well.

There are any number of situations which might mar your trip, perhaps a lost passport. Included in this is a medical emergency, of course.

Although I don't promise to answer all your questions, there is a variety of services available in both Copenhagen and the country you need to know about.

AMERICAN EXPRESS: "The pipeline" to America for many visitors, the American Express office in Copenhagen is at 18 Amagertorv (tel. 12-23-01).

BABYSITTING: If and when children become extra baggage on a trip, Denmark has a number of solutions to the problem. Perhaps more so than any other capital city in Europe. Copenhagen excels in facilities for keeping the kiddies occupied while their parents are off pursuing more sophisticated pleasures. Besides the many sights which seem designed with children in mind (the Tivoli, the Zoo), Copenhagen offers tot-tending services that may range from six hours to six weeks.

In the city, a top-notch babysitter service is run by the young women from Copenhagen University. It's called **Minerva Babysitters,** 52 A Smallegade (tel. 19-00-90). The office is open for you to make arrangements Monday to Friday from 7 to 9 a.m. and 2 to 7:30 p.m.; 2 to 6 p.m. on Saturday, and 5 to 7 p.m. on Sunday. The starting price for a babysitter is 20 kroner ($1.80), with 22 kroner ($1.98) per hour added.

Further, there is a supervised children's playground at Tivoli (open 10 a.m. to 6 p.m.), but a child shouldn't be left unattended by his parents. High school students will look after your child during the day—call the Minerva number. High school students are also available as sightseeing guides. You pay 20 kroner ($1.80) to start, then 22 kroner ($1.98) per hour (same telephone number).

BANKS: Check with your home bank before your departure, as many banks in Canada and the United States have affiliates in Denmark. In Denmark, banks, including the one at the airport, are open weekdays from 9:30 a.m. to 4 p.m. (on Thursday from 9:30 a.m. to 6 p.m.). They are closed on Saturday and Sunday. When the banks are closed, you can still get money exchanged by going to the office at the Central Railway Station. This kiosk is open seven days a week from 7 a.m. to 10 p.m. During the busy summer season, May 1 to mid-September, the Bank of Tivoli is open daily from noon till 11 p.m.

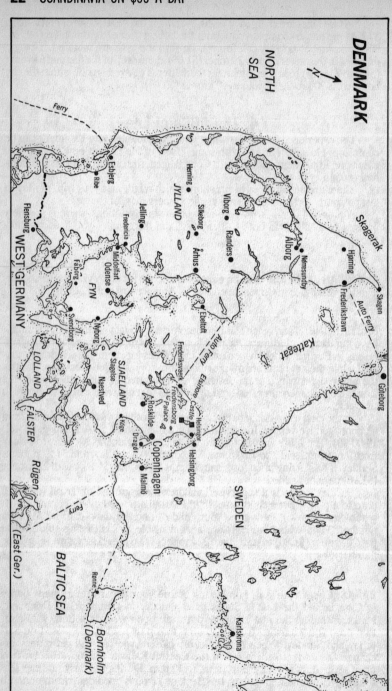

BATHS: The **Badstuen,** 63 Studiestraede (tel. 15-66-63), open to both men and women, is not only one of the finest of its kind in Scandinavia (carbon-lamp treatments, both dry and wet heat, massage, dips in cold pools), but it has numerous personal services as well, including on-duty pedicurists, barbers, and beauticians. The simple steambaths cost 30 kroner ($2.70); the luxury ones, lasting two hours, will run you around 90 kroner ($8.10). The baths are open weekdays from 10 a.m. to 7 p.m. (on Saturday from 9 a.m. to 5 p.m.). If you go at the end of the day you should enter an hour before closing.

BEACHES: The nearest beach to Copenhagen is **Bellevue** (take S-Train to Klampenborg), but the water is not recommended for swimming. If you like to swim at a sandy beach, take a trip (by train or car) to the beaches at North Zealand—Gilleleje, Hornbaek, Liseleje, and Tisvildeleje. Although these are all family-style beaches, the fashion these days is for minimum—if any—bathing attire. The swimming is also excellent here, although the water is somewhat cold.

To reach any of these beaches, take the train to Helsingør and then continue by bus. Or you can make connections by train to Hillerod and switch to a local train. Check at the railroad station for details. If you go by car, you may want to stay for the evening discos at the little beach resort towns dotting the north coast of Zealand.

CIGARETTES: American and British name brands are available in most stores in Denmark; however, they are very expensive. Count on spending 26 kroner ($2.34) for one pack of imported cigarettes.

CLIMATE: Denmark is mild for a Scandinavian country. The Yankee farmers of New England experience harsher winters than their Danish cousins. Summer temperatures average between 61 and 77 degrees Fahrenheit. Winter temperatures seldom go below 30 degrees Fahrenheit. The climate is so equable because of the warming waters of the Gulf Stream. Any time between mid-April and November is considered suitable for visiting this tiny nation.

CLOTHING SIZES: For the most part, Denmark uses the same clothing sizes as the continent of Europe. The sizes of women's stockings and men's socks are international.

For Women

Junior Miss		Regular Dresses		Shoes	
U.S.	*Denmark*	*U.S.*	*Denmark*	*U.S.*	*Denmark*
5	34	10	40	5	36
7	36	12	42	5½	36½
9	38	14	44	6½	37½
11	40	16	46	7½	38½
		18	48	8	39
		20	50	8½	39½
				9	40

For Men

Shirts		Slacks		Shoes	
U.S.	Denmark	U.S.	Denmark	U.S.	Denmark
14	36	32	42	5	36
14½	37	34	44	6	37
15	38	36	46	7	38
15½	39	38	48	7½	39
15¾	40	40	50	8	40
16	41			9	41
16½	42			10	42
17	43			10½	43
				11	44
				12	45

Warning: This chart should be followed only as a very general outline, as in the same country there are big differences in sizes. If possible, try on all clothing or shoes before making a purchase. You'll be glad you did.

CRIME: No particular caution, other than what a discreet person would maintain anywhere, is called for in Denmark. Compared to the rest of the world, Denmark remains safe. However, in Copenhagen you should beware of pickpockets in congested areas. Chances are, you'll need to be more careful of foreign visitors ripping you off than the Danes.

CURRENCY: In currency, the Danes use the **krone** (crown) which breaks down into 100 øre. At the time of publication, 1 krone is equal to approximately $.09 in U.S. coinage, there being approximately 11.04 kroner to the U.S. dollar. Of course, the devaluations and revaluations, the floating and floundering of world currencies, may change all that.

Notes are issued in denominations of 5, 10, 50, 100, and 500 kroner and coins in 1, 2, 5, 10, and 25 øre, as well as 1 and 2 kroner.

Kroner	U.S.$	Kroner	U.S.$
0.25	$ .02	60	$ 5.40
0.50	.05	70	6.30
1	.09	80	7.20
5	.45	90	8.10
10	.90	100	9.00
15	1.35	125	11.25
20	1.80	150	13.50
25	2.25	175	15.75
30	2.70	200	18.00
40	3.60	250	22.50
50	4.50	300	27.00

CUSTOMS: Denmark has very liberal Customs regulations. Nearly all items that can safely be viewed as "personal" are allowed in duty-free—that is, sports equipment, clothing, jewelry, typewriters. Cigarettes are limited, however; you can bring in either 400 cigarettes or 100 cigars. You can also bring in 1½ liters (a standard bottle) of spirits or 2 to 3 liters of strong wine, depending on whether you are coming into Denmark from a non-EEC country or from such a country. There are no restrictions on the import of currency into Denmark. Residents of Denmark may take out of the country only 5000 kroner, but nonresidents can take a higher amount if they can prove that the Danish kroner were brought in with them or obtained by conversion of foreign currency they imported.

Upon leaving Denmark, citizens of the United States who have been outside their home country for the past 48 hours or more are allowed to take home $400 worth of merchandise free—that is, if they have claimed no similar exemption within the past 30 days. If you make purchases in Denmark (and who doesn't?), it's important to keep your receipts.

DENTAL TREATMENT: In an *emergency only,* go to **Tandlaegevagten,** 14 Oslo Plads, near Østerport Station and the American Embassy. It is open week nights from 8 to 9:30 p.m. and on Saturday, Sunday, and holidays from 10 a.m. to noon and 8 to 9:30 p.m. Go in person (no telephone), and know that the dentist's fee is paid in cash. During regular business hours, you can ask your hotel to call the nearest English-speaking dentist. In the rest of the country, ask your hotel or host to phone **Falck** for information about local dental emergency service.

DOCTORS: For house calls, dial 0041 in Copenhagen. Doctors are on call 24 hours. In the suburbs, weekday emergency hours are 4 p.m. to 7:30 a.m.; on Saturday, Sunday, and holidays, 24 hours a day. The doctor's fee is paid in cash. Similar arrangements exist in all towns out of normal hours. If you cannot get a doctor in an emergency situation, dial 0-0-0 (alarm).

There are also wards for emergencies in Copenhagen and other towns throughout the country that function 24 hours a day. **Kommunehospitalet,** 5 Øster Farimagsgade, has such a ward in Copenhagen.

DOCUMENTS FOR ENTRY: Candaians, Americans, and the British need only a valid passport to enter Denmark for a stay up to three months.

DRUGSTORES: In Denmark they're known as **apoteker,** and are open Monday to Thursday from 9 a.m. to 5:30 p.m.; on Friday, from 9 a.m. to 7 p.m.; and on Saturday from 9 a.m. to 1 p.m. A 24-hour druggist in downtown Copenhagen is the **Steno Apotek,** 6C Vesterbrogade (tel. 14-82-66).

ELECTRIC CURRENT: The voltage is generally 220 volts A.C., but in many camping sites, 110-volt power plugs are also available. Adapters and transformers may be purchased once you're in Copenhagen. It's always best to check at your hotel desk before plugging in any electrical equipment.

EMBASSIES: I hope you'll not need such services. But in case of an emergency, such as a lost passport, these addresses will come in handy. The **U.S. Embassy** is at 24 Dag Hammarskjölds Allé (tel. 42-31-44), the **British Embassy** at 36-40 Kastelsvej (tel. 26-46-00), and the **Canadian Embassy** at 1 Kr. Berniskowsgade (tel. 12-22-99).

EMERGENCY: Dial 0-0-0 for the fire department, the police, to call an ambulance, or to report a sea or air accident. State your address and telephone number, and speak clearly. Emergency calls from public telephone kiosks are free (no coins). In case of a car breakdown on the road, you can get emergency help and towing in Zealand by calling **Falck** (tel. 01/14-22-22), Copenhagen.

FILM: This is so expensive that I suggest you bring in what you'll need since Customs is very liberal in this regard. It is also very expensive to have film processed in Denmark, so I suggest that you wait until you return home. There are no special restrictions on taking photographs, except in certain museums where signs are generally posted. When in doubt, ask.

GAS: It's readily available, and stations are frequent, so touring in the countryside is no problem. The rub is the expense. As an indication of what you'll pay, count on shelling out about 7 kroner (63¢) per liter for super-grade.

GEOGRAPHY: If a chauvinistic Norwegian sailor has had enough schnapps, he might tell a visitor that his country and Sweden are the *only* true Scandinavian countries, that little Denmark really belongs "down there with Germany." He would be very foolish, or very drunk, to suggest that in Nyhavn, the rowdy seamen's quarter of Copenhagen, but he does have a point.

Denmark is the only Scandinavian country attached to the mainland of Europe. Jutland shares a common border with Germany. Despite the geographic connection, Denmark is spiritually and culturally linked to its more isolated northern neighbors (in fact, Scandinavia more or less used to belong, however reluctantly, to Denmark).

Mainland **Jutland** is the largest land area of Denmark, followed by the island of **Zealand** (graced by Copenhagen), and both are separated by the second-largest island, **Funen.** Funen and Zealand are only two of more than 480 Danish islands, most of which are uninhabited. Despite its small size, Denmark has more than 4500 miles of irregular coastline.

Denmark is one of the low-lying countries. Yet the Danes, with their characteristic good humor, will often tell visitors about their "mountains" (the highest hill on Jutland is around 550 feet).

Essentially, Denmark is a land of manicured fields, medieval timbered houses, thatched-roof cottages, historic castles, manor homes, fishing villages, sand-duned coasts, and step-gabled churches. Functional modern architecture abounds as well.

GOVERNMENT: The country is a kingdom (technically speaking, a constitutional monarchy), and it's one of the most democratic nations on earth. The king or queen exercises power through the State Council and the Folketing (parliament). Prime ministers and other ministers are appointed by the king or queen, but approved by the parliament. There are dozens of Lower Courts of Justice, two Higher Courts, and a Supreme Court. An Ombudsman, an independent official, supervises the constitution and investigates complaints made by citizens against government authorities.

If you don't commit an infraction of the law, such as drunken driving, you'll encounter practically no interference from government authorities in touring this very liberal, freedom-loving nation.

HEALTH INSURANCE: All tourists in Denmark who become suddenly sick or suffer from worsening of a chronic illness have a right to free treatment in Danish hospitals or emergency wards. This does not apply to those whose aim in coming to Denmark is free medical treatment, and it is a condition that the patient is not strong enough to be moved to his or her home country. Home transport is at the patient's own expense.

HOLIDAYS: From year to year, there may be slight variations in some of these dates, so it's best to check with a local tourist office. Danish public holidays (and dates of those which do not vary) are: New Year's Day (January 1), Maundy Thursday, Good Friday, Easter Sunday, Easter Monday, Labor Day (May 1), Common Prayers Day, Ascension Day, Whit Sunday, Whit Monday, Constitution Day (June 5), Christmas Day (December 25), and Boxing Day (December 26).

LANGUAGE: Danish, the national tongue, is a rather guttural language, one of the Teutonic tongues. But this doesn't mean that Germans understand it. A Swede—not exactly an unbiased authority—said that "Danish is not a language. It's a pathological condition of the pharynx." More so than nearly any other country in continental Europe, English is commonly spoken in Denmark, especially among young people. You should have few, if any, language barriers.

LAUNDRY: Self-service laundromats are all over Copenhagen. A convenient one, open seven days a week from 6 a.m. to 10 p.m., is the **Vascomat** at 2 Borgergade, near Gothersgade. You can also leave your laundry to be washed for you. Hours for that service are Monday to Friday from 8 a.m. to 5:30 p.m.

METRIC MEASURES: Here's your chance to learn metric measures before they become popular in America.

Weights		Measures	
U.S.	*Denmark*	*U.S.*	*Denmark*
1 ounce	28.3 grams	1 inch	2.54 centimeters
1 pound	454 grams	1 foot	0.3 meters
2.2 pounds	1 kilo (1000 grams)	1 yard	0.91 meters
1 pint	0.47 liter	1.09 yards	1 meter
1 quart	0.94 liter	1 mile	1.61 kilometers
1 gallon	3.78 liters	0.62 mile	1 kilometer
		1 acre	0.40 hectare
		2.47 acres	1 hectare

NEWS BROADCASTS: All year, Program 3 (in English) is broadcast in Denmark, Monday to Saturday at 8:30 a.m. You'll hear news and announcements about events of interest to foreign visitors.

NEWSPAPERS: Foreign newspapers, particularly *The International Herald Tribune,* are on sale in Copenhagen at the Central Railway Station; in front of the cinema theater, Palladium, on Vesterbrogade; in Strøget, opposite the Ceylon Tea Centre; and at the newstands of the big hotels.

POST OFFICE: In general, post offices in Denmark are open weekdays from 9 or 10 a.m. to either 5 or 6 p.m., and from 9 a.m. to noon on Saturday. They are closed on Sunday. If you're seeking information in Copenhagen, telephone 14-62-98.

If you want your mail sent general delivery—that is, *poste restante*—it will be delivered to the main post office in Copenhagen at 35 Tietgensgade unless it is specifically addressed to some other post office in the country. The post office at the Central Railroad Station keeps the longest hours: Monday to Friday from 9 a.m. to 9 p.m.; Saturday from 9 a.m. to 6 p.m.; and Sunday from 10 a.m. to 4 p.m.

It costs 3.70 kroner (33¢) to send a regular letter by surface mail (up to 20 grams) to either the United States or Canada. But it'll take forever to get there. To send airmail letters, you pay 4.20 kroner (38¢) for 20 grams. It costs 2.70 kroner (25¢) to send a regular postcard to Canada and the United States.

Know that these rates are likely to change by the time you read this. Inquire before mailing.

RELIGIOUS SERVICES: Most Danes belong to the **Lutheran** church, but all minority religions enjoy complete freedom. The Danish church is therefore Protestant, and most of these Evangelical-Lutheran services are held on Sunday at 10 a.m. and again at 5 p.m. in churches in both Copenhagen and around the country.

In Copenhagen, other denominations you will want to know of are the **Roman Catholic** St. Ansgar's Church, 64 Bredgade; the **English** church (Anglican-Episcopalian) of St. Alban's on Langelinie; the **American** church (Protestant and Interdenominational) at the American Embassy, 24 Dag Hammarskjölds Allé; and the **synagogue** at 12 Krystalgade. Further information about these and other denominations is available at the Danish tourist offices.

RESTROOMS: All big plazas, such as Town Hall Square in Copenhagen, have public lavatories. In small towns and villages, head for the marketplace. Hygienic standards are usually adequate. Sometimes both men and women patronize the same toilets, so don't be surprised. Otherwise, men head for "Herrer" or simply "H," and women patronize the doors marked "Damer" or "D."

SENIOR CITIZEN DISCOUNTS: Refer to travel under "Railway" and "Buses."

SHOPPING HOURS: In general, shopping hours are Monday to Thursday from 9 a.m. to 5:30 p.m., till 7 p.m. on Friday, till 1 p.m. on Saturday. All shops are closed on Sunday. However, shopping hours vary widely, so look at signs on the main doors of the stores. On Sunday you'll find the kiosks and supermarket at the Central Railroad Station open, and there you can purchase food daily until 10 p.m. or midnight. The Central Station's bakery is open until 9 p.m., and one of the kiosks at the Rådhuspladsen, selling papers, film, and souvenirs, is open 24 hours.

STUDENTS: Students who can flash an International Student Identity Card can get a number of travel breaks in Copenhagen, particularly in intra-European charter flights, as well as slashed-to-the-bone railway reductions to such points as Germany and England. A card may be purchased in the U.S. from the **Council on International Educational Exchange (CIEE)**. Write to 205 East 42nd St., New York, NY 10017 (tel. 1-212/661-1414).

For information about low-cost air on train trips, go to **D.I.S.** (Students' International Committee), 28 Skindergade (tel. 11-00-44), in Copenhagen.

More than any other city, Copenhagen has special facilities for young people. One popular center for gathering and entertainment is a multifaceted establishment known simply as **Huset** (The House). In the basement, entrance at 13 Råhusstraede, is a bar, Café Rosa Luxemburg, open from noon to 1 a.m. daily. In the main building, entrance at 14 Magstraede (tel. 15-65-18), you'll find a jazz club on the ground floor (Vognporten), an information office for young tourists, "Use-It" (second floor), as well as a restaurant, an art cinema, and exhibition room on the third floor, another music club on the fourth floor, and other electrical music and a theater on the fifth and top floor. Music clubs open daily from 9 p.m. to 2 a.m. "Use-It" is open from June 15 to mid-September daily from 10 a.m. to 8 p.m. Off-season it is open from 10 a.m. to 4 p.m. on Monday, Wednesday, and Friday, and on Tuesday and Thursday from 10 a.m. to 8 p.m. At this center you can obtain information on youth camps, sleep-ins, camping, hostels, traveling, cheap places to eat, sightseeing attractions. The people are helpful and friendly. This youth center also offers information, free baggage checking, a bulletin board for messages, snacks, and an outdoor patio. It's a good clearinghouse for young persons on the road.

In the heart of Christianshavn (the old quarter of the city) is a youth settlement known as **Christiania.** Making use of former army barracks and buildings, Christiania features Copenhagen's liveliest communes (called collectives here), a bakery selling loaves of healthful bread, and often a free disco on weekends. For information, consult the "Use-It" Center, as the program changes daily. Take bus 8 from Town Hall to the end of the line.

Don't miss the highlight of the summer season—free open-air concerts from the first of May to the end of August in the **Faelledpark** (the Commons). Danish rock bands play to an enraptured audience of young people, who lie on the grass. On sunny days, partial undressing is the style for both sexes. This friendly setting provides an ideal mixing ground for Scandinavians and foreigners. On the outskirts of the crowd, young craftspeople and entrepreneurs of all nationalities show their wares—usually on blankets. You can purchase homemade jewelry, hashish pipes (hashish is nonetheless illegal in Denmark), health-food snacks, and other goodies at a fair price. Information about this can be obtained from **Café Pavillionen** (tel. 26-04-50).

Come early to get a good seat, because the crowd is huge on a warm day. Starting time is 3 p.m., every Sunday from June through August.

Take bus 1, 3, 6, or 14 to Trianglen, then follow the crowd. Or walk from the center of town (about 1½ miles) across the Fredensbro (the Peace Bridge).

SWIMMING POOLS: The top indoor swimming pool in Copenhagen (complete with sauna) is the **Øbrohallen,** at 1 Stauningsplads (tel. 42-30-65), just off Østerbrogade, at the Stadium, a short walk from Trianglen. For 12 kroner ($1.08), you can rent a bathing suit, towel, and get the works here.

Second choice is **Frederiksberg Svømmehall** (tel. 34-40-02) at 29 Helgesvej in the Frederiksberg section. This one is cheaper, but it has a smaller pool and lacks the elegant Roman-bath decor of the Øbrohallen. As you swim under the glass roof of Øbro, you will be surrounded by Greek and Roman statues. Warning: Both of these may be closed for repairs during three weeks in July, so check with the tourist office or telephone the pools.

Outdoor pools (frilufts bad) are also good. The largest one is **Bellahøj** (tel. 60-16-66), near the Bellahøj Youth Hostel. The entrance fee is 8 kroner (72¢). Take bus 5, 7, 8, 63, or 68. A smaller, suburban-type pool is **Emdrup Svømmebad,** at 5 Bredelandsvej, also costing 8 kroner (72¢), children 40 kroner (36¢). Take the 43 or 21 bus.

TAXES: As noted in the introduction, Denmark imposes 22% tax on goods and services. This is called a "Value Added Tax," and is known in Denmark as *Moms* (pronounced "mumps").

This tax, however, can be refunded for articles whose price exceeds 2300 kroner ($207), inclusive of Moms. This is no longer a complicated procedure, and you can take your purchase with you from the shop and all such articles out of Denmark when you go. Moms (or VAT) is 22% of the price of the article, so you can realize a substantial saving on your purchases. You buy and pay for an article as usual. The shop assistant helps you fill in the papers required for a repayment, and the refund of the tax will be made to your bank at home or sent by check to you at your home address. Stores will also often help you with shipment of purchases against payment of freight and other costs, but they're not obliged to do so.

TELEGRAMS: The main telegraph office in Copenhagen is at 37 Kømagergade, and it's open daily from 9 a.m. to 10 p.m., including Sunday.

TELEPHONES: All Danish phones are fully automatic. Dial the six-digit number for calls in the same area. Every district has its two-digit area code. Dial it first when calling from one area to another. Most of Copenhagen has an 01 area code; the suburbs, 02. The rest of Zealand and the nearby islands have an 03 area code.

At public telephone booths, use two 25-øre, 1-krone, or 5-krone coins only. No coins are returned, even if the number is busy. So begin with the smallest payment. You can make more than one call on the same payment if your time hasn't run out. Remember that it can be very expensive to telephone from your hotel room.

Need help in phoning? Dial 0030. For information, dial 0033.

TELEX: To send a Telex in Copenhagen, go to the Telex booths at the main telegraph office, 37 Købmagergade, which is open daily, including Sunday, from 9 a.m. to 10 p.m.

TIME: Denmark operates on Central European Time—that is, one hour before Greenwich. Daylight Saving Time is observed from the end of March until the end of September.

TIPPING: At last a country where tipping has been practically abolished! Tips are expected on very, very few occasions, and even then you should give only 1 or 2 kroner, for example in a public toilet when you wash your hands and there is an attendant. Only special services should be rewarded separately. Some Danes, in fact, are insulted if you offer them a tip.

Porters charge according to fixed prices, and neither hairdressers/barbers nor movie ushers are usually tipped.

But unless I sound too optimistic a note, know that hotels and restaurants, along with other establishments, even taxis, impose a 15% service charge in the rates they quote. Service is "built into" the system. Not only that, but with the 22% Moms, you'll end up paying an additional 37% for some services.

TOURIST INFORMATION: In Copenhagen head for the **Danmarks Turistråd,** by far the most helpful tourist bureau I've encountered in any country. It's at 22 H. C. Andersens Boulevard (opposite City Hall) (tel. 11-13-25). From May 1 to June 30, it is open weekdays from 9 a.m. to 6 p.m. (on Sunday from 9 a.m. to 1 p.m.). From July 1 to August 31, it is open weekdays from 9 a.m. to 8 p.m. (on Sunday from 9 a.m. to 1 p.m.). For the month of September, hours are weekdays from 9 a.m. to 6 p.m. (on Sunday, 9 a.m. to 1 p.m.). Off-season (that is, October 1 to April 30) hours are Monday to Friday, 9 a.m. to 5 p.m.; on Saturday, 9 a.m. to noon; closed Sunday.

Before you leave the States, you may want to call upon the **Danish National Tourist Office,** 655 Third Ave., New York, NY 10017 (tel. 1/212/949-2333).

YOUTH HOSTELS: From the sand dunes on the North Sea to the château country in Funen, Denmark has approximately 80 youth hostels. Guests of all ages are accommodated (usually for stays of not more than three days) for approximately 140 kroner ($12.60) to 160 kroner ($14.40) for a comfortable bed and three complete meals a day (bed linen needed). Even cheaper arrangements are available when hostelers take advantage of "do-it-youself" kitchens.

Types of accommodations vary considerably—from a renovated old manor farm in Odense to a big, sprawling, modern lodge in Jutland.

Dormitory-type regulations, such as "no smoking in the bedrooms," are enforced. It is customary to shut down the hostels from 1 to 4 p.m.; the lights go out at 11 p.m. Most hostels have small bedrooms, generally with four beds in each, also available for families.

The catch? A guest must be a member, but that's easy enough to arrange. In the United States, information may be obtained from the headquarters of the **American Youth Hostels, Inc.** The national headquarters is at 1332 I St. NW, Washington, DC 20005 (tel. 1/202/347-3125). In Canada, you can get in touch with the **Canadian Hosteling Association,** 333 River Rd., Vanier, ON KIL 8H9 (tel. 1/613/746-3844). A membership for seniors, those 18 and over, costs $20; juniors, under 18, pay $10. Family memberships are $30, and a life membership can be purchased at $200.

Chapter II

SETTLING INTO COPENHAGEN

1. The Budget Hotels
2. Private Homes
3. Hostels
4. Meals, from Budget to Splurge
5. Shopping in Copenhagen

AGE HAS MELLOWED this Danish capital on the sea, and centuries of dust have settled comfortably on some of the old gabled houses—but nothing has stricken the eternal bloom of the city. Each spring arrives as if it's the first one in this merchants harbor. When flower vendors with their Zealand red roses cluster around the statue of Bishop Absalon, legendary founder of the city, it's not hard to imagine a twinkle in the venerated old castle-builder's left eye.

In a city that never forgot its heart, don't be surprised to witness the following events:

—A Cupid-mouthed honey blonde pulls a cheroot out of her purse and asks: "Got a light, mister?" (The Copenhageners, especially the sweet young things, speak American, you know.)

—A man stopped casually on the street corner and asked for directions replies: "You're an American. C'mon, I'll buy you a Carlsberg. My relatives own half the cows in Minnesota." (Incidentally, "Americans," in this context, means any man, woman, or child living within flying distances of Tallulah, Louisiana, or Moose Jaw, Saskatchewan.)

That—and a lot more—is Copenhagen.

"KIOSK P" AND ROOMS IN PRIVATE HOMES: The first problem greeting a visitor to Copenhagen is that of finding a suitable accommodation. This can be difficult for those cavalier souls who don't make reservations and arrive during the peak summer months when the no-vacancy signs can be as plentiful as ants at a picnic. But the **Copenhagen Tourist Association** has tried to make the search as painless as possible. Visitors to Copenhagen are guaranteed space, even if the Queen has to put an extra cot in the dungeon of Amalienborg.

At the Central Railway Station, the tourist office maintains the ever-popular Kiosk P, a lifesaving hotel-booking service that has kept many a Düsseldorf dandy or a Kansas farmer from sleeping on the park bench when the hotels in Copenhagen were stuffed as thick as a Danish sausage. This is where a sort of "meet the Danes" program begins for many budget-conscious visitors shortly after their arrival in Copenhagen.

Dozens of Copenhagen homemakers, seeking extra money for cheroots and Tivoli splurges, have agreed to rent out their freshly scrubbed extra rooms to tourists. Rooms in some of these private homes are often the best accommodations provided in Copenhagen. Without question, they are the cheapest, averaging around 87.50 kroner ($7.88) per person nightly.

Visitors fill out a card at the kiosk, checking off the price they want to pay, then hand this card to one of the young men or women behind the desk who seem to speak every language from King's English to pure Swahili, and are super-skilled at quickly evaluating a customer's needs and wishes. After one or two swallowed-syllable telephone calls, a homeless foreigner is booked into a suitable hotel or into the home of a private family. In addition, the attendants provide guests with a map of their city, on which they indicate bus connections. The charge for this service, whether you have booked a youth hostel or a luxury hotel, is 12 kroner ($1.08) per person. A deposit must be paid at the kiosk, which will later be deducted from the room rent. For a luxury hotel room, you must pay 20 kroner ($1.80); for a medium room, 10 kroner (90¢); and for a simple accommodation in a hotel, 8 kroner (72¢).

The kiosk is open from May 1 to mid-September daily from 9 a.m. to midnight, a welcome relief to late-arriving passengers from the Continent. For the rest of September, the office closes at 10 p.m. In October the weekday hours are 9 a.m. to 5 p.m. From November 1 through March, the bureau is open weekdays from 9 a.m. to 5 p.m. (to noon on Saturday). In April, the kiosk remains open until 5 p.m. as well, weekdays only.

The kiosk will not accept reservations in advance. Kiosk P can secure private accommodations only when the hotels in the price range, which the guest can and will pay, are fully booked.

A new organization called **Hotelbooking København** has been set up, which enables the individual tourist to reserve hotel rooms in advance. This cannot be done by a travel agency. Either write the service at the tourist office or telephone 01-12-28-80. No advance bookings are taken for private homes. There is no extra cost to the traveler for advance booking service by Hotelbooking København except the price of a stamp or a phone call.

Staying in a Private Home

While I'll include numerous budget hotel selections in this chapter, I heartily urge that a private room with a family be considered—not only for its comfort and reasonable cost, but often for warmth and hospitality that can't be matched in the more impersonal hotel setup.

Some years back an American couple arrived in Copenhagen on a rainy night when tourists and convention revelers had grabbed up all the hotel space. In desperation, they went to the kiosk and asked to be booked into a private home "as a last resort," figuring they'd be able to locate a hotel in a day or two. Plenty of hotel accommodations later became available, but their temporary arrangements in this private home stretched out for two weeks, the length of their stay in the Danish capital. The charming, motherly widow who took them in that night gave them a pleasantly spacious and immaculate room, overlooking a tree-lined square. A bus stopped nearby, whisking passengers to the heart of the city in eight minutes. The hostess, who spoke English, served a homestyle Danish breakfast and always kept a bowl of fruit in the dining room "in case you get hungry."

For a number of specific private home (or guest house) recommendations, mine and readers', see the end of Section 1 below.

WHERE THE HOTELS ARE: Most of the hotels lie in and around the Central Railway Station and the **Rådhuspladsen** (Town Hall Square), the hub of life in the Danish capital.

One of the most popular hotel streets in Copenhagen is **Helgolandsgade,** near the Central Station and off the main artery, **Vesterbrogade.** It lies within walking distance of the Tivoli, as well as the principal shopping promenade (the traffic-free, merchandise-loaded **Strøget),** many of the major museums, budget restaurants, and SAS Terminal. Another small but scattered grouping is on the fringes of the seamen's quarter of **Nyhavn,** within walking distance of Kongens Nytory.

In addition, Copenhagen has a number of youth hostels (suitable for student travelers). These rock-bottom-priced hostels, in many cases, offer bunk beds, but have a prevailing atmosphere of camaraderie—and are often the focal point of much student activity and fun (a curfew is imposed in some, but not all, of them).

1. The Budget Hotels

For those who want to search for a hotel on their own—or else write in advance for reservations—here are my recommendations. I've ignored the plush and super-expensive first-class hotels, offering instead more reasonable accommodations in the smaller hotels and pensions. The ones recommended are usually family owned and operated; thus, a staff of tip-grabbers is avoided, although personal attention is generally the hallmark of these budget choices.

The hotels, in the main, occupy one or more floors of older, lackluster (in most cases) buildings that may or may not have elevator service. Many of them have been modernized, although few offer private baths, relying instead on separate corridor baths and toilets (when these facilities are not up to par, this lack

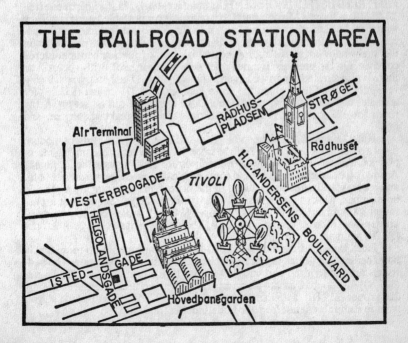

has been cited in the individual write-ups). As a rule, most of the bedrooms have their own sinks with hot and cold running water.

Throughout Scandinavia a chain of Mission hotels provides the food-and-lodging backbone to thousands of touring Swedes, Danes, Norwegians, and Finns who know they can get comfortable, immaculately clean rooms in well-run hotels . . . for a fair price. Copenhagen has several, each catering to a middle-class family trade. The hotels aren't as religiously oriented as they used to be, and they are open to people of all faiths. Although these hotels were originally founded by the old-fashioned Temperance society, which meant they were as bone dry as Dead Man's Gulch, now about 50% of the mission hotels in Denmark are fully licensed.

The Mission chain also operates restaurants in a number of its establishments, serving well-prepared meals at prices comparable to most medium-priced family restaurants. Since the Missions are heavily booked by visiting Scandinavians in the summer months, reservations are recommended.

Most of the establishments include the service charge in the rates they quote; others tack on 15% to the bill. Most quote a bed-and-breakfast rate; others charge extra for the morning meal. Throughout Denmark, in both its hotels and restaurants (and on virtually everything else), you'll find the word *Moms* on your bill. This is no maternal reference—rather, a government-imposed tax of 22% discussed earlier in the introductory section. Most hotels include the Moms tax in the rates they initially quote you; a few still surprise you by adding it onto the bill.

Caution: The 15% service charge and the 22% Moms mean that you'll pay 37% extra in addition to the room rate. Before checking into an establishment, ask the management to quote you the *total* rate to avoid unpleasant surprises when settling your account.

PREFERRED HOTELS IN THE CENTER: Comfort Hotel, 27 Løngangstraede (tel. 12-65-70), a former Mission hotel, contains 200 comfortable bedrooms, each with private bath and a streamlined, no-frills decor that includes contemporary Scandinavian furniture. You might want to relax with a newspaper in the big-windowed public rooms, seated on one of the leather-upholstered couches. On the premises is a pub offering a wide range of British beers, and there is also a restaurant as well as an in-house garage. The hotel, which is conveniently located just behind the Town Hall, charges 375 kroner ($33.75) for a single, 600 kroner ($54) for a double. An extra bed can be set up in any room for 125 kroner ($11.25) extra. Prices include breakfast, service, and tax.

Hotel Danmark, 89 Vester Voldgade (tel. 11-48-06), is a pleasant modern hotel a block behind the Town Hall, near the Tivoli Gardens. The smiling reception you'll receive in the sunny lobby is only one of the benefits at the Danmark. Among other amenities, clean and comfortable rooms, each with private bath, and a breakfast buffet are included in the price. This was formerly a Mission hotel annex, which since has established its independence. Singles rent for between 390 kroner ($35.10) and 450 kroner ($40.50), while doubles go for 630 kroner ($56.70) to 690 kroner ($62.10). The nearby garage charges 30 kroner ($2.70) per night for parking.

Hotel Dania, 3 Istedgade (tel. 22-11-00), is a comfortable, 50-room family hotel behind a red-brick façade, one minute from the railway station. The bedrooms are modernized and cost 320 kroner ($28.80) in a single, 420 kroner ($37.80) in a double, each with private bath. With no bath, a single costs only 220 kroner ($19.80), a double 310 kroner ($27.90). These rates include all you want to eat for breakfast from the buffet, service, and taxes.

Missionshotellet Nebo, 6 Istedgade (tel. 21-12-17), is set in the midst of a string of hotels that hover close to the railway station for survival, and it stands out like a blue bonnet in a patch of weeds. Indeed, it maintains its Salvation Army respectability and innocence among certain others on the same street that have lost theirs. Set back from the street, the Nebo is a quiet retreat from bustling traffic. Clean and up-to-date, it rents bathless doubles for 350 kroner ($31.50) to 410 kroner ($36.90), from 420 kroner ($37.80) to 500 kroner ($45) in a double with shower and toilet. Singles with hot and cold running water only are priced from 200 kroner ($18) to 240 kroner ($21.60). A single with shower and toilet costs 300 kroner ($27). All rates include taxes, service, and breakfast. It's difficult to entertain the royal family in the small lobby, but a lounge does open onto a side courtyard.

Hotel West, 11 Westend (tel. 24-27-61), is on two floors of a corner building about a four-minute walk from the railway station. Inside, you find a small public sitting room and rather basic bathless doubles that rent for 200 kroner ($18) to 220 kroner ($18.90) nightly, including service and tax. Parents traveling with a child can rent a triple room for 260 kroner ($23.40). Only a few singles are available, costing from 100 kroner ($9) to 120 kroner ($10.80). No breakfast is served.

Savoy Hotel, 34 Vesterbrogade (tel. 31-40-73), is one of Copenhagen's most central hotels, lying within minutes of the Tivoli Gardens, the City Hall Square, and the railway station. An old traditional hotel, it has been considerably modernized to keep pace with the changing demands of its clients. Cozy and comfortable, it has up-to-date furnishings and rooms that offer a range of plumbing. A bathless single rents for 250 kroner ($22.50), going up to 400 kroner ($36) for a single with shower. A bathless double (with hot and cold running water) costs from 350 kroner ($31.50) to 400 kroner ($36), although a double with shower will rent for as much as 600 kroner ($54) to 700 kroner ($63). The most expensive doubles, those with private bath and toilet, are 900 kroner ($81). A third person sharing a room pays an additional 125 kroner ($11.25). All these tariffs include Moms and service. Those in bathless rooms will find adequate showers and toilets on each floor. Breakfast, served downstairs in a pleasant morning room, costs an additional 45 kroner ($4.05) per person.

ON HELGOLANDSGADE: Now, still in the vicinity of the Central Station, we move to Helgolandsgade, running parallel to Colbjørnsensgade, the latter one of the principal streets for prostitution in Copenhagen. Helgolandsgade is called "Copenhagen's Sleeping Street," because it has five hotels, 650 rooms, and 1200 beds, which can be booked through only one office. The booking office is at 4 Helgolandsgade (tel. 31-43-44). By arrangement with two good restaurants on the same street, half- and full-board terms can be arranged. This can cut down on your food costs considerably in Copenhagen.

Hotel Absalon, 19 Helgolandsgade (tel. 24-22-11) is a six-story 200-room budget hotel, a few minutes' walk from the railway station. An elevator has been added and the lobby and reception area modernized. The bedrooms, too, are up-to-date, furnished with pleasant Nordic pieces and wall-to-wall carpeting. A number of shower rooms are available (free, of course), although many accommodations are complete with shower and toilet. The Absalon has added a cluster of units equipped with first-class baths, toilets, big mirrors, and proper ventilation. These are the most expensive, of course. In a bathless room, singles range from 300 kroner ($27) to 350 kroner ($31.50); doubles, from 400 kroner ($36) to 450 kroner ($40.50). With a private bath, singles cost from 400 kroner ($36) to 525 kroner ($47.25); doubles, 500 kroner ($54) to 700 kroner ($63). Families may want to ask about one of the triple accommodations, ranging in price from 600 kroner ($54) to 900 kroner ($81), depending on the plumbing.

Don't miss their wall of genuine Royal Copenhagen plates in the tiny reception lounge, the oldest one dating back to 1908.

Hotel Selandia, 12 Helgolandsgade (tel. 31-46-10), is an 81-room, immaculately kept family hotel, totally renovated in 1983. It is managed by veteran hotelman Eigil Hummelgaard, former general manager of the celebrated Hotel D'Angleterre. All rooms, with or without private baths, have telephones, radios, and color TV. A basic single without bath costs from 275 kroner ($24.75), a similar double going for 400 kroner ($36). With a private shower bath, a single ranges from 350 kroner ($31.50) to 500 kroner ($45), a double costing from 520 kroner ($46.80) to 625 kroner ($56.25). An extra bed can be placed in your room for another 150 kroner ($13.50). Rates include a Scandinavian breakfast buffet with Danish pastries, served in the inviting breakfast restaurant. The Selandia is centrally located right in the heart of Copenhagen, near the Tivoli, the Town Hall Square, the SAS air terminal, the Central Rail Station, and the shopping area, Strøget.

Triton, 7–11 Helgolandsgade (tel. 31-32-66), which was once known as the Kansas, has turned to Greek mythology for its new reincarnation. This hotel has been much improved in recent years, particularly after its 1979 takeover by a British hotel concern. A friendly and informal hotel right in the heart of the capital, it is large and expansive, with suitable rooms. Only a few rooms have complete private baths, although most are equipped with private showers and toilets which make them popular with visiting North Americans. Prices include a substantial Danish buffet breakfast, service, and VAT. Children under 12 who share a room with their parents get a 50% reduction. Rooms are graded basic, standard, and superior, and priced accordingly. When reserving, it's important to know that the basic rooms do not contain private baths or showers. A single ranges from 300 kroner ($27) to 500 kroner ($45), a twin-bedded unit costing from 500 kroner ($45) to 650 kroner ($58.50). An extra bed will be placed in your room for 150 kroner ($13.50).

Westend, 3 Helgolandsgade (tel. 31-48-01), is in the center of Copenhagen, only a short walk from the Central Station and Tivoli. A typical mid-city, brick Mission hotel, it contains modern, well-furnished rooms with Nordic blond pieces. Fifty are doubles, a surprising 79 singles. Some accommodations have refrigerators. The bathless singles range from 300 kroner ($27). The bathless doubles are 400 kroner ($36). However, if you insist on a double with private bath, expect to pay from 500 kroner ($45) to 675 kroner ($60.75), depending on the size and location. Breakfast, service, and tax are included in the rates. In the large lounge is a color TV. In the carpeted morning room, guests help themselves to a "Dansk breakfast."

Missionshotellet Hebron, 4 Helgolandsgade (tel. 31-69-06), competes with the best of the budget hotels. This 150-bed building has extended its lobby to cover a large area with seating for 26 persons. There is also a separate lounge for TV viewing. However, the attraction is its neatly kept, well-furnished rooms. These cost 210 kroner ($18.90) in a single without bath, going up to 320 kroner ($28.80) in a single with shower and toilet. A twin without bath costs 320 kroner ($28.80), rising to 510 kroner ($45.90) with shower and toilet. A large, help-yourself breakfast is included in the rates. The rates quoted are inclusive of Moms and service. On every floor are corridor baths which you can use without extra charge.

Centrum, 14 Helgolandsgade (tel. 31-82-65), is a 70-room hotel spread out on several floors. It offers solid, all-around comfort in units that are furnished with modern pieces and are freshly cleaned and polished every day. So close to the railway station that you can walk here (if you travel light), the hotel charges 230 kroner ($20.70) single, 330 kroner ($29.70) double, including breakfast, service, and Moms. Families may want to rent one of the three-bedded rooms for 500 kroner ($45). There's no charge for taking a shower in one of its public bathrooms.

ALONG COLBJØRNSENSGADE: Pick and choose your way carefully along this popular hotel street which rivals Helgolandsgade in offering accommodations. Some rooms along here are rented only for an hour or two. But a suitable selection follows.

Hotel Cosmopole, 9–11 Colbjørnsengade (tel. 21-33-33), used to be known to me as the incongruously named "Cuba." However, it is now operated by a chain hotel, Copenhagen Center, which is known for its series of budget hotels, including the Hotel Union nearby. In addition to tourists, the hotel also attracts a number of countryside Zealanders and the denizens of Funen and Jutland in the capital on either business or pleasure.

Housed in a tidy brick building, the hotel is contained on five floors, reached by elevator. Rooms have been updated considerably, and furnished along Nordic functional lines. The most expensive rooms are those doubles with private bath, costing 550 kroner ($49.50) nightly. If you can't afford that, you might ask for a double without bath, going for 400 kroner ($36). Single rooms with bath, always an expensive category, cost 400 kroner ($36) nightly, but only 250 kroner ($22.50) without bath. These tariffs include breakfast and all taxes. There is no hotel restaurant.

Hotel Union, 5–7 Colbjørnsengade (tel. 22-44-33), is an economy hotel in the very center of Copenhagen, only a few minutes' walk from the Central Railway Station, the Air Terminal, and the Tivoli Gardens. It's under the same management, Copenhagen Center Hotels, as the previously recommended Cosmopole. The interior design is modern Danish. Most of the rooms are equipped with phone, private shower, and toilet. A bathless double rents for 275 kroner ($24.75), going up to 545 kroner ($49.05) with shower. A single without bath goes for 275 kroner ($24.75), rising to 400 kroner ($36) with private bath or shower. It costs another 135 kroner ($17.55) per person to have an extra bed put into your room. Breakfast, service, and painful Moms are included in these tariffs. On the premises is an inexpensive restaurant, La Cave.

Hotel Excelsior, 4 Colbjørnsengade (tel. 24-50-85), offers 55 rooms behind an attractive façade of brown brick with white window trim. A wrought-iron stairwell and an elevator lead to the rooms, the quieter of which face the rear. The contemporary lobby contains warm colors, comfortable chairs, and a friendly and professional staff member who will check you in. Breakfast, which is included in the room price, is served in the Sukiyaki basement restaurant featuring Japanese food (see restaurant section). Depending on the plumbing and the season, doubles rent for between 480 kroner ($43.20) and 750 kroner ($67.50), with singles costing from 300 kroner ($27) to 570 kroner ($51.30).

Saga Hotel, 20 Colbjørnsengade (tel. 24-99-67), is perhaps your safest bet along this sometimes troublesome hotel street. A budget hotel, it is run by English-speaking Torben Bredwig, who welcomes the family trade. You walk up one flight to reach the reception area. The rooms are on the upper floors, and there is no elevator service. If that is no problem for you, you'll find pleasantly furnished and comfortable singles without bath renting for 190 kroner ($17.10) to 240 kroner ($21.60), doubles for 320 kroner ($28.80) to 400 kroner ($36), also without bath. If you prefer a room with bath, the single tariff is 380 kroner ($34.20), rising to 490 kroner ($44.10) to 530 kroner ($47.70) in a double with bath. An extra bed such as a cot for a child will cost 140 kroner ($12.60). Prices include Moms, service, and a continental breakfast.

Missionshotellet Ansgar, 29 Colbjørnsengade (tel. 21-21-96), is comfortable and cozy as well as much improved. After a major repair and much reconstruction, it now offers 87 bedrooms, 36 of which are equipped with showers and toilets. All the units, furnished in Danish modern, have central heating and hot and cold running water, plus phones. For those in units without private plumbing, there are showers and baths on each floor (no charge for use). In addition,

the hotel has a dozen large family rooms, each accommodating up to six guests in beds or on sofas. Families (if they are large enough) can always negotiate a special rate from the management. A bathless single room rents for 250 kroner ($22.50), going up to 385 kroner ($34.65) with shower and toilet. A bathless double costs 385 kroner ($34.65), rising to 550 kroner ($49.50) with shower and toilet. An extra bed in a room costs another 125 kroner ($11.25). Children under 3 years stay free when no bed is required, and children under 12 years pay half price in an extra bed. Breakfast, served up to 10 a.m., is included in the tariffs, and consists of a self-service buffet.

The hotel lies on a one-way street without any busy traffic, near the Central Railway Station, the Tivoli, Town Hall Square, and the shopping street, Strøget. There is free parking 24 hours a day just outside the hotel. Guests coming from Kastrup Airport can take the SAS bus to the Air Terminal at the Central Station, walk through the station and be inside the hotel in less than four minutes.

NEAR KONGENS NYTORV AND NYHAVN: Visitors wanting to live near the seamen's quarter of Nyhavn, with its sailor joints and tattoo parlors, yet in the middle of a colorful and fast-rising "chic" section of Copenhagen, may want to try the following. For this location, you will pay considerably more than our budget will allow, but you'll make up for it in extra luxuries and amenities.

The canny Danes have transformed the neighborhood in recent years. Some of the more famous tattoo parlors are still there, but most of the sailors' bars and red-light hotels have disappeared, as Nyhavn has turned into one of the most desirable areas of Copenhagen. The central canal at Nyhavn is filled with 19th-century boats, and the 18th-century façades of the buildings give the section much local color. Several hotels have opened up here, and my first recommendation offers the most value for the money, although the others are worthy of consideration, too.

The **Admiral,** 24–28 Toldbodgade (tel. 11-82-82), lies only two short blocks from the Nyhavn Canal, about a three-minute stroll from the ocean-liner size boats which steam almost daily to Oslo and Stockholm. Set inside the massively thick walls of what used to be a warehouse, the hotel appears like a brooding mass of unadorned windows, repetitive arches, and half-chiseled stones and bricks. Once inside, guests navigate between the thick timbers and the stone arches of the hotel infrastructure, around which partitions have been set up for the creation of the clean and functional bedrooms. About half of them have desirable views over the harbor, while all of them come with fully equipped baths where the water faucets are controlled with a single high-tech spigot.

The breakfast buffet is included in the room price, which ranges from 450 kroner ($40.50) to 600 kroner ($54) in a single and from 625 kroner ($56.25) to 750 kroner ($67.50) in a double. Later in the day, the same heavily timbered room doubles as the focal point for one of the best luncheon buffets in town. Guests are served an all-you-can-eat buffet of elaborately arranged fish dishes, meats, and Danish cheeses.

71 Nyhavn Hotel, 71 Nyhavn (tel. 11-85-85). This hotel, although beyond the budget of many readers of this guide, is so special that it might be the kind of place you'll be glad you robbed the piggy-bank to enjoy. Its award-winning design incorporated a slickly modern arrangement of space into the framework of a 200-year-old warehouse whose red-brick walls rise imposingly above the wooden hulls of the ancient ships anchored in the adjacent canal. The building is one of the few in the neighborhood to have escaped the British bombardment of Copenhagen in 1807, and as such, it retains even more cultural cachet than its neighbor.

Each of the 82 bedrooms has a goodly share of exposed timbers crisscrossing some of the living spaces almost randomly. The rooms are filled with sumptuous leather couches, smallish arched windows, comfortable baths, and plush gray carpeting. The public rooms include a small bar area and an elegant restaurant, Pakhuskaelderen, serving gourmet French and Danish specialties. The name of the hotel is a linkage between the year of its inauguration, 1971, and its address, No. 71, in what has been transformed from one of the roughest into one of the chicest neighborhoods in Copenhagen. Single rooms range from around 650 kroner ($58.50) to 900 kroner ($81), with doubles going from 825 kroner ($74.25) to 1050 kroner ($94.50). An extra bed can be set up in any room for an additional 180 kroner ($16.20). A Danish breakfast buffet is included in the room prices.

Hotel Codan, 21 St. Annae Plads (tel. 13-34-00), is a glistening white hotel near the ferryboat station to Oslo and the hydrofoil station to Sweden. Built about 30 years ago in a kind of international modern style, with handsome detailing and large sliding windows opening onto very tiny balconies, the hotel offers 134 contemporary bedrooms, each with colorful carpeting, private bath, phone, air conditioning, color TV, and radio. Clients have the use of the Codan bar, as well as the bar and restaurant of the more historic Hotel Admiral, which is connected to the Codan via a covered passageway. Depending on the view, singles range from 300 kroner ($54) to 635 kroner ($57.15), with doubles going for from 720 kroner ($64.80) to 760 kroner ($68.40). Here, too, you'll only be a few steps from the Nyhavn area.

Hotel Neptun, 18 St. Annae Plads (tel. 13-89-00), was originally built around 1850 to house the masses of emigrants waiting for a ship at the nearby piers to take them to the New World. It has a white-brick façade gracefully adorned with a single neoclassical pediment jutting toward the tree-lined square on which the hotel sits. The interior is tastefully decorated to look like someone's upper-class living room, with English-style furniture, warm colors, paneling, and even a corner chessboard set up for play.

Some of the rooms are arranged around a quiet interior courtyard, which, in summer, offers a place for a drink. The bedrooms are tastefully contemporary, equipped with private baths, color TV, radios, and phones. The Neptun is ideally situated a block from the Nyhavn Canal, near many of the city's chief attractions. Singles rent for between 420 kroner ($37.80) and 500 kroner ($45), while doubles cost from 625 kroner ($56.25) to 750 kroner ($67.50), depending on the plumbing and the accommodations. Breakfast is included in the room prices.

Hotel City, 24 Peder Skrams Gade (tel. 13-06-66), is a remodeled town house built around 1900, done in a rather severe Nordic modern, within an easy walk of the nighttime section of Nyhavn. It's reached by bus 41 from the Central Station, and you can also take the hydrofoil nearby to Malmö, Sweden, if you're interested in a day's outing. In the old business quarter of Copenhagen, the hotel has 95 rooms in all, many of which contain private baths and toilets. All are equipped with phones, and there are two bathrooms on each floor if you're housed in a unit without plumbing. A bathless single rents for 250 kroner ($22.50) nightly, the tariff going up to 380 kroner ($34.20) with shower or toilet. Bathless doubles range in price from 410 kroner ($36.90). However, you'll pay 570 kroner ($46.80) to 620 kroner ($55.80) in a double with complete private bath. The little restaurant is open for breakfast only, a continental selection included in the rates quoted, as are service and taxes.

Søfolkenes Mindehotel, 19 Peder Skrams Gade (tel. 13-48-82), lies only two blocks from the heartbeat Kongens Nytorv and in the vicinity of Nyhavn. Rising five stories, it has a modern façade. In summer, the flags of the Scandinavian countries wave from its top balcony. Accommodations are small, furnished in a simple, functional Nordic modern. A double room rents for 200 kroner ($18) to 350 kroner ($31.50), a single costing 150 kroner ($13.50) to 250 kroner ($22.50).

In a cafeteria downstairs, you can order not only breakfast, but a two-course hot meal for 85 kroner ($7.65) and up. Just 100 meters from the hotel, a ferry leaves for Sweden and Bornholm.

BRANCHING OUT: If you take bus 16 from the Central Station, you'll be delivered to **Ibsens Hotel,** 25 Vendersgade (tel. 13-19-13), which is preferred by many of my older readers and families traveling with children. English-speaking Mrs. Bertram will welcome you into her nicely old-fashioned place. She is a kind and accommodating hostess, charging 190 kroner ($17.10) in a single, from 320 kroner ($27.90) in a double, these prices including breakfast. No other meals are served. Showers are free. If you have a child, she'll add another cot for 110 kroner ($9.90).

Hotel Kong Arthur, 11 Nørre Søgade (tel. 11-12-12), is a gracefully proportioned building which has seen many transformations since it was first constructed as a home for Danish orphans in 1882. It sits behind a private courtyard next to a tree-lined canal in a residential part of town, which is about as idyllic a setting as anything in Copenhagen. It's been completely overhauled into a contemporary hostelry of modern comfort, although the antique double stairwell leading to the upper floors has been retained. Each of the blue-carpeted rooms is kept freshly painted, with sloping ceilings on the upper floors corresponding to the slope of the roof. Each contains TV, in-house video, mini-bar, leather-upholstered chairs, telephone, and private bath. The 55 bedrooms rent for 600 kroner ($54) to 900 kroner ($81) in a double, 480 kroner ($43.20) to 550 kroner ($49.50) in a single, with breakfast included in all tariffs.

Park Hotel, 3 Jarmers Plads (tel. 13-30-00), is a 19th-century building, a part of which is renovated every winter. It contains my favorite breakfast room in the entire city. In it, the owner, whose hobby is antique cars, has adorned one wall with the handsome radiator covers from six vintage automobiles. On other walls, you'll see an airplane propellor from 1916, a collection of antique auto headlights, and lots of machine-age posters and engravings, including one of an ancient car spattering mud over a wedding party leaving a French church. There's even an old big-wheeled "penny farthing" bicycle hanging below the skylight.

The bedrooms are lovely arrangements of tasteful furniture, marble-covered baths, thick carpeting, and lithographs. Bathless singles rent for 250 kroner ($22.50) to 480 kroner ($43.20), while singles with bath cost from 375 kroner ($33.75) to 600 kroner ($54). Bathless doubles rent for 330 kroner ($29.70) to 430 kroner ($38.70), while doubles with bath cost from 480 kroner ($43.20) to 720 kroner ($64.80). Breakfast is an additional 50 kroner ($4.50).

Hotel Carlton, 14 Halmtorvet (tel. 21-25-51), is a pleasantly modern hotel only a four-minute walk from the Central Train Station. The decor is stream-lined, fairly clean, and comfortable, with rooms ranging from 400 kroner ($36) to 600 kroner ($54) for a double with bath, from 265 kroner ($23.85) to 330 kroner ($29.70) for a single with bath. Bathless rooms cost from 250 kroner ($22.50) to 460 kroner ($41.40) in a double, from 150 kroner ($13.50) to 240 kroner ($21.60) in a single.

Hotel Viking, 65 Bredgade (tel. 12-45-50), is a 19th-century hotel with elaborately detailed windows and some surprisingly grand antique furniture scattered among its hallways and stairwells. There's an elevator, although most visitors prefer to use the gracefully winding wooden steps leading to the kind of 1960s-style rooms that many Scandinavian business visitors make their home during extended stays in Copenhagen. Since the hotel has an all-night bar, it attracts lots of salty seafaring types, watching television over half a dozen Carlsbergs. The 170 bedrooms come with breakfast included in the price, going for 335 kroner ($30.15) for a single with bath, 300 kroner ($27) in a bathless single. Doubles rent for 600 kroner ($54) with bath, 450 kroner ($40.50) bathless. This unusual hotel is near Amalienborg Castle, not far from the harbor and the Little Mermaid.

NEAR COPENHAGEN UNIVERSITY: Hotel Sonne, 33 Egilsgade (tel. 54-44-44), was deliberately built as a budget hotel in 1970. Even though into its second decade, it is still one of the newest looking of Copenhagen's family hotels. Rooms are modernized along Nordic lines, and each unit has hot and cold running water. I've found the shower baths and toilets on each floor adequate. Although costs have been rising, the manager tries to keep prices within reason—from 340 kroner ($30.60) for a double room, from 220 kroner ($19.80) in a single, these tariffs including breakfast, service, and tax. No lunch or dinner is served. Guests enjoy the central location, the modernity, and the polite reception. The location is across the canal, Sydhavnen. The Lange Bro (bridge) leads across the canal from the Tivoli.

2. Private Homes

Mrs. Anna Petersen, 7 Gentoftegade, 2820 Gentofte (tel. 65-82-71), was called "the warmest, friendliest person in all of Scandinavia" by reader Sandra Bromfield, and I heartily concur. She offers a great welcome to guests at her cozy villa in an exclusive northern suburb of Copenhagen. Her house is a 15-minute train ride from the Central Station (you can use your Eurailpass); the A train leaves about every 20 minutes, heading for Gentofte, from either Track 9 or Track 10. The house opens onto an attractive garden. Both double and triple rooms are available, double for 200 kroner ($18), including breakfast and shower. Mrs. Petersen, who speaks excellent English, is only too happy to give helpful travel hints to make your visit more enjoyable. Frequently guests are invited to share a midday coffee and pastry with her family. Besides being close enough to the sights of Copenhagen, her home is a good base from which to visit the castles at Hillerod and Helsingør.

Mr. and Mrs. Spühler, 44 Brønshøjholms Allé, Brønshøj (tel. 60-11-40), are among the friendliest hosts in Denmark. These warm, gracious people welcome you into their home and will house you in their guest room, which is light and pleasant with two large windows (one overlooks a large parklike area where there are many opportunities for lovely walks). The room is of fair size and has two large, comfortable beds, and the rent is 150 kroner ($13.50) per night. They enjoy receiving American and Canadian guests in their immaculate home. Often these proud Danes invite you to join them in their garden for schnapps and coffee.

Mrs. Gerda Oslev, 62 Brønshøjvej, 2700 Brønshøj (tel. 28-74-56), and her husband are friendly and gracious hosts who have provided hospitality to many readers. In a residential section, their home is in an attractive red-brick style, typically Danish. Rooms are pleasantly furnished. One has a balcony opening onto the garden. A single rents for 100 kroner ($9), a double going for 180 kroner ($16.20)—a superb bargain. A Danish breakfast costs yet another 40 kroner ($3.60). There is no charge for use of the bath.

READERS' GUESTHOUSE SELECTIONS: "We would like to mention the hospitality and warmth of **Mrs. Else Rathje,** 5 Jyllandsvej (tel. 86-45-02). We were accommodated in a pleasant situation, near the beautiful Frederiksberg Castle. Mrs. Rathje has a Danish ability of making complete strangers feel comfortable in her home. The double room amounted to 125 kroner ($13.15) per night" (B. V. Vanberg and J. Fleming, Minneapolis, Minn.). . . . —"Your acclamation of Danish people as warm, friendly, and hospitable is borne out by **Hanne Iversen,** and her mother, **Inga Mathiesen,** who rent double rooms in their modern, attractive homes in the inner suburb of Valby. The clean, fully furnished

doubles and twins go for a reasonable 160 kroner ($14.40) to 200 kroner ($18), 140 kroner ($12.60) for a single, while a small extra fee of 40 kroner ($3.60) will buy you a breakfast bigger than you can eat. The homes, at 12 and 20 Englodden Street, are only four stations or eight minutes' journey by the frequent and fast S-Tog train from Copenhagen's Central Station. The telephone is 46-46-36 or 30-45-05" (Frank Rolley, New York, N.Y.). . . .
"The two most helpful people in Copenhagen have got to be **Arthur and Minna Allin.** If you don't mind walking four flights of stairs, you'll get a genuinely warm welcome at their casual, informal apartment at 49 Gammel Kongevej (tel. 24-95-62). You are permitted to use the kitchen for making coffee or tea, and to watch the color TV in the living room. Their apartment is beautifully situated three minutes from the center. A no. 1 or no. 14 bus takes you right to the door. It's 140 kroner ($12.60) for a double, including free showers" (Kevin and Karen Vaughar, Fostoria, Ohio).

3. Hostels

HOSTELS: Vesterbro Ungdomsgaard, 8 Absalonsgade (tel. 31-20-70), is more of a small country hotel than a hostel. Hidden in its own parklike gardens (which face the back of the Copenhagen City Museum), it is a quiet, two-story, ranch-style retreat, off the Vesterbrogade (which leads to the railway station). During the off-season months, from the beginning of September to May 5, it serves as an idealistic youth center. But otherwise it undergoes a quick change: beds are hauled out and a night's sleep is offered to young people from all over the world at a flat fee of 80 kroner ($7.20) per person per night, including Moms as well as an all-you-can-eat breakfast. Bed sheets are rented for 23 kroner ($2.07) extra. Here are some positive negatives about the hostel: no service charge, no age limit, no membership required, no curfew. Most of the beds are grouped dormitory fashion. Showers, washrooms, and individual lockers are provided, but you must provide your own padlock. Don't miss the artwork on the walls (created by young Danes in winter). Take bus 28, 6, or 41 from the Rådhuspladsen—but it's a fairly short and pleasant walk on a good day.

Bellahøj Youth Hostel, 8 Herbergvejen, Brønshøj (tel. 28-97-15), was rated by the national tourist board as the cleanest and best organized hostel for youths in the Danish capital. It lies a 20-minute ride from Town Hall Square on bus 2 to Fuglsang Allé. It is open all year, except the month of December, and requires hostel membership. Guest cards valid for one night only cost 20 kroner ($1.80) per person. The overnight charge is 40 kroner ($3.60) per person, plus an additional 30 kroner ($2.70) for breakfast. A dinner is also available at an additional cost of 42 kroner ($3.78). Accommodations are provided mainly in eight-bedded rooms, although six areas house 12 beds. The hostel is closed from 10 a.m. till noon, and a 1:30 a.m. curfew is imposed.

Copenhagen Hostel, 55 Sjællandsbroen (tel. 52-29-08), is a dormitory as well as a modern hotel, offering 144 well-furnished and immaculately kept double rooms. In all, the hostel accommodates up to 448 guests, and it also has special facilities for some 56 handicapped persons. The overnight charge is 40 kroner ($3.60). Breakfast is 30 kroner ($2.70) and dinner 42 kroner ($3.78). It is open all year, except the month of January, and it does not shut down at night. Hostel membership is required. Guest card valid for one night only costs 20 kroner ($1.80) per person. Take bus 37 or 38E from Toftegårds Plads.

4. Meals, from Budget to Splurge

The food the Danes prepare is the best in Scandinavia. In fact, it's among the best in Europe, with no apologies to Switzerland or France.

Breakfast, to begin with, is usually big and hearty, fit fortification for a day of sightseeing. You may prefer, however, simply the continental breakfast of two pieces of Danish pastry (wienerbrød) and coffee. The "Danish" is moist, airy, and rich, a delicacy, not like the heavy dried-up bread too often disguised as pastry in North America. The Danes are hit-and-miss when brewing their coffee (too often miss). But it's easy to ignore this one gastronomic slipup when the other treats are hauled in. Those with sensitive stomachs can stick to tea in the morning.

But a usual Danish breakfast consists of an assortment of homemade breads, a selection of the incomparable Danish cheeses, and often a boiled egg, salami, or whatever. In most establishments, you may order bacon and eggs, two items with which this country is well stocked.

At **lunch,** the national institution, the ubiquitous smørrebrød, open-face sandwiches, is introduced. Literally, this means bread and butter, but the Danes pay little attention to literal meanings. They stack this sandwich as if it were the Leaning Tower of Pisa—then they throw in a slice of curled cucumber and bits of parsley, maybe pimiento, or perhaps sliced peaches or a mushroom for added color. The way these sandwiches are made separates the culinary artist from Hash House Harry.

Two of these sandwiches can make a more-than-filling lunch. They are seen in the grandest dining salons of the poshest hotels all the way down to the lowliest pushcart. Many restaurants offer a wide selection; guests inspect a checklist and then mark the ones they want. Some are made with sliced pork (perhaps a prune or peaches on top), roast beef with béarnaise sauce and crispy fried bits of onion, or liverpaste adorned with an olive or cucumber slice and a gelatin made from strong beef stock.

Smørrebrød is often served as an hors d'oeuvre. The most popular, most tempting, and usually most expensive of these delicacies is prepared with a mound of tiny Danish shrimp, on which a lemon slice and caviar often perch, sometimes fresh dill. The "ugly duckling" of the smørrebrød family: anything with a cold sunny-side-up egg on top of it.

The Danes keep farmers' hours for **dinner:** 6:30 p.m. is common, although restaurants remain open much later. Many main-course dishes are commonly known to North Americans, although they are prepared with a distinct flourish in Denmark—dishes such as lever med løg (liver and fried onion), bøf (beef in a thousand different ways), lammesteg (roast lamb), or that old reliable, flaeskesteg med rødkål (roast pork with red cabbage).

The country's cooks are really noted for their fresh-tasting fish dishes. North Americans readily agree on the splendid taste of the tiny Danish shrimp (rejer), although herring and kippers meet with less enthusiasm. Really topnotch fish dishes include plaice (rødspaette), salmon (laks), mackerel (makrel), and boiled cod (kogt torsk).

When the Danes smile and say "ost" (cheese), they're not posing for a camera. They are ordering one of the many Danish varieties of cheese, which are exported to decorate the before- or after-dinner tables of the world. It is also consumed domestically at any of the three meals a day, then eaten on a premidnight smørrebrød at the Tivoli. Danish bleu is too familiar to need definition. Want something softer and milder? Try Havarti.

Don't expect fresh vegetables. Vegetables are one of the least imaginative items in Mother Denmark's cupboard. A booklet put out by the National Travel Association of Denmark makes this statement: "Many Danes look upon them as intended for cows, sheep, and rabbits."

Danish specialties most worth sampling: frikadeller, the Danish meatballs or rissoles, prepared in umpteen and 28½ different ways. Also try a Danish omelet with a rasher of bacon covered with chopped chives and served in a skillet. A familiar dish—palatable to North American tastes—is Danish hamburger patties topped with fried onions and coated with a rich brown gravy.

Choice desserts: Danish apple charlotte, best when decorated with whipped cream, dried breadcrumbs, and chopped almonds. Another treat is rødgrød med fløde—prepared in numerous ways, but basically a jellied fruit-studded juice, over which the diner pours thick cream.

As for your drink, Carlsberg or Tuborg (take your choice) beer is the national beverage of Denmark. Knowing the vital statistics about their consumption by the Danes would turn the beet-colored face of any local citizen of Munich even redder. Profits from this golden brew go into the promotion of arts and science, so Danes have a justification for their excessive beer-drinking.

In one of the few masochistic streaks in the Danish character, however, they have socked this foaming stuff with so many petty taxes that it's all the low-income Dane can do to keep the sustenance of life flowing.

A bottle of pilsner, however, costs about half the price of the stronger, more decoratively labeled export beer. To keep from flattening his bank account, a Dane relies on the low-prices fadøl (draft beer). Foreigners on skimpy budgets are advised to do the same.

Lost-weekenders may gravitate more to aquavit (schnapps to the English), which comes from the city of Aalborg in northern Jutland. The Danes, who usually drink it at mealtime, follow it with a beer chaser. Go easy on the stuff. Made from a distilling process using potatoes, aquavit should only be served icy cold.

For those with daintier taste, the world-famous Danish liqueur, Cherry Heering, is a delightful drink, made from cherries as the name implies, and it's for consumption at any time other than during meals.

The more traditional imported hard-liquor drinks are not recommended—not for temperance reasons, but because of their expense. Denmark, seemingly, is locked in a conspiracy with AA. Such favorites as a martini and a scotch and soda are taxed so heavily that an imbiber who orders one is, in reality, putting an orphaned Danish kid through school. These drinks, therefore, are to be avoided, except by the most philanthropic.

Copenhagen is a dining festival. Recommended are a wide range of places, all of which have one thing in common: good food at moderate prices. Listed also are a number of restaurants with special atmosphere, where leisurely dining is the rule of the day—everything from Nordic bistros to chain restaurants. But along with these recommendations are included many quickie establishments, offering self-service and good, substantial hot meals at decent prices. At the latter, you avoid the 15% service charge. At most Danish restaurants, however, Moms (the government tax) and the 15% service charge are included in the price of the item on the menu. No further tipping is required. Of course, this added 37% makes many food items appear unreasonably high.

MEDIUM-PRICED MEALS: Let's start out where we should, with the best values—

Anva Cafeteria, 2E Vesterbrogade, is on the second floor of this all-glass department store and dishes up stark-bargain, good-tasting meals during shopping hours. Meal prices are kept low to tempt krone-conscious Copenhagen shoppers, who like the speedy self-service (and no tips, of course). A recent selection consisted of a hearty stewed veal, served in its own juices, and the inevitable potatoes—but also asparagus as an added treat. The cost? Just 65 kroner ($5.85). Smaller appetites make do with one or two of the wide selections of smørrebrød offerings. From the large windows of the softly draped cafeteria, you can see the old Circus building.

Det Grønne Køkken ("The Green Kitchen"), 10 Larsbjørnsstraede (tel. 12-70-68). Every day lots of local actors, authors, musicians, and visiting tourists fill this place with a kind of convivial community feeling, despite the somewhat forbidding entrance. You'll pass through a covered passageway and climb a cement-block staircase that may remind you of your freshman dormitory at college. At the top, however, you reach an amazingly attractive room with black accents, verdant palms, and a long ice table loaded with a vegetarian buffet priced at 60 kroner ($5.40) from noon to 4 p.m. and at 75 kroner ($6.75) for dinner. The owner is blond, blue-eyed, and bearded Alex Jørgensen, who seems to know well his repeat customers. If you're not interested in the salad buffet (many people come for that exclusively), you might enjoy the pizza with tomato and Emmenthaler cheese, the omelet with olives, the seaweed salad with Japanese dressing, or one of the soups, which include gazpacho. The establishment is open from noon to 10 p.m. daily except Sunday.

McDonald's, 25 Frederiksberggade (tel. 15-20-14). American parents with children in tow always head for McDonald's on the popular shopping street, Strøget, lying right off the Town Hall Square. Here they find a fast-food place that is far cheaper than the Tivoli restaurants. A Big Mac costs only 22 kroner ($1.98), and for another 7 kroner (63¢) you can get a side order of french fries.

The **DSB Bistro** operates right out of the Central Railway Station, 7 Banegårdspladsen (call 14-12-32 and ask for extension 12 to reserve a table). Go through the main door of the station, passing through the coffeeshop on your left. The staff here serves from 11:30 a.m. to 9:30 p.m., offering a good, moderately priced lunch and dinner smörgåsbord. You're always given a choice of two hot soups, followed by a cold plate consisting of ham, roast beef, sausages, and other cold cuts, plus an appropriate sauce, and vegetables. Danish pastries aren't offered, but you get a good selection of desserts, such as layer cake, lemon mousse, cookies, and a choice of different cheeses. The price? 85 kroner ($7.65), plus another 19 kroner ($1.71) for a beer.

Puk's Pub, 6 Vandkunsten (tel. 11-14-17), is across the street from Tokanten (see below). Much like a 1925 speakeasy, Puk's Pub is in the basement. During the day substantial hot plates are offered, including half a chicken with salad and french fries. You can also order French onion soup, wienerschnitzel, and spring chicken. Count on spending from 170 kroner ($15.30). Later in the evening, you may want to sample one of the smørrebrød offerings. "The Pub" is frequented predominantly by young beer-drinkers who listen to a piano player, often till 5 a.m. The commotion reaches its peak on weekends.

Tokanten, 1 Vandkunsten, at the corner of Rådhusstrade and Longangsstrade (tel. 12-73-09) a short walk from the Town Hall Square, is my favorite watering spa and eating house in all of Copenhagen. It's made so by the remarkable Bent K. Gylling, who opened Tokanten after World War II. A newspaper correspondent summed it up this way: "The lunch and dinner crowd may represent the most mixed company in all of Scandinavia, ranging from fur-faced revolutionaries to apple-cheeked, stern-faced executives, from office girls to fashion models." A look through the windows of this Left Bankish bistro-type restaurant, with its mad and wonderful mélange, is enough to draw you in. Touches of what used to be called "sophisticated bohemia" abound, including a pennyfarthing bicycle (circa 1870s) suspended in the window. The daily menu is printed on a blackboard. Meals cost from 150 kroner ($13.50) and might include salmon with dressing and a sourdough bread or else pickled herring with bread or roast beef with potato salad. You can also order a club sandwich or a hamburger steak with a salad and garlic butter. Fried camembert is served here with jam, and, to top off your meal, you might try Tokanten's famous apple pie.

Axelborg Bodega, 1 Axeltorv (tel. 11-06-38), across from the Circus and near Tivoli, is an old, well-established Danish café with outdoor tables. Order the dagens ret (daily special). Typical Danish dishes are featured, including frikadeller and bikesemad. For about 68 kroner ($6.12) you can select a two-course luncheon or dinner. A wide selection of smørrebrød is always available as well.

Skindbuksen, 4 Lille Kongensgade (tel. 12-90-37), off Kongens Nytorv, is an atmospheric landmark well known among the beer-drinkers of the city, who also know about a hot stew called lobscouse—a concoction of meat and potatoes (mainly potatoes). This popular dish frequently is sold out by noon, so plan to come early. Smørrebrød is available for 25 kroner ($2.25), and you can also order substantial meals from 85 kroner ($7.65) up. Established in 1728, the "Leather Trousers" was once a drinking cellar for coachmen.

Illums Bolighus, Amagertorv (tel. 14-19-41). Inside this department store, a showcase of Danish design, you'll find a third-floor restaurant where full meals cost from 200 kroner ($18). You can also order a full English breakfast, served between 9 and 10 a.m. daily except Sunday, costing 45 kroner ($4.05). Smørrebrød sandwiches later in the day begin at 11 kroner (99¢). Specialties include smoked leg of venison with scrambled eggs, among other tasty viands.

Grøn Mad City, 14 Linnésgade (tel. 14-29-96). The theme of the health food store in the basement of his unusual restaurant is repeated in the cuisine served upstairs. The menus are served from a long cafeteria line directed by some of the most charming and unpretentious restaurateurs in town. The fare is strictly kosher, strictly vegetarian, and strictly supervised by an articulate graduate of the Cornell Hotel School. The Jewish community provides many of the patrons, even though the owners are members of the Seventh-Day Adventist Church, who located their sunny establishment near the Israels Plads. No animal fats or cheeses are used in the food, which includes a different soup every day, simple vegetable dishes, hazelnut pâté, and vegetarian moussaka. The carrot juice is about the most delicious drink is all of Copenhagen, in my opinion. Full meals cost around 60 kroner ($5.40), although no one will object if you simply help yourself at the salad bar or the fruit salad table, priced at 24 kroner ($2.16) and 37 kroner ($3.13), according to the size of your helping. The establishment is closed on weekends. Monday through Thursday, it's open from 11:30 a.m. till 7:30 p.m. On Friday in winter, its hours are from 11:30 a.m. to 2:30 p.m., and in summer from 11:30 a.m. to 6:30 p.m.

Arne Cohn, 2 Rørholmsgade (tel. 13-30-12). If you're absolutely driven to find a kosher restaurant serving meat in Copenhagen, you can head for this hole-in-the-wall butcher's shop, where hamburgers, roast chicken, and steak filets can be eaten in a tiny side room that holds no more than three slightly chipped tables. The decor is rock-bottom basic, and the establishment is actually more interested in catering than in running a restaurant. The countermen are friendly, however, and speak English, so if you'd like, you might strike up a conversation. Cold-cut sandwiches cost around 18 kroner ($1.62) each, while platters of the foods mentioned above go for 75 kroner ($6.75) to 115 kroner ($10.35). The restaurant is open from 9:30 a.m. till 4 p.m. Monday through Thursday and from 9:30 a.m. to noon on Friday. It's closed weekends.

Café Nikolaj, 12 Nikolaj Plads (tel. 11-63-13). The dadoed, white-painted paneling of the entryway may remind you of your old Sunday School, and the soaring ceilings and broken-arch windows will give you a distinct feeling of being in church. That's no wonder, since this unusual café is located within the walls of the monument which, around 1530, was the scene of the thundering sermons of Hans Tausen, one of the fathers of the Danish Reformation. A different section of the lovely building shelters a rotating series of art exhibitions, although the real life will be found at one of the restaurant's indoor tables in the pale light of the old glass or, in summer, at one of the café tables which ring the venerable bricks of the weathered exterior. Inexpensive meals are served for around 100 kroner ($9), although if you're not hungry, someone will bring you your choice of all the standard café drinks. Its hours are erratic, so check first to see when it can be visited.

Café Restaurant Bee Cee, Pistolstraede (tel. 15-02-77). The position of this basement café on a traffic-free extension of the town's most celebrated shopping street (the Strøget) makes it seem like a quiet corner of a country village. The entrance is marked by a curved staircase lined with verdant, orange-berried plants and an iron railing. The establishment spills onto the pavement in summer. The rest of the year, you can eat and drink at marble-topped tables inside.

The café, open only from 11 a.m. to 4 p.m., serves a three-course fixed-price menu for 120 kroner ($10.80) and à la carte meals for 145 kroner ($13.05) and up. Herring salad, crab soup, and salmon prepared several different ways should be included in your meal.

Streckers Café, 3 Frederiksberggade (tel. 13-73-74). Everything is self-service in this well-known café on the Strøget, a pedestrian-only shopping street near the Town Hall. That doesn't prevent it from attracting an endless array of well-heeled shoppers, who, along with the marble tables, the bentwood chairs, and the gilded mirrors, give it an undeniable elegance. After selecting a sandwich, from 28 kroner ($2.52); a pastry, from 6.50 kroner (59¢) to 11 kroner (99¢); or a full meal, from 60 kroner ($5.40), you can proceed to one of the cushioned banquettes or, in summer, up a flight of stairs to the sun-drenched terrace. The café is open from 9 a.m. to midnight daily except Sunday, when the hours are 11 a.m. to midnight.

Restaurant Ostehjørnet, 56 St. Kongensgade (tel. 15-85-77). Although no one would discourage you from buying one of the hundreds of cheeses for sale in the downstairs section of this restaurant, the real gastronomic attraction is at the top of a short flight of steps leading from the street below. The establishment is so popular that at an average lunchtime, perhaps a dozen or so shoppers must be turned away. The secret is to show up fairly early or fairly late during the lunch hour for the Danish specialties prepared by the Swiss-trained owners, Steen and Ingelise Norrild.

The decor is a lot like that of a French café. You'll read the daily specials on a blackboard, and if you can't translate some of them, the English-speaking hosts will be glad to do it for you. I prefer, however, simply to choose from among the seafood salads, which are made fresh every morning and are good enough to have been invented in Asgård, where the old Scandinavian gods hung out. Each portion costs around 35 kroner ($3.15), and you can order as many different varieties as you want, which will be served in the exact order you requested them. The herring is superb, as are the mussel salad, the quiche Lorraine, the veal cordon bleu, the smoked turkey, the sweetbreads, or the ham and cheese omelets. Full meals begin at around 170 kroner ($15.30). To end your meal, why not try a delectable fruit tart with just a hint of chocolate?

The Foreign Colony

It may seem strange to recommend that you visit the Danish capital and dine in either a Chinese or a Japanese cafeteria. Yet for the most budget-conscious visitor to Copenhagen, the Oriental cafeterias—which serve up Western fare as well—provide the best value in food. These cafeterias—"Kinesisk" in Danish—are run by transplanted Orientals who, somehow, have mastered the Danish language (and often English, too). They often do not have a lavish decor, and they are more generous with noodles and rice than with chicken and beef, but they are not to be overlooked if you're struggling to keep costs bone-trim.

My preferred choice (based on price and value) is Cheung-Kau Fung's **Mandarin Grill,** at two locations—1 Istegade (tel. 22-52-36) and 74 Østerbrogade (tel. 26-21-92). One reader, Marvin A. Freadman of Pittsfield, Mass., put it bluntly: "I got tired of getting ripped off by the high food prices and chanced into the Mandarin Grill. Mr. Cheung-Kau Fung offers the cheapest prices for food and drinks in all of Copenhagen." Most diners patronize the Istegade address, which is near the railroad station and several of my previously recommended hotels, even though they have to pass a few porno shops on the way there. The menu is in English, and the grill stays open from 10 a.m. to 2 a.m. every day of the week. You can order a roast whole chicken. Main courses include such specialties as a beef steak dinner, with rice and salad, or chow mein. If you're snacking, sandwiches with a variety of fillings are offered. The best bargain is a main dish, with coffee or tea as well as a salad included, costing about 35 kroner ($3.15) per person. Ask about this daily special. Otherwise, count on spending from 80 kroner ($7.20) up. The moment the white-clad waiter spots you, he'll hand you a menu in English, and you haven't said a word. How does he know?

Asia Restaurant, 15 Farvergade (tel. 11-28-86), two blocks off the Rådhuspladsen, offers some of the finest, and most attractively priced, Chinese cooking in Copenhagen. Zealand bankers and Funen farmers come here for exotic treats, such as the luncheon specials (10 a.m. to 4 p.m.) that might include pork soup with vegetables, tender slices of beef immersed in Chinese vegetables —most filling. In the evening (till 11 p.m.), a larger dinner is served. It might begin with noodle soup with fresh vegetables floating in it, followed by an eggroll, then a choice of a main dish, Chinese tea, and fortune cookie. Full meals cost from 160 kroner ($14.40). Piped music in the background is to be expected, but Chinese women speaking Danish . . . ?

Ristorante Italiano, 2 Fiolstraede (tel. 11-12-95). I've given the phone number for this establishment, but the owner assures me that there is no need to phone. He claims his staff is far too busy to answer the phone. However, he says that you are almost assured of a seat—"possibly on an empty beer crate or somebody else's lap." As you may have gathered, this is a fun and amusing restaurant. It's patronized mainly by students from the nearby University of Copenhagen. Pizzas (Danish-Italian style) are featured, and, of course, the chef makes lots of spaghetti every night. Draft beer is only 18 kroner ($1.62), but you can also order the more expensive wine. You get a filling meal for about 90 kroner ($8.10). Hours are from 11 a.m. to 2 p.m.

Pizzeria Napoli, 63–65 Købmagergade (tel. 12-56-24), off Kultorvet in the students' quarter, is a Mediterranean-style trattoria built behind a huge stone arch that looks as if it served at one time as a carriage house. If funds are low, you can order one of eight kinds of pizza or spaghetti in tomato sauce. Otherwise, Italian meals, from minestrone to lasagne, go for around 75 kroner ($6.75). Tablecloths are appropriately red-and-white-checked, and candles cast a warm glow.

Restaurant Bali, 4 Lille Kongensgade (tel. 11-08-08), stands at the corner of Kongens Nytorv, just opposite the Royal Theater. It is open from noon to 1 a.m., serving an original Indonesian rijsttafel (literally "rice table") at a cost of 95 kroner ($8.55). The banquet features a dozen different meat and vegetable dishes, including seasoned meatballs with toasted coconut and grilled meat on a stick with soya-and-peanut sauce. You can make your rice table as spicy as you want; some prefer it with seasoned red pepper. At least that's another excuse to order a mellow-tasting Danish beer. The place is decorated with Indonesian artifacts. Hours are noon to midnight daily; however, the kitchen shuts down at 11:30 p.m.

La Tour, 3 Jarmers Plads (tel. 13-00-01), in the Park Hotel, is one of the two leading Lebanese restaurants in town. It's open from 11 a.m. to 11 p.m. But it's recommended mainly for its impressive buffet, which is served daily from 5 p.m. at a cost of 130 kroner ($11.70). The buffet also includes dessert and fruit. You get good value here, lots of well-prepared food, and friendly service. You can also rub elbows with the expatriate Arab colony of Copenhagen. The restaurant features Lebanese specialties served with pita bread, and these are likely to include shish kebab along with marinated grilled beef and lamb with Oriental spices.

Papa's, 15 Kultorvet (tel. 15-09-84), is probably the best, and it's definitely the most colorful, of the moderately priced foreign restaurants of Copenhagen. Standing on a pleasant, tree-lined square near the Nørreport station, the restaurant is a self-contained world of intricately spaced dining areas on at least three different levels, including two courtyards open to the summer air. The premises begin at a darkly stained bar area, which is the only section owned outright by the hardworking English/Danish proprietor, Mike Holm, who rents the rest of the premises from no fewer than five landlords. Each owns part of a separate house, the oldest of which dates from the 1880s. They all combine to form a restaurant loaded with richly decorated crannies, nooks, and cubbyholes.

My favorite corner is near a converted forge, where a mammoth bellows hangs idly above the red-and-white-covered tables. Be careful not to slip in the winding passages, whose decor evokes the homelands of the chefs, usually Italian; the waiters, usually Spanish; and the customers, who seek this place out when they come from all over Denmark. Full meals range from 180 kroner ($16.20) and could include pizzas, spaghetti dishes, minestrone, paella, scaloppine marsala, and cappuccino with cognac. If you just want a drink at the carved standup bar near the entrance, a beer, priced at from 16 kroner ($1.44) to 18 kroner ($1.62), will be served by the articulate and miltilingual barman, Rafael Ordoñéz. Although the kitchen closes at midnight, the restaurant is open every day from 11 a.m. to 2 a.m.

Restaurant Sukiyaki, 4 Colbjørnsensgade (tel. 24-98-33), is a Japanese restaurant in the basement of the Hotel Excelsior. Amid a decor of bamboo and exposed wood, it welcomes members of the Japanese Embassy staff, the local staff of Japanese Airlines, and visiting tourists for a set meal which offers good healthy value at 170 kroner ($15.30) per person. The restaurant is open daily for both lunch and dinner, except Saturday and Sunday when it's open only for dinner.

RESTAURANTS AT NYHAVN (BUDGET TO SPLURGE): Café Charlottenborg, 2
Nyhavn (tel. 13-11-58), sits on the Nyhavn Canal in the inner recesses of the School of Art and Architecture, behind a stately courtyard dotted with futuristic sculpture. The decor of the café is as avant garde as the exterior of the place is neoclassic. With its stark white walls, extremely high ceilings, and heat and drainage pipes as sculpture, the place looks almost like a piece of minimalist architecture which members of the student body might have worked up as a class project. The customers usually come from the art lovers' community of Copenhagen, while the English-speaking waitresses are as charming and informative as anyone in town. The establishment is open from 10 a.m. to 5 p.m. only during those times when there's an actual exhibition at the art school in progress, which means most of the time. Hot meals, costing from 100 kroner ($9), are served from 11:30 a.m. to 3:30 p.m., and excellent salads and sandwiches are available during the rest of the open hours. Lunch planners include venison ragoût with potatoes, smoked haunch of venison, frikadeller, and dessert pears in red wine with berries.

Mary Rose, 41 Nyhavn (tel. 12-71-41). As recently as 1981, the building housing this courteous and trendy restaurant contained one of the toughest bars in town. Today, you'll step past a glass vestibule into a warmly decorated room where the massive ceiling beams have been painted mariner's gray and the candlelit tablecloths are an attractive shade of maroon. Leif Evensen, the owner, is a former sailor who used to be a customer of the bar that was here. By many accounts, he was a pioneer of the real-estate change that swept over Nyhavn. Today, he directs a battalion of vested waiters who navigate among the lithographs, plants, and spotlights, delivering the well-prepared specialties to the well-dressed diners. A 210-krone ($18.90) fixed-price meal might include a soufflé of coalfish with salmon mousse, cutlet of venison chasseur with mandarin salad, and figs flamed in Pernod for dessert. À la carte meals are slightly more expensive. The restaurant welcomes visitors from 11 a.m. till midnight every day of the week.

Restaurant Gilleleje, 10 Nyhavn (tel. 12-58-58). Many years ago, *Gilleleje* was the name of a boat which moved potatoes from northern Zealand to a spot near No. 10 Nyhavn. Rumor says that there was an illegal—and notorious—

floating tavern aboard the boat, which created a minor legend in the sailors' repertoire of the time. Today, the considerably more respectable restaurant which bears the name and some of the fittings of the old boat sits on the Nyhavn Canal just as its namesake once did. The decor is one of the most attractive in the entire city, the kind of place guaranteed to make even a landlubber feel nautical. Among the well-oiled hardwoods and brass fittings of the interior are tabletops crafted from inlaid remnants of a boat which sank in the early 19th century.

Many clients come for the elaborate rijstafel (rice table), which offers well-flavored rice with an endless procession of meats, fish, spices, garnishes, and sauces, all with touches of curry. A full meal of rijstafel might take as long as two hours to consume. If you have the time to enjoy it, you can let it evoke thoughts of the Danish sailors wending (and wenching) their way to the Orient in the candlelit hold of a smoke-stained ship. The meal costs 225 kroner ($20.25) per person, although if you prefer, you can compose your own fixed-price meal from 270 kroner ($24.30) from the wide range of à la carte offerings on the menu. Specialties include a whisky steak flambé with grilled tomatoes, excellent fish soup, a Danish herring platter, huge portions of the captain's hash, and desserts such as papaya and passion-fruit sorbets. The restaurant is open from 11 a.m. till 3 p.m. and from 5 till 11 p.m.

THE SPLURGE RESTAURANTS: Restaurant Parnas, 16 Lille Kongensgade (tel. 11-48-10), offers a pleasant ambience where the dark interior sets off the vividly unusual paintings. It's really a perfect restaurant to escape into from a cold night outside, especially since each of the closely arranged tables has a welcoming candle, and since many of the well-dressed and seemingly successful smart set of town appear to congregate here. From noon until 5 p.m., a Parnas *platte* is served, which includes smoked salmon, roast beef, fish filet, and cheese. The other menu items are offered at both lunch and dinner, among them a savory and richly flavored hot pot concocted of sirloin medallions, roast vegetables, mushrooms, and bacon. This is accompanied by béarnaise sauce and pommes frites. If you prefer a simpler main course, you might enjoy the French onion or the turtle soup with sherry, followed by wienerschnitzel. The cheapest meal begins at around 210 kroner ($18.90). Your dinner will be accompanied by live music from an enthusiastic piano player illuminated with a single, dramatic spotlight. The restaurant is open from 11 a.m. to 2 p.m.

Ida Davidsen, 70 St. Kongensgade (tel. 11-36-55). Ida Davidsen, whose trademark is a friendly smile accompanied by a forthright manner and a chef's hat, is something of a legend throughout Copenhagen. Her father was acclaimed for selling what were said to be the best open-faced sandwiches in Denmark, and Ida today maintains a well-deserved place as the fourth generation of her family to direct a business established in 1888.

The ground-floor restaurant is identified by a wooden board painted with a chef's hat hanging in front of the dark-green façade's big windows. You step into an intimately lit restaurant where Ida herself might happen to be behind the glass smørrebrød case. If you don't want sandwiches, hot food is available. Specialties are crab or crayfish soup with cognac, pastrami with sauerkraut, crab salad, and a splendid smoked roast duckling served with pink salad (the ingredients are beets and endive, among other items) and horseradish.

A full dinner might cost around 180 kroner ($16.20), although many lunchtime visitors consider the open-faced sandwiches to be the real reason for coming here. The list is endless. A preferred choice is the Hans Christian Andersen (with liverpaste, bacon, tomatoes, horseradish, and jellied consommé), but you might like a highly unusual (and very expensive) one loaded with tiny Norwegian shrimp meticulously peeled and seasoned. Sandwiches range in price from 20 kroner ($1.80) to 115 kroner ($10.35).

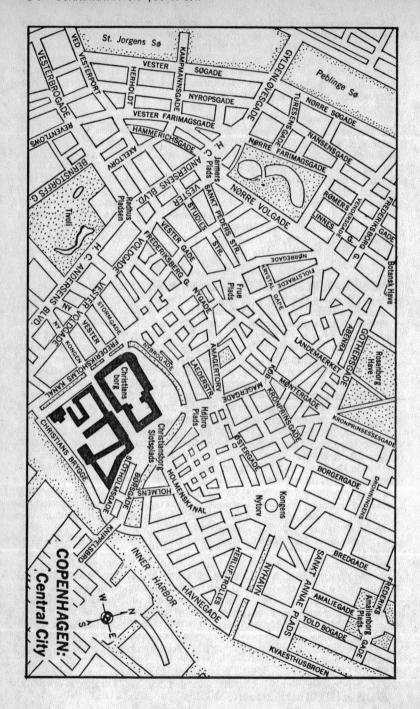

COPENHAGEN: Central City

Heering, 19–25 Pilestraede (tel. 15-22-40). The decor here is as red as the cherry liqueur which gives the place its name. The owner, who's a member of the distiller's family, has made further use of the fact by painting the walls a difficult-to-identify shade of red. Perhaps the suggestion of sitting inside what looks like the center of a well-ripened cherry helps to promote the sales of the Danish national liqueur. Games and laughter seem to be in order in what was definitely established as a fun restaurant.

The cucumber soup is a pleasant (and relieving) color contrast and might precede other specialties such as pâté of sweetbreads, filet of lemon sole stuffed with salmon, roast chicken with flap mushrooms, smoked salmon and spinach in puff pastry, salted duck, and steak of wild boar. Meals, which cost around 145 kroner ($13.05) for a three-course menu and around 125 kroner ($11.25) for a two-course lunch or dinner, are served from noon to 2:30 p.m. and from 5:30 to 9:30 p.m.

If you don't want a full meal, there's a café section to the right as you enter, where, naturally, Cherry Heering in several different combinations is a specialty.

Den Gyldne Fortun, 18 Ved Stranden (tel. 12-20-11), is extremely popular at lunchtime, a real "golden fortune," as the name translates, for those who stumble on it. The attractive stone building at the edge of a canal dates from 1796. In another era, it attracted such celebrated people as Jenny Lind and Hans Christian Andersen, when it was known as the Hotel Royal. Nowadays, the kolde bord at lunchtime is likely to draw a crowd from many of the business centers of Copenhagen.

You climb a wide flight of green marble stairs after entering from the street and find yourself in a surprisingly formal ambience a lot like an English club. Amid crystal chandeliers and modern lithographs, you'll enjoy a smörgåsbord of meats and fish served every weekday about 11:30 a.m. to 3 p.m. It represents good value at 180 kroner ($16.20) per person, drinks not included. At night and during all of July, the establishment is usually reserved for private gatherings or is closed altogether.

However, if you're in the neighborhood after dark, another restaurant under the same management is in the same building, in the basement. Reachable through a door set into the corner is **Fiskekaelderen,** 18 Ved Stranden (tel. 12-20-11), a warmly decorated restaurant specializing in seafood fresh from the icy waters around Greenland and Denmark. The decor includes a generous use of dark paneling, fish nets dangling from a dimly lit ceiling, terra-cotta floors, immaculate napery, and, at the entrance, a large ice tray filled with live lobsters and a wide range of seafood.

Your candlelit meal might consist of mussels poached in white wine, a variety of Danish herring, pine-smoked Danish salmon, poached trout in sauterne sauce, or a Scandinavian bouillabaisse for two. On the blackboards, you'll find the specialties of the day or of the season listed. Fiskekaelderen is open noon to midnight every day except Sunday, when its hours are from 5 to 11 p.m. It's closed holidays. A lunch menu is offered for a fixed price of around 100 kroner ($9) for a two-course meal, 125 kroner ($11.25) for three courses. In the evening, however, you can spend a minimum of around 300 kroner ($27) and up for an à la carte menu.

TIVOLI RESTAURANTS: A headwaiter who has worked at four different restaurants in Tivoli—and knows it well—estimates that food prices inside the pleasure garden are 30% more expensive than those outside the fantasy land. (Major reason: Restaurants, rented as concessions, have to pay back a goodly percentage of the meal price to their landlords.) Therefore, those on the strictest of budgets may want to eat outside.

Tip: A cost-cutting suggestion is to dine at one of the regular restaurants, skipping the dessert, then to pick up a less expensive sweet treat at one of the numerous stands in Tivoli. How about an oversize sugar cone, stacked high with vanilla ice cream and a blob of raspberry preserves (in the middle is a chocolate-covered marshmallow), and crowned by a cloud of whipped cream?

The Best for the Budget

Grøften (tel. 12-11-25), for my purposes and taste, is the best economy restaurant in Tivoli, offering a tourist meal in an attractive setting (lit by a festoon of colored light bulbs). It's just next to the Peacock Theater (where pantomime and ballet are presented). Most diners eat outside under leafy linden trees and a crescent-shaped, log pergola (some privacy is provided by ivy screens). The daily special could be a cup of bright-red tomato soup accompanied by hunks of crisp yet moist french bread, followed by a plate of tender ground beef, with such side dishes as grilled mushrooms and a separate bowl of gravy as well as tiny new potatoes. The price: 75 kroner ($6.75). In the afternoon, a three-sandwich combination is one of the most popular items: 30 kroner ($2.70). Note the polyphony of Danish voices mingled with a multitude of chirping and singing sparrows, which feed off crumbs on the table.

Faergekroen (tel. 11-65-21) is a small chalet with a wooden terrace overlooking a tiny lake. The salmon-colored inn is half timbered, and it features light hot meals, sandwiches, and beer. The inside dining room maintains its traditional characteristics. When sunny, the dining terrace is packed with the Danes, enjoying a small smörgåsbord. Another favorite dish is a kroplatte, a selection of cold cuts. A specialty is lobscouse, a meat-and-potato dish spiced with butter, bay leaf, and pepper. The fried plaice—practically the size of a plate—is also good. With a mug of beer, you'll become a Copenhagener by osmosis. Count on spending from 180 kroner ($16.20).

Divan I, Bordbestilling (tel. 11-42-42), was born the same year as the Tivoli. Ever since then Copenhageners and visitors from all over the world have enjoyed its Danish and international cuisine. From one of its tables, you have a good view of the Tivoli Gardens. The enclosed restaurant is like an indoor garden with fresh green plants. Divan I has been run by the same family for generations. You're assured of good food and service. Tables are offered both indoors and out in the garden. Meal prices range from 140 kroner ($12.50) to 250 kroner ($22.50). The restaurant is open in season only—May 1 to mid-September—from 11:30 a.m. to 10:30 p.m. However, you can visit for drinks until midnight.

Paletten (tel. 13-07-47) is a family-type beerhall and cafeteria in a garden setting opposite the Pantomime Theater. Each day, a menu special is offered. For example, on my most recent visit, I enjoyed a large order of roast pork, with a lot of vegetables, for 42 kroner ($3.78). Drinks start at 20 kroner ($1.80) for a mug of beer. There is also a selection of grilled dishes, along with open-face sandwiches. In the afternoon, many guests drop in to sample one of their cakes.

CAFÉS ALONG THE STRGØET: La Glace, 3–5 Skoubogade (tel. 14-46-46). A wise-looking portrait of the Queen of Denmark is displayed in the window of this time-honored pastry shop which, since 1870, has provided cakes and chocolates to successive generations of the reserved, affluent Danes. The decor is what you'd expect from an establishment dedicated to preserving a taste for another era. The furnishings are conservatively expensive, covered with leather accompanied by well-polished wood and scattered with flickering silver candlesticks. Lacy curtains filter the light, and it's not at all inappropriate to request a glass of sherry or cognac to go with the richly caloric and vastly tempting pastries that have given Copenhagen a reputation as one of the most fattening cities of Europe.

A pot of coffee or chocolate costs around 18 kroner ($1.62), while petit fours go for 13 kroner ($1.17) each. If you want to know what kept Søren Kierkegaard's insulin busy while he was composing his treatises, try a slice of sportsman's cake (sportskage), composed of whipped cream, crumbled nougat, macaroons, and profiteroles, which has been glazed in caramel. If chocolate is your greatest temptation, you'll appreciate how the Othellokage (meringue, whipped cream, and outrageous amounts of chocolate) got its name. The shop is open Monday to Friday from 8:30 a.m. till 5:30 p.m. and Saturday from 8:30 a.m. till 1 p.m.

Restaurant Amagertorv, 8 Amagertorv (tel. 13-71-01), is near the stork fountain off the Strøget. You proceed through an elaborately crafted wrought-iron gate and down a passage until you reach this dove-gray restaurant at the top of a solid 18th-century building, whose walls are as old as some of the pastry recipes followed by the chefs inside. The lower floors contain the showrooms for Royal Copenhagen porcelain, whose china covers the small tables inside the restaurant. You probably won't want to be seated until you survey the heavily laden pastry table, the combined total of which is an elaborate tour de force of the pastrymaker's art. Examples include almond wreaths filled with rose-hip jam and Sarah Bernhardts (macaroon cakes filled with chocolate cream and showered with candied violets). There's music by a pianist every afternoon starting at 2 p.m., which may help the customers to better enjoy their cheroots and cognac. Tea is served in the courtyard in pleasant weather. Pastries cost from 11 kroner (99¢) to 28 kroner ($2.52), and coffee goes for around 17 kroner ($1.53) a pot. The establishment welcomes clients from 10 a.m. till 5 p.m. Monday through Friday and from 10 a.m. to 1 p.m. on Saturday.

Self-Service Snacks

Paraplyen (tel. 15-16-15), perched off a colorful hidden alleyway in Tivoli, is really two restaurants in one: an inexpensive self-service cafeteria downstairs, a more expensive, but still economical, table-service establishment upstairs. After making a selection in the cafeteria, perhaps fish filet for 44 kroner ($3.96), guests take their trays onto the courtyard patio to have a view of the funtime beer hall and adjoining merry-go-round with miniature Viking ships. The Paraplyen is thus recommended to those who like to sup to the cacophony of happy screams. Upstairs, one may dine along the balcony (hanging baskets filled with summer flowers). My most recent meal consisted of the tourist middag special for 65 kroner ($5.85): two courses, including a choice of several kinds of meat or fish, plus salad and vegetables, and dessert. The name of the restaurant—French (sort of) for umbrella—comes from a decorative theme: witness the miniature parasols serving as light fixtures.

Restaurant Bixen (tel. 14-06-99) is like a smallish beer garden; guests pick up their self-service trays and take them into the courtyard, where they dine under trees. You can also order your own dinner and cook it over an open-air grill. Meals are from 90 kroner ($8.10). By night, garlands of colored lights make it festive. A typical meal is frikadeller with plenty of sauce and potatoes, or one of the daily specials offered from 4 p.m. A good smørrebrød selection is featured, many of them priced from 25 kroner ($2.25) up. Hot dogs and pizzas are also sold. It's a good place for a Carlsberg or Tuborg—or an orange soda. The Bixen is easy to find—opposite a park where motorists drive around in vintage cars.

TIME OUT FOR FOOD TIPS: For good and inexpensive on-the-run meals, Copenhagen abounds in unusually satisfying hot-dog stands, chicken and fish grills, as well as smørrebrød counters.

Don't belittle the pushcart **hot-dog stands** that dot the city, particularly in the area around the Rådhuspladsen. The hot dogs (polser) served here, which taste much better than our own variety in America, come either steamed or grilled (ristede), with a topping of crinkly toasted and shredded onion. Most of them cost only 10 kroner (90¢) and often french fries (pommes frites) may be ordered as a supplement.

The traveler's best bet is the bakery (**bageri** or **konditori**) usually found on almost every block in Copenhagen. Fresh bread, rolls, and Danish pastries (called wienerbrød—Viennese bread) . . . better and fresher than you can usually get at home.

Next, stop in at any of the small food shops—labeled **Viktualiehandler**— found throughout the city. They're the closest thing to a New York deli. Here you can buy roast beef; ask for the fried onions, løg, included free. With the fresh, soft roll you've purchased for a few pennies at the local bakery, you're set for a tasty lunch. You can also buy lunch meats such as ham and tongue at the Viktualiehandler. Best buy is the smoked fish. Ask the friendly counterman for a Bornholmer, a large, boneless sardine from the Danish island of Bornholm, usually costing 6 kroner (54¢) apiece. Want a new taste in cheese? Try the popular smoked cheese (røgost), very inexpensive.

Yogurt fans will be delighted to know that the Danish variety is cheap and tasty. It comes in small containers, five fruit flavors and plain, for only 5 kroner (45¢) in any dairy (**mejeri**). No spoon needed; just peel off the aluminum cover and drink it right out of the cup. Cottage cheese is also good and cheap, but it's only sold in Irma stores. Ask for *hytte ret,* about 5 kroner (45¢).

Want a cheap, heavy, filling dish? Try biksemad at any cafeteria or restaurant in town—a stewlike mixture of meat, potatoes, and onions; it's commonly called *bix.* In the fancier places, a fried egg rests on top.

Liver is relatively inexpensive in Denmark (ask for *stagt lever),* but if you want to live cheaply, you'll have to make it on fish and dairy products.

For fresh fruit and vegetables, try the folksy open-air **Grøn Torv** (Green Market) near Valby station. Local tomatoes in season are good buys, and carrots are usually reasonable. Buy a pound of fresh green peas and eat them straight from the pod the way the Danes do. Peaches, oranges, apples, and bananas can be purchased in large, wholesale quantities, in case you're traveling in a group.

There are quite a few new shops selling health food products. Best buy in these places is a fruit stick, wrapped in cellophane, which comes in diverse flavors—figs, dates, and rose hips *(hyben).*

5. Shopping in Copenhagen

In a country famed for its designers and craftspeople, you'll find your best buys in stainless steel, porcelain, china, glassware (the Danes have infringed on Sweden's traditional domain), toys (Kay Bojesen's wooden animals in particular; available at Den Permanente), functionally designed furniture, textiles (napkins to rugs), and jewelry (decorative, silver, semiprecious stones).

Strøget

Copenhagen is in the vanguard of shopping buys in Europe and much of that action takes place on a traffic-free pedestrian street in the heart of the capital known as Strøget. The Strøget begins on Frederiksberggade, north of the Town Hall Square, and winds like a python to Østergade, which opens onto Kongens Nytorv. This jam-packed street can be a window-shopper's dream, a buyer's heaven. It is lined with stores, everything from the tiniest of specialty shops to emporiums sagging with merchandise—a vast array of Nordic modern furniture, jewelry, porcelain, enamelware, applied art, Danish fashions. Everything is sold on the Strøget—from the porcelain statue of *Youthful Boldness* to Greenland shrimps to Kay Bojesen's teak monkeys.

Here, too, you can shop, have a drink or tea at an outdoor café, or just sit on a free bench and watch the crowds.

Two other walking areas are nearby—**Grabrødertorv** and **Fiolstraede.** You may want to browse through their antique shops and bookshops.

A SHOWCASE OF DANISH DESIGN: When does a store, featuring handmade home furnishings and accessories, become a national treasure? The answer is to be found at **Den Permanente,** in the Vesterport, within walking distance of the Central Station (tel. 12-44-88). Since it was founded in 1931, the Permanent Exhibition of Danish Arts and Crafts has become a jury-approved showcase for the best of Denmark's craftspeople. In-the-know interior decorators, magazine editors, and buyers for exclusive home furnishings make a yearly pilgrimage to this exhibition. On three floors are displayed all kinds of contemporary furniture, pottery, glassware, pieces of textiles and wood, stainless steel, as well as sculpture and etchings. Since it is a sales exhibition for about 300 people, and has a large number of works, it seems impossible for Den Permanente to issue a catalog for prospective buyers, but they have done so. The institution also has a large jewelry department and a special section for gift articles and souvenirs. It packs and forwards articles anywhere in the world.

DEPARTMENT STORES: **Magasin,** 13 Kongens Nytorv (tel. 11-44-33), is not only the biggest department store in Denmark, but one of the most elegant. Even the Queen of Denmark shops here without a bodyguard. It offers a complete assortment of Danish design in fashion, along with plenty of souvenirs to appeal to the tourist trade. Naturally, it has a large selection of glass and porcelain items for those who don't have time to go to the specialty stores. Goods are shipped abroad tax free. The main entrance to the store is opposite the Royal Theater.

Illum, 52 Østergade (tel. 14-40-02), is the other leading department store, lying on the pedestrian street, the Strøget. You are invited to browse through its vast world of Danish design. The staff is very friendly, and nearly everybody speaks English. In addition, there is a Harrods shop, along with a choice of three restaurants.

HOME FURNISHINGS: **Illums Bolighus,** Amagertorv, on Strøget (tel. 14-19-41), is Europe's finest showcase for household furnishings and accessories. A sophisticated center of modern design, it is where the host or hostess with the mostest does his or her shopping. Every nook resembles a page ripped out of *House Beautiful.* It embraces not only the fertile field of interior design, but simply any significant area of interior design. Strolling at your leisure, you can enjoy the exhibitions of unique pieces of applied art as well as the best specimens of refined industrial design. That means not only furniture and home furnishings, but lamps, rugs, textiles, bedding, glassware, kitchenware, flatware, china, fashions for both men and women, jewelry, and ceramics.

For the serious collector of high-quality furniture and antiques, **Snedkerhuset,** 4 Bredgade (tel. 12-45-55), merits a visit. Its owner, Peter Krog, is a dedicated craftsman, turning out pieces for the home that are classic in line and graceful in form. Mr. Krog is always ready to assist foreign visitors and introduce them to his showroom.

Lysberg, Hansen, & Therp, 3 Bredgade (tel. 14-47-87), is one of the great interior decorating centers of Europe, well past its 75th birthday. It has a wealth of fabrics and furniture design represented. At their showroom you're allowed to wander at leisure through lushly decorated apartments which have been furnished in impeccable taste. The company manufactures its own furniture, both in modern Danish design and in traditional reproductions. Also, try to visit their giftshop which has many hard-to-find and imaginative creations.

PORCELAIN AND GLASSWARE: Bing & Grøndahl, 4 Amagertorv (tel. 12-26-86), lies on the pedestrian street, Strøget. At this location you can choose from the world's largest collection of B & G artware, dinnerware, and gift items. Rising two stories, the building is packed with collector's items. In the heart of Copenhagen, its factory has been a center of Danish porcelain production since the early 18th century. There, artisans have turned out the world-famous porcelain figurines, vases, and trays. Every piece is made entirely by hand. B&G was the originator in 1895 of the Christmas plate, which is still produced in a limited series each year (a different motif each time). Its most popular figurine is *Youthful Boldness,* showing a boy kissing a blushing girl on the cheek. Dinnerware comes in a stunning range, everything from Venus to Falling Leaves.

A. B. Schou, 1 Ny Østergade (tel. 13-80-95), displays both Royal Copenhagen works as well as those of Bing & Grøndahl. In addition it also features Waterford crystal, porcelain from the Porsgrund factory in Norway, Lalique from Paris, Orrefors from Sweden, Lladró from Spain, and Wedgwood from England. If you like to compare-shop among famous competitors, then this is the place. The exhibition of collector's plates is the largest in Scandinavia. To save money, you can order Royal Copenhagen and Bing & Grøndahl seconds. These figurines have only small variations in colors, or almost-invisible-spots which prevent them from being sold as first quality. But the price is 20% less.

Holmegaards Glasvaerker, 15 Østergade (tel. 12-44-77), is the only major producer of glasswork in Denmark. Its Wellington pattern, for example, was created in 1859 and is now available once again. It's sturdy, yet gracefully elegant. The Holmegaard glasses are hand-blown and handmade, designed by well-known artisans. The toddy glasses are designed for warm drinks on cold days. Its Regiment Bar set reflects solid craftsmanship, and the ring around the glass enables it to rest easily in the imbiber's hand. It is said in Denmark that a Holmegaard glass is more than just something to drink from.

Bjørn Wiinblads Hus, 11 Ny Østergade (tel. 15-12-45), is a name known all over Europe for its fine porcelain bowls and plates. But the establishment is, in effect, a showcase for Wiinblads creations, ranging from posters to greeting cards.

Royal Copenhagen Porcelain, 6 Amagertorv (tel. 13-71-81), was founded in 1775. Its trademark, three blue wavy lines, has come to symbolize quality in porcelain throughout the world. For a century the factory was in royal possession before passing into private hands in 1868. For decades the factory has enjoyed a reputation for its designs in underglaze decoration. Royal Copenhagen's Christmas plates are in great demand as collector's items. The factory has turned out a new plate each year since 1908, most of the motifs depicting the Danish countryside in winter. On the top floor is a *huge* selection of seconds, and unless you're an expert, you won't know many of them are seconds.

Frøsig, 9 Nørrebrogade (tel. 39-90-00), is a specialist in Danish porcelain, and has been since 1889. It has one of the largest selections of Royal Copenhagen and Bing & Grøndahl. The store sells both first and second gradings in figures and art pieces. It often requires an expert to distinguish slightly imperfect creations from the "perfect" pieces of porcelain. The shop also has a large collection of glassware and crystal. Goods are sent with a guarantee against breakage. Buses 5 and 7 go there.

SILVER: The most regal silversmith in Copenhagen is the legendary **Georg Jensen,** 40 Østergade (tel. 11-40-80). Denmark, of course, is known for its fine silver, and Georg Jensen is the best place at which to buy it. It is probably the only store where a customer can have delivered immediately all the place settings in current patterns. For the connoisseur, there is no better address, for what they display is the biggest and best collection of Jensen hollowware in Europe. The jewelry, in gold and silver, comes in both traditional and modern Danish design. Tables are laid with many celebrated patterns in stainless steel and sterling silver. Many silver objects are the work of more contemporary Jensen designers, both male and female, who continue to win international awards. They have also opened a department specializing in old Georg Jensen pieces with old hallmarks—in other words, Georg Jensen secondhand pieces of special interest.

Less expensive, **Hans Hansen Silver,** 16 Amagertorv (tel. 15-60-67), lies on the Strøget. One of the best silver shops in the country, it has been run by the same family for several generations. A high level of craftsmanship is reflected in the pieces of contemporary silver on sale. You are faced with an array of sterling-silver rings, hollowware, cigarette boxes, whatever. Some items are made of rosewood and inlaid with sterling silver.

NEEDLEWORK: **Eva Rosenstand** sells Danish-designed cross-stitch embroideries in several locations in Copenhagen, including 23 Frederiksberggade (tel. 13-64-41), 42 Østergade (tel. 13-29-40), and 111 Amagerbrogade (tel. 58-48-87). The material is usually linen in medium or coarser grades, but pure wool and cotton materials are also used. The yarns employed are mainly embroidery cottons, and pure wool.

HAND-KNITS: **Sweater Market,** 15 Frederiksberggade (tel. 15-27-73), will stock your supply of cardigans, pullovers, hats, scarves, and mittens, hand-knitted in Denmark of 100% wool. There is also a large selection of Icelandic jackets and coats in stock, made from Icelandic natural wool. A catalog will be sent on request.

ANTIQUE PRINTS: If you're interested in the treasure of print, such as engravings and woodcuts, the best place in Copenhagen for this type of merchandise is **Sjaeldne Boger Antikvariat,** 10 Bredgade (tel. 15-91-87). The shop, which also sells maps and rare books, was founded in 1900.

PEWTER: **Tin-Centret/The Pewter Centre,** 2 Ny Østergade (by-street to Østergade, just behind the Hôtel d'Angleterre; tel. 14-82-00), will welcome you to its showrooms, where you will find Scandinavia's largest collection of beautiful handmade pewter.

MODEL THEATERS: To many adults, the model theater is a hobby and to children an imaginative toy. Once, such small fry as Hans Christian Andersen were attracted to this type of toy theater which had spread rapidly in Denmark during his boyhood. **Priors Dukke Teatre,** 52 Købmagergade (tel. 15-15-79), keeps alive the tradition of the model theater which came into existence in England around 1800. Lithograph-printed sheets painted by artists and stage-painters are for sale. This second-floor shop also sells marionettes and puppets.

FABRICS: **Gera Stoffer,** 36–38 Østergade (tel. 15-33-62), is a treasurehouse unmatched in Scandinavia for the quality, beauty, and excellence of its haute-couture fabrics. Fashion-conscious visitors—both men and women—will seek it out.

The challenger is **Per Reumert,** 33 Amagertorv (tel. 15-30-36), where John Frandsen will show you the marvelous woven wares found at this establishment.

CLOTHING: **Brødrene Andersen,** 7–9 Østergade (tel. 15-15-77), is one of the finest clothing stores in Denmark. A distinguished purveyor of "personal furnishings for gentlemen" (and increasingly for women, too), it has an atmosphere of quiet dignity. An unshakable status symbol in Denmark, it is well stocked with attractively designed and well-made clothing which has used very fine fabrics. Pleasantly displayed are items of haberdashery and all sorts of accessories for the male sophisticate who wants to have that continental flair.

ART GALLERIES: **Galerie Asbaek,** 8–10 Ny Adelgade (tel. 15-40-04), is the most sophisticated art gallery in Copenhagen. In their new location, Mr. and Mrs. Asbaek have taken over two marvelously restored old houses. One is situated on the site of the first theater in Copenhagen. There is not only a permanent exhibition of the best artists in Denmark today, but changing exhibitions of Scandinavian and foreign artists. Graphics and posters are offered for sale as well. In addition to the gallery, there is also a bookshop, along with a video room and restaurant. Mr. and Mrs. Asbaek have put a lot of imagination, work, and energy into creating the place, and they've made something special out of it. From Monday to Friday, the hours are 11 a.m. to 6 p.m., on Saturday from 11 a.m. to 4 p.m.; closed Sunday.

Galerie Birch, 25 Admiralgade (tel. 13-16-16), presents a foremost collection, catering to serious collectors. Whether the art that is shown here appeals to you or not, you'll find the competence of the painters beyond dispute.

Court Gallery, 24 Østergade (tel. 11-20-50), is a showcase of contemporary art, and it usually holds summer exhibits of its graphics, oils, acrylics, sculpture, gouache, watercolors, and drawings. Its owner, Sam Kaner, is an American. It is open Tuesday through Friday from 10 a.m. to 5:30 p.m.; Saturday from 10 a.m. to 3 p.m.; closed Sunday and Monday. Admission is free.

ART AUCTION HOUSES: **Arne Bruun Rasmussen,** 33 Bredgade (tel. 13-69-11), is an auctioneer of fine art. It doesn't usually have activities in July, preferring to begin its new season in August with an auction of paintings and fine works of art. Viewing time is allowed before the auction. On recent occasions, auctions have been devoted to modern art or else coins and medals, perhaps books and manuscripts.

Another recommendable auction house is **Kunsthallens Kunstauktioner,** 11 Købmagergade (tel. 13-85-69). It closes during the whole month of July.

PIPES: The **House of Pipe Dan,** 13 Vestergade (tel. 12-31-32), lies just off the Town Hall Square, beside Strøget. It was founded during the darkest days of World War II (1943), and its present director is I. Dan Christensen. The patroness of the shop is the Queen of Denmark. The selection on view here is enormous, including pipes by some of the new Danish designers. Pipe Dan will even give you a long list of pipe hints. Pipes come in many shapes and sizes, with names ranging from bulldog to chimney.

A SHOP IN NYHAVN: Vari-Art, 12 Nyhavn (tel. 12-07-84), offers an intriguing blend of antiques with hypermodern household accessories destined for a fashion plate. I liked best the array of old cast-iron stoves (which can be shipped) and the odds and ends that might not have been considered worth saving only a decade ago.

Chapter III

COPENHAGEN: WHAT TO SEE AND DO

1. The Major Attractions
2. Copenhagen After Dark
3. Louisiana
4. Elsinore (Helsingør)
5. Fredensborg Palace
6. Frederiksborg Castle
7. Dragør
8. Roskilde
9. Køge

IN SIGHTS AND NIGHTLIFE, perennially youthful Copenhagen is an Open Sesame to the charm of the past, the magic of the present, the promise of the future.

For all of the tourist propaganda emphasis on "life-seeing," amusement parks, shopping expeditions, beer-drinking cellars and gardens, and bustling nighttime spots, Copenhagen is also proud of its vast storehouse of antiquities, holding its own with the other capitals of Europe.

The "fun, fun" slogans and the "wonderful, wonderful" Copenhagen melodies tend to detract from this important fact: that the Danish capital is an excellent center not only for pleasure seekers, but for the serious visitor who wants to inspect art galleries, museums, and castles.

In the morning, museum trotters can wander back to the classical or Renaissance days in such showcases of art as Thorvaldsen's Museum. He and she can stroll down corridors, brushing the dust off such diverse sculptured creatures as Cupid driving two wild boars, a she-wolf, even Apollo Belvedere.

Then in the afternoon, they can head north of the city, along the so-called Danish Riviera, to Louisiana. Here, at this museum of Danish art, they can see a successful wedding of nature and architecture—one of the high points of modern Scandinavian architecture, a blazing look at the promise of the future. Incidentally, there's an ever-changing exhibit of modern art (on one occasion, a fully explosive outdoor sculpture, *The End of the World*) for those who don't wax enthusiastic over what one architect described as "black impregnated pillars . . . glued laminated girders."

On a summer evening, our imaginary visitors can stroll through the Tivoli pleasure gardens, which seem to have emerged intact from the days when the world was young . . . and so were we. Apparently, the Danes loved childhood too much to abandon it forever, no matter how old they got—so Tivoli keeps alive the magic of fairy-lights and the wonder of yesteryear.

One marvelous aspect of the Danish capital is that it has so many little hidden nooks of charm awaiting explorers. But to speed up the process for those who constantly have to face the harassment of time, I've covered the major sights.

In addition, the important attractions on the island of Zealand—by far not limited to "Hamlet's Castle"—are also surveyed, including one-day trips to the white chalky cliffs, the glacial deposits on the island of Møn, a geologist's field trip.

1. The Major Attractions

THE TOP TEN: From the standpoint of today's traveler, there's almost too much to see in Copenhagen. So, for those who have to be back at the office next Tuesday—or who have reservations in Paris next Friday—I've whittled the list down to ten.

(1) Tivoli Gardens

In 1843, on 20 acres of garden in the center of Copenhagen, a flower-filled world was created for the young at heart—be they toddlers or totterers with canes. It was an instant success, and has remained so ever since. Problems fade away within Tivoli's gates, as a visitor claps hands with Peter Pan . . . and believe again. In this amusement world everything has been done to make time fly over the rainbow.

Within the park grounds, funtime concessions flourish—but they are different (riders on a merry-go-round sail in a tiny fleet of Viking ships instead of on horses). Many concession are devoted to games of chance and skill (pin-table arcades, slot machines, shooting galleries), and a ferris wheel has *Around the World in 80 Days*-type balloons with cabin seats.

A playground for children is a veritable Rube Goldberg of modern design; and, in contrast, an overblown birthday cake—an Arabian-looking fantasy palace with towers and arches and strings of gaily colored lights—houses restaurants and dancing areas.

Interspersed among all this are more than two dozen different restaurants (in all price ranges), from a lakeside inn to a beer garden (see my restaurant recommendations in the preceding chapter). During the day all is laughter, brightness, and color. One of the pleasant diversions is to walk around the edge of the tiny lake with its ducks, swans, and boats.

The red-uniformed, busby-topped Tivoli Boys Guard, one of the traditional features of the amusement park, parades on weekends at 6:30 and at 8:30 p.m., and their regimental band gives concerts at 3:30 p.m. on Saturday on the open-air stage. The oldest building at Tivoli, the Chinese-style Pantomime Theater, with its peacock curtain, stages not only pantomimes but ballets in the evening.

For a closer and more specific look at all the nighttime offerings of Tivoli—fireworks displays, brass bands, orchestras, discos, variety acts—refer to the nightlife section below.

Tivoli is open from 10 a.m. until midnight from May 1 till a Sunday in mid-September; entrance fee, 16 kroner ($1.44) for adults, half price for children. Inside each of the entrances are large maps, outlining the plan of Tivoli. First-time visitors should simply ignore these diagrams—in other words, get lost in a fantasy world that has the realism of a Walt Disney miracle, but the spirit of a Hans Christian Andersen fairytale.

(2) The Royal Museum of Fine Arts

The huge state art museum, the **Statens Museum for Kunst,** Sølvgade (tel. 11-21-26), shelters the greatest collection ever assembled of Danish art, plus a representative selection of the old masters from other lands, including Rubens, Rembrandt, Cranach, Tintoretto, Mantegna, Titian, Hogarth, and the engravings of Albrecht Dürer. Donated to the museum were modern works by Braque, Matisse, and Picasso. The museum is open daily except Monday from 10 a.m. to 5 p.m., charging no admission.

The **Hirschsprung Collection (Den Hirschsprungske Samling)** displays Danish art from the 19th and the beginning of the 20th centuries. The rooms have furnishings from the homes of the artists, often designed by them. It is open every day from 1 to 4 p.m. (from October 1 to April 30, on Wednesday, also 7 to 10 p.m.); closed Monday and Tuesday. The address is 20 Stockholmsgade (tel. 42-03-36).

(3) Rosenborg Castle

This red-brick, Renaissance-style castle, founded by Christian IV in the 17th century, is the home of the "souvenirs" of the Danish royal family (everything from narwhal-tusked and ivory coronation chairs to Frederik VII's baby shoes). Officially, its biggest drawing card is the dazzling array of crown jewels and regalia in the Treasury in the basement, where also is shown in lavishly decorated coronation saddle from 1596, gleaming with gold and pearls—enough sparkle to burn the eyes of the most jaded of the sapphire-and-diamond viewers. Try to see the Knights Hall (room 21), with its coronation seat, three silver lions, and relics from the 1700s. One ofthe Rosenborg's most important attractions is the room (no. 3) used by founding father Christian IV (lucky in love, unlucky in war), who died in this bedroom with its Oriental lacquer art and stucco ceiling. Disillusioned, he was surrounded by sycophants, including nasty-tempered noblemen and bickering sons-in-law.

The slot (castle or palace) is at 4A Østervoldgade (take bus 14 or 16 from Town Hall Square). The King's Garden (Have) surrounds the castle, and the **Botanical Gardens** (many a rare plant) are across the street. Rosenborg is open from May 1 to May 31 and September 1 to October 20 from 11 a.m. to 3 p.m. daily; June 1 to August 31 from 10 a.m. to 3 p.m. daily; and October 21 to April 30 from 11 a.m. to 1 p.m. Tuesday and Friday, 11 a.m. to 2 p.m. Saturday. Admission is 18 kroner ($1.62). The Botanical Gardens are open daily from 8:30 a.m. to sunset (latest, 7:30 p.m.) and the hothouses daily from 10 a.m. to 3 p.m.

(4) Christiansborg Palace

Christiansborg Slot (Palace), Christiansborg Slotsplads (tel. 14-90-81), on the Slotsholmen—a small island that for more than 800 years has been the center of political power in Denmark—is a granite-masked, copper-sheathed palace housing the Danish parliament, the Supreme Court, the prime minister's department, and the Royal Reception Rooms, where the queen entertains her guests officially. The reception rooms are open to the public. Conducted tours in English leave at noon, 2 p.m., and 4 p.m., daily except Monday in June, July, and August. From September to June, the guided tour in English is given at 2 p.m. daily except Monday and Saturday. The entrance fee is 15 kroner ($1.35) for adults, 6 kroner (54¢) for children. The guide will conduct you through richly decorated rooms, including the Throne Room, the banqueting hall, and the

Queen's Library. Before entering the rooms, you will be asked to wear soft overshoes to protect the floors and to help polish them.

Under the palace—the entrance is beneath the tower—you will find well-preserved 12th-century ruins of **Bishop Absalon's Castle** (he was a famous Danish statesman and founder of Copenhagen) and of the old **Copenhagen Palace.** The history of these palaces as well as the history of the first, second, and present Christiansborg Palaces is told in the exhibition attached to the ruins. The ruins are open from 10 a.m. to 4 p.m. daily in June, July, and August; daily except Saturday from September to June. Admission is 7 kroner (63¢) for adults, 3 kroner (27¢) for children.

(5) Ny Carlsberg Glyptothek

The Glyptothek, on Dantes Plads (tel. 12-10-65), near the Tivoli, is one of the most important art museums in Scandinavia, chock full of modern paintings and French sculpture, as well as galleries rich in ancient art. The museum was founded by an extraordinary collector of art in the 19th century, Carl Jacobsen, Mr. Carlsberg himself. The Glyptothek until World War II was maintained by the revenue from the beer guzzled by the sailors of Nyhavn or by family men at the Tivoli, but today it is mainly run by the municipality and the state. Its Egyptian collection, on the ground floor, is particularly outstanding, ranging from the days of the pyramid builders to twilight time for Celopatra. Its most notable prize is a prehistoric hippopotamus. In addition, some of the finest Greek originals (headless Apollo, Niobe's tragic children), and Roman copies of original Greek bronzes (fourth-century Hercules) are displayed. Some of the noblest heads of Rome are here, too—men such as Pompey, Virgil, Augustus, Trajan. A favorite of mine is the display of Etruscan art (heads from sarcophagi, a winged lion, bronzes, pottery). Upstairs are several masterpieces of the French impressionists: highlights include works by Manet *(The Absinthe Drinker),* Monet (of water-lily fame), Degas (back with his ballet dancers and bathers), and Renoir (young girls and bathing boys). The son of the founder presented some important Gauguins. About 25 of his works appear here, as well as Cézanne's famous *Portrait of the Artist.*

Finally, French sculpture gives the Glyptothek added fame—particularly the fine works of Rodin, such as *The Citizens of Calais* and the Degas bronze set. The hours to visit, from May 1 to August 31 are 10 a.m. to 4 p.m.; September through April, the hours are from noon to 3 p.m. weekdays, 10 a.m. to 4 .m. on Sunday. Admission is 15 kroner ($1.35), but free on Sunday and Wednesday. Closed Monday.

(6) National Museum

This storehouse of treasures, self-billed as one of the oldest and largest in the world, is a gigantic repository of the cultural development of people down through the ages. The **Nationalmuseet** is at 12 Frederiksholms Kanal (tel. 13-44-11), opposite Christiansborg Palace (separate entrance; 10 Ny Vestergade). Primarily, it is divided into four departments, and the first-time visitor may want to concentrate on the Danish collections that date back to Stone Age times and leap forward to the present. Viking stones and helmets, fragments of battle gear left by these mightly warriors, and other remains are displayed. Don't miss seeing a "lur" horn, a Bronze Age musical instrument, among the most ancient of Europe. An elegant piece of pagan art, a Bronze Age "Sun Chariot," is world famous. Many ecclesiastical collections are featured, especially the 12th-century Lisbjerg Altar, a blending of pagan and Christian styles. The museum also houses the royal collections of medals and coins, and treasures that were imported to fill the Department of Egyptian, Asiatic (Western), Greek, and Roman Antiquities. See the third-century Gundestrup silver caldron, and the

Roman Hoby Cups, depicting Homeric legends. Finally, for specialized interest, there is the Ethnographical Department, with its relics of the Eskimo culture and that of Greenland. The admission-free museum is open from June 16 to September 15 from 10 a.m. to 4 p.m. (all galleries shut down on Monday); otherwise, from 11 a.m. to 3 p.m. weekdays, noon to 4 p.m. on Saturday and Sunday. Guided tours are conducted by 2 p.m. on Sunday.

(7) Thorvaldsen's Museum

This restrained yet decorated museum at 2 Porthusgade (tel. 12-15-32), on Slotsholmen next door to Christiansborg, houses the greatest collection of the works of Bertel Thorvaldsen (1770–1844), the most significant name in neoclassical sculpture. Thorvaldsen's life represented the romanticism of the 18th and 19th centuries: he rose from semipoverty to the pinnacle of success in his day. The sculptor is famous for his most typical, classically restrained works, taken from mythology: Cupid and Psyche, Adonis, Jason, Hercules, Ganymede, Mercury—all of which are displayed at the museum. In addition to the works of this latter-day exponent of Roman classicism, the museum also contains Thorvaldsen's personal, and quite extensive, collection, everything from the Egyptian relics of Ptolemy to the contemporary paintings he acquired during his lifetime (e.g., *Apollo Among the Thessalian Shepherds*). After many years of exile in Italy, Thorvaldsen returned in triumph to his native Copenhagen, where he died a national figure in 1844, and was buried in the courtyard of his own personal museum. The museum is open from May 2 to September 30 from 10 a.m. to 4 p.m.; October 1 to April 30 from 10 a.m. to 3 p.m. It is closed Tuesday in winter. Admission is free.

(8) The Museum of Denmark's Fight for Freedom (1940–1945)

This museum, *Museet for Danmarks Frihedskamp,* 1–4 Churchillparken (tel. 13-77-14), reveals the tools of espionage and sabotage that the Danes used to throw off the Nazi yoke in World War II. Beginning softly with peace marches in the early days of the war, the resistance movement grew from a fledging into a highly polished and skilled underground that eventually electrified and excited the Allied world: "Danes Fighting Germans!" blared the headlines.

The museum hightlights the workings of the outlaw press, the equipment used in the wireless and illegal films, relics of torture and concentration camps, British propaganda leaflets dropped in the country, satirical caricatures of Hitler, information about Danish Jews and conversely about Danish Nazis, the paralyzing nationwide strikes. In all, a highly enlightening and exciting moment in history is graphically and dramatically preserved. An armed car, used against Danish Nazi informers and collaborators, is displayed on the grounds.

The museum is open from May 1 to September 15, Tuesday to Saturday, 10 a.m. to 4 p.m. (on Sunday from 10 a.m. to 5 p.m.). During the rest of the year, it may be visited Tuesday to Saturday from 11 a.m. to 3 p.m. (on Sunday to 4 p.m.). Admission is free. Closed on Monday. Take bus 1, 6, or 9. Each Sunday and Thursday at 2 p.m., from May 1 to September 15, guided tours are conducted at no charge. An automatic guide will be switched on at request.

(9) Open-Air Museum

From the farmlands of Denmark and the former Danish possessions in the province of Skåne in southern Sweden and South Schleswig in northwest Germany, a village has been reassembled on the fringes of Copenhagen (Lyngby), capturing the long-ago country life of the tiny nation. The museum's statistics are staggering. It covers nearly 90 acres, requiring a two-mile walk around the compound. Obviously, even the most ambitious visitors won't be able to see the whole thing in one visit. Still, in about two hours, it's possible to visit a dozen authentic buildings—farmsteads, windmills, fishermen's cottages. The exhibits cover a wide range: a half-timbered 18th-century farmstead from one of the tiny windswept Danish islands; a primitive dwelling—long-house—from the remote Faroe Islands; thatched fishermen's huts from Jutland; tower windmills; a potter's workshop from the mid-19th century. The exhibits are chock full of the tools of the life of the past few centuries: churns, swan decoys, fiery crosses, hay gaffs.

On summer afternoons, a number of organized activities are staged: on a recent visit folk dances with native-costumed performers were presented, as were demonstrations of lace-making techniques and old-time loom weaving. The park, about nine miles from the Central Station, is open Tuesday through Sunday from mid-April through September from 10 a.m. to 5 p.m. (closed Monday); from October 1 to October 14, open from 10 a.m. to 3 p.m. (closed Monday); from October 15 to April 14 Sunday only, 10 a.m. to 3 p.m. Admission is 6 kroner (54¢). To reach the park, take the S-train from the Central Station to Sorgenfri (one leaves every 20 minutes). Conveniently perched at the entryway to the museum is an old-style restaurant (huge beams, casement windows), with tables placed so that diners may enjoy pastoral scenes such as sheep grazing in the pastures. For more information, telephone 85-02-92.

(10) A Visit to the Breweries

It has become a tourist tradition in Copenhagen to visit one—or both—of the world-famous Danish breweries: **Carlsberg** or **Tuborg** (tours that are followed by tasting the products). And they're free. The Calsberg tour is more popular, and it does seem to offer more sights, such as a museum and the tallest building in Denmark (a grain elevator)—all on more then 62 acres of grounds. On the other hand, Tuborg attracts smaller crowds and thus avoids the necessary regimentation of the Carlsberg tours.

Both tours are equally balanced in their presentation of how barley becomes beer. Visitors are escorted through the brew houses of the bottling plants, the yeasty cellars, the storage basements—and are given a look at the gigantic mash coppers. Esoteric information is picked up—including what happens to dirty beer yeast (it is sold to lipstick manufacturers).

Added note: The Carlsberg people are quck to point out that the now-abandoned swastika sign on the elephant didn't mean they were Nazi sympathizers. They had this sign long before Hitler's party adopted it. The Carlsberg breweries are at Ny Carlsberg Vej 140 (the Visitors' Reception is at the Elephant Gate). Take bus 6 or 18. Guided tours for individual visitors begin at 9 a.m., 11 a.m., and 2:30 p.m. Groups must book the tours in advance (tel. 21-12-21, extension 1312). Closed on Saturday and Sunday. But visitors may arrive any time (weekdays only) between 8:30 a.m. and 2:30 p.m. at the Tuborg Breweries, 54 Strandvejen (take bus 1). For information, phone 29-33-11. extension 2212.

OTHER MAJOR ATTRACTIONS: Now to the best of the rest.

Amalienborg Palace

These four 18th-century French-style rococo mansions—opening onto one of the most attractive squares (Amalienborg) in Europe—have been the home of the Danish royal family since the court fled the flames of Christiansborg in 1794. The rooms cannot be visited, but tourists flock here like pigeons to witness the changing of the guard ceremony when the queen is in residence (take bus 1). A swallowtail flag flapping in the wind signifies the queen is in Copenhagen— and not at her North Zealand summer home, Fredensborg Palace. The guardsmen mostly wear blue uniforms, reserving their red for state occasions or holidays, but they can always be counted on to march under their black bearskin busbies (like the hussars). Their traditional ceremony at noon is followed by a concert by the regimental band. The guards are not as formally rigid as the ones at Buckingham, but on occasion they will caution teenage girls to stop playing with their rifles.

Arsenal Museum (Tøjhusmuseet)

On the grounds of Christiansborg is the Royal Danish Arsenal Museum, 3 Tøjhusgade (tel. 11-60-37), sheltering a fantastic display of many of the weapons that man has used for hunting and to kill his fellow man. The building that houses the museum traces its origins back to Christian IV, who ordered it erected at the end of the 16th century (what is believed to be his armor is displayed here). On the main floor—the longest arched hall in Europe—is the Cannon Hall (mortars, tanks, 1909 airplanes suspended from the ceiling, howitzers, a 21-ton German armored car, a Nazi V-1 rocket). The Armory Hall upstairs is stacked with engraved 17th-century armor, rapiers, sabers, and ceremonial swords. A sniper rifle and submachine gun used in the Danish Resistance Movement are also displayed. In all, there are enough weapons to reconquer Norway and Sweden . . . at least. But above all, here you find one of the world's finest collections of old firearms. The admission-free arsenal is open from May 1 to September 30 from 1 to 4 p.m. weekdays (10 to 4 on Sunday); its off-season hours are from 1 to 3 p.m. weekdays and from 11 a.m. to 4 p.m. on Sunday. It is always closed on Monday.

Theater Museum

In the 1776 **Royal Court Theater,** on the grounds of Christiansborg at 18 Christiansborg Redebane (tel. 11-51-76), this museum traces the development —in pictures and exhibits—of the Danish theater from the time of Ludvig Holberg (1684–1754), the founder of the Danish national theater, through the Romantic movemet up to the present day. It is open Wednesday and Sunday from 2 to 4 p.m.; Friday also during June, July, August, and September. Admission is 6 kroner (54¢) for adults, 2 kroner (18¢) for children.

Theater devotees enter the Louis Philippe-style auditorium, walk on its sloping stage, and inspect its two-centuries-old former dressing rooms. The museum is stuffed with the mementos of yesteryear—including two ballet costumes and the slippers of Anna Pavlova, the pictures reminding us that Mlle Bernhardt came this way on her famous world tour, following her resignation from the Comédie Française in 1880.

King Christian VII once played a jealous Turkish sultan on these boards in 1768. But poor Hans Christian Andersen didn't fare as well. A rare ballet program from 1821 shows that his connection with the Court Theater was as an extra in the ballet *Armida*—that was the first time his name ever appeared in print.

Museum of Decorative Art

The **Kunstindustrimuseet,** 68 Bredgade (tel. 14-94-52), is in a rococo building consisting of four wings surrounding a garden, a part of the former Royal

Frederik Hospital built from 1752 to 1757 under King Frederik V. It was restored in the early 1920s and adapted to house the collections of the museum. These comprise mostly European decorative and applied art from the Middle Ages to the present, arranged in chronological order. The pride of the place is given to furniture, tapestries, and other textiles, pottery, porcelain, glass and silver. Furthermore, there are collections of Chinese and Japanese art and handicrafts. Several separate exhibitions are shown within the scope of the museum. The library contains around 60,000 books and periodicals dealing with arts and crafts, architecture, costumes, advertising, photography, and industrial design.

The museum is open daily except Monday from 1 to 4 p.m. (September to November and January to March on Tuesday from 1 to 9 p.m.). Admission is free on weekdays, but on Sunday, holidays, and in July and August, entrance costs 8 kroner (72¢). The library is open daily except Sunday and Monday from 10 a.m. to 4 p.m. (September to November and January to March on Tuesday from 10 a.m. to 9 p.m. Admission is free to the library. Take bus 1, 6, or 9. The nearest railway station is Østerport.

Bing & Grøndahl Museum

One of Copenhagen's newest museums, lying at 149 Vesterbrogade (tel. 21-26-69), displays B&G porcelain production from 1853 until today. B&G celebrated its 125th anniversary by opening this museum of historical porcelain. A glass-roofed palm lounge links the museum with the 19th-century factory, now used for offices.

In one of the long, sky-lit galleries is displayed a complete collection of the celebrated Christmas plates, issued every year. B&G's first Yuletide plate, reviving an old gift custom, was designed by F. A. Hallin in celebration of the Christmas of 1895. Through the arched glass roof of the palm lounge the old red-brick factory can be seen.

Among the outstanding exhibitions is a large porcelain vase by Benjamin Olsen, made in 1911 with an underglaze painting depicting the imperial German yacht *Hohenzollern* passing Elsinore, a 1918 pierced vase by Effie Hageremann-Lindencrone, and an unusual vase, *Bathing Boy,* made in 1897.

Seek out also an 1862 coffee service by Heinrich Hansen which celebrated the King Christian IV buildings, and a presentation cup from 1858 decorated by Andras Juuel. Pietro Krohn's unique Heron dinner service is also displayed, along with Heinrich Hansen's Rosenborg dinner service of 1871, inspired by 18th-century Meissen porcelain. Contemporary Danish design is represented in a 1962 service by Henning Koppel.

Charging no admission, the porcelain museum is open Monday to Friday from 10 a.m. to 3 p.m., on Saturday to 2 p.m., and on Sunday from 1 to 4 p.m.

Langelinie

This seaside promenade along the sound is the most heavily frequented pathway in Copenhagen, a stroller's delight, attracting half the local population as well as every tourist. The walk leads to the bronze, life-size *Little Mermaid,* once decapitated either by (I suspect) a full-fledged idiot or by some sane Dane tired of the fairytale myth spun around his country. Don't miss the Gefion Fountain. (Gefion, a Scandinavian mythological goddess, plowed Zealand away from Sweden by turning her sons into oxen. She's still whipping them on.) Langelinie may be tied in with a visit to Amalienborg Palace, to the south, or else to the nearby Danish Resistance Museum.

In summer, a special "Mermaid Bus," charging 8 kroner (72¢) round trip, leaves from Rådhuspladsen (Vester Volgade) at 10:30 a.m. (thereafter at half-hour intervals until 5:30 p.m.). On the coach marked "Langelinie," you'll be allowed a 20-minute stopover at the Mermaid.

The Zoo

The carefully mapped out Zoological Gardens, 32 Roskildevej (tel. 30-25-55), are home for a striking collection of animals—more than 2000—captured from such remote places as the snowy heights of Greenland or the dark depths of the heart of Africa. The zoo's planners are attempting to simulate the natural habitat of their hairy, furry, feathered denizens. Don't fail to see the open area where lions roam or the specious new enclosures for the elegant reindeer and the bulky musk ox. The zoo is mobbed on Sunday, when all the Danes and their offspring turn out, but it remains a perennial tourist adventure (take either bus 28 or 41). It is open every day from 9 a.m. to sunset. Admission is 25 kroner ($2.25), 10 kroner (90¢) for children. Don't miss taking a ride up the small wooden version of the Eiffel Tower. Across the street, youngsters can have a wonderful time in the specially arranged children's zoo, where they can play with the animals.

Denmark's Aquarium

The world beneath the sea—everything from sockeye salmon to the brown bullhead—swims at this modern aquarium on the Strandvejen (take the S-train from the Central Station to Charlottenlund, a 20-minute ride, or bus 1 or 27). The Akvarium, one of the most extensive in Europe, has large tanks which are famous for the beauty of their decoration and are devoted to hundreds of species—either saltwater fanciers or their freshwater cousins. The aquarium is open from 10 a.m. to sunset daily; admission is 20 kroner ($1.80) for adults, 10 kroner (90¢) for children.

Round Tower

This 17th-century public observatory, attached to a church on Købmagergade in the Students' Quarter, is visited by thousands who climb the spiral ramp (no steps) to the top for a view of Copenhagen. The Rundetårn is one of the crowning achievements of the architecture of Christian IV. Legend has it that Peter the Great, in Denmark for a state visit, galloped up the ramp on horseback, preceded by his carriage-drawn czarina. It costs 6 kroner (54¢) to climb to the top; the tower is open weekdays from 10 a.m. to 5 p.m., on Sunday from noon to 4 p.m. April through September; 11 a.m. to 4 p.m. November through March.

Copenhagen Cathedral (Vor Frue Kirke)

This is a Greek-Renaissance-style church, built in the early 19th century, Nørregade, near Copenhagen University. Although unimpressive from the outside, it is classically pure inside, featuring some of the white marble neoclassical works of Bertel Thorvaldsen, particularly his Christ and the 12 Apostles. The funeral of Hans Christian Andersen took place here in 1875, that of Søren Kierkegaard in 1855. Our Lady's Church is open on weekdays from 9 a.m. to 5 p.m. For information, telephone 14-41-28.

Marble Church (or Frederik's Church)

The two-century-old church, with a dome of (green) copper—among the largest in the world—lies at 4 Frederiksgade, only a short walk from Amalienborg Palace. In many ways, it is far more impressive than the Cathedral of

Copenhagen. After an unsuccessful start during the neoclassic revival of the 1750s in Denmark, the church was finally completed in Roman baroque style in 1894. Admission is free. It is open May 1 to September 30 from 9 a.m. to 4 p.m. (till noon on Wednesday and Saturday); closes an hour earlier off-season (tel. 15-37-63).

Louis Tussaud Wax Museum

At 22 H. C. Andersens Blvd., now a part of Tivoli, is one of the newest attractions in Copenhagen. It features more than 150 wax figures, among them, of course, the Royal Family. The fee is 35 kroner ($3.15) for adults, 15 kroner ($1.35) for children. For information, telephone 14-29-22.

The Circus

The **Benneweis Circus,** 8 Jernbanegade (tel. 14-59-92), opposite Tivoli Gardens, is one of the last grand-style circuses left in Europe. The Benneweis Circus family is Europe's oldest—five generations of Benneweises have run the circus nonstop in spite of two world wars. Bareback riders, tumblers, hordes of absurd and lovable clowns, aerialists, trained seals—this is the real thing. The Benneweis features its famous horses and stages performances Monday to Friday at 8 p.m.; Wednesday at 3 and 8 p.m.; and Saturday and Sunday at 3 and 7 p.m. Tickets range in price upward from 35 kroner ($3.15). The season begins in May, lasting till the end of October.

READERS' SIGHTSEEING TIPS: "In the large central hall of the **Copenhagen Town Hall,** at Rådhuspladsen, stand four impressive statues. Although this is a public building, none is of a political figure. Two of the four are of special interest to foreign visitors: Niels Bohr, the famous physicist who helped to give man so much physical power, and Hans Christian Andersen, whose wonderful stories may help to give us a little of the wisdom needed to use this power for good instead of harm. Free guided tours of the Town Hall are offered every hour, daily, and at 10 a.m., noon, and 2 p.m. on Sunday. It is open daily, but only for the guided tours on Sunday" (Richard A. Givens, New York, N.Y.). . . . "One of the high points on our stay in Copenhagen was a series of **guided walking tours.** Mr. Jacobsen, the tour guide, not only knows the history of the town, but also has a delightful sense of humor, enjoys what he's doing, and has entree to many places of historic interest. Our one regret is that time allowed us to take only four of the seven tours available. These walking tours are a real buy" (Mr. and Mrs. Bernard Luskin, Weston, Conn.).[*Author's Note:* The tours run every day except Friday from late June to early September, as well as on Saturday and Sunday in early and late season from April 1 to October 15. Prices are 15 kroner ($1.35) for adults, 10 kroner (90¢) for students; children free. For more specific information, write to *The Guide-Ring,* H. S. Jacobsen, 91 Kongelundsvej, 2300 Copenhagen S. (tel. 51-25-90); or when in Copenhagen, get the full program at the Tourist Information Center.]

2. Copenhagen After Dark

The Danish capital offers the most intriguing nightlife in Scandinavia, ranging from classical ballet to lively pubs. Star bet? Tivoli. But outside Tivoli's gates are jazz clubs, discos—and even something for the family man or woman.

TIVOLI AT NIGHT: At dusk (the festivities begin early), a special magic blankets Tivoli, as the firefly-gone-mad lighting goes on, bathing every fun-parlor, restaurant, tree and flower garden. The beauty intensifies—and so does the entertainment (discos, band and orchestra concerts, variety shows, fireworks display). Try to see:

Open-Air Stage

In the center of the gardens, this large stage books vaudevillian talents (tumbling clowns, acrobats, aerialists) who give two performances nightly, at 7 and 9 (extra show at 5 p.m. on weekend). Spectators have to go through the turnstiles for seats, but there's an unobstructed view from the outside for standees. Special arrangements with jazz, beat, and folklore groups take place during the season. Admission is free.

Pantomime Theatre

Quite near the Vesterbrogade entrance is this famed outdoor theater, with its Chinese-style stage and its peacock curtain that opens every evening, except Sunday at 7:45 p.m., revealing a repertory of 16 different Comedia dell' Arte productions (the eternally entertaining trio: Pierrot, Columbine, and Harlequin), authentic pantomimes that have been performed continuously in Copenhagen since 1801. Tickets cost only 7 kroner (63¢) but many stand and watch the show free. Classic ballets, accompanied by the Tivoli Promenade Orchestra, are performed on the stage at 10 p.m. This theater is more than 100 years old.

Concert Hall

This modern concert hall faces a formal plaza with a cluster of splashing fountains, and it is one of the best places in Denmark for hearing talented and famous artists, led by equally famous conductors. Performances of everything from symphony to opera are held nightly at 7:30. Good seats are available at prices ranging from 20 kroner ($1.80) to 175 kroner ($15.75) and up when major artists are performing—but most of the performances are free. Tickets are sold at the main booking office on Vesterbrogade.

Dancing at Tivoli

When the young man of Copenhagen wants to take his girl for a rocking reeling good time on the dance floor, he heads for **Dansetten** (tel. 14-06-99) in the Tivoli Gardens. Single women may ask Danish men to dance—and vice versa, of course. Various orchestras and bands play for dancing between 8 p.m. and midnight. The entrance is free, although beer begins at 20 kroner ($1.80).

CULTURAL: A great bargain in Copenhagen, if you're there in the winter months, is to see a performance of the world-renowned **Royal Danish Ballet** or **Royal Danish Opera.** Because the arts are subsidized by the state in Denmark, the best seats in the house usually cost no more than $10. Good seats are often available at the box office on the day before a performance (call 14-17-65 for advance bookings). On the day of the performance, telephone 14-17-66. The season lasts until May, and both companies perform at the **Royal Theatre** on Kongens Nytorv.

NYHAVN: This was once a strip of honky-tonks, bordering a canal, and guaranteed to take the starch out of the stiffest of collars. It is impishly situated only a short walk from the patrician Kongens Nytorv and the d'Angleterre luxury hotel. Once it was boisterous and filled with seafaring revelers and the prostitutes who entertained them. Nowadays, it has become one of the chicest restaurant colonies in Copenhagen. Some of the local places, such as the tattoo parlors, still exist, but most of the real low-down dives have gone.

However, there remains a favorite from the old days. It is the **Café Nyhavn 17,** 17 Nyhavn. There is a jukebox, but modern music is also played by a piano player who sings along. In summer, tables and chairs are placed outdoors. The club opens at 5 a.m. when it serves breakfast to the latest of the all-night revelers. A typical Danish lunch is also available. But mostly the people come at night when they can chat and dance until 1 a.m. Beer costs from 18 kroner ($1.62).

DISCO: Daddy's Dance Hall, 9 Axeltorv (tel. 11-46-79), is host to the city's top disco bands. It looks like a white castle, and is easy to find, lying in the vicinity of the Royal Hotel. Hours: Monday through Thursday from 10 p.m. to 4 a.m., on the popular Friday and Saturday nights from 10 p.m. to 5 a.m. In addition to just listening to the blaring music, you can also dance. Depending on the night and who's appearing, admission can range from a low of 16 kroner ($1.44) to a high of 40 kroner ($4.50) for a big blast on Friday and Saturday nights.

DANCING: Den Røde Pimpernel ("The Scarlet Pimpernel"), 7 H. C. Andersen Blvd., near the Town Hall Square (tel. 12-20-32), has a lively, clublike atmosphere. It's one of the best places in Copenhagen for dancing—for young people, who are admitted only after an inspection through a peephole. A live band plays for a variety of dance steps. On most nights the club is free; however, on the most popular Friday and Saturday nights, you pay an admission of 28 kroner ($2.52), and you must order at least one drink, which start incidentally, at 21 kroner ($1.89) for the potent aquavit, going up to 28 kroner ($2.52) for a half liter of draft beer. If you wish, you can order an open-face sandwich, starting at 17 kroner ($1.53), although it's unlikely you'll have enough elbow room in which to eat it. The club is open six days a week, from 8 p.m. to 2 a.m. (Friday and Saturday to 3 a.m.). Closed Sunday. The club's Leslie Howard bar stays open on Friday and Saturday nights until 4 a.m.

Club Exalon, 38 Frederiksberggade (tel. 11-08-66), has been in business for half a century, occupying a position both in the center of town on the Strøget, a pedestrian shopping street off the Rådhuspladsen, and in the hearts of the many Danes who have met here, fallen in love, and married. Once it was the scene of Big Band swing music, offering a showcase for Scandinavian actors and actresses who later starred in films. Today, there's still music for dancing, although in a drastically updated version, as well as lots of dark wood paneling, globe lighting, striped banquettes, and enough drinking glasses to stock a major hotel, placed in neat rows. The entrance fee varies from 25 kroner ($2.25) to 45 kroner ($4.05), depending on the day of the week. Once you're inside, you'll pay from 25 kroner ($2.25) for a drink of whisky.

LIVE MUSIC: Hand I Hanke, 20 Griffenfeldtsgade (tel. 37-20-70), is a popular hangout for young people, Danes and foreigners included, and it offers some of the best folk music (again, foreign and domestic) in the Danish capital. It's open from 9 p.m. to 1 a.m. Beer costs from 18 kroner ($1.62).

Rådhuskroen, 21 Longangsstraede (tel. 11-64-53), is a candlelit drinking and dining spot that offers a variety of meals for 35 kroner ($3.15)—liver, chicken, beef—and charges 19 kroner ($1.71) for large draft beer. The outside is modern and not aesthetically appealing, but inside the wooden tables give an air of comfort and relaxation. This is one of the most popular student hangouts in the city, offering live music from midnight to 4 a.m.

Purple Door Music Theatre, 28 Fiolstraede (tel. 13-66-28), is a place for some of the coolest jazz in Copenhagen. It also presents folk music, rock, and blues. For information about the current program, call the above number after 8:30 p.m. On Sunday a folk-music program is presented, and guest singers are welcome to join in. For the same price, another folk-music program is presented on Tuesday night. On Friday and Saturday, however it's rock, jazz, or blues. Depending on the artists appearing, admission is either 20 kroner ($1.80) or 40 kroner ($3.60).

(Underneath the Purple Door Music Theater is the **Banks Gallery,** entered by the blue door in the yard. This is a small gallery of arts and crafts. Most of the exhibitors are yet to be "discovered"; therefore, the prices are reasonable. The gallery is open daily from noon to 5:30 p.m., to 4 p.m. Saturday and Sunday. Coffee and tea are available. Another gallery, **Minigalleriet,** has opened in the yard, with exhibits of ceramics, small paintings, watercolors, and drawings, together with portraits by the American photographer Jo Banks. Hours are the same as for the Banks Gallery.)

Jazzclub Montmartre, 41 Nørregade (tel. 11-46-67), is the center of modern jazz in Denmark, if not Europe, drawing a string of Copenhageners, Americans, and Africans who know about flatted fifths and rhythmic accents. The club attracts the finest jazz musicians from all over the world, including some of the all-time jazz giants. The entertainment is first class from the time the club opens. Entrance fee most often begins at 40 kroner ($3.60), unless a very special group is appearing. This is a sophisticated, atmospheric place. Drinks cost from 20 kroner ($1.80). Hours are 8 p.m. to 1 a.m. Tuesday through Thursday, to 4 a.m. on Friday and Saturday; closed Sunday and Monday. Every Friday and Saturday night there is "progressive" disco, and on Sunday and Monday nights special events are staged, such as folk-rock evenings.

You can also head for the friendly atmosphere of **De Tre Musketerer** (The Three Musketeers), 25 Nikolaj Plads, near the Vingaarden (tel. 11-25-07). It is open daily except Sunday from 8 p.m. to 2 a.m., featuring a different jazz band every night. The entrance is 25 kroner ($2.25) and on weekends—worth the price if you like to dance. Beer is 18 kroner ($1.62).

Another place where you can dance to live music is **La Fontaine,** at 11 Kompagnistraede (tel. 11-60-98), where a three-piece Danish combo plays its version of jazz or dance music from 11 p.m. until 6 a.m. The doorman here is one of the friendliest in Copenhagen. Beer is from 20 kroner ($1.80).

Musik Cafe'n, 14 Magstraede (tel. 12-38-82), is the main center for rock and assorted electrical music in Copenhagen. Open from 9 p.m. to 2 a.m., the café is dedicated to promoting Danish progressive music such as funk, reggae, punk, and especially rock. Its monthly program is available at the entrance. On the top floor, **Foyer Scenen** specializes in experimental jazz music. It is open only on weekends. Both clubs charge an ordinary entrance of 45 kroner ($4.05), unless something extraordinary is happening.

DRINKING CELLARS: Det Lille Apotek, 15 Store Kannikestraede (tel. 12-56-06). As you enter from the street, a tiny and intimate bar envelopes you. It extends into a warren of serpentine drinking areas of deep red and forest green. The illumination comes from hanging green glass lamps, which reflect off the thick wood tables and handcrafted Windsor chairs. If you're not observing the dozens of students who pile in here on weekend evenings, you can study the oversize cartoons spanning a century between 1880 and 1980 which decorate the smoke-stained walls. This is a good bet for English-speaking foreign students who want to meet their Danish contemporaries.

You'll pay about 18 kroner ($1.62) for a beer. The place is open from 10 a.m. till 2 a.m. every day. During that time, platters of food, such as fish filet with asparagus and caviar, cold sliced salmon and caviar and chive sauce, seafood salad, or roast beef, cost from 22 kroner ($1.98) to 48 kroner ($4.32) each. Two-course fixed-price meals are offered as well, beginning at 75 kroner ($6.75). More formal viands are also available, including pepper steak with béarnaise sauce and salad, costing around 150 kroner ($13.50) for a full meal.

Hviids Vinstue, 19 Kongens Nytorv (tel. 11-10-64), built in 1670, is one of the oldest wine cellars in Copenhagen. During the great days of the clipper ships, it served Madeira and Málaga wines and punch to a rowdy group of sailors who appreciated the exotic character of practically anything imported into Denmark. Today the establishment maintains a reputation as the kind of dimly lit and safe labyrinth which can welcome everyone from a well-dressed woman in a fur hat to a local novelist drinking away some of his tension after a day at the typewriter. The tables, which have been worn smooth by the elbows of many generations of drinkers, are scattered through a rhythmic progression of rooms filled with "side-saddle" captain's chairs, grandfather clocks, dadoed half-paneling, and faded photographs of everything from churches to racehorses. In December only, a combination of red wine and cognac is served, heightened an unspoken camaraderie. You pay around 42 kroner ($3.78) for two export beers; it will be slightly cheaper if you order pilsner.

Vin & Olgod, 45 Skindergade (tel. 13-26-25), answers that question so feverishly asked by new arrivals in the Danish capital: "Where's all that friendly action Copenhagen is supposed to have?" Right here—in the cellar of the Rådhus Kaelderen (circa 1200), a dancing, drinking, singing, and snacking complex, with a taverna, a pub, a bodega, and a main beer hall through which the zany nighttime activity flows. Loners are quickly absorbed, as they settle in at one of the trestle tables and are served a stein of foaming fadøl (draft beer) by a waitress dressed in a leather apron and a student cap. The band plays on stage, and everybody sings along. Even if you don't know the words (printed on music sheets), you'll soon be ta-ra-ta-boom-trala-ing with the rest of the revelers. You may even join some of the more frivolous patrons, who prefer to do their dancing on the benches. The hours are 8 p.m. till 2 a.m. Admission is 20 kroner ($1.80) Monday through Thursday, 35 kroner ($3.15) on Friday and Saturday. Closed Sunday. In any room, light beer and a variety of snacks are available.

CAFÉS AFTER DARK: Café Victor, 8 Ny Østergade (tel. 13-36-13), contains a popular French-style café at one end and an inexpensive restaurant in the other. Founded in 1981, the Victor offers one of the most sophisticated gathering places in Copenhagen. You'll recognize it by the red awning with gilt lettering (à la Coupole in Paris), which attracts a good-looking and arts-oriented crowd around the curved and illuminated bar or at one of the tiny see-and-be-seen tables. Open from 10 a.m. to 2 a.m., the establishment sells cognac from 28 kroner ($2.52) and coffee from 12 kroner ($1.08). The Victor is always popular, although during the Sunday afternoon literary meetings (held at 3 p.m. in Danish, unless canceled at the last minute), the place is practically mobbed, and practically everyone will speak some English.

Victor's Garage Brasserie, Ny Østergade/Hovedvagtsgade (tel. 12-25-45). The Café Victor may be chic, but the real energy for the 20-and-under crowd comes from the café's annex, which abuts it on a side street. There's an aura of tongue-in-cheek punk here, which is made all the more acceptable by the drink specials written graffiti-style on the white tile walls and the folding garage doors which roll upward on overhead tracks to allow the summer air to come into the slickly illuminated hi-tech interior.

Despite the trendy decor, you can still buy copies of the *Financial Times* at a stand near the curving bar or discuss literature or the art forms of Boy George in several languages with the barman or just about any of the customers.

Light and flavorful meals are available for around 100 kroner ($9), while mixed drinks (Harvey Wallbangers, White Russians, and such) cost around 40 kroner ($3.60) each. While watching representatives of the Danish future parade past your table, you can enjoy roast beef sandwiches, tuna salad, gazpacho, and filet steak. The brasserie opens every day at 8 a.m. for breakfast (which is more in the nature of a brunch) and closes after a very long day at 2 a.m.

A NIGHTCLUB FOR EVERYBODY: By the turn of the century, **The Lorry,** 7–9 Allégade (tel. 34-33-23), had already become a traditional Copenhagen nightspot. Today it is one of Scandinavia's most impressive, large-scale, family-style nightclubs. Set back from a tree-lined boulevard, it is decked out with multicolored lights outside. Inside it's a world apart: on the ground floor a whole village —the "Landsbyen"—has been created, complete with half-timbered houses, a waterfall, and a ceiling of twinkling stars. The tables—dozens of them—are in the village "courtyard." Every evening except Monday, there's entertainment at 7 and 11 p.m., with a live band playing until 2 a.m. The 7 p.m. show is in Danish, while the 11 p.m. presentation is mostly musical. The whole evening, including both shows, costs 175 kroner ($15.75) to 250 kroner ($22.50), which covers the price of the celebrated smörgåsbord. On the first floor, at the Drachmannkroen, a genuine old-fashioned Danish inn, you can enjoy Danish gastronomy at reasonable prices. Dinner guests at Drachmannkroen have free entry to Landsbyen after 10 p.m. Night owls can continue until 5 a.m. at the Grock Jazz, listening to good musicians. Entry is free. You'll be charged 18 kroner ($1.62) for a beer, 35 kroner ($3.15) for mixed drinks. Hot and cold food is served until 3:30 a.m., costing from 30 kroner ($2.70) to 100 kroner ($9).

WHERE TO EAT, DRINK, AND MEET PEOPLE: A popular spot for young people who like to sit, drink, and talk is the **Pilegårdencafé,** 44 Pilestraede (tel. 15-48-80). You might be so distracted by the modern art hanging on the deep red walls that you never get around to ordering, which is fine since, if you're at a table, the barman may take his time getting around to serving you. In the meanwhile, you can listen to the rock music and watch the roughly masculine crowd rolling dice or talking English slang at the standup bar. The crowd is friendly and hard-drinking, and sometimes there's live music, which is listed to with great intensity. Export beer and wine cost 18 kroner ($1.62), draft beer around 17 kroner ($1.53).

Another popular late-night spot is the **Café Royal/Laurits Betjent,** 16 Ved Stranden (tel. 12-03-01), which has been entertaining crowds since 1850, when it was established and named after a popular local policeman. By no means assume that the ground floor is all there is to this place. Although pleasant and warmly decorated, it serves as a focal point only when the upper level is closed. When the upstairs is open, it's likely to attract drinkers of all walks of life, aged 20 to 60, who come for the conviviality engendered in the barnlike place by the foaming beer, which seems to be the favorite drink.

Tables are clustered around the trunks of two trees which, although cut almost 50 years ago, look as if they're growing out of the floor. The dim lighting is flattering to almost everyone, and while some people dance to the recorded or live music, many prefer to stand near the long bar. Live guitar music is featured every Thursday through Saturday upstairs. The café is open Wednesday through Sunday from 2 p.m. till 5 a.m., and the upstairs offers live music on Thursday, Friday, and Saturday. There's a 7 kroner (63¢) cover charge on Friday and Saturday. Once you get in, draft beer and wine can be purchased from 14 kroner ($1.26) a glass. The downstairs bar is open from 2 p.m. till 5 p.m. Wednesday through Saturday and from 2 p.m. till 5 a.m. Monday and Tuesday. On Sunday, both floors are closed.

Drop Inn, 34 Kompagnistraede, is a more refined and rather expensive eatery with a modern, American-style setting. It is popular with singles in the 20-to-30 age bracket, who come for beer, snacks, and conversation. Various omelets and pasta dishes are served. There is a large choice of sandwhiches as well. Count on spending 18 kroner ($1.62) for beer, 75 kroner ($6.75) for a light meal.

WHAT, ANOTHER AMUSEMENT PARK?: The **Bakken** amusement park, on the northern edge of Copenhagen, suffers by comparison with Tivoli. It is older, however—and loudly proclaims that it was created 35 years before the Pilgrims landed at Plymouth Rock. While it doesn't have the whimsy of Tivoli, it does provide facilities for a festive time. It's the Danes who take most advantage of the park, whizzing up and around on roller coasters, losing kroner at roulette wheels, dancing to the latest combo, riding through the tunnel of love, watching nude dancers. The merry-go-round twirls daily; open-air restaurants are plentiful, as are snackbars and ice-cream booths. Bakken is about a 20-minute ride from the Central Station (take the S-tog labeled "Klampenborg" at the Central Station, departures three times hourly). Get off at Klampenborg Station, then walk through the Deer Park, once an 18th-century hunting lodge. Proceeds from the amusements support this unspoiled nature preserve. Bicycles and horse-drawn carriages are used instead of automobiles. The park opens in the middle of April and closes around the end of August. No admission is charged. Bakken invites you in at 3 p.m., shutting down at midnight.

ONE-DAY TRIPS FROM THE CAPITAL

The most popular one-day trek from Copenhagen takes in three royal castles of North Zealand: Kronborg Castle at Shakespeare's Elsinore, the king's summer palace at Fredensborg, and the most treasure-filled of them all, the 17th-century castle of Frederiksborg at Hillerød. A popular stop along the way is the Louisiana Museum.

The Danish Railways offers a special ticket, allowing visitors to make the swing up the coastline to Elsinore, then back to Copenhagen via Fredensborg and Hillerød (you can do it in reverse order, too). There is fast and frequent train service from the Central Station in Copenhagen.

3. Louisiana

Louisiana, 20 miles north of Copenhagen on the Danish Riviera, is a museum of modern art (established 1958) that grew out of a 19th-century mansion. It is surrounded by elegantly planned and spacious gardens, opening directly onto the sound—and idyllic setting in which the old and the new are perfectly blended. Extensions have been added to the whitewashed brick building; they are connected to the main building by glassed-in corridors. Everywhere one wanders in this garden-museum maze of art, there are paintings and sculptures by the masters (Giacometti, Henry Moore) as well as by experimental artists. In particular, look for the paintings of Carl-Henning Pedersen, a modern artist worth remembering. Occasionally, exhibits from past civilizations (Chinese or Egyptian, perhaps) are shown in juxtaposition to today's sculpture. The pieces of sculpture are displayed in breathtaking settings. Besides its permanent and changing art collections, Louisiana is noted for its concerts. The hours are from

10 a.m. to 5 p.m. (Wednesday from 10 a.m. to 10 p.m.), and the entrance fee is 20 kroner ($1.80). To get to Louisiana, take bus 188 from Klampenborg to Humlebaek or the train from Copenhagen to Humlebaek (it's a ten-minute walk from there).

4. Elsinore (Helsingør)

This town (Helsingør in Danish), 25 miles north of Copenhagen, is visited chiefly for its "Hamlet's Castle." It has a certain charm in its own right: a quiet market square, medieval lanes, old half-timbered and brick buildings. Many of them remain from the golden days, when the town grew fat and prosperous (practically supporting Denmark) from the dues collected from ships passing through the narrow sound separating Denmark and Sweden. The hateful (to the Swedes and Americans) taxes were collected from 1428 to 1857. With the cannons of Kronborg trained on them, the ship captains had no choice but to pay up. Today ferries ply unthreatened across the sound to Sweden, 2½ miles away. On any clear day Swedish Helsingborg is visible.

KRONBORG CASTLE: This sandstone, copper-covered Dutch Renaissance-style castle (tel. 21-04-01), full of secret passages and casemates, is famous because of someone named Hamlet. As it happens, if Hamlet had really existed, he would have lived centuries before Kronborg was erected (1574–1585)—if we are to believe 12th-century historian Saxo Grammaticus. There is no evidence that Shakespeare ever saw the castle. No matter, modern visitors arrive by the busload to walk in the footsteps of Ophelia and the Prince of Denmark, real or imagined. And regardless of whether Hamlet ever wondered if he should or should not be at Kronborg, the castle was restored in 1629 by Christian IV after it was gutted by fire. It has been looted, bombarded, occupied by Swedes—and was used as a barracks from 1785 to 1922. It is bleak and austere, but that its drama. See in particular the starkly furnished Great Hall (the largest in Northern Europe), the church with its original oak furnishings, and the chambers once reserved for the king and queen. Kronborg also contains a collection of wood and silk tapestries, plus great old oaken chests and cupboards. In the basement sits Holger Danske, hero of mythology, who is supposed to pick up his sword and shield and come to the aid of Denmark when the country is threatened. The **Danish Maritime Museum** (tel. 21-06-85) is also on the premises. In it are displayed exhibits vividly illustrating the history of Danish shipping from prehistoric times.

To view the royal apartments, the chapel, and the casements, the cost is 10 kroner (90¢) for adults, 5 kroner (45¢) for children. To see the museum, the charge is the same, but if you want to see both the royal apartments and the museum, you can buy a joint ticket for 14 kroner ($1.26) for adults, 7 kroner (63¢) for children. From October to April, guided tours are conducted every half hour. In summer you can walk through the castle without a guide. Open May 1 to September 30 from 10 a.m. to 5 p.m.; from 11 a..m. to 4 p.m. in October and April; 11 a.m. to 3 p.m. the rest of the year. Closed Christmas Day; open Easter from 10 a.m. to 5 p.m.

OTHER ATTRACTIONS: **Vor Frue Kloster** is another attraction in Elsinore. This well-preserved 15th-century former Carmelite monastery is the best of its kind in Scandinavia. Open May 15 to September 15 from 11 a.m. to 2 p.m., the monastery charges 6 kroner (54¢) for adults, 2.50 kroner (23¢) for children.

See also **St. Mary's Church.** Admission is free; open from 1 to 4 p.m. daily.

Of special interest in the church's contents is the fine organ played by the church organist, baroque composer Diderik Buxtehude, from 1660 to 1668 and still in use.

Saint Olai Church on Sct. Annagade, was built between 1480 and 1559. The interior, with a fine christening chapel, is worth seeing. The church has been a cathedral since 1961. It's open daily from 10 a.m. to 3 p.m., with no admission charge.

The **Town Museum,** Hestemøllestraede, dating from about 1500, contains the town historic archives and exhibits of artifacts. You can visit it free from noon to 4 p.m.

Another town museum is at **Marienlyst Castle,** which was built in 1587 as a summer palace and rebuilt around 1760. Here you'll see many of Elsinore's historic relics here, and exhibits of arts and crafts are sometimes shown. The castle is open free of charge from June 1 to August 31 from noon to 5 p.m.

The **Technical Museum of Denmark,** whose main entrance is on Nordre Strandvej, has two separate sections in which are displayed technical industrial scientific and transportation examples, including the oldest airplanes of Denmark, railroad trains, trams, and buses, as well as the old Danish automobile, Hammelvognen from 1886. The museum is open daily from 10 a.m. to 5 p.m. and charges 14 kroner ($1.26) admission for adults, half price for children.

Guided tours of the city are held every Monday in July at 7 p.m. For information about these and other matters, go to the **Tourist Office,** Havnepladsen (tel. 21-13-33), which is open from 9 a.m. to 7 p.m.

FOOD AND LODGING: Typical Danish hot meals, such as hakkebof (hamburger steak), frikadeller (Danish rissoles), rib roast with red cabbage, cooked or fried flounder or herring, aeggekage (egg cake) with bacon, all cost about 50 kroner ($4.50). In Elsinore, several cozy little restaurants, all with different style, serve these meals, plus international dishes from an à la carte menu. Among them are **Anno 1880** on Kongensgade; **Faergegården** on Stengade; **Hos Anker** on Bramstraede; **Kabyssen** at the yacht harbor; **Klosercafeen,** Sct. Annagade; and **Sundkroen** at the railway station.

At most dining places you can get a *Danmenu,* a typical Danish meal plus something extra, for 65 kroner ($5.85). At lunch, many people prefer to select from the smørrebrød list, which offers around 60 different creations, ranging from herring to cheese. Many selections cost only about 18 kroner ($1.62).

In Elsinore, you'll also find many fast-food places, and you won't want to miss the celebrated Elsinore ice-cream wafers.

Cafeteria San Remo, 53 Stengade (tel. 21-00-15), on the corner of Bjergegade, a traffic-free shopping mall, might be your choice. Meals at this self-service establishment are down to earth despite the crystal chandeliers. Typical meals such as fried fish with rémoulade sauce and potatoes and the reliable frikadeller cost around 50 kroner ($4.50). In the center of town, half a block from the Hamlet Hotel and about two from the harbor, the cafeteria is in an old building with a heavy Dutch influence.

The **Hamlet Hotel,** 5 Bramstraede (tel. 21-05-91), is a classic corner building with a tiny lobby. It derives its special character from its paneling and pair of curving staircases. The remodeled bedrooms are simply furnished in the utilitarian manner. They are immaculately kept and rent for anywhere from 300 kroner ($27) to 450 kroner ($40.50) in a double, from 200 kroner ($18) in a single. These tariffs include breakfast, Moms, and service. A new restaurant has been opened in the cellar. Try to get an accommodation with a view over the harbor and the sound. The hotel is centrally located, only a short block from the harbor and a ten-minute stroll from Kronborg Castle.

NIGHTLIFE: The only international gambling **casino** in Denmark is at the Hotel Marienlyst (tel. 21-18-01), on the beach, Nordre Strandvej, with a high-class dining and dancing restaurant which is open all year.

5. Fredensborg Palace

This splendid Italian-style palace, built in the early 18th century, is the summer home of the royal family, and was particularly celebrated during the reign of the so-called father-in-law of Europe (Christian IX), who assembled the greats of European royalty here in the days when Queen Victoria ruled in England. Rooms shown are those actually used by the royal family when they stay here. The wings are for guests. The palace can be visited only in July from 1 to 5 p.m. for 7 kroner (63¢) admission—but its huge encircling park is open all summer. When the queen is in residence, visitors assemble at noon to watch the changing of the guard ceremony—just as interesting as it is in Amalienborg. On Thursday, except in July, the queen often appears to acknowledge a regimental band concert in her honor. Fredensborg Palace lies between Elsinore and Hillerød (about six miles from either).

Food and Lodging

If, after visiting the palace, you should desire either a room or meal, try **Store Kro**, 6 Slotsgade (tel. 28-00-47). Behind a handsome façade, the hotel is near the palace. Its well-furnished rooms are rich in character, and a friendly welcome is extended by the anxious-to-please staff. The hotel offers a total of 49 accommodations, all of which are equipped with private baths. Singles are rented for 410 kroner ($36.90), with doubles costing from 600 kroner ($54), a splurge but worth it to many readers. There is parking about one block behind the hotel. If you're stopping in just for lunch, count on spending from 150 kroner ($13.50).

6. Frederiksborg Castle

This moated slot (castle) at Hillerød, 22 miles northwest of Copenhagen, is perhaps the major castle in all of Scandinavia. It bears the hackneyed name of the Danish Versailles. Like Kronborg, it was built in the Dutch Renaissance style (red brick, copper roof, sandstone façade). Frederiksborg goes back to 1560, the time of Frederik II. However, his son, Christian IV, who was born at the castle, had some building ideas of his own. He had most of the original edifice torn down and rebuilt in the early part of the 17th century. In 1859, the castle was ravaged by fire, but was restored thanks to the generous assistance of brewer J. C. Jacobsen, the founder of the museum and of the Carlsberg Foundation. Now it is a major national history museum.

Among its many sights are the sumptuously decorated and gilded chapel (be sure to see the king's pew and the wooden organ built by Elias Compenius in 1610) where Danish kings were once crowned (a formality that has been dispensed with), and the Great Hall (over the chapel), which makes no apologies to ostentation. In addition, Frederiksborg houses an extensive collection of portraits and historical paintings and furnishings (ebony cabinets, four-posters, coronation tapestries, enameled miniatures, coats-of-arms). The castle is open every day from May 1 through September 30, 10 a.m. to 5 p.m.; to 4 p.m. in October; and 11 a.m. to 4 p.m. in April; 11 to 3 November through March. Admission: 18 kroner ($1.62) for adults, 4.50 kroner (41¢) for children. For more information, telephone 26-04-39.

A VIKING PAGEANT: Frederikssund (not to be confused with Fredensborg or Frederiksborg, also in North Zealand) is a little town about 25 miles northwest of Copenhagen that stages a two-week Viking festival each summer (usually in June). Nordic sagas, such as the adventures of Eric the Red and Leif Ericsson, are revived—and the record is set straight about who discovered America five centuries before that Johnny-come-lately from Spain. Check with Tourist Information in Copenhagen for dates and tickets. For an all-inclusive ticket (the upcoming price not known at press time), guests are transported there and back, shown the pageant, and beered and dined in the best of Viking tradition. In all, allow 5½ hours. Otherwise, if you don't want to pay for the cost of the Viking banquet, you can go on your own by taking a bus from Lurblaeserne at the Town Hall Square, departing at 7 p.m.

7. Dragør

This old seafaring town, three miles south of the Copenhagen airport, is Denmark in a nutshell. An imaginative public relations woman in Copenhagen once confided that when she's entertaining an important client who has only a short time for Denmark, she takes him or her to Dragør. In a setting far removed from the hustle and bustle of Copenhagen, this old Danish village offers a preview of the countryside for those who can't experience it in greater depth. A sleepy town on the water, it was an early 16th-century Dutch settlement. The community was established by Christian IV when he brought in Dutchmen to farm and provide vegetables for the royal family.

In addition to its Maritime Museum, Dragør is filled with half-timbered houses, many painted pink, which come under the protection of the National Trust. To reach it, take bus 33 from the Town Hall Square.

The **Strandhotellet** is the expensive eating place in town, a meal here costing from 180 kroner ($16.20) up for lunch.

But if you walk around the corner, the **Dragør Bodega** (with outdoor tables) offers the same food at lower prices, a lunch going for anywhere from 110 kroner ($9.90).

For eating and drinking in Dragør, go to the 2½-century-old **Dragør Kro,** 23 Kongevejen (tel. 53-01-87), where cheerful beer-drinkers populate the courtyard. The Kro, run by the Kjaer-Olsen family, is on the main walking street, about a block from the harbor. A good-tasting lunch here will cost from 45 kroner ($4.05) to 90 kroner ($8.10).

READER'S GUESTHOUSE SELECTION: "The best place we stayed anywhere in Europe was the home of **Nina Gertz** and her family, 172 Lundevej (tel. 53-10-28), in Dragør. Not only do they make you a part of their warm and hospitable Danish family, but their village is a vacation in itself. They were so kind, they subtracted the cost of the bus ride to their home from their usual rate because we had no car. Rates are 170 kroner ($15.30) per double room, and for another 35 kroner ($3.15) each you get a breakfast which is good and enormous" (Mr. and Mrs. Richard Wein, Boston, Mass.).

8. Roskilde

This provincial town, 20 miles west of Copenhagen, was once a great ecclesiastical seat and the country's leading city until the mid-15th century. Today it is the major pilgrimage center of Denmark because of its twin-spired cathedral, housing the bodies of 38 Danish kings and queens, most of them in sarcophagi, but not all. The sarcophagi are placed in four chapels and behind the altar (even old Harald Bluetooth of tenth-century fame is said to be interred here). The present Gothic-Romanesque cathedral traces its origins back to Bishop Absalon of the 12th century. In this checkerboard setting of marble and alabaster tombstones lie the worldly remains of the elegant and great in Danish history—figures such as Queen Margrethe, queen of Scandinavia, and that master-builder, Christian IV ("sitting in jugment"), as well as 14 bishops together with other clergy and noblemen. The tombstones are in the floor.

The cathedral was damaged by a fire that swept over it late in the summer of 1968, but it has since been restored, along with the magnificent altarpiece. The pantheon may be viewed daily from April 1 to October 1 from 9 a.m. to 5:45 p.m., for 5 kroner (45¢) admission. Winter hours are 10 a.m. to 3:45 p.m.

In the cathedral, above the entrance door, clock-work toys from around 1500 play a short tune while moving about.

Opened to the public in the spring of 1969, the **Viking Ship Museum** at Strandengen (tel. 35-65-55) displays five vessels which were found outside the town in Roskilde Fjord. The ships were painstakingly pieced together from hundreds upon hundreds of pieces of wreckage. It is presumed that the craft were deliberately sunk about 12½ miles north of Roskilde at the narrowest section of the fjord. Surprisingly, the discovery lay relatively unprotected and unpublicized until 1957 when the Danish National Museum carried out a series of underwater excavations. Every chip of the wood had to be saturated with chemicals to prevent disintegration.

Jan Sjöby wrote: "Resurrected in the main hall of the museum is a genuine knarr of the same type, and probably roughly contemporary with the ship Leif Ericsson sailed to the North American continent back in the year 1000. A knarr was a seagoing cargo and trading ship, heavily built and broad beamed, designed to carry heavy loads and take hard beatings." Until the Roskilde discovery, the knarr had remained a mystery. About 70% of the ship's timbers have been preserved, which is amazing considering that the vessel presumably dates from A.D. 1000–1050. Also displayed is a merchant ship of slender construction and elegant lines, used by the Vikings for carrying cargo across the Baltic, as well as a small ferry or fishing boat.

A Danish Viking warship is also on exhibit. This vessel is similar to the ones portrayed in the Bayeux Tapestry. Not yet assembled is a "longship," the Viking man-of-war that terrorized the coasts of Europe. Visitors calling on the museum can see the work in progress. Copies of Viking jewelry may be purchased at the museum.

The concrete and glass museum is open from June 1 to August 31 from 9 a.m. to 6 p.m.; 16 kroner ($1.44) for admission. In September and October and in April and May, it closes at 5 p.m. Otherwise, from November 1 through March 31, it opens at 10 a.m. and shuts down at 4 p.m.

What else to do? The Turistbureau, Fondens Bro v/Domkirken, arranges **Life-Seeing Tours**—that is, it matches North Americans with local people of similar interests. Trips are arranged to their homes, factories, and places of recreation. The catch is, these tours are only for groups and only by an appointment arranged well in advance with the Tourist Office.

The **Roskilde Museum,** 18 Sct. Olsgade (tel. 36-60-44), is well worth visiting. Occupying the home of a merchant of other days, the house contains a collection of the celebrated Hedebo embroidery, regional costumes from this part of Zealand, and an interesting collection of toys from the past. Exhibits also include an exceptional pair of axe-twins from the Bronze Age, a unique tomb of a woman from Viking days, and a large number of finds from the medieval times of this old cathedral town. In June, July, and August, the museum is open daily from 11 a.m. to 5 p.m. During the rest of the year, it's open weekdays from 2 to 4 p.m. and Sunday from 2 to 5 p.m. Admission is 6 kroner (54¢) for adults, free for children.

The museum also has a grocer's courtyard, with the shop in operation. **Brdr. Lützhøfts Købmandsgård,** 6–8 Ringstedgade (tel. 35-00-61), has a unique atmosphere of a Danish merchant's house from around 1910 to 1920. The same articles as the grocer had then are on sale now. The court of the merchant's house has an old coppersmith's workshop where copies of old copper jewelry are produced and sold. The shop is open from Monday to Friday from 11 a.m. to

5 p.m., Saturday from 9 a.m. to 2 p.m. In June, July, and August, it is also open on Sunday from 11 a.m. to 5 p.m. Admission is free.

The **St. Jørgensbjerg quarter** of Roskilde was originally a small fishing village, and a number of the old, half-timbered houses, some with thatched roofs, have been preserved. The houses cluster around St. Jørgensbjerg Church, which dates from about 1080. The church is open to visitors for part of June, all of July, and part of August weekdays from 10 a.m. to 2 p.m.

Roskilde has a number of old springs, some of which were once considered holy and thought to have a healing effect. For a short period during the last century, the biggest spring, **Maglekilde,** even formed the basis of a hydropathic establishment.

Roskilde Park has a fine view of the fjord, and during summer months concerts with contemporary music are held here every Tuesday night. Also during the summer, the steamship *Skjelskør* takes passengers on tours of the fjord on Saturday and Sunday at 2 and 3:30 p.m.

Throughout the year, a vegetable and flower market and a flea market are held at the Town Hall Square, Staendertorvet, on Wednesday and Saturday morning.

At the local tourist information office (tel. 35-27-00), you can obtain a pamphlet with a suggested walking route which takes you through all the Roskilde.

WHERE TO STAY: At **Lindenborg Kro,** 90 Holbaekvej (tel. 40-21-11), outside of town, two brothers, Bert and Boe Christensen, welcome you to what used to be one of the oldest inns in Denmark, tracing its origins back three centuries. However, that ancient "kro" burned to the ground, and a new one was rebuilt in 1967. What has emerged is one of the most attractive and best run inns in the country, where a healthy respect is paid to atmosphere and ambience.

Often you'll run into Danes holding family reunions here (some relatives come all the way from America to attend). Drinks are served in the Hunting Bar, where you can relax in armchairs, or else in the Golden Pheasant Inn, an English pub-style place with an open fireplace. The rooms are in a restrained Nordic modern, 15 in all, each very comfortable. All are doubles, and each unit contains a private bath, toilet, phone, and radio. The cost of all this is 400 kroner ($36) to 450 kroner ($40.50) for two persons, including a Danish breakfast.

Svogerslev Kro, 45 Hovedvejen (tel. 38-30-05), traces its origins back more than 250 years. But it has been skillfully restored, so that guests today are housed with all the benefits of modern comfort. Charmingly cozy and intimate, the inn is a typically Danish red-brick structure, resting under an old-fashioned roof. In summer, flowerboxes decorate the windows. Rooms are handsomely furnished and well kept, costing from 180 kroner ($16.20) in a single to a high of 300 kroner ($27) in a double, each unit equipped with a private shower. The kitchen serves those tempting Danish open-face sandwiches as well as an array of international dishes.

Hotel Prindsen, 13 Algade (tel. 35-80-10), is a good bet if your budget can afford it. A cozy, comfortable family hotel, it is small and attractive, smartly and suitably furnished. A single with shower goes for 275 kroner ($24.75), going up to 320 kroner ($28.80) with private bath. Depending on the plumbing, doubles rent from 410 kroner ($36.90) to 460 kroner ($41.40), breakfast included. The public rooms are sometimes full of the convivial chatter of a passing tourist party. From the pavement restaurant, you can watch the bustling life of this Danish cathedral town. You can also enjoy a wide selection of Danish dishes as well as an array of international specialties.

The **BP Motel,** 28 Motelvej (tel. 35-43-85), is a popular stopover on the motorway to Copenhagen. Prices range from 175 kroner ($15.75) in a single room without bath to 350 kroner ($31.50) in a double with bath. Breakfast is an additional 37 kroner ($3.33) per person.

At the lower end of the price range, you find the modern and comfortable **Hørgården Youth Hostel,** 61 Hørhusene (tel. 35-21-84), open to all age groups. A bed costs 45 kroner ($4.05) per night, with an additional 30 kroner ($2.70) if you rent bed linens also. If you don't have a youth hostel card, you pay an extra 22 kroner ($1.98) per night. The hostel has both large rooms with 15 beds per room and several family rooms with only four beds in each. It is open all year, but guests are not allowed inside between noon and 4 p.m. Take bus 601 or 604.

On the Outskirts

About 7½ miles north of Roskilde in the village of Jyllinge you'll find a small family hotel, **Hotel Søfryd,** Søfrydevej (tel. 38-80-11). Rooms and prices vary from 175 kroner ($15.75) for a small bathless single to 395 kroner ($35.55) for a large double room with private shower and a balcony overlooking Roskilde Fjord. The tariffs include a good Danish breakfast.

WHERE TO DINE: At **Restaurant Byparken** in Roskilde Park (tel. 35-05-72) you can enjoy the international cuisine while taking in a delightful view of Roskilde Fjord. Depending on whether you select a fish or meat dish for your main course, expect to pay from 100 kroner ($9) to 130 kroner ($11.70) for your meal.

Restaurant Toppen, Bymarken (tel. 36-04-11), is at the top of a water tower 274 feet above sea level. Here you can dine while enjoying a splendid view of the whole town and the surrounding country as well as Roskilde Fjord. A complete meal will cost from 120 kroner ($10.80) up.

The town has a number of smaller bodegas and restaurants, including a Chinese and a few Italian eating places with moderate prices.

Club 42, 42 Skomagergade (tel. 35-17-64), in the pedestrian street near the cathedral, is one of them. The restaurant, which is in one of the town's oldest houses, is richly decorated with antiques and has several small comfortable rooms, a magnificent covered garden, and a beautiful sidewalk restaurant. Club 42 specializes in good Danish food, with meals costing from 45 kroner ($4.05) to 110 kroner ($9.90). They also serve the Danmenu, two dishes of Danish food at 65 kroner ($5.85). End your meal in the Danish way, with an "endless" pot of coffee.

IRON AGE VILLAGE: At this unique **Archeological Research Center,** five miles west of Roskilde at Lejre Oldtidsbyen, an Iron Age village has been completely reconstructed. Scientists, historians, archeologists, as well as visitors flock to this 50-acre site to see how the industrious, ambitious young people and their advisers recreate the physical plant and the working conditions of primitive man. They thatch Iron Age huts, plow with "ards," harvent grain with flint sickles, weave, make primitive pottery by the open-fire method. At a shop at the entrance, some of the "ancient" handicrafts may be purchased.

The center is open May 1 to September 30 (closed the rest of the year), from 10 a.m. to 5 p.m.; admission is 30 kroner ($2.70). At the entrance to the village—deep in the woods, away from expressway traffic—is an old-style restaurant. Atop a wooded hill, with a terrace overlooking a lake, it offers light meals.

BRANCHING OUT FROM ROSKILDE: A baroque manor house, **Ledreborg Manor,** with a park laid out in French/English style, lies about 4⅓ miles southwest of Roskilde. It is open to the public on Sunday in June and August from 11 a.m. to 5 p.m. and in July daily from 11 a.m. to 5 p.m. Admission is 19 kroner ($1.71).

Not far from the manor is a **passage grave** dating from the late Stone Age, approximately 3000 B.C. This is one of the best preserved ancient monuments in Denmark.

Some 10 miles southwest of Roskilda, the **Tramway Museum Skjoldenaesholm** is situated in a pleasant woodland close to **Gyldenløveshøj,** the highest point on Zealand, 416 feet above sea level. To get to the museum, you board an old tram and travel about 1000 feet down the line to the main building.

9. Køge

This old market town, 25 miles south of Copenhagen, still retains a medieval aura, with its brick and half-timbered buildings. A new rail connection, an extension of the S-railway from Copenhagen, provides easy access to the historic town. It's our first stop on a projected one-day trek southward from Copenhagen to the island of Møn. For its dubious reputation as a witch-burning center, Køge ranks with Salem, Massachusetts.

Walk down **Kirkestraede,** filled with the graceful houses of a bygone era (a tiny building, no. 20, near the church, has a big reputation: "the oldest dated half-timbered house in Denmark"). It dates from 1527. A curiosity is **13 Smedegården**—note the twisted chimney. In front of the house, by an ancient tree, are a couple of porchstones from the Middle Ages, said to be the only pair in Denmark in their original position. Nearby is the attractively decorated **St. Nicolai Church,** which is open from 10 a.m. to noon and June 15 to September 15 from 2 to 4 p.m., except Sunday afternoon. Admission is free. Inside, look in particular for the carved angels, sans noses (thanks to Swedish troops who came this way), on the pews.

The **Museum of Køge,** 4 Norregade (tel. 65-02-62), is devoted to the history of culture in South Zealand. There are six well-furnished rooms and a kitchen with implements used between 1640 and 1899. Exhibited are special collections of costumes, textiles, carriages, farm implements, and crafts from artisans' guilds, as well as the prehistory of the area. The museum has a windowpane where Hans Christian Andersen scratched the words (translated, of course): "Oh, God, oh God in Kjøge." The museum displays a silver treasure which was found some years ago, a collection of 322 coins from all parts of Scandinavia (some from other European countries). It was the second largest find of old coins in Denmark, the oldest one a Palatinate Daler from 1548. In all, it is one of the finest provincial museums in Denmark. Texts in English clearly explain the exhibits. The museum also has a beautiful garden to which one of the oldest houses in Køge, dating from the early years of the 16th century, was moved from the main square.

Admission is 6 kroner (54¢) for adults, 2.50 kroner (23¢) for children. From June through August, the museum is open daily from 10 a.m. till 5 p.m. During the rest of the year, it may be visited daily from 2 to 5 p.m. (on Sunday from 10 a.m. till noon).

The **Køge Galleriet-Køge Skitsesamling,** 7 Brogade, are housed in an old granary on one of the most historic streets of Køge and can be visited daily except Monday from 11 a.m. to 5 p.m. An exhibition of sketches is on permanent display, whereas the gallery displays changing exhibitions of Danish art. After a visit there, you can also go to another building in Oluf I. Jensen's yard, where a non-profitmaking concern is located, turning out Danish handicrafts, including weaving. The group of dedicated craftspeople are trying to preserve the old occupations of Danes. Their arts and crafts are for sale, of course.

If you're interested in Danish arts and crafts, you might also want to visit **Vegnetslund Keramik,** 11 Teglvaerksvej (tel. 67-45-71), which was founded in 1892, and has had a turbulent history since then, flirting with bankruptcy several times. Fritz Jensen, the present owner, has developed a blue glaze that is celebrated locally. He offers stoneware, ceramics, terracotta pieces, and other products for sale in the display room. Visitors can also see the workshop. The factory is opposite an Esso station in Vordingborgvej. To reach it, go along Svansbjergvej and over the viaduct (the second road to the left is the street, Teglvaerksvej).

For guided sightseeing tours of the town, apply at the **Touristoffice,** 1 Vestergade (tel. 65-58-00), where English is spoken.

Food and Lodging

Hotel Hvide Hus, 111 Strandvejen (tel. 65-36-90), is your best all-around bet, either if you're planning to stop for the night or else you want to visit just for lunch, returning to Copenhagen by nightfall. It is an attractively modern and up-to-date hotel, containing a total of 118 rooms, each well furnished and equipped. All contain a private bath and color TV, and many units also have a balcony. The furnishings are in a severe Nordic style. The restaurant opens onto a view of Køge Bay, and there is also a bar and a lounge wih an open fireplace. Other facilities include a sauna and a solarium. Exotic birds can be seen in the reflection pool. Singles cost 330 kroner ($29.70), and doubles go for 475 kroner ($42.75).

An alternative possibility for a good room is **Søndergaard,** 15 Krogen, at Bjaeverskov, which lies between Køge and Ringsted. This was an old farmstead which has been successfully reconverted into a modern bed-and-breaksfast family-style hotel. The location is about 40 kilometers from Copenhagen. If you have a car, it is about a 10-minute drive to the beach. Next to a trotting course, Søndergaard is set on beautiful grounds, with a private garden. Children will delight in the playing field. Its most outstanding feature is its heated swimming pool (there is also a sauna). The hotel rents out two dozen bright and simply furnished bedrooms, only six of which contain private showers and toilets. Singles begin at 250 kroner ($22.50), with doubles costing from 350 kroner ($31.50). Your hosts are the friendly and helpful Inger and Viggo Snor.

FOR TRAVELERS ARRIVING FROM GERMANY: Hotel Saxkjøbing, 9 Torvet, 4990 Saxkjøbing (tel. 89-40-39), is a 17th-century inn in southern Zealand, about 16 miles from the Puttgarten/Rødbyhavn ferry landing. Travelers entering Denmark by way of the ferry from Germany find the hotel a delightful stopover before heading north to Copenhagen or other areas. The classic stucco-and-timber exterior of the inn belies the fact that inside you will find modern facilities, including comfortable rooms, many equipped with private bath or shower. A double room rents for about 240 kroner ($21.60) per night, including service. Singles cost 155 kroner ($13.95). For another 40 Kroner ($3.60), you'll get a hearty Danish breakfast of meat, cheeses, breads, and coffee. Dinner in the cozy dining room is a memorable experience, especially when you order the Danish plate—a huge array of smørrebrød—costing about 60 kroner ($8.04) per person. To reach Saxkjøbing, take the Europe Road E4 from Rødbyhavn.

VALLØ CASTLE: This castle with French-style gardens, 4 miles from Køge, was built between the 16th and 18th centuries, and once contained apartments for nearly a dozen aristocratic spinsters ("unmarried daughters of Danish nobility," if you prefer). The apartments cannot be visited as the castle has been converted to modern housing for old age pensioners. However, the sweeping gardens, with their lakes, moats, many rare trees, and flowerbeds containing mostly roses and dahlias can be visited for no charge. From April to October, the hours are 10 a.m. to sunset.

SELSØ SLOT: Denmark's first Renaissance slot (small castle), built in 1576 and converted to the baroque style in 1733 is open to the public. It's at Hornsherred, east of Skibby and south of the village of Skuldelev, 35 miles west of Copenhagen on Zealand (tel. 32-01-71).

Selsø is about the only private manor house on Zealand that tourists are allowed to inspect thoroughly, from the medieval kitchen under the basement vaults to the prison dungeons below. The baroque rooms are the most beautiful, and you can even see some of the oldest wallpaper extant in Denmark.

The last occupant of the manor house was Agathe Von Qualen Plessen, who left only one heir, but she owned, in addition to Selsø, many other estates and the heir never had time to occupy the Selsø property. The house remained unoccupied after 1829, falling into disrepair. But it was the very accumulation or rubbish over a century and a half of neglect that preserved the house's original interior. Annually the little castle stages such cultural events as Renaissance dancing and orchestra concerts.

Selsø Slot is open all week from mid-June to mid-August from 11 a.m. to 5 p.m. and all week for a week in mid-October from 1 to 4 p.m. Otherwise, it is open on Saturday and Sunday from 1 to 4 p.m. around Easter, from mid-May to mid-June, and from mid-August to mid-October. Admission is 17 kroner ($1.53) for adults, 10 kroner (90¢) for children.

Chapter IV

FUNEN AND JUTLAND

FUNEN IS THE SECOND-LARGEST Danish island, separating its bigger sister, Zealand, from the peninsula of Jutland, an extension of mainland Europe bordering on Germany. Although divided geographically, Funen and Jutland are one in charm and spirit—difficult to describe without lapsing into sentimentality. But lapse I shall, if only to tell a bittersweet story straight out of Funen:

Hans Christian Andersen was born in Odense, the son of a shoemaker. The years were oft unkind to young Hans, a poor storyteller. Still, he struggled onward, at last achieving such world renown that his tales were translated into 80 languages. But this is not the end of our story. Hans, it seems, had the heart of a swan, but he was, alas, an ugly duckling. So he lost his one true love, who was (oh fate!) the Swedish nightingale, Jenny Lind. . . .

Funen and Jutland are rich, treasure-filled (a Viking ship, runic stones) stamping grounds. What remains now is to outline in detail what to see and where to stay and dine, with our ever-present budget in mind.

FUNEN

LIFE ON A DANISH FARM: To get close to the heart of Denmark (the island of Funen) and to meet the Danes, there is no better way than by spending a week on one of their farms. Many rural homes throughout the country are prepared to receive paying guests. A minimum stay of seven days or more is desired, but this is not always mandatory. The price of a room and three meals a day, from Zealand to Jutland, is 175 kroner ($15.75) per person in season. Children from 4 to 12 are granted reductions of 25%. Farms never take more than eight paying guests, to preserve the family atmosphere.

Take a pin and stick it anywhere on a map of the island, go where the pin points, and you'll find a thatched and timbered farm, or perhaps a more modernized homestead. All are good bases—any point on the island can easily be reached on a day trip. Manor houses, museums, castles, woods, lakes—there is much to see and do in a week. Select the part of Denmark you'd like to explore, then write the local tourist office in that area, stating your requirements, the number in your party, the length of your stay, the ages of your children, if any, and whether you want full or half board.

Editorial postscript: The opportunity is golden to enjoy simple country-style cooking, with fresh vegetables, newly laid eggs, and richly churned butter. It's an exciting, offbeat adventure for those who can invest the time.

1. Nyborg

Visitors crossing on the Inter-City train ferries and the car ferries linking Zealand and Funen dock at this old seaport and market town, providing a good opportunity to explore historic Nyborg before rushing on to Odense or Copenhagen.

Nyborg Castle, founded in 1171, is the oldest royal seat in Scandinavia. The moated castle, with its ramparts intact, has seen revisions and expansions over the centuries. Denmark's first Constitution was signed here by King Erik Glipping in 1282, and Nyborg Castle was the seat of the Danish parliament, Danehof, until 1413. This medieval parliament formed an uneasy alliance between nobility and clergy. The present furnishings of the castle date primarily from the days of Christian IV, when Nyborg was a resplendent Renaissance-style palace. The castle is open from 10 a.m. to 3 p.m. March 1 to May 31 and September 1 to November 30; from 10 a.m. to 5 p.m. from June 1 to August 31. It's closed from December 1 to February 28. Admission is 7 kroner (63¢) for adults, 1.50 kroner (14¢) for children.

The **town square** of Nyborg came into existance when a block of houses was demolished in 1540 to make room for the royal tournaments of Christian III.

The **Church of Our Lady,** dating from the late 14th–early 15th centuries, has a fine Gothic spire, and the interior contains wood carvings, old epitaphs, candelabra, and ship's models. You enter through the door on the south side. Opposite the church is the 12th-century chapter house of the Order of St. John (Korsbrødregården), with a fine vaulted cellar which has been converted into a gift shop.

Nyborg Museum is housed in a well-preserved, half-timbered merchant's house built in 1601. In it, you'll see interesting artifacts of the region from prehistoric to modern times. For this and other information about Nyborg, go to the **Tourist Office,** 9 Torvet (tel. 31-02-80).

If you'd like to stay over in Nyborg, try **Hotel Nyborg,** 6 Adelgade (tel. 31-09-94), which is clean and comfortable, with an English-speaking management. The facilities are limited, but everything is well cared for. Rooms are in the style of a traditional provincial hotel of moderate quality. Depending on the plumbing, singles range from 140 kroner ($12.60) to 180 kroner ($16.20); doubles, from 250 kroner ($22.50).

2. Odense

This ancient town, the third largest in Denmark, doesn't look the way it did when its famous son, Hans Christian Andersen, walked its streets, his head spinning with fairytale fantasies of nightingales, duckponds, snow queens, little mermaids, and an emperor's lack of clothes. But industrious Odense has preserved much that is associated with its romantic past. It's still possible to discover a few unspoiled streets left over from yesteryear.

This Funen capital makes a good base for exploring the rest of the island—trips either north to the Viking ship at Ladby, or south to the château country and the archipelago.

The town has a very effective **Odense Tourist Association,** Rådhuset (tel. 12-75-20), which will aid in many problems and help arrange excursions. Here you can purchase tickets and receive information on a two-hour **sightseeing tour,** which is held daily except Sunday from July 1 to August 31. The charge is 40 kroner ($3.60) for adults, 15 kroner ($1.35) for children. A **Castle Tour** is offered every Saturday from July 1 to August 31, taking five hours, with adults being charged 95 kroner ($8.10) and children 45 kroner ($4.05). Also at the tourist office, you can find out about the **Hans Christian Andersen plays** in the open-air theater in the Funen Village, which are presented from mid-July to mid-August. Tickets cost 25 kroner ($2.25) for adults, 15 kroner ($1.35) for children.

During summer, Odense is overrun with fans of the storyteller. If no accommodations are available, the tourist office will also book guests into private homes.

HOTELS: The easy-to-find hotels in Odense cluster around the railway station like baby swans drawn to a protective but ugly mother duckling. I'll lead off with the pick of the moderately priced choices:

Hotel Windsor, 45 Vindegade (tel. 12-06-52), is a 19th-century corner building that offers the best Danish-style, modernized rooms for the money in Odense. All the rooms have both showers and toilets (most of the units also are equipped with TV sets). Its updated interior has a breath of autumn to it. From the lounge to the bedrooms upstairs, all is immaculate and pleasantly furnished. Singles begin at 315 kroner ($28.35), going up to 500 kroner ($45), and doubles begin at 480 kroner ($43.20), peaking at 610 kroner ($54.90) in a suite.

Ny Missionhotel, 24 Østre Stationsvej (tel. 11-77-45), directly across from the railway station, is a Victorian-style corner building, a monument to the comfort of the days when servants were cheaper by the dozen. This Mission's a tower of brick, crowned by a steeple; it offers medium-size doubles with semi-modern furnishings and private baths or showers for 400 kroner ($36), service and Moms included. Singles with bath or shower cost up to 245 kroner ($22.05). Bathless doubles cost from 350 kroner ($31.50). The least expensive singles, with hot and cold running water only, go for 195 kroner ($17.55). The staid middle-class family look has never been erased from the spacious public rooms, nor would anyone dare try—that's how the guests like it. The dining room is a good choice for adequate, typically Danish meals.

Missionhotellet Ansgar, 32 Østre Stationsvej (tel. 11-96-93), next to its Mission-chain sister, is smaller and more up to date. All year its doubles with bath rent for 350 kroner ($31.50) to 395 kroner ($35.55), the singles with bath from 220 kroner ($19.80) to 265 kroner ($23.85). The Ansgar is quieter than the bigger Mission, and it has two courtyards. There is also free parking. Meals, served in the spanking-clean dining room, are good and priced at 65 kroner ($5.85) for a two-course repast, including tips and taxes.

Motel Odense, 2 Hunderupgade (tel. 11-42-13), on Highway A-1 at the A-9 junction, one mile from the center of Odense, is an 82-bed motel in a half-timbered farmhouse. The farmhouse has, of course, been overhauled and decked out with modern comforts. Its attractively compact and well-furnished bedrooms appeal to many tastes. How much? From 405 kroner ($36.45) to 450 kroner ($40.50) in a double room, and from 305 kroner ($27.45) to 325 kroner ($29.25) in a single room. All prices include service and tax, and each unit is equipped with a shower, toilet, and TV. The motel also has a well-appointed first-class restaurant.

If you're ready for a splurge, you might enjoy staying at **Hotel H. C. Andersen,** 7 Claus Bergsgade (tel. 14-78-00), a new, first-class hostelry with 148 rooms, all of them with baths, toilets, phones, color TV, radios, and refrigerator brars. You can dine in the Hans Christian Restaurant, have your drinks in the Fairy-Tale bar, and be entertained in the Nightingale (Nattergalen) nightclub, which has live music. The hotel has an exercise room with billiard tables, table tennis, a sauna, a solarium, and lots of free parking. Single rooms cost 525 kroner ($47.25) and doubles 680 kroner ($61.20), with breakfast included.

READERS' GUESTHOUSE SELECTION: "A very special home at reasonable rates was found in Bogense, a short and easy drive from Odense. Here we luxuriated in large double rooms upstairs in the home of **Dr. and Mrs. Alfred Larsen,** 1 Aebeløgade (tel. 81-15-40). Rooms with wide windows overlooked large, secluded gardens. Double rooms are 200 kroner ($18) including breakfast, which consists of Mrs. Larsen's homemade breads, rolls, and pastries; large slabs of butter, marmalade, slices of cheese and sausage; pitchers of both milk and coffee; and a soft-boiled egg. Dr. Larsen, an M.D., speaks English, and his wife just a little. This was a most restful place to stay" (Mrs. Carl Skounborg, Chico, Calif.).

FUNEN FARE: Odense is a restaurant town—rich in variety but not necessarily in expense. Th old inns, of course, provide the most traditional Danish atmosphere.

Rode 7, 34 Østre Stationsvej (tel. 12-30-99), is near the railway station, but it is closer in spirit to the Opera House around the corner. Singers, writers, and musicians take their meals in one of the three dining rooms, and those who are on a budget make sure to eat before 8 p.m., when the à la carte menu takes over. It's easy to stack up a good, filling meal during the day from the smørrebrød checklist (these aren't just open-face sandwhiches—they're productions), from 28 kroner ($2.52). Hot meals are offered, ranging from 54 kroner ($4.86) to 138 ($12.42) for a three-course menu. Theater memorabilia cover the walls, and in all the atmosphere is jaunty, spicy, and friendly. The restaurant is closed in July.

Under Lindetraeet, 2 Ramsherred (tel. 12-92-86), is a 2½-centuries-old inn across the cobbled street from Hans Christian Andersen's house. Rut and Ebbe Hansen welcome you. Although popular, the little inn, with its hip-gabled roof and beam and plaster façade, is still unspoiled. Friendly and old world in its atmosphere, it's a fine place for a meal, a first-class restaurant serving both Danish and international selections. The simplest meal here is likely to cost 105 kroner ($9.45). The service is fine, too, matching the table settings and Danish china and stemware, silver candlesticks, and highly polished silver service plates. In summer, meals and light refreshments are served outside under linden trees. Artists often sit here, painting Andersen's house. The inn is open daily from 9 a.m. to midnight.

Den Gamle Kro, 23 Overgade (tel. 12-14-33), is a well-preserved old inn in the center of town. A wrought-iron-hinged oak door leads into two dining rooms—each cozy and rich with antiques. Cozier still is the brick-vaulted cellar, with its oak tables and antique chairs. Some are elaborately carved, others Empire. Lovers of quiet—or just plain lovers—congregate here under the spell cast by flickering candlelight. Menu sampling: beef Stroganoff, topped with crisp bacon and tomato wedges and served with french fries. Dinners are accompanied by a covered loaf of hot french bread, cutting board provided. Fresh strawberries, topped with whipped cream, are usually offered. Noontime is the occasion for 95-krone ($8.55) luncheon platter specials—featuring lobster salad, smoked salmon, herring, liverpaste with bacon, roast beef, hot filet of plaice, veal with mushrooms, plus cheese, pineapple, and peaches. In season, game dishes are a specialty. The house's dessert special is crêpes Andersen. A complete dinner will cost from 140 kroner ($12.60) up.

Sortebro Kro (tel. 13-28-26), outside the entrance to the regional culture museum (Funen Village), is a coaching inn that dates from 1807. Odense purchased it in 1943 and began the mammoth job of restoration. Today, it serves country meals in an engaging atmosphere. Waiters move about the two main dining rooms, lighting candles and directing diners to the sagging table where the popular all-you-can-eat Danish cold board is served for 105 kroner ($9.45) per person. Tip: Before partaking of this array of Danish specialties, starve for two days at least. A complete meal costs from 140 kroner ($12.60) up. The interior of Sortebro (open till 11 p.m.) is an attraction on its own: long refectory tables, sagging ceilings with overhead beams, three-legged chairs, florid handmade chests, and crockery cupboards.

THE MAJOR SIGHTS: The object of most pilgrimages here, of course, is the "hus" and museum of Hans Christian Andersen. **H. C. Andersen's Hus,** 39 Hans Jensensstraede (tel. 13-13-72), where dauntless tourist fight it out with the school kids to gain admission. Here is sheltered most of the H.C.A. memorabilia: his famous walking stick, top hat, battered portmanteau, plus letters to his dear friend Miss Jenny Lind and fellow-writer Charles Dickens. In addition, hundreds of documents, manuscripts, and reprints of his books in dozens of languages are displayed. The museum is open April 1 to May 31 from 10 a.m. to 5 p.m.; June 1 to August 31 from 9 a.m. to 6 p.m.; September 1 to September 30 from 10 a.m. to 5 p.m.; October 1 to March 31 from 10 a.m. to 3 p.m. The admission charged is 10 kroner (90¢).

Other principal sights include the following:

Andersen's Childhood Home (H. C. Andersens Barndomshjem): At 3 Munkemøllestraede is the humble "abode of my childhood," the house where the fairytale writer lived between the ages of 2 and 14. Someone once wrote that his "dearest memories of childhood" were attached to this house. But from what is known of Andersen's childhood, those memories weren't so dear; his mother was a drunken, superstitious washerwoman, and Andersen was a gawky boy—later to be referred to as an orangutang—lumbering and graceless, the victim of his fellow urchins' cruel jabs. However, all is serene at the cottage today; in fact, the little house has a certain unpretentious charm, and the "garden still blooms," as in the Snow Queen. Visiting hours are from 10 a.m. to 5 p.m., April 1 to September 30; from noon to 3 p.m., October 1 to March 31; admission is 4 kroner (36¢).

St. Canute's Cathedral, Klingenberg (tel. 12-03-92), is considered the most important Gothic-style building in Denmark, despite its unimpressive façade. The elegant triptych gold altar screen, carved by Calus Berg in 1526 at the request of Queen Christine, the widow of King Hans, alone draws many to the 13th-century brick building. Killed by angry Jutland taxpayers in 1086, King Canute, the patron of the church, was canonized 15 years later. From May 1 to August 31, St. Canute's may be visited from 10 a.m. to 5 p.m. weekdays, and 11:30 a.m. to 12:30 p.m. on Sunday. During the rest of the year, it is open from

10 a.m. to 4 p.m. weekdays (10 a.m. to noon on Saturday from November 1 to April 1).

Møntergården Museum, 48–50 Overgade (tel. 13-13-72), preserves the flavor of Odense that fast eroded when the town moved forward as a commercial center. Here, in a setting of 16th- and 17th-century buildings, authentically furnished, that past lives on—in a somewhat stilted fashion. One of the greatest Danish exhibitions of coins and metal is displayed in the museum. The Historical Museum is open from 10 a.m. to 4 p.m. Admission is 4 kroner (36¢).

Funen Village Den Fynske Landsby, Sejerskovvej (take bus 2 from Flakhaven to the museum, about 1½ miles from the center of Odense), is one of the biggest open-air regional culture museums in Denmark, vividly preserving Funen life of the 18th and 19th centuries. On this site in the Hunderup Woods, old buildings—among them a toll house, weaver's shop, windmill, farming homestead, jail, vicarage, a village school, even a brickworks—were reassembled and authentically furnished. Then farmers, sheep, and hogs moved in, and the village came alive. These days it is alive, too, with plays and folk dances, staged at the Greek-style theater. In addition, you can visit workshops, seeing a coppersmith at work, as well as a basketmaker, spoon cutter, blacksmith, and weaver. The museum is open April 1 to April 30 from 9 a.m. to 4:30 p.m.; May 1 to May 31 from 9 a.m. to 5:30 p.m.; June 1 to August 15 from 9 a.m. to 6:30 p.m.; August 16 to August 31 from 9 a.m. to 4:30 p.m.; September 1 to September 30 from 9 a.m. to 4:30 p.m.; October 1 to October 31 from 10 a.m. to 3:30 p.m.; November 1 to March 31 it is open on Sunday only, from 10 a.m. until 3:30 p.m. The admission charged is 6 kroner (54¢). The village inn, Sortebro Kro, however, is open every day all year round (see above).

The **Danish Railways Museum** has a cavalcade of original locomotives and carriages from the past century reflecting the railway history of the country. Denmark acquired at first railroad back in 1849. One of the oldest locomotives in the collection, an "A-Machine," dates from 1888. Also on display are two royal coaches and a double-decker carriage. Denmark's biggest model railway car can also be seen. The museum is just adjacent to the Odense Railway Station. (Incidentally, Hans Christian Andersen was an ardent railway fan.) The museum is open May 1 to September 30 from 10 a.m. to 4 p.m.; October 1 to April 30 on Sunday only from 10 a.m. to 3:30 p.m. Admission is 15 kroner ($1.35) for adults, 10 kroner (90¢) for children.

NIGHTLIFE: If you like dancing to live music, then the places to go are the **Nattergalen** (Nightingale) nightclub in the Hotel H. C. Andersen, 7 Claus Bergsgade (tel. 14-78-00), and the **Atlantic,** 45 Overgade (tel. 13-25-27), where Danes and foreigners of all ages trip the light fantastic. For your first drink, you pay from 20 kroner ($1.80) to 30 kroner ($2.70).

For dancing to disco music, the **Tiffany,** 45 Overgade (tel. 14-98-00), and the **Tordenskjold,** 7 Asylgade (tel. 13-77-08), are the most exclusive discos with light-and-sound shows. Drinks cost from 20 kroner ($1.80) to 30 kroner ($2.70).

BRANCHING OUT FROM ODENSE: Now, for some one-day excursions, we head north to:

The Viking Ship at Ladby

At Ladby, 12 miles northeast of Odense, is a Viking ship from the tenth century. The Ladby ship is a rare find, discovered in 1935. Visitors descend into an underground mound, where the remains of the 72-foot-long ship are displayed along with replicas from the excavation. The genuine articles are in the

National Museum in Copenhagen. The skeleton of the pagan chieftain who was buried in this looted ship was never found, but the bones of his stable of horses —nearly a dozen—and a pack of dogs were discovered. The burial mound, reached either by car or bus, is open daily except Monday from 10 a.m. to 4 p.m. all year. Admission is 7 kroner (63¢).

Egeskov Castle

This Renaissance castle, with its magnificent gardens, is the most romantic and splendid of the fortified manors of Denmark. The castle was built in 1554 on oak pillars in the middle of a moat or small lake. International experts consider it the best preserved Renaissance water-castle in Europe. Visitors, some 200,000 a year, can normally visit only the gardens and landscaped flower fields —but those are dazzling enough. Chamber-music concerts of high quality are held during summer in the magnificent great hall of the castle on ten summer Sundays, running at 3:30 p.m., starting the last Sunday in June. Tickets cost 60 kroner ($5.40), which includes the entrance fee to the gardens. Moated, spired, towered, and gabled Egeskov is certainly impressive from the outside, too.

The most dramatic story in the castle's history concerns an unfortunate maiden, Rigborg, who was seduced by a young nobleman and bore him a child out of wedlock. Banished to the castle, she was imprisoned by her father in a tower from 1599 to 1604.

The 30-acre park, on the main road between Faaborg and Nyborg, is open daily from 9 a.m. to 6 p.m. in July and August; from 10 a.m. to 5 p.m. in May, June, and September; weekends only from 10 a.m. to 5 p.m. in April and October. Admission to the park costs 17 kroner ($1.53) for adults, 8.50 kroner (77¢) for children under 12. There's an automobile, horse carriage, and airplane museum on the grounds as well. If adults go from the park to the gardens or vice versa, an extra charge of 15 kroner ($1.35) is levied; children pay an additional 7.50 kroner (68¢). The castle is a private home and cannot be visited, except during concerts. And then only the great hall and adjoining historical rooms are open for inspection.

3. Svendborg

This old port on Svendborg Sound has long been popular with the Danes as a boating center—you'll see everything from yachts to ketches and kayaks in the harbor. Foreigners generally find that Svendborg makes a good base for touring not only the château country but the South Funen archipelago as well.

Svendborg is a market town and anyone visiting on a Sunday morning should go to its cobblestoned central plaza, where the flowers and fish purveyed sort of cancel out each other's scents. The town still retains some of its medieval heritage, although much of the old part has been torn down in the name of progress.

Still, Svendborg has numerous winding streets and several brick and half-timbered structures. See, in particular, the oldest house, the 16th-century, half-timbered **Anne Hvides Home,** Fruestraede, in the town center, which now shelters a county museum of little more than passing interest. Also walk down **Bagergade,** inspecting the old homes of early seafarers. Svendborg has a Romanesque, late 12th-century **Church of St. Nicolai** that's definitely worth a visit.

Møllergade is one of the oldest streets in town, with about 100 different shops. Tradespeople here have created a pedestrian street so you can stroll at leisure. In between shopping, you can stop off at **Svendborgstuen,** 32 Møllergade (tel. 21-09-01), a bodega.

The city has one of the most helpful tourist offices in Denmark. The **Svendborg Tourist Office** is at 20 Møllergade, Torvet (tel. 21-09-80). From July 1 to

August 16 it is open Monday to Friday from 9 a.m. to 5:30 p.m.; Saturday from 9 a.m. to 3 p.m.; and Sunday from 10 a.m. to noon. From mid-March to mid-September, except for the period cited, it is open Monday to Friday from 9 a.m. to 5 p.m. (on Saturday to noon). From mid-September to mid-March, it is closed on Saturday.

In Svendborg you'll find the new **Dantourist,** which is a cooperative effort between local tourist associations, shipping companies, the Danish Tourist Association, and others. Together they offer you holiday trips on moderate terms. You can rent summer cottages or have farmhouse holidays where you can live with the local families, even take a bicycle holiday where the routes and hotels or youth hostels are arranged in advance.

Inexpensive tours of the South Funen archipelago, as well as of the manor houses inland, are arranged at the Tourist Bureau in Svendborg. I recommend especially a trip to the nearby island of **Taasinge,** to see the impressive **Valdemar Castle.** On Taasinge you can also see the shipping village of **Troense,** where more than 30 houses have been declared national historic monuments which can't be torn down or have their façades altered, and the church at **Bregninge.** A bridge connects Svendborg and Taasinge.

For those staying over, we turn now to:

ROOMS AND MEALS: **Missionshotellet Stella Maris,** 3 Kogtvedvaenget (tel. 21-38-91), is an old-fashioned, homey type of place that will appeal to many. Built along classic Danish architectural lines, it is set back from the water, and nearby you can take walks through a garden setting. The furniture may be dated, but all is comfortable, and the patina of time has given the hotel a certain dignity. Seaview units are more expensive, of course. Both singles and doubles are rented with and without baths. A single room with breakfast included rents for 165 kroner ($14.85) to 220 kroner ($19.80), with doubles going for 270 kroner ($24.30) to 390 kroner ($35.10). It's best to stay here on the half-board rate, ranging from 240 kroner ($21.60) to 285 kroner ($25.65) in a single, from 400 kroner ($36) to 520 kroner ($46.80) for two persons. The staple dishes of the local countryside are handled best. The service is smooth and welcoming.

Kogtvedstrand, 20 Sundvaenget (tel. 21-06-18), is an old-fashioned Danish house, with a fireplace, rocking chairs, a library, a piano waiting for some player, and superb hospitality provided by English-speaking Ellen and Holger B. Dorvil. The seashore location of the inn is about 1.8 miles from the center of the city. Beds are comfortable, and rooms are nicely furnished. No singles are rented out, but two persons can stay here at a cost of 235 kroner ($21.15) a night, including a Danish breakfast. Other meals can be prepared in the guest kitchen.

Hotel Royal, 5 Toldbodvej (tel. 21-21-13), is for those who prefer a central location. This corner brick structure stands near the station and is often used to lodge guests on those motorcoach tours of Denmark. The hotel is owned by a group of 14 young people, who have done their utmost to renovate and redecorate the house and the rooms and have succeeded. A hotel of modest comforts, the Royal has 20 comfortable rooms, each unit equipped with hot and cold running water. The furnishings in the bedrooms are very simple, and guests find adequate bathrooms on each floor. Singles are rented for 150 kroner ($13.50), with bathless doubles going for 245 kroner ($22.05). The most expensive rooms, the handful of doubles rented with bath, cost 305 kroner ($27.45) nightly. The Royal serves only breakfast, at a cost of 33 kroner ($2.97).

Hotel Aerø, 1 Brogade (tel. 21-07-60), is modest and good. It is a reasonably priced old-style but modernized hotel near the harbor. In a quiet position, it offers adequately furnished single rooms from 140 kroner ($12.60), the tariff rising to 245 kroner ($22.05) in a double. The hotel has a good chef who makes fresh fish a specialty. Dinners are from 65 kroner ($5.85).

Villa Strandbo, 13 Børges Allé, Rantzausminde (tel. 21-12-74), is a first-class boarding house, perched on the sound, about a mile and a half from the center of town. Carl Børge, who speaks English, is a gracious host and he'll welcome you to one of his comfortable and well-furnished rooms, where you can stay and enjoy his Danish cuisine, at a cost of 185 kroner ($16.65) per person nightly. Guests are accepted only from June 15 to August 15. The house stands on the water, and the furnishings inside are well selected in the traditional style. You'll have the feeling of living in a fairly luxurious and well-appointed private home.

Lodgings on Thurø

Hotel & Pension Røgeriet, Thurø (tel. 20-50-84), stands in a tranquil, waterside setting, just three miles from Svendborg and opening onto its own private beach. It's a lovely old Danish compound, furnished in a homey, personalized style, with terraces containing comfortable chairs set out so that you may soak in the view. The view, incidentally, is of the sound and the Isle of Taasinge. Most of the well-furnished bedrooms have private toilets, showers, and balconies opening onto the sea. It's best to stay here on the half-board plan. In a double, depending on the plumbing in your room, the half-board cost is from 230 kroner ($20.70) to 270 kroner ($24.30) per person. In a single, the demi-pension tariff ranges from 230 kroner ($20.70) to 280 kroner ($25.20). There are only 16 rooms, so reservations are imperative during the summer months. In the cozy dining room, first-class materials are used in the cooking. Dishes are served by a pleasant staff. If you base at the compound, you can set off on day excursions, exploring the islands south of Funen and many historic manor houses in the countryside. Your friendly, English-speaking hosts are a brother and sister, Dorthe Petersen and Niels Hansen. Thurø is a horseshoe-shaped island connected with Funen by a causeway. Its many orchards and well-cared-for gardens have earned for it the title of "The Garden of Denmark."

Your Own Apartment

Hotel Tre Roser, 90 Fåborgvej (tel. 21-64-26), is a holiday center which rents out 70 well-furnished and attractively decorated apartments suitable for one to five persons. Each of these well-equipped units comes with bath, toilet, and a fully stocked kitchen. You also have plenty of parking space as well as a patio. Most German and Danish guests stay here by the week; however, if available, apartments are rented on a daily basis, a single costing from 235 kroner ($21.15) to 245 kroner ($25.05), a double going for 340 kroner ($30.60) to 350 kroner ($31.50). The most expensive apartment costs 390 kroner ($35.10), and an extra bed will be added for 60 kroner ($5.40). In the main building is a well-appointed restaurant, and you'll also find a TV room, billiard room, and table tennis. Outside a big swimming pool, as well as paddling pool and playground for children. The location is about a mile from Svendborg and three miles from the nearest bathing beaches. A five-minute drive will take you to the Svendborg Golf Course, where Tre Roser guests play free.

A Kro (Inn) at Oure

Majorgården, 155 Landesvejen, Oure (tel. 28-18-49), on the coast road between Svendborg and Nyborg, is an out-of-the-way white-brick inn that has been cherished by such illustrious Danes as tenor Lauritz Melchior. Without meals, rooms cost 130 kroner ($11.70) single, 185 kroner ($16.65) double. If you're just driving by, stop in for a "plate of the inn"—two kinds of herring, plaice, meatballs, meat sausages, liverpaste, and cheese for 55 kroner ($4.95). A large selection of fish and meat dishes is also available for 38 kroner ($3.42) and up. Outside a bower of roses grows against the walls, low white tables are placed on the lawn for coffee, and a little pond at the rear is filled with ducks. An old horse stable has been turned into a bar, complete with bowling lanes.

Lodgings on Taasinge

The **Motel Troense,** 15 Badstuen (tel. 22-53-41), is a small, six-room motel built in the half-timbered style. It stands on the island of Taasinge, which is the biggest in the South Funen archipelago. It is connected to Funen by the Svendborg Sound Bridge. Only double rooms are rented, these costing from 260 kroner ($23.40) nightly, including a continental breakfast. Of course, a single person might occupy a double room, if available, and a special price will be quoted if the stay is for more than one night. Troense, from which the motel takes its name, is one of the best preserved villages in Denmark. Once upon a time, Taasinge skippers sailed the world's seven seas. If you have children, the staff will direct you to Vindebyøre, where there are many activities designed for youngsters.

Country Inn Dining on Taasinge

Bregninge Kro, in Bregninge, Taasinge, three miles south of Svendborg on the main road, is an old-fashioned country inn that has been serving abundant farm-style meals since the turn of the century. It offers a daily middag (Danmenu) for 65 kroner ($5.85) but also has a large variety of modern Danish cuisine. Bregninge Kro has a fresh, clean-scrubbed look to it. It is a plaster structure with a steep tile roof, set off the main road. It makes for a pleasant and restful interlude, enhanced by the thoughtful innkeepers.

READER'S HOTEL SELECTION: "We recommend the **Stenstrup Kro,** 2 Jernbaneveg (tel. 26-15-14), seven miles northwest of Svendborg. The dining rooms are in an old building that has been decorated most attractively with antiques, and the food is excellent. The rooms are in a newly constructed wing which is modern and most accommodations have baths. The proprietors speak no English, but they have a chef or waitress or someone about the place—perhaps a guest—who does, so one manages. To stay here on half board costs from 210 kroner ($18.90) to 235 kroner ($21.15) per person daily. An overnight stay in a double goes for 185 kroner ($16.65) if bathless, rising to 235 kroner ($21.15) with bath. Bathless singles rent for 110 kroner ($9.90). The kro is convenient for touring the southern portion of Funen and for ferries to such places as Aerø Island" (Allan V. Ven Cott, Santa Rosa, Calif.)

4. Faaborg

A good base for exploring southwestern Funen, Faaborg lies 17 miles from Svendborg. A small seaside town of red-roofed buildings, it is of interest to those who want to see one of the best collections of Funen painters and sculptors, particulary the work of Kai Nielsen, one of the most important of modern Danish sculptors. The town—crowned by an old belfry—has a number of well-preserved buildings, among them the medieval **Vesterport,** all that's left of Faaborg's walled fortifications.

Don't miss seeing the controversial piece of sculpture, the **Ymerbrønd** (Ymer Well), a work of Nielsen that has been denounced as obscene by some, praised by others. It is displayed in the market square (a copy is in the Museum of Faaborg). The sculpture depicts a man drinking from the udder of a bony cow while the cow licks a baby.

The **Faaborg Museum,** 75 Grønnegade (tel. 61-33-38), has a rich collection of the works of Kai Nielsen, showing that the artist has a sense of humor. In the octagonal rotunda of the museum is a huge statue, standing in a cascade of infants. This impressive work by Nielsen was commissioned by Mads Rasmussen, the town rich man and art patron who bore the nickname of "Mads Tomato."

Aside from Nielsen's works, the museum also contains paintings by such outstanding local artists as Peter Hansen, Johannes Larsen, and Fritz Syberg, who owe a debt to French impressionism. The gallery is open April 1 to October 31 from 10 a.m. to 4 p.m.; November 1 to March 31 only on weekends and holidays from 11 a.m. to 3 p.m. Admission is 10 kroner (90¢).

Den Gamle Gaard (The Old Merchant's House), 1 Holkegade (tel. 61-33-38), built in 1725, was established as a museum in 1932. The life of Faaborg in the 18th and 19th centuries is the subject of displays in the front building, with various furnishings, some of which were the property of an early love of Hans Christian Andersen, Riborg Voigt. You'll see glass, china, and faïences which are an indication of the extent of Faaborg's past importance as a trade and shipping center. Exhibits from Lyø are in the back, with beautiful textiles and embroidery. The house is open May 15 to September 15 daily from 10:30 a.m. to 4:30 p.m., charging 10 kroner (90¢) for adults. Children are admitted free.

The old belfry, **Klokketårnet,** Tårngade, is the landmark of Faaborg, the remains of the Church of Sct. Nicolai, the first church of the town which was built in the 13th century and demolished around 1600. The town's old fire sledge is to be seen here. The tower has the largest carillon of Funen, the bells playing hymns four times a day. The belfry may be visited from May 1 to September 30 from 9 to 11:30 a.m. and 2 to 5 p.m.; October 1 to March 31 from 2 to 4 p.m. Admission is 2 kroner (18¢).

Helligåndskirken, the Church of the Holy Ghost, Kirkestraede, is the parish church of Faaborg, dating from the 16th century, when it was constructed as part of a monastery of the Order of the Holy Ghost. It became the parish church after the Reformation. A Bible which belong to King Christian IV, circa 1632, lies on the altar. A church cabinet from 1500 may also be seen. The altarpiece was painted by W. Marstrand.

If you can plan to be in Faaborg during July, you may be there for the annual festival. Ask at the Faaborg and District Tourist Association, 2 Havnegade, for information.

WHERE TO STAY: Hotel **Faaborg Fjord,** 175 Svendborgvej (tel. 61-10-10), in its own park on the edge of town, is the newest year-round hotel of Funen, with comfortable rooms, each with a balcony/terrace, private bath, and telephone. Guests may use the indoor swimming pool and the sauna. Singles rent for 305 kroner ($27.45) and doubles for 460 kroner ($41.40). The restaurant of the hotel has a magnificent sea view and good food.

Hotel Strandgade, 2 Strandgade (tel. 61-20-12), is in the center of town, near the market and the old part of Faaborg. The building dates from 1814. It was restored in 1981 and now provides 11 modern double rooms with private baths and toilets. Single persons are charged 205 kroner ($18.45), while doubles rent for 315 kroner ($28.35), all tariffs including breakfast.

Hotel Pension Mosegaard, 31 Nabgyden (tel. 61-06-91), is a private little compound, completely surrounded by trees and opening onto the shoreline. Run by H. P. Andersen, it is an oasis of charm and Danish comfort. Most guests stay here on a weekly basis, exploring the sights of South Funen. Guests are received from March 1 to September 1, paying 205 kroner ($18.45) in a single without bath, 270 kroner ($24.30) in a single with bath, these rates including not only the room, but breakfast and dinner. On the same half-board terms, two persons in a room without bath are charged 390 kroner ($35.10) daily, the rate going up to 480 kroner ($43.20) in a room with bath and sea view. Full-board terms are also available, but most guests prefer to tour during the day.

ON THE OUTSKIRTS: Korinth Kro og Gaestgivergård (tel. 65-10-23), in Korinth, is a good base for exploring some of the attractions of South Funen, including the castles of Arreskov, Egeskov, Brahetrolleborg, and Holstenshus. Or else you may prefer to go motoring in the Svanninge hills. Grethe and Børge Hoffmann are your friendly innkeepers, and they are skilled at anticipating the needs of their guests. Under a red roof, the inn is painted white, and you'll usually find a row of parked cars lined up at the entrance. Larger than it seems, the kro actually accommodates 70 guests, and does so well, housing them in newly redecorated rooms, some of which contain private baths and toilets. A single room rents for 150 kroner ($13.50), a double for 200 kroner ($18). These are rates in bathless rooms which have hot and cold running water. In a double with private bath, the charge goes up to 270 kroner ($24.30). A big Danish breakfast is yet another 35 kroner ($3.15), and you can also stay here on half-board terms, costing from 200 kroner ($18) per person nightly. In the old garden is a children's playground. The inn also has a sauna and a solarium.

5. Aerø

Perhaps one of the most interesting excursions in Denmark is to the island of Aerø and the 17th-century skippers' town of **Aerøskøbing.** Few towns or villages in all of Scandinavia have retained their heritage as has Aerøskøbing. It's been called "a lilliputian souvenir of the past," with its gingerbread houses (you can practically reach up and touch the roof gutters), intricately carved wooden doors, and lamps of cast iron. In the heyday of the windjammer, nearly 100 commercial sailing ships made Aerøskøbing their home port.

If you're bringing an automobile from Copenhagen, you should have made a reservation for space on the car ferry, as it is usually crowded. The trip to Aerø is about an hour in duration, going for around $7 (U.S.) for each adult, although children pay half fare. For the average car, the cost is $15, a fee subject to change.

The ferry docks at **Soby,** which lies in the northwestern sector of this most charming of Danish islands. Before rushing to Aerøskøbing, as most motorists tend to do, you can visit a mellow manorial property, **Sobygård.** Now in ruins, this manor house is complete with moat and dank dungeons.

From Svendborg you can take a ferry to Aerøskøbing through the South Funen archipelago. Two ferries operate with ten daily round trips, carrying 700 passengers and 70 cars. There are first-class restaurants on board. For a timetable, ask at the tourist office or the ferry office at the harbor in Svendborg. Bookings are made through **A/S Dampskibsselskabet Aerø** in Aerøskøbing (tel. 52-10-18).

At Aerøskøbing visitors are fond of photographing the local church which goes back to about 1200, although it has seen many other additions and alterations over the centuries. See, in particular, Claus Berg's primitive rendition of the Crucifixion, a triptych. The town church is characterized by its octagonal steeple.

Today seafaring life is documented in the **Ship Museum,** a museum of ships in bottles which represents the life's work of Peter Jacobsen, a former cook. At his death in 1960 at the age of 84, he had crafted more than 1600 bottled ships and some 150 model sailing vessels built to scale. He earned a reputation in Aerøskøbing as "the ancient mariner." The museum has been extended by a collection made by a sculptor, H. C. Petersen, consisting of Aerø clocks, furniture, china, and carved works. The museum, 22 Smedegade (tel. 52-13-00), is open May and September from 10 a.m. to noon and 2 to 4 p.m.; in June, July, and August from 9 to 11:45 a.m. and 1 to 5 p.m. Entrance is 7 kroner (63¢) for adults, 4 kroner (36¢) for children.

It's also possible to visit **Hammerich House,** which is filled with 18th-century antiques and porcelain. Ask at the tourist office about visiting hours and expect to pay an admission of 5 kroner (45¢).

There are many good places on Aerø to eat and sleep—cozy inns in the country and comfortable little hotels in town. By all means try some of the local rye bread—it's said to be the best in Denmark. With your aquavit (schnapps), ask for a dash of Riga balsam bitters if you're being traditional. Aerø men sailed to Riga, where they brought back these bitters which they've used ever since in their aquavit.

Should you become completely absorbed in the pastel colors and cobble-stoned streets, you can spend the night at an inn.

WHERE TO STAY: Hotel Aerøhus, 38 Vestergade (tel. 52-10-03), is painted a salmon pink with typically Danish tile roofs and black half timbers. Dormer windows peer like all-seeing eyes through its steeply pitched roof. Inside, the place is one of mellowness, with many traditional features, such as copper kettles hanging from the ceiling and warm lamps glowing, lighting up the rooms. The price in a bathless double is 195 kroner ($17.55), dropping to just 125 kroner ($11.25) in a bathless single. If you want one of the few doubles with private bath, you'll have to pay from 290 kroner ($26.10) per night. You can also order good Danish meals here, dining in the large garden in summer.

ON THE OUTSKIRTS: Dunkaer Kro, 1 Dunkaervej at Dunkaer (tel. 52-15-54), stands in the middle of the island, and for six generations it's been owned by the Clausen family. In summer food is served in an attractive old garden. Quaintness prevails, from the thatched roof to the old grandfather clock standing in the dining room. If charm and antiquity appeal to you, then this inn is a winning candidate. Rooms are cozy and tidily furnished, costing from 185 kroner ($16.65) in a bathless double, from 110 kroner ($9.90) in a bathless single. If you're traveling with children, Ejvind Clausen will add an extra bed to your room for 70 kroner ($6.30). Pension rates are quoted only after stays of three days. Otherwise, you can order an old-fashioned Danish breakfast at 35 kroner ($3.15) or a hearty, filling dish of the day for 50 kroner ($4.50), complete with all the trimmings. This is a fine recommendation for the traditionalist.

JUTLAND

A peninsula of heather-covered moors, fjords, and farmland, hills and lakes, lonely sand dunes, Jutland differs dramatically from the rest of Denmark. It contains three major tourist centers—Ribe in the south, and the cities of Århus and Aalborg in the north—as well as countless old kros and off-the-beaten-path hamlets.

Those who are heading on to Germany after Denmark might want to make the northern swing first (Århus and Aalborg), stopping at Ribe on their jaunt south. On the other hand, those heading north to either Norway or Sweden would be better advised to cross the mainland of Jutland into Ribe in the southeast, then steer north for the major sight at the top of the peninsula.

The Little Belt Bridge at Middlefart connects the island of Funen with the mainland, leading to **Fredericia,** where our tour begins.

6. Fredericia

Denmark's most important railway junction, Fredericia is a seaport near the southeast corner of Jutland, on the western shore of Little Belt, opposite the island of Funen. Little Belt is a bridge of steel and concrete forming Route 1 in Denmark. Most readers who arrive in this seaport come from Hamburg, Germany. The average tourist seems to hurry through the town, in pursuit of far more attractive destinations in the hamlets of Funen and Jutland. However, some people, particularly late arrivals, may want to lodge in one of the private homes rented out (see a reader's tip below).

If you fancy Fredericia, you can use it as headquarters for exploring Jutland, branching out to Århus in the north or else taking the trek over to Funen in the west to pay your respects at the shrine of Hans Christian Andersen in Odense. You can also visit the already-previewed Svendborg in the south of Funen, and from there you can make connections to the island of Aerø and the picture-postcard town of Aerøskøbing.

Established about three centuries ago as a garrison town, Fredericia had the duty of protecting the Jutland peninsula from invasion. Ramparts of the old walled town still stand, and visitors like to take a stroll along these fortifications which command panoramic views. The 17th-century ramparts are unique, having both a powder tower from 1675 and cannon positions from 1849. Inside the ramparts, you find the celebrated statue, *The Valiant Foot Soldier,* a memorial of the battle on July 6, 1849, as well as other memorials of historic interest. These ramparts were stormed for the last time in 1864, and monuments at the seaport commemorate Danish soldiers who fell in an earlier battle against the invading Prussians in 1849.

The many churches in Fredericia attest to the fact that this town in the past was a refuge for many religions. The museum holds mementos of the past and the largest collection of lamps in the north.

READER'S ACCOMMODATION SELECTION: "We learned from a written inquiry that the very accommodating tourist office in Fredericia will make advance reservations for lodging in private homes there. They arranged for us to stay with the Gade family, 29 Odinsvej, where we had two upstairs bedrooms with adjoining bath all to ourselves for 75 kroner ($6.75) per person, including breakfast. The Gades speak little English but their son and daughter are fine interpreters. Their home is in a quiet neighborhood, about 1½ miles from the railway station. The Fredericia Tourist Office mailed us sightseeing information and maps. A deposit is required to reserve a room. Write: **Fredericia Turistforening,** Axeltorv, Postbox 68, 7000 Fredericia, Denmark (tel. 92-13-77)" (H. Deon Holt, Dallas, Texas).

7. Jelling

This is a sleepy little village that looms large in the history of Denmark. It was the tenth-century seat of Danish kings Gorm the Old and Harald Bluetooth, Gorm's son. In front of Jelling's village church stand two runic stones that practically mark the beginning of recorded Danish history, but don't expect Stonehenge. One stone commemorates Queen Thyre, Gorm's wife and "Denmark's ornament." The other, a bigger, triangular hunk of granite, was ordered sculpted by Bluetooth to honor his father, although in fact Bluetooth took up most of the lettering praising his own conquests and the conversion of the Danes to Christianity (his doing, or so he claimed, on a stone a thousand years ago). No one can fail to see the ancient tumuli (burial mounds) near the church. You may climb them. One is called **Gorm's Hill,** the other **Thyre's Hill,** but a recent excavation revealed another burial chamber, under the site of the first **Jelling Church,** built around A.D. 960. It contained skeletons and large quantities of gold thread; Viking artifacts included silver figurines—all of which lead archeologists to believe that this burial chamber once housed royalty, perhaps even the earthly remains of Gorm and Thyre.

WHERE TO STAY: Those spending the night in Jelling might want to consider the following:

Jelling Kro, 16 Gormsgade (tel. 87-10-06), is a simple country inn in the center of this tiny village that puts up travelers for 260 kroner ($23.40) double. Singles rent for 135 kroner ($12.15). Most of its handful of rooms are largish, comfortable in a superannuated way but equipped with up-to-date furniture, and many have private showers. The kro, across from the old church, overlooks the historic burial mounds. Dining is leisurely here, the kitchen staff small, but the food is good and wholesome. I recently paid 65 kroner ($5.85) for a Danmenu, plus an extra 35 kroner ($3.15) for breakfast.

Tøsby Kro, 12 Bredsten Landevej (tel. 88-11-30), is a simple little inn, actually a boarding house, run by Åge Andreasen. Most of the guests are Norwegian or Danish, but the owner looks forward to entertaining an American or Canadian. Six double rooms are for rent, each pleasantly furnished and well kept, costing 180 kroner ($16.20) nightly. If you're traveling with children, you can ask for an extra bed for 65 kroner ($5.85). Singles cost 100 kroner ($9). The Danish food I was recently served was well prepared and presented. You can ask about full-board terms, which are 220 kroner ($19.80) per person daily. Otherwise, a lunch or dinner, a big meal at that, costs 65 kroner ($5.85) extra. The inn stands only a few kilometers from the well-known Legoland i Billund and from the Lions Park in Givskud.

READERS' FOOD AND LODGING SELECTION: "Readers who visit either the chalk mines at Mønsted or the outdoor museum at Hejle Hede on Jutland will be given a warm welcome at **Sevel Kro** (tel. 44-80-11), in the village of Sevel in mid-Jutland, whether they want to stay here or to eat. Run by Rita and Aksel Jensen, who are extremely outgoing and accommodating, the inn offers bathless singles, containing wash basins, for 150 kroner ($13.50) and bathless doubles for 250 kroner ($22.50). A giant breakfast costs 35 kroner ($3.15), and in the evening the standard Danmenu (two courses) is offered for 65 kroner ($5.85). However, 'Gammel Kro' (Old Inn) specialties are also available, such as various pâtés and boiled eels at low prices" (Maureen and Les Foulds, Gainesville, Fla.).

8. Ribe

The dilemma in Denmark's oldest town is simply this: "Will the storks fly back in April?" Ribe became legendary because of the graceful storks which build their nests on top of its red-roof medieval houses. As long ago as the Spanish Civil War, stork-loving Danes reported a dwindling number of birds flying back from their southern winter homes. Hungry Spaniards were blamed. Now other causes are cited: storks eat frogs; frogs eat insects; insects are often poisoned. One of Denmark's beloved legends is threatened, but Ribe is used to change and upheaval.

This port was an important trading center of the Vikings as far back as the ninth century and became an episcopal seat in 948, with one of the first Christian churches in Denmark being established here. This was the royal residence of the ruling Valdemars around 1200.

In medieval days, Ribe was linked by sea trade routes to England, Germany, Friesland, the Mediterranean, and other ports, but then its waters receded. Today it is surrounded by marshes, much like a landlocked Moby Dick. The town watchman still makes his rounds—armed with his lantern and trusty staff —since the ancient custom was revived in 1936.

Ribe, a town of cobblestones, narrow lanes, half-timbered and crooked houses, can easily be explored on foot.

WHERE TO STAY: I'll cover the major sights, of course, but first let's take a look at the budget accommodations.

Hotel Dagmar, 1 Torvet (tel. 42-00-33), smack dab in the heart of town, wsa named after Queen Dagmar. It is Ribe's leading hotel, and charges 410 kroner ($36.90) for bathless doubles. Singles with hot and cold running water only go for 190 kroner ($17.10). If you're willing to splurge, ask for a double room with private bath—510 kroner ($45.90), including service and Moms. The hotel's exterior of restrained classic brick with a gabled and dormered roof belies the lush interior. Its four dining rooms are a decorator's dream palace: crystal chandeliers, furniture of white and gold; provincial, Victorian, Empire, and antiseptic modern style; Persian rugs, stained-glass windows—you name it and it's here. For those who aren't staying over—but would like to drop in for a visit— luncheon served in the hotel's restaurant is 50 kroner ($9). But you may enjoy the "plate of the day" at 50 kroner ($4.50) in the medieval vaulted cellar.

Hotel Sønderjylland, 22 Sønderjylland (tel. 42-04-66), is a typical Danish hotel, standing under a red tile roof studded with dormers. Right in the center of town, it rents out bedrooms heavy in style, but comfortable. A single rents for 130 kroner ($11.70), a double going for 250 kroner ($22.50). A better arrangement is to stay here on full-board terms, including the price of your room. The dining room is simply decorated, and the food is appetizing, of an acceptable general standard. The servings are large, incidentally. English is spoken.

Kalvslund Kro, 105 Koldingvej at Kalvslund (tel. 43-70-12), is a little Danish inn lying on the outskirts of Ribe, about six miles to the north. English-speaking Gitte Kalff runs a most acceptable place, with perfectly adequate rooms. The prices are much more reasonable than those encountered in Ribe. The tariff in a single without bath is 110 kroner ($9.90), rising to 160 kroner ($14.40) in a double without bath. A Danish breakfast is another 35 kroner ($3.15). Home-style cookery is the keynote of the place, and the food I've sampled here was very good, well prepared and presented. The dishes are straightforward, the meat of good quality. A lunch or dinner costs 45 kroner ($4.05) to 55 kroner ($4.95).

WHERE TO DINE: Weis' Stue, 2 Torvet (tel. 42-07-00), is a brick-and-timber Lilliput inn on the market square. In a setting of heavy black beams, a cast-iron stove, shelves of pewter plates, tiled dado paneling—and with a 400-year-old clock tick-tocking in the background—guests sit in high-backed settles and watch as the scrumptious food is spread out before them on crude wooden tables. My most recent dinner here consisted of marinated herring with raw onions, shrimp with mayonnaise and lemon, smoked Greenland halibut with scrambled eggs, liverpaste with mushrooms, sliced ham and Italian salad, filet with onions, two sorts of cheese with bread and butter—all for 80 kroner ($7.20). Four rooms are available renting for 110 kroner ($9.90) for single occupancy, 190 kroner ($17.10) to 210 kroner ($18.90) for doubles. Breakfast is 40 kroner ($3.60) per person.

Vaertshuset Saelhunden (The Seal Guesthouse), 13 Skibbroen, is a charming little inn at the harbor, where you can enjoy a meal from the à la carte menu costing around 75 kroner ($6.75) or more. A bottle of beer to accompany your repast costs 15 kroner ($1.35). A half-timbered house, painted white, "The Seal" dates from about 1600. Inside you'll find one of the cozy guesthouses of that day, with furniture in the original style, low ceilings, an assortment of different lamps, as well as pictures and other trappings evoking Ribe's connection with the sea.

READER'S INN SELECTION: "The **Thomashus Kro,** Hovedvej (tel. 52-22-33), is on the Autoroute E3 (main route between Flensburg in the northern part of Schleswig Holstein and Fredericia–Middlefart Bridge). As such it provides a convenient stopping place for motorists weary from the long drive to Jutland from Germany, and even a base for exploring west to Ribe or 14 miles north to Kolding and on to Jelling. We had the pleasure of dinner at the kro, and I can only describe the meal as Lucullan. The 50-krone ($4.50) 'kroplatte' is trundled to the table and in the pleasant atmosphere of antique auto prints, stained wood paneling, and carriage lanterns, one is tempted with several herring filets with onion; tender pork loin smothered with sautéed mushroom caps; cold rare roast beef slices with fresh horseradish and fried onions; beef tartare to be mixed at one's whim with fresh horseradish, chopped onions, egg yolk, and capers; a bowl of shrimp with lemon and parsley; and finally cheese with many slices of rugbrød (white bread) and that delicious Danish butter. If your appetite is not quite up to this, you can choose egg cake or filet of plaice with mounds of french fries and curried rémoulade. Smørrebrød selections are good. The trilingual (Dutch-English-German) woman who presides over dining activities tells us that for 210 kroner ($18.90), double rooms without bath are available. For 280 kroner ($25.20), you can have a double with bath, and for 310 kroner ($27.90), you get a grand, large double with bath. Singles start at 150 kroner ($13.50), going up to 175 kroner ($15.75) with some kind of plumbing. All prices include service and Moms. We didn't inspect the rooms, but if the spotlessness of the dining areas was any indication, have no qualms about the upstairs. Thomashus Kro is on A10 (E3), 1¼ miles north of Haderslev. The kro closes at 11 p.m." (Dr. Jon H. Kinne, Germany).

THE TOP SIGHTS: The stone and brick **Cathedral of Ribe** (tel. 42-06-19), inspired by Rhineland architecture, was completed in the mid-12th century, and it remains the crowning achievement of this little town. Further, it's a fit memorial to the Romanesque influence on Danish architecture, despite its Gothic arches. A century later a tower was added: climb if you want to see how the storks view Ribe—and if you have the stamina. Try to see the legendary "Cat's Head Door," once the principal entranceway to the church, and the granite-stoned tympanum—"Removal of the Cross"—the most significant piece of medieval sculpture left in Denmark. The church is open from mid-May until the end of September from 10 a.m. to 6 p.m. (on Sunday from noon to 6 p.m.); otherwise, from 10 a.m. to noon and 2 to 4 p.m. (2 to 4 p.m. on Sunday during the off-season).

Among the other sights are:

St. Catherine Church and Monastery: The Black Friars (Dominicans) came to Ribe in 1228 and began work at once on constructing a church and chapter house (the east wing of a monastery). The original church was only half as wide as the existing one, although parts of the older edifice can still be seen, especially the southern wall. The present church, with nave and aisles, dates from the first half of the 15th century, and the tower is from 1617. The weight of the church gave the friars trouble, a problem which continued until after World War I, when extensive restoration was carried out, so that this is now one of the best preserved abbeys in Scandinavia. Only the monks' stalls and the Romanesque font remain from the Middle Ages. The handsome pulpit dates from 1591 and the altarpiece from 1650. You can walk through the cloisters and also see models of ships hanging in the southern aisle, as well as religious paintings. Tombstones of Ribe citizens from the Reformation on are along the outer walls of the church. A small collection of coffin ornaments found when the edifice was restored can be seen in the guardroom at the end of the broad cloister against the church. The church and monastery are open from 10 a.m. to noon and 2 to 5 p.m. in summer. Admission is 3 kroner (27¢).

Across the street is the **smallest house in Ribe,** a brick-and-timber structure, a private home which is not open to the public.

Try to visit at least some of the five museums of Ribe which embrace different spheres of interest. You can get detailed information on them at the tourist office or at the office of the **Antiquarian Collection** (Den Antikvariske Samling i Ribe), 12 Overdammen (tel. 42-00-55). An 8-krone (72¢) admission ticket will admit you to all five (described below), which are Hans Tausen's House, the Antiquarian Collection in Quedens Gaard, the Town Hall Museum, the Museum of Art, and a ship replica at Skibbroen harbor.

Hans Tausen's House, a red-painted brick-and-timbered building facing the cathedral, is a museum with a new exhibition dealing with the history of the Ribe area from the Stone Age (some 10,000 years ago) up to today. This display is on the ground floor, while the first floor contains an exhibit of the rich and unique Viking Age, with finds dating from the earliest days of Ribe, between 700 and 800. Among the ancient artifacts is an old coffin carved out of a tree. The house is open from 10 a.m. to noon and 2 to 5 p.m. in summer, closing at 4 p.m. in winter. It is closed Monday from November 1 to March 31.

Also facing the cathedral is the **Antiquarian Collection** exhibited in Quedens Gaard, 10 Overdammen, next door to the office listed above. Here you'll see an interior from about 1600 of a merchant's house dating from 1582, together with displays of the life of Ribe in the early industrial era, 1830 to 1870. Hours are the same as for Hans Tausen's House.

The medieval **Town Hall Museum** (Ribe Raadhussamling) is worth a visit to see artifacts and archives of the town's past. Displayed is the executioner's sword from the 16th century, as well as ceremonial swords from the same period. The town's money chest, signs used as symbols of various trades, and a depiction of the "iron hand," which defined the limit of the town's jurisdiction and is still a symbol of police authority, are also on exhibit in the museum, which may be visisted weekdays May to October from 2 to 4 p.m.

An extensive collection of Danish art is to be seen in the **Museum of Art,** in a building lying in an attractive spot on the north side of the Ribe River. Works of the most acclaimed Danish artists, such as Eckersberg, Købke, C. A. Jensen, Hammershøj, and Juel, may be seen, including several masterpieces. The museum is open from 10 a.m. to noon and 2 to 5 p.m. in July and August. Otherwise, it's open from 2 to 5 p.m. only and closed entirely on Monday.

At **Skibbroen,** you can board a full-size replica of a special kind of ship, called an *evert,* which used to carry much of Ribe's seafaring goods. On board there is a small exhibition of artifacts connected with shipping. Skibbroen is the harbor on the river, used today only by pleasure craft and the excursion bota, *Riberhus,* which operates from May to September, taking passengers through the marshland around Ribe to the Kammerslusen (sluice) and the tidal flats.

READER'S SIGHTSEEING TIP: A lovely experience awaits all who include **Møgeltønder,** just west of Tønder, on their itinerary. Quaint buildings frame an idyllic cobbled main street, transporting all who tread thereupon into a more gentle era" (Jean Paula Paulsen, Chicago, Ill.).

9. Fanø

In 20 minutes, a ferry from the expanding modern port city of Esbjerg takes passengers to Nordby, their starting point for an exploration of the island of Fanø, with its heather-covered moors, windswept sand dunes, fir trees, wild deer, and bird sanctuaries. Fanø is a reigning summer resort with the Danes and English. Sønderho, on the southern tip, with its memorial to sailors drowned at sea, is my favorite spot . . . somewhat desolate, but that's its charm. Fanø makes for a day's excursion (or longer if there's time) from easily accessible Ribe.

A summer highlight on Fanø is the **Fannikerdagene** festival, which takes place on every first weekend in July. This is a festival which combines traditional dancing, costumes, and events connected with the dyays when sailing ships played a major part in the life of the community.

If you can't make the festival, you might try to be on Fanø the third Sunday in July for **Sønderho Day.** High point of the festive day is a wedding procession which passes through the town to the square by the old mill. Traditional costumes and bridal dances are among the attractions.

For information on these and other events taking place, ask at the **Fanø Turistbureau** (tourist office) in Nordby.

FOOD AND LODGING: Sønderho Kro, Sønderho (tel. 16-40-09), is a 1722 thatched-roof, ivy-covered inn that is nestled behind the sand dunes of this windswept island. For those with well-padded wallets, this National Trust House is the unbeatable choice on Fanø, but the prices may be a bit steep for some. The warmth of the hotel is immediately felt by guests as they enter the beamed and planked entrance hall with its huge open fireplace. The lounge on the first floor looks out on the tidal flats. A new wing was opened in 1977, and throughout each each of the rooms has its own distinctive character, yet all fit into the traditional atmosphere of the inn. The dining rooms are full of atmosphere as well, with lime-green beams, long trestle tables, candlelight, copper and brass fixtures, and, as throughout the crude inn, terracotta tiles or ancient plank flooring. The cuisine is superb and plentiful. Olga and Erik Jensen charge 360 kroner ($32.40) to 585 kroner ($52.65) for a double, depending on the room location. A single is priced from 310 kroner ($27.90). Breakfast, served in the dining room of the inn, consists of bread, butter, juice, cold meat, and cheese and costs 50 kroner ($4.50). From November 1 to April 1, the inn offers full board for 390 kroner ($35.10) per person per day.

Hotel Krogarden, Nordby (tel. 16-20-52), is a 300-year-old cozy inn, with a good restaurant and comfortable rooms. You can snuggle in here in a double for 340 kroner ($30.60) to 410 kroner ($36.90). A single will cost from 175 kroner ($15.75) to 230 kroner ($20.70).

If you're in the market for an apartment for a stay of a week or more, try Danland on Fanø Island, **Holiday Hotel Vesterhavet,** Fanø Bad (tel. 16-32-77), which has 146 two- and three-room accommodations, with a maximum of six beds. Rent per week is from 990 kroner ($89.10) to 3895 kroner ($350.55) per apartment. The hotel has a good restaurant and a cozy bar.

10. Århus

This capital city of Jutland, second-largest city in Denmark, is a university town and lively port, drawing ships from all over the world. It has many restaurants, hotels, and some nighttime amusements. In addition to the city's own attractions, such as the open-air museum, "The Old Town," it's a good base for day excursions to Silkeborg and Ebeltoft, or to moated manors and castles north of Århus. First, a survey of the East Jutland city's hostelry scene.

BUDGET HOTELS: The actual low-cost accommodations in this lively university city are extremely limited. Those on the strictest of budgets should go to the tourist office, in the Town Hall (tel. 12-16-00), where bookings in private homes can be obtained at a cost of 65 kroner ($5.85) per person. From June 15 to September 15, the office is open from 9 a.m. till 7 p.m. (on Saturday and Sunday from 9 a.m. till 1 p.m. and 5 to 7 p.m.). During the off-season, hours are from 9 a.m. till 5 p.m.

Missionshotellet Ansgar, 14 Banegaardsplads (tel. 12-41-22), is a great bulk of a hotel—dignified and traditional, convenient to the Town Hall. It offers a full range of rooms in different price ranges. In the older portion, bathless double rooms rent for 300 kroner ($27) to 360 kroner ($32.40), including a continental breakfast, service, and tax. In the new wing, all the bedrooms have private baths and rent for 360 kroner ($32.40) to 410 kroner ($36.90) double, inclusive. The hotel has 215 bedrooms, all tastefully decorated—many with modern furnishings. There's plenty of lounging room, and the food and service in the dining room are quite fine.

Eriksen's Hotel Garni, 6–8 Banegardsgade (tel. 13-62-96), is quite small, more of a rooming house than a hotel. Everything is totally utilitarian, but clean and recently modernized. No accommodations have private baths, but showers are found just outside the rooms. Singles range from 130 kroner ($11.70) to 140 kroner ($12.60); doubles go from 230 kroner ($20.70) to 250 kroner ($22.50).

Pavillonen Marienlundsvej (tel. 16-72-98) is a youth hostel at the edge of Risskov Forest. It's reached by taking bus 1 or 2 to the terminal at Marienlund. Prices are 50 kroner ($4.50) per person in a dormitory room for four, but you have to possess a membership card. It's open all year except from December 15 to January 15. Take bus 1 or 2 from the main railway station to the terminus at Marienlund.

In the environs, **Motel La Tour,** 139 Randersvej (tel. 16-78-88), is expensive by our standards, but many motorists will prefer it to lodgings in Århus center. This well-furnished and accommodating place lies on the main road, E3 and A10, between Randers and Århus. A contemporary structure, the motel has cozy, nicely equipped, and comfortable rooms, each with private bath, toilet, phone, radio, and TV. Singles are priced at 285 kroner ($25.65), doubles going for 360 kroner ($32.40), tax and service included. Breakfast is yet another 40 kroner ($3.60) per person. The lowest priced fare is served in a cafeteria on the premises, or, if you prefer, you can order both international and Danish specialties in the motel's restaurant, an intimate spot for dining.

ECONOMY DINING: Teater Bodega, 7 Skolegade (tel. 12-19-17), opposite the cathedral and near the Royal Hotel, is an intimate café. But surprisingly the meals are moderately priced—if one sticks to the well-selected daily specials. Smørrebrød selections are available for as low as 30 kroner ($2.70), fish platter with mushrooms in a cream sauce will tally up to 80 kroner ($7.20), and the ever-popular biksemad goes for 60 kroner ($1.35).

Flaskehallen, 12 Østergade, serves moderately priced meals in a comfortable setting. On walls are motifs of Hans Christian Andersen, and the various platters are named after the Danish writer's adventure stories. A hearty fish dinner with potatoes and vegetables costs 40 kroner ($3.60), and other meals range from 25 kroner ($2.25) to 65 kroner ($5.85).

Gadespejlet, at the harbor (on Skolegade), is a congenial place, people and atmosphere alike, serving luncheons from 35 kroner ($3.15) to 75 kroner ($6.75).

Another suggestion for the budget-minded tourist is to snack at the **Special Smørrebrød Shop,** 2 Sønder Allé (tel. 13-38-13), on the corner of the Park Allé. For 17.50 kroner ($1.59) and up, you can order one of the largest and most appetizing selections of smørrebrød in town. It's open until 11 p.m.

Bøsen, 2 Mindelbrogade (tel. 12-22-29), is one of the most popular and long-enduring favorites in town. Many of the recipes used were passed down by the original owners from 1893. However, the kitchen has kept abreast of the times, offering nouvelle Danish cuisine as well. The welcome is warm and gracious, and diners enjoy the homemade specialties, paying about 85 kroner ($7.65) and up for lunch, from 170 kroner ($15.30) at dinner.

Guldhornet, 10 Banegårdsplads (tel. 12-02-62), is centrally located, lying near the rail station. This corner restaurant is warm and cozy, with hanging lamps and brightly colored tables. At those tables, you get friendly, efficient service. Prices are very reasonable, costing from 85 kroner ($7.65) at lunch and from 150 kroner ($13.50) at dinner.

Munkestuen, 5 Klostertorv (tel. 12-95-67). You almost invariably stumble upon this charming old place if you're doing some serious sightseeing. It is in the old Klostertorv across from Frue Kloster Abbey. Lise Poulsen will welcome you and serve you both a Danish and international cuisine. Specialties depend on the fresh produce of the season. The inn is small and cozy, and there is also a courtyard. Food is served from noon to 8 p.m., although drinks are available for a longer period. You'll spend around 80 kroner ($7.20) for lunch, perhaps 125 kroner ($11.25) or more for an early dinner.

THE MAJOR SIGHTS: For the best introduction to Århus, head for the Town Hall's tourist office, **Århus Turistforening,** Rådhuset (tel. 12-16-00), from which sightseeing tours leave daily at 11 a.m. and 1 p.m. in summer, a 2½-hour trip taking in the whole town and costing 35 kroner ($3.15) per person.

The top sight is **Den Gamle By** ("The Old Town"), which re-creates in more than 60 buildings—all within a botanical garden—the life in Danish towns from the 16th to the mid-19th century. This open-air museum is different from the ones near Copenhagen and Odense, where the emphasis is on rural life. As visitors walk through the old workshops—bookbinder, carpenter, hatter, tanner, and others—the question often asked is: "Where did everybody go?" It's that realistic. Prime targets of strollers: the Burgomaster's House, a wealthy merchant's antique-stuffed, half-timbered home, built at the end of the 16th century; the Textile Collection and the Old Elsinore Theater, erected in the early 19th century. Inquire at the ticket office about summer programs staged here, chamber music, opera, and the like. There's a restaurant on the grounds. The museum, on Vesterbrogade (no. 3 or 5 bus), is open from 10 a.m. to 5 p.m. May to mid-October. Off-season it's open at 11 a.m., closing at 3 p.m. in spring and fall, 1 p.m. in winter.

Other major sights meriting a good inspection include:

The **Cathedral of St. Clemens:** This late-Gothic cathedral, crowned by a 315-foot spire, traces its origin back to the beginning of the 13th century, although the present building represents the architecture of the 15th century. It is the longest cathedral in Scandinavia, practically as deep as its spire is tall. Chief interest focuses on its Renaissance pulpit, 15th-century triptych, and 18th-century pipe organ. The red-brick, copper-roofed cathedral, at Bispetorvet, is open weekdays only (if no ceremonies are being held): May 1 to September 30, 9:30 a.m. to 4 p.m.; and October 1 to April 30, 10 a.m. to 3 p.m.

(After the cathedral, I'd suggest a visit to the medievalesque arcade nearby, 3 Vestergade, with its half-timbered buildings, rock garden, cobblestone courtyard, aviary, and excellent display of antique interiors.)

After visiting the cathedral, you can enter the **Andelsbanken,** 6 Skt. Clemens Torv (tel. 12-73-33). Down the steps on the left, you enter a Viking Museum where remains of old Viking walls of the town have been found. No admission is charged.

When visitors have seen the Viking Museum, they are invited to enter the bank itself. There is always an admission-free exhibition of Danish artists in the basement next to the storage room. The museum in the bank is open Monday to Friday from 9:30 a.m to 4 p.m., except on Thursday when its hours are 9:30 a.m. to 6 p.m.

Church of Our Lady: This 13th-century church, on Vestergade, was the abbey church of the Dominican brothers (1240). Worth an inspection is St. Nicholas Church under the chancel, the oldest stone church in Scandinavia. It dates back to Viking days (1060). *Vor Frue Kirke,* as the Danes call it, is open

Monday to Friday from 10 a.m. to 4 p.m.; on Saturday to 2 p.m. On Sunday there are services at 9 and again at 10 a.m.

Town Hall: A crowning architectural achievement in the center of Århus, the Rådhuset was built between 1936 and 1941 (Arne Jacobsen was one of the designers)—and it's been the subject of controversy ever since. It commemorated the 500th anniversary of the Århus charter. Ultramodern in design, the marble-plated structure (lots of airy space, plenty of glass) can be visited on a guided tour at 4 p.m. sharp from June 15 to September 15, except Sunday. The tour starts from the tourist office at the entrance of the tower, and it is free. But I prefer to take the elevator (346 steps for those who dare) to the top of the 197-foot tower, where a carillon rings every now and then. The tower is open from June 15 through September 15 at noon and 2 p.m. (on Saturday and Sunday, at noon only). From the tower, the entire city of Århus (250,000 inhabitants) and the much-trafficked harbor greet the gazer.

What was formerly the Århus Museum is now the **Archeological and Ethnographic Museum,** in a country setting about five miles from the town, at Moesgård Manor. (Take bus 6 from the railway station.) This museum of prehistoric times is a major attraction that brings visitors from all over the world. That's because it owns the incredibly well-preserved 1600-year-old Grauballe man who lay since the Iron Age in a bog in central Jutland. The museum has a 15-krone ($1.35) entrance fee for adults, free to children under 15 with adults. It's open April through September from 10 a.m. to 5 p.m. daily. During the off-season, it closes Monday. In the park and woods is an open-air museum, with prehistoric reconstructions and a prehistoric "trackway."

ÅRHUS AFTER DARK: Århus has its own version of Copenhagen's Tivoli, and fortunately this one, **Tivoli-Friheden,** Marselisborg Skov (tel. 14-73-00), has its own particular character, avoiding sterile imitation. Buried in a forest, it is designed in a bright, modern fashion (extremely angular buildings, colored plastics, spheres like moons and suns half hidden among the ferns and trees)—a fairyland at night. A number of amusements are offered—open-air theater, art shows, concerts, and clowns. The park is open June 1 to mid-August. Admission is 15 kroner ($1.35) for adults, 10 kroner (90¢) for children.

Tropicana, Ryesgade, near the tourist office, is a glittering fun-palace extravaganza. Decorated for a perpetual New Year's Eve party, this is the place for dancing and drinking in Århus. Beer is 17 kroner ($1.53). There's a live orchestra and plenty of dancing on the top, crowded floor. Guests select tables either on the lower, crescent-shaped level, or else at the oval bar at the back. Stags perch up here to people-watch. Those who have found their love of the evening often snare the tiered "royal boxes." It opens at 9:30 p.m.

For more dancing, the **Cabana,** 2 Klosterport, is a lively disco, this one with mirrors on the ceiling. A mid-20s, friendly crowd is attracted to its precincts. Entrance fee is 30 kroner ($2.70) weekdays, 40 kroner ($3.60) on weekends.

BRANCHING OUT FROM ÅRHUS: Using Århus as home base, you might want to consider the following jaunts into the countryside:

An Amusement Park

Legoland (tel. 33-13-33), at Billund, is an amusement park for the whole family. Its main attraction is the Miniland, built of approximately 25 million Lego bricks. Here you'll find a lot of famous landscapes and buildings, in miniature, from many countries all over the world. There is also a real Wild West town in which you will see a copy of the monument at Mount Rushmore. Also worth seeing are a world-famous antique doll and dollhouse collection, a theater for children, various educational exhibitions including one on energy, and, of course, a lot of adult and kiddie rides. Attractions include Titania's Palace, the largest and most expensive miniature palace in the world; and an antique collection of scraps. The season is from May 1 until mid-September. Hours are from 10 a.m. to 8 p.m. daily. The admission charged is 30 kroner ($2.70) for adults and 20 kroner ($1.80) for children.

READERS' SELECTION IN BILLUND: "Our 'discovery' is the home of **Mr. and Mrs. Victor Christensen** at 13 Baastlundvej (tel. 33-15-68). Mr. Christensen is a long-time employee of the Lego plant and speaks enough English to manage. Their home was the only one we found available in Billund. The charge for the two of us was 250 kroner ($22.50) for bed-and-breakfast. (This was actually the highest we paid for a room in Denmark, but the Christensens have a monopoly, and it was a lot more reasonable than the Legoland Hotel.) We found this home to be comfortable and well planned for guests. We had our own outside door and a lovely patio to share with other guests. In addition, the Christensens provide a table full of Lego pieces for the use of guests' children" (Ken and Jane Olson, Boulder, Colo.).

Jutland Car Museum

At Gjern, near Silkeborg, is the only automobile museum in Jutland, **Jysk Automobilmuseum** (tel. 87-50-50), exhibiting veteran and vintage automobiles. In all, 130 cars are presented, from 1900 to 1948, with 65 different makes. Among them are the V12 cylinder Auburn, V12 cylinder Cadillac, 1947 Crosley, the famous Renault Taxis de la Marne, Kissel, Hotchkiss, Jordan, Vivinus, Rolls-Royce, and Maserati. A number of motorcycles are also exhibited. From April 1 to November 1, the museum is open Saturday and Sunday from 10 a.m. to 6 p.m. From May 1 to September 15 it is open daily from 10 a.m. to 6 p.m. Admission is 30 kroner ($2.70) for adults, 15 kroner ($1.35) for children.

Øm Kloster Museum

At Emborg, on the north bank of a lake, lie the ruins of a Cistercian monastery dating from 1172. Skeletons from the monastery hospital intrigue those medically inclined. Besides the church site and monks' graves there is a medicinal herb garden. This historical attraction is open daily, except Monday, May to August from 9 a.m. to 6 p.m. Adults are charged 12 kroner ($1.08) for admission; children pay 7 kroner (63¢). In April and September hours are from 9 a.m. to 5 p.m., to 4 p.m in October.

AN INN ON THE OUTSKIRTS: **Årslev Kro & Motel,** at Brabrand (tel. 26-05-77), lies about seven miles from Århus. Part of it is a timbered and thatched-roof old-fashioned inn built in the year 1854. A modern motel wing, containing 110 beds in comfortable rooms, each equipped with private bath, toilet, and telephone, has been added. The price for a single is 270 kroner ($24.30), rising to 455 kroner ($40.95) in a double. Guests can make use of a pleasant lounge with color TV, or else enjoy games in the large basement. On Thursday, Friday, and Saturday nights, a pianist plays the Hammond organ from 6:30 p.m., and the chef prepares Charolais beef, which is carved right at your table. The old kro makes a good center for excursions to Legoland, the Lion Park, "Sky Mountain," the Silkeborg lakes, and Djurs Sommerland.

A YOUTH HOSTEL AT RØNDE: **Kalø Youth Hostel** (tel. 37-11-08), in Rønde on the main road, A15, between Århus and Grenå, is on top of a high hill, with an excellent view over the landscape encircled by the bay of Kalø and the Mols mountains. Many walks and bicycle tours are possible in the woods nearby and along the beach. A special experience is a walk along the medieval road to the ruins of Kalø Castle. The hostel has 28 beds in five rooms, plus two huts with four beds in each. Kitchen equipment is available. You can order breakfast, but no evening meal is served. The cost to stay here is 34 kroner ($3.06) per person.

READER'S SELECTION AT RØNDE: "**Randers Youth Hostel** is a lovely accommodation outside Rønde, which features family bungalows with gas ranges for cooking and complete kitchens, all for the bargain price of 34 kroner ($3.60) per person. The hostel is right in the woods, and the surroundings are beautiful. Getting here is a bit of a problem unless you have a car, but it's well worth the effort. Take bus 8 in Rønde to Fladbro. From there it is a half hour's walk" (Doron Weissbrod, Ramat-Gan, Israel).

11. Silkeborg

This riverside town is the center of the Danish Lake District, as well as the most important one-day jaunt west from Århus. Silkeborg lies in the midst of some of Denmark's most beautiful scenery, but it's principally a base for exploring **Himmelbjerget** (Sky Mountain), highest peak in low-lying Denmark. But be warned: the "mountain" is less than 500 feet high and won't dazzle readers who've just come from Norway. The most intriguing way to see Sky Mountain and the surroundinig countryside is aboard the paddle steamer *Hjejlen*, which has seen action since 1861. The steamer sails frequently in summer. For timetables and information, telephone **Hjejlen Co. Ltd.** (tel. 06/82-05-05 or 82-07-66). But the most important sightseeing attraction of Silkeborg—from the vantage point of the foreign visitor—is:

The Tollund Man: In an 18th-century manor by the Gudenå River is the **Silkeborg Cultural Museum,** drawing visitors from all over the world who come to gaze upon the face of the 2200-year-old Tollund Man (he lay in a peat bog until discovered in 1950). His face is considered the "most unspoiled" of all man's early ancestors. This body was so well preserved, in fact, that scientists could determine the contents of his last supper: flax, barley, and oats. His head capped by fur, the Tollund Man had been strangled by a plaited leather string— probably the victim of a ritual sacrifice. The Tollund Man recently acquired a girlfriend. An equally well-preserved body, known as "the Elling Girl," was found near the same spot where the Tollund Man was discovered. Scientists estimate she was about 30 to 40 years old when she died in 225 B.C. The museum also has a special exhibition of old Danish glass, a clogmaker's workshop, a collection of stone implements, antique jewelry, plus artifacts from the ruins of Silkeborg Castle. From April to October 20 it is open from 10 a.m. to 5 p.m., charging adults 10 kroner (90¢) for admission, 5 kroner (45¢) for children. From October 21 to April 1, it is open on Wednesday, Saturday, and Sunday from noon to 4 p.m.

The **Silkeborg Art Museum,** 7–9 Gundenåvej, offers unique exhibitions of Asgar Jorn's art (paintings and ceramics), the Cobra group, and modern European art. The museum is open daily except Monday April 1 to October 31 from 10 a.m. to 5 p.m., November 1 to March 31 from noon to 4 p.m. Admission is 15 kroner ($1.35) for adults, 8 kroner (72¢) for children.

WHERE TO STAY: Hotel Dania, 5 Torvet (tel. 82-01-11), stands right on the marketplace. It's an interesting old-style building with a lot of class. Many antiques have been placed in the corridors and in the reception lounge. However, the rooms are more functional and in the modern style. A few rooms don't have private baths or showers, and these are the cheapest, costing from 315 kroner ($28.35) to 335 kroner ($30.15) in a double, from 195 kroner ($17.55) to 205 kroner ($18.45) in a single. With private baths, doubles peak at 435 kroner

($39.15), singles at 315 kroner ($28.35), and triples at 520 kroner ($46.80). Included in the price, breakfast is large fortification for the day. You may dine outside on the square, pleasing yourself with such well-prepared food as fresh salmon with a choron sauce and fresh vegetables, finishing with a bowl of fresh strawberries with cream.

Missionshotellet Ansgar, 28–32 Drewsensvej (tel. 82-37-00), is large and pleasant, nearly as big as the Dania. You can get a simply furnished, bathless double at prices that range from 330 kroner ($29.70), and you pay from 390 kroner ($35.10) for a double with private bath. Breakfast is included.

Slightly out of town, the venerable **Svostrup Kro,** DK 8642 Grauballe (tel. 06/87-70-04), is a stylish place, a bargeman's inn at one time. Set in rolling farmland between the Guden River and the Gjern Hills, it offers comfortably styled rooms with modern furnishings costing from 160 kroner ($14.40) for singles, 310 kroner ($27.90)for doubles. The kro is right on a walking path winding along the river.

Silkeborg Turistbureau, the efficient tourist office, 9 Torvet (tel. 82-19-11), will book you into private homes in the vicinity. A double room costs about 160 kroner ($14.40). Breakfast is an additional 30 kroner ($2.70). The office is open from 9 a.m. to 5 p.m. weekdays, 9 a.m. to noon on Saturday.

Motorists may prefer to anchor on the outskirts at **Pension Syejboeklund,** at Svejbaek (tel. 84-60-36), which lies only 1½ miles from "Sky Mountain." The setting is tranquil, adjoining Lake Juulsø and surrounded by picture-postcard-type scenery. The owner, Johanne Hedegaard, has tastefully furnished the place, and the look is quite elegant, as in a private Danish country home. The drawing rooms, in particular, have charm and contain color television, a piano, as well as a library. But the two dozen bedrooms are cozy and comfortable as well, and half of them are equipped with private bath and toilet. Depending on the room, half-board terms begin at 195 kroner ($7.55) per person, rising to 210 kroner ($18.90) per person daily. If you give your exact date of arrival, you can be met at Silkeborg or Ry with a car. The house lies only a ten-minute walk from the Svejbaek ferry pier, and equipment for fishing can be rented as can boats.

READER'S DINING SELECTION IN SEJS: "For a super-good heaping platter of pork chops, cauliflower, peas, and carrots, and a large bowl of steamed potatoes, we suggest a 'find' of ours, the **Hedekro** in Sejs. A wonderful, patient woman served us and smiled at our struggle with the Danish language. She spoke no English, but a man at a nearby table stepped over and assisted us in ordering what proved to be a gourmet's delight. We highly recommend this dining place and that meal for 75 kroner ($6.75). Our money belts were too sizes too small when we'd eaten all we could hold" (Mrs. Carl Skounborg, Chico, Calif.).

A TRIPLE-TREAT MANOR TOUR: The triangle tour of three of East Jutlands's most attractive manor houses is one of the greatest treasure hunts awaiting the visitor on the Danish peninsula. The manors—in varying states of preservation—are Gammel Estrup, Clausholm, and Rosenholm. We'll begin with:

Rosenholm

Erected on an islet 13 miles north of Århus, the moated Renaissance manor has been the home of the Rosenkrantzes for four centuries. The four-winged castle, encircled by about 35 acres of parkland, houses a Great Hall (its most important room), as well as a large collection of French Gobelins, old paintings, Spanish furniture, a vaulted gallery walk, and pigskin-bound folios, to name only a few of its enrichments. Rosenholm Castle is open during the school holidays (June 20 to August 5) weekdays from 10 a.m. to 5 p.m. Admission is 22 kroner ($1.98) for adults, 8 kroner (72¢) for children.

Gammel Estrup

This Renaissance manor, near Auning, was owned by two families for six centuries, but today it houses the **Jutland Manor House Museum** (tel. 48-30-01). The origins of Gammel Estrup, built on medieval fortified grounds, go back to the 14th century, and the major rebuilding of the present structure took place in the early 1600s. The museum itself—from its Great Hall to its Komtesse Room —is richly furnished and decorated in Pomeranian pine, stucco ceilings, tapestries and paintings from the 17th and 18th centuries. It may be visited daily from 10 a.m. to 5 p.m. from May 1 to October 31; admission is 12 kroner ($1.08). The **Danish Agricultural Museum** (tel. 48-34-44) is now situated in the earlier "drifts-buildings." Visiting time there is the same as in the manor house. Admission is 6 kroner (54¢).

Clausholm

Built in the 17th century, Clausholm, eight miles southeast of Randers and 19 miles north Århus, is a splendid baroque palace—one of the earliest in Denmark. It was erected by King Frederick IV's chancellor, whose teenage daughter, Anna Sophie, married the king. When Frederick died, his son by another marriage banished the queen to Clausholm, where she lived with her own court until her death in 1743.

The rooms of the castle are basically unaltered since Anna Sophie's day, but few of the original furnishings remain. The salons and ballroom feature elaborate stucco ceilings and decorated panels. The castle also boasts an excellent collection of Danish rococo and Empire furnishings, replacing the original pieces. The Queen's Chapel, where Anna Sophie and her court worshipped, is unchanged and contains the recently restored organ, the oldest in Denmark.

In 1976 the Italian baroque gardens were reopened, complete with a fountain system laid out on the symmetrical axis of the castle and its grounds. Visitors can snack at the cafeteria in the vaulted cellars of the castle, open from 11 a.m. to 6 p.m., May through October. The castle is open from May 15 to September 15 daily from 10 a.m. to noon and 2 to 5:30 p.m. Both castle and cafeteria are open on weekends and holidays only during the spring and fall. The park and gardens are open year round from 10 a.m. to 6 p.m. Admission to the castle, which includes a guided tour, is 17 kroner ($1.53) for adults, 6 kroner (54¢) for children.

Lord and Lady Berner, the present owners of Clausholm, have devised a unique attraction to make your visit to the castle even more enjoyable. Given sufficient notice, special arrangements can be made which include a special tour of the castle conducted by Lady Berner herself, followed by various choices of lunch or dinner, served in the elaborate ballroom. Prices range from 150 kroner ($13.50) to 250 kroner ($22.50), depending on the type of arrangements made. If you arrange for it several months in advance, you may even reserve a concert on the old organ in the chapel, or a chamber music recital in the grand ballroom. Advance reservations and arrangements for concerts and tours can be made by telephoning 06/49-10-40, or by writing Clausholm Castle, Voldum, 8370 Hadsten, Denmark.

12. Ebeltoft

A well-preserved town of half-timbered buildings, 32 miles northeast of Århus, Ebeltoft is the capital of the Mols hill country. A veil of fantasy seems to cover the fishing village of cobblestone streets, hidden-away lanes, and old inns. Ruddy-faced fishermen carry on the profession of their ancestors, and the **Town Hall** looks as if it were erected just for kindergarten children to play in. Don't fail to go inside this 1789 building, now a museum housing an ethnographical collection from Thailand and an old post office. From March 1 through September, it is open daily from 10 a.m. to 5 p.m. Off-season, its hours are from 10 a.m. to 4 p.m. It is always closed on Monday, however, and the price of admission is 6 kroner (54¢) for adults, 3 kroner (27¢) for children.

Also try to visit the frigate *Jutland* moored in the harbor, which is the oldest man-of-war in Denmark, dating from 1860. The frigate may be visited daily, 10 a.m. to 5 p.m., May to September. Admission is 6 kroner (54¢) for adults, 3 kroner (27¢) for children.

Another sight is **Farvergården,** 13–15 Adelgade (tel. 34-13-82), which is a dye works dating from 1772. The oldest part is from 1683. Exhibits include the living quarters with original furniture, the dye facilities with a pressing room, a dye room with boilers, and a printing room, as well as a stable wing with a coach house which dates from the beginning of the 18 century. From April 1 to September 15, hours are 10 a.m. to 5 p.m., costing 10 kroner (90¢) for adults, 5 kroner (45¢) for children. Off-season, the museum shuts down at 4 p.m., and it is always closed on Monday.

If you have children accompanying you, take them over to the **Missers Dukkemuseum,** a doll museum at 17 Grønningen (tel. 34-21-40). This museum houses one of the largest private collections of dolls exhibited in the Scandinavian countries, circa 1820 to 1930 inclusive. On view are not only dolls, but doll prams, doll beds, dollhouses, toys, trains, cars, steam engines, and tin soldiers. Other items include doll dresses and handiwork from the 19th century. English is spoken. Admission is 8 kroner (72¢) for adults, 5 kroner (45¢) for children. The **Ebeltoft Turistbureau** is at 9–11 Torvet.

FOOD AND LODGING: **Hotel Hvide Hus,** Strandgardshøj (tel. 34-14-66), is a modern, elegant hotel with many recreational facilities, including an exercise room, sauna, solarium, swimming pool, golf course, and a nightclub, Molbostuen. All rooms have private baths, terraces, telephones, color TV, radios, and refrigerators. The charge for a double is 500 kroner ($45), while a single pays 350 kroner ($31.50).

Hotel Ebeltoft Strand, 3 Nordre Strandvej (tel. 34-33-00), is a pleasant hostelry with rooms overlooking Ebeltoft Bay. Centrally located, the hotel is also near a forest and offers numerous attractions, such as an 18-hole golf course, tennis courts, and horseback riding opportunities, as well as indoor activities. You can swim in the pool, steam in the sauna, or work out in an exercise room. Rent for a double is 550 kroner ($49.50), with a single costing 330 kroner ($29.70). All rooms have private baths, TV, and radios.

Ebeltoft Parkhotel, 4 Vibaek Strandvej (tel. 34-17-17), is a new holiday hotel, in pleasant surroundings, about a thousand feet from a fine, sandy beach, with a number of its rooms commanding bay views. All rooms have telephones, radios, TV, and private baths. Doubles range from 360 kroner ($32.40) to 420 kroner ($37.80), singles cost from 240 kroner ($21.60) to 280 kroner ($25.20). For recreation, you can use the solarium, swimming pool, bicycle trainers, and play table tennis and billiards.

Mols Kroen, Femmøller Strand (tel. 36-22-00), combines nostalgia with modernity. The architecture is in the half-timbered style, and the rooms are attractively decorated, most of them containing half-canopied beds and private baths and toilets. Some units open onto terraces, overlooking the fertile, undulating scenery of the Mols Hills. The finest white beach is just 330 feet from the hotel. In a bathless single, the tariff is 160 kroner ($14.40), going up to 270 kroner ($24.30) in a bathless double. Doubles with private showers or baths range from 330 kroner ($29.70) to 350 kroner ($31.50). An extra bed will cost another

90 kroner ($8.10). Since the hotel ranks as one of the finest eating places in the countryside, you may want to ask for the half-board rate of 275 kroner ($24.75) per person. The staff takes a lot of trouble here to present the food with some flourish, and the quality is first class.

Hotel Ebeltoft, 44 Adelgade (tel. 34-10-90), is an old house in the middle of town which rents out rooms. The building and the atmosphere may carry you back in time. The owners are hospitable and they speak English, too. Four double rooms and six singles are rented out, their price quotations including breakfast. No other meals are served. For a bathless single, the charge is 135 kroner ($12.15) nightly, increasing to 210 kroner ($18.90) for a double, also bathless.

13. Randers

The sixth largest town in Denmark, Randers with its present 60,000 inhabitants was first mentioned on coinage minted in 1086. It was founded at the point where Denmark's longest river, the Gudenaa, offered a natural fjord for the traffic between the northern and southern parts of Denmark.

Randers has some industry, but you're not aware of factories as you stroll through the medieval streets and lanes of its old town. Several beautiful and well-preserved half-timbered houses from the 16th and 17th centuries were first constructed by prosperous merchants. The most outstanding of these is the so-called House of the Holy Spirit, dating from 1490. On the roof of this house is a storks' nest.

Like Ribe, Randers was once long known for its storks, the national bird of the country. But in the past decades, this red-legged bird which was a harbinger of spring has slowly disappeared from Danish meadows. In and around Randers, the characteristic stork nests on top of the farmhouses have remained empty.

As this guide was researched, the stork population was pathetically reduced to a couple. The citizens of Randers eagerly look and wonder if the storks' offspring will honor their town with a return in the spring. The stork house is also the headquarters of the most helpful **Randers Tourist Office** (Hellgandshuset), 1 Erik Menveds Plads (tel. 42-44-77).

On your stroll through the old town, which has been turned into a charming pedestrian mall, you will come upon the following recommendation.

Food and Lodging

Hotel Randers, 11 Torvegade (tel. 42-34-22), dates from as early as 1856. The hotel has kept its original charm and is popular with American tourists, who enjoy the combination of elegant style and old Danish tradition. The appreciation of American tourists eventually led to an award from American Express. In 1981, the company gave the hotel an award for the finest hotel service rendered to its customers world-wide. Each of the pleasantly furnished rooms, 85 in all, contains a private bath. Singles rent for 350 kroner ($31.50), with doubles going for 525 kroner ($47.25).

If time allows, Randers has a number of green areas and parks, ideal for peaceful walks or jogging. In particular, the Gudenaa valley is idyllic.

DENMARK'S MOST FAMOUS INN: Hvidsten Kro, Hvidsten, 8981 Spentrup (between Randers and Mariager; tel. 47-70-22), is a thatched farmhouse beside the road that has doubled as a country inn since 1634. For an overnight's lodging, doubles with water basin cost 155 kroner ($13.95). For a stopover or a home-cooked, farm-style meal, Hvidsten Kro is unbeatable. The reason why is its famed five-course "Gudruns Recipe" that costs only 120 kroner ($10.50); it's possible too to order only a half recipe—herring, bacon omelet, and the Dansk koldt bord—for 70 kroner ($6.30), a huge meal. The furnishings at the five-room main inn, used only for dining, are memorable (pieces of copper, brass, ceramics, samovars, deep recessed windows, old sea chests, and walls painted with primitive murals), and the country-girl waitresses wear floor-length, cotton checked kitchen aprons. The bedrooms out back are bright and clean, but single and small. This kro is beloved by many Danes, who remember that during World War II the male members of the family were tortured and killed by Germans when they refused to name their associates in gun-smuggling activities. A walk through the gardens will lead visitors to two natural boulders, dedicated to their bravery.

14. Mariager

Following a meal or an overnight's stay at Hvidsten Kro, Aalborg-bound motorists with the time are advised to pay a call on Mariager, known as "the city of the roses." In a charming setting overlooking Mariager Fjord, the town is filled with cobblestoned streets and half-timbered, red-roof buildings, a bastion against the creeping industrialization and modernization that has tainted many of its North Jutland neighbors.

Lying eight miles east of Hobro, at the western end of the Mariager Fjord, Mariager (Maria's Field), the tiniest town in Denmark, was only a little fishing hamlet with ferry service on the way between Randers and Aalborg before the founding of the Brigettine Abbey around 1410, after which it became an active commercial and trading center. From this era, many buildings have been preserved, among them the abbey church, which may be seen as you walk around the paved streets of the town. A museum, in a building dating from 1750, and a maritime collection show artifacts from the town's more active periods.

If you're passing through Mariager, the road will take you right past the **Hotel Postgården,** 6A Torvet (tel. 54-10-12). It looks out onto the marketplace and the small Town Hall. Resting under a red-tile roof, the weavy half-timbered building is painted a buttercup yellow. Roses in summer grow at its entrance. This hotel, dating from 1710, was restored in 1982 and rents out eight lovely rooms with bath, TV, and telephones. The price for a double is 425 kroner ($38.25), with singles costing 280 kroner ($25.20). Breakfast is included. The hotel has a pub where people meet for drinks.

In Mariager, you will also find a new motel, **Landgangen,** Oxendalen, with a view over the inlet and the yacht harbor. This seven-bedroom hostelry charges 310 kroner ($27.90) for a double accommodation, 210 kroner ($18.90) for a single, both including breakfast.

If you can't find a hotel room, the **Mariager Tourist Association,** 4B Kirkegade (tel. 54-13-77), will help you secure accommodation in a private home.

The **Restaurant Skoven,** on the hill on the outskirts of town, has a magnificent view of the area. You can dine here in comfort for about 65 kroner ($5.85) to 100 kroner ($9).

15. Aalborg

Aalborg is the largest city of North Jutland, and it turns out the popular aquavit that has earned it a world reputation. Although essentially a shipping town and commercial center, it makes a good base for visitors, with its large number of comfortable hotels, sightseeing attractions (a blend of the old and new), its more than 200 restaurants, and its nightlife.

History is a living reality in Aalborg. The city was founded a thousand years ago when the Viking fleets assembled in these parts before sailing out on their predatory expeditions. The original atmosphere of Aalborg is preserved in old streets and alleys. Near the Church of Our Lady are many beautifully re-stored and reconstructed houses, some of which date back to the 16th century.

Aalborg is easily reached by train. In addition, the bus station, across from the railway terminus, has more than 50 routings daily. In the environs of Aal-borg is Denmark's largest forest, Rold, where robber-bandits once roamed, as they did in Sherwood. Also, **Rebild National Park** is the site every year of the American Fourth of July celebration.

Incidentally, not far from Aalborg are some of the finest beaches in North-ern Europe, on the west coast of northern Jutland, stretching from Slettestrand to Skagen. The beach resort towns of **Blokhus** and **Løkken** are especially popu-lar with Danes, and you will also see vacationers from Germany and Sweden basking on the sunny, sandy beach. From Aalborg to Blokhus is about 18 miles by car.

Finally, if you're interested in a farmhouse holiday in North Jutland, write to **Dantourist A/S,** 21 Hulgade, 5700 Svendborg. For half board, adults pay ap-proximately 150 kroner ($13.50) per day; children age 4 to 11, 80 kroner ($7.20); and younger children, 40 kroner ($3.60). Full board costs adults 175 kroner ($15.75); children age 4 to 11, 92.50 kroner ($8.33); and younger children, 51.25 kroner ($4.61) per day. In high season, the price for a self-catering holiday in the country in an apartment or a house is 1300 kroner ($117) per week. Off-season discounts are granted. Write to **Lønstrup Tourist Bureau,** 90 Strandvejen, Løn-strup, 9800 Hjørring; **Rebild-Skørping Tourist Bureau,** 1 Jyllandsgade, 9520 Skørping; or Dantourist A/S.

HOTELS: Aalborg has many good and reasonably priced hotels, many of which lie within an easy walk of the rail station. The newer ones contain private baths in most of the rooms; however, if you're on the strictest of budget you can stay at one of the older places and ask for a unit with hot and cold running water only.

Hotel Hafnia, J. F. Kennedy Plads (tel. 13-19-00), has long attracted pas-sengers who arrive by rail in Aalborg. But it manages to escape the dreary curse of many railway hotels. It is a long-established and well-maintained hostelry, known for both its service and friendly personnel. English is spoken, and guests are made to feel welcome. The Hafnia's rooms are pleasantly and adequately furnished, making for a comfortable overnight stop at 380 kroner ($34.20) in a double with bath, but only 320 kroner ($28.80) without bath. Depending on the plumbing and the size of the room, singles cost from 180 kroner ($16.20) to 200 kroner ($18).

Missionshotellet Ansgar, 14 Prinsengade (tel. 13-37-33), a half block from the railway station, is not an exceptional building (old-fashioned and solidly brick), but it does offer good basic accommodations: bathless doubles for 200 kroner ($18) to 260 kroner ($23.40), going up to 310 kroner ($27.90) with bath. Singles cost 100 kroner ($9) to 190 kroner ($17.10), depending on the plumbing. All the rooms have water basins, and there are plenty of corridor baths and toi-lets. The accommodations have been modernized somewhat, with helter-skelter furnishings. Breakfast, the only meal served, costs 35 kroner ($3.15).

Central Hotel, 38 Vesterbo (tel. 12-69-33), on Aalborg's main street, is a 70-room hotel that has been considerably modernized, although it was built in 1936. Bathless doubles cost around 380 kroner ($34.20), doubles with private baths are available for 470 kroner ($42.30). Breakfast, the only meal served, is included in the rates. The space-saving foyer and second-floor dining room don't give a fair idea of the convenience of the bedrooms, which have been fitted out with built-in motel-type conveniences (zebra-grain wood beds and cabinets —no tacky oddments here).

Aalborg Sømandshjem, 27 Østerbro (tel. 12-19-00), is an 80-bed choice that has a functional look and an exterior that is most businesslike. The public rooms are simple and welcoming, and the direction is by K. B. Clausen. Bathrooms are small and adequate, and rooms are light and airy, but not stylishly decorated. A bathless single rents for 160 kroner ($14.40), rising to 230 kroner ($20.70) in a single with shower. A double with shower goes for 330 kroner ($29.70). In the pleasant breakfast room, you can order a Danish morning meal for 35 kroner ($3.15). Good-tasting lunches and dinners are also served at a cost of 65 kroner ($5.85).

Limfjordshotellet, 14–16 Ved Stranden (tel. 16-43-33), is newer than the establishments I have considered previously. It's also one of the best hotels in Aalborg, and has caused many regular visitors to the city to desert their old favorites and come on over to the Limfjordshotellet. The location has a lot to do with the desirability of the hotel. It was built so that its units would open onto a view of both the harbor and the fjord. The hotel stands across from the Jomfru Anegade, which is the very heart of "Aalborg After Dark." The hotel is small enough to keep service personal, but big enough so that you have a reasonable chance of getting an accommodation here even in peak season. The management rents out nearly two dozens well-furnished singles and a total of 65 doubles, each unit complete with bath. I applaud the management's decision to construct five rooms for handicapped guests. A double room rents for 520 kroner ($46.80), a single going for 360 kroner ($32.40). Breakfast, included in the tariffs quoted, is the only meal served.

On the Outskirts

Hotel Scheelsminde, 35 Scheelsmindevej (tel. 18-23-33), is one of my favorite hotels in the city, and it should appeal to motorists in particular. The Scheelsminde became a hotel in 1960 when it was converted from a Danish manor house dating from 1814. In classic surroundings, you can escape the noise of Aalborg and wander at leisure through the hotel's large private grounds. Each of the rooms is attractively furnished and well maintained. There are 56 rooms in all, each with a private bath. Reservations are strongly advised in peak season, because of the popularity of this hotel. A double room costs from 500 kroner ($45), a single going for 360 kroner ($32.40), tariffs including a Danish breakfast. You might also like to dine here, as the hotel has employed a good chef who is equally at home in the Danish kitchen or else venturing into the international field.

WHERE TO DINE AND DRINK: Holles Vinstue, 57 Algade (tel. 13-84-88), a two-room family-run bar and tea room, is at the back of a former pastry shop. It's suitable only for a luncheon stopover, as it doesn't serve complete meals. You may enjoy smørrebrød, a trio of sandwiches for 32 kroner ($2.88), followed by a pot of coffee at 15 kroner ($1.35). The wine stube is not elaborately decorated, but few remember the decor, just the friendly atmosphere.

Other good dining spots include the **Fyrtøjet** (Tinderbox), 17 Jomfru Anegade (tel. 13-35-89), a cozy, small restaurant in 300-year-old surroundings in the center of town. The ambience is mellow, and half of Aalborg seems attracted to its precincts. The cooking, I've found, is some of the best in Jutland. Main dishes begin at 35 kroner ($3.15), although some are quite expensive. A Danish specialty, called almueplatte, at 40 kroner ($3.60), is a meal in itself. Beer starts at 17 kroner ($1.53) for a glass.

Other restaurants serving good food at reasonable prices are:

The **DSB** at the railway station (tel. 12-95-48). A daily special goes for 42.50 kroner ($3.83).

At **Restaurant Kniv & Gaffel,** 10 Maren Turis Gade (tel. 16-69-72), you can enjoy a good lunch for around 55 kroner ($4.95).

If you're in the mood for pasta, try the **Pizzeria Kunst & Spaghetti,** 65 Vesterbro (tel. 12-63-13), where you can choose from a variety of pizzas, starting at 40 kroner ($3.60). Other pasta dishes are good here, too.

Nørregade Salatbar, 20 Nørregade (tel. 12-41-42), as its name implies, specializes in salad dishes, which cost from 25 kroner ($2.25) and include an interesting variety of ingredients.

A number of restaurants throughout Denmark, including Aalborg, serve a Danmenu with a two-course lunch or dinner of traditional Danish food with local specialties going for 65 kroner ($5.85). A Danmenu restaurant is easy to find, identifiable by the special Danmenu sign.

An Adventure in a Wine Cellar

Duus Vinkjaelder, 9 Østeraagade (tel. 12-50-56), is an old-world cellar underneath one of the most famous private Renaissance mansions in Denmark (Jens Bang's Stonehouse). It features a selection of beer and wine (ever had Rainwater Madeira?), but it's a bit skimpy on the food. Snacks cost from 14 kroner ($1.26) to 25 kroner ($2.25). After a descent down steep steps, guests enter a brick-vaulted main room with crude provincial stools and chairs, and heavy oak tavern tables. It is dimly lit by candles and wrought-iron lanterns, and aged wooden wine casks stand nearly six feet high against the walls. Locals who don't want to miss any of the action usually select a seat in one of the three little "opera boxes."

SEEING THE TOWN: The major attraction of Aalborg is the above-mentioned **Jens Bang's Stonehouse,** on the major traffic artery of Østeraagade. This six-floor mansion once belonged to a wealthy merchant, who had it built in 1624—a glittering Renaissance-style celebration of the growing might of the bourgeoisie. On the ground floor is an old apothecary.

Also take a look at the **Budolfi Kirke,** Algade, an elaborately decorated (unusual pews, 16th- to 18th-century paintings, Renaissance pulpits, a baroque font) cathedral which dates back to 1500, although its spire was built in the late 1700s. The cathedral honors St. Botolph, patron saint of men at sea.

Nordjyllands Kunstmuseum (the North Jutland museum of modern and contemporary art), 50 Kong Cristians Allé (tel. 13-80-88), is a prime example of modern Scandinavian architecture, designed by Elissa and Alvar Aalto and Jean-Jacques Baruël and built from 1968 to 1972. It is a showplace for Danish and international art of the 20th century, with the principal emphasis being on contemporary Danish visual art. There is a varied program of exhibitions. The museum houses galleries, sculpture gardens, two auditoriums, an outdoor amphitheater, and a restaurant, the Museumscaféen. There's also a children's museum, which can be experienced by the senses reacting to the changing displays.

The museum and restaurant are open daily from 10 a.m. to 5 p.m.; closed Monday except in July and August. Admission is 7 kroner (63¢) for adults, with children and students admitted free.

From the **Aalborg Tower,** rising 325 feet above sea level, there is a perfect view of the city and the fjord. The tower is at Skovbakken, and is open from April to October, charging adults 6 kroner ($1.08) admission; children 6 kroner (54¢). For more information, telephone 12-01-02.

The **zoo,** Mølleparkvej (tel. 13-07-33), is the second largest one in Scandinavia, with animal specimens from all over the world, wandering freely in surroundings which duplicate as nearly as possible an open African range. Apes and beasts of prey are kept under minimal restrictions, however. The zoo is open from March to November, charging 30 kroner ($2.70) for adults, 15 kroner ($1.25) for children. There is a good restaurant, and you'll find snackbars here and there.

Møllenparken is a large park area with a lookout from which you can see most of Aalborg and the Isle of Egholm. Look for Roda Reilinger's sculpture, *Noah's Ark.*

As a final stopover, the vine-covered **Monastery of the Holy Ghost,** C. W. Obels Plads, is considered the oldest home for the sick and aged in Denmark, as well as the oldest building in Aalborg, dating back to 1431. This step-gabled monastery, in the heart of the shopping malls, is well preserved. See the refectory, the vaulted storage cellars and "prison," the whitewashed cloisters, and the chapter house with its 16th-century frescoes. Guided tours normally are conducted Monday to Thursday in July at 3 p.m. Cost is 12 kroner ($1.08) for adults and 6 kroner (54¢) for children. Off-season, arrangements are made through the Aalborg Tourist Bureau.

AALBORG AFTER DARK: Aalborg has long been known as a festive city with a lot of pubs and restaurants, some of which are open 24 hours a day. One street of old houses—known as **Jomfru Anegade**—has been equipped with a whole series of bars, discos, and restaurants, serving tasty food at reasonable prices.

The **Tivoliland** from April to September has lots of snap and sparkle, although it is but a mere protégé of the more famous gardens of Copenhagen. Still, it has many of the elements that make for fun times, such as a panoramic lift passing through the ages—from Paradise to the Space Age. There's a rotating stage for an international orchestra, plus good restaurants and a pizzeria, dancing, sing-alongs, a roller coaster with a loop, a roundabout which offers a vertical ride, and a cinema with a 180-degree screen.

Several nightspots are on Jomfru Anegade, one of the pedestrian streets in the heart of town. **Gaslight,** 23 Jomfru Anegade (tel. 13-94-29), is a leading disco. It's open from 9 p.m. till 4 a.m. (till 5 a.m. on Friday and Saturday), charging 25 kroner ($2.25) during the week, 35 kroner ($3.15) on Friday and Saturday. Beer is 22 kroner ($1.98). Closed Sunday.

The older singles crowd goes to **Dancing Palace,** 76 Vesterbro (tel. 12-62-22), the closest thing to a 1940s dance palace—advertised as "the largest of its kind in the city." The entrance fee is 25 kroner ($2.25), 35 kroner ($3.15) on Friday and Saturday. A beer goes for 22.50 kroner ($2.03), meals from 40 kroner ($3.60).

TOURS: You can rent a taxi with an English-speaking driver who takes you past the highlights of Aalborg, both old and new. The maximum number of passengers is four, and the tour lasts about 1½ hours. The price for four persons is approximately 200 kroner ($18) to 250 kroner ($22.50). Inquire for particulars at the extremely helpful **Aalborg Tourist Association,** 8 Østeraagade, 9000 Aalborg (tel. 08/12-60-22).

EXCURSIONS: The remains of a Viking hamlet and cemetery (more than 600 cremation graves) have been excavated at **Lindholm Høje,** near Nørresundby north of Aalborg. It is a ten-minute bus ride from the Aalborg town center, then another ten minutes on foot. Take bus 1, which leaves every ten minutes during the day. Set in park surroundings, the excavations are open to the public all year. Finds from the site are deposited in the Aalborg Historical Museum.

A private foundation in 1966 opened **Voergård Slot** to the public for the first time. It is a magnificent Renaissance castle dating from 1588, and it is filled with sculpture, Louis XVI furnishings, a banqueting hall, grand salon (works by Goya and Rubens)—in all, a most worthy sight. Open during school holidays (approximately June 20 to August 10), 2 to 5 p.m. weekdays, 10 a.m. to 5 p.m. on Sunday; from mid-May to mid-September, 2 to 5 p.m. on Saturday, and 10 a.m. to 5 p.m. Sunday and holidays; 10 a.m. to 5 p.m. during Easter holidays, 2 to 5 p.m. Easter Eve. Admission is 15 kroner ($1.35) for adults, 7 kroner (63¢)

for children. Inquire at the tourist bureau in Aalborg about ways of approaching the castle.

Americans who are in Jutland on the Fourth of July should make a beeline to the **Rebild National Park,** 18 miles south of Aalborg. On these heather dunes, Danes, Danish-Americans, and Americans celebrate American Independence Day. The program often features opera singers, folk dancers, choirs, and glee clubs, together with well-known speakers. On the occasion of the Rebild Golden Jubilee in 1962, the late President Kennedy said this annual celebration was "a most extraordinary example of international friendship when the people of another country celebrate American Independence Day on their own soil." In the park is the Lincoln Memorial Log Cabin and Immigrant Museum, devoted to mementos of Danish immigration to the United States.

A one-hour bus ride takes you to the resort town of **Blokhus** and the broad white beaches of the North Sea coast. Not far from here is **Fårup Sommerland,** a 124-acre amusement park which offers many possibilities of fun and relaxation for both children and adults. There's a 750-yard ride on a coastal railway, Icelandic ponies, canoeing, rowing, sailing, a firing range for air guns or saloon rifles, trampolines, bowling, and midget golf. Restaurant, grill bars, and barbecue facilities are available. Your entrance ticket, which costs 50 kroner ($4.50) for adults, 45 kroner ($4.05) for children, entitles you to the use of the park's attractions for the day. Children under 5 are admitted free.

16. Frederikshavn

This eastern coast town is, for many, a final stopover in Denmark. Its ferry connections with Sweden (Gothenburg) or Norway (Oslo, Fredrikstad, Moss, and Larvik) have earned it the title of a gateway city to these other Scandinavian countries. It's a port, business center, fishing base—and holds some tourist interest. The Swedish Stena line (tel. 42-43-66) maintains luxury ferry service, six sailings daily in summer from Frederikshavn to Gothenburg. It's a three-hour crossing; the adult one-way fare ranges from 90 kroner ($8.10) to 150 kroner ($13.50) per person, depending on the line and season. The cost of transporting a car depends on the season and the size of the vehicle, usually from 150 kroner ($13.50) up. In addition to boats to Sweden, there are also ferries to Norway, seven per week during the summer.

You can visit **Bangsbo Museum** in a typical Danish manor, lying in a wooded area at the edge of town beside the Deer Park. The buildings, dating from the 18th century, were constructed on the site of a manor house erected here in 1364. The old barn is from 1630, one of the oldest in Denmark, now containing antique farm equipment and implements. In the main house you'll see a collection of handicraft made using human hair, a large display of relics from World War II, and a nautical section which has ship models, figureheads, and other mementos. An early medieval ship similar to the vessels used by the Vikings is in one of the stable buildings. The museum is open daily March 1 to December 31 from 10 a.m. to 5 p.m.; January 1 to February 28 Monday to Friday from 10 a.m. to 5 p.m. Admission is 7 kroner (63¢) for adults, 2 kroner (18¢) for children.

Quite near the Bangsbo Museum, you can't miss seeing the **Cloostårnet,** a tower almost 200 feet high which gives you an extensive view from 528 feet above sea level. In good weather, most of Vendsyssel is visible. An elevator will take you up on Easter Saturday from 10 a.m. to 4 p.m.; Easter Sunday from 10 a.m. to 7 p.m.; from then until May 14 Monday to Friday from 1 to 6 p.m. and weekends from 10 a.m. to 6 p.m. From May 15 to June 14, you can go up daily from 1 to 7 p.m. and from June 15 to August 14 from 10 a.m. to 8 p.m. Hours from August 15 to September 30 are 1 to 6 p.m. daily except Monday. The charge is 6 kroner (54¢) for adults, 3 kroner (27¢) for children.

At Havneplad, right on the waterfront and shipping docks, stands the

Krudttårnsmuseet, the gun tower which was the main part of the fortification, Fladstrand, built in 1686–1690. The museum contains weapons and uniforms pertaining to the historical period of the fortification. It may be visited from April 1 to October 31 daily from 10 a.m. to 5 p.m., costing adults 4 kroner (36¢), children 1.50 kroner (14¢).

FOOD AND LODGING: The helpful tourist office, **Frederikshavn Turistbureau,** 1 Brotorvet (tel. 42-32-66), near the ferry dock, is open during the summer season from 8:30 a.m. until 8:30 p.m. (Sunday from 11 a.m. to 8:30 p.m.). In case you miss the boat and need a room, staff members will book you into a private home, costing around 150 kroner ($13.50) for a double.

There is a good youth hostel. **Vandrerhjemmet Fladstrand,** Fladstrand, 6 Buhlsvej (tel. 42-14-75), at the north end of town, about one mile from the center. This modern one-story brick building looks like a motel and has comfortable family rooms with four to six beds costing 50 kroner ($4.50) per person.

Hoffmanns Hotel, 1 Tordenskjoldsgade (tel. 42-21-66), is smack in the heart of Frederikshavn (car park at the rear is convenient for ferry departures). A double with bath costs from 415 kroner ($37.35). The Danish food is top-notch. A typical dinner averages 65 kroner ($5.85).

Motel Lisboa, 248 Søndergade (tel. 42-21-33), is one of the most modern and up-to-date accommodations in the north of Jutland. On the outskirts of town, it is a two-story motel with rooms that are bright, airy, and color-coordinated in a tasteful Danish design. Units contain up-to-date baths, and the motel is well run and most comfortable. A single costs 250 kroner ($22.50) nightly, a double going for 450 kroner ($40.50) with color TV. If you're traveling with children, the management will put in an extra bed at a cost of 150 kroner ($13.50). Breakfast is an additional 35 kroner ($3.15). At the Lisboa's restaurant, you can also order dinner until 10 p.m.

Hotel Jutlandia, Havnepladsen (tel. 42-42-00), just opposite the harbor with a splendid view, rents doubles with bath for 600 kroner ($54), including breakfast. You can be sure your car is safe, as it will be placed in a locked basement garage for the night.

Right in the heart of Frederikshavn, **Hotel Mariehønen,** 40 Danmarksgade (tel. 42-01-22), is an elderly but still nice hostelry. Singles with bath cost 210 kroner ($18.90), doubles with bath going for from 400 kroner ($36). Breakfast is included in the tariffs. You can't buy beer or alcoholic beverages in this hotel. It's closed Sunday from September to May.

Park Hotel, 7 Jernbanegade (tel. 42-22-55), is another old hotel in the city center, this one recently restored so you're provided with up-to-date accommodation. Singles range from 190 kroner ($17.10) to 310 kroner ($27.90), the latter price for rooms with bath. Doubles cost from 360 kroner ($32.40) in a bathless unit to 510 kroner ($45.90) with bath. Breakfast is included.

Frederikshavn has several good restaurants, most specializing in fish dishes. My favorite is **Hyttefad II,** Trindelen, in Fiskerihavnen (tel. 42-52-22). I always enjoy the savory Frederikshavner-plaice, prepared especially well here. Expect to pay from 150 kroner ($13.50) up for a complete meal. The restaurant is open Monday to Friday from 11 a.m. to 2 p.m. and 5 to 8 p.m.

16. Hirtshals

There is daily steamer service from this port to Norway across the Skagerrak.

Of particular interest is the **North Sea Museum,** a modern center for fisheries and marine biology as well as a living museum and information center providing an insight into the situation faced by fishermen today, the fisheries industry, and fishery research. In the enormous octagonal aquarium, the ocean's secrets can be studied at close quarters. It holds large, rare fish and many smaller sea creatures. There is also a huge outdoor tank for such large sea animals as dolphins and seals. You can watch them through observation windows and galleries around the tank. The museum is open daily from 9 a.m. to 8 p.m. from mid-June to mid-August. The rest of the year, hours are from 9 a.m. to 4 p.m. Monday to Friday and 10 a.m. to 5 p.m. Saturday, Sunday, and public holidays. Admission is 25 kroner for adults ($2.25), 10 kroner (90¢) for children 7 to 16.

The **Hirtshals Museum** is set up in a typical fisherman's house, built of granite in 1880. The interior is a reproduction of a 1915 fisherman's family home. The museum is open daily from June to August from 10 a.m. to 5 p.m.; September to May Monday to Friday from 1 to 4 p.m.. Admission is 6 kroner (54¢) for adults, 3 kroner (27¢) for children.

WHERE TO STAY: Reservations can be made through the **Hirtshals Turistbureau,** 32 Vestergade (tel. 94-22-20), for either a private home or a hotel. If you prefer to make your own selection, try the following:

Munchs Badehotel, Tornby Strand (tel. 97-71-15), is open only from May 1 to October 1. Attracting mainly a summer business, it rents out only 12 doubles, for which it charges 145 kroner ($13.05) a night. It's also possible to stay here on full-pension terms at a rate of 165 kroner ($14.85) per person.

Hotel Strandlyst, Tornby (tel. 97-70-76), is another summer possibility, receiving guests from the first of June until the end of August. It is much larger, containing a total of 45 adequately furnished bedrooms, of which only 13 are equipped with private facilities. Singles rent for 100 kroner ($9), while doubles, depending on the plumbing, cost from 200 kroner ($18) to 240 kroner ($21.60).

On the Outskirts

You might enjoy spending the night at the home of a marvelous Danish lady, **Karla Pedersen,** 15 Stationsvej, Tornby DK, 9850 Hirtshals (tel. 08/97-70-25). She provides rooms with bath in her home in Tornby, just five miles south of Hirtshals. Look for a "Zimmer/Rooms" sign on the main road through Tornby.

Her lovely, modern, one-story brick home is quiet and beautifully furnished, and it's kept sparkling clean. The cost is 100 kroner ($9) in a double room, plus another 25 kroner ($2.25) for a Danish breakfast. Mrs. Pedersen speaks a little English, enough to get by in and welcome you, of course.

She treats guests as one of the family, and some readers have reported that they've never "felt more welcome in all of Europe." She asks her guests to sign a large book which she has kept for many years.

Those motorists catching a ferry at Hirtshals, Hanstholm, or Frederikshavn may need to know of Mrs. Pedersen.

Chapter V

A PREVIEW OF NORWAY

1. Getting There
2. Getting Around
3. Transportation in Oslo
4. Cutting Accommodation Costs
5. The ABCs of Life

AT A CAFÉ IN OSLO, the wife of my host picked up a fork, leaned over the table, and tapped her husband on the knuckles: "Keep your eyes off the huldre, darling."

The "huldre" was a tall blonde in pants at least three sizes too small.

In Norwegian folklore, a huldre is supposed to be a most beautiful woman —but she has a cow's tail tucked under her skirt, perhaps tied around her waist. And this bovine appendage is always dropping out at the most inopportune times. For her tail to drop off completely, she has to marry a man in a church.

The huldre makes a clever housewife and is resented—for that and other reasons—by Norwegian women. The Anna, Nora, or Birgit who wants to hang onto her husband is not averse to warning him against accepting an invitation to go home with a huldre for the night. The huldre has the power of stretching that night out for seven years. At least that's what many an errant Olav has claimed when he finally stumbles back to his much older spouse.

Frankly, the tall blonde singled out probably wasn't a real huldre. It was impossible for her to conceal anything under those pants. But that didn't matter. The wife knew her to be a huldre—and that was that.

LEGENDS, MOUNTAINS, AND NATURE: As children, Norwegians grow up on stories, not only of huldres but of trolls. These extremely large creatures—who can be both good and evil—have become a part of the folklore of the country. And in their secret hearts, many Norwegians still believe in them.

Trolls have very long noses—but often only one eye per family. To compensate for this lack of vision, some trolls possess as many as seven heads. In case a Norwegian farmer should chop off one of the troll's heads, three more will grow back in its place. Mrs. Troll has a bigger nose than her husband. She uses it for everything from stirring porridge to whipping the children. Trolls never come out in sunlight. If they should happen to make a sudden appearance during the day, they burst and are petrified as mountains. That's why Norway has so many mountains, so the legend goes.

And mountains Norway has—and fjords and waterfalls unique in Europe.

Go to Norway for an experience not only with folklore, but with the great outdoors. Spain and Italy overflow with legendary, treasure-filled cities. Norway has nothing to equal them. England has preserved the crooked old architecture from the days of Samuel Johnson. Norway's wooden villages have burned to the ground for the most part. Many of its towns along the coast—such as Bodø—were destroyed during World War II. But in sheer scenic beauty, Norway is about the greatest thing this side of Valhalla.

Norway is a blend of the ancient and the modern. How curious to see a Lapp grandmother—attired in a brightly colored braided costume, bonnet, and deer-hide moccasins with turned-up toes—waiting to board an airplane at the Tromsø airport.

Search long and hard enough, and you might turn up a sod-roofed house, where old Grandfather Per—wearing high trousers—sits in a tub-chair in the corner downing his curds-and-whey. On the other hand, his grandson, clad in a male bikini, will probably be sunning himself on a rock listening to American music on his transistor radio.

1. Getting There

Scandinavia's major airline, SAS, flies into Oslo, and in several previous editions I have recommended it. For a change of pace, I recently flew a Minneapolis-based airline, **Northwest Orient,** to the Norwegian capital.

Their modern fleet of 747s makes frequent runs from both New York's JFK and Minneapolis/St. Paul once a week during winter and five times weekly from New York and Minneapolis. In summer, some of the airline's runs from the midwest are nonstop, making Norwegian descendants' return to the land of their ancestors faster than would have been dreamed by their forebears making the trip west a century ago.

Many fare options are available, the cheapest being a round-trip basic season special excursion fare. This requires that passengers book their reservations within 20 days (and not more) of their departure. They also need to stay at least seven days out of this country before using the return half of their ticket.

Fares from New York, as of this writing, range from $628 in low season to $809 in high season, while fares from Minneapolis range from $802 in low season to $893 in high season. All takeoffs from North America require a $3 departure tax. These fares could change radically by the time you read this, so you should know that the best way to investigate Northwest's tariffs would be to call them at whatever toll-free number is listed in your telephone directory.

For travelers wanting to plan their trips and their takeoff from North America many weeks in advance, the special excursion fare might not suit their needs. In that case, a regular APEX fare would be appropriate. While slightly more expensive, it would guarantee a specific departure date many weeks in advance. That ticket, of course, must be paid for more than 21 days prior to departure and requires a minimum stay of between 5 and 10 days (depending on the season) and a maximum stay of three months.

2. Getting Around

From reindeer sleigh to electric train, the choice of transport in Norway is vast. I'll survey the most popular means for getting about.

AIR SERVICE: Norway has excellent air service, both from SAS and an independent airline, which provide a quick and convenient means of getting there in a vast country with its many hard-to-reach centers.

SAS crisscrosses Norway with a number of regularly scheduled domestic flights, such as the common jaunt between Bergen and Oslo, but Trondheim and Bodø are other popular destinations. It's also possible to fly to the Arctic gateway of Tromsø; to Alta in Finnmark, the heart of Lapland; and to Kirkenes, near the Russian border.

A top-notch independent airline, offering supplementary service, is fast-rising Braathens S.A.F.E. This small company operates many worldwide charter flights, but has regularly scheduled routings inside Norway, linking major tourist centers as well as more remote places not covered by other airlines. Its air routes have the pattern of half a wagon wheel, with Oslo as the hub, and along the rim are such important destinations as Stavanger, Bergen, Ålesund, Kristiansand, Molde, and Trondheim. The airline also covers Bodø, Evenes, and Tromsø in northern Norway. More than 100 daily jet services (Boeing 737 and Fokker 28) cover 13 main cities all over the country. For information or assistance, contact the Oslo booking office for **Braathens S.A.F.E.**, 2 Haakon VII's Gate (tel. 41-10-20).

BUSES IN THE COUNTRY: Where the train or coastal steamer stops, a scenic bus is usually waiting to take passengers the rest of the way. The crisscrossing bus system of Norway is excellent, linking up remote, but beautiful, off-the-beaten-path hamlets along the fjords. Numerous conducted, all-inclusive motorcoach tours—often combined with steamer travel—are offered from either Bergen or Oslo in summer. As mentioned, the train ends its northward run in Bodø, but it's possible to take the Polar Express bus, 39 miles east of Bodø in Fauske. This most fascinating of bus trips spans the distance along the Arctic Highway through Finnmark (Lapland) to Kirkenes near the Russian border—and back. The Kirkenes run operates from June to October; but the service is all year from Fauske to Alta in Finnmark. Passengers are guaranteed hotel accommodations along the way.

CAR FERRIES: Mostly privately run, the car ferries in the western fjord country and in the north are essential to transportation. Motorists in particular should go to the nearest tourist bureau and ask for a free map, "Norway By Car." With it, you should pick up a timetable outlining car-ferry services in Norway. Some ferries will accept advance reservations; others will not. Since the ferries are vital to the transportation system—and are mostly used by the Norwegians themselves—the cost for passengers or for car transport is kept low.

CAR RENTALS: A drive through Norway is likely to be one of the most scenic you find in Europe. If you want to rent a car, Hertz and Avis are well represented in Norway, and **Budget Rent-a-Car,** for example, maintains about 18 Norwegian offices, each staffed with courteous personnel and stocked with a variety of well-maintained vehicles.

The least expensive arrangements always include a rental of at least seven days or more and require an advance reservation of at least three business days. The cheapest car is a Honda Civic or a Ford Fiesta with manual transmission. Capable of seating four passengers with their luggage, they rent for around $180 per week, with additional days costing around $25 each. For a slightly bigger model, you might opt for a Ford Escort, costing about $200 per week, with each additional day costing another $30. This model is usually suitable for most travelers, unless a five-passenger car with automatic transmission is required. This would cost around $250 per week, with $36 for each additional day, for a Honda Accord or a similar vehicle.

You should keep in mind that the Norwegian government requires all rental customers to be at least 23 years old and to possess a valid driver's license.

You should also know that the government will impose a 20% tax on the final bill of your car rental, which, unless you're aware of it in advance, could raise the price of a four-wheeled jaunt to more than you bargained for.

Unless you purchase an optional collision damage waiver, you'll be responsible for the first 2500 kroner ($300) worth of damage to your car in case of an accident. Costing around 40 kroner ($4.80) per day, it usually proves worth the money.

Luggage and ski racks are available if you reserve them in advance, for no additional charge. In winter, all of Budget's cars are equipped with spiked snow tires.

If you're interested in making a circuit into other regions of Scandinavia, Budget won't charge you a dropoff fee if you pick up your car in Oslo and drop it off in Copenhagen. Likewise, there's no charge if you pick up a car at Oslo, Bergen, or Stavanger and then drop it off at the Budget office at either of the other two cities.

For more information on how to rent a car from Budget, you can call toll-free during extended day or nighttime hours to their reservations center in Dallas, Texas, at 1/800/527-0700.

You might also try **Avis Rent a Car,** which has an office at Fornebu airport in Oslo (tel. 53-05-57). It is also represented at 27 Munkedamsveien (tel. 41-00-60) and at 115 Økernveien (tel. 68-00-90). Hertz is represented in Oslo by **Kjøles Car Rental,** with offices at Fornebu airport (tel. 53-36-47). In Oslo, Kjøles is at 16 General Birchsgate (tel. 46-68-36) and at Holbergsgate (tel. 20-01-21).

HITCHHIKING: I've seen many people hitchhiking on the roads of Norway, although I'd recommend this at best as a summertime enterprise (otherwise, you might freeze to death before you get a ride). Norwegians are friendly and helpful to most hitchhikers, and since many of them speak English, language should not be a barrier.

MOTORING: Dazzling scenery awaits you at nearly every turn. Some of the roads are less than perfect (often dirt or gravel), although passable. Most mountain roads are open by the first of June; the so-called motoring season lasts from mid-May to the end of September. In western Norway, hairpin curves are common. A guide once said, "Norwegian drivers are either good or dead." But most foreigners who are willing to settle for doing less than 150 miles a day needn't fear. You can drive to the North Cape by car (at least a seven-day trip from Oslo). The easiest and most convenient touring territory is in and around Oslo and the trek southward, going from the capital to Stavanger. Final warning: If a policeman catches a motorist with as much as a drop of aquavit or even beer on his or her breath, the driver is slammed into jail for three weeks —and can't be rescued by a fine! All the big-drinking Scandinavian countries are fanatically strict not only about drunken drivers, but one-shotters, too.

To enter Norway with a car does not require many formalities. Motorists must have their national driving license, car registration book, "warning-triangle," and an insurance "Green Card" (obtainable from Customs upon entering Norway if you don't have one).

STEAMERS: For a look at the fjords of western Norway, nothing tops the indomitable steamer. In North Norway, too, those with the time can take one of the tiny cargo and mail steamers to one of the remote offshore fishing villages, a marvelously cheap and offbeat adventure. Some of the most popular sea trips in Europe are the 11-day, all-inclusive, round-trip steamer trips from Bergen to Kirkenes, near the Russian border, an estimated 2500 miles of scenic coastline. Thrift-conscious travelers book passage in the spring (April), early summer, late summer, and autumn, when the fares are considerably reduced. From May 21 to July 31, you pay $1000 per person for the trip, including first-class passage and three abundant meals a day. From August 1 to August 31, the fare is $970 per person. You can take the trip in early May for $762 per person. Bookings are tight during peak months, so reserve in advance. The tours are offered by the **Bergen Line,** and reservations may be made at their New York City agent's office at 505 Fifth Avenue (tel. 212/986-2711).

TRAINS: Norway is crisscrossed by a network of excellent electric and diesel-electric trains. They run as far as Bodø, 62 miles beyond the Arctic Circle. (After that, visitors have to take a coastal steamer, plane, or bus along the run to Tromsø and the North Cape.) The scenery is splashy on the 300-mile ride between Oslo and Bergen, the most popular run. Friendly conductors recognize the fact that visitors like to see the sights. Stops at major scenic views are commonplace (the stops, not the views).

Second-class travel on Norwegian trains is recommended. Present-day Norse people have made rapid scrubbing progress since the days of their Viking ancestors. The second-class fare to Bergen from Oslo, for instance, costs 300 kroner ($36) one way. The express trains are called *hurtigtägl ekspress,* while regular trains are called *persontog* (usually second-class seats only). There are special compartments for the physically handicapped on most medium and long-distance trains. These may be used by persons in wheelchairs and others with physical handicaps as well as their companions. Be specific about this. Children under 4 travel free if they do not occupy a separate seat. Passengers between 4 and 15 years of age pay half-fare. In express and other main trains reservation of seats is compulsory, handled at the train's starting station. Reservation fee is 10 kroner ($1.20). Sleepers and seats may be reserved up to a year in advance of your trip. The cost of sleepers first class (a one-berth compartment) is 170 kroner ($20.40). In second class, you can have either a two-berth compartment for 85 kroner ($10.20) or one with three berths for 50 kroner ($6).

There's a **Nordturist** ticket which allows unlimited travel by train in Denmark, Finland, Norway, and Sweden during a 21-day period costing 1080 kroner ($129.60) in second class, 1620 kroner ($194.40) in first class. You can plan your own route or just go when you feel the urge. There are also special **Interrail** tickets, which allow travel in 16 European countries for a period of one month as well as allowing reduced rates on some steamer services.

Norway defines a senior citizen as a person over 67. Travelers who have reached that age are entitled to a 50% discount on train tickets for Norwegian railways. It's called an Honnørrabatt. The distance traveled must be at least 31 miles. No reductions are offered on the popular coastal steamers.

Another rail ticket you may want to use is the **Norwegian Bargain Rail Pass.** Two versions of this ticket can be purchased at any train station in Norway. A one-way ticket valid for seven days and good for travel of up to 470 miles costs about $32 (U.S.). A similar ticket good for unlimited travel is priced at $43. You can stop over when and where you wish on this ticket, although it is not valid during some peak travel and holiday periods.

3. Transportation in Oslo

Whether you visit the Munch Museum or the Viking ships on the Bygdøy peninsula, you'll find Oslo well serviced by an efficient citywide network of buses, trams (streetcars), or the East–West subway system. Either buses or electric trains whisk visitors and Norwegians alike to the suburbs. Most local trains leave from the Vestbanestasjonen, near the City Hall (also ferry departures from here to Bygdøy). The subways, as well as many trains to the environs, pull out from near the National Theater and Students' Grove.

AIRPORTS/AIR TERMINALS: The Oslo domestic airport, **Fornebu,** lies at Snarøya, 5½ miles from the center of Oslo, while the international airport is **Gardermoen,** one hour from the city center. There is airport bus service from the two terminals to the Central Railway Station and other points in the city every 20 minutes. The fare is about $6 to and from Gardermoen and about $3 to connect with Fornebu. Public transport, costing about $2, is by bus 31 from the center of Oslo to Fornebu, leaving every 30 minutes. The bus also stops at Wessels Plass and National Theater. There is also an airport bus leaving every 20 minutes from the Central Station, SAS Hotel, and the Braathens S.A.F.E. booking office.

BUSES AND TRAMS: Jernbanetorget is the major terminal stop in Oslo. The average bus and tram passing through the heart of town stops at Wessels Plass, next to the Parliament, or at Stortorget, the main marketplace. Many also stop at the National Theater or University Square in Karl Johans Gate. Underground, the T-banen has four branch lines east and the Western Suburban route (including Holmenkillen) has four lines to the residential sections and recreation grounds west and north of the city. For information about timetables and fares, get in touch with the main inquiry office of **A/S Oslo Sporveier,** 27 Dronningens Gate, next to Stortorget and Domkirken. This is open weekdays between 8 a.m. and 7 p.m. and Sunday between 10 a.m. and 3 p.m. Telephone calls are handled daily between 8 a.m. and 10 p.m. at 41-70-30.

The system consists mainly of one-man-operated vehicles or trains with self-service machines which cancel pre-bought tickets. These are applicable on all modes of transport with free transfer within one hour of purchasing. The tickets are sold as books of either four coupons for 26 kroner ($3.12) or 10 tickets for 65 kroner ($7.80). Single-journey tickets are also sold by the drivers at 9 kroner ($1.08). Children travel at half-fare.

Most convenient for visitors is the 24-hour **Tourist Ticket,** which lets you travel anywhere you like in Oslo whenever you wish, by bus, tram, underground, local railways, or boat, including the Bygdøy ferries in summer. The tourist ticket costs 30 kroner ($3.60) for adults, half-fare for children under 16 (children under 4 travel free). The ticket will be stamped when it's used for the first time and will then be good for the next 24 hours.

The prices given above, although current at press time, will surely rise during the lifetime of this edition.

TAXIS: Dial 348 if you want a taxi. If you want to order a taxi in advance, such as for a trip to one of the airports, reserve at least one hour in advance by calling 38-80-70 daily between 9 a.m. and 3 p.m. and from 6 to 11 p.m. The approximate fare from Gardermoen into Oslo is $44 and from Fornebu $8. (The fare for Gardermoen can be greatly reduced if you order the taxi in advance.) All taxis are equipped with an official taximeter, and Norwegian cab drivers are honest. When a car is free, a light goes on on its roof. Taxis can be hailed on the street, providing they are more than 100 meters from a rank.

FERRIES: In summer, beginning in mid-April, ferries go to Bygdøy with its many museums, departing from Pier 3 in front of City Hall (for information about departures, telephone 41-72-65). Because of crowded parking conditions on Bygdøy, it's recommended that you use either a ferry or bus to get to these museums.

RAILWAY: Oslo has two main railway stations: Oslo Central Station (Oslo S) with connections to the continent via Copenhagen, to Sweden, and to such destinations recommended in this guide as Åndalsnes, Trondheim, Bodø, and Bergen. From Oslo West Railway Station (Oslo V), trains go in the direction of Tønsberg, Kristiansand, and Stavanger.

BICYCLES: This is a perfectly acceptable method of getting about. **Den Rustne Eike,** 32 Oscarsgate (tel. 44-18-80), right behind the Royal Palace, rents bicycles at moderate rates, complete with 20-kroner ($2.40) maps of interesting routes in Oslo and its environs.

The Oslo Card (Oslo-Kortet): Although Oslo is not a big city, it nevertheless has a rich cultural life, and most people find it exciting and beautiful. The Oslo Card is offered to help you become acquainted with the city at a fraction of normal costs. It allows you free travel on public transport; free admittance to famous museums and other top sights; favorable rates on sightseeing buses and boats; a rebate on your car rental; special treats in restaurants; and reduced rates in any of 23 hotels in the Oslo area, including some of the finest. You may purchase the card in hotels, fine stores, from travel agents, at tourist information offices and in the branches of Sparebanken Oslo Akershus.

Adults may purchase the card for 50 kroner ($6) for one day, 75 kroner ($9) for two days, and 100 kroner ($12) for three days. Children's tickets are half-price. At the time of your visit, you may pay more for this card, but it will still be a bargain way to see Oslo.

4. Cutting Accommodation Costs

In addition to the budget hotels, previewed in this guide, Norway also has several other imaginative lodging suggestions, some of which are described below.

CHALET HOLIDAYS: Norway offers one of the least expensive vacation bargains in all of Europe. Ideal for outdoors-loving families or friendly groups, log-cabin-style chalets are available throughout the country, on the side of a mountain or by the sea, in a protected valley or woodland, or by a freshwater lake. Some lie in what is known as chalet colonies; others are set on remote and lofty peaks. At night, by paraffin lamplight or the glow of a log fire, you can enjoy aquavit or an early supper, as many Norwegians do. Some cabins are fully equipped with hot and cold running water, showers, and electricity; others are more primitive, evoking pioneer living. Naturally, the price of the rental varies according to the amenities, as well as the size (some with as many as three bedrooms, most with tiered bunks). The price range is from $100 to $1000 (U.S.) weekly, the latter price for completely modern structures with fairly luxurious facilities. There are chalets in most parts of the country—in the mountains, near lakes, along the coast, and in the fjord country. For a catalog giving prices, locations, and other data, write to **Den Norske Hytteformidling Bergen A/S,** 10 Kaigaten, 500 Bergen (tel. 31-66-30); **Nordisk Fene-Novasd A/S,** 28 Bogstadveien, W-0355 Oslo 3; **Den Norske Hytteformidling A/S,** Box 3207 Sagene, N-0462 Oslo 4; **Nordisk Hyttelene,** 8 Storgate, W-2600 Lillehammer; or A/S Trønderreiser, 30 Kongensgate, W-7000, Trondheim.

FARMHOUSE HOLIDAYS: In all the travel adventures possible in Europe, few equal time spent on a fjord farm in Norway. I spent part of one summer at one, completing a novel, and found it a tranquil oasis. I also expanded my culinary repertoire, never having tasted reindeer salami before.

The accommodations are most often simple, but almost invariably the setting is magnificent. Opportunities for walking, fishing, climbing, hiking, horseback riding, and breathing the sparkling mountain air are unlimited. It's also the cheapest way to stay in Norway. Adults can stay at one of these farms for about 165 kroner ($19.80) per person, including meals, and children are charged around 75 kroner ($9).

Don't expect a private bath or luxury in any way. However, my room was filled with hand-carved wooden heirlooms of the family. Usually at least one member of the host family will speak English.

The food is homemade—it's rarely Cordon Bleu, but it is good and hearty fare. If you like wine or liquor, it's better to bring along your own supply. A packed lunch will be provided, because many visitors like to spend the day exploring fjord and mountain scenery. Sometimes you'll come upon reindeer or elk.

The most popular month for booking a farm is July, so reservations are tight then and should be made as far in advance as possible.

For this type of holiday, get in touch with **Den Norske Hytteformidling,** Post Office Box 3207, Sagene, N-0462 Oslo 4, Norway (tel. 35-67-10), which, for the most part, handles bookings for farms in the south of Norway. However, those seeking rustic accommodations in the Gudbrandsal Valley should write to the **Lillehammer Tourist Office,** Post Office Box 181, Storgaten 56, N-2601, Lillehammer, Norway (tel. 51098).

YOUTH HOSTELS: From the mountain peaks to the fjord valleys, Norway maintains about 5000 youth hostels, many of them newly built and offering quite good accommodations and decent meals. The hostels are well organized in Norway and are used by many who generally shun the idea of hostel living. Many Norwegian youth hostels have separate accommodations for families. Usually it costs only 70 kroner ($8.40) to 75 kroner ($9) a night for a bed. Sheet sleeping sacks may be rented. Reasonable meals—averaging from 25 kroner ($3)—are served in most of them, although many maintain do-it-yourself kitchen facilities. Membership cards are accepted without formality at all hostels in Norway. The most popular youth hostels—those in Oslo, Bergen, and other major tourist centers—will be surveyed in this guide.

To join the **American Youth Hostels, Inc.,** the membership fee is $20 per year for a person over 18 years of age. Those under 18 need pay only half that fee. The U.S. hostel headquarters, to which you should write for membership, is at 1332 I St. NW, Washington, DC 20005 (tel. 202/347-3125). Canadians can get in touch with the **Canadian Hosteling Association,** 333 River Rd., Vanier, ON K1L 8H9 (tel. 613/746-3844).

CAMPING: There are more than 1400 authorized camping sites in Norway, classified, according to standards and amenities, as one-, two-, and three-star camps. Charges vary according to the number of stars. Most campers perfer to live in tents and prepare their own meals, and this is without a doubt the cheapest way to go. Facilities depend on whether the camp in question caters for one night only, for weekend guests, or for those who intend to stay for longer periods. Norwegian campsites are comfortable and maintain high standards. Most have rental cabins/chalets, which are becoming increasingly popular. If you want to stay at one of these, you should make your reservation early in the afternoon. This can be done by telephone. Camping chalets are usually fitted with four bunk beds with mattresses, chairs and tables, and are electrically heated with a hotplate for cooking. Other necessary equipment, such as pillows and blankets, must be provided by the camper. If you wish more detailed information on camping, apply to the Norwegian Automobile Club, **NAF Turistavdelingen,** 2 Storgata, N-Oslo 1, for its inexpensive manual.

5. The ABCs of Life

Norway will require you to make some adjustments in simple ordinary activities of life. A krone here will no longer have the same value it had in the chapters on Denmark. In this section, I have compiled an alphabetical listing of certain basic facts that the visitor will need to know to adjust more readily to the pace of the country. These facts pertain not only to Norway in general but specifically to Oslo, which I assume will be your "gateway" to this fascinating country.

BANKS: Normal business hours for most banks are Monday to Friday from 8:15 a.m. to 3:30 p.m.; Thursday, from 8:15 a.m. to 5 p.m.; closed Saturday and Sunday. The **Fellesbanken's Exchange** at the Oslo Central Railway Station (tel. 41-26-11) is open Monday to Friday from 8 a.m. to midnight, on Saturday from 8 a.m. to 7 p.m., and on Sunday from 8 a.m. to noon. As mentioned, there's a bank at Fornebu, one of Oslo's airports, and it's open from 7 a.m. to 10:30 p.m. daily. There is also a bank at Gardermoen, the military airport where Northwest Orient jumbo jets arrive.

BATHS AND SWIMMING POOLS: The most centrally located municipal bath is **Vestkantbadet,** 1 Sommerogate; it offers Finnish sauna or Roman baths from 7:30 a.m. to 7:30 p.m. for about 40 kroner ($4.80) for "the works." Vestkantbadet is usually closed the last week in July and the first three weeks in August (tel. 44-07-26). . . . For outdoor swimming, try **Frogner Park's** open-air pool, near the Vigeland sculptures (take streetcar 2 from National Theater). The entrance fee is 8 kroner (96¢), 4 kroner (48¢) for children, and the hours are

7 a.m. to 8 p.m. weekdays from mid-May to mid-September, 10 a.m. to 5 p.m. on Sunday.

CHARACTER: A number of Norwegians look askance at the more "frivolous" Danes or the "materialistic" Swedes. Rugged individualists, the Norwegians live by choice in relative isolation. They love their mountain and fjords, and nearly everyone has—in addition to his or her home—a little hut tucked away somewhere in the wilderness.

CIGARETTES: Tobacco kiosks carry Norwegian brands of American-blended cigarettes which are cheaper than the British and American brands on sale. To save money, it's best to buy these local brands, a package of 20 costing from 20 kroner ($2.40).

CLIMATE: The Norwegian climate need not make foreign visitors from sunnier lands quake in their thermal underwear. In summer the average temperature in Oslo ranges from 57 to 63 degrees Fahrenheit. The western coast of Norway is warmed by the Gulf Stream, and winters tend to be temperate. Rainfall is heavy, however. Oslo in January hovers around 25 degrees Fahrenheit—but the temperature is ideal for winter sports.

Above the Arctic Circle, the sun shines night and day from mid-May until the end of July. The residents retreat behind black shades to get some shut-eye, while tourists stay up to bay at the midnight sun. In contrast, the North Cape is plunged into darkness for about two months in winter.

CLOTHING: Your everyday clothes should be adequate. However, bring a waterproof jacket, a sweater, and a stout pair of walking shoes. It's likely to be chilly at high altitudes, so dress accordingly. Warm underclothing is a good protection. Except on holidays, most hotels don't require you to change your clothing for dinner. What you wore during the day should suffice.

CLOTHING SIZES: Norway follows the lead of continental Europe. For a chart for both women and men, look under the listing in Chapter I, "A Preview of Denmark."

CRIME: The Norwegians are noted for their honesty and integrity. They have now taken to locking hotel doors, but that could be due to the tourist invasion. With their strong and sustained values, they appear to be the most traditional of Scandinavian people, if I can exclude Iceland from that generalization. Always take the usual precautions, but know that you can travel around the country without fear of molestation. Violent crime is relatively rare.

CURRENCY: The currency—based on **kroner** and **öre**—is simple for those who have mastered the Danish system. In Norway, a krone is worth about $.12 in U.S. coinage, as of this writing. It takes about 8.57 kroner equal $1 U.S. Banknotes are issued in 10, 50, 100, 500, and 1000 kroner. Nickel coins are issued in 10 and 50 öre, 1 krone, 5 kroner, and 10 kroner.

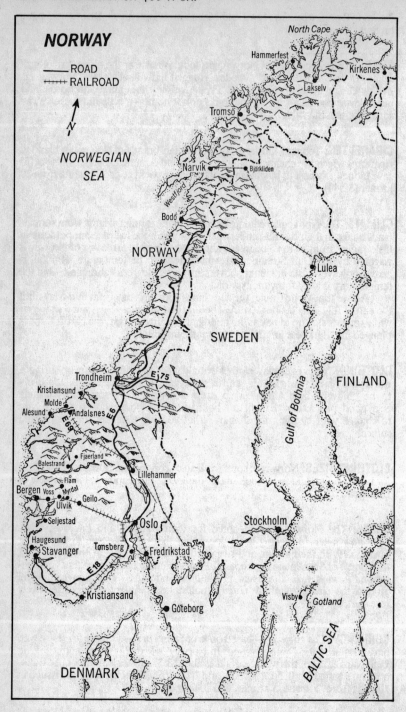

Kroner	U.S.$	Kroner	U.S.$
0.25	$ .03	60	$ 7.20
0.50	.06	70	8.40
1	.12	80	9.60
5	.60	90	10.80
10	1.20	100	12.00
15	1.80	125	15.00
20	2.40	150	18.00
25	3.00	175	21.00
30	3.60	200	24.00
40	4.80	250	30.00
50	6.00	300	36.00

CUSTOMS: With certain food exceptions, personal effects intended for your use can be brought into Norway. If you take them with you when you leave, you can also bring in cameras, binoculars, radios, portable TV sets, and the like, as well as the usual run of fishing and camping equipment. Americans or Canadians can bring in 400 cigarettes or 500 grams of tobacco and 200 sheets of cigarette paper or 50 cigars and one liter of spirits or one liter of wine. Britons can bring in 200 cigarettes or 250 grams of tobacco and 200 sheets of cigarette paper, one liter of spirits, and one liter of wine.

On leaving you can hold up to 5000 kroner in Norwegian cash, but banknotes of denominations higher than 100 kroner may not be taken out.

DENTISTS: In an emergency, get in touch with **Tøyen Senter,** 18 Kolstadgate (tel. 67-48-46), in Oslo, which is open daily from 8 p.m. to 11 p.m., on Saturday, Sunday, and holidays from 11 a.m. to 2 p.m. Private dentists may also be called if you can wait. There is rarely a language barrier. In the phone directory, volume 1 B, look under *Tannleger.*

DOCTORS: In Oslo there are two clinics for emergency cases. The **Oslo Municipal Casualty Clinic** is at 40 Storgata (tel. 20-10-90). Equipped with ambulances, it handles mainly accident cases on a 24-hour basis. There's a **Red Cross Clinic,** entered at Gabelsgate (tel. 44-39-80), which is open weekdays from 8 a.m. to 7 p.m. and on Sunday and public holidays from 1 to 7 p.m. Otherwise, you may visit private doctors, as there is rarely a language barrier. See the telephone directory, volume 1 B, under *Leger.*

DOCUMENTS FOR ENTRY: For a stay up to three months, all a British, American, or Canadian citizen needs is a valid passport. No visa or vaccination certificates are required of these nationals.

ELECTRICITY: Norway has 200 volts, 50 cycles A.C., and continental standard two-pin plugs are used. Adapters will be needed with Canadian, American, and British equipment. Always inquire at your hotel before plugging in any electrical equipment.

EMBASSIES: In case you lose your passport or have some other such emergency, you may need to get in touch with your national embassy. If so, the **U.S. Embassy** is at 18 Drammensveien (tel. 44-85-50), the **British Embassy** at 8

Thomas Heftyes Gate (tel. 56-38-90), and the **Canadian Embassy** at 20 Oscarsgate (tel. 46-69-55).

EMERGENCY TELEPHONES: For immediate assistance, dial the Oslo police at 11-00-11; report a fire at 42-99-00; call an ambulance at 20-10-90.

GASOLINE: In and around Oslo you'll find plenty of gasoline stations. However, if you're planning long drives on offbeat roads (of which Norway has many), always inquire where the next station is. For a liter of super-grade gasoline in Norway, expect to pay from 6 kroner (72¢). Prices are likely to be higher in the north. In Oslo the Esso station, **Abelhaugen**, 9 Haakon VII Gate (tel. 11-23-26), is open day and night.

GEOGRAPHY: Imagine a headless sea horse hanging over Denmark, with an elongated tail curving northward along the Swedish border—beyond the Arctic Circle—the tip of its tail brushing against Russian Lapland. This is the shape of Norway, a land that features porcupine ridges of mountains broken in spots by unladylike fingers—fjords—that gouge into the rocky surfaces of the earth.

Norway measures some 1100 miles in length, but it is an extremely narrow country.

In all, it is a land of waterfalls and rapids, majestic mountains, forbidding glaciers, green islands, crystal lakes, pine and spruce forests, steep-sloped farmsteads, secluded valleys, craggy cliffs, peaceful fjords, and fishing villages.

The Norwegian lives in one of the most thinly populated (per square mile) countries in Europe. Most of the rugged Norwegians reside in the swag-bellied southern part, which has the largest amount of land suitable for cultivation. But Norsemen still depend on the sea.

In the north the coastline is dotted with brightly painted houses, their sparkling colors contrasting with the somber grandeur of fjords and mountains. The northern slice of Norway—Finnmark, or Lapland—is low and hilly, bleak and forlorn, peopled in part by nomadic Lapps with reindeer herds.

GOVERNMENT: Norway is a constitutional monarchy, with the 150-member National Assembly (**Storting**) exercising legislative power. But the country is in the vanguard of the advanced socialized nations (compulsory national insurance, old-age pensions, unemployment insurance, family allowances, holidays with pay for all workers).

HOLIDAYS: Norway celebrates the following public holidays: New Year's Day, Maundy Thursday, Good Friday, Easter, Labor Day (May 1), Ascension Day, Independence Day (May 17), Whitmonday, Christmas, and Boxing Day (December 26).

INFORMATION: Tourist Information is dispensed at Rådhuset, the City Hall of Oslo (tel. 42-71-70); entrance is on the harborside. Services include not only providing information and giving out free maps and brochures, but selling sightseeing tickets and hiring guide services. From June 1 till the end of August, hours are from 8 a.m. to 5 p.m. weekdays, from 8 a.m. to 2 p.m. on

Saturday, and from 9 a.m. to 1 p.m. on Sunday. Otherwise, weekday hours are from 8:30 a.m. to 3:30 p.m., but the bureau is closed on Saturday and Sunday.

For inquiries about discounts in student travels, see the **Universitetenes Reisebyrå,** Norwegian Student Travel Office, Universitetssentret, Blindern (tel. 02/45-50-55). Branch offices are in Bergen (tel. 32-64-00), Ås (tel. 02/94-11-20), Stavanger (tel. 55-60-13), and Tromsø (tel. 083/84820).

Some vacationers like to meet people while working. If this is your bent, contact the **LNU,** the Norwegian Youth Council, 18 Rolf Hofmosgate, Oslo 6 (tel. 67-00-43). Apply from your home country. The staff there can arrange stays for you at Norwegian farms, where you live as a member of the family, get free board and lodgings, and some pocket money. You must pay a 200-krone ($24) registration.

In Oslo the city also runs the **Municipal Information Office for Youth,** 28 Pilestredet (tel. 11-04-09), which assists young people from all over the world in finding reasonably priced accommodations. In addition, information is dispensed about inexpensive eating places and activities of particular interest to youth. The office is open Monday to Friday from 9 a.m. to 4 p.m., and on Thursday it stays open until 6 p.m. However, it is closed on Saturday and Sunday.

LANGUAGE: A nationwide controversy. Something called Danish-Norwegian (riksmaal) is commonly spoken, but a rise of patriotic spirit has caused many of the people of Norway to turn to what is known as New Norwegian (landsmaal). But these controversies over dialect need not concern us. English is spoken almost universally in Norway, certainly by most persons engaged in the tourist business.

LAUNDROMATS: Majorstua Mynstvaskeri, 15 Vibes Gate in Oslo (tel. 69-43-17), is open Monday to Friday from 9 a.m. to 8 p.m. and on Saturday from 9 a.m. to 3 p.m. It's self-service, and washing and drying is usually finished in one hour. However, you must have your coins ready to put in the machines.

LIBRARY: The Oslo municipal library, **Deichmann Library,** lies at 1 Henrik Ibsens Gate (tel. 20-43-63), and is the largest in the country. It has many volumes in English, and there's also a children's department. The library is open from 8:15 a.m. to 8 p.m. Monday to Friday, 8:15 a.m. to 3 p.m. Saturday.

MEAL HOURS: Most workaday Norwegians seldom eat lunch, grabbing a quick open-face sandwich (smørrebrød) at their offices. But in the major towns and cities, lunch is generally served from 1 to 3 p.m. By the time the waiters in Spain are hauling out the luncheon desserts, Norwegians are quitting work and heading home for the *middag,* the main meal of the day, eaten generally between 4:30 and 6 p.m. Many restaurants serve this popular middag from 1 to 8 p.m. Of course, in certain late-closing restaurants it's possible to dine much later, until around midnight in Oslo. Long after middag time —in the seclusion of a summer hut in the wilderness—a Norwegian family will partake of *aftens,* a smørrebrød supper that will see them through the night.

NEWSPAPERS: English-language newspapers and magazines are sold (at least in the summer months) at newsstands (kiosks) throughout Oslo. International editions, including **The International Herald Tribune,** are always available at Narvesens Kiosk.

PETS: Leave your pet at home. Fearing the risk of rabies, Norway does not allow dogs, cats, and other domestic animals into the country without a permit from the Ministry of Agriculture. The quarantine period for dogs and cats is four months. Not only that, but the Ministry of Agriculture advises foreign visitors who are in constant contact with domestic animals to keep away from domestic animals in Norway.

PHARMACIES: An all-night pharmacy in Oslo is **Jernbanetorvets Apotek,** 4A Jernbanetorget (tel. 41-24-82).

PHOTOGRAPHY: All towns and cities have photo shops selling most major brands of film and photographic equipment at fairly high rates.

POST OFFICE: The **Oslo General Post Office** is at 15 Dronningensgate, with its entrance at the corner of Prinsensgate. It is open weekdays from 8 a.m. to 8 p.m., on Saturday from 9 a.m. to 3 p.m.; closed Sunday and public holidays. If you've sent your mail general delivery (mark it *"Poste Restante"*), you can collect it here at counters 37–41, providing you have your passport. For further information, telephone 40-88-70. Postage stamps are on sale in Narvensens Kiosk. As of this writing, air-mail letters to the United States and Canada cost 3.50 kroner (42¢) for up to 20 grams. Postcards are sent for 3 kroner (36¢).

RELIGIOUS SERVICES: Evangelical-Lutheran is the official state religion, but there is complete religious freedom for all. There's an **American Lutheran church** at 15 Fritznersgate (tel. 44-35-84), and an **American Community Chapel** (a military chapel) at the American School, 53 Gamle Ringeriksvei, at Bekkestua (tel. 17-01-90, ext. 53). Masses are said in English at **Eikeli Catholic Church,** 18 Veståsen (tel. 24-25-69). Other churches (with services held in Norwegian) include **St. Olav's Church,** which has mass for Roman Catholics, at 5 Åkersveien (tel. 20-72-26). There's a Baptist church, **Baptistmenighet,** at 22 Hausmannsgate (tel. 20-76-49), and a Methodist church, **Centralkirken,** 28 St. Olavsgate (tel. 20-03-01). A **Synagogue** is at 13–15 Bergstien (tel. 69-29-66).

REST ROOMS: Oslo is well supplied with clean public toilets in the center. They are also found in parks, and all terminals, such as bus, rail, and air. For a detailed list, get in touch with the Tourist Information Office.

SHOPPING HOURS: Shops are generally open from 9 a.m. to 5 p.m. (in summer until 4 p.m.). On Saturday most of them close by 1 p.m. (to 2 p.m. or 3 p.m. in some bigger stores in larger stores), and they are closed on Sunday.

SKIING: In Norway whole families go skiing together. The best times for skiing are in February and March (the first two weeks in April are usually good also). Two of the principal resorts, **Geilo** and **Voss,** lie on the Oslo-Bergen rail line. Perhaps the most famous resort is **Lillehammer,** easily accessible, to the north of Oslo. In and around the Norwegian capital skiing is common; the deservingly famed ski jump, **Holmenkollen,** with its companion ski museum, is reached in minutes from the heart of Oslo. The yearly ski championship meet here in March draws the curious, as well as crack skiers from all over Europe and North America.

The one outstanding quality found in Norwegian ski resorts is the naturalness evident both in the informal ski schools and in the atmosphere. Simple folklore and hearty good fun replace the sophisticated après-ski life often found in alpine resorts. Incidentally, *ski* is an old Norse word, as is *slalom.* Norwegians have a 4000-year-old rock carving (discovered near Trondheim) depicting a skier.

A great part of the skiing in Norway is cross country, easily suitable for the amateur who is just getting familiar with the term "stem christie." But there is plentiful terrain for the more skilled. Curling, sleigh rides, and skating also are popular winter sports. All the major centers have ski lifts. The equipment in Norway is much cheaper to rent than it is in such established luxury resorts as St. Moritz.

TAXES: Norway is not a member of the European Common Market, but it imposes a "Value Added Tax" on most goods and services which is figured into your final bill. If the purchases you make in one shop cost more than 1000 kroner ($120), you are entitled to a VAT refund of 16.67%. Before leaving the country, obtain Form 135 from the Customs authorities. This will be stamped at your time of departure. The form is then sent to the shop where your purchases were made, which will then send your refund to you.

TELEPHONE/TELEGRAPH: Phone calls, telegrams, and Telex can be sent in Oslo from 8 a.m. to 10 p.m. at 12 Kongensgate and at night (from 10 p.m. to 8 a.m.) at 21 Kongensgate. The entrance is from Nedre Slottsgate. When using the international direct-dial service, dial without interruption the international prefix 095 + the country code + the national trunk code + the local telephone number. For codes, see pages 5 to 7 in the Oslo phone directory 1 A. For operator assistance in English, dial 093. To send telegrams, dial 013. Try, if possible, not to call long distance from your hotel, where the charges are often doubled or tripled.

TIME: At noon, Eastern Standard Time (EST) in New York City, it is 6 p.m. in Norway. Norway goes on summer time around March 28 (the date varies every year), lasting until around September 26.

TIPPING: For years the Norwegians never practiced much tipping, but the custom has grown with the influx of millions of tourists, especially Americans. Hotels, depending on their classification, add some 10% to 15% to your bill, which handles most matters, unless someone on the staff, such as the concierge or head porter, has done some special service for you. Most bellhops get at least 3 kroner (36¢) per suitcase. Like hotels, nearly all restaurants add a service charge up to 15% to your bill, but it's still customary to leave the small change. Bartenders get about 5% of the bill. Surprisingly, barbers and hairdressers aren't usually tipped. However, toilet attendants and hatcheck people expect at least 2 kroner (24¢). It's not the custom to tip theater ushers.

WEIGHTS AND MEASURES: As do most countries of the world, Norway uses the international metric system. For a chart, refer to the listing in Chapter I, "A Preview of Denmark."

Chapter VI

SETTLING INTO OSLO

1. Moderately Priced Lodgings
2. Big Splurge Hotels
3. Where to Dine

DESPITE ITS MODERN ARCHITECTURE and expanding suburbs, Oslo remains much the country town. But not in size. In a seam-splitting postwar expansion the Oslovians stretched out their boundaries to encompass 175 square miles. Then these Norse people announced that their city was one of the ten largest capital cities in the world in sheer physical size.

In branching out, the city fathers incorporated more than people. They ended up with the most heavily forested capital on earth. And Oslo is a municipality that encompasses both nightclubs and farmlands, there being hogs, cows, and chickens within its boundaries.

In all this square mileage, fewer than half a million Norwegians live and work—so Oslo is not faced with immediate extinction due to overpopulation.

Oslo was founded in the mid-11th century by a Viking king. Around 1300 it became the capital under King Haakon V. In the course of its history the city burned down several times, and was completely destroyed by fire in 1824. However, the master builder, Christian IV, king of both Denmark and Norway, ordered the town rebuilt under the Akershus Fortress. He named the new town Christiania, after himself, and that was its official name until 1924 when the city celebrated its 300-year-old jubilee. At that time it was decided to revert to the old name of Oslo.

In 1814 Norway was separated from Denmark and united with Sweden, that union lasting until 1905. During this period, the capital got most of its representative buildings, such as the Royal Palace, the House of Parliament, the old University, the National Theater, and the National Gallery.

GETTING ORIENTED: At the mouth of the 60-mile-long, island-studded Oslo Fjord, the capital city of Norway makes up in physical beauty what it lacks in architectural distinction.

Opening onto the harbor is **Raadhusplassen,** dominated by its modern **City Hall,** a major attraction. The guided motorcoach tours leave from this point, and the launches that cruise the fjords embark from the pier facing the municipal building.

Jutting out on a promontory to the east (facing City Hall from the harbor) is **Akershus Castle,** the ancient guardian that protected Oslo from an invasion from the sea. The much larger peninsula of Bygdøy juts out to the west (it's

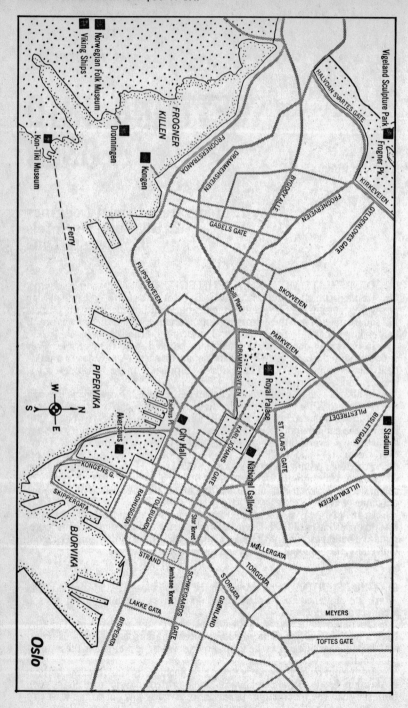

possible to catch Bygdøy-bound ferries from the quay at Raadhusplassen). On the peninsula are to be found four of Oslo's major attractions: the **Viking ships,** the **Fram Museum, Kon-Tiki raft,** and the **Folk Museum.**

To the north of the City Hall Square runs **Karl Johans Gate,** the closest that Oslo comes to having a main street. This boulevard begins at Østbanesstasjonen (East Station) and stretches all the way to the 19th-century **Royal Palace** at the western end. A major artery, Karl Johans Gate is used primarily for strolling and shopping. At the Central Station is a hotel accommodation service (more about this coming up), and at the western frontier visitors gather to watch the changing of the guard at 1:30 p.m., followed by a regimental band concert when the king is in residence.

A short walk from the palace is the famed **Students' Grove** (the University of Oslo is nearby), where everybody gathers on a summer day to talk, snack, and be seen. Dominating this center is the famed **National Theater,** guarded over by statues of Ibsen and Bjørnson, the two greatest names in the Norwegian theater (forgive me, Mr. Holberg) whose plays have been performed here countless times. South of the theater, closer to the harbor and running parallel to (but much shorter than) Karl Johans Gate, is **Stortingsgate,** another shop-filled street.

Now, with some downtown orientation, visitors may have the courage to strike out for one of the mountains surrounding Oslo. At a subway stop near the National Theater, it's possible to head out for **Tryvässtaarnet,** the loftiest lookout town in Scandinavia, and to the **Holmenkollen** ski jump.

THE HOTEL OUTLOOK: A potential stygian nightmare for reservationless pilgrims who arrive with eight kids in tow during certain peak months, Oslo simply doesn't have enough hotels to meet its ever-increasing popularity. All the doubling and tripling of beds in single rooms helps but doesn't solve the problem. Don't despair. There are compensating factors.

First, the kiosk at the East Railway Station will book overflow guests into hotels or private homes of Norwegian families. The latter is a highly recommended means of not only securing a comfortable lodging, but of getting to know the Norwegians. Further, the Hotel Accommodation Office of the Oslo Tourist Board will make reservations for you three weeks in advance.

The worst months for finding a place to stay, according to the Oslo Tourist Board, are May, June, September, and October. Many conferences and conventions are held in Oslo during those months. In July, there's a fighting chance, even though that is a peak month of the summer tourist invasion.

First, let's take care of the emergency cases with:

A Room in a Hurry on Arrival

The **Innkvartering** kiosk at the Central Station (tel. 41-62-21) keeps many a visitor from having to break into Akershus Castle to find some old Renaissance bed for the night. If the attendants at the station can't find a hotel in the price range specified, they book guests into private homes or apartments—usually charging from 220 kroner ($26.40) for a bathless double, 85 kroner ($10.20) to 120 kroner ($14.40) for a single. The service charge for on-the-spot booking: 10 kroner ($1.20) per person, plus a small deposit.

In summer, a large number of European visitors request accommodations in homes in the suburbs, which actually remain within the wide-ranging Oslo city boundaries. North Americans, on the other hand, tend to prefer to be in the heart of things.

Hours are from 8:30 a.m. to 11 p.m. weekdays (from 8:30 till 11 a.m. and 6 to 11 p.m. on Sunday during the season). In the off-season this office is open from 6 to 11 p.m. weekdays; closed Sunday. Otherwise, you have to report to the **Tourist Information Center** at City Hall, seaside entrance (tel. 42-71-70), which is open from 8 a.m. to 3:30 p.m. in the off-season. In season, it's open from 8 a.m. to 7 p.m. on weekdays, from 8 a.m. to 2 p.m. on Saturday or 9 a.m. to 1 p.m. on Sunday.

Reservations for Hotels in Advance

The Oslo Tourist Board can assist in providing visitors with overnight accommodation in hotels and pensions. Advance booking must be sent in a written application to the **Oslo Tourist Board,** 19 Raadhusgaten, Oslo 1, at least 21 days before your arrival date and must contain the following: name and address, date of arrival and departure, required standard and price class, and a bank draft for 100 kroner ($12) per person. This payment includes a booking fee of 25 kroner ($3) due the board and a deposit to the establishment in which your rooms are reserved. The deposit will be deducted from your bill on departure. Cancellations must be made in writing at least eight days before the date of arrival and sent direct to the accommodation address. A full refund cannot be guaranteed. Visitors will receive a written confirmation of their reservations with a receipt for the advance payment. Hotel rates are given in the board's price list. Pensions cost from 110 kroner ($13.20) to 175 kroner ($21) for a single room, 180 kroner ($21.60) to 280 kroner ($33.60) for a double. Private home accommodations cannot be booked in advance.

The office is open Monday to Friday from 8 a.m. to 4 p.m. It's closed Saturday and Sunday.

A Survey of Oslo Accommodations

For the lowest priced living in Oslo, the private homes are an excellent choice. But also highly rated for economy is the **hospits** or **pension,** usually a family-operated establishment occupying one or more floors of walk-up and older buildings. Elevators are offered in some cases, but don't count on it. These modest, informal places are furnished simply, but are well maintained and kept clean (at least my recommendations).

I'll survey the pick of the moderately priced hotels, and concluding will be splurge recommendations which exceed the $35-a-day allotment for a double room. These latter establishments are recommended for those seeking better amenities and plumbing facilities than those found in the typical hospits.

1. Moderately Priced Lodgings

Sta Katarinahjemmet, 21B Majorstuveien (tel. 60-13-70), is a red-brick building, the newest part built in 1976, run as a hospits from June till September by Dominican sisters who accept both men and women. All the rooms have hot and cold running water. In the new building, every room has a balcony. Showers and toilets are in the corridors. Singles rent for 165 kroner ($19.80), the price going up to 225 kroner ($27) in a double. You can get a big Norwegian breakfast here for 40 kroner ($4.80). The hospits, run as a boarding house for girls in winter, is an interesting place in which to stay, and it's kept clean. The compound is tucked away in its own private world—at the base of a towering modern apartment building. It's in the middle of Oslo but situated away from traffic on the busy Bogstadveien. Take tram or streetcar 11 or 1, getting off at Vibes Gate. Walk a little bit farther in the same direction, passing the traffic light on the left-hand side of Bogstadveien. There you'll find a small street leading up to Katarinahjemmet. Motorists have to come from Majorstuveien.

Hotel-Pensjon Hall, 21 Fritznesgate (tel. 56-44-80), is one of the most charming inexpensive hotels in Oslo. It's owned by Karl Victor Hall, whose family, the original founders, transformed a solid stone building originally intended to house out-of-town members of the Norwegian Parliament into a high-ceilinged pension in 1929. The second-floor reception area is at the top of a staircase leading from a side street's entrance. The room is a carpeted, freshly painted area with a fireplace, a sunny bay window lined with plants, a 19th-century heroic painting, and a collection of turn-of-the-century chairs pulled into comfortable conversation groups. Each of the hotel's four floors has its own sitting room. All the bedrooms are bathless, but they contain TV, phones, and sinks. The shared showers and toilets in the hallways are clean and adequate. There's no elevator. Singles rent from 300 kroner ($36), while doubles go for 420 kroner ($50.40). English is spoken, and you're received in friendly fashion.

Hotel Fønix, 19 Dronningensgate (tel. 42-59-57), a three-minute walk from the railway station, is better than its unimpressive entryway would indicate. It offers a bright, airy place to stay in an eight-story building, for 170 kroner ($20.40) in a bathless single, rising to 240 kroner ($28.80) in a single with bath. For the lone traveler, the Fønix is perhaps the best bet in Oslo, especially since most of its rooms (41 to be exact) are singles. The handful of double rooms with private bath rent for 390 kroner ($46.80), but couples settling for only a water basin pay the lower rates of 270 kroner ($32.40) to 290 kroner ($34.80). Most of the medium-size rooms have bed-sitting arrangements. Breakfast, served from 7 to 10 a.m., is included in the tariffs quoted. It's served in a pine-paneled room.

City Hotel, 19 Skippergata (tel. 41-36-10), is a remodeled and renovated building, about a three-minute walk from the railway station. Owned by the Salvation Army, the well-run, 60-room hotel has bathless doubles with water basins that rent for around 320 kroner ($38.40). A bathless single is 210 kroner ($25.20). In rooms with bath or shower, two persons pay 360 kroner ($43.20); one person, 260 kroner ($31.20). When the self-service elevator whisks you to the fourth floor, all becomes pleasant, respectable, and immaculate. A Norwegian special breakfast is served, the cost included in the tariffs quoted. The spacious corner living room is homelike, with large windows, homespun draperies, modern furnishings, and lots of green-thumb touches.

Seminarheimen, 3 B Josefines Gate (tel. 69-10-06), is open only in summer, from mid-May until about mid-August. The host speaks English, and he has about a dozen handsomely maintained and nicely furnished bedchambers to rent. For these, he charges from 250 kroner ($30) to 295 kroner ($35.40) in a double. Breakfast, the only meal served, is yet another 40 kroner ($4.80). Rooms are equipped with hot and cold water, and you make use of the bath in the corridor. Guests are especially fond of the old-fashioned sitting room with its fireplace, grandfather clock, woodcarvings, and piano. Take tram 7 to the Bislet stop to reach this little oasis.

Oslo Sjomannshjemmet, entrance on Fred Oslensgate between Raadhusgate and Tollbugate (tel. 41-20-05), is a Seamen's Hotel in Oslo, but also patronized by the family trade as well. Reader Lee Carlsen of Pasadena, California, writes: "Norwegians told us that at the seaman's hotel we'd see just a bunch of drunks. Not so! Women alone stay there, middle-age ones anyway, and it's in a quiet location." The rooms, at least most of them, are large and spacious, lying on the sixth floor. Some are equipped with private shower, costing from 210 kroner ($25.10) in a double per night. Singles cost from 180 kroner ($21.60). For another 35 kroner ($4.20) you can partake of a buffet breakfast.

OSLO'S YEAR-ROUND YOUTH HOSTEL: Haraldsheim, 4 Haraldsheimun (tel. 15-50-43), Oslo's prininipal youth hostel, lies about two miles from the heart of the city in the eastern suburbs, on the rise of Grefsenaasen hill. This 300-bed hostel—six to a room with individual lockers—charges 75 kroner ($9) for overnight stopovers, plus an all-you-can-eat Norwegian breakfast. A lunch or hot supper (middag) taken separately in the self-service dining room costs 45 kroner

($5.40). Haraldsheim is built like a modern Southern California hacienda, sprawling and open to the sun, with open-beamed ceilings, a large lounge with picture windows and a fireplace, and a TV room. Guests of all ages gather here from all over the world. Guitars often accompany spontaneous folk singing. There are bathrooms on each floor. An extra bonus is the fully equipped laundry room, and a special kitchen is available to do-it-yourselfers. A minimum of regulations is imposed: make your bed, closed from 10 a.m. to 4 p.m.; no alcohol, 1 a.m. curfew. Open year round, the steam-heated hostel becomes a ski center in winter, and it's within walking distance of slopes and a lift. From Oslo's Central Station, take streetcar 1 or 7 to Sinsen, a four-minute walk from there. The hostel is jam-packed in summer—so call before making the trek.

2. Big-Splurge Hotels

Hotel Gabelshus, 16 Gabelsgate (tel. 56-25-90), is a pleasant hotel which has earned a respected reputation since it was built in 1912 on a quiet, tree-lined street. The façade, greatly expanded since it was purchased by the present owner in 1945, looks very much like an English manor house built of dark brick and laced with climbing ivy. Inside, the English theme continues with public rooms filled with antiques, unusual art, burnished copper, working fireplaces, and a kind of country-style, 17th-century ambience. The staff is conservatively correct, as is the clientele. The operation is directed by Agathe Riekeles. Each of the bedrooms is filled with tasteful colors and textiles, and some have private balconies or terraces. All the units are air conditioned. Singles cost 540 kroner ($64.80), while doubles rent for from 690 kroner ($82.80) to 720 kroner ($86.40). Rates include breakfast. The hotel is a brisk 15-minute walk from the center of town, although nearby trams or a taxi would make the time shorter.

The in-house restaurant contains elegantly tasteful Empire tables and chairs, lots of space between the tables, pink napery, big sun-drenched windows, and what may be the most beautiful antique silver candelabra in Oslo. It's open seven days a week for à la carte lunches and dinners, priced at around 200 kroner ($24) for a substantial meal.

Ritz Hotel, 3 Frederick Stangs Gate (tel. 44-39-80). The acquisition of this 1915 white and pastel hotel by the owners of the nearby Gabelshus Hotel turned this duo of well-managed buildings into one of the city's best values for good overnight accommodations. The manager, Morten Mowinckel-Amundsen, added full private baths to all the establishment's rooms. The hotel shares its parking lot with the Gabelshus, whose back you can see through the rear windows of the Ritz. Room prices are sometimes cheaper than at the Gabelshus. With breakfast included, singles cost 525 kroner ($63) and doubles 690 kroner ($82.80). An extra bed can be set up in any room for an additional 120 kroner ($14.40). Each of the rooms is air conditioned.

Müllerhotel Astoria, 21 Akersgate (tel. 33-67-00), is in the center of town, behind a dignified brick façade with strong vertical lines. The hotel was built in the 1930s and has many ups and downs in its history, but today the quality seems to be fairly even, thanks to its management by one of Scandinavia's largest hotel chains. There's a contemporary interpretation of a mother and child, adding soft curves to the sober and angular lobby. There are also a bar on the premises and a starkly dramatic restaurant with a single stained-glass window filling most of one wall. The furnishings in the bedrooms are modern, and each has a private bath, phone, and toilet. Tariffs are 620 kroner ($75.60) in a single, dropping to 335 kroner ($40.20) on Friday and Saturday. A double costs 830 kroner ($99.60) on weekdays, 480 kroner ($57.60) on Friday and Saturday. Breakfast is included in the prices.

Norum Hotel, 53 Bygdøy Allé (tel. 44-79-90), was built in 1912 in a style that looks like a turreted castle in Holland, with baroque copper-covered towers, a steep roofline, arched and embellished windows, and walls of yellow brick. The entrance lies through a triangular rose garden near a busy street on the west side of town. The neighborhood is residential, lined with trees, and a brisk walk to the Vigeland Park. In summer a cascade of vines falls across the façade of the hotel, although the 60 functionally modern bedrooms, while clean and comfortable, are more pedestrian. The price is between 565 kroner ($67.80) and 590 kroner ($70.80) for a single, for 675 kroner ($81) in a double. Ellen and Per Mathisen are the resident owners. The in-house bar with its adjoining restaurant is lined with unusual stained-glass windows and wood paneling. Bus 30 reaches the hotel from the center of town,while bus 31 passes nearby from both the airport and the center of town.

West Hotel, 15 Skovveien (tel. 56-29-95). In 1968, an old apartment building was transformed into a hotel by a Norwegian hotel chain. Since that time, the hostelry, now under independent ownership, has received several facelifts which have gradually changed many of the bedrooms into gracefully stylish examples of modern design. A few remain to be renovated, but even they are comfortable and clean. Relatively small singles rent for 660 kroner ($79.20), doubles costing 840 kroner ($100.80), breakfast included. Each of the units contains TV with video, a mini-bar, radio, and private bath. In the newer ones, beds are sometimes contained in foldaway couches, presenting a living room/bedroom format. The hotel has a ground-floor bar where people from the rather well-heeled area nearby congregate. The stylish restaurant serves French food, a fixed-price lunch going for 75 kroner ($9). Trams 1 and 2 go to the center of town, about a 12-minute walk from the hotel, if you step out briskly.

White House, 18 President Harbitzgatan (tel. 44-19-60), looks surprisingly like a steep-roofed and iron-accented country house set in a residential neighborhood only 15 minutes on foot from the center of town. The white-walled building, standing on a low hill at the end of a tree-studded lawn, was built around 1910. However, the dazzling white lobby and most of the pleasant but simple bedrooms were renovated in 1981. The 21 units contain private baths and, with breakfast included, cost from 480 kroner ($57.60) in a single, 630 kroner ($75.60) in a double during the week. As in many other Oslo hotels, weekend prices go down, dropping to 330 kroner ($39.60) in a single, 480 kroner ($57.60) in a double at the White House. There's a simple fondue restaurant (the only one I know of in Oslo), where you can dine on an outdoor wooden platform overlooking the street in summer. It's open from 4 p.m. to midnight daily except Sunday, charging from 90 kroner ($10.80) to 100 kroner ($12) for cheese fondue, from 130 kroner ($15.60) to 175 kroner ($21) for the meat dish. The restaurant is called Den Lille Fondue. Walther Hammod-Hurleen, owns both the hotel and the eating place.

Hotel Munch, 5 Munchsgate (tel. 42-42-75), is one of the newest as well as one of the best bargains in downtown Oslo. It opened for business in 1984 and is known throughout the town for its angular modern design of red brick and severe windows. There are a total of 180 rooms, the first two floors being more or less permanently occupied by enlisted men in the Norwegian army. The rooms are simple, decorated in neutral colors, and contain private baths, TV phones, and mini-bars which you'll have to stock yourself if you want something other than mineral water. As the name of the hotel would lead you to surmise, you'll see some of the works of Edvard Munch here—a lobbyful of framed reproductions of his paintings, dozens of which are for sale. The hotel has no bar or restaurant, but the surrounding neighborhood is well supplied. Singles here rent for 450 kroner ($54), while doubles cost 570 kroner ($68.40), breakfast included.

Bondeheimen, 8 Rosenkrantzgate (tel. 33-16-90), is a modern hotel on the upper floors of a building. It's in the city center, only a short block from Students' Grove. The rooms are well furnished, but prices vary depending on facilities. All rooms contain private baths and cost 450 kroner ($54) in a single, 550 kroner ($66) in a double. Friday to Sunday, special discounts are granted, with singles costing 300 kroner ($36), doubles 400 kroner ($48) per night. Those same prices are charged from June 15 to August 15. All tariffs include breakfast, served in a dining room on the second floor, where you also find a popular Kaffistova. The hotel is operated by a Rural Youth Organization devoted to cultural activities and folklore.

Gyldenløve, 20 Bogsladveien (tel. 60-10-90), is an eight-story establishment—in true Nordic modern, with balconies, and large glass doors and windows to let in the precious sunlight. This hospits has been considerably modernized, with much additional plumbing. The accommodations, for the most part, are generous in size and suitably designed for a comfortable stay. Depending on the plumbing, the single rate is 250 kroner ($30), and doubles are charged from 500 kroner ($60). The bedrooms, for the most part, are compactly furnished, with wood-grained units that form sitting areas (sofas, black leather armchairs, and teak coffee tables, plus wall-to-wall draperies). Guests gather in the lounge, in comfortable chairs by the fireplace. The Gyldenløve is a ten-minute walk from the grounds of the Royal Palace (or else a tram ride on no. 1 or 11).

THE MISSION CHAIN: This is a chain of well-run, alcohol-free hotels.

Stefan Hotel, 1 Rosenkrantzgate (tel. 42-92-50), is clean, comfortable, and unpretentious and benefits from an excellent location in the very heart of town. Its eighth-floor restaurant is one of the city's lunchtime landmarks (see "Where to Dine" section). The bedrooms are simple but accommodating and more spacious than many rooms in similarly priced hotels. Each of the 131 units has its own phone and private bath, with facilities for the handicapped available in two of the bedrooms. Both families and the business community are attracted to the Stefan, where weekday prices are 575 kroner ($69) in a single, 380 kroner ($45.60) per person in a double. Weekend prices are considerably cheaper: from 325 kroner ($39) in a single to 250 kroner ($30) per person in a double. The hotel is owned and maintained by a Christian organization.

Ansgar Hotell, 26 Møllergaten, off Youngstorget (tel. 20-47-35), a well-built and decorated establishment, draws a conservative clientele who want good, plain comfort. It is popular with Americans visiting relatives in Norway. Modern bathless doubles go from 350 kroner ($42) to 525 kroner ($63) in high season, including service and a big buffet breakfast. Bathless singles range from 200 kroner ($24) to 330 kroner ($39.60). Special reduced weekend rates are quoted all year for guests arriving Friday, Saturday, and Sunday: from 325 kroner ($39) per night in a double. There's a private indoor garage.

Norrøna Misjonshotell, 19 Grensen (tel. 42-64-00), in the heart of the old section of Oslo, is one of the best of the Mission chain (handy for both sightseeing and shopping). It offers well-equipped bedrooms furnished in Scandinavian modern. The hotel in recent years has been considerably improved and upgraded. Much new plumbing has been added which, regrettably, is revealed in the rates—from 400 kroner ($48) to 445 kroner ($53.40) in a double, from 300 kroner ($36) to 345 kroner ($41.40) in a single. Breakfast, service, and taxes are included. The hotel occupies the upper floors of a modernized building. The lounge is homey and informal. A few of the rooms have private balconies. A cafeteria in the same building serves hot meals until 6 p.m.

Forbundshotellet, 1 Holsbergs Plass (tel. 20-88-55), is a dignified, 104-bedroom corner hotel, opposite the city air terminal, within easy walking distance of the Royal Palace, and its gardens and park. A new wing has been added, with 24 handsomely furnished doubles, and in 1982 two floors were reconstructed. The hotel's rooms each have a private bath and toilet. The Mission treads the line between a simple hotel and an upper bracket one. The lounges are attractive and gracious, but I prefer the bedrooms (some with living room areas), with their Nordic modern furnishings. Units have color TV and radios. Singles with private baths are priced from 550 kroner ($66), and doubles with private facilities cost from 650 kroner ($78). Breakfast is included. All three meals are served in the bright, airy dining room which features parquet floors, crystal chandeliers, and paintings. A complete lunch goes for 75 kroner ($9), the cost rising to 100 kroner ($12) for dinner.

Hotel Imi, 4 Staffeldts Gate (tel. 20-53-30), is a popular 60-bedroom Mission hotel a half block from the Royal Palace grounds. Children under 18 are free if they occupy a room with their parents. Doubles with bath cost 650 kroner ($78), while singles go for 500 kroner ($60) to 550 kroner ($66) Monday through Friday. Special weekend rates for Friday through Sunday are 450 kroner ($54) in a double, 350 kroner ($42) in a single. Breakfast is included in the prices. Three meals a day are served in the recently remodeled restaurant, with a Norwegian cold table buffet being offered from noon to 4 p.m. for 85 kroner ($10.20), with the dishes being à la carte from 4 to 9 p.m. You can order a packed lunch to take with you on your excursions. The Imi is near the airport bus terminal, taxi stand, and a tram stop.

STUDENT-RUN HOTELS: **Fjellhaug Sommerhotell,** 15 Sinsensveien (tel. 37-70-90), is a comfortable student hotel, with singles priced at 280 kroner ($33.60) and doubles at 390 kroner ($46.80). These tariffs include breakfast and taxes. Each of the 80 rooms has a shower. The staff has on display many decorations from all over the world around the lobby. The place has its own gardens, and from its perch, it enjoys a panoramic view. Guests are received from June 10 to September 1. Take the Sinsen tram from the cathedral.

Bibelskolens Sommerhotell, 4 Staffeldts Gate (tel. 20-53-30), is open from June 10 to August 20. There are no dormitory accommodations, as this is more like a true hotel, with 100 rooms. Doubles without private bath cost 330 kroner ($39.60), bathless singles going for 245 kroner ($29.40). With private bath and toilet, doubles are priced at 450 kroner ($54), singles at 350 kroner ($42). The hotel shares restaurant facilities with the Hotel Imi of the same address and phone number.

Panorama Sommerhotell, 218 Sognsveien (tel. 18-70-80), is a modern 800-bed student dorm open all year but with hotel status from June 1 to September 1. Special prices are quoted for students with university ID cards as well as for senior citizens and children under 12. Single rooms with semi-private shower and toilet cost from 330 kroner ($39.60) to 360 kroner ($43.20), while doubles go for 200 kroner ($24) to 285 kroner ($34.20) per person. The prices include breakfast. Self-catering apartments and camping rooms are also offered. The hotel is about 15 minutes from downtown by tram to Kringsjå Station by Sognsvannsbanen. On the hotel's premises, you'll find a supermarket, newsstand, post office, and laundromats, and there's a bank nearby. Lake swimming is possible in beautiful surroundings. The hotel has a restaurant and cafeteria. There's ample free parking. The hotel also operates a winter residence, but not as many units are available then. In the off-season months, it's known as the **Pan Hostel.**

Anker Sommerhotell, 55 Storgaten (tel. 11-40-05), is one of Oslo's better equipped summer hotels open from the first of May to August 31. It rises tall and proud, only five minutes by subway from the center of the city. Of the 176 rooms, 42 are actually "mini-suites," and all units are complete with shower and toilet. A continental breakfast is included in the tariffs. Singles cost from 300 kroner ($36) to 325 kroner ($39), and combination rooms housing two persons go for from 400 kroner ($48) to 440 kroner ($52.80). A luncheon is available at 60 kroner ($7.20). Facilities include an open-air restaurant and a café. The hotel also rents out about 64 rooms in the winter months, when it is known as **Hybel-**

hushotellet. The management charges from 250 kroner ($30) in a single to 350 kroner ($42) in a double then.

AN OASIS ON A MOUNTAIN PLATEAU: Voksenåsen, Voksenkollen (tel. 14-30-90), is a Nordic Shangri-la, perched in a choice location, on the ledge of a mountain a 20-minute subway ride on the Holmenkollen line from the National Theater to the station Voksenkollen (ten-minute walk from there). With heavy luggage, it's best to take a taxi. For a double room with private bath, two persons are charged a splurgy 700 kroner ($84). Singles rent for 575 kroner ($69). Breakfast is included in the price. Originally, Voksenåsen was created by the Norwegians as a tribute to the Swedes for their help during World War II. The bedrooms are semi-luxurious, with grained wood, hand-woven textiles, and a crow's-nest view of the harbor and mountains. A cantilevered roof provides shelter for outside terraces. Vast sitting rooms in a modern style abound with picture windows. Quiet retreats are found beside fireplaces, and fine furniture, original paintings, and sculpture are seen everywhere.

CAMPING: About 5½ miles from the center of Oslo, the **Bogstad Camp og Turistsenter** (tel. 24-76-19) is operated by the Norwegian Automobile Association, and is about one of the cheapest ways of living in Oslo. Manager Per Brun, Jr., rents out 1200 tents and 20 chalets. The chalets, suitable for parties of about four, are fully equipped, costing about 350 kroner ($42) daily per hut. You pay another 35 kroner ($4.20) to rent bed sheets. Close to the Bogstad Golf Course, the site is open all year, and it's reached by bus 41 "Sørkedalen" from the National Theater. On the grounds are Bogstad Kro where lunches and dinners cost from 45 kroner ($5.40), a laundromat, kitchen, post office, bank, and filling station.

READER'S MOTEL SELECTION: "We were jubilant to find the charming **Busy Butlers Kafeteria and Motel** (tel. 32-05-34), a short distance northeast of Oslo. The well-appointed, modern, and comfortable rooms are priced at 350 kroner ($42) for doubles, 290 kroner ($34.80) for singles. All rooms have either a shower or bathtub. Easy ordering of tasty and reasonable meals is facilitated through the use of a pictorial menu board at the inviting Kafeteria. Take E6 toward Hamar to 159; go under the viaduct, turn right at the first street, Per Krohgs Vei, from where the Motel and Kafeteria are visible on the right. A great find for motorists" (Mrs. J. H. Paulsen, Chicago, Ill.).

READERS' GUESTHOUSE SELECTIONS: "Mrs. Tollefsen, 12 Johan Svendsens Vei, 1410 Kolbotn (tel. 80-20-09), charges 60 kroner ($7.20) per person. She is warm and helpful and speaks English well. Her home is an upper-middle-class suburban house, 15 minutes by train from the central station in Oslo, via trains marked Ski-Westley on tracks 18–20. Then it's a ten-minute walk from Kolbotn station. Your Eurailpass will take you there free. Mrs. Tollefsen is as meticulous a person as I've ever met. The house is spotlessly clean and beautifully decorated. However, it's not possible for her to reserve a room in advance for only one or two nights. No breakfast is served, but a cafeteria right next to the Kolbotn train stop provides an excellent morning meal" (Jerry and Kathi Peterson, Denver, Col.). . . . "At **Ellingson Pensionat,** 25 Holtegate, I had a single for 150 kroner ($18), without breakfast. The rooms have running water and are spotlessly clean, and there are good tram connections to the city center, or a 15-minute walk" (Rolf Hepke, Achim, West Germany).

READER'S HOTEL SELECTION: "The **KFUK-Hjemmet** (the Norwegian version of the YWCA), 3 B Neuberggatan (tel. 44-17-87), rents singles for 175 kroner ($21), doubles for 280 kroner ($33.60), including breakfast. It's open only in summer. In spite of its name, it gives accommodation to male and female travelers. The service is performed by some of the young women who normally live there during the rest of the year. There is even a garden, and it's close to Frogner Park with its sculptures and the open-air swimming pool" (Rolf Hepke, Achim, West Germany).

3. Where to Dine

What's the truth about Norwegian cooking? The chief criticism leveled against it—as against the English variety—is that it's too bland. The food is always abundant (the Norwegians are known for their second helpings), substantial, and well prepared—but no threat to the French for a Cordon Bleu prize.

Norwegians are proud—and rightly so—of many of their tempting specialties, ranging from boiled cod (believe it or not, this is considered a delicacy) to reindeer steak smothered in brown gravy and accompanied by tart little lingonberries (like wild cranberries).

As a seafaring nation, Norway relies for much of its food supply on fish, both fresh- and saltwater. Prepared in countless ways, fish is usually well cooked—and always fresh. A good bet indeed. Try in particular the aforementioned boiled cod (whenever there's an "R" in the month); it's always—but always—served with boiled potatoes.

In early summer, kokt laks (boiled salmon) is a highly rated delicacy. Kreps (crawfish) is another big production number, as it is in Finland. Ørret (mountain trout)—preferably broiled and served with fresh lemon—is a guaranteed treat. A recommendation for top-notch fare: fiske-gratin (fish soufflé), delicately seasoned.

Norwegians love their fatty smoked eel (røket ål), although many foreigners have a tendency to whip by this one on the smörgåsbord table. Likewise, the national appetizer, brine-cured herring with raw onions, wins few friends, Germans excluded.

Besides the already mentioned reindeer steak, you may want to try an unappetizing-sounding specialty; faar-i-kaal, the national dish, a heavily peppered cabbage and mutton stew served with butterless boiled potatoes. A fisherman's or a farmer's favorite is lapskus (hash to us), prepared with whatever's left over in the kitchen. The North American palate seems to take kindly to kjøttkaker, the Norwegian hamburger—often pork patties—served with sautéed onions, brown gravy, and boiled potatoes.

The boiled potato is ubiquitous. Incidentally, the Norwegian prefers the vegetable without butter—just a bit of parsley—and assumes the foreigner likes it that way, too. Increasingly, fresh vegetables and crisp salads have become a regular feature of the Norwegian diet as well.

Except for cakes, desserts tend to be unimaginative, consisting as they often do of plain ice cream—adorned with a cookie—or canned fruit cocktail. But don't miss rømmegrøt: a sour-cream porridge covered with melted butter, brown sugar, and cinnamon. If they're in season, try the good-tasting, amber-colored multer (cloudberries). An additional treat, well made in Norway, is a pancake accompanied by lingonberries.

Frokost (breakfast) is often a whopping "koldtbord," the famous cold board consisting of herring and goat's cheese, but also more appetizing fare, such as salmon and soft-boiled eggs, plus wienerbrød (Danish pastry). At this time, most tourists encounter the ever-popular flatbrød, paper-thin crisp rye bread. Many visitors may not want to spend the extra kroner for this big spread, but those going on glacier expeditions need this early-morning fortification.

Incidentally, smörgåsbord and smørrebrød are very popular in Norway, although they seem to be served here without the elaborate ritual typical of Denmark and Sweden. Customarily, smörgåsbord in Norway is only a prelude to the main meal.

Norway has strict laws regarding the sale of alcohol—but not for reasons that would put a gleam in the eye of ax-swinging prohibitionist Carrie Nation.

Beer and wine may be served in hotels and restaurants seven days a week, but hard liquor can be sold only between 3 and 11:45 p.m.—and never on Sunday.

Visitors who like to imbibe can buy the precious stuff from the "Vinmonopolet," the big-brother state liquor and wine monopoly. The restriction on hard liquor may be a bonus for budgeteers, since Norwegian prices are skyhigh, in line with all the Scandinavian countries. *Warning:* Unless a visitor asks for a favorite-brand gin or scotch, he or she may be served a Norwegian home brew that tastes as if Mother Troll concocted it one night on Rattlesnake Mountain, using wood-grain alcohol and toad liver.

The Norwegians, like the Danes, are essentially beer drinkers. Low in alcohol content is pils, a light lager, but the lagerøl is so low in alcoholic content (less than 2.5%) that it's a substitute for water only. The stronger Norwegian beer is the export, available at higher prices. Two other newer types of beer that have been introduced are called Brigg and Zero.

The other national drink is aquavit. Who would ever think that potatoes and caraway seeds could knock a person under the table? It's that potent, although it's misnamed the "water of life." Norwegians gulp down beer as a chaser. Aquavit (try Linie Akevitt) is sloshed around in oak vats all the way to Australia and back—for added flavor.

Vinmonopolet, the monopoly that sells wines and spirits, is open Monday to Wednesday from 10 a.m. to 5 p.m., on Thursday from 9 a.m. to 6 p.m., and on Friday from 9 a.m. to 5 p.m. The Vinmonopolet is closed on Saturday in all towns except Kirkenes, Bodø, Ålesund, Trondheim, Haugesund, and Arendal. Alcoholic beverages are not sold to persons under 20 years of age.

From reindeer cutlets to Norwegian hash, from self-service cafeterias to elegant pubs, Oslo offers a surprising range of dining choices, for the $35-a-day'er. First, I'll spotlight the least expensive recommendations, the Kaffistova chain, then turn to other good choices in and around the Students' Grove and East Station. A special feature of Oslo is a number of "two-in-one" establishments, which usually combine a self-service cafeteria with an old Norse restaurant at higher prices.

Except in the cafeterias, a service charge of 12½% is usually added to the bill.

KAFFISTOVAS—THE BEST FOOD BARGAINS: The Kaffistova chain of cafeterias is known for its authentic Norwegian cooking, generous portions, pleasant atmosphere—and prices that appeal. The Kaffistovas are like a gravy train, with boxcars filled with food values. The chain is owned by the League of Country Youth, which prints its menus in the more obscure New Norwegian, as opposed to the Danish Norwegian usually spoken in the cities.

Storstova, 8 Rosenkrantzgate (tel. 42-99-74), is on the first floor of the modernized Hotel Bondeheimen in the center of Oslo. You'll find it at the top of a flight of marble-covered stairs in a room with spacious windows where a young, informal crowd gathers to enjoy fresh salads daily and a good selection of smørrebrød. A ham and cheese salad, bread, and coffee costs 22 kroner ($2.64), with a full dinner and coffee going for 45 kroner ($5.40). No alcohol is served here. The place is open from 7 a.m. to 7:30 p.m. weekdays, closing at 3:30 p.m. on Saturday and at 7 p.m. on Sunday.

Torgstova, 13 Karl Johans Gate, is one flight up in a turn-of-the-century building where you can overlook the flower market and the Oslo cathedral. You can enjoy tasty Norwegian food in typically Norwegian surroundings at this plain, basic restaurant. On the menu are such dishes as lapkus (the seafood favorite) and fish pudding. You can have a Norwegian cheese sandwich, salad, and coffee for 38 kroner ($3.36). A set dinner with coffee costs 42 kroner ($5.04). The coffee is very good here. The Torgstova is open Monday to Friday from 7:45 a.m. to 10:15 p.m., Saturday from 11 a.m. to 3:30 p.m., and Sunday from noon to 6 p.m.

OTHER CAFETERIA-STYLE MEALS: Stratos, 2 Youngstorget (tel. 33-11-53), is on the 12th floor of a modern building, offering an extensive view of the city and a simple cafeteria-style format. The restaurant does not serve alcoholic beverages, but you get a large choice of well-cooked food here. For example, several kinds of soup are offered, and main dishes range from fresh flounder to a hamburger plate. Desserts include fruit with cream. You'll spend from 60 kroner ($7.20) up for a meal. The Stratos is open from 10 a.m. to 5 p.m. weekdays, from 10 a.m. to 2 p.m. on Saturday. Closed Sunday.

Samson, 21 Övre Slottsgate (tel. 56-56-80), corner of Karl Johans Gate, is yet another cafeteria-type restaurant housed in a building dating from 1894. You climb a flight of stairs into a modernized setting in warm orange and blue, with big windows overlooking a pedestrian street. You pay for your meal at a counter, and a waitress will carry it to your table. Main-dish specialties include such familiar dishes as filet mignon, peppersteak, wienerschnitzel, and beef Stroganoff. Count on spending from 90 kroner ($10.80) for a meal. It's closed on Sunday but open weekdays from 8 a.m. to 7 p.m. On Thursday it stays open till 8 p.m. However, it closes at 4 p.m. on Saturday.

Norrona Café, 19 Grensen (tel. 42-72-88), is a self-service cafeteria in a simple series of paneled rooms one floor above street level in the commercial center of town. From your unpretentious table, you'll be able to see sections of Oslo's street traffic through the establishment's enormous windows. Many elderly shoppers prefer this place for a mid-morning smørrebrød, priced at between 10 kroner ($1.20) and 30 kroner ($3.60). The place gets busier between noon and 6 p.m. when full hot meals are served, beginning at 70 kroner ($8.40). The selections include simple and wholesome dishes such as Norwegian fish soup, pork cutlets, and salads, and you might finish it off with a sugared dessert.

VEGETARIAN FOOD: Friskeporten (Vegeta Vertshus), 3B Munkedamsveien (tel. 41-29-13). If you're looking for one of the city's strongholds of vegetarianism, social activism, and budget dining, you might enjoy this basement-level cafeteria near City Hall. The street level is devoted to a green and white café, while the lower section is outfitted with natural-grained vertical planking, ceramic wall sculptures, macramé, and a community bulletin board listing many of the city's counterculture festivities. You can have a large order of soup, salad, and meat-free hot dishes for around 50 kroner ($6) or a smaller selection for 42 kromer ($5.04). Although this restaurant moved into its woodsily romantic new quarters in 1984, it's been an Oslo institution since 1938. It's open from 10 a.m. to 10:30 p.m. daily.

Kurbadets Vegetarrestaurant, 74 Akersgaten (tel. 20-64-14); entrance on Thor Olsengaten. For vegetarians or those who like an occasional vegetarian meal, this well-known bathhouse runs a fine restaurant, offering wholesome dishes at reasonable prices. Only vegetarian dishes are served, including uncooked fruit, vegetables, and juices, along with solely nonalcoholic drinks. I'd advise that your meal begin with a bowl of bortch. The omelets are good, usually made with mushrooms and asparagus and served with a cucumber salad. You can order a three-course meal—that is, soup, main dish, and dessert—for about 60 kroner ($7.20). In this quiet atmosphere, no smoking is allowed. The cafeteria is open Monday to Thursday from noon to 7 p.m., its Friday hours are always posted on the bulletin board; it serves on Sunday from noon to 5:30 p.m., and is closed all day on Saturday.

DEPARTMENT STORE DINING: At **Steen & Strøm Magasin,** 23 Kongensgate (tel. 41-68-00), on the top floor of Norway's largest department store, you'll find several other top-notch places to eat: a self-service cafeteria, as well as three Old Norse-style dining rooms. The cafeteria has a wide selection of open-face sandwiches. I recently had a roast beef delight with rémoulade sauce, and also a wide selection of cakes. A meal here will cost from 60 kroner ($7.20). Next to the cafeteria are the three old dining rooms of Gamlestua, each one specializing in Norwegian recipes. Meals cost from 110 kroner ($13.20) and include such typical fare as schnitzel with peas or beefsteak, finished off with either Norwegian sour-cream pudding or almond cake. The furnishings and decorations of the Gamlestua were gathered from old chalets across Norway (rose-painted hope chests, wooden kegs, natural wood trestle tables, wormy wood paneling). Hours are Monday from 10 a.m. to 4:30 p.m., Tuesday to Friday, from 9 a.m. to 4:30 p.m., and Saturday from 9 a.m. to 2 p.m.

SALAD AND SANDWICH BUFFETS: **Tivoligrillen,** 26 Stortingsgaten (tel. 41-90-60), entrance around the corner on Roald Amundsens Gate, in the Hotel Continental, near the National Theater, serves three meals a day. The specialties of the house change daily but are likely to include such food items as boiled fresh brisket of beef or roast leg of lamb with a salad. These dishes, which are served from 3 to 7 p.m., cost from 120 kroner ($14.40). However, the establishment is also frequented by those who wish to patronize its salad and sandwich buffet offered daily except Sunday from 11 a.m. to 2 p.m. Meals cost from 90 kroner ($10.80) up.

    Handverkeran Bar and Grill, 7 Rosenkrantzgate (tel. 33-10-00). The entrance to this place is actually around the corner from the street it prefers to give as its address. However, a well-lit sign makes it easy to spot. The bar and grill, often frequented by the press, is best recommended as a lunchtime restaurant, where a fixed-price buffet costs 42 kroner ($5.04), making it one of the best bargains of the neighborhood. Amid a decor of textured stucco, repeating arches, stained glass, and secluded cubbyholes, the lunch is served from Monday through Saturday from 11 a.m. to 2 p.m. Later in the day and at night, the place takes on a more masculine ambience of flowing beer and amicable, loud conversations. Draft beer costs from 30 kroner ($3.60).

ITALIAN FOOD: **Restaurant Mamma Rosa,** 12 Övre Slottsgate (tel. 42-01-30). This Italian trattoria is about the best example of changing taste of the Nordic palate in all of Oslo. Today, the "reproduction rococo" second-floor room with the blazing chandeliers and globe lights draws a volume of business that would make many of the restaurants of Naples green with envy. The clients tend to be conservatively dressed Oslovians who apparently enjoy the waiters' Mediterranean bravado along with the Italian food specialties. Dishes include 10 kinds of pizzas, fried scampi and squid, fettuccine Seventh Heaven, spaghetti marinara, grilled steaks, and Italian ice creams. Full meals cost from 120 kroner ($14.40). The establishment is open from 11 a.m. to 11 p.m. daily except Sunday, when hours are from 1 to 10 p.m.

GRAND CAFÉ DINING: Maybe Oslo doesn't possess the grandeur of the cafés of fin-de-siècle Vienna, but one or two are still around to draw the devotee. Those of you who admire *A Doll's House* and *Hedda Gabler* can have a pleasant evening experience while paying tribute to Norway's premier dramatist by going to the **Grand Café** at the legendary Grand Hotel, 31 Karl Johans Gate (tel. 33-48-70). Ibsen used to patronize this place, and the chair he sat in, even the glass from which he drank, have been zealously preserved. Most of the furnishings are warmly contemporary, yet the tall ceiling and glowing paneling, brass hanging lamps, and palm trees give the feeling of a more antique decor. If you're versed in Norway's artistic life of the late 19th century, you may recognize some of the faces in the large mural at the end of the room, supposedly showing many members of the Grand Café's original clientele.

Food is served on beautifully formal blue-and-white china by red-vested waitresses and might include everything from a Napoleon with coffee to a full meal. Seafood specialties range from a platter of whale meat to fried sting ray, while meats comprise a selection from standard veal and beef dishes to reindeer steaks and elk stew. A three-course dinner costs 95 kroner ($11.40) and up. If you want just a light meal, you can help yourself to the salad bar for 45 kroner ($5.40). Sandwiches are also available.

Theatercafeen, Hotel Continental, 24 Stortingsgate (tel. 41-90-60), competes with the Grand Café for the patronage of theatergoers, present-day *boulevardiers,* and business persons who always seem to look better in the soft light of antique bronze and cut-glass lighting fixtures. The café is large, sophisticated, and beautiful, containing beneath its arched ceilings a battalion of vested employees and a bar area whose art nouveau mirrors fit snugly under the vaulting, plus a musicians' gallery. As you dine the strains of a string quartet will float down from the orchestra there, one of whose members was a hale and hearty 95 when I last was there. The music usually lasts from 4 to 6 p.m. and from 8 to 11 p.m.

Daily specials, served only from 3 to 7 p.m., include a fixed-price meal for 60 kroner ($7.20). Otherwise, you can spend from 170 kroner ($20.40) or more, particularly at night ordering à la carte. You can enjoy shrimp cocktails, frog legs with tarragon sauce, reindeer with mushrooms, filet of hare in juniperberry sauce, mussels with white wine in sour cream, and a "fish and sea fruit" pot. The establishment is open from Monday through Saturday from 10:30 a.m. to 11:30 p.m. and on Sunday from noon to 11:30 p.m.

THE ATMOSPHERE OF THE PAST: Stortorvets Gjaestgiveri, 1 Grensen (tel. 42-88-63), near the Oslo cathedral and flower market, is a three-centuries-old inn that specializes in the favorite dishes of Norway. The inn has an inner courtyard—a symphony of oranges and yellows—for fair-weather dining. But inside are large rooms with antique touches (carved ceiling, fireplace, circular wrought-iron stove, antique chairs). Norwegian dishes are served, and in the courtyard, entrecôte, lamb chops, and trout chops are barbecued. Meals cost from 100 kroner ($12). Jazz is featured from 8 p.m. to midnight on Friday and from 2 to 5 p.m. on Saturday. Under the same management and at the same address is Gamle Christiania (see section on "Oslo After Dark").

Restaurant Gamla Raadhus (Old Town Hall), 1 Nedre Slottsgate (tel. 42-01-07), is the old-style restaurant and bar established within the weathered brick walls of what used to be Oslo's Town Hall. After checking your coat, you can turn left into the timbered and paneled Kroen Bar for a drink or turn right into the dining room, a high-ceilinged, spacious area where a fixed-price noon meal is served for 60 kroner ($7.20) and where there's a full array of smørrebrød. À la carte selections can be made from a menu of fresh mussels poached in white wine with cream, crab tails with mussels in cream sauce, reindeer schnitzel with stewed mushrooms and cranberries, and peppersteak with cognac sauce. A full meal will cost 280 kroner ($33.60) and up, although if you're watching your budget, you can be served a plate of food with a glass of beer or mineral water in the bar. The best seats are the leather-covered banquettes which alternate with captains' chairs. On the upper floor, there's a museum and a theater which presents different plays, usually in Norwegian, on a to-be-announced basis.

Traktørstedet Restaurant Statholdergaarden, 11 Rådhusgatan (tel. 41-48-25). This establishment benefits from a double blessinig of offering one of the best reasonably priced luncheon buffets in town and being one of the oldest restaurants inside one of the oldest buildings in Norway. The entrance lies around the corner from a truck-filled thoroughfare. The present-day restaurant was the residence of the Danish governor when Denmark ruled Norway a few hundred years ago. You enter a richly papered and paneled room whose crowning glory is an inner room whose allegorical stucco ceiling, which dates from the construction of the building around 1640, is said to be the only one of its kind in the country.

The luncheon buffet, set out on a table near the bar, is served every weekday from 11 a.m. to 3 p.m. and costs 90 kroner ($10.80) per person. A la carte dinners, priced at between 100 kroner ($12) and 180 kroner ($21.60), are available until 10 p.m. weekdays only. The restaurant is closed Saturday and Sunday. The owners of this establishment are Abraham Ben Avi and his wife Liv, who, before they migrated to Norway in 1980, lived near Tel Aviv.

NOUVELLE CUISINE: Restaurant Bagatelle, 3 Bygdøy (tel. 44-63-97). There's been a French restaurant on this site for the past 50 years, its most recent incarnation dating from 1982 when Ole Petter Rostad and chef Elvind Hellstrom transformed it into the best nouvelle cuisine restaurant in Oslo. It isn't as expensive as you might fear, particularly if you order the carefully prepared, fixed-price three-course lunch for 145 kroner ($17.40) or the two-course meal for 110 kroner ($13.20). At night, three courses cost 240 kroner ($28.88), and a seven-course nouvelle cuisine extravanganza goes for 360 kroner ($43.20). In Paris, meals like these would easily cost three times as much.

The service is as sunny and gracious as the decor is sophisticated. You may be so impressed with the sculptured zinc and the rattan chairs of the bar that you'll want to stay there, but you shouldn't miss the interior with its Chinese Chippendale-style whitewashed furniture and the garden setting. There's even a colorful collection of lithographs and a 10-foot-long collage by one of Scandinavia's leading artists in vivid Hindu red and black. The restaurant is closed Saturday and Sunday, but it's open weekdays from 11:30 a.m. to 2 p.m. and from 6 to 10 p.m. The menu changes daily, depending on the market availability of fresh ingredients.

"CABIN-IN-THE SKY" DINING: Frognerseteren Hovedrestaurant (tel. 14-37-36), on a mountaain ledge, is a log Norse lodge, authentically furnished like a grand chalet. Its commanding view of Oslo and fjord must rank (at least) with Nero's choice seat to witness the burning of Rome. Go early (opens noon), stay late (closes 10:30 p.m.)—it's that spectacular. In daylight there's scenic beauty; at night the glittering lights below provide their own magic. The lodge has a breezy outside terrace, either for snacks or beer for those who come just to drink in the view. The dining room on the left (lower level) is ornately decorated. There is also a café which charges prices about 10% lower than the restaurant. The chef specializes in game, including pheasant pâté with Cumberland sauce, smoked reindeer tongue with horseradish sauce, and filet of elk fried in honey and nuts. You can also order Norwegian salmon prepared in a number of ways. An average meal here will range in price from 175 kroner ($21). To finish your dinner, you can quietly sip your coffee and enjoy the vista or else ask for the chef's well-known applecake. At certain times of the year, you can also order the acclaimed cloudberries with whipped cream. In winter every guest here seems to be a skier, and the logs in the hooded fireplace burn brightly. To reach the restaurant, take the subway, Holmenkollen, near the National Theater. It's a 30-minute ride to the terminal stop some 1600 feet above sea level. *Be warned:* It is about 1000 feet downhill over a poorly maintained dirt path to the restaurant from the Holmenkollen railway stop. In daylight, aim for the buiding flying three flags. At night, the path has lights. Don't let the similarity of names (Frognerseteren) mislead you into thinking this restaurant is near Frogner Park.

PUB DINING: **Den Runde Tonne** (The Round Barrel), 4 Pløensgate (tel. 42-79-12), shares a spacious square with the severely modern Opera House. The proximity of the two buildings seems to encourage the kind of singing which at night includes a balladeer, many customers, a few of the motherly waitresses, and an occasional troll. The decor is rustic, looking like a cross between a half-timbered barn and an English pub with a coffered ceiling. As you sit on an adaptation of an alpine chair, you might hear everything sung from "Trink, trink, Brüderlein, trink" to "Waltzing Matilda."

Beer costs from 30 kroner ($3.60), while a simple set meal goes for either 50 kroner ($6) or 75 kroner ($9), depending on which of the two you select. Full à la carte meals usually cost from 120 kroner ($14.40) up. The chef specializes in steak. This establishment has been entertaining Oslovians since 1890. It's open daily from 10 a.m. to 11:30 p.m.

FOR SMÖRGÅSBORD: Everyone has heard of smörgåsbord in Sweden, for which that country is widely known. However, the Norwegians are also skilled at preparing this delectable array of dishes. The **Stefan Hotel,** 1 Rosenkrantzgate (42-92-50), previous recommended as a Mission hotel, is widely known for its luncheon smörgåsbord—at least 50 different dishes—which is served Monday to Saturday from noon to 2 p.m. Go early, as I've found it's better to get there when the food is first put on the table. The cost is about 125 kroner ($15), but you can eat so much that only a sandwich or bowl of soup might suffice for a light supper. No alcoholic beverages are served in the dining room (ask about their alcohol-free wines).

My Norwegian friends consider this the best luncheon buffet in the capital, and I concur. The assortment includes (usually) cucumber salad, fish and meat salads, sausages, meatballs, potato salad, smoked fish, and a selection of Norwegian cheese. Desserts are also good.

The **Forbundshotellet,** 1 Holbergs Plass (tel. 20-88-55), offers a cold buffet with hot dishes Monday to Friday from 4 to 8 p.m. for 125 kroner ($15). It's good and plenty filling, although not as large as the one offered at the Stefan Hotel.

READER'S RESTAURANT SUGGESTION: "Bella Napoli Restaurant, 26 Storgaten (tel. 41-00-52), has delicious food at reasonable prices. It is a ten-minute walk from the cental train station. Prices range from about 65 kroner ($7.80) to 100 kroner ($12). Pizza costs 45 kroner ($5.40) and lasagne goes for 45 kroner ($5.40). The food was so good we went back a second time. The restaurant is open Monday through Saturday, 2:30 to 11:30 p.m." (Joanna Ficaro, Cambridge, Mass.).

OSLO: WHAT TO SEE AND DO

ONCE CONSIDERED the far frontier—the other side of Valhalla—Oslo is now a mainline tourist center.

Among other "events," it has dusted off and opened up its greatest medieval site, Akershus Castle, and has preserved more contemporary greatness in the sparkling modern museum devoted to the works of Scandinavia's most famous painter, Edvard Munch.

In keeping with Oslo's outdoor orientation, its tops sights are, for the most part, situated in the great outdoors (Holmenkollen ski jump, Folk Museum, Vigeland sculptures)—or else now housed inside, but related to seafaring exploits *(Kon-Tiki* and the polar ship *Fram,* or the Viking burial vessels).

Suitable either for one- or two-day excursions are Lillehammer, both a summer resort and winter ski center; the 16th-century Old Town in Fredrikstad, known for its arts and crafts; and the old whaling and shipping towns of Tønsberg and Sandefjord to the south. All of these centers have good train and bus connections.

Before striking out for the hills, I'll survey the attractions within the city, beginning with:

1. The Top Sights

THE VIKING SHIPS: Of the ships that symbolized terror (the Vikings are coming)—or of the ships that sailed to Leif Ericsson's *Vinland*—all that remain in a well-preserved shape are the three Viking burial vessels displayed at the hall at 35 Huk Aveny, on the Bygdøy peninsula (tel. 55-86-36).

Excavated on the shores of the Oslofjord, all three ships have been preserved in varying degrees by clay. In many ways the most spectacular find is the ninth-century **Oseberg**, discovered as late as 1904 near Norway's oldest town. This 64-foot dragon ship, containing a wealth of ornament, is believed to have been the burial chamber of Harald Fairhair's grandmother and her slave, along with her entourage of 15 horses, an ox, and four dogs, plus numerous artifacts— everything from a sea chest to a cauldron.

But since it was in a better state of preservation, the **Gokstad** find is considered to be the best example of the Viking era in all of the Nordic countries. In greater disrepair than the other two, the smaller **Tune** ship was never restored, but is exhibited in somewhat the same condition as when it was discovered. Look for the Oseberg animal-head post, the elegantly carved sleigh used by Viking royalty, and the Oseberg four-wheeled cart.

The museum is open May through August, daily from 10 a.m. to 6 p.m; in September, from 11 a.m. to 5 p.m.; from October through April, 11 a.m. to 3 p.m. The admission is 5 kroner (60¢) for adults, 2.50 kroner (30¢) for children.

To reach the Viking ships or the three sights that follow, take a ferry in summer, leaving from Pier 3 facing the City Hall, or else bus 30 at the National Theater which goes all the way to *Fram* and *Kon-Tiki*, previewed below.

THE POLAR SHIP FRAM:
An anchor away from the Viking ships is a great relic of modern explorers, the stout and sturdy exploration ship *Fram*. Its claim to fame: it has been farther north and farther south than any other ship. The fully rigged *Fram* is housed, fittingly enough, in a triangular, slope-roofed structure based on the principle of the old Norse boathouses.

The vessel is forever linked to the exploits of Roald Amundsen and Fridtjof Nansen, who run a close second to Leif Ericsson as Norway's most lengendary explorers. Nansen was also a statesman, winner of the Nobel Peace Prize in 1922. He sailed across the Arctic in 1893–1896 in the *Fram*, and the vessel was later used by Amundsen, the first man to reach the South Pole (1911). He planted a Norwegian flag on the southern wastelands, a heartbreaking sight to Scott who arrived a month later. With its rounded-off and thick wooden hull, the *Fram* had a buoyancy that could lift it up on the packed ice, as happened many times.

The museum at Bygdøynes is open May 15 through August, daily, from 10 a.m. to 6 p.m.; from 1 a.m. to 5 p.m. in September, from noon to 3 p.m. in October; Sunday in November from noon to 3 p.m.; daily from noon to 3 p.m. from April 15 to April 30; daily from 11 a.m. to 5 p.m. for the first two weeks in May. The admission is 5 kroner (60¢) for adults, 2 kroner (24¢) for students and children. For information, call 55-84-00.

KON-TIKI MUSEUM:
Also in this compound of sea relics is the balsa-log raft, the world-famed *Kon-Tiki*, that the young Norwegian scientist, Thor Heyerdahl, and his five comrades sailed 4300 miles in 1947—all the way from Callao, Peru, to Raroia, Polynesia. Despite the hazards, Heyerdahl proved his theory: that pre-Inca Indians could have crossed from South America to populate Polynesia.

The museum displays the raft, plus other exhibits from Heyerdahl's subsequent visit to Easter Island: casts of stone giants and small originals, a facsimile of the whale shark, and an Easter Island family cave, with a collection of sacred lava figurines of the kind hoarded in secret underground storage passages on that island.

The museum also houses the original papyrus *Ra II* in which Heyerdahl crossed the Atlantic in 1970. His book, *Kon-Tiki,* was translated into 64 languages.

The museum is open from 10 a.m. to 6 p.m. daily from May 16 to August 31; from 10:30 a.m. to 5 p.m. from September 1 to October 31 and April 1 to May 15; and from 10:30 a.m. to 4 p.m. November 1 to March 31. Admission is 5 kroner (60¢) for adults, 2 kroner (24¢) for children. For more information, telephone 55-65-52.

NORWEGIAN FOLK MUSEUM: From all over Norway, 170 old buildings (no reproductions) have been transported and reassembled on 35 acres on the Bygdøy Peninsula at 10 Museumsveien (tel. 55-80-90). This open-air section of the Norwegian Folk Museum is the oldest of its kind in the country, and includes a number of buildings from the Middle Ages, such as the Raulandstua, one of the oldest wooden dwellings still standing in Norway, and a stave church from about 1200. The rural buildings are grouped together by region of origin, while the urban houses have been laid out in the form of an old town.

The indoor section of the museum is made up of about 180,000 exhibits, capturing every imaginable facet of Norwegian life, past and present. Furniture, household utensils, clothing, woven fabrics, and tapestries abound. You can see fine examples of rose painting and woodcarving as well. Farming implements and logging gear pay tribute to the development of agriculture and forestry in Norway. One of the most celebrated displays is Henrik Ibsen's completely reassembled study, transported from his home at 1 Arbiens St. in Oslo, where he lived until his death in 1906. The study appears as if the dramatist had just stepped out for a few minutes.

The museum also contains a fascinating musical and ecclesiastical section. Recitals are frequently held here using the historic instruments from the museum collection. Finally, don't miss the outstanding Lapp exhibition, which pays tribute to Norway's Lappish population who mainly inhabit the Arctic regions and traditionally survived by hunting, fishing, and reindeer herding.

Visiting hours for the museum vary according to season, but generally summer hours are from 10 a.m. to 6 p.m. and winter hours from 11 a.m. to 4 p.m. Sunday hours usually begin at noon. Admission is 12 kroner ($1.44) for adults, 5 kroner (60¢) for children. To reach the museum, take bus 30 "Bygdøy" from the National Theater or the ferry in front of the Town Hall to Dronningen Pier.

THE VIGELAND SCULPTURES: In the 75-acre **Frogner Park** in western Oslo sprawls the lifetime work of Gustav Vigeland, Norway's greatest sculptor, whose outstanding one-man show draws tourists from around the world. In nearly 175 sculptures in granite, bronze, and iron, he depicted the embryo-to-death struggle of humanity, recapturing the rages and joys, the sorrows and happiness of life. At one time the works were immensely controversial—"raze the park to the ground," the Oslo press once suggested. One critic found the nudity "disgraceful." However, the Vigeland sculptures would hardly be considered disgraceful by today's standards. In fact, Vigeland survived his critical reception and went on to become hailed as "one of the master sculptors of modern times."

Financed by the city of Oslo—unique in itself—Vigeland struggled for three decades, until his death in 1943, to create these works. See in particular his four granite columns, symbolizing the fight between man and evil (a dragon, the embodiment of evil, embraces a woman, and her smiling face reveals that she enjoys it). Six men carrying a huge bowl—a splashing fountain—symbolize the burden of life (some men are not carrying their equal load, but the statue representing Vigeland is saddled with the heaviest share). The angry boy is perhaps the most photographed statue in the park. But the really celebrated work is the 52-foot-high monolith, comprising 121 figures of colossal size—all carved into one piece of stone, a writhing mass presenting the struggle of life (Vigeland did the plaster model, but it took three men 14 years to carve it).

The municipally owned park is open all year. To reach it, take the subway (Frogner) from the National Theater, then get off at the main entrance, the geometrically patterned—twisting dragons—gates of Kirkeveien. Nearby at 32 Nobelsgate is the sculptor's former studio, containing more of his works, along with sketches and woodcuts. The admission-free museum is open daily (closed Monday) from 1 to 7 p.m.

EDVARD MUNCH MUSEUM: A modern museum at 53 Tøyengate (tel. 67-37-74) is devoted exclusively to the works of Edvard Munch (1863–1944), considered the leading painter of Scandinavia. Chronologically arranged, the exhibit, his gift to the city, traces his work from early realism to his latter-day expressionism. Love and death (the fear of the latter haunted him) form the paramount elements in his paintings, which also reveal the artist's ambivalent attitude toward woman; he was frightened by her (see the vampire sucking blood from her victim) and he adored her at the same time. Critic Michel Ragon appraised Munch's work this way: "In it we find the melancholy, the irony, the bitterness, and the anguish of Kierkegaard; the pessimism of Ibsen; Strindberg's morbid misogyny and detestation of love; Hamsun's savage sensuality." The collection comprises 1100 paintings, 4500 drawings, around 18,000 prints, numerous graphic plates, and six sculptures, as well as important documentary material. The exhibition shows a selection of this vast collection, but the pictures are changed periodically.

The admission-free museum, opened in 1963, may be visited from 10 a.m. to 8 p.m. every day except Monday. On Sunday, it's open from noon to 8 p.m. Take bus 29 from Rådhusplassen or the subway from Central Station to Tøyen Station.

THE CITY HALL: Called everything from "aggressively ugly" to the "pride of Norway," the modern city hall, the Oslo Kommune, a mere idea in 1915, a reality in 1950—must be seen to be judged properly. Its plain and simple brick exterior, despite its double towers, doesn't suggest the wealth of decoration inside (the work of Norwegian artists and craftspeople). In the courtyard, don't miss the astronomical clock and Dyre Vaa's swan fountain. Greeting visitors inside is the stunning troll-size (85 by 43 feet) wall painted by Henrik Sørensen. The rest of the City Hall is a virtual Milky Way of Norwegian art: tapestries, frescoes, sculpture, and woodcarvings.

The admission-free city hall at Rådhusplassen (tel. 41-00-90) is open weekdays from 10 a.m. to 2 p.m. from April 1 to September 30. During this time, it is also open Monday and Wednesday evenings from 6 to 8 p.m. (on Sunday from noon to 3 p.m.). From October 1 to March 31 it is open from 11 a.m. to 2 p.m. (on Sunday from noon to 3 p.m.).

AKERSHUS CASTLE: One of the oldest historical monuments in Oslo, Akershus Castle is on the top of a steep cliff jutting into the water of the inner Oslofjord. Built in 1300 by King Haakon V Magnusson, it was an impregnable fortress as well as a royal residence for several hundred years. Although subjected to nine sieges, it was never conquered. A fire swept over the castle in 1527, leaving the northern wing in ruins—even the great keep, the Daredevil's Tower—almost reduced to shambles. Under the Danish-Norwegian king, Christian IV, the castle was rebuilt and transformed into a royal Renaissance palace. Now restored, the castle is used by the Norwegian government for state occasions. From the bastions and "curtain walls," views open onto Oslo and the fjord.

The castle is open in summer from 10 a.m. to 4 p.m., on Sunday from 12:30 to 4 p.m. Guided tours are at 11 a.m., and 1 and 3 p.m. (Sunday 1 and 3 p.m.). In spring and fall, it's open on Sunday only. Closed in winter. Entrance is 5 kroner (60¢) for adults, 2 kroner (24¢) for children.

On the grounds is a monument dedicated to Norwegian patriots, many of whom were executed at this spot by the Nazis in World War II. Next to the monument is **Norway's Resistance Museum (Norges Hjemmefrontmuseum)** (tel. 41-43-79), documenting the dramatic events beginning with the German attack in 1940 until the liberation in 1945. From underground printing presses to radio transmitters, the constant resistance of the Norwegian people to their German conquerors is revealed in exhibits. The museum is open April 15 to September 30 daily from 10 a.m. to 4 p.m. Otherwise the hours are weekdays from 10 a.m. to 3 p.m. (Sunday from 11 a.m. to 4 p.m.). Admission is 5 kroner (60¢) for adults, 1 krone (12¢) for children.

LOOKOUT TOWER AND SKI JUMP: At some point, I suggest that Viking ships and balsa rafts be deserted long enough to take the Holmenkollen subway near the National Theater to the end of the line. A 30-minute trek by electric train takes passengers to the country, the end-of-the-line stop at Voksenkollen. From here, it's a 15-minute walk up the hill (for the energetic only) to **Tryvannstårnet** (tel. 14-67-11), loftiest lookout tower in Scandinavia. On a clear day, forever is only part of what the viewers see (the gallery is approximately 1900 feet above sea level. The tower is open Tuesday to Sunday from 10 a.m. to 6 p.m. in March and April; daily from 10 a.m. to 8 p.m. in May and from August 16 to September 9; daily from 9:30 a.m. to 10 p.m. from June 1 to August 15; daily from 10 a.m. to 6 p.m. in September; and Tuesday to Sunday from 10 a.m. to 4 p.m. in October. Adults pay an admission of 7 kroner (84¢); children, 4 kroner (48¢).

A walk down the hill takes us back to Frognerseteren (see the restaurant recommendations). The athletic take another 20-minute walk down the hill to the Holmenkollen ski jump, one of the most famous in the world, the site of the Olympic competitions in 1952. The highlight of the winter sports season in Norway is the annual **Holmenkollen Ski Festival** here, which gathers the elite skiers of the world for competitions in downhill, slalom, and giant slalom, cross-country ski races, and jumping, climaxed by the Holmenkollen ski-jumping contest on Holmenkollen Sunday, an event which gathers thousands of spectators, headed by the king and the royal family.

At Holmenkollen, an elevator takes visitors up another tower for a view of Oslo and the fjord. At the base of the ski jump is the **Ski Museum (Skimuseet)** (tel. 14-20-18), opened in 1923, displaying a wide range of exhibits from the 2500-year-old Overbø ski to equipment used on the polar explorations of Nansen and Amundsen. The museum is open daily from 10 a.m. to 9 p.m.; from August 16, it closes at 8 p.m.; from September 1, it shuts down at 6 p.m. In October, November, March, and April to mid-May, it is open only on weekends and holidays from 10 a.m. to 4 p.m. Otherwise, it remains closed from

December through February. The combined price of admission to both the lift and the museum is 15 kroner ($1.80) for adults, 9 kroner ($1.08) for children.

2. Other Major Sights

THE NATIONAL GALLERY: This state museum of art, at 13 Universitetsgaten (tel. 20-04-04), a short walk from Students' Grove, contains a good collection of the work of world artists, such as Cézanne and Matisse, but it is recommended chiefly for its paintings by Norwegians—particularly the leading romantic landscape painter, Johan Christian Dahl, who flourished in the early 19th century, and his contemporaries. In addition, a special room is devoted to Edvard Munch. His self-portrait hardly reveals why he was considered "the handsomest man in Norway." See his much-reproduced *The Scream*, painted in 1893. Munch was lionized in Europe, but three other outstanding Norwegian artists were highly valued in their own bailiwick for their realistic works: Harriet Backer (a leading painter in the 1880s; interior portraits of Norwegian life); Christian Krohg (seafarers to prostitutes); and Erik Werenskiold (see his *Peasant Funeral).* On the ground floor is Norwegian art of the last generation or so. On the main staircase there is a display of Norwegian sculpture. See particularly the works of Gustav Vigeland.

The admission-free museum is open Monday to Friday, 10 a.m. to 4 p.m. (on Saturday from 10 a.m. to 3 p.m., and on Sunday from noon to 3 p.m.). It may also be visited on Wednesday and Thursday evenings from 6 to 8 p.m.

OSLO CATHEDRAL: At Stortovet (the Marketplace), Oslo's 17th-century cathedral, Oslo Domkirche (tel. 41-27-93), was restored as recently as 1950, when its modern tempera ceiling decorations were completed by Hugo Lous Mohr. Like the city hall, the cathedral contains works by 20th-century Norwegian artists, including bronze doors by Dagfin Werenskiold, son of the famed 19th-century artist, Erik. In addition, don't miss the pulpit and altar from the cathedral's earliest days, its stained-glass windows by Emanuel Vigeland (not to be confused with the sculptor, Gustav) in the choir and Borgar Hauglid in the transepts, and its organ that rises five floors.

The cathedral may be visited weekdays from 11 a.m. to 1 p.m. from October 1 to April 30 (closed Saturday and Sunday). In May and in September, it is open daily except Sunday from 9 a.m. to 1 p.m. From June 1 to August 31, it is open weekdays from 9 a.m. to 2 p.m. (from 9 a.m. to 1 p.m. on Saturday). Admission is free. Services are held on Sunday at 11 a.m. and 7:30 p.m., with church music and prayer on Saturday at noon and Wednesday at 7:30 p.m.

THE HISTORICAL MUSEUM: At 2 Frederiksgate (tel. 41-63-00), a polevaulter's leap from the Students' Grove, is a three-in-one museum operated by the University of Oslo Universitetets Oldsaksamling. Different wings are devoted to ethnography, antiquities, and numismatics. By far the most interesting is the Collection of Antiquities on the ground floor, presenting artifacts from the Viking era—remote links to the legendary Scandinavians of yore—including armor, combs, blades, swords, jewelry, tools, shields, and spears—even a collection of gold and silver from the 5th through the 13th centuries displayed in the aptly named Treasure House. But this collection also contains relics of even more remote Scandinavian forefathers. For example, Cases 19 through 35 illustrate what is known as the Migration Period (about A.D. 400 to 600). This is an interesting exhibit of gold objects that found their way to Northern Europe all the way from the fading Roman Empire in the East. Cases 36 through 39 illustrate a later period, from about A.D. 600 to 800 (known as the Merovingian epoch). Iron objects were typical of this period. Like the Vikings who followed them, Merovingian men buried the tools of craftsmen along with their bodies, affording later generations a keen glimpse of what otherwise might have been a blank page in history. In addition to some of the exhibits already cited, don't miss the reddish Ringerike Strand Stone (in the entrance hall), which was carved in relief; and the Dynna Stone, an old runic stone from around the 11th century, honoring the fairest maiden in Hadeland, whoever she was. Finally, for medievalists, the museum contains a rich collection of ecclesiastical art in a series of portals of stave churches, up to the 15th century. The collection may be visited daily from 11 a.m. to 3 p.m. in summer; off-season, noon to 3 p.m. It's closed on Monday. Admission is free.

HENIE-ONSTAD FOUNDATIONS: An art center (tel. 54-30-50) on a handsome site beside Oslofjord at Høvikodden, Baerum, seven miles from Oslo, opened in the summer of 1968. Who could forget Sonja Henie? She was that blond, curly-haired, smiling-faced darling who (as writ in *The Movies*) "added new millions to those she already had" when Zanuck offered her a film contract. She skated through one flick after another, while Ray Milland or John Payne stood agonizingly by. Before her death, Miss Henie was married to the shipping tycoon, Niels Onstad.

The ex-movie star and her magnate spouse decided to share some of their money (about $7 million) and some of their art treasures with the world, so they opened a museum. As an art patron, Mr. Onstad donated an especially good collection of the works of 20th-century artists, not only paintings by home-grown Edvard Munch, but by Picasso, Pierre Bonnard, Miró, and many others as well. Miss Henie made her contribution, too, to be seen in her Trophy Room (three Olympic gold medals—she was the star at the 1936 competition—and ten world skating championships).

Besides the permanent collection, there are plays, concerts, films, and special exhibitions. Plans call for the open-air theater-in-the-round to be used in summer for folklore programs, jazz concerts, and song recitals.

On the premises is a top-notch, partly self-service, grill restaurant, the **Piruetten,** for the budget traveler. The free-fanning, five-leaf building is of advanced design, the creative statement of two young architects of Norway who won the contract by scoring over their rivals in a competition.

The ideal way to go is by taking bus 36, 37, or 32 from the old university at Karl Johans Gate; the fare is 10 kroner ($1.20). It's about a five-minute walk from where the bus lets you off to the entrance at the musuem. The museum is open daily from 9 a.m. to 10 p.m., charging 15 kroner ($1.35) admission for adults, 8 kroner (96¢) for children.

THE OSLOFJORD: Chances are, you may get to see your first fjord on a boat trip from Oslo. I highly recommend the trip for the first-time visitor. At the head of the fjord, Oslo lies in a natural setting of unspoiled hills and woodland, rivers and lakes, arable lands and farms. Some, but certainly not all, of these farms are disappearing as the city suburbs spread ever outward. Since the city extends southward, down the eastern and western shores of Oslofjord, it is easy to reach some of Norway's finest scenery of forest and fjord in a short amount of time.

Oslofjord extends for 70 miles, and the coast is fringed with many islands. In summer, boating and bathing are major attractions. Since the dawn of recorded history, people have lived on this fjord, and traces of early days remain in rock carvings, burial graves of Viking ships, stone churches, fortresses, and rock carvings.

If you're exploring the fjord by car, refer to individual descriptions of some of the sightseeing goals (Fredrikstad and Tønsberg, in particular) in this same chapter under "One-Day Excursions." However, if you're pressed for time, you'll get plenty of scenery by taking one of the boat tours from Oslo.

Those most pressed for time can take the 50-minute tour of the bustling harbor, going among the islands. From mid-May till around mid-August, departures are from Pier 3 in front of Rådhuset (City Hall) on the hour from 10 a.m. to 9 p.m. during the peak vacation months. Price is 30 kroner ($3.60) for adults, 15 kroner ($1.80) for children.

Otherwise, take the two-hour Oslofjord cruise of the western reaches of the fjord. While you sit back and soak up the scenery, refreshments can be ordered. Departures are daily in the peak season from Pier 3 in front of Rådhuset (City Hall). The vessel leaves at 10:30 a.m., and 1, 3:30, and 5:45 p.m. Tours operate from May 1 to about mid-September, costing adults 60 kroner ($7.20) and children 30 kroner ($3.60).

Both tours are operated by **Båtservice Sightseeing A/S,** Terminal, Pier 3 (tel. 20-07-15).

ORGANIZED TOURS: HMK tours has been showing visitors around Oslo for more than a century. From April 1 to October 31, they have a three-hour morning sightseeing jaunt that costs 75 kroner ($9) for adults and 35 kroner ($4.20) for children. The bus visits Akershus and goes to Frogner Park where visitors get out to see the Vigeland sculptures. Later the coach climbs up to the Holmenkollen ski jump for a view of Oslo and its fjord, before going on to the Munch museum.

You might also want to take the three-hour afternoon tour for the same price. Leaving at 2:30 p.m., it concentrates on the museums at Bygdøy, including the Museum of Norwegian Folklore and the Viking ships, as well as *Fram* and *Kon-Tiki.*

Starting point is the harbor side of city hall, and passengers should arrive 15 minutes before departure. Authorized guides speak English, of course. The tours are operated by **H. M. Kristiansens Automobilbyrå,** 73B Akersgate (tel. 20-83-02).

3. Shopping in Oslo

Whether you're seeking graceful functionalism or provincial handicrafts little changed in centuries, the best buys in the "northern outpost of Europe" include sportswear (top-grade materials, exciting colors), silver and enamelware (high degree of technical skill, moderate prices), traditional handicrafts, pewter, glass by **Hadelands Glassverk** (founded in 1762), teak furniture, and stainless steel.

Oslo has a series of traffic-free streets lined with strollers and shoppers. The heart of this district is the Strøget (dubbed the "smile of the town"). On this street, almost a dozen restored 19th-century buildings and backyards shelter more than two dozen shops selling everything from Norwegian handicrafts to enameled silver jewelry. At the marketplace on Strøget, you can, in fair weather, stop for a glass of beer at an open-air restaurant. Strøget's reconstruction and subsequent popularity in 1970 has led to the creation of other streets for pedestrians only in midcity.

ARTS AND CRAFTS: Your preliminary shopping jaunt might begin at the **Forum,** 7 Rosenkrantzgate (tel. 42-38-70), the permanent exhibition of Norwegian arts and crafts and industrial design. Opposite the Hotel Bristol, the center displays merchandise which has been jury approved. It's comparable to Den Permanente in Copenhagen. You can wander at leisure through a wealthy array of hand-woven rugs, functional furnishings, hand-knitted sweaters, coming up with some stunning little item such as a crystal "eiderduck" representing the fine craftmanship of the Hadelands Glassverk. The place is run as a nonprofit organization to promote the crafts of Norway's leading artists and artisans. Nearly all the merchandise is of a unique character, so exhibitions are likely to be different every season.

Norway Designs, 28 Stortingsgaten (tel. 42-70-50), is the country's largest headquarters for the exhibition and sale of high-quality Norwegian and Scandinavian arts and crafts, With its 7000 square feet of floor space, it is an ideal shopping center for ceramics, glassware, pottery, textiles (there's a fashion shop), rugs, souvenirs, silverware, and furniture. All the crafts that have made Norwegians known internationally as outstanding designers are displayed here.

Den Norske Husflidsforening (Husfliden, for short), 4 Møllergate (tel. 42-10-75), stands near the Marketplace and the cathedral. It is the display and retail center for the Norwegian Association of Home Arts and Crafts. Experts scan the rural areas, selecting the best works, particularly those items which show skill and artistry. Here you'll find beautiful handicrafts with up to 1000 years of tradition, displayed side by side with modern Nordic design. The store offers specialist departments for embroidery, furniture, gifts, hand-woven textiles, knitwear and yarns, knotted Rya rugs, national costumes, and woodware; and goods are sent all over the world. Hours are daily from 9 a.m. to 4:30 p.m. (Saturday until 1 p.m.).

Heimen, 14 Karl Augusts Gate (tel. 11-11-25), is where a lot of Norway—at least its regional handicrafts—comes together in one shop. Its products, in general, are made by skilled individuals who have mastered their craft all over the country, turning out items both modern and traditional. The store is open Monday to Friday from 8:30 a.m. to 4 p.m. (Saturday from 8:45 a.m. to 1 p.m.).

DEPARTMENT STORES: Oslo has strong opinions about where to buy the widest selection of glassware, ceramics, pewter, silver plate, wood, and textiles. Claiming that smaller boutiques tend to charge more, local people usually head for one of the biggest department stores in town, which specializes in unusual accessories for the home, the table, and the kitchen and which might qualify as the biggest outlet of the Hadelands Glassverk (Glassworks) in all of Norway. The establishment is the **Glasmagasinet,** 9 Stortorvet (tel. 11-40-80). It also contains a ground-floor coffeeshop and shopper-oriented restaurants on both the second and third floors.

Steen & Strøm, 23 Kongensgate (tel. 41-68-00), is the largest department store in Norway, a treasure house of hundreds of Nordic bargains—spread out from the ground-floor souvenir shop to the sales departments on the top floors. Look for hand-knitted sweaters, hand-painted wooden dishes reflecting traditional Norwegian art, hand-knitted caps, and pewter dinner plates made from old molds.

NORWEGIAN SOUVENIRS: **William Schmidt,** 41 Karl Johans Gate, was established in 1853 and quickly became a leading purveyor of interesting and unique souvenirs, including items made from whale teeth, pewter (everything from Viking ships to beer goblets), Norwegian dolls in national costumes, woodcarvings (the troll collection is the most outstanding in Oslo), and sealskin items such as moccasins and handbags. The house specializes in hand-knitted cardigans, pullovers, gloves, and caps. Sweaters are made from 100% Norwegian wool which has been mothproofed. The store is open daily from 9 a.m. to 5 p.m. (till 2 p.m. on Saturday).

JEWELRY, ENAMELWARE, AND SILVER: The most outstanding jeweler in Norway, **David-Andersen,** 20 Karl Johans Gate (tel. 41-69-55), distributes those enameled demitasse spoons that many smart shoppers like to take back home with them. These mocca spoons usually are delivered in gift boxes, coming in six assorted colors. Bracelets in sterling silver with enamel are presented in many stunning colors such as turquoise and dark blue. Some have painted flower motifs. The muticolored butterfly pins are another popular item, in sterling silver (gold-plated) with enamel. David-Andersen's collection of Saga silver is inspired by traditional features in Norwegian folklore, combined with the simple beauty of today's design. The Saga jewelry is based on copies of original pieces at present in Oslo's Historical Museum. David-Andersen has revived the old pewter casters' working methods, and now offers for sale an exquisite collection of items in pewter which reflect both high-quality workmanship and artistic design.

PEWTER: Tinnboden, 7 Tordenskioldsgate (tel. 42-24-61). Time was when only kings ate from pewter plates. But today the world can dine on pewter dinnerware, and some of the best available in Oslo is offered at Tinnboden, near the city hall. Hours are daily from 9 a.m. to 4 p.m. (on Saturday until 1 p.m.).

BOUTIQUE: Marjatta Butikk og Galleri, 14 Kongensgate (tel. 42-31-67), one of the best boutiques in Oslo, offers a wide selection of jewelry, textiles, women's wear, glass, pottery, and arts and crafts, based on quality and good design from not only Scandinavia, but many countries all over the world. This shop is open from 9 a.m. to 5 p.m. weekdays (Saturday, to 1 p.m.).

SWEATERS: Oslo Sweater Shop, SAS Hotel Scandinavia, 5 Tullinsgate (tel. 11-29-22). The models for this shop's publicity photos are fair-skinned, blond, and smiling in much the way many of the establishment's customers smile after bringing one of the handcrafted sweaters back to the New World. Peter and Ulla Grusd buy the work of knitters throughout Norway, in all the colors of a Norse forest. Since the sweaters are handmade, it's important to try them on before you buy. The sales staff is helpful and forthright about their advice. In all, you'll find a stock of around 5000 sweaters, one of the best collections in Norway.

BOOKS: Damms Antikvariat, 25 Tollbodgate (tel. 41-04-02), has been a bookseller since 1843. It specializes in both old and rare books, as well as atlases, maps, and prints, the latter dealing heavily with nautical themes. Claes Nyegaard is the director, and he sees that the store is open from 9 a.m. to 4:30 p.m., in summer to 4 p.m. He has yet another store at 14 Eckersbergsgate (tel. 56-45-33).

ANTIQUES AND MODERN ART: Try **Kaare Berntsen,** 12 Universitetsgaten (tel. 20-34-29), one of the best bets for Norwegian antiques and modern art. Among items likely to intrigue are dram bottles from 18th-century Norway as well as illustrated wooden tankards, also from the 18th century. In its department, the

Galleri KB, it shows only contemporary art. Artists are likely to range from a master such as Edvard Munch to one of the younger Norwegian artists of today. The shop and gallery are open Monday to Friday from 9 a.m. to 4 p.m. (on Saturday till 1 p.m.).

Hammerlunds Kunsthandel, 3 Tordenskioldsgate (tel. 42-36-26), is yet another good possibility for the serious antique hunter.

4. Oslo After Dark

Oslovians aren't apologetic about their lack of sparkling nightlife. Apparently, summer nights are to be savored in the out-of-doors—not wasted inside a smoke-filled nightclub. Nevertheless, the tourist may seek—and find—a little action, although nothing naughty. Tame fare: folklore for the less adventurous, a few dancing spots, English-language films. Young people have charted their own nighttime diversions in a few student nightclubs. For simple social gettogethers, beer drinking, and talk, the ever-reigning choice is the milling Students' Grove, near the National Theater.

A NIGHTCLUB COMPLEX: The most complete collection of nightclub facilities in Norway is owned and under the direction of the **Hotel Bristol,** 7 Kristan IV Gate, whose severe stone walls are city landmarks and whose richly upholstered neo-Moorish public rooms have given it the reputation of being the most desirable hotel in the Norwegian capital. It contains no less than five nighttime amusement centers, any one of which might fill your need for distraction in the depths of a cool Norse night. For information, the central switchboard of the hotel (tel. 41-58-40) is the number to call. Each of the nightlife facilities is open every night except Sunday.

The **Library Bar** may be the best spot in the Bristol for watching the comings and goings of a lobby reminiscent of Grand Hotel. You'll be sheltered behind racks and racks of leather-bound books, which you can actually remove and read if you're alone and want to study your Scandinavian diphthongs. The total effect is like being inside a well-furnished private club, and whether you sit near the bar or in one of the lobby's chairs below the ornately carved arches, you'll be able to hear the music from the live pianist as it drifts around the potted palms, stuffed bears, and crystal chandeliers. Beer costs from 30 kroner ($3.60).

El Toro. The entrance is clearly visible from the sidewalk near the main entrance to the hotel. As both the name and the presence of a large statue of a bull near the enormous coatroom might suggest, the decor of this place looks like a cold-climate version of something you'd find on the plains of southern Spain. It combines a popular bar with an intimately lit restaurant and a dance floor near the instruments of a frequently changing live band. This has become one of the most popular places in Oslo for members of the business community, their clients, and their friends to meet. The carpeting, of course, is red and the lighting fixtures Iberian-style wrought iron. Drinks cost between 27 kroner ($3.24) and 48 kroner ($5.76). There is no cover charge other than paying to check your coat, and if you decide to stay for an evening of dining and dancing, your meal will cost around 230 kroner ($27.60). Reservations are suggested, as is conservative dress. Most of the men who come here wear jackets and ties. The establishment is open daily except Sunday from 7 p.m. to 1:30 a.m.

Backstage is the newest club to join the Bristol's collection, and it's by far the most unusual. On Friday and Saturday nights, there's likely to be a line stretching along the street outside, sometimes waiting time running to as much as an hour, so eager are Oslovians to get a look and a feeling for the two-level club. Some of Europe's most popular bands come here to play. The clients on any given night could include Bjorn Borg and Eric Heiden. After you pay the cover charge of 40 kroner ($4.80) and enter, you'll be treated to a view of photographs of Marilyn Monroe and the Marx brothers, some occasionally bizarre and always humorous sculptured heads, kilometers of colored neon tubing, a decorative roulette table, and dozens of cubbyhole seating areas, some of them shaped into circular banquettes that look suspiciously like red-velvet canopy beds. What may be best about this place is that a different musical group will be playing on each of the two levels, each with its own dance floor. (One looks like an assortment of dozens of colored ping pong balls arranged into an illuminated pie, covered with shatterproof glass.)

Overall, you'll find an attractive, well-dressed crowd here. The average age is probably betwen 25 and 45, and the most popular drink is beer, priced from 30 kroner ($3.60) a glass. Of all the clubs at the Bristol, this is my favorite. It even serves dinner under a type of verandah on the uppermost level, if you're hungry. The entrance to Backstage is on a side street, around the corner from the main entrance to the hotel, the Library Bar, the Leopard, and El Toro.

Leopard Club is the Bristol's answer to the interests of the young punk community of Oslo. There's never any live music here, but the disco sounds include the most recently released songs from England and America. The D.J. counts as one of the city's minor celebrities, sitting in lonely isolation above the crowded dance floor. Customers who enjoy a standup beer at the long expanses of bar are not allowed into the Backstage, which is connected by a swinging door, without paying an additional cover charge of 30 kroner ($3.60) on weekdays, 35 kroner ($4.20) on Friday and Saturday. Unlike the other Bristol Hotel clubs, the Leopard is open on Sunday, when entrance is free, and no one particularly cares what the patrons wear. This is without question the least formal of the Bristol's clubs, attracting just about every teenager, no matter how bizarre in appearance, who wants to see and be seen amid the painted leopards and the blood-red decor. It's open from 10 p.m. to 3:30 a.m. seven days a week.

Trafalgar looks like an English pub with a small dance floor near the D.J.'s booth. On crowded nights, the staff opens an upper-level balcony with a separate bar and enough oiled hardwood to outfit a private yacht. On less crowded nights, the conservative clientele stays on the bottom level, trying to navigate through a paneled room which is dramatically lit, disco-style, with flashing colored lights and neon. There's no cover charge here, and beer costs from 30 kroner ($3.60) a glass. Since one of the several entrances is through the hotel lobby, the Trafalgar gives disco exposure to business people unwilling to mingle with the teenagers in the Leopard. The Trafalgar is open from 7 p.m. to 1:30 a.m. daily except Sunday.

DANCING: The best all-year-round, all-around spot for the post-25 set is the **Humla,** 26 Universitetsgaten (tel. 33-23-33), where a live combo plays music for dancing until 2 a.m. You can also order food at night, meals beginning at 100 kroner ($12). Drinks begin at 40 kroner ($4.80). Late arrivals may have a problem getting across the threshold on jammed-tight weekends. Closed Sunday.

Loftet, 26 Stortingsgaten, entrance on Roald Amundsens Gate (tel. 41-90-60), which was opened late in 1977, is a disco in the Hotel Continental, with a unique setting. Five small rooms were built as a loft, each with a different decor. You will find the bar-loft, the dancing-loft, the small-loft, the play-loft with billiards, and the nice-loft. The fuly licensed Loftet requires its patrons to be at least 22 years of age. A half liter of pils costs 30 kroner ($3.60). Expect to pay 30 kroner ($3.60) cover charge on Friday and Saturday nights. On weekends you must arrive at the door by 8 p.m., or else face an hour wait in line just to get in. The club is closed Sunday and Monday.

Riddarhallen, 5 Torgatan (tel. 42-72-68), is one of the leading dance halls of Oslo, advertising (and living up to its promise) "nonstop action every night."

The theme, as the name suggests, is that of a knights' drinking hall from the Middle Ages. The decor, in the vicinity of the Cathedral of Oslo, is one of heraldry, with suits of armor, helmets, and swords. Both disco music and live bands play for the throngs of young Norwegians attracted here at night. On Monday and Tuesday, there is no admission charge. However, you'll pay from 15 kroner ($1.80) on midweek nights and from 25 kroner ($3) to 30 kroner ($3.60) on weekend nights. Sometimes, especially on Friday and Saturday night, there is a long line waiting to get in. You can order meals or else settle for a pizza, costing from 35 kroner ($4.20) and a beer from 35 kroner also.

Bonanza Bar, at the Grand Hotel, 31 Karl Johans Gate (tel. 42-93-90), is the very crowded bar, restaurant, and disco inside the vaulted cellars of the hotel. After checking your coat in the upstairs vestibule, you descend a stairway into a candlelit series of rooms where each has been carefully designed as to its purpose—for eating, drinking, or dancing. The D.J., whose music influences an over-35 crowd of jacketed businessmen or conservatively dressed women, is amenable to playing almost any request the crowd may make. There's a 30-krone ($3.60) entrance fee collected every Monday through Thursday and a 35-krone ($4.20) fee every Friday and Saturday between 8 p.m. and 2:30 a.m. The last call for drinks is strictly maintained at 1:30 a.m. Once inside, drinks cost from 30 kroner ($3.60) each. The place is closed on Sunday.

Another place for young people in Oslo is the old student club, **Kroa,** 22 Storgata (tel. 42-53-73). It is still in existence and features crowded dancing to disco music every night except Sunday and Monday. The energetic crowd here is aged 18 to 25, and you'd better get there early (7:30 p.m.) if you want to get in Admission is 20 kroner ($2.40) weekdays, rising to 30 kroner ($3.60) on weekends. Drinks begin at 35 kroner ($4.20).

A more modern dance spot is the **Château Neuf,** 7 Slemdalsveien (tel. 69-37-94), Oslo's student club. You'll find first of all a disco, but also a grill and pizza bar and a concert hall. Usally Scandinavian acts perform in the disco and in the grill bar, activity being confined to Friday and Saturday during the school term. Beer costs 25 kroner ($3), soft drinks 10 kroner ($1.20), and hamburgers 10 kroner also. The place is open from 8 p.m. to 1 a.m. Concerts are frequently arranged in the Château Neuf's concert hall, with artists such as Eurythmics, Culture Club, Nina Hagen, Pretenders, Clash, and other British or American acts. An evening here is likely to cost from 85 kroner ($10.20) to 175 kroner ($21). Take the subway to Majorstua.

For the older crowd, my recommendation is **Jegerhallen** (appropriately translated as "Hunting Hall"), 38 Akersgata (tel. 33-68-20), across the street from the *Aftenposten* newspaper headquarters. The age range here is from 25 to 45, and there are lots of single men and women. Dancing every night is in a style reminiscent of an old German bierstube (beer hall). You can eat a middag here for 60 kroner ($7.20) to 80 kroner ($9.60), or just have a beer for 35 kroner ($4.20) and pizza from 35 kroner also.

READER'S DISCO SELECTION: "**Club Remember,** 10 Karl Johans Gate (tel. 42-96-52) is a great disco only one block from the central train station. The club is on the third and fourth floors and is open daily from 8 p.m. to 3 a.m. There is a 20-krone ($2.40) to 40-krone ($4.80) cover charge. The minimum age to enter is 23, but most of the crowd seems to be 25 to 30. This singles' disco is filled with friendly Norwegians and many travelers, all of whom love to dance. We went there several times, enjoying it more each time" (Joanna Ficaro, Cambridge, Mass.).

LIVE MUSIC: Gamle Christiania, 1 Grensen (tel. 33-56-20), is a popular nightspot whose entrance lies around the corner from a previously recommended restaurant, the Stortorvets Gjaestgiveri. Both establishments are contained within the same historic brick building, although the Gamle Christiania offers live country/western music, while its neighbor features occasional jazz. In this establishment, the stage area is at the far end of a baronial sitting room whose banquettes are arranged like the seats for some dignified governing body. The enthusiastic crowd which comes here, however, is far from being overly digni-fied, especially when the music begins after 8:45. If you drop in for lunch, a cafeteria-style collection of sandwiches or snacks such as warm bacon quiche are offered for 25 kroner ($3) each. A medium-size glass of beer costs 32 kroner ($3.84) all day and night, although there's a cover charge imposed in the evening of 20 kroner ($2.40) on week nights, 35 kroner ($4.20) on Friday and Saturday. Full meals are offered if you wish.

Rosenkrantz Hot House, 158 Pilestredet (tel. 20-22-27), is the place for jazz, offering live music all week. Maybe not the greatest names in jazz appear here, but it's "hot" nevertheless. It has a pleasant, comfortable atmosphere where you can order good, hearty food and drink. It's open for lunch from noon, but after 8 p.m. when the music begins, there's an entrance fee of 10 kroner ($1.20) on Sunday, Monday, and Tuesday, rising to 35 kroner ($4.20) to 50 kroner ($6) Wednesday through Saturday. It is open daily until 2 a.m. from May 15 to September 15. Otherwise, it closes at 1 a.m. Monday through Thursday and at 2 a.m. on weekends during the winter months.

A PUB: Andy's Pub, 8 Stortingsgaten (unlisted phone). Once inside this English-style pub, you can stand on any of three sides of a central bar and quaff as much beer as you like for 30 kroner ($3.60) a glass. Above the well-polished bar, you may find the currency of even the most obscure countries encased within plexiglass "sandwiches." The place is one of the most crowded in the downtown area so it's not exactly quiet, but if you're with someone you like, it can be a lot of fun. It's open from 10 a.m. to 11 p.m. daily except Sunday, when the hours are from noon to 11 p.m.

CINEMAS: American or British import films are shown in English, with Norwegian subtitles. Patrons line up at the cinemas for tickets in the same way that Americans might frequent Broadway shows. Tickets are sold for specific performances only. Many theaters have three showings nightly, at 5, 7, and 9, but the big road show specials usually are shown only once in an evening, generally at 7:30. One of the most centrally located cinemas, showing first-run features, is the domed **Colosseum,** 8 Fridtjof Nansensvei (tel. 46-39-60).

CULTURAL ACTIVITIES: The landmark **Nationaltheatret** (National Theater), 15 Stortingsgaten (tel. 41-27-10), the upper end of the Students' Grove, is closed in summer. But it opens in August—so may be of interest to off-season theater-lovers who want to hear Ibsen and Bjørnson in the original. Seats range from a low of 50 kroner ($6) to a high of 75 ($9). Norse theater people haven't discovered Broadway prices, primarily because theaters are partially supported by the state. Avant-garde productions get a fair trial at the new **Amfiscenen** in the same building.

In summer, there are concerts in the courtyard of the **Vigeland Museum,** 32 Nobelsgate (take streetcar 2). Performances are at 7 p.m. on Wednesday, 1 p.m. on Sunday.

At the **Munch Museum,** 53 Tøyengata, concerts are held on Tuesday at 8 p.m. See *Oslo This Week* for details.

The **Norwegian National Opera** (Den Norske Opera), 23C Storgaten (tel.

42-94-75), has a September-to-May program of opera, operetta, and ballet. Tickets range in price from 30 kroner ($3.60) to 120 kroner ($14.40).

Kunstnernes Hus, 17 Wergelandsveien (tel. 60-74-23), is the "Artists' House" of Oslo. It's open from 10 a.m. to 6 p.m. Tuesday to Saturday and from noon to 6 p.m. on Sunday (always closed on Monday). Not only can you view some of the latest exhibitions of contemporary Norwegian and international art, but you can meet and talk with the local artists (all of whom speak English, at least all those I've encountered).

On the first floor is a snackbar where the conversation is lively and the companions fun. In the galleries upstairs the temporary exhibitions of contemporary art are displayed. The government sponsorship doesn't inhibit the nature of the art. I've found much of it quite "revolutionary," or at least provocative.

Students' Grove: Paris has its Champs-Élysées, Rome its Via Veneto—and Oslo its Students' Grove (Studenter Lunden), near the National Theater on Karl Johans Gate. A narrow, tree-shaded park, the grove has promenades with benches on either side. In an atmosphere like a musical-comedy beer garden, tables and chairs are set out, some under parasols. Soft drinks, tea, coffee, beer, meals, and other refreshments are served. But talk is the main fare.

Club 7, 15 Munkedamsveien (tel. 33-37-32), in the same building as the Oslo Concert Hall, is the spearhead of the younger people of Oslo (ages 20 to 40) and the largest music center in town—a club featuring rock music, jazz, folk singing, poetry recitations, avant-garde theatrical productions, experimental films and opportunities for the exchange of ideas. It was created in 1963 by Attila Horvath, a native Hungarian transplanted to Norwegian soil. The club has today expanded into full cultural bloom. The building is designed like an almost indestructible concrete and glass cube, with dramatic open spaces for sculpture and painting exhibitions, several metal catwalks stretching toward gallery-like views of a lower floor, and the kind of undistinguished furniture you find in the student center of a large university. But for any visiting artist or music lover, this place should be a must on an itinerary, particularly since the food served cafeteria-style in the street-level restaurant is cheap, plentiful, and good.

Between 1 and 8 p.m. (unless the hours are extended because of a concert in the lower level), the sophisticated and charming bar manager, Anka Ness, will describe the upcoming functions as well as serve steaming plates of the daily special. Long, well-filled sandwiches cost 23 kroner ($2.76). Downstairs is an enormous low-ceilinged room which can hold as many as 900 concert-goers who appreciate some of the trendiest musical groups passing through Scandinavia. Live music is presented in the lower level almost daily from 8 p.m. till 2 a.m. On Friday and Saturday, there's often live music in both the upstairs restaurant and the downstairs bar.

If you plan to stay in Oslo for a while, it might pay to purchase a membership in the club, since the cover charges are somewhat cheaper if you do. On Tuesday, Wednesday, and Thursday, members pay 25 kroner ($3), while nonmembers are charged 40 kroner ($4.80). On Friday and Saturday, these prices rise to 30 kroner ($3.60) for members, 45 kroner ($5.40) for non-members. Once you're inside, you'll be charged 30 kroner ($3.60) for an export beer. The lower level is usually closed on Monday unless there's a special (well-publicized) concert.

ONE-DAY EXCURSIONS

The environs of Oslo offer an array of one-day excursions. Those who want to seek out the best will head south for an old fortress town, former whaling ports, and remains of the Viking days. The chief center is Fredrikstad in Østfold. A trip here can be combined—in one day—with visits to the ports of Sandefjord and Tønsberg by crossing over the ferry from Moss to Horten, then traveling south. Finally, Lillehammer, to the north of Oslo, in "Peer Gynt" country, is the chief center for those who want to get a preview of the rugged mountains and scenic grandeur of eastern Norway, or who want to go skiing in winter.

5. Fredrikstad

Straddling the banks of the Glomma River is this split-personality town: a modern industrial section on the west bank is linked by a half-mile-long bridge to a unique fortified Old Town with turreted ramparts, a drawbridge, and moat. However, if you're walking, the most feasible way to reach the Old Town is by ferry across the river, costing 2 kroner (24¢) each way. The ferry plies back and forth continuously, and is utilized by a large number of local people with bicycles. The departure point is about four blocks from the railroad station. To reach it, simply follow the crowd out of the main door of the station. Make an obvious turn to the left and continue down to the shore of the river.

Fredrikstad, easily reached by express train or car from Oslo, lies about 60 miles south of the capital in the historic section of Østfold, near the Swedish border.

In recent years Fredrikstad has become a major tourist center, thanks to the old town and its fortifications. Most such defenses have been demolished in Norway in the name of progress, but in Fredrikstad, the 17th-century fortress and its precincts have been preserved. Take a guided tour while in the old town to visit the church, the museum, and the glass-blowing and textile-printing operations belonging to the arts and crafts organization, **PLUS**, a society of artists and artisans. Tours are at 9:30 and 11 a.m. and at 12:30 and 2 p.m. Monday to Friday; at 11:30 a.m. and 1:30 p.m. Saturday; and at 12:30 and 2:30 p.m. from June 1 to August 15. The glass-blowing and textile-printing workshops are closed on Saturday and Sunday, however. The tour, taking just about an hour, costs 12 kroner ($1.44). Afterward you can buy locally made handicrafts at one of the sales centers.

Inside the fortified town are two good restaurants. Outside its gates are a modern youth hostel and the 17th-century **Kongsten Fort** (secret passages, dank underground chambers). But the west bank is the spot for other restaurants and my major budget accommodations.

Coming from Denmark? A ferry from Fredrikshavn, Denmark, plies its way to Fredrikstad in about eight hours.

STAYING OVER: Fredrikstad offers limited but suitable accommodations to fit most purses.

The **Victoria,** 3 Turngate (tel. 11-165), is an attractive, modern hostelry with 59 well-furnish rooms, most of which have private baths or showers and toilets. Singles cost from 220 kroner ($26.40), while doubles go for 330 kroner ($39.60) upward. The tariffs include breakfast.

Hotel City, 44–46 Nygaardsgate (tel. 17-750), has pleasant, modern bedrooms, all with private baths, toilets, TV, and video. Singles are priced from 385 kroner ($46.20) and doubles from 540 kroner ($64.80), breakfast included. In summer, from June 23 to the end of August, prices are a bit cheaper.

Britannia Hotel, 4 Agentgate (tel. 11-131), near the docks and the center of town, is a former large private home (with a later addition) that has been successfully converted into a modest hotel. Year round, its bathless doubles with water basins cost from 280 kroner ($33.60); singles go for 210 kroner ($25.20). The front entrance is deceivingly shabby, but it picks up inside, despite ill-matched furnishings. The dining room, painted white, with ornate wood paneling, suggests faded glory, but still offers good meals.

Fredrikstad Motel and Camping, on the outskirts of the Old Town (tel. 20-315), is a two-in-one combination: a rambling, one-story motel, plus a camping site. The motel, built in the American style with staggered car spaces in front of each unit, charges 175 kroner ($21) for a double, 230 kroner ($27.60) for a three-bedded room, and 390 kroner ($34.80) for four beds. The rooms contain water basins. Breakfast is offered for 35 kroner ($4.20). Both the motel and camping site are within walking distance of Kongsten Fort and near an open-air swimming pool. The place is open from June 1 till September 1.

WHERE TO EAT: The best all-around dining choice is an old inn, **Tamburen,** 78 Ferjeportgate, in the Old Town on a tiny plaza. A well-preserved, two-story brick building, it features dining on two levels: the downstairs is simple and rustic with tables outside for refreshments, while the upper level is formal with crystal and candlelight. The food is well prepared. Many hot dishes are served, and there is an impressive selection of open-face sandwiches. Traditional Norwegian cooking, such as grilled pork chops with cabbage and parsley potatoes, is offered. Meals cost from 100 kroner ($12).

On the west side, there are several restaurants, including those at the previously recommended Victoria Hotel and Hotel City. Both places offer lunches for 95 kroner ($11.40) and dinners from 120 kroner ($14.40).

6. Tønsberg

Norway's oldest town was founded a year before King Harald the Fairhaired united the country in 872. In 1971, Tønsberg celebrated its birthday: it was 11 centuries old. Bordering the western bank of the Oslofjord, lying 64 miles south of Oslo, Tønsberg still maintains a lot of well-preserved old clapboard houses, making it an interesting stopover. Once Vikings walked its streets, and it has been the coronation site of what one Norwegian called "a brace of bold kings." Svend Foyn, the man who invented modern whaling and seal hunting, was born here. **Slottsfjellet,** a huge hill fortress, is called the Acropolis of Norway. This is one of the Nordic countries' largest collections of ruins of early fortifications. From the lookout tower, built in 1888, a striking view of the surrounding country is possible. The major attraction is the—

VESTFOLD FOLK MUSEUM: At the entrance to Tønsberg, this museum contains many treasures related to the once-great whaling industry, as well as reminders that Viking chieftains roamed this Vestfold district. One of the chief sights is the skeleton of the blue whale, the biggest animal the world has ever known (sometimes weighing up to 150 tons). It's easy to see how Jonah might have created a spacious modern living room in its belly. In the main exhibit room are large collections of model ships and seafaring relics, such as figureheads. On the lower level is an archeological section with the late medieval ecclesiastical and profane carvings from Tønsberg. There is also a real Viking ship displayed, the *Klåstad* from Tjölling, built in or about A.D. 800. Another exhibit in a nearby building shows the city life in Vestfold from 1880 to 1960, with trade, industry, social life, politics, and costumes being depicted. On the lower level are iron sculptures from the mills in Vestfold as well as traditional Norwegian furnishings.

In the rural section you can visit the Vestfold Farm, which includes a 1600 Hynne House, a timbered barn from Bøen, a storehouse from Fadum (with the characteristic apron), the Heierstadloft (oldest preserved timbered building in Vestfold, circa 1350), a smithy with charcoal shed, a grain-drying house, a mountain farmstead, and two cow-sheds. The old rural culture of Vestfold is well preserved. Admission is 5 kroner (60¢) During the summer season, the museum is open from 10 a.m. to 7 p.m. on weekdays, from 1 to 7 p.m. on Sunday and holidays.

In the center of these attractions, you can have lunch at a real mountain farmstead—a typical collation, with rømmegrøt (porridge made with sour cream) and other farm foods. The area is also perfect for a picnic.

Tønsberg is not just the Slottsfjellet. As Scandinavia's oldest town, it has a fascinating historical walk. The old Nordbyen is a preserved area, with all the houses restored to their original look. You should also see Fjerdingen, which is near the mountain farmstead. Charming old, restored houses stand on a street where the residents have established their own preservation group.

Tønsberg was also a Hanseatic town during the Middle Ages. It was originally established at the harbor. Here the citizens lived and worked. Some of these houses have been restored in the typical Hanseatic style.

Tønsberg, although small and concentrated, can be divided into two parts: the historian area and the shopping center, where you will find the marketplace.

WHERE TO STAY: The Hotel Klubben, 49 Nedre Langgaten (tel. 15-111), is in the center of town, overlooking the harbor. The comfortable, well-furnished bedrooms—95 in all—have views of the park, harbor, and sea. A first-class double costs 700 kroner ($84) with full bath. Singles go for 485 kroner ($58.20). Breakfast is included in the rates. The hotel has attractive restaurants, bistros, discos, and cocktail bars, as well as its own garage for the vehicles of guests.

The **Grand Hotel**, Møllegaten (te. 12-203), is also in the center of town, but its prices are more suitable for budget travelers. It charges 500 kroner ($60) for its staidly comfortable double rooms with bath. Singles with bath go for 375 kroner ($45). A Norwegian buffet breakfast is included in these tariffs. The dining room, conservatively appropriate with brass chandeliers and carved chairs, serves à la carte lunches and dinners, costing around 120 kroner ($14.40).

If you don't want to be in the center, you might consider the **Borge Hotel** (tel. 23-801) on the island of Husøy in the Oslo Fjord, about six kilometers from Tønsberg. The welcome is hearty, and the scenery is attractive. In summer, there is a bathing beach in use, along with a private garden and tennis court with a swimming pool (it's heated with salt sea water). It's possible to arrange fishing and boating trips. The hotel receives guests from June 1 to October, charging 150 kroner ($18) to 170 kroner ($20.40) in a single, from 195 kroner ($23.40) to 240 kroner ($28.80) in a double. Full board ranges from 210 kroner ($25.20) per person daily. Ordered separately, a main meal costs from 75 kroner ($9) and up. There are bus connections to the railway station at Tønsberg.

WHERE TO EAT: The most popular eating places are either at the above-mentioned **Grand,** or across the street at **Håndverkeren,** 6 Kammengaten, where you can enjoy meals in an L-shaped dining room and an open paved courtyard. I recently dined here, ordering a big plate of the famed Norwegian hash, complete with a green vegetable and mashed potatoes, for 65 kroner ($7.80). But the best buy is a three-course luncheon, 65 kroner also. Housed in a frame building, the restaurant is on a small triangular area. Umbrellas offer daytime shade, while garlands of colored lights make it festive at night, attracting Tønsberg youth.

READER'S RESTAURANT SUGGESTIONS: "A restaurant with fair prices is **Vagteren**, in an old restored house, done in typical country style. The prices are around 65 kroner ($7.80) to 100 kroner ($12), and I promise you to get really full. Two rather cozy pizza restaurants are **Kong Svenne** and **Pizza Hi-Hi**, both with a nice atmosphere. **Fregatten Restaurant**, in the center like the others I have mentioned, is the place to go if you have decided to spend the evening dining" (Ruth Severenson, Chicago, Ill.).

7. Sandefjord

"Where have all the blue whales gone?" is the sad lament of Norway's attractive old whaling town. "Gone to blubber factories every one," to paraphrase a song. So many Japanese and Russian Ahabs have gotten in on the act that all of Moby Dick's children are threatened with extinction. In the autumn of 1968, the industrialist Anders Jahre announced that Norway would no longer send expeditions to the Antarctic. As reported in *Time,* "When Jahre tied up his factory ship, *Kosmos IV,* it marked the end of an enterprise that made millionaires out of owners and national heroes out of the top gunners who manned the harpoons."

Sandefjord hasn't relied on blubber for some time. It has built up the third-largest merchant fleet in Norway. In addition, the small town is fast rising as a summer resort. Sandefjord lies about two hours' drive from Oslo, but is also easily reached by one of five daily express trains from the capital.

Many are drawn to **Commander Christensen's Whaling Museum** at 39 Museumsgaten (tel. 63-251). The museum has a replica of the mighty blue whale (its tongue weighs 3½ tons). Old whalers work here as guides, relating stories about the catches and the exotic stuffed animals captured on the expeditions. Near the marketplace, the great Whaling Monument attracts, with water from the fountains splashing over the whale attacking a boat. Visiting hours are from 11 a.m. to 4 p.m. daily from May to October (in winter, Sunday only). Admission is 10 kroner ($1.20).

ACCOMMODATIONS: Hotel Kong Carl, 9 Torggaten (tel. 63-117), is as clean, comfortable, and inviting as a country tavern. It offers well-outfitted doubles with private bath for 340 kroner ($40.80) to 425 kroner ($51); singles also with bath cost from 230 kroner ($27.60) to 325 kroner ($39). These prices include a buffet-style Norwegian breakfast. The management is pleasant, the food is good —and the hotel is in the center of Sandefjord. Oldtimers like to come here for an authentic Norwegian meal ordered from an à la carte menu.

8. Lillehammer

A three-hour ride north of Oslo, past blue waters and fields of farmland and larkspur, delivers us to Norway's leading resort. The holiday center is easily reached by rail and is accessible by automobile, even though the road is unpaved in parts. You have a choice of eight trains leaving Oslo daily. The faster one takes two hours and 20 minutes, the slower one making the trip in three hours.

Surrounded by mountains, Lillehammer is at the head of Lake Mjøsa. The pine-scented air is so great that many Europeans make this their holiday center at vacation time; but in-a-hurry foreigners skip in and out of town to see the open-air museum, one of the finest collections of folk art and culture in Scandinavia.

Nobel Prize winner Sigrid Undset resided in the environs of Lillehammer. Mrs. Undset's daughter-in-law lives in her former home, Bjerkebaek, which is closed to the public.

I'll look first at the major sights for those visiting for the day, then survey the accommodations.

THE SANDVIG COLLECTIONS: At Maihaugen (May Hill) (tel. 50-135) is a museum of peasant culture, containing old farmsteads, heirlooms, and native art. It was created by a visionary dentist, Anders Sandvig, an antique dealer in the days when it was considered idiosyncratic rather than fashionable to collect regional art. Assembled on a hill are 150 buildings (more than 30,000 exhibits), ranging from manor farms to the cottage of the poorest yeoman worker. The houses, reassembled here and furnished in 17th- to 18th-century styles, came from all over the Gudbrandsdal Valley. See, in particular, the Garmo Stave Church and the Old Workshops. The latter, housed in a modern building, cover a wide range: gunsmith and wood-engraver's shop to a glass furnace. During the summer the museum, charging 15 kroner ($1.80) for admission, is open from 10 a.m. to 4 p.m. In the winter the Old Workshops remain open from 11 a.m. to 2 p.m.

ART MUSEUM: Lillehammer Art Museum *(Lillehammer Bys Maler-isamling)*, Stortorget (tel. 51-944), with about 650 works of art is one of the most important galleries in Norway. A visit here gives you an excellent impression of Norwegian art from the beginning of the 19th century up until today. During the season, from September to April, lectures and various music performances are given here. The museum is open weekdays from 10 a.m. to 3 p.m., Sunday from noon to 4 p.m., and closed Monday. Admission is 10 kroner ($1.20), half-price for children.

FOR THE CHILDREN: Øyer Gjestegard's model town **Lilleputthammer,** is 10½ miles north of Lillehammer. It is a miniature of the shopping street, Storgaten, and consists of 62 miniature houses of turn-of-the-century style. Some are populated with mechanical dolls in old-fashioned costumes. In one of the houses, children can play, paint, and draw and in another is a small moving picture theater. A mini-train goes through the park, which has play areas for very small children and ponies to ride, plus a cafeteria and gift shop. There's a carnival for children on Sunday. It's open from mid-June to mid-August from 10 a.m. to 6 p.m., costing 25 kroner ($3).

Hunderfossen Playland, about 7½ miles north of Lillehammer, has a 40-foot troll at the gate to welcome visitors. There are various activities for both children and adults and lots of space just to roam around. It's open from mid-June to mid-August from 9 a.m. to 8 p.m. Admission is 25 kroner ($3).

TRANSPORT MUSEUM: Norway's only vehicle museum, showing the development of this method of transportation from the first sledges and wagons to the car of today, is the **Museum of Norwegian Historical Vehicles.** It's open from 10 a.m. to 6 p.m. weekdays from mid-June to mid-August; from 10 a.m. to 2 p.m. from September to mid-June; and on Saturday and Sunday from 10 a.m. to 4 p.m. Admission is 20 kroner ($2.40) for adults, half-price for children.

VARIETY PROGRAMS: During the peak of the summer season, usually June 20 to August 20, the tourist bureau schedules several excursions. Included are such activities as a visit to the Maihaugen Open-Air Museum, or an excursion on Lake Mjøsa on board the *White Swan of Lake Mjøsa,* a 128-year-old paddle steamer. Drop in at the tourist bureau at 56 Storgata (tel. 51-098) for a list of activities.

SKIING: After a fall lull, Lillehammer comes out of hibernation in December and starts stirring up activities for its winter sports season. Ideal as a center for both professional and neophyte skiers, Lillehammer has a 307-foot slope for the show-offs, but a smaller jump suitable for amateurs. Skiers have relative luxury in Lillehammer, with its long ski lifts that whisk sports people 1500 feet above sea level up the slalom slope at Lillehammer Ski Center. Daily skiing classes are offered at the Lillehammer Ski School; several cross-country tours are held weekly. More than 250 miles of marked skiing trails are packed by machines.

In addition, Lillehammer has a leading admission-free skating rink (closed Saturday but otherwise open from 11 a.m. to 9 p.m., except on Sunday, when it shuts down at 5). All of this activity is supplemented in winter by festivals, folklore nights, and ski races.

At Follebu

Only 12 miles from Lillehammer, in Follebu, is **Aulestad,** the home of Norway's Nobel Prize winning poet, Bjornstjerne Bjornson (1832–1910). He purchased the farm in 1875 and with the help of his wife, Karoline, turned it into an attractive home. He was living here when he learned of his selection for the Nobel laurels in 1903. Now a national museum, the home is open from September to May from 11 a.m. to 3 p.m.; from June to August from 10 a.m. to 4 p.m., and in July from 10 a.m. to 6 p.m. Admission is 6 kroner (72¢) for adults, 3 kroner (36¢) for children.

WHERE TO STAY: Lillehammer is well equipped to handle an influx of visitors either in winter or summer. Prices remain comparable for both seasons.

The Budget Range

Breiseth Hotel, 5 Jernbanegaten (tel. 50-060), a block from the tourist office, is undistinguished architecturally (gray cement), but it warms up considerably inside, attracting a basically Norwegian clientele (mayors of small villages, business people, and artists). The walls of the two living rooms, foyer, and staircase are lined with original paintings, apparently left by artists who painted for their supper. The bedrooms, redecorated and modernized, are comfortable. Bathless doubles range in price from 285 kroner ($34.20). Singles pay 150 kroner ($18). These tariffs include a large Norwegian breakfast. The public furnishings are a mixture of mahogany and rosewood. Good meals are served in the dining room, with its Queen Anne oak chairs.

Longva House, 6 Kirkegaten (tel. 50-580), is a private home run as a pension by two sisters, who come from an old Norwegian family of creative artists. The pension consists of two Dutch-roofed wooden houses, surrounded by a large hillside garden. The sisters offer bed and breakfast for 125 kroner ($15) per person. Most of the homey bedrooms—some with sitting areas—are furnished with sofas, armchairs, and coffee tables; some have balconies. The artistry of the family is reflected in the natural textures: the handmade implements, and the antiques that are scattered throughout the house. In the main living room is a small version of the typical raised hearth, where a fire burns brightly most of the year.

Bellevue Sportell og Helseheim (tel. 50-400) stands on wooded grounds on the outskirts of town, convenient for ski trails and footpaths. It's a popular, homelike, friendly place for cross-country skiers, hikers, and young-minded travelers of any age. From the front you have a view of Lake Mjøsa and the forested hills in the distance. Sportell, incidentally, is a new Scandinavian name for pensions serving "sporty" travelers. Beds are available from 75 kroner ($9) per night.

Dølaheimen Hotell & Kafeteria, 3 Jernbanegt (tel. 50-430), is a band-boxy modern hotel and cafeteria, standing right by the railway and bus station in the center of Lillehammer. Built in 1968, it is usually heavily booked in July and for the first part of August, so reservations are important. The receptionist speaks English and does much to make a guest's stay here pleasant. An informal, family-type atmosphere prevails, and children are welcome. The rooms are sleek, functional, and comfortable. Five family rooms, each containing three or four beds and a shower and toilet, are rented at a rate of 340 kroner ($40.80). The more expensive double rooms with shower and toilet go for 295 kroner ($35.40), and singles pay 85 kroner ($22.20). On the ground floor is a large cafeteria with air conditioning and a separate room for nonsmokers. The cafeteria was renovated in 1984. On the second floor are the bedrooms as well as the sitting rooms and a TV lounge.

Ersgård (tel. 50-684) is a pleasant but simple family-style hotel just on the outskirts of town, sitting high atop a Norwegian mountain which overlooks not only the resort but the largest lake in the country, Mjøsa. If you have a car, it's far preferable to stay here than at some of the dreary concrete piles around the station. Bedrooms are modest but adequately furnished. The cheapest way to stay here is to get a single without bath, costing from 150 kroner ($18); however, singles with shower go for 210 kroner ($15.20). Bathless doubles are priced at 225 kroner ($27), rising to 330 kroner ($39.60) with private shower. For 45 kroner ($5.40), you'll be served a typical Norwegian breakfast, a buffet with a tempting assortment of jams, along with cheese (even goat), many types of Norwegian herring, cold cuts, fresh bread, boiled eggs, a choice of cereal, and, naturally, coffee, tea, milk, or juice. The cookery is plain; I found nothing badly done. A complete lunch or dinner will cost from 85 kroner ($10.20) to 100 kroner ($12).

A Summer Hotel

Smestad Turistheim og Motell, 14 Smestadveien (tel. 50-987), is occupied by students during term-time, but otherwise accepts transient guests from June 10 to August 20. The summer hotel, really a student dormitory, stands on E6, about two kilometers north from the center of Lillehammer. The bed-and-breakfast rate is from 175 kroner ($21) per person. Each of the well-furnished 117 rooms contains a private bath with toilet. There are also 25 complete apartments, consisting of a bedroom, sitting room, kitchen, shower, and toilet, as well as equipment for self-catering. On the premises is a cafeteria as well as a TV room. There's plenty of parking.

A Modern Youth Hostel

Birkebeiner'n Turistcenter (tel. 51-994), is on hillside grounds near the foot of the ski lift, within walking distance of the town. Built in the old wooden-frame style, its central part is painted barn red but its other wings are contrasty buttercup yellow. It accommodates 88 hostelers, mostly four in a room, all accommodations with hot and cold running water. The cost is 85 kroner ($10.20) for bed and breakfast. Lunch or dinner costs from 55 kroner ($6.60). To stay here, you must have an international hostel membership card. The wood-paneled lounges are spacious, cheerful, and comfortable, with a corner fireplace where logs burn on cold days. The hostel, open December 26 to April 17 and June 1 to September 15, attracts skiers in winter, hikers and mountain climbers in summer (no age limit). An outdoor swimming pool adjoins the hotel.

WHERE TO STAY ON THE OUTSKIRTS: Lillehammer is so established as a resort it is surrounded by satellite mountain centers. Those with cars might want to anchor in the wilderness at my favorite spot outside Lillehammer, about 14 miles north at the **Rustad Fjellstue** in Sjusjøen (tel. 63-408). Built in a rustic log-and-timber style, the chalet is on the edge of a lake (there's a dock for swimming and boats) and surrounded by rugged fir trees and private grounds. There's horseback riding in summer months. Guest stay here on a half-board rate of 175 kroner ($21) in summer (based on a three-day stay). Many of the well-furnished bedrooms have views of the lake or mountains. More than half of them have private showers and toilets (all come equipped with hot and cold running water). The living room is furnished with antiques. In winter, the younger crowd gravitates to a den for dancing to music by a three-piece band. Country-style meals are served.

DINING AT MAIHAUGEN: The tourist for the day should head for the **Kirkestuen Cafeteria** (tel. 50-135), in an old countryside inn on a hillside, among the ancient buildings of the folk museum. Traditional Norwegian dishes cost about 55 kroner ($6.60). A wide selection of open-face sandwiches is also offered, going for 30 kroner ($3.60) to 5 kroner ($6).

9. The Peer Gynt Road

This road is so called because it takes you right into the heart of the Peer Gynt country, where for centuries the inhabitants have cultivated the soil of sunny hillsides. Henrik Ibsen came this way when he was researching what was to become a masterpiece, *Peer Gynt,* which was published in 1867 and set to music by Edvard Grieg later in the century. Ibsen based his tale, in part, on the exploits of one Per (spelled with only one *e),* a real-life Norwegian folk hero noted for his exploits such as riding on the backs of reindeer at breakneck speed.

In Gudrandsdal (Gudrands Valley), you can travel the route and experience the same sense of adventure and contact with nature that bewitched the original hero. You can see the mountains of Rondane, Dovrefjell, and Jotunheimen spread around the horizon of this unspoiled bit of Norwegian countryside, with its gentle hills, desolate mountains, old farmsteads, fish-filled lakes, wild game, and alpine flowers. The grave or Per Gynt Hågå, the Peer Gynt prototype, and the district where he lived near Vinstra, at the north end of the valley are visited by thousands of pilgrims every year. Along the road, you'll find the first-class Peer Gynt hotels, many good small hotels, mountain lodges, and holiday farms.

FOOD AND LODGING AT PEER GYNT HOTELS: Gausdal **Høifjellshotell** at Gausdal (tel. 28-500). The central core of this rambling hotel is one of the oldest in this part of Norway, although with its many additions and renovations, it looks fairly modern. On the premises are facilities for tennis, swimming, downhill and cross-country skiing, horseback riding, and hill climbing. Miles of trails surround the hotel, which includes a sauna and a recently constructed pool. This is especially popular as a ski center in winter. Clients take the train to the Tretten station, some 10 miles from the hotel, to which owners Lise and Andreas Smith-Erichsen will send a hotel car for the arrival of guests. In summer, bed-and-breakfast rates range from 300 kroner ($36) for a single to 500 kroner ($60) in a double. Lunch or dinner costs about 120 kroner ($14.40) per person. In winter, because of the popularity of skiing, full pension bookings are required for a minimum stay of five nights. Full board costs from 450 kroner ($54) per person per day.

Dalseter Høyfjellshotell at Dalseter (tel. 99-910) is a contemporary hotel set on a hillside overlooking a forested wilderness against a backdrop of mountains. Its design includes a central white-walled core flanked with symmetrical red-brick wings, each turned to permit the best possible view. On the premises is a warmly contemporary dining room with curved rows of big windows, an indoor swimming pool, a gymnasium, an intricate network of well-marked hiking or skiing trails, fishing and riding facilities, and evening dance music. Although the hotel attracts many families and their children, dark jackets are the requested attire for men during the winter evenings, when a well-prepared cuisine contributes to the ambience. In summer, singles rent for from 250 kroner ($30) to 300 kroner ($36), with doubles going for from 420 kroner ($50.40) to 460 kroner ($55.20). In winter, the owners, Elso and Erik Gillebo, require full pension and a minimum stopover of five days, during which period daily per-person rates range from 380 kroner ($45.60) to 420 kroner ($50.40).

Fefor Høifjellshotell at Fefor (tel. 90-099) is blessed with one of the most interesting façades of any hotel in the region, partly because it's the oldest. When it was founded in 1903, it was the first hotel in Norway to cater to winter visitors. Its design includes an older wing with wood siding in a deep red, Nordic dragons above the roof peaks, and white-trimmed windows. The hotel has been owned by the Walter family since it was sixteen years old, and today it contains a modern addition that has the best rooms. The high-ceilinged walls of the public rooms are covered with half-rounded pine and have fireplaces, heavy iron chandeliers, and lots of comfortable nooks and cubbyholes. There's an outdoor swimming pool, many ski runs, boating facilities, organized children's activities, four ice skating rinks, and magnificent mountain views. Robert Scott trained in this region, staying at this hotel, in preparation for his expedition to the South Pole. In summer, single rooms cost 250 kroner ($30), while doubles range from 330 kroner ($39.60) to 420 kroner ($50.40). In winter, guests book for five nights, always with full board, for between 330 kroner ($39.60) and 400 kroner ($48) per person.

Golå Høifjellshotell at Golå (tel. 98-109). Many of the public rooms of this red and white hotel are sheathed in natural-finish birch wood, which should come as no surprise, what with the miles of birch forest which surround the hostelry. Nestled among the trees are some 20 duplex chalets, offering lakeside seclusion, with evening sallies into the public rooms of the main building. Many guests arrive with their skis at the Vinstra station, where they are met by a hotel car. Outdoor activities here center around either the lake or the ski slopes, although there's a large outdoor pool near the base of the main building. The attractive bedrooms, filled with Scandinavian furniture and colorful textiles, are maintained by the owners, Anne Sofie and Jan Erik Kielland. In summer, with breakfast included, singles cost 225 kroner ($27), while doubles rent for 440 kroner ($52.80). Lunch or dinner costs about 120 kroner ($14.40).

Wadahl Høgfjellshotell at Wadahl (tel. 98-300). The view from the windows of this recently expanded hotel includes the large outdoor pool and row upon row of conifers leading down to a lake. There's also an indoor pool, tennis courts, horseback riding facilities, saunas, a year-round sun terrace, and a landing strip for light aircraft. Men are requested to wear dinner jackets for the twice-weekly banquets, although dress is considerably less formal on the ski runs, of course. Patrons usually spend parts of their days outdoors, but they all seem genuinely to enjoy coming into the well-warmed interior for the tasty dinner and the evening dance music. In summer, single rooms cost 335 kroner ($40.20), while doubles rent for between 460 kroner ($55.20) and 520 kroner ($62.40). Breakfast costs an additional 55 kroner ($6.60). In winter, five-night bookings are required, costing between 420 kroner ($50.40) and 480 kroner ($57.60) per person for full board.

Skeikampen Høifjellshotell at Skeikampen (tel. 28-505). In many ways, this is the best of the hotels in the region, and guests checking in are as interested in the good life indoors as they are in the miles of woodland scenery stretching in all directions. The interior is filled with both antique and contemporary furnishings as well as a collection of modern Scandinavian paintings, good Oriental rugs, and wintertime fireplaces. Sports lovers will find an indoor pool, the ubiquitous sauna, a ski lift adjacent to a smaller rope tow for beginners, and a ski school with child-care facilities. As the hotel is right at the timber line, both forested and rocky paths are well marked for climbers.

On the premises is a Spanish-influenced bodega, whose wine stock, in racks surrounding the tables and chairs, is one of the best in the region. Wine-tasting parties as well as semiformal dinners are held here at least three times a week. At lunch, a 120-krone ($14.40) buffet is an attraction that few guests like to miss. In summer, with breakfast included, single rooms cost from 325 kroner ($39), while doubles go for from 560 kroner ($67.20). No pension rates are quoted during this season. In winter, however, guests are required to take full pension for a minimum of five days. Depending on the time of the year, this ranges from 360 kroner ($43.20) to 460 kroner ($55.20) per person. The resident proprietor are Erikka and Alf-Christian Anderssen.

Farm Holidays

In the valley, Gudbrandsdal, five farms receive guests. All have rooms with hot and cold running water, showers and toilets on the same floor as bedrooms, which are comfortable and welcoming. For further information, get in touch with the Lillehammer tourist office, **Lillehammer Turistkontor** (tel. 51-098). Full board per day, including breakfast, a packed lunch, and dinner, costs around 175 kroner ($21).

One farm I like is **Glomstad Gård og Pensjonat,** 2635 Tretten, Gudbrandsdalen (tel. 76-257), a blend of modern comfort and old-fashioned rural culture. Jøda and Janna Glomstad welcome you to this manor farm that dates back to the 16th century. You can stay here and have full board at terms ranging from 155 kroner ($18.60) per person daily. Half board is 150 kroner ($18) per person. Fifty guests are accommodated in rooms with hot and cold running water. The farm lies only a short distance from mountain moors where summer pastures reach a height of 3250 feet. The winter season is from December 6 to May 1 and the summer season from June 1 to October 10. The E6 highway runs through Gudbrandsdal.

10. Gjøvik

This small industrial city is known as "the white town by Lake Mjøsa" because of its white wooden buildings and choice location. Since the early 19th century, more and more industry has been attracted here, although it was not until the coming of the railroad in 1902 that it really blossomed in the world of commerce. It is a center of trade for the district, and a variety of schools and colleges are here, particularly in technology and business administration, with various professional training facilities.

Gjøvik is suitable for vacations and recreation in both winter and summer, with the lake drawing warm-weather crowds and the ski facilities attracting winter visitors.

A collection of glass from the first industry started in Gjøvik, Caspar Kauffeldt's glassworks (it only lasted 40 years), is in **City Hall.** An 1807, well-preserved glassworks building can be seen in Kauffeldtgården.

You can see **Gjøvik Gård,** an old farm turned into a cultural center, with a large park containing interesting old buildings.

Eiktunet Museum, four miles from the center of town, has a collection of old, rustic buildings from the district. Guided tours are given from June 15 to August 15 daily from noon to 6 p.m.

Another collection of old farmhouses, arts and crafts, and an interesting old church inventory is at **Toten Museum** at Stenberg. The structures date from the 1790s. Tours daily between noon and 5 p.m. are given from June 1 to September 1.

Some 24 miles south of Gjøvik, **Balke Church,** Østre Toten, built around 100, contains more well-preserved pictures of saints than almost any other church in Norway.

WHERE TO STAY: Nye Grand Hotel, Jernbanegate (tel. 72-180), is an old, restored building with modern bedrooms, a restaurant, and a pub. In the center of town, it charges 380 kroner ($45.60) for a single with bath, 520 kroner ($62.40) for a double with bath. Tariffs include breakfast.

Strand Rica Hotel, 15 Strandgate (tel. 72-120), is a pleasant modern hotel in the center of town. Well-furnished bedrooms with baths rent for 380 kroner ($45.60) to 480 kroner ($57.60) in a single, 600 kroner ($72) to 630 kroner ($75.60) in a double. The hotel has restaurants, a bar, a disco, an indoor swimming pool, and a sauna.

Tranberg Gjestegaard (tel. 72-950), one of Gjøvik's oldest farms on a hilltop with a beautiful view over the lake, has been turned into a hotel. It lies about 1¼ miles from the center of town. Bathless singles cost 180 kroner ($21.60) to 210 kroner ($25.20), while bathless doubles go for from 225 kroner ($27) to 250 kroner ($30).

A youth hostel, **Hovdetun Ungdomsherberge** (tel. 71-011), near the town's big out-door swimming pool, Hovdetjernet (Fastland), has full pension from 175 kroner ($21) per person. Howver, board is not required to stay in one of the 134 beds of the hostel, which is divided up into cabins. It's open all year. If you're only renting a bed, you can enjoy a meal for from 75 kroner ($9).

11. Beito/Beitostølen

Beito is an attractive little alpine village in the Norwegian mountains from which you can take a ski lift up to Beitostølen, on the fringe of Jotunheimen, 2800 feet above sea level. In the summer this is a good area for walking, with various tracks for hikers who find the scenery breathtaking. Beitostølen is a good base for those who intend to climb Bitihorn (5000 feet).

From Beito, you can take an interesting boat trip on **Bygdin,** northern Europe's highest inland waterway, lying 3000 feet above sea level.

Weather conditions are stable in this area, both in winter and in summer. There is normally snow from October on, with skiing lasting until May. In the summer season, you can use Beito/Beitostølen as a base to places of interest such as the **Valdres Folk Museum,** with its 70 restored buildings, its 13th-century stave churches with magnificent wood carvings, and its burial mounds and runic stones.

WHERE TO STAY: Beito Høyfjellshotell (tel. 41-050) is a first-class Norwegian mountain hotel offering every comfort. The pleasant rooms all have phones and bathrooms with heated floors. The Beito has two saunas, two lounges, playrooms for children, and other recreation facilities, including a huge swimming pool. Singles with bath rent for 275 kroner ($33), and doubles with bath go for 620 kroner ($74.40), all rates including breakfast. The hotel has a large dining room, a bar, and a ballroom where there is dancing plus entertainment.

Beitostølen Høyfjellshotell (tel. 41-028) is up the mountain somewhat from the Beito. Its homey, relaxed atmosphere has made it a favorite with many visitors. This modern structure has intimate Loft and Lounge Bars, both fully licensed. Six days a week, there is live music on the two dance floors. The bright, spacious dining room has a view of the heights of Mugnatind to the west. Singles with bath cost 330 kroner ($39.60), doubles with bath 400 kroner ($48). Breakfast costs 55 kroner ($6.60) extra. Ragnhild and Sven-Aage Jonsbråten are the capable managers.

Bergo Fjellstogo (tel. 41-045), directed by Liv and Ansgar Sande, is a recently redecorated mountain lodge with 29 high-standard rooms, each with its own shower and toilet. Singles are priced at 160 kroner ($19.20) to 220 kroner ($26.40), with doubles going for 240 kroner ($28.80) to 320 kroner ($38.40). A fully licensed pub is on the premises, and you'll find a playroom, sauna, and a lounge with an open fireplace for après-ski festivities. In summer you can take boat trips by Bygdin and Gjende. The food here is good Norwegian cuisine. Breakfast costs 45 kroner ($5.40), while lunch goes for 65 kroner ($7.80) and dinner for 120 kroner ($14.40).

12. Heddal's Stave Church

Those wishing to see a genuine Norwegian stave church can do so at Heddal, southwest of Oslo. This is the largest of the old Norwegian stavekirker. Once hundreds of these churches dotted the countryside, but now only 32 remain.

The church dates from the mid-13th century, although it was restored in the mid-19th century. The structure is 85 feet high and 65 feet long, and contains a dozen columns inside. On the portals dragons and serpents play peek-a-boo among the tendrils. An occasional human face can be seen peering out. Some interesting 14th-century murals can also be viewed inside.

To reach Heddal, take the route from Oslo to Drammen. From Drammen, Highway E76 leads to Kongsberg, known for its old silver mines. From there, head to **Notodden,** a town noted for its saltpeter industry. The stave church is on the highway on the far side of Notodden.

If you leave early enough, you can continue on to **Eidsborg,** on Route 10, where you'll see yet another stave church. Along the way, you'll view the scenic Seljord district, with its lake and mountains and valleys.

Chapter VIII

BERGEN AND THE FJORD DISTRICT

MIGHTY FJORD FINGERS rip into rugged, snow-capped mountains; cascading waterfalls teach rainbows how to waltz; canyon-like secluded valleys lie at the end of corkscrewing roads; glaciers—opaline and irridescent—glitter in all their brilliance in western Norway, a star-spangled attraction of Europe.

Fjords, fjords, fjords, seemingly endless in all directions—enough to satisfy the appetite of the most insatiable scenic gulper. Especially recommended, because of both their beauty and easy accessibility from Bergen, are the famous fjord of Hardanger (best at blossom time, May and early June); Sogne, Norway's longest fjord, to the north of Bergen; and the Nord fjord cutting through an area that contains what is perhaps some of the finest scenery in all of Norway. One of the most popular excursions is from Loen to Olden along rivers and lakes to the Brixdal Glacier.

Readers with a packed itinerary will, of course, have to settle for a quick glimpse on a day trip from Bergen; others can anchor in at one of the sheltered fjord resorts, such as Ulvik or Lofthus. From many vantage points, it's possible to view the Folgefonn Glacier, spanning more than 100 square miles, Norway's second-largest ice field.

Other stopover centers include Stavanger and Haugesund, two fjord towns and fishing ports south of Bergen. And when fjord fever starts to wane, visitors can hit the folklore trail and go to the summer resorts (winter ski centers) of Voss and Geilo.

Bergen, of course, with its many sightseeing attractions, moderately priced hotels, pensions, and restaurants, its good boat, rail, and coach connections, makes the best center in the fjord district. We'll go there first.

1. Bergen

The soft tones of a Grieg recital floating on the perfume of blossom-scented air, the musty smell of Hanseatic warehouses along the wharf, oilskin-clad fishermen hawking their herring in the open-air market, rain lashing against the funicular to Fløien, broad avenues and medieval lanes in the old quarter—all this is Bergen, set against a backdrop of seven mountains.

Bergen is ancient, a city that looms large in Viking sagas. Until the dawn of the 14th century, it was the seat of the medieval kingdom of Norway. The Hanseatic merchants established a major trading post here, holding sway till the 18th century.

A series of fires has hit the city (the most recent, a minor one in 1955, destroyed some of the old wooden houses at Bryggen). In World War II, a Nazi ship loaded with nitroglycerin blew up in the harbor, killing or blinding many Bergenese and damaging many buildings. But Bergen always bounces back; it's survived so many disasters.

The Bergenese once found it easier to go to England than to Oslo, but in 1909 Norway's two leading cities were linked by rail. Still, as any citizen will volunteer, "Oslo never developed our cosmopolitan air." Carl O. Gram Gjesdal once expressed the special character of the resident of Bergen, writing that he's a "lover of sunshine and poet of the gray weather, free bird of the mountains and bold rider of the waves, a canny merchant and art lover, man of the world and local patriot."

Some North American first-time visitors regard Bergen as a village. Actually, it's larger than it appears, although it does seem to tie in with the preconceived conception of a Scandinavian town. It's not only a center for research in many fields, but a town with important traditions in shipping, banking, and insurance. Its modern industries are expanding rapidly (visits to plants can sometimes be arranged through the tourist office). Its airport is increasingly gaining importance with its intercontinental routes (e.g., New York, Los Angeles, Seattle, Chicago, and Montréal). Finally, many visitors head out from Bergen on the express coastal steamer that goes beyond the North Cape to Kirkenes.

From Bergen there are international shipping routes to Newcastle, England; Cuxhaven, Germany; and Amsterdam. Call Bergen Line, 21-00-20.

Bergen is a lively university town. Thousands of students are enrolled at University of Bergen and the School of Economics and Business Administration. The local student club is closed in July and August, but the **Universitetenes Reisebyrå** (The Universities' Travel Bureau), 1 Parkvei (G4), remains open throughout the summer. Call 32-64-00.

TRANSPORTATION TIP: At the tourist bureau, at Torgalmenning, visitors can purchase for 30 kroner ($3.60) a special Tourist Ticket, allowing 48 hours of unlimited travel on the buses and streetcars of Bergen (within the city limits, of course). The ticket is sold from May 1 to September.

ROOM IN A HURRY: The **tourist bureau,** easily found in a kiosk in the center of Torgalmenning (tel. 32-14-80), not only books guests into hotels, but secures accommodations in private homes. More than 50 families take in guests during the summer months.

The booking service charges 12 kroner ($1.44), but prospective guests also pay a deposit, which is deducted from the final bill. Rooms in private homes are usually priced at 90 kroner ($10.80) to 150 kroner ($18) per person, with no service charge. Breakfast costs approximately 35 kroner ($4.20) extra.

During the busy tourist season, from mid-May until September 5, the office is open weekdays from 8:30 a.m. to 10 p.m. and on Sunday from 9:30 a.m. to 10 p.m. In the early spring, mid-April to mid-May, it is open daily from 9:30 a.m. to 8 p.m. It is also open from September 6 to mid-October—daily from 9:30 a.m. to 8 p.m. From mid-October to mid-December, it is open weekdays only from 10 a.m. to 3 p.m., closing on Sunday. It reopens January 3, weekdays from 10 a.m. to 3 p.m. (closed Sunday).

The tourist bureau will also exchange foreign currency and cash travelers checks when the banks are closed.

ACCOMMODATIONS: A full array of rooms—suitable for most budgets—is available in Bergen. And thus my listings will range from a modern student-run summer hotel to a youth hostel, from pensions and hospitses to private homes to moderately priced hotels. I'll lead off with the cream of the recommendations, in the heart of the city, then follow with some pensions on the outskirts for those who don't mind taking a bus.

Medium-Priced Hotels and Pensions

Fagerheim Pensjon, 49 Kalvedalsvei (tel. 31-01-72), is an attractively old-fashioned hillside house, about six minutes from the center of town (bus 2 from the post office), that rents bathless doubles at prices that range from 175 kroner ($21) per day. Singles cost from 100 kroner ($12). A few of the homey bedrooms have small kitchens, especially suitable for those with dietary problems. Most of the accommodations have a view of the water and city, and a terrace lawn is ideal for sunbathing. The pension receives guests from June 1 to August 31.

Park Pensjon, 22 Parkvei and 35 Harald Hårfagersgt (tel. 32-09-60), is one of the finest guest houses in Bergen, a converted town house in an attractive university area. Run by the Klohs family, the pension has 50 beds in comfortable rooms. Most contain private baths. Bathless singles rent for 225 kroner ($27); bathless doubles, 340 kroner ($40.80), breakfast included. In the summer season, guests are advised to reserve well in advance. They will get a prompt reply, with instructions for a deposit to cover the first night's rent. The Park is a ten-minute walk from the train and bus station.

One of the best bargains in town is **Kloster Pension,** 12 Klosteret (F4) (tel. 31-86-66), a cozy little centrally located hotel with friendly management and comfortable rooms. Singles cost 180 kroner ($21.60), with doubles going for 275 kroner ($33). A family room is available also. Breakfast is included in all the tariffs.

Augustin Hotel, 24 C. Sundstgate (tel. 23-00-25), is a family favorite not quite a mile from the railway station. The 40 recently remodeled rooms contain phones, TV, and video. About a dozen of them have private showers, and all are pleasantly furnished. Doubles without bath cost 380 kroner ($45.60), while doubles with bath go for 480 kroner ($57.60). Bathless singles rent for 225 kroner ($27), singles with bath for 320 kroner ($38.40). The hotel

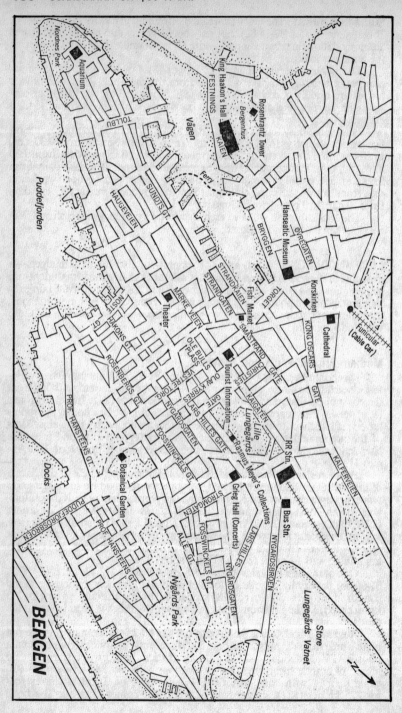

has an attractive coffeeshop where you can have breakfast or light lunches, even hot meals and pizzas if you're too hungry to settle for sandwiches and salads.

Hotel Hordaheimen, 18 C. Sundstgate (tel. 23-23-20), sits right by the harbor, offering a Nordic salt-air flavor. It's operated by the Bondeungdomslaget i Bergen, an association that sponsors cultural and folklore programs. As such, the hotel has become a Bergen base for many fjord-farming youths who come in from the nearby districts. By lodging here, therefore, overseas guests have an opportunity to "know the Norwegians." The lounge and dining rooms have been tastefully designed and coordinated, and the bedrooms—simple and utilitarian—are maintained immaculately. In high season (May 1 to September 30), a bathless double goes for 200 kroner ($24) per person. A single without bath is 240 kroner ($28.80). These rooms have hot and cold running water. A few of the accommodations contain showers and toilets, renting for 320 kroner ($38.40) in a single, 245 kroner ($29.40) per person in a double, these tariffs including service and tax. A Norwegian breakfast is another 42 kroner ($5.04). A better bargain is the hotel annex, around the corner, where the rooms have modern furnishings and curtains, and there is no street noise.

Strand Hotel, 2–4 Strandkaien (tel. 31-08-15), occupies the fourth, fifth, and sixth floors of an office building overlooking the harbor and fish and flower market of Bergen. In recent times, the Strand has been modernized, and its bedchambers promote confidence and provide good comfort. Most of them are fairly spacious. The cheapest way to stay here is to take one of the units with hot and cold running water, but no private baths. These rent for 250 kroner ($30) in a single, going up to 400 kroner ($48) in a double. If you're extravagant, you'll take the singles with private bath or shower at 310 kroner ($37.20), the tariff rising to 480 kroner ($57.60) in a double. Adequate showers are available in the corridors.

To check in, take an elevator to the fifth floor. Breakfast is included in the rates quoted, but the place is really a "bed-and-breakfast" establishment, serving no other main meals. Still, it's possible to order sandwiches and refreshments throughout the day. The Strand is also licensed for beer and wine.

In summer tourists fill up the rooms, but there's also a lot of patronage by men connected to offshore oil drilling and the merchant marine. The Strand is just a few minutes from the rail terminal, as well as the bus terminal. The airport bus leaves from nearby, as do many fjord and coastal steamers.

Student-Run Hotels on the Outskirts

Hotel Hatleberg, 5 Hatleveien (tel. 25-60-10), provides yet another opportunity to take advantage of a student-run accommodation, open to outsiders from July 1 till mid-August. Some 420 rooms are avilable to the public. The bed-sitting rooms are streamlined modern. The hotel has a spacious lounge and dining hall. For a double with shower, guests pay 180 kroner ($21.60), although singles with shower rent for a high 110 kroner ($13.20). However, these rates include taxes and the standard service charge.

Also rented out are some family apartments, costing 240 kroner ($28.80) for three persons, 260 kroner ($31.20) for four persons. After a stay of three days, special rooms rates are quoted. Breakfast in the cafeteria is à la carte. The hotel lies 3½ miles from the center of Bergen, and the setting is tranquil, with views of a shipping lane. There is good bus service into the center of Bergen.

Fantoft Sommerhotel, postal address 5000 Bergen (tel. 28-29-10), an 18-

floor concrete building off the main road E68 to Bergen (north), reflects an advanced Norwegian design concept. Used by students during the school term, Fantoft accepts transients from June 1 to August 25. The public rooms are generous—not only a lounge and fully licensed bar, but several places for meals, including the regular dining room. There are quiet reading rooms as well. All of the accommodations are equipped with a private shower and toilet, the tariffs including a continental breakfast, tax, and service charges. Singles are 275 kroner ($33); doubles, 380 kroner ($45.60). These latter rooms are actually singles, but extra beds are added. The furnishings are simple and pure, with a use of light modern wood pieces, wall-to-wall draperies, hanging contemporary lights, and prints on the walls.

Family apartments, with showers and toilets, rent for 420 kroner ($50.40) for three persons, 480 kroner ($57.60) for four persons. You can also stay here on half-board rates.

Recommended Private Homes

Mr. and Mrs. Gaupholm, 5 Nyhavnsbakken (tel. 25-87-86), are the genial owners of this yellow frame house in an outlying rural section of Bergen (only a ten-minute bus ride on no. 1 or 8 from the city center). They charge 150 kroner ($18) nightly for double rooms. The accommodations are furnished in a tidy, homelike fashion. On the second floor, two double rooms share another large kitchen. There are a number of conveniences: a place to wash your clothes, a telephone in the hallway, a semi-private toilet and shower, and a place to park your car. Mr. and Mrs. Gaupholm assist visitors (they speak English rather well), offering tips and aid—even, on special occasions, escorting guests on sightseeing trips.

Solang Spord, 2 Sydneskleiven (tel. 32-71-73), is a neat, well-kept house in the center of Bergen. Rooms are pleasantly furnished, and Mr. Spord speaks English. The price for a single room is 110 kroner ($13.20), going up 180 kroner ($21.60) in a double. A public shower is available. The house lies about a five-minute walk from the fish market and aquarium. Parking is available just outside the house.

At the tourist bureau kiosk, a map can be picked up, and the young staff will indicate the easiest ways of reaching this or other private dwellings.

READERS' HOTEL SELECTION: "I stayed in a very nice single room for 120 kroner ($14.40) per night at the **Mariakroa Sommerhotel,** on Klostergat near the city center. The hotel has a television set, Ping-Pong facilities, Scrabble sets, and a nice lounge for guests to enjoy" (Barry Isaac, Chicago, Ill.). . . . "The Tourist Bureau in the downtown kiosk arranged for us to stay with **Emely and Johannes Holsen** at 86 Hardagaten (tel. 29-79-41), about a ten-minute drive from the center of town. These are super people who have a nice home and who serve unbelievable breakfasts. Emely bakes all of her own goodies. She brings them with coffee to your room at night. The table is set differently every morning, with fine silver, candles, and a different menu every day. It is an uplifting experience to have breakfast with the Holsens, who bend over backward to make you feel welcome. We had a bedroom, sitting room, and private bath with shower. The charge is 150 kroner ($18) per day, and 30 kroner ($3.60) extra per person for breakfast. Staying at the Holsens was the best investment we made on our travels" (The Stratings, Colorado Springs, Colo.). . . . "We stayed at the **Myklebust Pension,** 19 Rosenbergs Gate (tel. 31-13-28), where the owners are very nice and extremely helpful. For 255 kroner ($30.60) for a double, we got a large room pleasantly furnished in contemporary Scandinavian, with a sink with hot and cold water and the shower and toilet only steps away. In a central hallway, there is a stove, refrigerator, washing machine (soap was provided), and all the dishes and utensils necessary for a small meal. For an additional 35 kroner ($4.20) per person, breakfast is provided, brought to your room at the time you request. We had ham and cheese, bread, rolls, marmalade, butter, jam, coffee, milk, juice, and a soft-boiled egg. We couldn't finish it all!" (Martha and John Annoni, Buffalo, N.Y.). . . . "**Edel and Svein** have a lovely home at 11 Blaauwsvei (tel. 31-15-27). The roof of the house contains a beautiful stained-glass skylight, and the view of Bergen from their balcony is breathtaking. They have a fully-equipped kitchen and a living room with a television, for their guests' use. Their home is less than a mile from the railway station, and if a guest phones, Svein will pick him or her up on arrival. Showers are included in the very reasonable rates, but breakfast is extra. Two persons pay about 150 kroner ($18) for a pleasant room. Svein and Edel both speak English and are quite willing to supply Bergen tourist information and maps to their guests" (Gail Cohen and Gary Godwin, Tulsa, Okla., and Brenda and Lars Nissen, Saskatoon, Sask., Canada).

DINING IN BERGEN: Bergen has a good choice of restaurants and cafeterias—at moderate prices. Fresh fish is the big specialty in all the restaurants. I'll lead off with a selection of self-service cafeterias in and around the harbor (many close around 7 p.m. so the most stringently budgeted readers will plan to have their middag early). The splurge choices, some of which stay open till midnight, will follow.

The Harbor Cafeterias

Lido, 1 Torgalmenningen (tel. 31-01-20), a second-floor cafeteria, is the queen of the dockside dining rooms, serving well-prepared food. Ceiling-to-floor picture windows overlook the harbor, and guests walk across carpets to sit in white Windsor-style chairs. A typical meal might begin with a bowl of fish soup, then followed with a pan-fried pork chop accompanied by boiled potatoes, caraway seed cabbage, and carrots, and be topped off by one of the tasty desserts. Meals cost from 90 kroner ($10.80) up. To have dinner here, you'll have to keep the same dining hours as the cows (before 4:30 p.m.).

Cafeteria Kaffistova, 1 Torget (Marketplace) (tel. 31-66-27), is a three-story building overlooking the harbor that is one of the best all-around choices for economy dining in Bergen. Quality isn't sacrificed at this establishment, run by Bondeungdomslaget i Bergen, a Norwegian association devoted to cultural activities and folklore. A self-service cafeteria is on the lower floor—all modern, spick and span. The decor is unfrivolous, and the room is compensatingly graced with a picture-postcard view of the harbor. Many of the most interesting smørrebrød concoctions are priced from 35 kroner ($4.20). The cafeteria is open from 8 a.m. till 10 p.m. On the third floor is a moderately priced café, serving hot meals till 7:30 p.m. The cheapest way to dine here is to order either the 55-krone ($6.60) luncheon or the 75-krone ($9) middag. Many interesting Norwegian dishes are offered on the à la carte menu as well, including rømmegraut (sour cream porridge), cured mutton, trout, ham, potato salad, scrambled eggs, and desserts from 2 to 9 p.m.

Yang Tse Kiang, 3 Torget (tel. 31-66-66), stands next to the already recommended Cafeteria Kaffistova on the Marketplace, which sells everything from fish to flowers. It features an unusual combination of Chinese and Norwegian dishes in a typical Shanghai atmosphere. The red-and-gold dining room overlooks the harbor, but instead of coolies you see bearded Norwegian fishermen wearing yellow raincoats. Otherwise, the illusion inside the restaurant would be perfect. The food is pleasant, but unspectacular, and meals run from 100 kroner ($12).

Dining for Splurgers

Holberg-Stuen, 6 Torgalmenningen (tel. 31-80-15), is a second-floor tavern, typically Old Bergen, that recaptures the flavor of a country inn (beamed ceilings, open log fire, leaded-glass casement windows, high-back settles and armchairs, sage-green walls). The decor is from the time of Ludwig Holberg. To the discreet accompaniment of organ music, hearty appetites devour such dishes as fish filet in white wine sauce, accompanied by prawns, mushrooms, and asparagus. The restaurant, a good gathering spot for late-night diners, stays open till 11:30 p.m. But from 12:30 till 6 p.m., the Holberg-Stuen serves its daily middag selections, such as a two-course main meal for 75 kroner ($9). Dinner is from 120 kroner ($14.40).

Villa Amorini, 5 Rasmus Meyers Allé (tel. 31-00-39), isn't an Italian restaurant, despite the name. It's Inni-Carine Holm's House of Cupids, done up in cheerful yellow walls, green seat covers, and blue touches which please the eye even as the stomach is pleased by a variety of seafood, salads, and grill specialties. You can enjoy reindeer filet with blackberry and madeira sauce, poached lemon sole, and salmon slices, accompanied by outstanding wines from France, Italy, and the United States. The modern decor and the food have made this place popular with locals and visitors alike. Meals cost from 120 kroner ($14.40) up. The villa is open daily from noon to midnight.

The Teahouse of the Bergen Moon

Reimers (tel. 32-05-59), in the Telegraph Building by the Town Park, is informal and tea-roomy. The English love it here, as do visitors drawn by its tempting selection of homemade cakes (especially the pineapple cream), as well as by its open-face sandwiches. A typical one might contain meat patties. Inexpensive luncheon plates, such as wienerschnitzel or a hamburger plate, are also served. Meals begin at 80 kroner ($9.60). Within walking distance of the tour buses, this pâtisserie, open from 8:30 a.m. to 4:30 p.m., makes a good stopover between sightseeing excursions. While munching and sipping, you can see a statue of Grieg in the park, but he rudely has his back turned. Just beyond the composer is an ornate old bandstand.

READER'S RESTAURANT SUGGESTION: "We found a neat café on the port, an old mariners eating place built in the 19th century, **Børs Café,** 15 Strandgaten (tel. 32-47-19), near Vågen and the fish market. It offers huge meals at 80 kroner ($9.60)" (Mary D. Radcliffe, APO New York).

THE MAJOR ATTRACTIONS: Eleven for the asking.

Bryggen

This row of Hanseatic timbered houses, rebuilt along the waterfront after the disastrous fire of 1702, is what remains of medieval Bergen. The northern half burned to the ground as late as 1955.

Hanseatic Museum

In one of the best preserved wooden buildings along Bryggen, this museum illustrates commercial life on the wharf in Bergen centuries ago. German merchants, representatives of the Hanseatic League centered in Lübeck, lived in these medieval houses built in long rows up from the harbor. With dried cod, grain, and salt as articles of exchange, fishermen from northern Norway met German traders during the busy summer season. Furnished with authentic trappings dating from 1704, the museum is open from 10 a.m. to 4 p.m. in June, July, and August. In May and September, the hours change, from 11 a.m. to 2 p.m. Off-season, it is open Sunday, Monday, Wednesday, and Friday from 11 a.m. to 2 p.m. Admission is 6 kroner (72¢) for adults, 3 kroner (36¢) for children during the season. Off-season, it's free.

St. Mary's Church

The oldest building in Bergen (exact date unknown, perhaps mid-12th century) is a Romanesque church, considered one of the most beautiful in Norway. Its altar is the most ancient ornament in the church; a baroque pulpit was donated by Hanseatic merchants: carved figures depict everything from Chastity to Naked Truth. The church, on Dreggen, is open weekdays (except Saturday) from May 1 to September 30, 11 a.m. to 4 p.m. (daily and Sunday off season, except Monday and Saturday from noon to 1:30 p.m.). Free organ concerts are given at 8 p.m. every Thursday during the summer.

Rasmus Meyer's Collections

Within walking distance of the fish market, this museum (tel. 31-11-20) houses an excellent display of paintings by Norwegians. The star attraction is the elongated, egg-shaped figures of Edvard Munch, but two important 19th-century artists, Christian Krohg and Harriet Backer, are also represented. The collection is open from mid-Mary to September 15, 11 a.m. to 4 p.m. weekdays; on Sunday from noon to 3 p.m.; off-season, except Tuesday, from noon to 3 p.m. Admission is 5 kroner (60¢).

Haakonshallen and Rosenkrantz Tower

A long walk along the water from Bryggen are two ancient landmarks that were badly damaged when a Nazi boat loaded with nitroglycerin exploded in the harbor in 1944. Haakonshallen (King Haakon's Hall; tel. 31-69-67) was built in the 13th century, and has been restored. Likewise Rosenkrantz Tower (tel. 31-43-80), once a fortified royal residence from the 13th century, but rebuilt and enlarged in the 16th century, has been restored. Both are open from mid-May to mid-September, 10 a.m. to 4 p.m. Admission is 4 kroner (48¢) for each site. Off-season, Haakonshallen is open from noon to 3 p.m. (3 to 6 p.m. on Thursday); Rosenkrantz Tower is open Sunday only from noon to 3 p.m.

The Fish Market

Once a visitor has smelled out this place, there can be no doubt that Bergen is a city of fish-lovers and sea-lovers. To watch the women of Bergen appraise the latest merchandise from the sea and haggle with the fishmongers is worth the trip. Fortunes have been made for Kodak with the rolls used up here.

Funicular to Fløien

A short walk from the fish market is the station where the funicular heads up to Fløien, the most famous of Bergen's seven hills. The ride, operating till midnight, costs 16 kroner ($1.92) round trip, 8 kroner (96¢) one way (you can walk down), and the subsequent view of the city, the neighboring hills, and the harbor is worth every öre.

Cable Car to Mount Ulriken

For a glorious view of Bergen and its suburbs, the ocean and islands, fjords and high mountains, Mount Ulriken (2000 feet) can't be beat. Many footpaths lead to unspoiled mountain terrain. There's frequent bus service (no. 2) to Haukeland Hospital, or you can go by car to this point where you board the cable car. The cost to go up is 20 kroner ($2.40); to come down, 15 kroner ($1.80) for adults. Children pay 7 kroner (84¢) to ascend, 5 kroner (60¢) for the descent. A combination bus/cable car ticket costs 25 kroner ($3) for adults, 10 kroner ($1.20) for children.

Bergen Aquarium

This aquarium, one of the largest and finest in Scandinavia, contains tank after tank of marine life, ingeniously displayed. Two large outdoor ponds contain diving seabirds and seals. The aquarium, reached by bus 4 from the center of town, is open from May 1 to September 30, 9 a.m. to 8 p.m. (off season, 10 a.m. to 6 p.m.). The aquarium is a ten-minute walk from the Centrum. The admission charged is 15 kroner ($1.80).

One California magazine writer had an extreme reaction after being conducted through the Aquarium. He writes, "You watch, and the horrible thought comes to you that your favorite food may be sentient life. You stumble out into the daylight, ready for a diet of vegetables and vitamin pills."

For information, telephone 32-77-60.

Fantoft Stave Church

Constructed on the principle of a Viking ship, this well-preserved stave church at Fantoft, near Grieg's home, was built in 1150. Richly decorated with both pagan and Christian elements, it was described aptly by a Norwegian: "Simple interiors with beautiful paintings on wood are outdone by ornate exteriors with roof upon roof, gable interlocking gable, pinnacled with dragons, serpents, or crosses, finally topped off with a cupola in two or three layers. The church is so well built that it actually bends with the winter winds." It may be visited (take the bus from the station at Bergen to Paradise) from 10 a.m. to 1 p.m. on Tuesday, Thursday, and weekends (every day in July). From May 15 to September 15, it is also open daily from 3 to 6 p.m. Admission is 5 kroner (60¢) for adults, 2.50 kroner (30¢) for children. For information, telephone 28-17-04.

Troldhaugen (Trolls' Hill)

This house, in beautiful, rural surroundings at Hop, near Bergen, was the summer villa of the composer Edvard Grieg from the time it was constructed in 1885 until he died in Bergen in 1907. The Victorian house still contains Grieg's own furniture, paintings, and other mementos. His Steinway grand piano of 1892, still in excellent condition, is frequently used at concerts given in the house during the annual Bergen Festival, as well as at Troldhaugen's own summer concerts. The former kitchen is today a memory room, holding several original music manuscripts, letters, and other articles worth seeing. Both Grieg and his wife are buried in a cliff grotto on the estate. At his cottage by the sea, he composed many of his famous works. Grieg's home is open daily from May 2 to October 1, 11 a.m. to 2 p.m. and 3 to 6 p.m. Admission is 6 kroner (72¢) for adults, 3 kroner (36¢) for children. For information, telephone 13-54-38.

Old Bergen

At Elsero and Sandviken is a collection of old houses from the 18th and 19th centuries—giving you an idea of how your great-grandparents lived, if they came from Norway. The old town's complete with streets, an open square, and narrow alleyways. Open from May 12 to September 14, the museum (tel. 25-63-07) has guided tours every hour from 10 a.m. to 7 p.m. for 10 kroner ($1.20). The park and restaurant are open from 11 a.m. to 10 p.m. Bus 1 from the Bergen post office leaves every ten minutes. Reader Mrs. James E. Sell writes: "We had one of our most delicious meals here in cozy surroundings. The Bergen beef broth was out of this world, and you could really get by with ordering only one serving. We also enjoyed the fricassée of lamb." For the restaurant call 25-70-34.

MOTORCOACH CITY TOURS: Bergen has a top-notch list of conducted sightseeing tours by coach. All buses depart from the tourist bureau in the heart of the city at Torgalmenning. A quick-orientation nonstop preview of Bergen, both old and new, is offered every day throughout the year. Lasting 1½ hours, the tour departs at 9:30 a.m. and costs 35 kroner ($4.20) per person. But the best tour of Bergen is the 11 a.m., 2½-hour tour of the city, covering all the major sightseeing attractions, among them the Hanseatic Museum and St. Mary's 12th-century church. The tour operates from May 2 to September 30 and costs 70 kroner ($8.40).

Another tour—same price, same season, same length—leaves at 3:30 p.m. and calls at Grieg's home and the Fantoft stave church.

For a look at historical Bergen, including the Old Bergen Museum, the cost is 70 kroner ($8.40), the price of a guide and the entrance fee included. This popular tour departs daily at 10:30 a.m., June 1 to September 7. A small concert will be given in the house of Grieg's parents.

SHOPPING IN BERGEN: A particularly good city for shopping, the gateway port of Bergen not only has unusual merchandise, but offers many moderately priced buys as well. To survey the types of items offered, head first for:

Sundt & Co., 14 Torgalmenningen, (tel. 38-80-20), the leading department store, lying near the tourist information booth. Excellent buys include rough linen tablecloths, purses for women, and Norwegian knitwear, plus a vast array of souvenirs (half the trolls in the mountains must have posed).

Kløverhuset, 10 Strandkaien (tel. 32-77-20), by the fish market on the harbor, is Bergen's largest fashion store. Besides the latest in modern design, it also offers good bargains, such as moderately priced and attractively designed knitted sweaters, gloves, and Lapp jackets. There's also a special giftshop open only in summer. When cruise ships arrive in Bergen harbor, Kløverhuset's giftshop is open on Sunday and in the evening on weekdays.

Prydkunst Hjertholm, 8 Torgalmenningen (tel. 21-78-60), is the permanent exhibition of Norwegian artists and artisans who work in such traditional forms as jewelry and enamelware, ceramics, pewter, and rugs.

Marketplace: Real bargain sleuths head here where many local handicrafts from the western fjord district are displayed, including rugs and handmade tablecloths. This is one of the few places in Norway where bargaining isn't objectionable.

In and around **Bryggen Brukskunst,** the restored old town near the wharf, many craftspeople are taking old houses to ply the ancient Norwegian trades. Crafts boutiques here often display Bergen souvenirs, many of which are based on designs 300 to 1500 years old. For example, I recently purchased a reproduction of a cruciform pilgrim's badge (Romanesque in style). Other tempting items are likely to include sheepskin-lined booties or exquisitely styled handwoven woolen dresses.

Norway's leading jeweler, **David-Andersen,** 10 Torgalmenningen (tel. 21-74-74), is represented in Bergen as well. (Refer to the Oslo shopping section for more details.)

For glassware and ceramics, the leading merchant in Bergen is **Bergens Glasmagasin,** 9 Olav Kyrres Gate (tel. 21-57-98). The store is open 8:30 a.m. to 4 p.m. on Monday, Tuesday, Wednesday, and Friday; Thursday from 8:30 a.m. to 7 p.m.; and Saturday from 9 a.m. to 1 p.m.

For national handicrafts, the widest and most impeccable presentation is at **Husfliden I Bergen,** 3 Vågsalmenning (tel. 31-78-70). The firm also maintains a branch at 8 Østre Skostredet. The finest hand-knitwear from the western fjord district, along with rugs in beautiful colors and designs, are just some of the merchandise offered for sale. Hours are 9 a.m. to 4 p.m. on Monday, Tuesday, Wednesday, and Friday; from 9 a.m. to 7 p.m. on Thursday; and from 9 a.m. to 1 p.m. on Sunday.

BERGEN AFTER DARK: Las Vegas it isn't. Bergen is too much of an outdoorsy city in summer to have nightclubs. But it has six movie theaters—such as **Konsertpaleet,** 3 Neumannsgate, and **Engen,** 39 Engen that show English-language films. The earliest performance is at 11 a.m., the latest at 11 p.m.

Cultural Note: September to June is in season for **Den Nationale Scene,** Bergen. Call the booking office at 31-19-20. The country's oldest theater, it was founded in the mid-19th century. Its repertoire consists of classical Norwegian and international drama, contemporary plays, frequent productions of music drama, as well as visiting productions of opera and ballet.

The **Bergen Symphony Orchestra,** which is more than two centuries old, performs in season from August to May, on Thursday at 7:30 p.m. and also often on Saturday at 12:30 p.m. at the Grieghallen, 3A Lars Hilles Gate. Its repertoire consists of classical and contemporary music as well as visiting productions of opera. International conductors and soloists perform. Call the booking office (tel. 31-31-04).

Wedding Festival: For centuries the wedding festival in the country districts of Norway has been a great social event. Guests arrived in colorful costumes with rose-painted baskets and carved pails of wedding food. The procession to the church was led by a fiddle player. The bridal pair, relatives, and neighbors wore regional costumes with silver brooches, belts, and ribbons, silver buttons and buckles. The festival was a long celebration, lasting several days and nights.

Today **Fana Folklore** invites you to a wedding festival in simplified form. You are taken to an 800-year-old Fana church where the organist plays old hymns instead of the wedding march. Then you are received in a private home where you are treated like friends of the family in true Norwegian farm hospitality, enjoying their festivals which follow old customs, accompanied by plenty of food, songs, music, and lively dances. You are invited to join these activities.

Buses leave from Festplassen in Bergen from June 1 to August 31 on Monday, Tuesday, Thursday, and Friday at 7 p.m. The price, which includes everything—and that means a full meal—is 130 kroner ($15.60). Tickets are available from your hotel, the Brødr. Lie, 12 Torgalmenningen, from travel agents, or direct from the operators: Fana Folklore, N 5047 Stend-Bergen (tel. 11-72-40).

GRIEG HALL: Opened in mid-1978, the strikingly modern Grieg Hall is Bergen's monumental showcase for music, drama, and a host of other cultural events. The building is a composite of architecture and design, reflecting the genius of a number of different builders, designers, and architects. The main auditorium can seat 1420 people for concerts, and will hold 100 more when the orchestra pit is raised to stage level. The stage is large enough to accommodate an entire grand opera production, and the main foyer will comfortably seat 1500 guests for lunch or dinner. Snackbars provide drinks and light snacks throughout the performances. On the street level, the building features an arcade of shops, and the upper floors house the offices of the Philharmonic Orchestra and the Bergen International Festival.

BERGEN INTERNATIONAL FESTIVAL: This jam-packed festival, most often scheduled during the last week in May and the first days in June, has become famous for its offerings of music, drama, opera, ballet, and folklore. The works of native son Edvard Grieg dominate the festivities. Concerts are held every day at his former home, Troldhaugen, and the modern concert hall bearing his name, but current-day international artists, such as André Previn, Oscar Peterson, Judith Blegen, and Murray Perahia, are also featured. Den Nationale Scene performs Ibsen plays as well as contemporary ones. Concerts are given in the 700-year-old Haakonshallen or in the 12th-century St. Mary's Church, and folklore performances round out the events. The last few years, concerts have also been held at Lysøen, the former home of the 19th-century Bergen-born violin virtuoso Ole Bull. Details are available at the festival office, Grieghallen, 3A Lars Hilles Gate, P.O. Box 183, 5001 Bergen (tel. 32-04-00).

SWIMMING AND FISHING: Fishing in Western Norway? Permits with all details may be obtained from the **Bergen Angling Club,** 4 Magnus Barfotsgate (tel. 32-11-64). Sea fishing is free. . . . swim in the heated saltwater pool at the **Sentral-badet,** 9 Teatersgaten (tel. 23-10-34). For open hours; check with the tourist office. The cost is 8 kroner (96¢) for adults, 6 kroner (72¢) for children. . . . For open-air swimming, take the bus to Tømmersvagen, 15 minutes from the center.

EXPLORING THE FJORDS: Two of Norway's most famous fjords, **Hardanger** and **Sognefjord,** can easily be explored from Bergen. The least expensive way to see the blue waters of the Hardanger fjord and the **Folgefonn glacier** is to take a round-trip coach from the Central Bus Station, 8 Strømgaten, leaving daily at 9 a.m. from May 1 to October 1. The full-day independent tour includes a luncheon stopover at **Norheimsund** and delivers guests back to Bergen around 8 p.m.; round-trip fare is 130 kroner ($15.60). Platform 22.

A third coach tour of Hardanger, departing at 8 a.m., visits **Ulvik** and **Norheimsund,** two spectacularly scenic fjord resorts, and makes a stopover at Voss. This highly recommended trip leaves from Norheimsund by fjord steamer; it's possible to have meals on board. Total cost is 265 kroner ($31.80). Platform 1.

Norway's longest fjord, Sognefjord, can be traversed by the express steamer to **Gudvangen.** From Gudvangen, passengers go by bus to **Voss.** From Voss, a train runs to Bergen. The round-trip fare, including an "airline meal," is 310 kroner ($37.20) per person. The departure from Bergen is daily at 7:45 a.m. June 1 to August 3.

Norway in a Nutshell: This 12-hour Do-It-Yourself tour may not be Norway in a nutshell; rather it is a capsule of some of its five-star scenic highlights, encompassing two arms of Sognefjord, and the train ride from **Myrdal** down to **Flåm** (a drop of 2900 feet, past seemingly endless waterfalls). From April 28 to September 3, the tour leaves at 8:35 a.m. from the Bergen railway station; guests have lunch at Flåm, then board a river steamer for Gudvangen, where they hop a bus to Voss, then a train back to Bergen. The round-trip fare, excluding meals, is 210 kroner ($25.10): Norway in a Nutshell is the single most exciting one-day tour in the country.

Having explored Bergen and environs, the hydrofoil is ready to whisk us south to:

2. Rogaland

Rogaland, the southern part of Norway, is called Norway in a nutshell because of its great variety of nature. Fjords, endless mountains, lush green valleys, miles of sandy beaches, colorful towns and villages, great fishing possibilities, a mild climate, and a hospitable atmosphere combine to make this area, with its 300,000 inhabitants, a part of Norway well worth visiting.

The district lives today in the technological future, thanks to its oil industry, but it also harks back to the country's oldest inhabitants. Here, the Viking king, Harald Fairhair, gathered Norway into one kingdom in 872. The locals say it was from here that the Vikings sailed to discover America.

Rogaland consists of the hilly Dalane in the south, the flat Jaeren (farm land), the beautiful Ryfylke, and, in the north, Karmøy with Haugesund.

EGERSUND: A gleaming white town in bare, gray surroundings, the white houses of Egersund cover the slopes up from the long narrow harbor. The history and development of the town is closely connected with fishing and shipping, as Egersund has the only natural harbor, irrespective of weather conditions, along the whole coast between Fedafjorden and Boknafjorden. In ancient sagas, reports are given of gatherings here of people from eastern and western Norway for trade purposes. Herring was once an important product sold here for the markets of the world, but even though that has not been so since the 1950s, there is still a great interest in fishing, although today most of it is of the sport variety.

The great King Canute of Denmark and England, who also claimed Norway against its wishes, was probably not welcome when he put into the sound for the protection of his fleet in 1028, but the Danes today are held in high esteem, particularly since establishment of a ferry service from Hanstholm, Denmark, to Egersund in the summer of 1984. There are also train connections with Oslo and Stavanger.

WHERE TO STAY: **Eiger Hotell,** 3 Johan Feyers Gate (tel. 49-18-11), is a new, modern hostelry with 28 well-furnished rooms, all with complete bathrooms, radios, and TV. Singles rent for 275 kroner ($33) and doubles for 400 kroner ($48), with breakfast included. The hotel has its own pub and restaurant.

If you're driving, you might like the **Eiger Motell** (tel. 49-02-00), a modern, comfortable motel on the outskirts of Egersund on highway 44 toward Flekkefjord. The motel has 20 pleasant rooms, all with showers and toilets. You'll pay 275 kroner ($33) for a single, 400 kroner ($48) for a double room. Breakfast is included in the rates. The motel has a comfortable lounge, a cafeteria serving low-cost meals, and good parking facilities.

HAUGESUND: Some 35 miles north of Stavanger is a shipping and fishing port with century-old herring fisheries that is beginning to lure visitors with its peaceful setting and good facilities. Surrounded by fjords Hardanger and Ryfylke, Haugesund is relatively undiscovered and unspoiled, despite the fact that it is only two hours from Bergen by hydrofoil.

The most interesting sight inside town is the raspberry-pink **Town Hall,** which boasts a flower-filled square and cobbled marketplace. The gift of a local shipping magnate, the Haugesund Town Hall continues a Norwegian tradition —local artists decorate municipal buildings.

About a mile north of the town is a 55-foot granite obelisk, erected in 1872 in honor of Norway's unification a thousand years before under Harald Fairhair (the burial mound of this warrior king is believed to be on the spot). Each country, called *fylke,* contributed a stone pillar.

For information about any number of day tours from Haugesund, go to the tourist bureau at the bus station. A popular round-trip excursion is to Norway's most populated island, **Karmøy.** South of Haugesund, this island was strategic in Viking times, and is linked to the mainland today by Karmsund Bridge, one of the largest in the country.

Food and Lodging

The least expensive accommodations in town are offered at the **Skeisvang Ungdomsherberge** (tel. 12-146), a youth hostel on the edge of town beside the water. It has the look of a fraternity house, offering rooms for couples or quartets. It's possible for a family to book an entire room; otherwise, the sexes are separated. The cost is only 85 kroner ($10.20) per bed. A self-service kitchen can be used by the hostelers, who buy supplies at a nearby store.

If you're more flush, check into the **Haugaland Hotell,** 215 Karmsundgate (tel. 13-146), which is as slick and compact as a luxury cruiser. It's dubbed by locals "as the smallest hotel in Norway." Small though it is, it still packs a powerful punch. Its situation for bus passengers is ideal—right at the terminal (which is the cleanest bus station I've seen in Norway). Rooms have coordinated colors and fabrics; each has its own combination writing desk and dressing table, sofa, armchairs, radio, electric sockets for shaving, and abundant wardrobe space.

Singles without bath rent for 225 kroner ($27), going up to 380 kroner ($45.60) with private shower. Bathless doubles cost 280 kroner ($33.60), rising to 520 kroner ($62.40) with private bath. A Norwegian breakfast is included.

In the intimate modern dining room, lunches or dinners are served, a complete one going for 120 kroner ($14.40). However, an added feature is the ground-floor, self-service cafeteria which provides money-saving meals, such as frikadeller with vegetables, for 55 kroner ($6.60) and up. It's a fresh and airy place, attracting the townspeople as well as the transient.

3. Stavanger

This seaport—unequaled in Norway as a fish-canning center—slaps anything in a tin from sprats to anchovies. Oil discovered in the North Sea has given it somewhat of a boomtown air, but as a tourist center and base for fjord excursions and North Sea bathing beaches, it is just beginning to develop (the English, as usual, have already discovered it).

In Stavanger, the charm of the past meets the modernity of the present. The result is a pleasant, often romantic-looking port. The old marketplace, where fish and fruit have been sold since the ninth century, is set against a backdrop of a gleaming modern bank.

Unlike Bergen, Stavanger hasn't seen a fire since the 17th century; consequently, in its heart lies one of Norway's best preserved old wooden towns. On an irregular terrain cobbled streets run uphill—and hours can be spent walking along the quays, promenading around a lake, and exploring hidden alleyways.

Stavanger, Norway's fourth-largest town, 100 miles south of Bergen, is a center for many excursions, including such popular trips as one to the Lyse and Ryfylke fjords.

The hydrofoil from Bergen is the fastest way to reach Stavanger.

ACCOMMODATIONS: It is customary to anchor into one of the moderately priced hotels in the "satellites" of the town (such as Madla, Sola, Randaberg, or Tananger). Each of these points is easily reached by buses that leave regularly from the bus station, near the railway station in Stavanger. For the most part, the hotels in the environs are by the sea.

Stavanger is a booming and prosperous city now, thanks to the already-mentioned Norwegian oil strikes in the North Sea. Thus, you may find the hotels filled (at high prices, too) due to the recent influx of engineers and business people—many of them Americans.

The local tourist office (tel. 52-84-37), next to the railway station, will book you into a private home, at rates beginning at 125 kroner ($15) per person and up for a night's lodging.

Rogalandsheimen Gjestgiveri, 18 Musegatan (tel. 52-01-88), is a friendly, old-style Norwegian guest house, run by English-speaking Alfhild and Leonard Roalkvam. He was the chef of the kitchen of the Atlantic Hotel for 13 years. They take in paying guests, bedding them down in one of their old-fashioned, comfortable rooms. They'll rent you a double for 250 kroner ($30), the price dropping to 180 kroner ($21.60) in a single. Families may want to rent a three-bedded room costing 280 kroner ($33.60) or a four-bedded unit going for 320 kroner ($38.40). A buffet breakfast is served for 45 kroner ($5.40), but no other meals. However, their guest house lies only a few minutes' walk to the center of Stavanger, where you can find many restaurants. The hosts are kind, inviting people and do much to make your stay enjoyable.

Rex Hospits, 11 Wesselsgate (tel. 52-45-70), is modesty itself, with a relaxed, friendly atmosphere where English is spoken. Recommended only as an overnight stopover, it rents out simply furnished, clean rooms at a rate of 175 kroner ($21) in a single without bath, 450 kroner ($54) in a double with bath. No meals are served.

READER'S PENSION SELECTION: "In Stavanger, we found a modest pension in a quiet residential area, a five-minute walk from the center. It's **Bergeland Hospits,** 1A Vikedalsgate (tel. 52-84-85). The charge is 325 kroner ($39) for a double room with bath. There are ample showers. Breakfasts, served in the bedrooms, cost 35 kroner ($6.23) and are quite filling. The rooms, incidentally, are nice, all containing water basins with hot and cold running water" (Dr. and Mrs. Gerald D. Fox, Brooklyn, N.Y.).

Lodgings in the Environs

Stavanger Sommerhotell, 6 Madlamarkveien in Madla (tel. 55-70-00), houses students at term-time but receives foreign visitors from all over the world from June 1 to September 1. Since housing for Norwegian students is among the highest in the world, you get very good comfort and facilities here and avoid the sky-high prices within the heart of Stavanger. Like its fellow student summer hotels, it is modern, with a simple but tasteful interior.

Single rooms with private showers rent for 240 kroner ($28.80) to 280 kroner ($33.60), and doubles, also with private showers, cost from 380 kroner ($45.60) to 500 kroner ($60), all these tariffs including a buffet-style breakfast. The hotel caters to groups, but also welcomes the individual tourist.

Hummeren Hotel, in Tananger, eight miles from Stavanger (tel. 59-61-31), receives guests from mid-May to mid-September, charging 350 kroner ($42) for bathless doubles, 300 kroner ($36) for singles, these tariffs including a continental breakfast. A two-story wooden-frame hotel, it stands on a little harbor, practically on the sea. A desire for informal living is a must here—definitely no frills. Guests dance to piano music every night except Monday in a large room overlooking the harbor (a combo often plays). One of the joys of eating here is the privilege of being able to net one's own lobster from a pit on the terrace. Tananger is a popular fishing village.

Viste Beach Hotel, Randaberg, six miles from Stavanger (tel. 59-70-22), is a sprawling white hotel built right by the sea. In addition, it has separate bungalows with picture windows and private terraces. Offering a private beach and lawns for sunbathing, it is popular with the family trade. Doubles with bath go for 550 kroner ($66), including breakfast, but you may prefer to rent a bungalow on the beach, accommodating four to five persons. The hotel rooms, sparsely furnished, offer good views. The bungalows are furnished motel style, all compact and up-to-date. A lunch costs 85 kroner ($10.20); a dinner, 110 kroner ($13.20). The hotel is open from May 1 to September 30.

Fjelltun Gjesteheim, 4 Gulaksveien (tel. 58-50-46), bills itself as a "studentheim" and a "Bibelskole." Attracting a very international clientele, this summer hotel lies 2½ miles south of Stavanger, in attractive surroundings near a beach and swimming hall. Its 58 guest rooms are furnished in immaculate Nordic taste, each equipped with phone, shower, and toilet. Guests are allowed access to a kitchen and a TV room. The hotel accepts bookings only from June 1 to August 15 and charges from 220 kroner ($26.40) in a single, from 350 kroner ($42) in a double, including breakfast. Try to make reservations as far in advance as possible, as this boxy modern hotel tends to fill up quickly.

A Youth Hostel

Mosvangen Youth Hostel/Tourist Center, 21 Henrik Ibsengate (tel. 53-29-76), lies in beautiful surroundings less than two miles from the center of Stavanger. All buildings were modernized in 1983. The prices vary from 90 kroner ($10.80) to 320 kroner ($38.40) per night per person. The price includes breakfast.

DINING CHOICES: **Sjøhuset Skagen,** Skagenkaien (tel. 52-61-90), is a first-class restaurant, packed with antiques, that operates from an old timbered "boathouse," adding atmosphere and charm to the site. The old maritime warehouse has many rooms on different levels, and residents of Stavanger have long ago selected their favorite nook or cranny. The decor is nautical, ranging from models of sailing ships to fishing equipment. Naturally, the kitchen specializes in fresh-tasting fish dishes, a meal costing from 120 kroner ($14.40).

Elisabeth Restaurant, 41 Kongsgate (tel. 53-29-67), lies in the center of town near the train station. Here Elisabeth Aune serves a superb French cuisine. Attracting the "oil barons" of Stavanger, this restaurant makes for a marvelous change of pace from Norwegian fare if you can afford the prices. Both the staff and the service are outstanding. The specialties served are of good quality and tastily prepared. Excluding wine, prices begin at 140 kroner ($16.80).

Café Ajax, Atlantic Hotel, 1 Jernbaneveien (tel. 52-75-20), is for those who enjoy taking their meals in a top-level atmosphere in a first-class hotel. The location is ideal: in the center of Stavanger, opening onto Breiavatnet (Swan Lake), near the tourist bureau. The café is the least expensive dining spot at this well-run hotel. The setting is light and airy, handsomely decorated. Under the glow of globe lighting, guests enjoy light lunches, snacks, and salads. There is always a tempting selection of smørrebrød, including roast beef. Count on spending from 75 kroner ($9). It is open from 11 a.m. to 6 p.m. weekdays and Saturday (closed Sunday).

La Gondola A/S Steakhouse and Pizzeria, 8 Nytorget (tel. 53-42-35), is an Italian restaurant with a warm atmosphere. A fixed-price lunch here costs 38 kroner ($4.56), while a dinner goes for from 65 kroner ($7.80). If you just want pizza, expect to pay from 45 kroner ($5.40).

You can also purchase cooked seafood or picnic delights in the **Skagenkaien**

Market right on the waterfront. You'll have a lot of choices for making your own tasty sandwiches, at costs ranging from 25 kroner ($3) up.

THE CHIEF SIGHTS: The **Stavanger Cathedral,** facing the marketplace, retains many of its original features, and is indisputably one of Norway's most outstanding ecclesiastical monuments to the Middle Ages. The cathedral was probably dedicated around 1125, when a bishopric was established. After a fire in 1272, the chancel was built in the Gothic style. The larger part of the church, the magnificent nave, remains as it was built before 1125 in the Norman style. If you visit the church, seek out the fine memorial tablets and the enormous pulpit, outstanding examples of baroque art in Norway. The cathedral, restored most recently during the early 1940s, is open from 9 a.m. to 9 p.m., mid-May to mid-September (10:30 a.m. to 6 p.m. on Sunday). Worship services are on Sunday at 11 a.m., on Wednesday at 7 p.m.

There are many opportunities to see goldsmiths, silversmiths, and enamel workers at their crafts in and around Stavanger. For details, call the tourist office at 52-84-37 or 52-72-54.

The **Stavanger Museum and Maritime Museum,** 16 Muségate (tel. 52-60-35), contains archeological, historical, zoological, and maritime collections. It is open daily from 11 a.m. to 3 p.m. June 1 to August 31; 11 a.m. to 2 p.m. Saturday; and 11 a.m. to 3 p.m. Sunday only from September 1 to May 31. Admission is 6 kroner (72¢) for adults, 2 kroner (24¢) for children.

The **Ullandhaugh Tower,** three miles from the center, offers one of the best views. You can reach it by taking bus 10, departing from St. Olaf's Garden and going to Gosen. The cost of the one-way fare is 8 kroner (96¢).

Ledaal is a famous mansion built in 1800 for the Kielland family. It is now the local royal residence, belonging to the Stavanger Museum. If you wish to view its antique furniture and decorations, you have to get in touch with the museum (tel. 52-60-35). The mansion can be reached on foot by walking a quarter of a mile from the railway station. It is open weekdays from 11 a.m. to 1 p.m. June 1 to August 31; 11 a.m. to 2 p.m. on Sunday. Admission is 6 kroner (72¢) for adults, 2 kroner (24¢) for children.

Breidablikk, the other patrician mansion, this one built in 1880, is also run by the Stavanger Museum and keeps the same hours and charges the same admission as Ledaal.

TOURS: For a two-hour view of the sights of Stavanger, including vistas of the Ryfylke fjord arms, a guided motorcoach tour leaves daily (except Sunday) at 11 a.m. from June 1 to August 31 in front of the cathedral (visited at the end of the tour). Cost is 70 kroner ($8.40), half fare for children.

For a real economy special, take bus 10, 12, 17, 40, or 50 from St. Olavsgaarden for a circular ride around Stavanger (no guide). You get 30 minutes for 8 kroner (96¢).

A staggering number of fjord cruises are offered, but the star choice is the three-hour Clipper cruise along the Lysefjord. Passengers generally reach for tranquilizers as they pass under the famed **Pulpit Rock,** towering precariously 1800 feet above the fjord. The sightseeing boat leaves daily at 10:30 a.m. and 4:30 p.m. from Strandkaien. The price is 125 kroner ($15).

Finally, you can take any number of independent fjord excursions on one of the ships of the White Fleet that traverse the Ryfylke fjords. For tickets and help with itineraries, go to the **Stavanger Steamship Co.,** Ryfylkekaien (tel. 52-00-20). Tours are generally run from April 1 to mid-September.

AFTER DARK: The Cobra Club, Atlantic Hotel, 1 Jernbaneveien (tel. 52-75-20), is a leading nighttime rendezvous, billing itself as an "adult disco." Fully licensed, it is sleekly and elegantly decorated. Many local people are members; otherwise, visitors are charged a cover of around 50 kroner ($6). Drinks begin at 40 kroner ($4.80). You can dance to the latest music or else drink in a richly textured setting.

4. Solfonn/Seljestad

Fast rising as both a summer excursion center and a winter ski resort, Solfonn, 80 miles from Haugesund, is easily reached on a cross-country bus ride. In the Hardanger district, Solfonn lies on the route linking the fjord district of the west with Telemark in the east.

Not-to-be-missed natural phenomena include the view of the **Folgefonn glacier,** the **Seljestad gorge** split by a highway, and the much-photographed **Laatefoss waterfall** on the road to **Odda.**

A ski slope, suitable either for downhill or slalom, makes Solfonn an ideal winter resort. The chair lift also operates in summer, whisking visitors up for a magnificent view of the surrounding area for a charge of 12 kroner ($2.14).

The community of **Seljestad** is in the extreme southern part of Hardanger, 15 miles south of Odda, 2000 feet above sea level. Its traditions as a tourist center go back for more than a century. Once guest houses and a coaching inn stood to greet visitors in the 19th century, but now you'll find modern hotels and motels. The most popular months to visit are from May deep into September.

ACCOMMODATIONS: Solfonn Turisthotell, Skarde (tel. 45-122), is a mountain-ledge hotel on an inland route halfway between Voss and Stavanger. Built just after the war, it is surrounded by snow-covered mountains and has its own ski lift. Not much in decor is needed here, just windows to embrace the view. Facilities include an indoor heated swimming pool, a sun terrace, sauna bath, and hairdresser for women. Solfonn is open all year. Because of a change of owners, its prices were unavailable at press time.

Seljestad Hotel and Motel, Seljestad, Hardanger (tel. 45-155), is a modern hotel/motel complex owned and operated by Marit and Svein Thorsen, who are constantly adding to and experimenting with their establishment—trying to make the rooms distinctive and interesting and the services memorable for their guests. The hotel has 47 rooms, 43 with private bath or shower.

Although the Seljestad is open year round, it charges high-season rates from June 1 to August 31. During high season, the bed-and-breakfast rate in a single room is 320 kroner ($38.40). Doubles range from 180 kroner ($21.60) to 240 kroner ($28.80) per person. Breakfast is included. Motel units, which feature private balconies and built-in closets and desks, cost about 175 kroner ($21) per person for a four-bedded room. Full-board rates in season range from 325 kroner ($39) per person per day.

À la carte lunches and three-course dinners are served in the dining room. Music and dancing are a nightly feature. The hotel is an ideal base for day tours of the area, and the staff is happy to arrange special excursions for its guests.

5. Lofthus

A favorite spot in all the Hardanger district is the sleepy hamlet of **Lofthus,** once the haunt of Edvard Grieg and other artists. Rich in tradition, it is pervaded by a melancholy peacefulness. On a fjord, the resort is enveloped by snow-capped mountains, farms, and orchards that form a galaxy of blossoms in early summer. Hovering in the background is the Folgefonn glacier.

From Solfonn, it's possible to catch a morning bus to the industrial town of Odda. From there, a bus leaves at 1 p.m. for Lofthus, about an hour's ride. This trip is exceptional, even for the most jaded of the scenic set. The driver daringly winds along a narrow road skirting the fjords, slips in and out of several tunnels blasted through the mountains, and whizzes past cascading waterfalls. In other words, it's not the best time to be reading *War and Peace*.

WHERE TO STAY: For the lucky few who get to stay over, Lofthus has a hotel famous for its orchard blossoms, and it's been run by the same family for four generations. Excursionists for the day might want to stop here for lunch. It is served at the **Hotel Ullensvang** (tel. Lofthus 61-100), a romantically located inn on the edge of the misty blue Hardanger Fjord. Ullensvang was once the retreat of Grieg (his piano rests peacefully in a tiny cottage on the grounds).

To the old inn a bedroom extension of contemporary, streamlined, and efficiently up-to-date rooms was added in the 1970s, and staying in the new wing is more expensive. Bed and breakfast in the standard rooms is 325 kroner ($39) per person with bath (some of these contain private balconies as well). Deluxe accommodations in the new wing are budget breaking, of course.

A good and hearty Norwegian lunch, three courses, is served for 175 kroner ($21). Most guests, however, are drawn to the buffet at dinner, served in a dining room which has poles angled along the wall like a Viking ship. At least 65 dishes are spread out—everything from jellied salmon to homemade cakes. The price of the buffet at night is 165 kroner ($19.80).

Throughout the antique part of Ullensvang are prize hand-painted chests, wooden implements, copper pots and pans, old china. Lounges are traditionally furnished; some have a corner fireplace (lit in the evenings). Occasionally, folk dancing is staged, and guests are invited to join in. Six nights a week a band plays for dancing. During the day, rowboats and fishing equipment—belonging to the hotel—may be used freely. A speed boat may be rented as well. A newer extension features an indoor heated swimming pool, two sauna baths, a hairdresser, and souvenir shop.

Ullensvang Gjesteheim (tel. 61-236) is a cozy, homey guesthouse, furnished with warm, personalized touches by its owners. Their rooms are attractively decorated, costing 180 kroner ($21.60) in a single, the price rising to 220 kroner ($26.40) in a double. You may relish their home-cooked food which is made even nicer because of the company and the pleasant surroundings. Breakfast is an additional 45 kroner ($5.40), and either lunch or dinner goes for 95 kroner ($11.40).

6. Utne

Utne is a compact community with an attractive position, having a view of the entrances to three fjords: Indre Samla, Granvin, and Eid. Across Utnefjorden, the formidable bulk of Oksen (7953 feet) rises from the shoreline of the headland separating the Granvin and the Eid fjords. A great ravine breaches the steep slope of Oksen, its sinister shape sharply revealed as the shadows lengthen. Utnefjorden is almost two miles wide opposite Utne and nearly 2700 feet deep in places, making it deeper than any other part of the Hardangerfjord.

Utne is at the center of the broad base of the northern end of the Folgefonn peninsula, with mountaiin heights looming nearby. Two valleys converge on the town, Utnedalen to the east and Fossdalen to the west. The river through Fossdalen forms fine falls as it drops through the woods toward the end of its course, dividing into two branches as it reached the fjord.

The **Hardanger Folk Museum,** on a rocky promontory at the northwest end of the village, was founded in 1911 and is owned and financed by seven communities of the area. Old timber buildings from several parts of Inner Hardanger have been erected in the grounds and equipped according to their eras. By the fjord are old boathouses and a general store that once stood on the quayside.

When fjords were the highways of western Norway, Utne was an important junction, and it was the first place in Inner Hardanger to offer board and lodging to travelers. **Utne Hotel** (see below) opened in 1722 and has belonged to the same family since 1789. It first became internationally known among tourists when it was managed by Torbjørg Utne (1812–1903), affectionately known as Mor (Mother) Utne for her warm hospitality.

The handsome original bank building, founded iin 1846, still stands at the edge of the quay, although the bank business has moved several times since that construction.

About 10 miles away from Utne lies the **Agatun,** one of the oldest preserved farms in Norway. Here you can see Norwegian farming culture and rural arts and crafts.

As road systems were developed in western Norway, Utne lost some of its commercial importance, although this has been partially regained by construction of a road along the west side of Sørfjordent to Odda and the development of Kvanndal and Kinsarvik (see below) as the largest car-ferry terminals in this part of the country.

Utne Hotel (tel. 66-983) is still in business, and if you'd like to relax in a comfortable atmosphere of hospitality, this is the place for you. For five generations, the proprietors of this hotel have had an unbroken tradition of service and consideration for their guests. There are no other hotels or pensions in Utne. Bed-and-breakfast in a bathless room costs 225 kroner ($27) per person, while a room with bath goes for 285 kroner ($34.20) per person. You can have lunch for 90 kroner ($10.80) and dinner for 125 kroner ($15) and up. The hotel is just a few minutes from the road and the ferry quay.

7. Eidfjord

At the northern extremity of the Hardangerfjord lies the Eidfjord district. There are approximately 1000 people living in the community of Eidfjord, their economy based mainly on agriculture, tourism, and cottage industries. As nearly 45 miles of the Oslo-Bergen highway cuts its way through this district, there's lots of mountain traffic in summer.

The county of Eidfjord contains nearly one-quarter of **Hardangervidda National Park,** which is on the largest high mountain plateau in Europe, home to the continent's largest herd of wild reindeer (20,000). On the plateau, you'll find well-marked footpaths to follow from one to another of the 15 tourist huts. These can offer accommodation with full board from about 225 kroner ($27) per person. Their specialty in the kitchen is mountain trout with heavy sour cream, a feast for a gourmet.

Several canyons lead down from the plateau to the fjords, the most renowned one being the **Måbø Valley.** In this canyon, the famous Vøringsfoss waterfall can be seen. The free fall of this cataract is 550 feet, but there are even higher ones in Eidfjord. The Valurefoss in Hjømo Valley has a free fall of almost 800 feet.

More than 1000 years ago, the east-west road across Norway passed through Eidfjord. Part of it up the Måbø Valley was steep and challenging, with 124 curves and 1300 steps. Part of this road has been restored for hardy hikers.

In Sima Valley, about 3¾ miles from the center of Eidfjord, the **Sima Power Plant** can be visited. This is one of the largest hydroelectric plants in Europe, and guided tours are given. In connection with the construction of the power plant, several dams were built, one of which, the enormous Sysendam, can be seen from the R7 road.

A small mountain farm, **Kjeaasen,** nearly 2000 feet above sea level, can be reached by car, although until eight years ago, people who lived there had to climb up an extremely steep footpath. From Kjeaasen you have a splendid view. The footpath is recommended only to those in good physical condition and with strong nerves.

Eidfjord Old Church is a stone building from the 14th century. Visits with a guide can be arranged with the tourist office (tel. 65-177).

Numerous lakes and rivers offer good trout fishing, and in two rivers, Eio and Bjoreio, as well as in the Eidfjord Lake, you can fish for salmon. The local tourist office has rowboats and bicycles to rent.

WHERE TO STAY: In Eidfjord, you can find all types of accommodation—hotels, motels, tourist huts, and camping huts of various sizes, standards, and prices.

Hotell Vøringsfoss (tel. 65-184) lies by the fjord in Nedre Eidfjord. The hotel represents a pleasing combination of the old and the new. It has 58 rooms, most of them with baths. A double with bath costs from 380 kroner ($45.60) to 440 kroner ($52.80), with breakfast included. In the dining room with its excellent view to the fjord you can have lunch for 85 kroner ($10.20) and dinner for 110 kroner ($13.20).

Ingrids Appartements (tel. 65-154) is also by the fjord in Nedre Eidfjord, renting 22 beds to travelers. The view of the fjord is outstanding. The facilities here are modern, self-contained apartments with high standards. You can have a room for two persons for 290 kroner ($34.80) or for four for 350 kroner ($42).

About 18½ miles from Eidfjord on the R7 road isi **Dyranut Touristhut,** which has a special mountain atmosphere characteristic of accommodations in days gone by but nevertheless pleasant. A double room costs 200 kroner ($24), a room with three beds going for 260 kroner ($31.20). Breakfast is an extra 45 kroner ($5.40). Dinner costs 85 kroner ($10.20) and will give you the chance to enjoy Norwegian dishes such as sour-cream porridge and cured meats.

8. Kinsarvik

The main village of Kinsarvik is on a glacier-formed ridge at the mouth of the Kinso River, which rises in the heart of the Hardangervidda and forms four magnificent waterfalls as it drops from the plateau to Husedalen on its way to the sea. An early settlement in Kinsarvik was the marketplace for the region and attracted merchants from eastern Norway, who exchanged bog-iron and furs for salt extracted from the sea by local farmers.

The plot of grass which slopes to a stony beach near the Kinsarvik ferry terminal is **Skiperstod,** site of a boathouse for naval longships from about 900 until 1350.

Borstova, the building on the fjord side of the green facing the church, was constructed on the site and partly from the timbers of St. Olav's Guildhall, the meeting place of the local guild until 1680. It is now a council chamber and social center.

Kinsarvik Church, said to have been built by Scottish masterbuilders at the end of the 12th century, is one of the oldest stone churches in Norway. The interior was restored in 1961 to its pre-Reformation condition. It has a 17th-century pulpit painted by Peter Reimers, a painted and carved altarpiece, and medieval frescoes. Until Utne Church was built in 1896, Kinsarvik Church drew worshippers from a wide area along both sides of Utnefjorden and Eidfjorden. Many came to the services by church boats, no doubt providing a wonderful spectacle in the bay as they converged on Kinsarvik.

The stone column *(minnestein)* on the green commemorates the local men who fought in the wars which led to the end of the union with Denmark in 1814.

Kinsarvik was the principal timber port of Hardanger in the 17th and early 18th centuries, the main customers being Scots. When the export of timber was transferred to Bergen in 1750, Kinsarvik developed a shipbuilding industry which continued until 1870. It became a center for woodcarving when Lars Kinsarvik (1846–1925), painter, fiddler, and poet, revived the traditional forms of the craft.

The early service boats from Bergen to the Inner Hardangerfjord called at Lofthus and Utne but not at Kinsarvik, and, for some time, the village lost some of its importance. This was restored by the opening of the road to Eidfjord, followed by the completion of the road along Sørfjorden half a century ago, and finally by the establishment of car-ferry links with Utne and Kvanndal. It is now one of the busiest traffic junctions in western Norway. A pewter factory is one of its principal industries.

WHERE TO STAY: Kinsarvik Fjord Hotel (tel. 63-100) is a modern and well-equipped family hotel, with 75 well-appointed rooms, 62 with bath/shower and toilet. A room with bath on the bed-and-breakfast rate rents for 300 kroner ($36) per person. Even if you don't stay here, you might like to have lunch, 120 kroner ($14.40), or dinner, 135 kroner ($16.20), in its pleasant dining room. There's a fully licensed bar, and an international orchestra plays for the guests' pleasure.

9. Ulvik

That rare institution—an unspoiled resort—Ulvik lies like a fist at the end of an arm of the Hardangerfjord. This summer tourist center is graced with misty peaks and fruit farms. The fresh-air-loving English flock here in late May and early June when drifts of blossoms perfume the air along the apple-tree walk, and again at harvest time in September when the hills are saffron.

The village's century-old church is attractively decorated in the style of the region ("English organist needed to play at church services" is a common sign).

The serenity of Ulvik is overwhelming. Wars seem far removed, almost inconceivable. But the newness, the freshness of the wooden houses, is a painful reminder that the village was partially destroyed during World War II.

The Ulvik tourist office, in the center, is helpful in arranging any number of excursions—from trips on fjord steamers to rides on a milk boat as it stops along the shore at various dairy farms.

From Bergen, Ulvik is reached by taking a train to Voss, then connecting with a bus. Those who are following our "circuitous" route to Oslo can board a steamer at the last stop in Lofthus, a 1½-hour ride to Ulvik.

ACCOMMODATIONS: For accommodations, you have a choice of traditional or modern.

Strand Hotel og Motel (tel. 26-305) is a waterside, low-constructed motel in the center of town with its own private beach. All the bedrooms are completely modern and overlook the fjord. The owners have extended the building, adding a motel with a dozen rooms, all with bath, shower, and toilet. Seven of these newer units contain private balconies, and four of them come equipped with private terraces. In the high season, a single with bath rents for 200 kroner ($48), a double going for 620 kroner ($74.40), with bath, these tariffs including breakfast. A five-minute walk from the steamer dock, the motel is open from April 1 to October 10. It is licensed for beer and wine, and has a dining room where you can order lunches and dinners for 110 kroner ($13.20). Waterskiing, motorboat rides, and rowing are popular pastimes. There's a large hall over the heated swimming pool which can be used in spring and autumn. On top of this hall is a roof garden which can be reached directly from the reception hall and which has an entry to the garden.

Bjotveit Hotel (tel. 26-300) is a 60-bed, year-round hotel and annex, opposite the Ulvik church and about a 150-yard walk from the quayside. Mrs. Arthea Hovde is the secret behind the warmth, success, and vitality of this modernized hotel, catering primarily to the family trade. The compact, well-furnished bedrooms along the front have balconies and good views of the fjords and mountains. The wee rooms in back are for latecomers without reservations. Mrs. Hovde charges 280 kroner ($33.60) for her bathless doubles in high season, June 10 to August 31. For a double with shower or toilet, the rate increases to 350 kroner ($42). A single room costs 180 kroner ($21.60). The meals served here, 85 kroner ($10.20) for a complete dinner, are home-cooked. The waitresses bring large silver platters loaded with good-tasting Norwegian dishes. Guests take coffee in the living room—one set gathering around the fireplace, the other watching television.

Ulvik Fjord Pensjonat (tel. 26-170) is one of the finest guesthouses along Hardangerfjord. A wooden-frame structure, painted white, the guesthouse has been in operation since 1974. It was built about 700 yards from the center of Ulvik. However, a separate, one-story bedroom wing, with spacious, pleasantly furnished rooms, was completed in 1977. Four bathless doubles are rented at a cost of 340 kroner ($40.80). For a double with bath the cost goes up to 400 kroner ($48). A single with shower and toilet is priced at 260 kroner ($31.20), but drops to just 210 kroner ($25.20) without bath. All these tariffs include a Norwegian breakfast. After stays of three days, half-board rates will be quoted. If you're visiting just for a meal, a dinner costs around 100 kroner ($12). Guests enjoy use of the garden and the house lies just a short distance fom the fjord. Lilly and Odd H. Hammer are your hosts, and they run a hospitable, satisfactory operation, serving good food and, if you wish, wine and beer as well. They also have a sauna.

10. Voss

A train ride of less than two hours takes visitors from Bergen to this summer resort and winter ski center, lying in a district between two fjords, Sogne and Hardanger. Voss, on the shores of Lake Vangsvatn, is known for its wealth of folklore. Maybe the trolls don't strike fear into the hearts of farm children any more, but they are still called out of hiding to give the visitors a little fun. Voss is a good center, with many excursions and tour possibilities.

WHERE TO STAY: Voss has been discovered, and Bergen bankers may soon erect vast luxury hotels on mountainsides. But in the meantime, the town offers many moderately priced living arrangements—a good range for many purses.

Hotel Jarl (tel. 51-19-33) is centrally situated. Opened in 1961, it added a new wing in 1972 and an indoor swimming pool in 1979. The Jarl now has 110 beds, most of them in rooms with private baths and toilets. There are singles, doubles, suites, and family rooms. You can take your meals in the spacious and pleasant dining room, relax in comfortable lounges or at an intimate bistro and bar. The hotel also has attractive public rooms, a sauna bath, games room, and disco. Single rooms rent for 380 kroner ($45.60), depending on the plumbing, two-bedded accommodations for 600 kroner ($72). Dinner is 110 kroner ($13.20), but a Norwegian breakfast is included in the rates. A popular disco, Knight's Club, is on the premises, attracting a young, most often noisy clientele.

Fleischers Hotel (tel. 51-11-55), a first class-hotel, was built the year that John Wilkes Booth was shooting it up at the Ford Theatre, and it's seen a long line of portmanteau-carriers all through the Victorian era up to the present-day rise of Voss as a resort. On the lakefront, Fleischers couldn't be more convenient; the Bergen-Oslo train stops out back. This gracious old frame hotel—resplendent with gables and towers—added a modern wing that stands in stark contrast with the old. Doubles with bath cost 650 kroner ($78) in high season, and singles are charged 430 kroner ($51.60) with bath. Breakfast is included in these tariffs. The motel section has 30 units, all with private showers, toilets, kitchenettes, and terraces overlooking the lake. In the old part of the hotel, the rooms are consistently old-fashioned, with a wealth of furniture and plenty of room to store hoop skirts. Room after room in this part is wood paneled; the drawing room, library, lounges, and billiard room retain nostalgic furnishings—but the grandest of all is the dining room, dominated by an orante carved-wood serving counter, from which Norwegian meals are brought to the tables. The fully licensed hotel features two bars, dancing to a band, films, and occasional folk dancing.

Hotel Vossegangen (tel. 51-21-44), rebuilt in 1951 after having been bombed during the war, is a top-quality lakeside hotel whose origins go back to the first half of the 19th century. Re-created with all the modern conveniences, it offers 160 beds; many of the rooms have lounge chairs and sofas. Depending on the season, singles cost from 330 kroner ($39.60) to 360 kroner ($43.20); doubles from 225 kroner ($27) to 250 kroner ($30) per person. In ski season, guests stay on full pension terms, costing from 310 kroner ($37.20) to 350 kroner ($42). The lounges at the Vossegangen are sensibly constructed to capture the view. The hotel has its own park opening onto a lake, where there are boats for guests.

Nøring Pension (tel. 51-12-11), is a 45-bed, first-class pension near the river, about a ten-minute walk from the center of town. Opened in the postwar years, the Nøring provides a modernized accommodation, with well-furnished, pleasant-looking doubles at 330 kroner ($39.60) per person daily. Licensed for beer and wine, the pension serves good meals, with generous portions. If you're dropping in just for a meal, a complete dinner costs 85 kroner ($10.20). The Nøring is open in both summer and winter (ski boots are available). The lounge opens onto a terrace with summer garden furniture.

Vang Pensjonat, 31 Uttrågate (tel. 51-21-45), stands right in the center of town, a modern (built in 1967) pension with severe Nordic styling. Everything is of a high, acceptable standard, and the lounges are comfortable. The pension, which receives guests from right after Christmas until the end of October, has small, cozy rooms. A single rents for 225 kroner ($27), a double goes for 330 kroner ($39.60), and some three-bedded units cost 400 kroner ($48). For stays of three days or more, you'll be quoted modestly priced pension or half-board rates. Otherwise, the tariffs quoted include a Norwegian breakfast, and a lunch or dinner will cost from 85 kroner ($7.80). You might ask for a room with a balcony.

Kringsjå Pension (tel. 51-16-27) is a friendly, inviting modern guesthouse, right in the center of Voss, owned and run by Liv and Knut Klemetzen. The public rooms are spacious and airy, and the bedrooms are plainly decorated and furnished in a functional style. In a room with toilet, the charge is 180 kroner ($21.60) per person daily, rising to 190 kroner ($22.80) per person daily if you want a toilet and shower. An extra bed will be placed in your room for another 110 kroner ($13.20). Singles pay a supplement of 50 kroner ($6). After three days, half-board rates will be quoted; otherwise, you'll pay an extra 85 kroner ($10.20) for lunch or dinner. A Norwegian breakfast, however, is included in the tariffs quoted. If you stay here you'll be away from traffic, yet just a two-minute walk from the shopping center.

Voss Turistheim (tel. 51-16-13), about a mile from the rail station in the direction of Bulken, is really the Voss High School, but in summer it is converted into a 110-bed pension, offering one of the least expensive accommodations in Voss. The Turistheim is a collection of framed cranberry-red buildings that look like a compound of New England farmhouses. All rooms have hot and cold running water. The cost is 280 kroner ($33.60) for two persons, 195 kroner ($23.40) for a single. Three meals a day—good basic cooking—are offered, with full-board terms priced from 250 kroner ($30) per person daily. However, pension rates apply only after a stay of three days. Ordered separately, a luncheon costs 75 kroner ($9); a middag, 95 kroner ($11.40). The Turistheim receives guests from June 1 to August 20.

The Voss Ungdomsherberge (youth hostel), **Skulestadmo** (tel. 51-20-17), is open year round and charges 80 kroner ($9.60) for a bed, breakfast included, to members of the Y.H.A. About two miles from the railroad and bus station, the hostel offers a special winter rate for ski enthusiasts: 150 kroner ($18) per person for half board. There are 56 beds. The hostel is closed for cleanup between 11 a.m. and 4 p.m. daily.

READERS' PENSION SELECTION: "We were directed by the local tourist service to the new **Bavallstova Pensjonat** (tel. 51-18-76), about 3¾ miles from the center of Voss. Here all the rooms have showers and toilets, there is a large lounge with an open fireplace, and the bright, shiny cafeteria has a panoramic view of Voss, the lake below, and the mountains beyond. It is close to the Bavallen ski lift and mountaineering. Our hostess spoke English and was very helpful and pleasant. Her daughter was our guide for the Norway in a Nutshell trip. We had a comfortable room, an excellent breakfast selection, and a good supper. Doubles rent for from 250 kroner ($30)" (George F. and Jan Bauer, Golden, Colo.).

WHERE TO EAT: Most visitors seem to prefer to dine at their hotels or pensions, but on Vansgate, in the center of town, are some moderately priced cafés.

The **Vangen Café,** Vangen Super-Market, Vangen Souvenirs, 42 Vangsgate (tel. 51-12-05), is right in the heart of the shopping center. Simple and unpretentious, it is a favorite of working people and visiting foreigners alike. Simple meals begin at 60 kroner ($7.20).

A good bargain is **Arnes Kro** (corner café), 47 Vangsgate (tel. 51-15-61). The decor is familiar—wooden tables and seats. The food is excellent and the portions large. Half a chicken with french fries and salad costs 45 kroner ($5.40), and a large pizza, suitable for four, goes for 65 kroner ($7.80). A lot of Norwegian specialties are offered also. Arne Wie is the proprietor.

THE MAJOR SIGHTS: In the center of Voss is a 13th-century church, Vangskyrkja, with a timbered tower. Completely restored, the early Gothic structure is open from 9 a.m. to 7 p.m. in summer (admission free). Of note are the Renaissance-style pulpit, the stone altar and triptych, the woodcarvings, and the painted ceiling. Luckily, the church escaped bombing in World War II.

St. Olav's Cross, near the cinema, is the oldest historic relic in Voss. The stone cross is believed to have been raised when the people of the town adopted Christianity in 1023.

Finnesloftet (tel. 51-11-00), lying about a mile west of Voss in Finne, is one of the oldest timbered houses in Norway, dating from the mid-13th century. In summer the visiting hours are from 10 a.m. to 3:30 p.m., and the admission is 8 kroner (96¢).

The **Folk Museum of Mølster** (tel. 51-11-05) is a compound of authentic houses and furnishings, tracing the daily farmlife of the early ancestors of the district. On a guided tour many fascinating items are displayed and explained, including a milk strainer made of cow's hair and implements used to make beer out of corn. A taxi is recommended for the uphill climb: those whose grandfathers are part goat can attempt to walk it. From May 1 to October 1, it is open from 10 a.m. to 5 p.m. (closing an hour for lunch at 1 p.m.). Off-season it is open weekdays from 11 a.m. to 3 p.m. Admission is 6 kroner (72¢) for adults, 3 kroner (36¢) for children.

A ride on the **Hangursbanen Cable** (tel. 51-18-17) is fun. For 20 kroner ($2.40) round trip for adults, 15 kroner ($1.80) for children, you ascend the mountain for a view of Voss and the environs. Refreshments or meals are available at a mountain-clinging restaurant. The hardy take the cable up, then spend the rest of the afternoon strolling leisurely down the mountain.

ORGANIZED SCENIC TOURS: Voss offers any number of excellent excursions, including **Norway in a Nutshell** (the Myrdal–Flåm valley train ride is only a slice of it). This tour usually leaves five days a week from Voss. The price: 150 kroner ($18). On every weekday, a full-day tour is slated either to **Hardanger** or to **Sognefjord** (these trips often include waterfalls, a stave church, and fjord hamlets). Prices average around 175 kroner ($21) for a day's excursion. For tickets and information about any of these tours, go to the tourist bureau. All these excursions leave from the NSB Travel Agency, 32 Uttrågata (tel. 51-18-35), at times ranging from 9 a.m. to 11 a.m. Reservations have to be made one day in advance.

VOSS AFTER DARK: **Fleischers Top Spot** bar at Vossevangen (tel. .51-11-55) is open for dancing every day from 8:30 p.m. except on Sunday. A band plays music, and the cover charge ranges from 45 kroner ($5.40) to 50 kroner ($6). No jeans are allowed.

SKIING: Voss is sprucing up, continually adding to its facilities—and is definitely in the ski race to overtake Geilo and Lillehammer as Norway's most popular winter playground. With its chair lifts, ski lifts, and aerial cableway that carries passengers up 2625 feet, Voss is prepared as never before to welcome skiers.

The town offers what it calls a "ski circus": beginners take the Hangur cable car; one ski lift (3600 feet long) goes from Traastølen to the top of Slettafjell (wide choice of downhill runs); the Bavallen lift is for the slalom slopes, and the downhill runs are at Lønehorgi.

The Ski School, at the end of the cable-car run, is packed with experienced instructors who make it all seem so easy—and the lessons are inexpensive. The tourist office and hotels can book you into the ski school.

Parents can park children, ages 3 to 7, in a "snow nursery," while they're spending the day skiing. After a child reaches the age of 7, Voss-ites consider that it's high time he or she gets on skis. A special branch of the Ski School handles these youngsters. Ski equipment—everything from boots to touring skis—can be rented cheaply.

Après-ski life, such as tea dances and folklore evenings, flourishes in Voss. The happenings are particularly successful in that they draw on heritage ("Have you ever met a troll?") and don't try to imitate the nighttime activities of more sophisticated ski centers.

A TRIP TO SOGNEFJORD: Motorists with more time may want to take the following trip to the Sognefjord district, the largest of all Norwegian fjords. From Voss the northern route leads to **Vik.** The scenery is beautiful, and the road goes along for miles across a desolate tableland at an altitude averaging 3000 feet above sea level. The lakes on a summer day appear green, and on the distant slopes is snow.

In Vik, try to see the stave church, one of the most attractive in Norway. After visiting the church, you can take the road until you reach **Vangsnes.** From there you can make ferry connections across the Sognefjord to either **Balestrand** or **Dragsvik.** Once across, you can take road no. 5 north. The highway is steep, bringing you through pleasant countryside with waterfalls until you reach the hamlet of **Viksdalen,** about 40 miles from Dragsvik.

Those journeying on the long road to Ålesund may want to stop over here for the night. My recommendation is **Viken Pensjonat,** Viksdalen (tel. 16-706), right on the roadside. Gunhild Viken Tjønneland will welcome you, offering her hospitality in large and clean rooms with hot and cold running water. The scenery is pastoral, and the site is convenient for anglers or boating enthusiasts. A single costs 140 kroner ($16.80); a double, 210 kroner ($25.20). The breakfast at 45 kroner ($5.40) remains one of the best I've ever had in Scandinavia. The dinner at 75 kroner ($9) is served in a large guest room and often features trout from the brook outside the house.

11. Balestrand

Long known for its arts and crafts, Balestrand, on the Sognefjord, is a good stopover on the trip from Bergen to Flåm. The little town lies on the northern shore of the fjord, at the junction of the Vetlefjord, the Esefjord, and the Fjaerlandsfjord. The nearest railway station with boat connections is Flåm, 53 miles away. Both day and night there is express boat service between Bergen and Balestrand. There is also express boat service between Balestrand and Flåm.

If you're interested in doing some exploring, you might visit the tourist office in the town first. The staff there can also put you in touch with local crafts-people. While there, you can pick up an excursion program and purchase tickets for a number of scheduled 1½-day tours. It's possible to take a taxi plane across the Jostedal Glacier.

Kaiser Wilhelm II was a frequent visitor to Balestrand in days gone by, and he presented to the district two statues of old Norse heroes, King Bele and Fridt-jof the Bold. The English church of St. Olav in Balestrand is a tiny wooden building, dating from 1897.

You can explore by setting out in nearly every direction, as there are good country lanes with little traffic, as well as a wide choice of marked trails and upland farm tracks. A touring map may be purchased at the tourist office. There is good sea fishing, as well as lake and river trout fishing. Fishing tackle can be rented, as can rowboats and bicycles.

WHERE TO STAY: Midtnes Pensjonat (tel. 91-133) stands close to the road in the center of Balestrand. This well-run and reasonably priced boarding house rents out 70 beds for guests. It's family owned and managed. The rooms are pleasant-ly furnished and well kept, most of them opening onto Sognefjord. Units in the older building are equipped with hot and cold running water, and those in the newer extension have showers and toilets. Depending on the plumbing, singles range in price from 115 kroner ($13.80) to 185 kroner ($22.20), and doubles go for 160 kroner ($19.20) and 225 kroner ($27). The pension, which is fully li-censed, also offers good food, a full luncheon or dinner going for about 70 kro-ner ($8.40) to 75 kroner ($9). A Norwegian breakfast will add another 32 kroner ($3.84) to your final bill. Meals are served in a dining room opening onto a view of the fjord.

Balestrand Pensjonat (tel. 91-138) is both old and new. Run by Nils Rendedal, it offers good rooms in the old section which are cheaper, or else in a boxy new block where all units come with private facilities. Most of the accom-modations have excellent views. With its rebuilding and modernization program finished, the pensjonat isn't small anymore—rather, a total of 74 beds. Of course, the new section faces the fjord, and most guests like to book in here. The rates are reasonable. Mr. Rendedal asks from 110 kroner ($13.20) to 175 kroner ($21) in a single, from 160 kroner ($19.20) to 220 kroner ($26.40) in a double. It's best to check in here on half-board terms, costing from 160 kroner ($19.20) to 220 kroner ($26.40) per person daily, the higher tariff for those units in the modern block, of course.

Breakfast is served at a large buffet table. Dinner is simple but good. My most recent meal began with a bowl of asparagus soup, followed with roast pork and vegetables (I could have had fresh fish), and was topped with a baked fruit pudding and then coffee.

About 5½ miles from Balestrand, **Dragsvik Pensjonat** (tel. 91-293) is a comfortable, moderately priced place to stay, owned and managed by Turid and Sigurd Farnes. In a new wing, there are 10 double rooms with private bathrooms. All the other 21 rooms have hot and cold running water and toilet facilities in the corridor. The charge for a double without bath is 190 kroner ($22.80), going up to 260 kroner ($31.20) with bath. Breakfast costs 35 kroner ($4.20) per person, and you can have a middag for 95 kroner ($11.40). The large dining room offers a spectacular view of the Fjaerlandsfjord. The pension has a private swimming area. You can rent bicycles and rowboats for exploring the district. The Dragsvik ferry quay is close to the Dragsvik Pensjonat.

READERS' SELECTIONS: "We stayed at the **Bøyum Pensjonat** (tel. 91-114), the least pretentious of several spots the tourist office at the wharf directed us to. Breakfast was enough for the whole day—caviar, cheese, eggs, meats, assorted fish and breads, cucumbers and tomatoes, cereals—and dinner was equally tremendous. A double room with a balcony but no bath costs 150 kroner ($18) to 160 kroner ($19.20). Bathless singles rent for 110 kroner ($13.20) to 120 kroner ($14.40). A full dinner goes for 70 kroner ($8.40), with breakfast costing another 35 kroner ($4.20) per person. Full-pension rates are 170 kroner ($20.40) to 180 kroner ($21.60) per person per day. It's open from June 20 to September 1. The Balestrand area is noted for its strawberries, which kids sell, freshly picked, at the ferry" (Paul and Beth Wilson, Bakersfield, Calif.).

"The north side of the Sognefjord is a beautiful fruit-growing area. Besides Balestrand, another major tourist center is **Sogndal/Kaupanger** in the east. Trips into mountain passes and along idyllic fjord inlets are scheduled from both places. Be sure to see the **Sogn Folkmuseum** in Kaupanger, especially the enormous collection of old farm implements housed in several buildings.

"**Elveseter Hotel**, 8A Bøverdal (tel. 12-000), off the mountain road from Sogndal to Lom, is unique and worth visiting just to see, if not to stay. It is an old family farm, converted and added to, with buildings and rooms named after legendary places and characters. Several lounges are richly decorated with carved, painted, woven furnishings—many by members of the Elveseter family. There's an indoor heated swimming pool and folk dancing in season. The hotel is set near a river with views of the valley and mountains. In season, a double with bath or shower goes for 150 kroner ($18) to 180 kroner ($21.60), inclusive. Half board is 200 kroner ($24) per person daily.

"The adventurous and hardy can take the special bus to **Gjuvasshytta**, 6000 feet high, and then with guide cross the glacier and climb to Scandinavia's highest mountain, more than 8000 feet high" (Alex E. Friedlander, Brooklyn, N.Y.).

12. Turtagrø

If you'd like to find an area of untamed beauty which has been a source of inspiration to any number of Norwegian and foreign artists, I'd suggest Turtagrø. Attracting a rugged clientele, the center is a starting point for hiking in the Jotunheimen mountains and for rock-climbing in the Horungane. At Turtagrø the slender Fortun Valley cleaves its way down to the Sognefjord.

Turtagrø is considered the rock-climbing center of the Skagastø peaks. The grandest group of the Jotunheimen mountains is Horunger, where the Skagastø peaks consist of hard gabbro scooped out by great glaciers. Rock-climbers make their way across these narrow ledges and sharp peaks.

For your center, I'd recommend the **Hotel Turtagrø**, Sogn (tel. 86-116). There the director will extend a welcome in English, inviting you to inspect one of the immaculate rooms. A bathless single rents for 200 kroner ($24), the rate going up to 235 kroner ($28.20) in a single with bath. A bathless double costs 250 kroner ($30), the tariff rising to 300 kroner ($36) with bath, breakfast included. For longer stays, pension terms will be quoted.

Rising on the crest of a hill, the hotel has pleasantly furnished lounges decorated in the typical style of the region as well as an open fireplace. From the windows you'll enjoy views of the Skagastø peaks. A three-course hot dinner in the evening costs 100 kroner ($12).

The location is certainly remote, 68 miles by road from Balestrand with one ferry crossing, or else 77 miles from Voss with one ferry crossing. There is a bus connection with Otta, Lom, Sogndal, and Leikanger, and an express-boat connection (Bergen-Leikanger), with a direct bus connection. The nearest railway station with a direct bus connection is Otta.

13. Fjaerland

This fertile farming district lies at the top of the tributary fjord, just under the Jostedak Glacier. It can be reached by boat along the 17-mile Fjaerland fjord (1½ hours). The nearest railway station with a boat connection is Flåm. The express-boat service running from Bergen to Balestrand takes four hours. The Flåm–Balestrand connection takes two hours. When the tunnel opens in 1986, Fjaerland can be reached by road from Skei in Jölster.

Fjaerland is an excellent starting point for tours of the Jostedal Glacier, and there is a wide range of marked trails and upland farm tracks. Fishing tackle can be rented to guests who want to try the sea fishing as well as the river trout fishing.

The preferred choice for lodgings is **Hotel Mundala**, Fjaerland, Sogn (tel. 93-101), run by the Orheim family. This attractive hotel dates back to the 19th century, although it has been much modernized since then. Nevertheless, its old-fashioned atmosphere has been carefully preserved. The hotel was built by the grandparents of the present owners, who welcome their guests and house them in comfort. The food is excellent and has been praised by magazines such as *Gourmet*. The family will be available to assist visitors with information on glaciology, geology, botany, local traditions, and handcraft. The hotel also has a well-stocked library on all these subjects and more.

No two bedrooms are alike, and the living rooms are spacious and attractively furnished, partly with antiques. A single room, bathless, costs 225 kroner ($27), the rate going up to 300 kroner ($36) in a single with bath. Bathless doubles are rented for 340 kroner ($40.80), the price rising to 450 kroner ($54) in a double with bath. Board terms are quoted for stays of three days or more. Otherwise, you must pay an additional 55 kroner ($6.60) for a Norwegian breakfast or else 120 kroner ($14.40) to 130 kroner ($15.60) for one of the satisfying lunches or dinners.

The Hotel Mundal is a favorite with Walter F. Mondale, unsuccessful candidate for President of the United States in 1984. Mondale's grandfather left Fjaerland for America in 1856. Norman Rockwell also visited the hotel (1972) and like many other artists was inspired by the scenery. The Mundal opens May 20 and closes September 15.

I'd also suggest **Fjaerland Pensjonat**, Fjaerland, Sogn (tel. 93-161), where Ansgar Mundal also extends a hearty welcome, housing you in his fjord-front home. Just right for a sporting hotel, the atmosphere is cheerful and friendly. Tourists come and go here, enjoying the rowing, badminton, and fishing for both the sea trout and the brown trout. Fishing gear may be rented, and guides are available for tours over the mountains. Rooms are adequately furnished and pleasant enough, costing 175 kroner ($21) in a bathless single, the cost rising to

235 kroner ($28.20) in a single with bath. A bathless double goes for 310 kroner ($37.10), going up to 360 kroner ($43.20) in a double with bath, including breakfast. Board terms are quoted for stays of three days or more; otherwise, you'll pay about 125 kroner ($15) extra for a big Norwegian meal, usually featuring trout. The pension is licensed for beer and wine.

14. Luster

On the Sognefjord, Luster is a little hamlet set in a region widely known for the rugged beauty of its landscape. The village forms a natural bridgehead between the towering peaks of the Sognefjord and the wild, untamed scenery of Jostedalen and Jotunheimen.

Tours can be arranged to the Jostedalen Glacier, largest in Northern Europe. Excursions are also arranged to the unique stave churches in the district. One, the Urnes church, for example, dates back to the year 1000. Another, the Dale stone church, traces its origins back to 1230. In addition, the Heiberg Museum at Kaupanger displays a collection of old tools and agricultural implements from the surrounding area.

Luster may be reached by speedboat (known as a westamaran) from Bergen to Leikanger, where it is possible to make bus connections to Luster. It can also be reached by air. Guests fly first to Sogndal airport where bus connections are made to Luster. Luster can be reached from either Oslo or Bergen in only one day.

Once there, you can find rooms and meals at **Solstrand Pensjonat** (tel. 85-450). The fjord-fronting complex consists of both an older wooden-frame building and a modern annex. A double room at the inn costs 320 kroner ($38.40) to 400 kroner ($48), but only 220 kroner ($26.40) at the annex. Singles at the inn rent for 175 kroner ($21), but only 150 kroner ($18) at the annex. For 220 kroner ($26.40) to 290 kroner ($34.80) per person, you can stay here on full-board terms. Accommodations are simple but adequate, and the standard of cookery is quite satisfying. For the expert angler, there's good sport.

A SIDE TRIP TO SOLVORN: In the municipality of Luster, Solvorn is a tiny fjordside hamlet, which was once an important trading post. If you decide to visit, I'd suggest a call first at the tourist office, where you can learn about a number of half-day and full-day excursions. The most interesting is to the Urnes stave church, about ten minutes away by boat. This is considered to be Norway's oldest and best preserved stave church, dating in part from 1050. From Solvorn, there is easy access to the glaciers and to Sognefjell where the Norwegian Mountain Touring Association has many marked trails. Guided tours of the Nigard Glacier can be organized upon request. Solvorn lies on Lusterfjord, an arm of Sognefjord, about 11 miles from Sogndal.

For your room and lodging, I'd suggest **Walaker Hotell og Motell** (tel. 84-207). This is a complex consisting of a mellow-appearing old wooden-frame building, painted a buttercup yellow, and a series of 11 apartments in a terraced row set in a garden overlooking the fjord. These units have showers and toilets, plus a kitchen area with electric hotplates and a refrigerator. Two beds are built into the wall and curtained off, and two sofa beds have been placed in the lounge area, which has a picture window and a door leading to the lawn.

The owner and manager, Hermod Nitter Walaker, also rents out four singles with shower and toilet and eight doubles with the same plumbing. There is only one bathless single as well as two bathless doubles. A bathless single rents for 150 kroner ($18), a bathless double going for 210 kroner ($25.20). A single with shower and toilet costs 190 kroner ($22.80), and a double with the same plumbing goes for 230 kroner ($27.60) to 300 kroner ($36). Two persons can occupy one of the mini-apartments for 300 kroner ($36). After stays of three days, half-board rates will be quoted. Otherwise, if you're stopping by, you can order a breakfast for 40 kroner ($4.80) and a good-tasting Norwegian dinner, including coffee, for 110 kroner ($13.20).

There are several boat trips a day from Solvorn to Urnes, which offers one of the biggest attractions in the Sognefjord, the **Urnes Stavchurch** (stave church), built 1130–1150. The north wall is one of the most excellent of its kind in the world in the field of woodcarving. Urnes Stavchurch is reckoned to be the oldest and best preserved stave church in Norway.

15. Flåm

This village lies on the Aurlands Fjord, a tip of the more famous Sognefjord. The best—and most exciting—approach to Flåm is by the Bergen railway to Myrdal, where guests then hop aboard an electric train that takes them on a 2844-foot drop (all in only 12 miles) to Flåm (pronounced Flawm). The train follows a serpentine path in and out of tunnels, halting periodically for passengers to photograph spectacular waterfalls and the like. At Flåm, you can visit the old church which dates from 1667, with painted walls done in the typical Norwegian country style.

WHERE TO STAY: If you want to stay over and savor the scenic delights, there is this excellent accommodation:

The **Heimly Lodge and Marina,** Flåm, Sogn (tel. 32-241), near the end of the electric railway, was created by Dr. Tokvam some 35 years ago as a ski school. But under pressure to provide accommodations for the large number of visitors who flock to Flåm, he enlarged it into a pension of 35 rooms—all with hot and cold running water (a few with private baths). Heimly, open from May 1 to October 30, charges 220 kroner ($26.40) for a double room. A single rents for 160 kroner ($19.20). With a private bath, there is a supplement of 15 kroner ($1.80) per day. A complete dinner, including coffee, tallies up to 95 kroner ($11.40), and breakfast is an extra 42 kroner ($4.04). Dr. Tokvam, educated in Paris and in England, has furnished the rooms in part with antiques and old-fashioned pieces. Heimly is a frame chalet, with views in many directions. Badminton, swimming, waterskiing, salmon and trout fishing, motorboating along the fjords, and gazing at the mountain scenery will occupy many an hour. The facilities also include a cafeteria, which is a popular place for light meals and snacks at reasonable prices. There is also a tennis court.

READERS' PENSION SELECTIONS: "The best bargain at Flåm is **Svingen Herberge** (tel. 32-116). It charges 100 kroner ($13.20) to 130 kroner ($15.60) in a double. Showers are free, and breakfast is 35 kroner ($4.20). A complete dinner can be ordered for 85 kroner ($10.20). The breakfast is great, including sliced tomatoes, goat cheese, regular cheese, bread, butter, jam, milk, and all the coffee you can drink. Mrs. A. Vangan, who runs it, is friendly and knows the ferry times for trips on the fjord. The pension is right at the end of the fjord, and the rooms are on the second story, looking right out at the scenery" (Larry Thompson, Clymer, N.Y.). . . . "We stayed in the home of **Nelly and Knut Brekke** (tel. 32-121), where the cost of a bathless double is 120 kroner ($14.40). Showers are free. People with their own bedding can have a place in a cabin for 30 kroner ($3.60). There is also a campground where, for a reasonable price, you can pitch a tent. This is a real find in Norway. Mr. Brekke will be waiting as the 10:05 a.m. train from Oslo comes in, with a cart to haul luggage. We can't say enough for his kindness" (Bill and Jeannie Kaye Beaushaw, Franklin, La.).

16. Geilo

One of Norway's best known ski resorts, Geilo is our last stopover on the Bergen Railway to Oslo, which lies about four hours away. Geilo's position in the Hol mountain district—2600 feet above sea level—makes it a good summer excursion center as well.

With its chair lift, ski tows, and slalom runs, plus more hotel beds than any other ski resort in Norway, it bustles with fun-loving skiers January through March, although some come earlier and others stay a month later. The Ski School has more than two dozen highly skilled instructors, known for their patience with amateurs. In lieu of a highly organized après-ski life, Geilo guests amuse themselvles with sleigh rides, curling, and skating at the Geilo Stadium.

In summer pay a call at the extremely active tourist bureau, in the center of town, to inquire about the weekly program, a list chock full of interesting and relaxing things to do.

Day excursions in the surrounding mountain country are ever popular. Organized trips vary throughout the year, but include such targets as Hol, six miles northeast of Geilo, containing an historical museum with 16th-century woodcarvings, as well as a 12th-century stave church. Another destination is an ancient Viking burial ground at Fekjo.

Of course, the chair-lift ride is good for scenery—mountain plateau and fjord. The terminal for the lift is a short walk from the railway station. The fare is 15 kroner ($1.80).

ACCOMMODATIONS: For such a major international resort and ski center, Geilo offers a number of hotels and pensions with low rates. Their comfort, cleanliness, and friendliness make them worthy, and provide a good reason for stopping over.

Geilo Høyfjellspensjonat (tel. 85-036), 500 yards from the station, is a small but immaculately clean Norwegian pension, one of the friendliest and most homelike in Norway. The owner is Mrs. Konnerth. A single without bath costs 175 kroner ($21). Depending on the plumbing, doubles rent for 225 kroner ($27) to 245 kroner ($29.40). Good Middle European cooking is offered in the restaurant. Lunch is not served—rather, Norwegian open-face sandwiches, with coffee or tea. The pension has an attractive dining room and lounge, opening onto good views.

The house is still partly of the old Norwegian loghouse style, the interior being decorated with the traditional *rosmaling*. The Høyfjellspensjonat staff will arrange adventure holidays for guests, including canoe tours, Jeep tours, hunting, and more.

Geilo Hotel (tel. 85-511) is an informal family-style pension, about a six-minute walk from the center of town. The hotel is open the whole year. A well-appointed double room costs 460 kroner ($55.20), while singles go for 365 kroner ($43.80). All the renewed rooms contain private baths or showers. The food is generously served and well prepared. In winter skiers might want to take the full-board rate for a minimum of five days, ranging from 395 kroner ($47.40) to 550 kroner ($66) per person daily. Many of the bedrooms are large enough to put in an extra bed. A fire burns nightly in an open fireplace. In the nightclub on the premises, guests dance to orchestra music, generally from 9 p.m. till 12:30 a.m.

Hotel Alpin (tel. 85-544), renovated and modernized, stands right in the center of the village. The intimate and cozy atmosphere is apparent from the soft lighting and wood paneling in the halls and smaller lounges. The larger lounge is luxuriously appointed with comfortable sofas, cozy corners, and piped-in-music. The 31 guest rooms are equipped with baths or showers and toilets and cost from 185 kroner ($22.20) for a single and from 265 kroner ($31.80) for a double. Breakfast costs an additional 40 kroner ($4.80). The international restaurant offers an excellent à la carte menu. The hotel is open year round and features music and dancing during the evening in season.

Lia Fjellstue og Motel, Skurdalen (tel. 87-912), lies nine miles from the

Geilo railway station. Owned and managed by English-speaking Karin and Knut Lia, this establishment is a combined mountain lodge and motel, with a view of Hardangervidda. The owners keep the running of the hotel very personal, and they have picked a small but capable staff. They rent out 14 double rooms, along with 14 family rooms, these latter units containing three and four beds. Each of these contain private showers and toilets. In addition, they have four single rooms with shower and toilet. Serious economizers will ask about one of four additional single rooms or one of six double rooms, containing hot and cold running water. Guests usually book in here on the half-board plan, staying a minimum of three days. Depending on the room assignment, singles in summer range from 100 kroner ($12) to 160 kroner ($19.20); doubles from 150 kroner ($18) to 280 kroner ($33.60). In winter, guests can stay here on half-pension terms at rates going from 180 kroner ($21.60) to 260 kroner ($31.20) per person. In winter, skiers use the ski tow with a 1980-foot-long slalom hill, or else follow the marked ski trails in the neighboring forest and mountain terrain. Trout fishing in mountain lakes is popular in the warmer month, and rowboats may be rented.

The **Geilo Youth Hostel** (tel. 85-300) is in a central spot, a five-minute walk from the railroad station. The hostel, with four-bedded rooms, is near the railway and halfway between Oslo and Bergen. Summer rates are 75 kroner ($9) for bed-and-breakfast, 150 kroner ($18) for full board, based on dormitory rooming. In winter, full board costs 165 kroner ($19.80) per person.

WHERE TO DINE: Café Alpin (tel. 85-544), on the second floor above the bank and next to the tourist bureau, is the best all-around economy dining choice in town. Decorated in an Austrian style, it's good for coffee, sandwiches, or a hot meal. The cafeteria serves a three-course dinner from noon, and diners may order from the à la carte menu till 10 p.m. in the grill room. If it's on the menu, try the creamed fish soup. For main dishes, you may want to try Norwegian specialties such as chopped reindeer meatcakes with mixed vegetables or cured herring with sliced beets, raw onions, and boiled potatoes. For dessert, a tempting selection of Norwegian pastries is offered, or perhaps chocolate pudding. Meals cost around 85 kroner ($10.20). In the winter, the cafeteria is popular for after-ski chats. Sometimes "ski sock dances" are held between 5 and 6 p.m. Incidentally, Café Alpin is the most frequented "Kafeteria" on the main road between Oslo and Bergen (east and west), as it lies at the halfway point.

In addition, a cozy little grill is on the premises. Called **Grill Alpin,** it offers à la carte dishes every day from 3 to 10 p.m. (music during the season). The specialty here is steak. Other selections include lamb chops, followed by hot apple pie with ice cream. Expect to spend from 120 kroner ($14.40) up.

17. Kristiansand

Those returning to Bergen may want to take the route along the southern coast. If you do, the town to head for is Kristiansand (not to be confused with Kristiansund, near Trondheim). The biggest city and one of the most important ports of Sørlandet (the south coast), Kristiansand has been called "the pearl of the Norwegian Riviera." It is built on a peninsula.

Many visitors land here from Harwich, England, or Hirtshals, Denmark. Others take the Sørland railway from either Oslo or Stavanger. It's also possible to arrive by bus or else fly into the Kristiansand Municipal Airport at Kjevik, lying ten miles from the center of town. Both Braathen's SAFE and SAS airlines service the town.

Founded by King Christian in 1641, Kristiansand is a busy port and industrial center, yet it has many charming old streets and antique houses clustered cozily together. Water surrounds the city—in fact, Kristiansand is said to have the biggest fleet of pleasure craft in relation to its population of any Norwegian town.

It's worth a visit to **Christiansholm Fort**, at Østre Havn, dating back to 1674 and often the center of local handicraft exhibitions; the **Fish Quay**, with its troughs and tanks full of live fish; and **Kristiansand Cathedral**, one of the largest churches in Norway. Built in the neo-Gothic style, it was dedicated in 1885. If you're interested in churches, try also to visit the **Church of Oddernes**, one mile from the center. It was built around the middle of the 11th century, but much later reconstructed. Its baroque pulpit, for example, is from 1704. From May 1 to September 9, the church is open daily from 9 a.m. to 2 p.m. (otherwise, from 9 a.m. to noon).

One of the largest open-air museums in Norway, **Vest Agder County Museum** contains nearly 30 buildings moved to the site. Some of these farm buildings and city dwellings are equipped with provincial furnishings, glass, and stoneware. The museum is open from June 20 to August 20, daily from 11 a.m. to 7 p.m. (on Sunday from noon to 7 p.m.). It's at Kongsgard, a short distance east of the center of town. Admission for adults is 5 kroner (60¢) and for children 2 kroner (24¢). For information, telephone 90-228.

The **Setesdal Railway** runs a steam train along three miles of a disused narrow-gauge track. The locomotive, dating from 1894, starts its run at Grovane, 12½ miles from Kristiansand. Departures are at 11:30 a.m. and 1 and 2:30 p.m. Sunday from mid-June to the end of August; 1 and 2:30 p.m. Saturday in July. Fares are 25 kroner ($3) for adults and 15 kroner ($1.80) for children along the Grovane-Beihølen run.

Covering some 50 acres, the **Kristiansand Zoo** contains many exotic specimens, including some Nordic species. Animals are allowed to roam in large open enclosures. The zoo and park are open daily from 10 a.m. to 8 p.m. (till 4 p.m. in winter), and it lies seven miles east of Kristiansand on the E18. Norway's biggest amusement park was opened recently in connection with the zoo. It contains a section known as "Troll Valley," along with a playland, bob track, amphitheater, and a gold digger town.

If time remains, I'd also suggest you do some exploring in the countryside around Kristiansand. Many motorists like to view the coast and skerries, but if you dip inland, you'll find a countryside of rolling meadows, birch-clad hills, deep valleys, and mountain moors. Leaving Kristiansand, drive along E18.

West of **Mandal** stands Norway's southernmost point with its lighthouse, originally erected in 1655. Seek out, in particular, the Dutch town of **Flekkefjord** on the Grise Fjord, with its low wooden buildings, narrow twisting streets, and warehouses.

Much scenic variety is offered by driving on Highway 9 toward the Setesdal and Sirdal moors. Amid delightful scenery, oldtime customs and costumes still prevail.

Kristsiansand's new sightseeing boat, M/B *Maarten,* offers tours between the idyllic islands outside the town. Departure is from the fish quay.

WHERE TO STAY: The hotels in Kristiansand offer reduced prices with up to 40% rebate in the summer season, from mid-June to mid-August. The prices include rooms with bath or shower, toilet, and breakfast. Some hotels also include the big Norwegian cold table at lunch time.

Throughout the year, **Savoy Hotell**, 1 Kristian IVsgate (tel. 24-175), offers comfortably furnished single rooms from 275 kroner ($33) to 375 kroner ($45) and double rooms from 375 kroner ($45) to 500 kroner ($60). The staff is friendly and accommodating.

Bondeheimen, 15 Kirkegaten (tel. 24-440), lies in the heart of town, near the bus terminal. A corner hotel, it offers 36 rooms, most of which have been refurbished. Rooms are comfortable and adequately furnished. Depending on the plumbing, doubles cost from 375 kroner ($45) to 420 kroner ($50.40); singles, 215 kroner ($25.80) to 290 kroner ($34.80). These tariffs do not include breakfast, which is an additional 42 kroner ($5.04). There's a car park connected to the hotel, and the English-speaking staff will help you make restaurant reservations and in the evening will direct you to local dance spots. The hotel has lounges, as well as a cafeteria offering routine Norwegian food all day long. After 6 p.m., hot meals are served.

For something cheaper, try **Roligheden Ungdomsherberge,** South Kristiansand (tel. 94-947), a youth hostel on the outskirts. Campers often pitch their tents on its grounds. If you're a member you pay 67 kroner ($8.04) for its simple, dormitory-style accommodations. Otherwise, the charge for nonmembers goes up to 79 kroner ($9.48). There are also rooms for families. Breakfast is served every day, and dinner, too, providing that enough people request it. Breakfast is included in the rates, but dinner is another 43 kroner ($5.16). The beach is about 1000 feet away.

Chapter IX

Chapter IX

THE TRAIL TO THE NORTH CAPE

REGARDLESS OF ALL the waterfalls, mountains, and fjords that we've explored, the exploration of Norway in terms of mileage hasn't reached the halfway mark yet. The great stretch along the coast—beyond the Arctic Circle to the North Cape and Norwegian Lapland (Finnmark)—is one of the most rewarding treks in Europe.

As discussed earlier, the easiest way to do this is to take one of the coastal steamers out of Bergen that stops off at the North Cape, that hunk of granite that won't win any beauty contests, but draws a constant stream of summer visitors who like to gaze upon the northernmost extension of Europe, lit by the Midnight Sun.

Our exploration begins to the north of Bergen—often called the top of the fjord country. Four ring-around-the-water centers make ideal headquarters, both for their own beauty and sights, as well as for a starting point for excursion. They are Ålesund, Geiranger, Andalsnes, and Molde.

After visiting this scenic land, the northward journey eventually continues to medieval Trondheim, one of the three favorite tourist cities in Norway. After leaving Trondheim, the land of sunlit nights comes into view. The first county, Nordland, is above the Arctic Circle (Bodø makes the best center). Troms comes next, with a center at Tromsø. Polar explorers set out from this city. Both Bodø and Tromsø have airports, as the airplane is the easiest means of transportation for crossing this vast expanse of land.

The Nordland rail line ends in Bodø, but it's possible to travel from Stockholm to Narvik, Norway, north of Bodø, by railroad—originally built to carry iron-ore shipments from Kiruna, Sweden.

From Tromsø, the final province is reached—Finnmark, home of most of the world's Lapps, the aborigines of Scandinavia, who still herd reindeer across these northern wilds. In summer the Lapps often move their camps nearer to the coast and are more accessible to tourists who wish to see them (yes, they sell handmade trinkets).

In Finnmark there are airports at Alta, Lakselv, Vadsø, and Kirkenes, near the Russian border. Those with the time, however, can travel by bus.

Do-it-yourselfers exploring Finnmark by bus may find Honningsvåg the best center for viewing the North Cape.

July seems to be the most crowded month in northern Norway. Not enough facilities exist as yet, but it's somewhat of a miracle that the land is even as built up as it is. The Nazis razed almost everything to the ground in their scorched-earth retreat in 1944. Everything in Finnmark has been built since the war.

Since not enough hotels or guest houses exist to handle the summer crowds (Finns are among the most prevalent tourists), reservations are imperative, although a little juggling here and there may work in emergencies.

But we're a long way from Lapland. First, a look much closer to Bergen, at:

1. Ålesund

At the top of the fjord country, Norway's "big-catch" fishing town spreads over three islands in an archipelago that is further dramatized by the snow-capped Sunnmøre Alps in the background. The islanders are graphically as well as symbolically accurate in pointing out that the shape of the town resembles a fishing hook.

This harbor town was almost totally rebuilt after a fire in 1904. Today it is teeming with sights—the works of nature and of humanity. Seagulls screech along the harbor where trawlers bob up and down; elongated spears of pink on a summer night split open the sky; clouds hover over mountains that resemble gray-haired Father Trolls with gigantic noses; three-toed kittiwakes perch on a bird rock in the center of town, and the fading sun turns the rebuilt stone buildings saffron.

The guardian of Ålesund is lofty **Aksla** (600 feet), a scenic sanctuary with a terrace restaurant, offering a view of fjord landscape, ancient Viking islands, and the Sunnmøre mountains. In the harbor nestles the flat island of **Giske,** which is believed to have been the native soil of Rollo, tenth-century founder of the Duchy of Normandy, the father of William the Conqueror. The island today is inhabited by farmers and people who earn their living from the sea.

Inquire at the **tourist bureau,** in the Town Hall at the bus station (tel. 21-202), about tours in and around the area, as well as daily excursions to the fjords of Romsdal, Geiranger, and Hjørund.

The most popular excursion is to **Fjellstua** (see my mountaintop dining recommendation), coming up. You can take a taxi there which costs 100 kroner ($12), including a 30-minute stopover (tel. 43-801).

A longer journey via public transport to Geiranger, considered the most scenic fjord in the world, is a nine-hour bus/ferry round trip costing 200 kroner ($24). It takes you from Ålesund to Magerholm, Sykkylven, Stranda, Hellesylt, Geiranger, Eidsdal, Valldal, Sjøholt, and back to Ålesund. The trip is offered from May 8 to September 20, leaving Ålesund at 8:50 a.m.. Of course, you can hire a car to take you on this jaunt, if you prefer.

In addition, a ferry leaves Ålesund to the island of **Giske**, where you can visit an old Viking chapel. Departures are 10 times daily from Skateflua quay, and the cost of the two-hour boat tour is 20 kroner ($2.40). You can extend your ferryboat ride on to Godøy and back for the same 20 kroner.

Birdwatchers head for **Runde**, Norway's southernmost bird rock. Åle-sunders estimate that half a million birds inhabit the rock. The cost of the five-hour tour, weather permitting, is 135 kroner ($16.20), but it is only conducted between June 1 and August 1. Get in touch with the tourist bureau for more details.

On the outskirts of town, the **Sunnmøre Museum** (tel. 44-024) is a major attraction of Ålesund. The main exhibition hall houses an extensive collection of Viking-inspired fishing boats, many in use as late as 1900. A 60-foot sixth-century Viking ship—a model based on one excavated—is also displayed. Three boats seen here were used by Norwegian saboteurs in World War II. The museum is open daily from 11 a.m. to 6 p.m. (noon to 5 p.m. on Sunday), charging 7 kroner (84¢) for admission. On the grounds are some 40 wooden buildings, moved to this site and reconstructed to illustrate the early days of the inhabitants of the district. Guided tours leave every second hour.

A permanent exhibition in the main building shows prehistoric life in the district from the Stone Age to the Vikings, A.D. 1000, as well as displays on local cultural history. Buses leave every 15 minutes going to the museum, costing 12 kroner ($1.44) per person.

Near the museum are the remains of a town from the Middle Ages.

The **Ålesund Aquarium** has on display in near-natural surroundings a wide variety of fish and marine animals from the North Sea from the wharves of Åle-sund to the ocean depths. Admission is 5 kroner (60¢).

Ålesund is reached by airplane either from Bergen or Oslo. The airport is at Vigra, where there are bus and ferry connections into town. The train runs to Åndalsnes, which has good bus connections with Ålesund, and coastal steamers from Bergen stop off. The highway from Borgund leads to the chain of islands.

WHERE TO STAY: Hotel Noreg, 27 Kongensgate (tel. 22-938), only 100 yards from the steamer dock, is a neat, compactly modern, five-story corner building that offers pleasantly and comfortably furnished rooms. The hotel was recently extended with more accommodations, along with a swimming pool with salt water. Units are both bathless and with complete bath, the rate in a single going from 300 kroner ($36) to 525 kroner ($63). Prices in a double begin at 400 kroner ($48) in the bathless accommodations, climbing all the way to 650 kroner ($78) for the most expensive doubles with bath. These rates include service and breakfast. The hotel, built in 1954, is the largest in Ålesund. The bedrooms have glass walls and look out on views of the boat-filled habor. A lively orchestra plays nightly except Monday for dancing in the Maritime room. The fish dishes here are well prepared, a complete dinner costing around 120 kroner ($14.40). In summer the north light pours through the skylight overhead—even at midnight.

Havly, 4 Rasmus Rønnebergsgate (tel. 24-960), is a good little hotel in the center of town. Although the facade is boxy modern and impersonal in style, the rooms are clean and comfortable. Furnishings are in a severe Nordic modern, but the compensating factor is that units open onto views of fjords and mountains. Most of the rooms in this 75-bed hotel, which was enlarged and modernized in 1972, are equipped with phones, radios, showers. Depending on the plumbing, doubles range from 350 kroner ($42) to 510 kroner ($61.20) and singles begin at 225 kroner ($27), peaking at 420 kroner ($50.40), breakfast included. You can take your meals at the cafeteria on the ground floor.

MOUNTAINTOP DINING: The **Restaurant Fjellstua** offers mountaintop dining and an incredible view (described earlier). The restaurant is divided into two parts—one a self-service cafeteria and another a more formal dining section, where fish specialties, such as the excellent sauteed trout in burnt-butter sauce with lemon, are served. The fish platters are a popular choice, followed by fresh strawberries with cream and sugar, a favorite dessert here. Meals cost from 100 kroner ($12). In the cafeteria, sandwiches and snacks are available.

If you're hungry and your budget is really low, you can find a snack in front of the Shell station of Nesgaten. There, sausage costs 10 kroner ($1.20); a plate of french fries, an extra 10 kroner.

READER'S TOURING RECOMMENDATION: "**Olden** is one of a trio of villages (Strym and Loen are the other two) on the lovely Nordfjord. Each has a lake in a valley of pastoral beauty. The biggest attraction here, besides the many fine walks, is the trip by bus, boat, and foot (or pony cart for the foot-weary, but it's expensive) to the edge of the Briksdalbre, an arm of the Jostedal Glacier, Europe's largest. You can watch chunks of the glacier break off, and wade in the icy waters at its base. There are several places to stay, and as usual one or more cafeterias and cafés with $35-a-day prices and $100-a-day quality" (Alex E. Friedlander, Brooklyn, N.Y.).

[*Author's Note:* **Yris Pensjonat** (tel. 73-245) in Olden is a small, clean, country-like hotel providing bathless singles for as low as 150 kroner ($18) and bathless doubles for as little as 250 kroner ($30). A large Norwegian breakfast is an extra 45 kroner ($5.40), with lunch or dinner in the 65-krone ($7.80) to 85-krone ($10.20) range.]

2. Geiranger

Most Norwegians consider Geiranger fjord, a favorite body of water for cruises, their most majestic, and well they should. The village of Geiranger is set at the very head of this narrow fjord, and it's one of the most famous resorts in the fjord country.

Perched on rocky ledges, high above the fjord, are a number of small farmsteads. Waterfalls, such as the celebrated Seven Sisters (Syr Søstre), the Wooer, and the Bridal Veil, send their shimmering veils cascading down the rock face.

Excursions by bus, boat, and car can be arranged, as can fishing trips on the fjord. Rowboats and fishing tackle are also available for rent.

You can leave Geiranger by boat for a three-hour cruise along the fjord, with its vertically rising cliffs, tiny farms, and rocky ledges. On this tour you'll past the already-mentioned Seven Sisters, a waterfall plunging down over a sheer wall, en route to Valldal.

From Valldal, which is also connected by car-ferry to the village of Geiranger, you can continue by bus, a two-hour trip, over the mountains on Trollstig Road (Giant's Path) that zigzags down to the village of Åndalsnes, our next stopover.

Or else you can return to Geiranger by bus on the Eagle's Road, which was opened to traffic in 1955. Reader Alex E. Friedlander, of Brooklyn, N.Y., who made this trip, writes: "The climb, about one hour from the road above town, takes you to just under the top of a ferocious plunging waterfall. You stand *behind* it! If you are lucky, you will meet a flock of 50 mountain goats on the way. The descent from the mountain into Geiranger in 10½ miles takes you down 3280 feet with 11 hairpin bends. From the top (Djupvasshytta), a toll road, open around mid-July, climbs to the summit of Dalsnibba (4757 feet) for a breathtaking panorama."

Almost daily in summer, large cruising liners anchor up in the Geiranger fjord. Occasionally some of the world's best known vessels are moored here at the same time.

The nearest railway station with direct bus connections is Åndalsnes, 50 miles away. The Bergen–Nordfjordeid has express boat connections (with direct bus hookups), and the nearest airport is Vigra, Ålesund, 81 miles away.

Geiranger also has bus connections with Åndalsnes, Ålesund, Otta, Stryn, and Nordfjordeid. In addition, car-ferries call several times during the summer season.

Back at Geiranger, if you're spending the night, you should have reserved a room if visiting during the peak months. And be prepared to dig deep into your wallet.

WHERE TO STAY: Geiranger Hotel (tel. 63-005) is the traditional favorite. Overlooking the fjord, it probably has the most scenic situation. The better units, facing the fjord, contain balconies from which you can soak up the scenery. The hotel has existed for some time, but in the '60s it added a new wing to expand its bed capacity. Singles with private baths or showers range in price from 450 kroner ($54); doubles, also with private plumbing, go for 600 kroner ($72); and even more for the units overlook the fjord.

From the big roof garden, another view of the fjord unfolds. The hotel is licensed, with a cafeteria and a pizza bar, and is known for its good food, a meal costing from 85 kroner ($10.20). One public room has dancing and an open fireplace (nights can be chilly here even in summer). Rowing boats are rented, and licenses can be easily obtained for fishing on the fjord. The hotel staff will book you on excursions to the waterfalls, glaciers, and mountain farms.

Built above the sea at the head of the fjord, the **Union Turisthotell** (tel. 63-000) is an old family-style hotel which has been brought up-to-date in the past few years. Like the Geiranger Hotel, it has also added a new wing which gives it a total of 80 beds, equipped with bath, shower, and toilet. Including a Norwegian breakfast, a single room rents for 430 kroner ($51.60) to 460 kroner ($55.20), with doubles going for 600 kroner ($72) to 630 kroner ($75.60).

The public rooms, especially one done in the old style, are comfortable and pleasantly furnished. The Union is fully licensed, and in the peak season folk dancing is presented two or three nights a week. Dinners are served, costing from 120 kroner ($14.40).

The staff can arrange for you to go out in a rowing boat with or without outboard motors, and cars, owned by the hotel, can be rented for excursions.

At the edge of the fjord, you can also book into the **Meroks Fjord Hotel** (tel. 63-002), where adequately furnished bedrooms overlook the waters. It's attractive and clean, and guests are received from May 1 to October 1. With a Norwegian breakfast included, tariffs are from 380 kroner ($45.60) to 420 kroner ($50.40) in a single, from 510 kroner ($61.20) to 600 kroner ($72) in a double, each accommodation equipped with either private bath or shower.

There's a cheerful, informal atmosphere, with guests mixing and talking freely about mountain sights and fishing. A friendliness and camaraderie prevail. The cookery is wholesome and satisfying, lunches going for 85 kroner ($10.20), dinners for 130 kroner ($15.60).

Meroks has been run by the same family ever since 1868, first as an inn and later in this century as a hotel. Of course, it has been extended and modernized a number of times.

3. Åndalsnes

A summer resort at the foot of mountains and at the head of the **Romsdal Fjord,** Åndalsnes is easily reached by bus from Ålesund, about 80 miles away.

Bombed in 1940, it has been rebuilt into one of the best resorts along the coast, attracting rock climbers and fishermen (trout and salmon in the Rauma River).

One of the most exciting approaches to the village—and worth a day's excursion—is the zigzagging **Trollstien** (Troll Road), with hairpen bends through the mountains. Excursions are arranged in July to the **Geiranger Fjord** (past the Seven Sisters waterfall), to **Romsdal Valley,** and to **Eikesdal** (the fairest of vales), including a look at **Mardal Foss,** the highest falling water in Northern Europe, a drop of 1000 feet.

Andalsnes is the end of the line for the **Rauma Railway,** about an eight-hour run from Oslo.

READER'S TRAVEL TIP: "We left Åndalsnes in the morning and took the public transportation bus to the ferry that made connections with a bus to Geiranger. This was not a tour but transport for the locals. All connections were synchronized so there was almost no waiting. The trip cost only about 66 kroner ($7.92) and took about five hours. The bus ride from Åndalsnes to the ferry was along the Troll Road, with many hairpin turns and countless waterfalls on either side. All bus drivers stop along the way so you can take pictures. They also stop on the top of the mountain at a gift shop and restaurant" (Johanna Ficaro, Cambridge, Mass.).

ACCOMMODATIONS: For such a tiny village, Åndalsnes has a fair range of good and attractive accommodations. It's also possible to obtain lodgings with private families by going to the tourist office.

Budget Pensions

Rauma Pensjonat (tel. 21-233), a short walk from the rail station, is for those seeking a bone-bare economy place—clean and friendly—with many compensatory factors, such as views of mountaintops from the bedroom windows. A three-story corner building with little dormer windows, the 20-bed pensjonat has been run by Mr. and Mrs. Hans Tomter ever since it was built in 1945. They charge 230 kroner ($27.60) for bathless doubles, 135 kroner ($16.20) for singles. A double with bath costs 290 kroner ($34.80). A breakfast is served for 40 kroner ($4.80).

Setnes Gård og Pensjonat (tel. 21-383), in Veblungsnes, five minutes from Åndalsnes, is a white farmhouse built by Mr. and Mrs. Setnes many years ago. Prophetically, they added extra rooms (30 beds) to accommodate paying guests, since they realized that Åndalsnes might one day be a booming tourist resort. From June 1 to September 1, they charge 200 kroner ($24) for bathless doubles, 150 kroner ($18) for bathless singles. The rooms have well-selected furnishings and rugs made from leftover bits of brilliantly colored cotton. Breakfast is the only meal served, costing 45 kroner ($5.40). Living here is like being in a private Norwegian home. It's also one of the best bargains in town. Mr. and Mrs. Setnes like to have their guests join them around a brick fireplace in the evenings.

An Untypical Youth Hostel

Setnes Ungdomsherberge (tel. 21-382), is a simple wooden building, surrounded by lawns and trees, with views of the fjord and mountains. The hostel is one mile from the railway station. Setnes is dominated by the kindliness and warmth of its director. The low cost of staying at this 75-bed hostel is 45 kroner ($5.40) per person in rooms that may contain anywhere from one to six beds. Ideally an entire room may be rented by one family. The rooms, with coordinated colors and plaids, are most inviting. The director knows about home-cooking, and the meals are well prepared and nutritious, costing 45 kroner

($5.40) for a big spread, such as soup, fried fish with butter sauce, string beans, potatoes, and cole slaw. A big Norwegian breakfast goes for yet another 35 kroner ($4.20). There's even a do-it-yourself kitchen for guests who want to turn out their own specialties. In the evening, life centers around the fireside. Guests don't seem to mind the 11 p.m. curfew.

Another youth hostel building opened in 1982. It contains eight big four-bedded rooms and two large six-bedded rooms. All units have hot and cold running water.

Out on the Outskirts

A good bargain is **Lensmannsgarden** (tel. 28-120), which lies in Innfjorden, a small village just seven miles from Åndalsnes. It's a rather quiet place in beautiful surroundings. There Dagny Hage will welcome you, housing you in one of the guesthouse's small, pleasantly furnished bedrooms, renting for 120 kroner ($14.40) in a single, from 160 kroner ($19.20) in a double. Good meals with bountiful portions are also served. The big Norwegian breakfast costs the same as lunch, 50 kroner ($6). For dinner, you'll be served a fine meal for just 65 kroner ($7.80).

If you're seeking a little guesthouse in idyllic surroundings, try **Gjerset Pensjonat,** 6325 Torvik (tel. 25-966), which is set at the head of the lake in this sparsely settled Norwegian hamlet. The rooms are pleasant, the food is good, and you can even catch your dinner in the lake, taking it back to the guesthouse to be prepared for you. For a double room, the charge is 160 kroner ($19.20), dropping to only 90 kroner ($10.80) in a single, plus another 40 kroner ($4.80) for breakfast. You'll enjoy the good home cooking and the Norwegian hospitality. English is spoken. At the tourist office in Åndalsnes, you'll be given detailed instructions on how to reach this pension.

4. Molde

Norway's "town of roses" is famed for its view of 87 white-capped Romsdal Alps. This summer tourist center and industrial town turning out ready-made clothes sprang from the ashes left by the German bombings in 1940, when the king and crown prince fled here, hotly pursued by the Nazis.

The town is reached from our stopover in Åndalsnes by taking a bus to Vikebukt, where a ferry connection is made across the Molde Fjord to the north bank. It's also possible to visit Molde directly from Ålesund by coastal steamer and by plane from Oslo, Bergen, and Trondheim several times a day.

ACCOMMODATIONS: Since Molde was severely bombed and then rebuilt, all of its accommodations have one feature in common: they're post-war structures. But in price and style, they vary considerably. I'll lead off with the medium-priced selections, then include the more expensive and better appointed hotels.

A Mission Pension

Norrøna Kafe & Pensjonat A/S (tel. 51-824), a Mission establishment, stands right in the heart of town. It offers 20 immaculate and well-kept bedrooms, with bathless doubles going for 250 kroner ($30) to 325 kroner ($39), singles for 170 kroner ($20.40) to 235 kroner ($28.20), plus another 40 kroner ($4.80) for breakfast. Many of the rooms have glass doors leading out onto private balconies; all have armchairs and sinks. The morning devotionals in the lounge are optional, of course. Meals are in the 45-krone ($5.40) to 75-krone ($9) range.

A Student Hostel

Rimo Hostel, summer quarter youth hostel, 4 Fabrikkveien (tel. 54-330 during term time; otherwise, 51-077), is open only from June 18 to August 23, providing 236 beds in rooms occupied by students during school sessions. Accommodations house one or two or three persons in well-furnished rooms. All rooms are equipped with hot and cold water. There are no private baths, but corridor showers are adequate. Singles in summer quarter cost 160 kroner ($19.20) to 180 kroner ($21.60), and twin-bedded rooms, 240 kroner ($28.80) to 280 kroner ($33.60). The youth hostel charge is 50 kroner ($6) for members of national or international youth hostel organizations. Meals are not included but are available in the cafeteria. The Norwegian breakfast table costs 32 kroner ($3.84), and a two-course lunch or dinner goes for 55 kroner ($6.60).

Medium-Priced Hotels

Romsdalsheimen Hotell (tel. 51-711) is a 38-room hotel in the commercial center of town, behind an imposing corner façade with a three-story additional wing stretching off to the side. The public rooms contain a minimum of glamour, except for the semicircular modern fireplace which illuminates a nearby seating area in winter.

Not all of the comfortably functional rooms contain private baths, but those that do cost 300 kroner ($36) in a single and 390 kroner ($46.80) in a double. Bathless rooms cost 280 kroner ($33.60) in a single, 350 kroner ($42) in a double.

Hotel Nobel (tel. 51-555), a few minutes' walk from the wharf and the main street, is a combination of old and new architecture, offering widely varied accommodations and prices. The entire hotel was remodeled in 1982 into a style which reflects Old Norway, especially in the rustic café-bar, the Butler Kro. The modern restaurant is Danish in style, the grill room being slightly less formal. The bedrooms are tastefully elegant statements of contemporary simplicity, done in pleasingly light colors and rattan furniture. Singles with bath cost between 300 kroner ($36) and 400 kroner ($48), while doubles with bath cost from 400 kroner ($48) to 500 kroner ($60).

In addition to the clean and pleasant accommodations, the hotel will arrange guided tours to surrounding regions of scenic beauty.

Hotel Alexandra (tel. 51-133), one of the largest hotels in the region, rises impressively in an angular concrete format of recessed loggias, strong horizontal lines, and an obvious difference between the older wing and a new addition, which was constructed in 1975. In addition to containing 115 conservatively simple bedrooms, the hotel has a first-class restaurant, a resident dance orchestra, a cafeteria and bistro, and a bar done in turquoise and black. There's also an indoor pool, a sauna, a gymnasium, a solarium, and a sun terrace.

From Monday to Friday, singles rent for 600 kroner ($72), doubles for 720 kroner ($86.40). However, on weekends, singles drop to 310 kroner ($37.20) and doubles to 500 kroner ($60). All tariffs include breakfast.

On the Outskirts

Knausen Hotell-Motell, N-6400 Molde (tel. 51-577), lies about two miles from the heart of Molde and the Arø airport. Set against a country landscape, it commands views over the Romsdals mountains and the Fanne Fjord. Knausen moved into a new hotel in 1984, and in addition to that, it consists of two parts—one a superbly modern motel, another a cluster of wood-frame chalet buildings insulated for winter living. There is, as well, a campsite on the grounds, complete with power points. In the motel, two persons are charged 280 kroner ($33.60) for a stay of one night in units complete with bath and toilet. Even cheaper are the bathless doubles, costing 220 kroner ($26.40) nightly. Singles without bath cost 180 kroner ($21.60). A double with bath and toilet goes for 290 kroner ($34.80), a similar single priced at 260 kroner ($31.20).

The chalets—called "hutts"—are the bargain of the resort. Two persons pay 110 kroner ($13.20) on a daily basis; four persons, 175 kroner ($21); and five persons, 190 kroner ($22.80). Breakfast costs another 40 kroner ($4.80) per person, and you can also order other meals throughout the day until 9:30 p.m. Incidentally, the motel section is equipped with its own kitchen facilities. Knausen is a temperance establishment, and if that is no problem for you, you'll find it a good base for exploring Bjørnsund, the Troll Road, Geiranger, and the Mardalsfossen Falls.

WHAT TO SEE: The **Molde Cathedral,** in the heart of town, was erected in 1957 —the largest postwar cathedral to be built in Norway. Done in an unusually advanced and successful style, it features huge shafts of open glass running skyward. It has a simplicity and purity of line, with white brick walls, deeply recessed mullion windows, blue and beige ceiling, and a rose window behind a pipe organ. Over the baptismal font is an old charred cross and an old altarpiece —both rescued from the bombed ruins. The church, open all year, may be visited free from 10 a.m. to 5 p.m.

The modern **Town Hall,** a short walk away, is probably one of the most stunning, well-conceived municipal buildings in the world. Its executive offices on the upper level open onto a winter garden with hanging baskets, marble floors and stone walls blend harmoniously, domes and skylights capture the northern lights, and the roof terrace is filled with raised flower beds. It may be visited free during the working days.

Romsdal Museum *(Romsdalmuseet):* From the Romsdal district about 25 wooden houses were carefully torn down and reassembled on the outskirts of Molde, a ten-minute walk from the center of town. In summer, children in regional costumes perform folk dances here, much to the delight of cruise-ship passengers. One museum houses a representative collection for those who want to get a quick whiff of Romsdal tradition; but other buildings range from a 15th-century *aarestue* (log cabin) to a medieval-style chapel. From mid-June to August 15, the museum is open from 10 a.m. to 6 p.m.; in other months, 10 a.m. to 2 p.m.

Finally, don't miss the view of those already-mentioned 87 peaks, or the island-studded fjord, as seen from the deck of the **Vardestua Restaurant,** a dazzling 1300 feet high. Eventually, a ski lift may be built to this sky-high restaurant, but in the meantime tourists can take a taxi up and get the driver to wait for 20 minutes. That will leave enough time to have a cup of coffee at the café while enjoying the view.

EXCURSIONS: The Molde Tourist Traffic Association, near the main church, is open in summer from 10 a.m. to 6 p.m. weekdays and from 2 to 6 p.m. on Sunday. It will give you detailed information about how to take the following excursions.

Bjørset is about 1½ miles from the center of Molde. Behind a yellow wooden house are three rock carvings dating from prehistoric times. Admission is free.

The so-called **Troll Church** is a natural wonder. At this site are several underground caves and grottos, many of them unexplored. The effect is stunning. There's also a 45-foot waterfall. To get there by car, take road no. 67 in the direction of Eide, stopping at the "Trolkyrkja" sign. From there you have to walk for 1½ hours over a steep path. Incidentally, you can catch a bus heading for Eide at the Molde terminal.

The **Veøy Stone Church** on **Veøy Island** dates from 13th century. Its little village of Kaupangen was until the 14th century the center of Romsdal. To reach it, you have to get in touch with Karsten Flovikholm, 6370 Nesjestranda (tel. 41-562). He takes visitors over on his boat.

The **Fisheries Museum** on the island of Hjertøya is part of the Romsdal Museum in Molde. Its collections consist of about 15 old buildings from the western coast of Romsdal, including dwellings, boathouses, and other maritime buildings. There are a number of authentic old fishing boats and fishing gear, and you can see how the Norwegian coastal fishermen lived, as well as sealers and whalers. The museum has a natural and beautiful location on the seaside. The water taxi leaves from the marketplace in the center of Molde during the museum's open hours, from 10 a.m. to 3:30 p.m. weekdays and from noon to 3:30 p.m. on Sunday from mid-June to August 15. The round-trip fare on the boat is 10 kroner ($1.20) for adults, 6 kroner (72¢) for children. The museum costs adults 6 kroner (72¢), children 3 kroner (39¢).

INTERNATIONAL JAZZ FESTIVAL: Molde horns in on Antibes and Newport by staging its annual jazz festival the last week in July. It is considered a main European jazz festival. Although the town may not attract the top-drawer names of the other two festivals, a group of talented and dedicated artists—from pianists to drummers—plays on till midnight. During the festival, two concerts a day are given in the town cinema, followed by festival club sessions at **Jazz Kro,** Distrikshøyskolen. Admission is 75 kroner ($9) to 20 kroner ($24) for the concerts. The festival has been broadened to include poetry, folk songs, theater presentations, and painting exhibitions. For further information about this year's program or for ticket reservations, write to the Molde Jazz Festival, Box 261, 6401 Molde (tel. 53-779).

NORTH TOWARD TRONDHEIM: Molde is our last stop in this part of the fjord country. After visiting it, we continue our northward trek to Trondheim. For that purpose, direct plane connections from Aaroe Airport in Molde are made to Trondheim (flight time 30 minutes). Trondheim is also reached by coastal steamer from Bergen and by train from Oslo, eight hours away, as well as by plane from both Bergen and Oslo several times a day. But before Trondheim, those with the time can make an excursion to Kristiansund.

5. Kristiansund

Almost entirely destroyed in World War II, this coastal town on three islands has been attractively rebuilt into a modern city. According to Norwegian authorities, it is designated as the main service base for oil activities on the mid-Norwegian continental shelf. The city has good connections with the mainland, with car ferries running continuously. The Kvernberget Airport connects Kristiansund with the domestic air route network in all directions.

Despite the newness of the town today, its history has not been allowed to vanish. **Nordmøre Museum** (tel. 71-578), by the Atlanten Stadium, follows and preserves the heritage of the district of Nordmøre. Archeological exhibits show

how people have lived here through 9000 years, from the first settlers, the Fosna people, through the Viking age. Fishing has always been an important economic factor in Nordmøre, with codfish being perhaps the most sought-after product of the North Sea before the discovery of oil there. In the museum, you can see how fish was treated and dried on rocks all over the islands of this area to produce "klippfish," a major export to other parts of Europe.

Woldbrygga at the Vaagen (harbor) is a part of the museum where you can see a complete barrelmaking operation, ropemaking equipment, and some old boats from the area, all connected with an old building which was a klippfishhouse.

Another part of the museum, **Mellomvaerftet,** lies at the same harbor, where you can park your car and walk along the seaside. The shipyard (vaerftet) takes care of old boats, restoring them when possible.

The museum by the station is open Tuesday to Friday from 10 a.m. to 2 p.m., Sunday from noon to 3 p.m., and closed Saturday and Monday. Admission is 5 kroner (60¢) for adults, 2.50 kroner (30¢) for children. You can see Woldbrygga and Mellomvaerftet from June 26 to August 3 or by appointment made through the Nordmøre Museum.

The **Kirkelander Church** of Kristiansund is a look into the future, not the past. With a fan-shaped ground plan and side walls that slope in toward the choir, this church marks a definite break with traditional ecclesiastical architecture. The slope to the west of the main entrance is a vast rosarium, and the entire structure blends in well with its site.

Kristiansund is a town of music-lovers, known as the opera town of Norway, with a special Opera Week in early February in the *Festiviteten* culture center where ballets, concerts, and theater productions are staged. Jazz concerts are sometimes presented.

EXCURSIONS: Grip, near Kristiansund, is one of the most fascinating of all Norway's offshore islands, often likened to Scotland's St. Kilda. Of the more than 80 such islands, this was the only one permanently occupied until its abandonment by year-round inhabitants within the last 20 years. Now it is only lived on during the summer months, when there is regular boat service from Kristiansund, costing adults 66 kroner ($7.92) and children 33 kroner ($3.96) for a round trip.

Of special interest on this flat, rocky piece of ocean land is the 14th-century stave church. The walls of the choir were repainted and decorated in 1621 with motifs from the Old and New Testaments. The beautiful little altar chalice from 1320 is one of only two such cups in the country. The church has withstood tempests and tidal waves throughout the centuries, some of which almost wiped out all other island buildings. Grip, once the smallest parish in Norway, is now united with Kristiansund. Similar small stave churches in the islands of Brattvaer and Odden were built between 1470 and 1500.

Grip was an important source of klippfish during its productive life. The group of islands, islets, and skerries of which Grip is a part lies about nine miles out from Kristiansund in the open sea.

Another of the islands which can be visited is **Smøla.** Take the ferry from Kristiansund to Straumen, going through the tight straits of Tustna. Pass Edøy with its stone church from about 1250 and catch the bus from Straumen. Drive to Veidholmen, Norway's most active fishing village with an old tradition like that of Grip. You'll see the other side of Smøla on your return, with the flat inner part contrasting with the landscape of islets and rocks in the western and southern part.

For information on these excursions, get in touch with the Nordmøre Travel Association in Kristiansund.

WHERE TO STAY: Kristiansund has several modest pensions, where your budget can be stretched, and of course there are more expensive and better equipped accommodations.

Central Pensjon, 6 Floyveien (tel. 75-120), offers 14 beds and a simple restaurant. It is open all year. Functional but clean bathless singles cost 150 kroner ($18) and bathless doubles cost 230 kroner ($27.60). Breakfast is an extra 35 kroner ($4.20), and either lunch or dinner costs upward of 75 kroner ($9).

Utsyn Guest House, 4 Kongens Plass (tel. 73-305), is a very small house about 150 yards from the steamship quay. Open all year, this unlicensed hotel offers only one corridor bath. However, those who can survive with a minimum of plumbing will find singles going for 175 kroner ($21), doubles for 280 kroner ($33.60), breakfast included.

Grand Hotel, 142 Postboks (tel. 73-011), is a hotel with traditions but is at the same time a modern city hostelry. The 115 comfortable bedrooms have complete baths, radios, and color TV. Singles cost from 530 kroner ($63.60) to 555 kroner ($66.60), with doubles going from 700 kroner ($84) to 720 kroner ($86.40), all with breakfast included. However, weekend reductions are given, with singles renting for 275 kroner ($33) and doubles for 420 kroner ($50.40). The hotel has an intimate first-class restaurant, where guests can dance to the music of international orchestras. You'll also get good food in the bistro/pub.

Hotel Fosna Atlantic, 16 Hauggate (tel. 74-011), is small but has a personalized and friendly atmosphere. It was renovated in 1980, and the restaurant was completely redone in 1984. Some rooms have fantastic views over the Kristiansund Harbor. Singles cost 480 kroner ($57.60), and all have complete baths. Doubles, which also include color TV in their amenities, rent for 580 kroner ($69.60). Breakfast is included in all the tariffs.

6. Trondheim

Founded by the Viking king Olav Tryggvason in the tenth century, Trondheim is Norway's third-largest city, ranking only behind Bergen and Oslo as a major attraction. It is a scenic, pleasant city as well as an active university center. Noted for its timbered architecture, Trondheim has retained many of its medieval aspects, the most notable example of which is the Gothic-style **Nidaros Cathedral** (more about this later). After the city's last disastrous fire, some three centuries ago, enterprising Trondheimers widened their streets to prevent further devastation. Until the early 1200s, Trondheim was the medieval capital of Norway. It was also the Canterbury of Scandinavia: pilgrims came from all over Europe to worship at the shrine of Olav, who was canonized in 1031. But with the coming of the Reformation, the fortunes of the city declined.

The city lies on the south bay of the Trondheim Fjord, and at the mouth of the Nid River, some 425 miles north of Bergen.

From Oslo to Trondheim by car is seven or eight hours. For intrepid souls planning to drive all the way from Oslo to the North Cape, Trondheim is a convenient resting place on the main European route (E6) north.

The coastal steamers plying their way from Bergen to the North Cape make 35 stops en route. These steamers may be seen in Trondheim every day, one heading north and the other going south. The round trip takes 11 days and (subject to change) costs $724 (U.S.) in second class and $937 in first class from May 1 to May 22; $950 in second and $1254 in first from May 22 to July 31; and $921 in second, $1215 in first from August 1 to August 31. For detailed information in the United States, get in touch with the general agent of Bergen Line, Inc, 515 Fifth Ave., New York, NY 10020 (tel. 1/212/986-2711).

Vaernes Airport lies 20 miles from Trondheim. Bus service to the center of the city costs 25 kroner ($3) and takes about 30 minutes.

The **Trondheim Tourist Office,** 7 Kongensgate (tel. 51-14-66) (entrance on the marketplace), is open from 9 a.m. to 8 p.m. on weekdays, from 1 to 6 p.m. on Sunday. Off-season hours are 9 a.m. to 4 p.m. Monday to Friday, 9 a.m. to 1 p.m. on Saturday. The tourist office will help you with your hotel accommodations, and staff members may also be able to place you in a private home at a cost of 90 kroner ($10.80) and up per bed.

ACCOMMODATIONS: Trondheim is well equipped to handle the influx of thousands every summer. If the greater number of its hotels—most of them in the moderately priced category—don't ooze with chicness and elegance, they do offer sober value. Most recommendations are within walking distance of the center of town.

Student-Run Summer Hotel

Singsaker Studenterhjem, 1 Rogertsgate (tel. 52-00-92), is a student residential hall that converts into a choice bargain hotel from mid-June till mid-August. Surrounded by a village green, the student home is about a 15-minute walk from the center of Trondheim or by bus 63. Used to house German officers during the war, the hotel is one of the largest wooden buildings in Scandinavia, rivaling the Royal Palace.

Bathless singles rent for 190 kroner ($22.80), increasing to 245 kroner ($29.40) with shower and toilet. Doubles are 275 kroner ($33) for bathless rooms, 350 kroner ($42) for rooms with bath. Families or friendly groups may want to rent a room with four beds, complete with shower and toilet, costing from 475 kroner ($57). All prices include a Norwegian breakfast, service, and taxes. The bedrooms, not large, are comfortably cozy—and all have water basins. The dining room is plainly decorated and serves good, wholesome food. In the evening, attractive young people gather around the open fireplace, watch television, and play billiards or other games.

Other Medium-Priced Hotels

Imi Misjonshotellet, 26 Kongensgate (tel. 52-83-48), across the street from Prinsen Hotel, is supremely somber, with attractive old-world architecture, sort of Williamsburg Dutch. The good-size rooms contain both antique and modern furniture. Doubles with bath or shower cost 620 kroner ($74.40) and up. With a bath or shower, a single rents for 500 kroner ($60). Breakfast is included in the price. Solid meals are served in the staid dining room, and a separate café on the premises serves cheaper meals.

Norrøna Kafe og Misjonshospits, 20 Thomas Angells Gate (tel. 53-20-20), despite its somber, impersonal mission appearance, is a good choice, offering bathless doubles for 420 kroner ($50.40), singles for 300 kroner ($36), and doubles with private bath for 500 kroner ($60) to 530 kroner ($63.60), breakfast included. The most functional of Nordic modern furniture abounds. The rooms are too often small but they're functionally designed. The restaurant is spacious, and the service and food are good.

Gildevagen Hotell, 22 Söndre Gate (tel. 52-83-40), looks like a New York City arsenal from the outside, but inside it is most functional, offering newly renovated clean and sedately comfortable living. The hotel bears a distinguishing mark of conservatism. Its bedrooms, for the most part, are quite large. Singles with toilets and showers cost 280 kroner ($33.60). Doubles with bath and toilet go for 450 kroner ($54). All prices include breakfast. Most rooms have phones, TV, and video. Summer discounts are granted from May 15 to September 15. The rooms, both the private and public, are functional and serviceable. Meals, including the big Norwegian cold-table breakfast, are served in the old-fashioned dining room, but there is a cheaper cafeteria on the premises.

Hotel Residence, 26 Munkegate (tel. 52-83-80), is an old-fashioned hotel with many intriguing architectural features. It boasts opera-red draperies, gilt mirrors, and crystal chandeliers. Across the street from the Royal Palace, the Residence charges 420 kroner ($50.40) to 750 kroner ($90) for doubles, depending on the plumbing. Singles, on the same basis, cost 330 kroner ($39.60) to 620 kroner ($74.40). Breakfast is included. In and around the hotel are many extra features that add up to a comfortable stopover. The American Bar is the popular watering hole in the evening; outside is the Wintergarden, a café where both refreshments and food are served. Next to the bar, you find an excellent gourmet restaurant with an exceptional wine cellar. A dinner in the restaurant costs from 175 kroner ($21).

Larssens Hoteli, 10B Thomas Angells Gate (tel. 52-88-51), is of sober appearance. Centrally located, the hotel has been modernized in recent years, attracting both the high-speed tourist racing to the North Cape or the business person. Tor Wessel, the manager, has a well-trained staff. The public rooms strike a better note than the private units, although the bedrooms are reasonably comfortable. A single with private bath rents for 275 kroner ($33), a double, also with bath, going for 400 kroner ($48). These rates include an all-you-can-eat breakfast. The hotel also serves good food (dinners between 5 and 8 p.m.), and it's licensed for beer and wine.

A Youth Hostel

Ungdomsherberget (Youth Hostel), 41 Weidemannsveien (tel. 53-04-90), on a hill right in town, offers a splendid view of Trondheim—if you can make the climb. Take the Singsaker bus from the center of town. Bed-and-breakfast here will cost you 90 kroner ($10.80) in a dormitory accommodation, 160 kroner ($19.20) in a private single room, 250 kroner ($30) in a private double. Middag, served in a large modern cafeteria, costs from 35 kroner ($4.20). The price of full board ranges from 170 kroner ($20.40) to 250 kroner ($30) per person. The hostel is open year round. Toward the end of summer, it is filled with Europeans and other foreigners making their way south from the North Cape. The hostel is closed in the daytime from 10 a.m. to 3 p.m. for cleaning.

On the Outskirts

Parapeten Bed and Breakfast, 26 Brøsetveien (tel. 91-90-15), lies less than two miles from the center of the town. The charge is 325 kroner ($39) to 350 kroner ($42) for a bathless double room, 375 kroner ($45) to 425 kroner ($51) for a double with a private bath. A single room without bath costs 250 kroner ($30), a single with bath going for 325 kroner ($39). Breakfast is 40 kroner ($4.80) per person. The hotel is in a quiet place near Leangen, and it's relatively easy to reach by car or public transportation.

Camping Sites

Trondheim offers convenient cabins for campers, outside of town. These quaint wooden structures are each fitted with four beds and rent for 200 kroner ($24) per night. Information is available from the Trondheim tourist office.

READER'S PENSION SELECTION: "At **Nanna Thomassen Pensjonat,** 1 Museum Plass, you'll find Mrs. Thomassen to be a very friendly person who speaks enough English to make it interesting. Her rooms are large and comfortable, with the bathroom nearby. The price is

275 kroner ($33), including breakfast, for a double, 150 kroner ($18) in a single, in this expensive city. The most remarkable thing about the place is the breakfast. Mrs. Thomassen bakes all her own bread. On the table were several kinds of fish, including Norwegian fish cakes. There were also different kinds of cheese, cold cuts, sausages, jams, preserves, cold cereal, hot cereal, and plenty of coffee. This was undoubtedly the largest and best breakfast we found on our trip. We stayed in 51 different places during the 74 days we traveled through Scandinavia and Western Europe" (John W. Cummins, Escondido, Calif.).

WHERE TO EAT: Try a local specialty, waffle and cheese (vafler med ost), sold at most cafeterias and restaurants in town.

Tavern på Sverresborg (tel. 52-09-32) near the Folk Museum, has been moved up on the hill and reassembled. The wood-frame tavern, built in 1739, was once a merchant's home. In 1841 it was considered the best inn in Trondheim when the *Kun folk* of the "first society" came here. It escaped the great fire and is now a national shrine, offering authentic Trønder specialties at reasonable prices. When ordering, try the blandet spekemat, the kind of meal—served with flatbrød—that a Norwegian mother would serve her family in the early evening in their mountain hut. The platter, costing 92 kroner ($11.04), consists of thinly sliced smoked ham, diced meat, slices of salami, smoked mutton, and little garnishes of lettuce and tomato. Lots of other comparably priced items are offered to those who consider this fare too simple. Meals cost from 130 kroner ($15.60). The restaurant is open until midnight from April 1 to December 31.

Naustlofet Fish Restaurant, 42 Prinsensgate (tel. 21-800), is a licensed establishment offering food and drink on three levels. First and foremost, it's a fish restaurant, built like an old boathouse, with lots of kettles, captain's chairs, copper and brass, plus wooden implements. It overlooks the fjord, so everyone dashes for the window seats. The fish here—fresh from the sea—is prepared with tender, loving care. Fried halibut with rémoulade sauce is invariably featured. Meals cost from 175 kroner ($21) up. In the 300-year-old cellar is a bar, and there is also a nightclub.

The Theatregrill and Wine Lounge in Prinsen Hotel, 30 Kongensgate (tel. 53-06-50), is a place rich in tradition, where the chef makes sure that the food lives up to the expectations of old and new guests alike. As Trøndelag Theatre is nearby, a special theater platter is served on show nights. Meals cost from 150 kroner ($18).

The Bryggen (tel. 53-40-55), near Gamle Bybro (the Old Town Bridge), is where Turid and Arvid Skogseth serve good food according to the ingredients available during particular seasons of the year. The fully licensed restaurant has a wine and cheese room, a bistro, and a bar. It is open at 11 a.m., when you can enjoy sandwiches and light meals. Dinner is served from 3 p.m. Meals cost from 120 kroner ($14.40). The Bryggen is closed Sunday.

If you're hungry for a salad, you can enjoy the freshest ones in town, either to eat on the premises or to take with you, at the town's salad bar. **Den Grønne Bølge A/S,** 21 Kjøpmannsgate (tel. 53-36-32). Salads cost from 75 kroner ($9), depending on your choice of ingredients. It's open Monday to Friday from 10 a.m. to 7 p.m., Saturday from 10 a.m. to 3 p.m.

Snappy's Burger House, 13 Olav Trygvassonsgate, is the place to go if you want a quick meal, particularly one centered around an American-style hamburger. Your meal will cost from 75 kroner ($9). Snappy's is open weekdays from 10 a.m. to 11 p.m., Sunday from 1 to 11 p.m.

READER'S RESTAURANT SELECTION: "**Braseriet Pizzeria Grill,** 11 Nordregt (tel. 52-47-30), is an economy restaurant about two blocks from the Viking statue. The food is good and reasonably priced. Pizza costs from 45 kroner ($5.40), depending on the size and the topping. Fish and chips are offered for 35 kroner ($4.20). The grill is open from 10 a.m. to midnight daily" (Johanna Ficaro, Cambridge, Mass.).

READER'S FOOD TIP: "In Trondheim while visiting the **Fish Market,** we noticed people buying shrimp and eating them right outside the market on the jetty. We did the same, enjoying the cold drinks from the automat in the market. We were delighted with the fresh, tasty shrimp. Only 25 kroner ($3) buys 15 to 20 large ones" (Hanna and Yizchak Dar, Haifa, Israel).

NIGHTLIFE: Trondheim is one of the liveliest of Norwegian towns in terms of nighttime activity. ID is usually required. The big place to go is the **Student Restaurant and Club,** 1 Elgestergate (Tel. 52-21-57). In a large round red building, originally a circus, at the edge of the park behind the cathedral, it's a ten-minute walk from the main square, just across the bridge. Concerts are held from September through May, and many other events take place in this huge funhouse. Summer hours vary. In a cellar, Strossa is a magnet. A friendly crowd of people —approximately ages 18 to 25—dances to pop and rock music seven nights a week from 8 p.m. until 1 a.m.

Studio Hjorten, 73 Kjøpmannsgate (tel. 53-40-10), at the Royal Garden Hotel, is a nightclub where the decor and ambience provide a fine framework for a relaxing and fun evening. Here you can dance into the wee hours of the morning surrounded by silvery columns branching out across a midnight-blue ceiling. Disco music is played. It's open Thursday to Sunday from 9 p.m. to 2 a.m. A cover charge of 45 kroner ($5.40) is levied.

Hollywood, on the fourth floor of Handelsstandens Hus (tel. 52-24-23), is a swinging disco with exceptional light and sound effects. The minimum age here is 19, and jackets are required. Entry costs from 45 kroner ($5.40).

WHAT TO SEE: Nidaros Cathedral (tel. 52-12-53)—the goal of the medieval pilgrim—is the crowning ecclesiastical building of Scandinavia. Dating back to the 11th century, it has witnessed many changes over the years, decay, then ultimate restoration. Once the burial place of medieval Norwegian kings, it was also the site of the coronation of King Haakon VII in 1906, an event that marked the beginning of modern Norway. Nidaros is a classical European cathedral in that it represents different blends of architecture, including Gothic and Romanesque. The intricate rose window of the west front is stunning. Gustav Vigeland used his chisel to carve the gargoyles and grotesques for the head tower and northern transept. The cathedral may be visited May 1 to May 14 and September 1 to September 14 from 10 a.m. to 2:30 p.m. Monday to Friday; from 10 a.m. to 2 p.m. Saturday; and from 1:30 to 3 p.m. Sunday. May 15 to June 14, hours are 9:30 a.m. to 3 p.m. Monday to Friday, 9:30 a.m. to 2 p.m. Saturday, and 1:30 to 4 p.m. Sunday. June 15 to August 31: 9:30 a.m. to 5:30 p.m. Monday to Friday, 9:30 a.m. to 2 p.m. Saturday, and 1:30 to 4 p.m. Sunday. September 15 to April 30: noon to 2:30 p.m. Monday to Friday, 11:30 a.m. to 2 p.m. Saturday, and 1:30 to 3 p.m. Sunday. Admission is 6 kroner (72¢).

Behind the cathedral is the **Archbishop's Palace,** Erkebispegaarden, which can be visited for 3 kroner (36¢). This residence dates from the end of the 12th century. It is open only during the summer, from June 16 until August 15.

Stiftsgaarden

This buttercup-yellow Royal Palace was built as a private home by a rich merchant's widow in the 1770s, when Trondheim began to regain its prosperity. It is the largest wooden building in Scandinavia, perhaps in Northern Europe.

The furnishings inside are unpretentious, presenting various styles of design. Near the marketplace (Torvet), the mansion (tel. 52-24-73) may be visited from 11 a.m. to 2 p.m., June 1 to September 15. Closed Sunday. Admission is 5 kroner (60¢) for adults, 2.50 kroner (30¢) for children.

Museum of Music History

At Ringve Manor (tel. 91-45-15), this museum—the highlight of many a visit to Trondheim—may be viewed only on conducted tours. At specified times musical selections (a sonata, perhaps) are performed on the old, carefully preserved instruments, which include an impressive collection of keyboard instruments, such as spinets, harpsichords, clavichords, and pianofortes, in addition to string and wind instruments and other musical instruments. From May 20 to September 30, guided tours are offered at noon and again at 2 p.m. In October, only the noon tour is conducted. To reach Ringve, take a taxi from the marketplace, a two-mile ride, or else catch streetcar 1 to Lade Church, then walk the rest of the way. Also on the premises is an old kro (inn), where guests enjoy waffles, or settle for light refreshments and coffee instead. The mansion was the birthplace of Admiral Tordenskiold, the Norwegian sea hero.

The Trøndelag Folk Museum at Sverresborg

Outside the city is a good collection of old timbered houses from the Trøndelag district. Be sure to see the old farmhouse and barn-red church, as well as the merchant's house from the 18th-century Trondheim. A tiny, gold-colored stave church here is one of the oldest in Norway. The folk museum at Sverresborg may be visited from 11 a.m. to 6 p.m. in summer; admission is 12 kroner ($1.44). Take bus 8 or 12 from Dronningens Gate to Wullumsgaarden.

The University of Trondheim Museum

At 47 Erling Skakkesgate (tel 59-21-45), this collection contains a fine exhibition of zoological art, including a bird diorama with recorded commentary. Of great interest are the artifacts and relics of the area, dating back to prehistoric times. There are also Lapp and Eskimo arts and crafts, plus a numismatic collection. The museum (tel. 59-22-26) is open on Sunday all year from noon until 3 p.m. From May 2 to May 31, weekdays from noon to 3 p.m.; June 1 to August 31, weekdays from 11 a.m. to 3 p.m.; September 1 to September 30, noon to 3 p.m. Admission for adults is 2 kroner (24¢), for children, 1 krone (12¢).

Organized Tours

From June 1 through August, a 1 p.m. bus tour departs daily from the marketplace, lasting 1½ hours and costing 50 kroner ($6). Its main attraction is a guided trek through the cathedral (not included in price).

In addition to the bus tour, there are boat trips daily, leaving Ravnkloa. The trip to **Munkholmen Island** leaves daily at 10 a.m. and every half hour thereafter until 5 p.m. You're given a guided tour of the island's historical fortress. Lunch, not included in the tariff, is available at Munkholmen.

Do-it-Yourself Tour

For a quick tour of Trondheim, start from the cathedral and walk toward the water on Munkegaten, the main street in town. You'll pass by the modernistic statue of a tall Viking king (Olav Tryggvason) and the Torvet (market square) where outdoor vendors sell vegetables and fruit. On your left is the Residence Hotel and on your right the old wooden building. Keep walking and you come to the fish market at the dock. From there you can take a ferry to the little island of **Munkholmen,** which was formerly a fortress, a monastery, and a prison, and is now a resort spot with a beach and restaurant. A round-trip ticket on the ferry costs 15 kroner ($1.80) for adults, 8 kroner (96¢) for children. A half-hour conducted tour is held between 10 a.m. and 6 p.m., costing adults 5 kroner (60¢); children 3 kroner (36¢).

Excursions

Trondheim can be the center of some rugged one- and two-day trips, many of which will appeal to adventurous readers.

HITRA AND FRØYA: By fast steamer from Trondheim, operating daily all year, you can go to Ansnes (Hitra), a trip taking about three hours and costing 125 kroner ($15) each way, and to Sistranda (Frøya), also about three hours, priced at 150 kroner ($18) each way.

Hitra is one of Norway's largest islands. It offers a variety of scenery: forests, wooded hills, well-stocked lakes, weathered rocks, and small fjords. It is also known for the large herds of red deer, the Dolm Church, and Dolmen town, a miniature community designed and built by a Dolmøy crofter and fisherman. When you have reached Hitra, you should make the hop across to neighboring Frøya by ferry. With the ocean as their constant companion, these islands have a weatherbeaten but widely varied landscape.

RØROS: Of all the old Norwegian mining town, Røros, is perhaps the most characteristic. It is more than 300 years old, with some 80 preserved houses still in use. Communications are excellent by road and railway from Oslo and Trondheim, and the town airport is almost in its center. There are daily flights to and from Oslo and Trondheim.

You can take conducted tours of the Quintus and Olav Mines, the Røros Museum, the Old Miners Village, Rørus Church, and Ratvollen, home of author Johan Falkberget, who died in 1967. You'll find easy mountain rambling, excursions and boat trips on Lake Femunden, visits to Funäsdalen in Sweden, fishing in rivers and lakes, and good shopping and walking in the town center.

The **Røros Tourist Office** (tel. 11-165) will be pleased to advise on making your stay pleasant, summer or winter.

Where To Stay in Røros

Bergstaden Turisthotel (tel. 11-111) is a rather bleak structure, which is about the best of the lot. At least, all its adequately furnished rooms contain private bath. Rut and Leif Ericson are the efficient managers, renting a single room for 350 kroner ($42); a double for 435 kroner ($52.20). However, prices are lowered in summer until the rate is quoted at 150 kroner ($18) per person for an overnight stay. Breakfast costs another 45 kroner ($5.40), and you can order a main meal for around 100 kroner ($12).

Another possibility is the **Røros Turisthotell** (tel. 11-011), run by Kristin and Knut R. Strøm. They also offer all rooms with bath. A single costs from 425 kroner ($51), a double going for 500 kroner ($60). There is a motel section where a double costs from 350 kroner ($42), and a section of *hytter* or cabins, renting for 235 kroner ($28.20) for two. Breakfast is 40 kroner ($4.80), and you can order a lunch at 85 kroner ($10.20).

HORSEBACK TOURS IN THE TYDAL MOUNTAINS: At the head of the Tydal Valley, about 85 miles southeast of Trondheim stands **Vaektarstua Tourist Lodge,** the starting point for horseback trips in the Tydal and Sylene Mountains. Oddmund Dyrhaug, who runs the riding center, has a string of some 20 Scandic ponies and organizes regular pony-trekking tours. A one-day course as well as treks lasting several days, with the nights spent at tourist lodges, are included in the program. Tours are scheduled in June, July, and August. The seven-day all-inclusive treks cost around 2500 kroner ($300) per person, with a one-day trip priced from 200 kroner ($24) per person. For details, write to Oddmund Dyrhaug, N-7590, Tydal.

OPPDAL: A number of holiday activities and attractions make Oppdal a good choice for visitors who seek changing countryside, physical recreation, and healthy mountain air. Oppdal is 75 miles south of Trondheim on the E6 and the Trondheim–Oslo railway, set amid parts of the Dovrefjell and Trollheimen massifs. The River Driva, one of Norway's best sources of salmon, runs like a silver ribbon through the narrow valley. The surrounding mountain areas are a paradise for brown trout fishermen, and lodging is offered in charming mountain huts. The center of Oppdal has all the amenities of an up and coming village where the main sources of livelihood are agriculture and forestry augmented by slate-stone, woodwork, glass-making, and the tourist industry.

You can arrange a week's tour on horseback in the Trollheimen massif through **Kvåles Ridesenter,** 7320 Fannrem. The overnight stays are in mountain chalets (check with the tourist office). Prices quoted are for full board, a horse, and a leader. The week's tours start every Sunday, costing 2200 kroner ($264) and up.

Mountain rambles along marked trails on the hillside or in the mountains can be made, as well as excursions by car or bus to the fjords and into valleys and mountain areas.

The local tourist office can provide information about a variety of matters, including permits for salmon and trout fishing. You may find the local museum of interest, and shopping for local products is good here.

7. Bodø

This seaport, the terminus of the Nordland railway, lies north of the Arctic Circle. Because of its unique location visitors flock here for a glimpse of the Midnight Sun. Bodø is the capital of Nordland, lying just north of the Arctic Circle.

The train ride from Trondheim to Bodø takes 13 hours and might well be called the Midnight Sun Special (few passengers sleep—they keep their eyes glued to the windows). Bodø can also be reached on one of the daily flights from Trondheim in about an hour. You can walk from the SAS Royal Hotel (in the heart of town) to the airport in 15 minutes. Flights from Oslo are also possible, but many visitors take the coastal steamer from Bergen.

The Midnight Sun shines brightly in Bodø from June 1 to July 12. Warning: Don't always expect to have a clear view of it at this time, as many nights are rainy or hazy. Bodø citizens eventually pay for this extra daylight: the sun completely disappears from December 19 to January 9.

But Bodø has more claims to being a tourist center than simply a sun which doesn't know when to go down. Excursions are possible in many directions—to both glaciers and bird islands, but, most important, to the **Lofoten Islands.**

On May 27, 1940, German bombers swept over Bodø, leveling it. But it has since been rebuilt into a modern town. The most notable of its postwar buildings is the **Bodø Cathedral,** completed in 1956. Its most outstanding architectural feature is a spire that stands completely separated from the main building. The interior boasts tufted rugs depicting ecclesiastical themes, wall hangings, and a stained-glass window that captures the northern lights. A memorial outside honors those killed in the war: "No one mentioned, no one forgotten."

ACCOMMODATIONS: The **tourist office** is in the center of the town, 16 Storgata (tel. 21-240). In summer, it's open from 9 a.m. to 8 p.m. Monday through Saturday, from 5 to 8 p.m. Sunday. You can arrange for a room in a private home here or make reservations.

At the **Norrøna Bed and Breakfast,** run by SAS Royal Hotel, 2 Storgata (tel. 24-118), you can get a well-furnished and comfortable bathless single for 210 kroner ($25.20), a single with bath for 280 kroner ($33.60). A bathless double goes for 310 kroner ($37.20), a double with bath costing 380 kroner ($45.60). Breakfast is included in all tariffs.

Central Hotel, 6 Professor Schyttesgate (tel. 23-585), lies 2½ blocks from the harbor, in the shadow of the rebuilt cathedral. A first-class hotel, it rents out well-furnished rooms, each with private bath, TV, radio, and phone. The cost ranges from 420 kroner ($50.40) to 450 kroner ($54) in a single and from 540 kroner ($64.80) to 600 kroner ($72) in a double. Its restaurant, The Beef, serves fresh fish (try the fried halibut), steaks, and crisp salads. Every day a sandwich buffet is featured, with all the sandwiches you can eat. The best news for last. In summer, a special tourist rate of 200 kroner ($24) per person is charged nightly, the most economical way to stay here.

Park Pensjonat, 54 Storgata (tel. 24-596), on the main street, has undergone complete modernization in recent years, and now offers 31 rooms, 13 of which are doubles. The Park offers bathless singles for 240 kroner ($28.80) and bathless doubles for 385 kroner ($46.20). Some three-bedded family rooms are rented for 530 kroner ($63.30). A few units have private shower/toilet, costing an extra 80 kroner ($9.60) per room. Breakfast is included in the prices. This is a good place to rest if you've been roughing it on the way to or from the Nordkapp.

Midnattsol Guesthouse, 65 Storgata (tel. 21-926). English-speaking Finn Aurdal welcomes you to this simple, boxy modern house, standing on the main street at the junction with Highway 80. Particularly popular with motorists, it rents out 16 adequately furnished rooms, none of which has a private bath. For a single, the charge is 180 kroner ($21.60), going up to 230 kroner ($27.60) in a double, breakfast included. Parking facilities are available, and the location is 100 yards from the railway terminal, 300 yards from both the bus and boat terminals, and just ten minutes by taxi from the airport. The guesthouse, incidentally, is licensed to serve beer and wine.

Kristensens Pensjonat, 45 Rensagate (tel. 21-699), has good, clean rooms at reasonable rates: 150 kroner ($18) to 175 kroner ($21) in a single, 180 kroner ($21.60) to 200 kroner ($24) in a double, and 275 kroner ($33) to 300 kroner ($36) in a triple. All rooms have color TV. The English-speaking Kristensens have only 12 beds to rent, and are interested in meeting foreign travelers from all over the world. A breakfast, Norwegian style, will be served to you for 30 kroner ($3.36). There are no private baths.

A Youth Hostel

The **Flatvold Youth Hostel,** Rønvikkrysset (tel. 25-666), is the only such accommodation in Bodø. It is a series of student homes which are rented to transients from June 20 to August 16, about two miles from the town center or 20 minutes' walking distance from the railway station. City buses run regularly from the bus station in the city, stopping almost at the door of the hostel. The charge for members is 50 kroner ($6) per person nightly, with the use of kitchen facilities included. Use of sleeping bags is not allowed, but a sheet bag is. Guests usually share rooms with at least one other person. The only meal offered is breakfast in a box. The hostel shuts down daily between noon and 5 p.m.

FOR DESSERT—THE MIDNIGHT SUN: Turisthytta (tel. 217-131), on the top of a mountain, is the most popular excursion point for those who come to dine while watching the Midnight Sun. Reached by a taxi, the restaurant is open only in summer. Budgeteers are warned to pick and choose carefully from the à la carte menu. Many come here just for drinks and snacks (wide selection of open-face sandwiches), since the view is the big treat. Coalfish, a popular Norwegian dish is always featured. Meals cost from 120 kroner ($14.40).

For other food in Bodø (and a view of the harbor and mountains), go to **Løvold's Cafeteria,** a second-floor eatery on the quay, offering home-style "norsk" food from 8:30 a.m. until 6 p.m. weekdays, on Saturday from 8:30 a.m. to 4:30 p.m., and on Sunday from noon until 6 p.m. The daily special may be meat cakes with peas and cabbage. Broiled cod is served in a small platter or a larger portion, which is enough for two. For dessert, try the traditional Norwegian hot fruit soup. The town's young people congregate here to stare at the foreigners.

READER'S CAFÉ SELECTION: "A marvelous café, about two blocks from the tourist information center, called the **Fønix,** serves excellent lunches (dinners are two or three times as expensive) in an elegant atmosphere on silver serving dishes. We paid 45 kroner ($5.40) each for exquisitely prepared fish filets, potatoes in butter, and salad. It was the best meal I had in Europe" (Mrs. Patricia A. Colburn, Redding, Calif.).

ORGANIZED TOURS: A bus tour is offered to the mighty maelstrom, the **Saltstraumen Eddy,** some 20 miles from Bodø. The coach trip takes one hour each way. It leaves daily, but the tourist bureau will provide the exact time, as treks are limited to catch the most powerful current. Cost is 45 kroner ($5.40).

SEA EXCURSIONS: As mentioned earlier, one of the reasons for coming to Bodø is to take one of the local steamers along the fjord or to some of the offshore islands. The tourists information office, 16 Storgata (tel. 21-240), will furnish complete information and times of departure (they vary considerably). Depending on the weather, there is a boat trip to the **Vaeran Islands,** west of Bodø. Book through Salten Steamship Co. (tel. 21-020), across from the SAS Royal Hotel. Early risers can take this tour daily. Round trips on coastal express boats to the Vaeran Islands cost 80 kroner ($9.60) for adults, half-price for children. For longer journeys, you can go by bus to **Narvik**—scene of tremendous naval fighting in World War II. One leaves Bodø twice a day, the trip lasting nine hours.

A highly recommended tour for those with the time is to the jagged peaks of the **Lofoten** and **Vesterålen Islands,** which offers some of North Norway's most dramatic scenery. The Lofotens also have the largest codfish catches in the world. A coastal express steamer to Stamsund in the Lofoten leaves every day. The trip costs 124 kroner ($14.88) in second class.

For an offbeat adventure, you may rent a fisherman's cottage in summer in one of the remote Lofoten villages, even as far away as the islands of **Vaerøy** and

Røst. These cottages, some built on piles, are more or less abandoned in summer, as they are used by fishermen only during the season, which begins in January and lasts only until the end of April. Most of those for rent are timbered structures, with combination living rooms and kitchens (often with bunks for eight to ten persons). For the most part, the cottages have running water (some only a tap outside). A few—but not all—have inside toilets. Prospective renters must have ordinary camping gear. At any rate, you'll be on the sea wherever you rent, and more than likely there will be a jetty on your doorstep. Fishing tackle and rowboats are easy to rent once you're there. Village stores sell other equipment you may need. Fishermen's cottages may be booked through the tourist office. Write Tourist Information, P.O. Box 514, N-8001 Bodø, Norway. Prices range from 100 kroner ($12) to 200 kroner ($24) per cabin (accommodating four to six persons) or from 30 kroner ($3.60) to 50 kroner ($6) per bed. You reach the islands after about four to six hours, the boat leaving Bodø on frequently scheduled runs. The cost is 87 kroner ($10.44) one way. Helicopter service is operated from April 1 to October 31, a one-way ticket costing 295 kroner ($35.40). Two planes leave Bodø daily, heading for both Vaerøy and Røst.

In addition, air service has opened between Bodø and the Lofoten Islands, where Edgar Allan Poe spent several months writing "A Descent into the Maelstrom." These planes fly from Bodø to **Svolvoer** and **Leknes** several times daily, costing about 315 kroner ($37.80) for a one-way flight. Service is year round.

BODØ MISCELLANY: Horseback riding? The **Bodø Hestecenter** (14-148) rents horses, for riding into the Midnight Sun. The charge is 50 kroner ($6) per hour or 70 kroner ($8.40) for two hours of riding. The horse center is a little more than nine miles from Bodø. Buses go there Monday to Friday morning and evening. For more information, call the **Bodø Tourist Information Office** (tel. 21240).

The town's swimming pool and sauna offer the works for 10 kroner ($1.20).

NIGHTLIFE: For a grand view of Bodø and environs, go to the **Top 13,** at the top of the SAS Royal Hotel, 2 Storgata (tel. 24-100). You can order a drink from the friendly bartender or just gaze out at the mountains and the sea. Take the elevator to the 12th floor and walk up one flight. There is bar service till midnight.

The **Pizzakjeller'n** (Pizza Parlor), in the SAS Royal Hotel, 2 Storgata (tel. 24-100), is a steak and pizza place, offering pizza from 45 kroner ($5.40) and steaks from 75 kroner ($9). It's open from noon to 1 a.m. It's downstairs in the lobby of the hotel.

8. Narvik

This ice-free seaport on the Ofot Fjord is in Nordland fylke, 250 miles north of the Arctic Circle. It dates from 1903 when the Ofoten railway line was completed, its initial purpose being to transport iron ore from the Kiruna Gällivare region of Sweden for shipment around the world. However, it it also a magnificent scenic line through precipitous mountain terrain north of the Arctic Circle. It is still the northernmost electrified railway line in the world. It climbs through mountains and tunnels, along ridges, and across tall stone embankments. Only 6½ miles from Narvik, Straumsnes station is the last permanent habitation as you go east. The last Norwegian station, Bjørnfjell, is well above the timber line and about three hours from Kiruna, Sweden, about 87 miles north of the Arctic Circle. From there, you can go on by train to Stockholm, 982 miles from where you boarded at Narvik. In 1984, a road was opened from Kiruna to Narvik.

Narvik boasts Europe's most modern shipping harbor for iron ore, built to accommodate ships of up to 350,000 tons dead weight. However, smaller ore carriers are a more frequent sight in the harbor. Narvik is no longer entirely dependent on the transport of iron ore for its economic survival, having developed a rich and varied economy.

To get a good look at Narvik, take the cable car which operates from March to October. In just 13 minutes, it takes you to an altitude of 2100 feet, where you can admire the impressive panorama of the town and its surroundings.

The Germans seized Narvik in 1940, and it was the scene of two naval battles in World War II. Many Nazi ships were lost, but so was most of Narvik in the process. Today, one of the most important sights of Narvik is the **War Museum,** owned by the Nordland Section of the Norwegian Red Cross. The museum displays concentrate on the events of 1940–1945 in Narvik, when most of the town was destroyed by the Germans, who occupied it until the end of World War II. Events of that era are depicted as well as experiences of the civilian population and the foreign POWs.

The **Ofoten Museum** preserves the cultural history of the area. It is in Parkhallen, entrance at the back.

In the **Bifrost Museum,** in the gardens at the railway station, you can see what may be the only surviving specimen of a series of train engines constructed in Trollhattan, Sweden, in 1882.

Narvik is industrial, with large harbor installations, yet it is surrounded by fjord and mountain scenery. The Midnight Sun shines from May 26 to July 19, but August is noted for its "mysterious lighting."

WHERE TO STAY: As the hotels of Narvik tend to be expensive, your best bet is to book a room in a private home through the tourist office, 66 Kongensgate (tel. 43-309). The average cost is from 110 kroner ($13.20) per person nightly.

Breidablikk Gjestgiveri, 41 Tore Hundsgatan (tel. 41-418), lies about 15 minutes from the station, or a six-block walk uphill. For 210 kroner ($25.20), you are given a double room, well furnished, with a view over Narvik and the snow-covered mountains in the distance. Plenty of hot water (and plenty of towels) are provided. The hotel has more than 20 rooms, and the English-speaking hosts are most accommodating. As a thoughtful extra, they have provided a lounge with TV for their guests. Some singles are also rented, most of which cost from 150 kroner ($18) per night.

You could stay at a youth hostel, **Nordkalotten Ungdomsherberge,** 3 Havnegaten (tel. 42-598), where in bone-bare, simple surroundings, you can get a dormitory-style accommodation at a cost of 78 kroner ($9.36) if you are a member of a recognized youth hosteling association. Otherwise, the cost is 90 kroner ($10.80) per person. It is almost impossible to obtain a single room in the summer season. Breakfast is served at the hostel and is included in the price. You can order an adequate dinner for 45 kroner ($5.40).

EXCURSION TO THE LOFOTEN ISLANDS: From Narvik, you can go on one of the most scenic rides in Norway, taking a boat to **Svolvaer** in the already mentioned **Lofoten Islands.** You sail through a large number of the islands and can visit some of the smaller ones, meeting the local fishermen and occasionally their wives. Passengers can inspect fish nurseries and see metal cages in the harbor where fish are grown. Reader Edward Karpoff says that the vessel on which he rode for this island excursion was "a two-hull catamaran, modern, and possibly brand-new. Principal passenger accommodation was in a room like a section of a 747, with about 80 comfortable seats." This boat makes the trip in four hours. It leaves Narvik on Saturday at 1 p.m. The return boat leaves Svolvaer at 6 a.m., arriving in Narvik the next morning at 10 a.m. The one-way fare is 160 kroner ($19.20) per person.

9. Tromsø

This is a real boomtown—and an expensive one, with prices comparable to those of Alaska in the gold rush days. Partially because of the recent discovery of oil in the North Sea, Tromsø is prospering, bursting at its seams; the population is expected to double in the near future. A university, the world's northernmost, opened in 1972. In case you choose not to stay in a hotel, you can ask for a room in a private home. These private accommodations are obtained through the tourist office, 18 Parkgata (tel. 84-776).

Lying some 250 miles north of the Arctic Circle, Tromsø gets the Midnight Sun from May 21 to July 23—but not one ray comes through from November 25 to January 21.

The town is quickly reached from Bodø by plane; otherwise, bus and coastal steamer connections can be made either from Narvik or Bodø. It does not have rail service.

ACCOMMODATIONS: If you arrive from June through August, your best bet is in one of the summer hotels, providing friendly accommodation in a Nordic setting. Practically all of them have the same atmosphere and prices. Singles are hard to find, but doubles are available. Most of these hotels are open from June till the end of August.

Prestvann Turistheim, 8 Olastien (tel. 86-486), is a summer hotel lying at the top of Tromsø island, halfway between the airport and the center of town. It stands close to Prestvannet, from which it takes its name, an attractive little lake noted for its bird life. Since 1973 this hotel has been accepting international guests from June 20 to August 20, otherwise, in the off-season, it becomes a home for university students. It offers 100 tastefully furnished combination and family rooms, each with wall-to-wall carpeting, phone, shower, and sink. A single rents for 250 kroner ($30), a double going for 320 kroner ($38.40). Families might want to ask for one of the three-bedded rooms costing 400 kroner ($48) or a four-bedded room going for 450 kroner ($54). The family units consist of two rooms and a kitchenette with stove and refrigerator. In the cafeteria you can order dinner or sandwiches from 1 to 9 p.m., although on Sunday only breakfast is served.

Also recommendable is **Tromsdal Gjestgiveri,** Elvestrand, Tromsdalen (tel. 35-944), offering a bathless double for 300 kroner ($36), a double with bath for 400 kroner ($48). With bath, a single costs 285 kroner ($34.20), dropping to 225 kroner ($27) if bathless. Breakfast is included in the tariffs. A dinner can be another 95 kroner ($11.40) in the dining room. There is also a cafeteria.

Another possibility, if you're watching your kroner, is the **Skipperhuset Pensjonat,** 112 Storgata (tel. 81-660), which offers 35 beds in simply furnished rooms. None of the accommodation contains a private bath, but you can rent a single for 200 kroner ($24), with a double going for 225 kroner ($27). Breakfast is included, and you can also order a lunch at 45 kroner ($5.40).

The least expensive place to stay in Tromsø is the **Tromsø Ungdomsherberge,** the youth hostel at 7 Rödhettestien, Övre Breivang (tel. 85-735), which operates only from June 20 to August 20. In addition, the hostel closes down for cleaning at 10 a.m., not reopening for guests until 4 p.m. So if you stay here plan to be off on an excursion for the day. All rooms at this bone-bare place are with three beds, each with a private bath and a small kitchenette. The price is 85 kroner ($10.20) per night for nonmembers, although this charge is reduced to just 75 kroner ($9) for members. Breakfast is not served, but you can prepare your own in your kitchenette.

WHERE TO DINE: At the **Peppermøllen,** 42 Storgata (tel. 86-260), you can order the local specialty, reindeer steak, for 125 kroner ($15).

However, you may prefer **Fiskekrogen,** 42 Storgata (tel. 85-234), next door, where a wide variety of fish platters cost from 65 kroner ($7.80). The timber on the walls is from the mid-19th century.

The cafeterias and pizza restaurant at the **SAS Royal Hotel,** 9 Sjøgate, will serve you with a meal for about 65 kroner ($7.80).

WHAT TO SEE: The **Arctic Church,** across the longest (approximately 1100 yards) suspension bridge in Scandinavia, was built in the shape of an iceberg, with aluminum on the outside that glistens in the Midnight Sun. A stunning design in modern architecture, it is open June 15 to August 15 from 10 a.m. to noon and 4 to 5 p.m.

Beyond the church is the entry station to a **funicular** that takes passengers on a lofty ride to a perch 1400 feet above sea level. Here is an unparalleled view of Tromsø and its environs, and there is a restaurant "upstairs." The cable car operates daily throughout summer from 9 a.m. to 2 p.m. A round trip costs 25 kroner ($3).

In complete contrast to the Arctic Church (see above) is **Tromsø Cathedral,** which is one of Norway's largest wooden churches. The 19th-century house of worship is open daily from noon to 1 p.m. and 5 to 6 p.m. from mid-June to mid-August.

The **Tromsø Museum,** University of Tromsø, a 20-minute walk from the center of town, or a 6-krone (72¢) bus ride, traces the life—both animal and humankind—carved out of the wilderness north of the Arctic Circle. Of special interest to foreigners is an exhibition on Lapp culture, which aims to present as extensive a picture of these people as possible in the space available. In addition, a good assortment of medieval church art and furnishings is exhibited. The museum is open daily from 9 a.m. to 6 p.m. in summer, charging 5 kroner (60¢) for admission.

A **tour** of the sights described, plus a ride past Tromsø's old timbered buildings, leaves from the Grand Hotel on summer mornings at 10:30 a.m. The guided tour takes 2½ hours and costs 75 kroner ($9) for adults, half-price for children. Many sightseeing tours by boat can be made for as little as 75 kroner ($9) to 100 kroner ($12). Check at the tourist office for schedules.

Sea fishing trips are arranged throughout the summer. You will be taken to places where catches are guaranteed. Fishing equipment may be rented on board for the three-hour trip. Departure is at 5 p.m. every day except Sunday. For information, go to the Tromsø Travel Association, 312 Postboks.

NIGHTLIFE: The town's nightlife, such as it is, can be found at the **SAS Royal,** 7 Sjøgate (tel. 83-606). There you can usually dance in the hotel's restaurant, Caravelle, or else enjoy drinks in Charly Bar, which features live music.

10. Harstad

Harstad, with 22,000 population, is one of the biggest towns in North Norway, lying in the center of the island of Hinnøya, the country's largest island, which is connected to the mainland by Tjelsund Bridge. It is linked to the E6 by highways 19 and 83 across the bridge, and it is possible to cross Lodingen or to take a route north by ferry.

Shipbuilding and repair yards are Harstad's main economic base, and the town was selected as the main point from which offshore oil prospecting was mounted in the north. The harbor is usually thronged with shipping. Northbound and southbound coastal express steamers call daily, while a network of express boats provide a link with outlying districts.

Harstad has two major summer events, the North Norway Festival in the last week of June and an International Ocean-Fishing Festival in July.

The early history of Harstad harks back to the time of the sagas, as a visit to **Trondenes Church** will impress on you. The world's northernmost medieval stone church, this house of worship is one of Norway's major cultural treasures. A church was built on this spot in 1100, the present one being erected on the same spot in 1250, where it provided a landmark for seafarers for centuries. The church is open daily during the tourist season. For details, ask at the tourist office.

Worth seeing is **Slottet** (the Palace), a prominent rocky bastion, situated in the built-up area and one of North Norway's two prehistoric hill forts. It can be reached from the Vocational Training School (Yrkesskilen).

On the west side, a wide fjord thrusts its way in from the sea, and the innermost section, nearest Trondenes, is known as **Altevågen,** where you can see three or four small burial mounds and two large dwelling sites set in an east-west direction.

Nupen excursion point is one of the best spots from which to see the Midnight Sun. It's about 9¼ miles from the center of Harstad.

WHERE TO STAY: Gullstad Guesthouse, 83 St. Olavsgate (tel. 63-057), rents out only 20 beds in simply furnished rooms. A single with bath costs 160 kroner ($19.20), while a double with bath goes from 210 kroner ($25.20). Breakfast is another 40 kroner ($4.80).

Høilands Hospits, 4 Magnusgate (tel. 64-960), is one of the smallest guesthouses in town, with only seven beds. Rooms are well furnished and comfortable, costing 180 kroner ($21.60) in a single, 230 kroner ($27.60) in a double, plus another 45 kroner ($5.40) for breakfast.

Harstad also has a youth hostel, **Stangnes Ungdomsherberge,** at Stangnes (tel. 63-446), which has 80 beds, costing only 70 kroner ($8.40) each.

11. Alta

A well-built town of thousands of hearty souls, Alta is a major airport terminal for the north of Norway. It has a limited number of accommodations, and is a center for offbeat excursions to the Lapp village of **Masi,** on the main road to Finland, about 44 miles from Alta. In the village, which has a Lapp school, the natives don't live in tents, but on most occasions wear their colorful costumes. The excursion is best done by car. Inquire at the local tourist bureau in Alta about rentals.

From the Lapp village, it's possible to take a riverboat excursion on a long, flat-bottom boat with an outboard motor, driven by costumed Lapps. The boat can be rented and the excursion usually lasts four hours. The cost depends on your skill at negotiation and the number in your party. Obviously this trip—from the standpoint of the budgeteer—is only possible if four or five guests at the hotel can be convinced to join together on a one-day excursion. But it does offer a rare and intimate contact with the Lapps.

Guests take a packed lunch from their hotel with them, then stop along the way—preferably in a secluded spot by the riverbank—for a picnic.

While in northern Norway, try a reindeer meat sandwich, called Lappbiff. Another specialty of Finnmark is almond cake (furstekake).

From Alta, it's possible to take a riverboat excursion along the Alta river up to the biggest and most beautiful canyon in northern Europe. Get in touch with Alta Riverboat Service (tel. 33-378).

You should take time to visit the rock carvings in **Hjemmeluft,** dating from 2000 to 5000 years ago.

See the local tourist office for further information about the sights and to arrange a guide for your tours.

WHERE TO STAY: Many spending the night in Alta head for the **Altafjord Turisthotell** (tel. 34-055), one of the many guesthouses that sprang up after the war, when Norwegians, returned to find that some of their hometowns—such as Hammerfest—didn't exist any longer. This establishment, like Topsy, just grew and grew. Today, with its new wings—California hacienda style—the hotel is one of the stars of a chain of hotels of North Norway. A couple can stay here, with private bath, for 700 kroner ($84) a night, breakfast included. Singles with bath cost 495 kroner ($59.40). Most of the rooms are attractively furnished, compact and comfortable, with coordinated color schemes. The food is quite good. The hotel, open all year, is about five miles from the airport.

The **Alta Hotel** (tel. 35-311) is a modern hostelry, centrally located in Alta, only 2½ miles from the airport. Here you'll find good food, a friendly environment, and personal service. All rooms have private baths. Doubles rent for 400 kroner ($48) per person, while singles cost 545 kroner ($65.40). All tariffs include breakfast. The hotel has a restaurant, a bar, and a disco.

Gargia Fjellstue (tel 33-351) provides 40 simply but sufficiently furnished rooms with corridor baths. Bathless doubles peak at 280 kroner ($33.60). Breakfast is an extra 40 kroner ($4.80). Gargia Fjellstue also offers cabins for rent.

In the Alta area, there are seven campgrounds.

12. Kautokeino

A visit here is recommended as an offbeat adventure. This village, with mostly a Lapp population, is at the end of a main road running south from Alta. It is set in a wilderness inhabited for the most part by Lapps. The enveloping countryside is a land of unpolluted rivers, lakes, and mountains. Reindeer herds cross the plains. Camping is discouraged in Finnmark countryside. In September, when the vegetation is red and gold, the countryside is at its most beautiful, although nights tend to be cold.

Today Kautokeino is one of the most important centers of Lappish culture. With municipal boundaries enclosing an area of 3860 square miles, it is Norway's largest township and its most important reindeer district. The population numbers 2500 inhabitants and some 70,000 head of reindeer.

In this remote village, you may be surprised to find fine silver jewelry, the product of **Frank and Regine Juhls** in whose showroom you can see ornaments used by the Lapps as part of their national costumes, bowls and beakers designed from ancient pieces, and striking contemporary jewelry. Particularly sought by visitors is an abstract ptarmigan pin, one of the oldest Lapp ornaments which the Juhls make in two sizes. Frank is from Copenhagen and Regine from East Prussia, but they chose this place for their work because of his desire not to be affected by the work of other artists. From repairing the Lapps' silver jewelry as a favor to his neighbors, Mr. Juhls went on to learn silversmithing and now has a number of other smiths working in his studio. Mrs. Juhls is responsible for designing the contemporary pieces. Besides the silver, in the 25 years of their operation, the Juhlses have added Oriental rugs and other stock which is unusual for Finnmark, as well as traditional Lapp spoons and vessels. The shop is open from 10 a.m. to 10 p.m. daily.

From Alta you can take a bus ride to Kautokeino. Bus 9800 on weekdays leaves Alta at 4 p.m., reaching Kautokeino at 6:50 p.m. On Sunday the bus pulls out of Alta at 6:30 p.m. The one-way fare is about 100 kroner ($12).

WHERE TO STAY: You'll have to spend the night, and your best bet is at **Kautokeino Turisthotell** (tel. 56-205), the preferred place to stay, although, like so many other accommodations in this Far North world, it's over the budget. Singles with private bath rent for 400 kroner ($48), doubles with bath for 540 kroner ($64.80). Breakfast is included in the rates. The hotel has a restaurant and a disco.

Alfreds Kro and Overnatting (tel. 56-118) has basic furnishings but might be a good stopover if you're searching. A single room without bath rents for 180 kroner ($21.60), with a bathless double costing 280 kroner ($33.60). Lunch or dinner here costs from 40 kroner ($4.80) to 65 kroner ($7.80). This establishment works in conjunction with:

Kautokeino Ungdomsherberge, a youth hostel of moderate comfort. Although bleak by some tastes, the place is warm and friendly and often attracts a pleasant crowd of international youths. If you have your own bedclothes, the charge is just 50 kroner ($6) for an overnight stay. Otherwise, if you want a readymade bed, you'll pay 70 kroner ($8.40). The cookery is simple, very basic, but nutritious. A breakfast costs 32 kroner ($3.84). Lunch is the big meal of the day.

13. Lakselv (Banak)

Wandering in the wilds of Finnmark, you might find yourself at the terminus of Banak, which is part of Lakselv, lying at the south end of Porsangerfjord, with a small airport on the main plane route with daily flights to all Norway.

One of the few buildings here which survived World War II is Kistrand Church, 125 years old. At Trollholmsund, you can see many strange stone formations, which a Norwegian saga says are trolls turned to stone when they were caught out in the sun.

Valdakmyra is a wetlands area on the fjord which is an important breeding fround for birds. You can see it from the main road between Lakselv and Stabbursnes. The tourist information office will direct you to these and other natural wonders in the area.

The **Banak Hotell** (tel. 61-377) is centrally situated by National Route 6, only one kilometer from Banak airport. Anne Siri Brandrud offers 70 beds, each with phone and hot and cold running water. Most units also have a private shower and toilet. In a single the tariff is 350 kroner ($42), going up to 450 kroner ($54) in a double, including breakfast.

In the large cafeteria, beer and wine are served, and a grill room offers dancing every evening. A simple meal goes for 90 kroner ($10.80). It's best to stay here on full-board terms at a rate of 480 kroner ($57.60) per person daily. The hotel is open all year.

The staff will help you with bus connections to the following points: Finland through Karasjok, 60 miles; Kirkeness, 221 miles; Hammerfest, 90 miles; and Alta, 107 miles. At Kåfjord, 60 miles from Banak, you can make ferry connections to the North Cape.

Lakselv Gjestgiveri (tel. 61-066) is in the heart of Finnmark. Here you'll find a warm and friendly atmosphere at one of the oldest inns in the county. Room prices are from 250 kroner ($30) to 425 kroner ($51) per person.

14. Karasjok

The capital of the Lapps was razed during World War II, but it has been rebuilt. Near the Finnish border, the town lies in a loop of the Karasjokka

River. The Lapp population is hearty, because the temperature is freezing for most of the year. In the middle of winter, lows of 50 degrees *below* zero Fahrenheit are not uncommon. Summers are short and surprisingly hot, particularly in July.

In the village you can see a Lapp museum with a collection of handicrafts and a 150-year-old church, the only building left standing in Karasjok after World War II. Ask someone to direct you to the studio of Iver Jåks, a well-known Lapp artist who does paintings and drawings as well as carvings.

Totaling an area of 145 square miles, Karasjok is the second-largest municipality in Norway. The world's nothernmost pine forest lies in the southern part of the municipality, the National Park of Anarjokka.

Karasjok can be reached from Lakselv, Norway, or from Kamanen, Finland. From Lakselv, catch bus 9800, leaving twice daily in summer, at 11:45 a.m. and 8:45 p.m. From Karasjok it's possible to continue by bus to Rovaniemi, Finland.

WHERE TO STAY: Those spending the night in Karasjok will find good accommodation at **Karasjok Turisthotell** (tel. 66-203). This hotel is furnished in traditional style. A light, airy feeling prevails and much use is made of wood. A single with bath cost 450 kroner ($54); a double with bath, 600 kroner ($72), breakfast included. Meals here are expensive, because seemingly everything except reindeer meat has to be shipped in. Therefore, expect to pay 85 kroner ($10.20) for a lunch, 110 kroner ($13.20) for dinner.

Karakroa Motell & Campinghytter (tel. 66-446) offers 17 cabins, most of which are insulated for use in cold weather. Each unit contains not only kitchen facilities, but a bedroom as well. Guests must go to a separate building for use of the showers, toilets, and the sauna, which has a whirlpool. Prices are from 65 kroner ($7.80) per person. Those explorers in this part of the world who want to live better can rent one of the four double motel rooms, complete with showers and toilets, at a cost of 240 kroner ($28.80) in a double, 160 kroner ($19.20) in a single, with breakfast an extra 35 kroner ($4.20). English is spoken, and the establishment lies about a five-minute walk from the center of the village.

You can join in a wide range of outdoor activities arranged by the motel, including riverboating, canoeing, panning for gold, fishing, and cross-country and slalom skiing. The disco and tavern provide warm relaxation after your outings.

15. Hammerfest

This is the most northerly town in the world of any major size. A port of call for North Cape steamers, it was destroyed in World War II, but has long since been rebuilt. Lapps from surrounding camps often come into town to shop. Count yourself lucky if they bring their reindeer with them.

The port is ice-free year round, and the shipping and exporting of fish is a major industry. The sun doesn't set from May 17 to July 28. On the other hand it doesn't rise from November 21 to January 23.

Why not take time to do as 70,000 others have done and join the Royal and Ancient Polar Bear Society here in the right climate? Apply in person and get a membership while you're in Hammerfest. For further information, get in touch with the Hammerfest Tourist Office (tel. 12-185).

WHERE TO STAY: Accommodations are very expensive in Hammerfest. The preferred spot is **Rica Hotel** (tel. 11-333), which is quite modern and well equipped. Bathless singles cost from 400 kroner ($48), singles with bath from

500 kroner ($60) to 545 kroner ($65.40). Doubles with bath cost from 750 kroner ($90). All room rates include breakfast. The hotel has a bar and a restaurant.

Also preferred by many visitors is **Finnmarksbo Gjestehus**, 2–4 Strandgate (tel. 11-622), which stands right on the town hall square known as Raadhusplassen. Rooms open onto the harbor of Hammerfest. The manager, Odd Evensen, rent out rooms with bath, TV, and fridge. Singles with shower or toilet go for 500 kroner ($60) nightly, going up to 720 kroner ($86.40) in a double with similar plumbing. On the premises is a cafeteria and lounge, although 70 guests are seated in the main dining room, where the service is helpful and well managed, and the menu has some excellent items. A lunch or dinner costs 110 kroner ($13.20), and if you want to fortify yourself with a Norwegian breakfast, it is included in the rates.

Larsens Gjestiveri/Brassica tel. 11-822) has simple, basic furnishings but might do if you're looking for a place to lay your head. A double without bath costs 420 kroner ($50.40), a similar single going for 325 kroner ($39). Breakfast is included in the rates.

16. Honningsvåg

The world's northernmost village—called the gateway to the North Cape —is a completely modern fishing harbor (only the chapel withstood the German destruction of 1944). It is on the southern side of the island of Magerøy, but is connected by a road to the North Cape, a 22-mile run. A bus leaves from the marketplace every evening at 10:40 in summer. Guests—dazed by the Midnight Sun—return to their hotel in Honningsvåg around 2 a.m. Round-trip fare is 100 kroner ($12). On the road to the cape is a Lapp encampment—a bit contrived perhaps, but visitors do get to go inside one of the tents, and they come away with an idea of how nomadic Lapps used to live.

The **North Cape Festival** is held in the middle of June each year, with a wide display of local culture, lasting one week. During the festival, the **North Cape March** is held from Honningsvåg to the North Cape and back, a total of around 44 miles. For further information concerning the festival or the march, get in touch with the tourist office (tel. 72-894). You can also ask for information about sightseeing boat trips, museums, walks, and deep-sea fishing.

WHERE TO STAY: Those staying over have the following choice of accommodations—with the most expensive lodgings coming first. Incidentally, the first recommendation is considered the world's northernmost hotel. The **SAS Nordkapp Hotell** (tel. 72-333) is fairly modern, lying downtown a few minutes' walk from the quay and 21 miles from the North Cape. The hotel contains 133 rooms, 100 of which have private baths with toilets. Doubles with bath, a Norwegian breakfast included, are offered for 720 kroner ($86.40). A complete dinner in the large restaurant costs 125 kroner ($15). Early reservations at this hotel is strongly advised.

Havly Guesthouse (tel. 72-966) offers clean and quiet accommodations at 225 kroner ($27) for bathless singles and 200 kroner ($24) per person for bathless doubles. The most expensive rooms—those units equipped with a private bath—cost 320 kroner ($38.40) in a single, 250 kroner ($30) per person in a double. A continental breakfast is 45 kroner ($5.40). The food is good and hearty, and many guests ask for the half-board terms of 300 kroner ($36) per person.

This is primarily a hotel, although it also doubles as a seamen's home. It's also in the center of town on the water.

Sifi Sommerhospits (tel. 72-817) is an offbeat accommodation. Actually it's a residential quarters of the Herring and Fish Industry, a Norwegian herring-oil refinery, which produces herring meal and herring oil. However, the fishing is seasonal, and there are many empty rooms during summer. Since the North Cape has a severe shortage of rooms in the tourist season, the refinery was asked to turn over its empty rooms to visitors. If you don't mind the bone-bare accommodations, and are used to roughing it a bit, then you can seek a room here. Units have hot and cold running water, and showers and saunas are on the ground floor. The bed-and-breakfast rate is 250 kroner ($30) per person. You can also book into a double room on half-board terms of 310 kroner ($37.20) per person.

Betania Hospits (tel. 72-501) rents out basic rooms, costing 220 kroner ($26.40) in a single without bath, 175 kroner ($21) per person in a bathless double. The room rates include breakfast.

Rogers Inn (tel. 72-465). It's the simple life here, but it's clean. The price varies from 160 kroner ($19.20) per person up to 280 kroner ($33.60) per person.

Valanbo Gjestehus (tel. 73-026) has basic, low-cost accommodations. At the guesthouse, the price is from 210 kroner ($25.20) per person up to 320 kroner ($38.40) per person.

17. Vadsø

Vadsø, also called the capital of Finnmark, is on the southern coast of Varanger Peninsula. In this part of the North, this town has a lot to offer the vacationer, and if you want to visit, you can reach it by car, plane, bus, or the coastal express steamer.

In spring, summer, and autumn, Vadsø offers unforgettable experiences for nature lovers, anglers, and birdwatchers.

Norway's largest herring-oil factory is here, but public administration is the largest employer. Vadsø has built 6000 inhabitants.

Vadsø Museum includes the Toumainengård estate, built in Finnish style, and the Esbensengård estate, in Coast-Norwegian style, both from the middle of the 19th century. The Vadsø Library is the central library for Eastern Finnmark and contains a large collection of North Norwegian publications and Finnish literature.

WHERE TO STAY: **Vadsøhotel** (tel. 51-681) is a new and modern hotel in the center of town, offering 72 rooms. Singles without bath rent for 400 kroner ($48), while singles with bath go for 480 kroner ($57.60). Doubles, all with bath, cost from 500 kroner ($60) to 595 kroner ($71.40). All tariffs include breakfast. The hotel has a restaurant, grill, bar, pub, and disco.

18. Vardø

Norway's easternmost town, Vardø, also has the easternmost point in the country, the island of Hornøya. Here the climate is hard, with Norway's lowest mean average temperature and the most stormy days being recorded. But don't let the climate frighten you off. Vardø, on the island of Vardøy, is worth a visit. A submarine tunnel, the first one in Norway, allows you to reach Vardø by car, bus, or the coastal expess steamer. It's some 44 miles from the airport in Vadsø, but there are bus connections. Today, the population of this chilly place is about 3900.

When you visit Vardø, take time to visit the old and preserved fishing village just over 20 miles away, crossing a fascinating landscape to get there.

Vardøhus Fort on Vardøy, was built in 1737 as the northernmost and easternmost fort in Norway.

At **Vardøhus Museum** there's a *kongestokken* where you'll find the signatures of several kings.

ACCOMMODATIONS: Vardø City Hotell (tel. 87-761) is in the center of town, a new and modern establishment with 42 rooms. The pleasant, quiet dining room becomes a place for dinner-dances in the evening. The hotel also has a bar, a lounge with an open fireplace, saunas, a keep-fit room, a billiards room, and, of course, a disco. It is fully licensed, and has accommodations for handicapped persons.

Singles with bath cost 395 kroner ($47.40), doubles with bath going for 550 kroner ($66). All tariffs include breakfast. For a big lunch, you'll pay 115 kroner ($13.80) and for dinner from 85 kroner ($10.20) up.

Nerunias Overnatting (tel. 87-529), with very basic rooms, is the best bargain in town. Prices vary from 130 kroner ($15.60) to 90 kroner ($22.80) per person, with breakfast costing an extra 35 kroner ($4.20).

19. Skaidi

Skaidi is a small village in the heart of Finnmark, with road connections to all other parts of the district. You'll find splendid surroundings for hiking, skiing, fishing, and hunting here. The name *Skaidi* is Lappish and means "where the rivers meet."

WHERE TO STAY: Repparfjord Turisthotell (tel. 16-121) is a pleasant hotel in the heart of Finnmark. Bathless singles cost 350 kroner ($42), while singles with bath go for 425 kroner ($51). Doubles, bathless, rent for 450 kroner ($54) and doubles with bath are priced at 550 kroner ($66), breakfast included. The fully licensed hotel has a dining room, cafeteria, bar, and pub. You can rent bicycles, skis, and snow scooters, use the sauna or solarium, play table tennis, or just enjoy the scenery.

Skaidi Gjestehus (tel. 16-120). Prices range from 170 kroner ($20.40) to 460 kroner ($55.20) per person. The more expensive rooms have private baths.

20. Kirkenes

This iron-ore mining town is the end of the line for travelers in Norway, 170 miles north of the Arctic Circle. The Soviet Union prevents explorations much farther. Kirkenes is reached by plane or via the long Polar Bus referred to earlier. A coastal steamer also calls daily.

The Midnight Sun shines on Kirkenes from May 20 to July 25, and what it reveals is a completely modern town, but from November to January, the people live in darkness. Fortified by the Nazis, Kirkenes was bombed repeatedly during World War II, 307 raids in all, until nearly all the town was destroyed by 1944. That same year, during the infamous German retreat from Finnmark, the surviving parts were also razed by evacuating Nazis who didn't want to leave anything behind for the Russians.

The **Sør-Varanger Museum** may be visited, including Bygdetunet Bjørklund farm at Svanvik, Noatun at Vaffetem, and St. Georg's chapel in Neiden. You can also see King Oskar's Chapel at Grense-Jakobselv, a stone church built in 1869, as well as the wooden Neiden Chapel at Neiden.

There's a **Monument to the Red Army** at Kirkenes, erected in memory of the liberation of Finnmark by the Russians, as Western Allies, in 1944. It's a statue of a Russian soldier. There are also several memorials for Finnish and Norwegian soldiers killed in the war.

South of the town you can head to the **Pasvik Valley,** a distance of 75 miles. The trip takes you through the easternmost national park of Norway. The Pasvik River marks the boundary between Russia and Norway. Known for its special flora and fauna, the Pasvik Valley is the meeting place of two different biological worlds, Asia and Europe. Along the way you go by **Svanvik**, 25 miles from Kirkenes. There you can visit the beautiful Svanvik chapel and see a state experimental station.

To take a bus trip to the Russian border, consult the tourist bureau (tel. 91-751). Kirkenes is only seven kilometers from the Russian border and only eight hours by train from Murmansk, a large Russian seaport. The Finnish border is also nearby. The border between Norway and the U.S.S.R. is 121 miles long. It is NATO's only border with the Soviet Union.

The **Sør-Varanger** open-pit mines, near Lake Bjørnevatn, may be visited, as can the plant inside Kirkenes. Arrangements can be made at the tourist bureau.

WHERE TO STAY: Kirkenes Rica Hotel (tel. 91-491), a splurge recommendation, sits on top of a hill overlooking the town, a 68-bedroom hotel that looks like a midwestern country club. Completely modern, it offers an attractive double with bath for 650 kroner ($78) to 760 kroner ($91.20), 445 kroner ($53.40) in a bathless double. Singles with bath rent for 450 kroner ($54) and bathless singles for 360 kroner ($43.20); breakfast included. The hotel is better looking inside than outside. The Kirkenes bleakness is compensated somewhat by the hotel's heavy emphasis on color; stained glass and tapestries add an elegant touch. Guests dance at night to the sounds of a combo. This licensed hotel also has a tennis and badminton court. Reindeer meat is a specialty of the dining room.

Sollia Gjestgiveri (tel. 90-820) lies about ten miles east of Kirkenes, just 66 feet from the Russian border. The guesthouse is small, only 16 beds, but the welcome in this bleak part of the world is big. The house is very modestly furnished, and most guests reach it by renting a car in Kirkenes and driving here (the Kirkenes tourist office will arm you with a map). Reservations are needed, of course. In a double room, the charge is 250 kroner ($30), dropping to 190 kroner ($22.80) in a single. Full meals are served at the guesthouse and, somewhat surprisingly, you pay the same for breakfast (a big Norwegian one at that) as you do for either dinner or supper: 45 kroner ($5.40.).

Another possibility for lodging in the area is the **Neiden Mountain Lodge,** at Neiden (tel. 96-141), which rents log cabins for 140 kroner ($16.80) per night. Rooms can also be obtained at 140 kroner ($16.80) for a double. Breakfast is 40 kroner ($4.80). Beer and wine are served in the dining room. Neiden is about 23 miles from Kirkenes on the Neiden River.

Back in Kirkenes, **Stenbys Overnatting** (tel. 91-162) can offer you a double without private bath but with breakfast for 240 kroner ($28.80).

Chapter X

A PREVIEW OF SWEDEN

1. Flying to Sweden
2. Getting Around
3. Cutting Accommodation Costs
4. The ABCs of Life

YOU'VE HEARD all that cocktail-party talk about Sweden. You know—suicides, unwed mothers, cradle-to-the-grave socialism, blondes scampering around in the nude. And now you want to know if it's true. Answers are hard to come by, since Sweden is one of the most paradoxical nations on earth. An essentially conservative country, Sweden is nonetheless a leader in social welfare, prison reform, and laws regarding sex.

The miracle of Sweden—a late-bloomer among European nations—is that it shot out of nowhere to usher in a country with the highest wages and the best standard of living in Europe. Of course, these are material gains, and there are those who have suggested that there is trouble in paradise.

Sweden's critics are fond of pointing to its supposedly high suicide rate; it is commonly considered that Sweden has the highest suicide rate in the world. This isn't true. The Danes, fun-loving though they are, grow disenchanted with smørrebrød and Tivoli and kill themselves at a higher rate than their northern neighbors. And the people most intent on doing themselves in are Austrians and Hungarians.

A great deal of what the world knows of Sweden comes from the old films of Ingmar Bergman, yet it is the Swedes themselves who have been most critical of Bergman, considering his cinematic brooding and the introversion of his characters a throwback to medievalism.

Then there are those other films, the ones dealing with what one writer called the "demimonde" of Sweden—electric, erotic, forever moving with the latest what's happening tide that washes up on its shores.

Each person looks at Sweden through his or her own kaleidoscope, and what he or she sees is an ever-changing rotation of diverse impressions. Some call the Swedes cold, unfriendly, as uncommunicative as the hired hand in Katherine Anne Porter's *Noon Wine*.

So I cannot answer your questions. You must go and see for your-self.

1. Flying to Sweden

Two major airlines, SAS and Northwest Orient, fly direct and nonstop from North America to Stockholm, and TWA also makes frequent connections through London or Paris. Because I prefer to patronize U.S. airlines whenever possible, and because the routings were fairly easy, I selected **Northwest Orient** as the carrier for my most recent trip to Stockholm.

Northwest's 747s fly across the Atlantic to the Swedish capital from Minneapolis/St. Paul and New York's JFK airport at intervals which average five times a week in summer and about twice a week in winter.

A wide range of fare options is available, with an executive class splurge being the most comfortable and the most pampered. However, most budget-conscious travelers gravitate toward the Super APEX fare. The conditions of this fare option include reserving and paying for a seat at least 21 days prior to departure and a delay of between 10 days and three months before using the return half of the ticket. This fare ranges from $713 round trip in low season to $964 during high season from New York and from $863 during low season to $1112 in high season from Minneapolis/St. Paul. Each takeoff from the U.S. requires a $3 departure tax.

These prices, of course, were valid during the writing of this guide, and they could easily change prior to your departure.

If things don't work out for you to fly Northwest Orient, you might consider SAS, the Scandinavian Airlines System, which is composed of financial backing by Denmark, Sweden, and Norway. English is the official language of this airline, whose five gateways to Scandinavia are New York, Chicago, Los Angeles, Seattle, and Anchorage, Alaska.

2. Getting Around

Sweden is one of the largest countries of Europe, but traveling long distances is relatively easy because of the sophisticated network of public transportation, which is previewed in this section.

AIR SERVICE: The airports of Gothenburg and Stockholm are the major gateways to Sweden. Scandinavian Airlines System (SAS), and the Swedish domestic airlines (LIN) maintain good domestic routings inside Sweden, with connections to 31 airports, including Kiruna (Swedish Lapland); Visby (on the island of Gotland); Malmö (capital of the château country); Karlstad (center for Värmland); and Kalmar, the latter a good base for exploring the glassworks district. From around the first of June to mid-July, Midnight Sun flights depart from Stockholm, winging their way north to Swedish Lapland.

Air travel in Sweden is a moderately priced means of getting around because of the fares offered by **SAS/LIN** (Linjeflyg). In the summer months, these airlines offer what they call their mini-fares, effective from the end of June until mid-August, when most Scandinavian commercial travelers resume their flights and the demand the for seats goes up.

During this low-priced summertime, a passenger is charged only a one-way fare on a round-trip ticket! The accompanying spouse (either male or female) pays only 200 kronor ($24) to travel to and from Stockholm to any place in the country, regardless of the actual distance, with one exception. Children aged 2 to 11 travel free, and those from 12 to 26 (yes, 26 years old) pay only the 200 kronor.

The exception cited is between southern and northern Sweden (which includes Lapland, of course). For a change of aircraft in Stockholm and for nonstop travel between Gothenburg and Sundsvall, a surcharge of 150 kronor ($18) is assessed for each accompanying family member. Children under age 2 travel

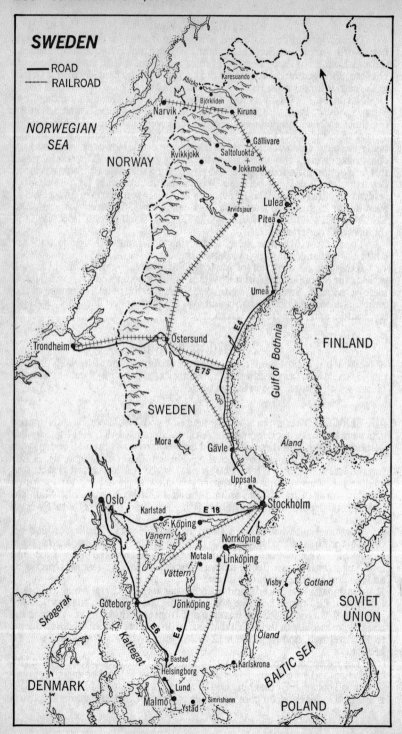

SWEDEN

— ROAD
----- RAILROAD

NORWEGIAN SEA

NORWAY

Abisko
Karesuando
Björkliden
Narvik
Kiruna
Gällivare
Kvikkjokk
Saltoluokta
Jokkmokk
Lulea
Arvidsjaur
Piteå
Umeå
E4
Östersund
Trondheim
E75
SWEDEN
Mora
Gävle
Åland
FINLAND
Gulf of Bothnia
Uppsala
Oslo
Karlstad
E 18
Stockholm
Köping
Vänern
Norrköping
Motala
Linköping
Vättern
Visby
Gotland
Göteborg
Jönköping
SOVIET UNION
E6
E4
Skagerak
Kattegat
Öland
Bastad
Karlskrona
Helsingborg
BALTIC SEA
Lund
DENMARK
Malmö
Simrishann
Ystad
POLAND

free. A minimum two-night stay is required for these mini-fares, unless a passenger's domestic trip begins on a Saturday.

A great advantage is granted to people under 26 years of age. They are allowed to travel stand-by to and from Stockholm to destinations in the country for only 150 kronor ($18). A senior citizen over 65 can purchase a single reserved-seat ticket to and from Stockholm for 200 kronor ($24). For any other connections, a surcharge of 100 kronor ($12) is assessed.

BOATS AND HYDROFOILS: The major means of traveling between Denmark and Sweden is by hydrofoil, running from Copenhagen to Malmö. They run frequently, and the entire trip takes only 38 minutes, costing 45 Swedish kronor ($5.40). The frequent ferry crossing between Copenhagen and Malmö takes 1½ hours and costs 25 kronor ($3). This ferry runs six to ten times daily, depending on the season. Cars are transported at a cost of 135 kronor ($16.20).

Another heavily traveled route is that between the mainland of Sweden (Nynashämn) and Visby on the island of Gotland. From June to August, crossings are daily. After that, more limited schedules take effect. The fares are 94 kronor ($11.28) per passenger. Most cars are transported for about 132 kronor ($15.84).

The most important boat trip in summer—and one of Sweden's major attractions—is the three-day Göta Canal ride, a distance of 350 miles, from Gothenburg (Göteborg) in the west to Stockholm in the east, or vice versa. The trip, capturing the essence of Sweden, takes you through 65 locks (the highest more than 300 feet above sea level), and includes stopovers at Vadstena and Motala.

When still a poor nation, Sweden launched the Göta Canal project in the early 17th century. It was built by 58,000 conscripts and some Russian deserters. Its military value dried up with Sweden's neutrality stance. However, in 1832, the final link was completed.

Arrangements for this trip can be made through the **Göta Canal Steamship Company,** 2 Hotellplatsen, Box 272, S-40124, Göteborg, Sweden (tel. 31/17-76-15). Tours operate between the middle of May and the beginning of September. The cheapest way to take this trip is to rent a small cabin on the main deck for about 1350 kronor ($162) per person. Meals for the whole trip cost around 350 kronor ($42) per person.

BUSES: This is a second popular means of travel, particularly for reaching some of the more remote villages. In summer the Swedish State Railways (which also operates buses) arranges a number of motor-coach tours. A two-day tour, for example, takes passengers from Copenhagen to Stockholm (or vice versa). The tour covers such areas as the glassworks district, the lake section, the château country.

Express buses operate between many places in Sweden. You can leave the bus on the way home and take a train instead if that is your wish. There is no extra charge for booking. These express buses are a reasonable means of travel.

In the northernmost parts of the country, the buses are operated by the post office. These are a low-cost way of seeing the countryside. For example, a bus will take you along the Sjöfall Road from Gällivare to Ritsem, a distance of 114 miles. If you're an old-age pensioner, you can buy a round-trip ticket for the price of a single.

CAR RENTALS: Sweden has a fair highway system, particularly in the southern provinces and the central lake district. Swedish Customs issues an insurance card for cars or motorcycles brought into the country (the "Green Card" will do), and driver's licenses from Canada, Great Britain, and the United States are acceptable in Sweden.

Since the roads are good, many travelers appreciate the freedom that only a rental car can give them (Sweden long ago switched to driving on the right-hand side of the road).

All the major car-rental firms, including Hertz and Avis, are represented in Sweden. **Budget Rent-a-Car,** for example, maintains more offices in Sweden than it does in any other country in Scandinavia, a total of 57.

The least expensive option would be for a traveler to take advantage of the weekly rates which apply only if a reservation is made at least three business days before actual pickup of the car. Reservations can be made through Budget's phone center in Dallas, Texas, which you can call toll-free at 1/800/527-0700 during extended hours throughout the day or night.

The least expensive car in Budget's Swedish fleet is a Ford Fiesta with manual transmission, capable of holding up to four passengers with their luggage. Of course, if you're a professional basketball player traveling with three of your teammates, you might want to take advantage of the free luggage rack which Budget will provide if you reserve it in advance. Even so, Budget finds that many families of four or less appreciate the smallest size car without any particular inconvenience.

A Fiesta rents for around $120 per week, with unlimited mileage included. Each additional day costs an extra $17. Travelers who prefer a bigger car can opt for a four-passenger manual-transmission Ford Escort, which, with unlimited mileage, rents for $190 per week, plus $29 for each additional day of rental.

For most readers, however, the most luxurious vehicle they need is a five-passenger Volvo 240 SO. Among all the fleet of Budget's Sweden-based cars, this is the least expensive model containing an automatic transmission. This, as it does throughout, adds to the rental price. Holding up to five passengers comfortably with their luggage, and with unlimited mileage included, this model costs around $245 per week, with each additional day costing an extra $35.

The Swedish government will garnish your eventual bill with a whopping 23.46% tax.

You can drive with assurance knowing that all winter rentals are equipped with spiked snow tires. Also, unless you want to be financially responsible for the first 2500 kronor ($300) worth of damages to your car in the unfortunate event of an accident, you can purchase a collision damage waiver for around 36 kronor ($4.32) additional per day. Additional personal accident insurance is also available for an extra 12 kronor ($1.44) per day.

Finally, if your rental-car itinerary begins in either Stockholm or Gothenburg, Budget will allow you to drop off most cars (after a seven-day rental) in Copenhagen for no additional charge. Dropoffs in some Swedish and Norwegian cities are free as well, depending on the length of rental.

A local firm, **Netto Biluthyrning,** 33 Klarabergsgatan (tel. 24-26-55), in downtown Stockholm, opposite the big Åhens department store, is a reliable establishment. It can deliver you a car to Arlanda airport upon advance reservation. All major credit cards are accepted.

HITCHHIKING: It's perfectly acceptable here. Contrary to their reputation, Swedes, I've found, are warm, friendly, and hospitable. They often pick up presentably dressed hitchhikers along the roadside, and usually speak English, too. Because of weather conditions, hitchhiking isn't recommended in the colder months.

RAILWAYS: Most of Sweden's vast network of railways is electric. Modern coaches, roomy and comfortable, are the earmark of the Swedish State Railways. Second class (adjustable seats, no less) can be heartily recommended. Lots of minor conveniences have been installed, showing Swedish concern for detail.

Sweden, as mentioned in Chapter I, is a member of the Eurailpass agreement that allows unlimited first-class travel across the country. Those without a Eurailpass will find train fares in Sweden reasonable. The longer the run, the shorter the charge.

Nordic Touristticket by train gives you a unique opportunity to know the Scandinavian countries at close range. The entire state railway in the four countries—Denmark, Norway, Sweden, and Finland—is at your service with this mode of travel, except for Stockholm's local train system. You may break your journey whenever you like and continue when you wish. You will be able to plan your trip to your own tastes and interests, choosing rustic scenery of busy capitals.

Nordic Touristticket by train also gives you a 50% discount on the following ship travel: Gothenburg–Frederikshavn (Sessan Line), Stockholm–Helsinki (Silja Line), Stockholm–Turku (Silja Line), Kristiansand–Hirtshals (KDS), as well as Hirtshals–Hjørring by Hjørring Private Railway. The ticket by train is valid for 21 days and costs 1250 kronor ($150) for second class, 1860 kronor ($223.20) in first class. Children between 4 and 12 travel for half-price. Reservation of seats, couchette carriage, and sleeping car can be made at the regular prices. Cost of fares is subject to change, of course.

Swedish trains follow tight schedules. Trains leave Malmö/Helsingborg for Stockholm every hour throughout the day, Monday to Friday. The same applies to trains leaving Gothenburg for Stockholm. In fact, there are trains every hour, or every other hour, to most of the big towns of Sweden.

On expresståg runs, it is necessary to reserve a seat at a cost of 12 kronor ($1.44).

On long journey's, couchette and sleeping-car facilities are provided. Sleeper charges are 80 kroner ($9.60) per person in a three-bed compartment for second-class travel. Couchettes in second class are available on many routes —that is, Stockholm–Kiruna–Narvik (Norway)—at a cost of 50 kronor ($6).

A voucher, known as **Lågpriskort,** costs only 115 kronor ($13.80) in second class, giving you a 45% discount on all railway trips within Sweden. The voucher is valid for 12 months, but not for travel on Friday, Sunday, and major holidays. For example, a regular one-way second-class fare from Stockholm to Gothenburg is 215 kroner ($25.80). With the use of the reduced-rate card, the fare is just 120 kroner ($14.40). The card may be purchased at any Swedish railway station.

Families (a minimum of three passengers) can travel on a reduced fare all days of the week without buying the voucher. Accompanying children between the ages of 6 and 12 pay only half the fare. For infants under 6 years of age, there is no charge.

SENIOR CITIZEN DISCOUNTS: Sweden grants visitors over 65 years of age 50% reductions on train tickets, good for either first- or second-class travel. Some buses and ferries run by the Swedish State Railway also honor this reduction. During such holidays as Easter and Christmas, and on summer weekends, the discount is not granted.

TRANSPORTATION IN STOCKHOLM: Stockholm has a good transportation network—buses and a streamlined subway system, in addition to taxis. The basic fare on all public vehicles is about 6 kronor (72¢). But on the purchase of a regular bus ticket, the passenger may get a second ride, providing that he or she boards the second bus within one hour after purchase of the initial ticket. After midnight, the fares in Stockholm are doubled, so krona-watchers pull a Cinderella act.

Before entering the subway, passengers tell the ticket seller the destination, then purchase tickets which they surrender when they get off at their station (any discrepancies will be ironed out by the ticket-taker at the other end).

Your best transportation bet is to purchase one of the **tourist season tickets.** A one-day card, costing 16 kronor ($1.92), is valid for 24 hours of unlimited travel by metro, bus, and commuter train within Stockholm and the ferry to Djurgården. A one-day card for 25 kronor ($3) is valid for traveling within Stockholm county and the ferry to Djurgården. Most visitors will want the three-day card for 45 kronor ($5.40) which is valid for 72 hours in both Stockholm and the county. It is also valid for admission to Skansen, Kahnastornet, and Gröna Lund. Children under the age of 16 pay half-price, and two children up to 7 years of age can travel free.

Tickets are offered at tourist information offices as well as in subway stations and at most news vendors. Naturally, the prices may vary somewhat in the lifetime of this edition, but this transportation tip should prove to be a bargain, regardless of the actual price in effect at the time of your visit.

Taxis are insufficient in number and priced so high as to make them unappetizing to economy-minded tourists. For example, a ride in from **Arlanda** airport into the center of Stockholm costs about 270 kronor ($32.40). Better take the SAS bus for about 30 kronor ($3.60). Still, there may be an occasion when a taxi is imperative. If so, those that have the sign *Ledig* may be hailed. Or telephone 15-00-00.

Stockholm has two airports. **Bromma** is small and used mainly for private aircraft. All international and domestic flights leave from the larger Arlanda airport, mentioned above, 30 miles from town. Take the airport bus from the special terminal across the street from the main train station.

3. Cutting Accommodation Costs

Sweden has many alternatives to high-priced hotels, some of which will be reviewed here.

FARMHOUSE HOLIDAYS: About 60 Swedish farms scattered throughout the country accept English-speaking guests in summer. None of them is particularly fancy, but all of their owners have one thing in common: a desire to meet people and extend their hospitality. The cost is low. For example, the bed-and-breakfast rate is about 85 kronor ($10.20) per person daily. Children under 12 pay half price. In some of the farms all meals are prepared and served for guests, but you must pay extra for this, of course. Separate kitchens are available to guests, or else they may share the kitchens of the hosts. These holidays are arranged by the Federation of Swedish Farmers (LRF) with its member paper, *Land,* as well as the local tourist offices. Accommodations can be booked by writing to the farm directly or through the local tourist offices. A list with details and addresses of the farms is available from LRF, Bondgårdssemester, 10533 Stockholm (tel. 787-50-00).

SWED-CHEQUE: An economical way for motorists to travel is to avail themselves of the "Swedish Hotel Cheque" program, called Swed-Cheque for short. This plan offers a savings at hotels throughout the country. Readers of this book may be particularly interested in the "Swedish Budget Hotel Cheque," one of the two plans offered.

On the budget plan, hotels participating charge about 135 kronor ($16.20) per person, based on double occupancy. Breakfast, service, and taxes are included, and children under 12 sharing their parents' room are permitted to do so without charge. Only the first night must be booked in advance.

These rooms do not contain private baths. However, for those willing to pay 185 kronor ($22.20) per person nightly, a private bath will be included. The staff at each hotel help you book ahead for the following night. The Swedish Hotel Cheque is valid at about 200 hotels throughout the country.

For further information, get in touch with the Swedish Tourist Board, 655 Third Ave., New York, NY 10017 (tel. 1/212/949-2333).

LOG CABINS AND CHALETS: Gerry Brenes and his wife Joan spent a week in a little red and white cottage (a *stuga*) in West Sweden: "It was a little short of midnight, all very quiet except for the slight sounds of small animals in the undergrowth, and yet light enough to be able to read a newspaper on the veranda without artificial light. We walked along in the eerie twilight for a while and then traced our steps back to the lake. Suddenly we noticed something out of the ordinary—orchids!" British families long ago discovered the advantage of log cabin and chalet rentals. For many North Americans as well, especially families, it can be an ideal way of keeping costs trimmed, plus enjoying one of the last frontiers in Europe.

Chalets and cottages can be rented in Sweden by the week. Prices are based on the dwelling, the situation, and the standard of comfort. For example, a holiday cottage with four beds in high season (mid-June to mid-August) rents for anywhere from 800 kronor ($96) to 2000 kronor ($240). Bookings are made through local agents.

YOUTH HOSTELS: Sweden has about 250 youth hostels and Touring Club Lodges, offering a varied range of accommodations that includes a manor house on the Baltic, a boat in Stockholm harbor, a converted stable in the château district, or a mountain hut in the northern highlands. Most hostels have rooms with two or four beds, some with hot and cold running water in the rooms, and some with separate wash-rooms. In most cases, traveling families can have a room of their own, but these are best booked in advance.

Fortunately, you don't have to be a youth to stay at a youth hostel (there's no age limit), and you can travel by car if you wish (some countries forbid the use of youth hostels facilities to travelers unless they arrive on foot or by bicycle). Nearly all hostels have a members' kitchen, where you can prepare your own meals at no extra charge. Pots and pans are usually provided, but you must bring your own dishes and cutlery.

All foreign visitors to Swedish Youth Hostels must have either a Youth Hostel Membership Card or an International Guest Card. If you do not already belong to a youth hostel organization, you can purchase one of these membership cards at the Swedish Touring Club or at most youth hostels. Overnight charges at most hostels range from 30 kronor ($3.60) to 45 kronor ($5.40), although a few establishments charge a higher fee. If you did not bring your own bedsheets, you'll pay an additional 20 kronor ($2.40) to rent the unwoven sheets provided by the hostel. Most hostels close down during the day from about 9:30 a.m. to 5 p.m. Silence is strictly maintained at night from 11 p.m. to 6 a.m. Each guest is responsible for keeping his or her bed, sleeping room, and washroom neat and clean. During the busy season, each guest's stay is limited to not more than five days.

To book at a youth hostel in advance, use the International Advance Booking Card, available at most Youth Hostel Associations or from the youth hostels. Mail the booking card directly to the hostel where you wish to stay, enclosing an International Reply Coupon. The coupon which is returned to you is your confirmation of a reservation and must be presented when you register at the hostel. Beds booked in advance must be claimed before 6 p.m on the day of arrival.

Youth hostel members are also granted a reduction on overnight fees at Swedish Touring Club and Highland Stations, and in the northern mountain huts. Members also receive a reduction in fare on the Touring Club boat service on highland lakes.

Further information on the Swedish Touring Club and Youth Hostel Association can be obtained by writing the Swedish Touring Club, Box 25 S-101 20, Stockholm.

4. The ABCs of Life

Many things are done quite differently in Sweden from the other Scandinavian countries. For example, the Swedes even spell their currency—kronor—with an *o* instead of an *e* as in the kroner of Denmark and Norway. There are many, many other differences as well, and knowing what they are can ease your adjustment in Stockholm and prepare you for an eventual plunge into the countryside.

BANKS: Stockholm's banks are open for regular service, including the exchange of foreign currency, from 9:30 a.m. to 3 p.m. Monday to Friday. Some bank offices in the center of Stockholm are open from 9:30 a.m. to 5:30 p.m, and others have an evening service from 4:30 to 6 p.m. The bank at Arlanda airport is open daily from 7 a.m. to 10 p.m.

BUSINESS HOURS: Most offices are open from 8:30 or 9 a.m. to 5 p.m. on weekdays (sometimes in the summer to 3 or 4 p.m.). On Saturday, offices and factories are closed completely or else open only for a half day.

CIGARETTES: Most tobacco stores sell a good assortment of British and American cigarettes. A package of 20 sells for 14 kronor ($1.68) to 18 kronor ($2.16).

CLIMATE: In climate, Sweden is hard to classify, as temperatures, aided by the Gulf Stream, vary considerably from the fields of Skåne to the wilderness of Lapland (the upper tenth of Sweden lies north of the Arctic Circle). The country as a whole has many days of sun in summer, but visitors don't exactly drop dead of heat exhaustion. July is the warmest month, with temperatures in both Stockholm and Gothenburg averaging around 62 degrees Fahrenheit. On the other hand, February is strictly for polar bears, with the temperature in Stockholm averaging around 26 degrees Fahrenheit (Gothenburg a few degrees warmer). In late spring and summer, long days are common, and the evening sky, like love, is a many-splendored thing.

It ain't necessarily so that the farther north the cooler. It happens, and not seldom, that during summer the northern parts of the country may suddenly have the warmest weather and the bluest skies. The "north" very often stands for the province of Hälsingland and the northern section of Dalecarlia and up to the northernmost parts of Lapland. Do check the weather forecasts, which are claimed by the Swedes to be 99% reliable. Swedish television and one of the biggest nationwide daily newspapers give frequent five-day prognoses all year, the latter daily during the summer.

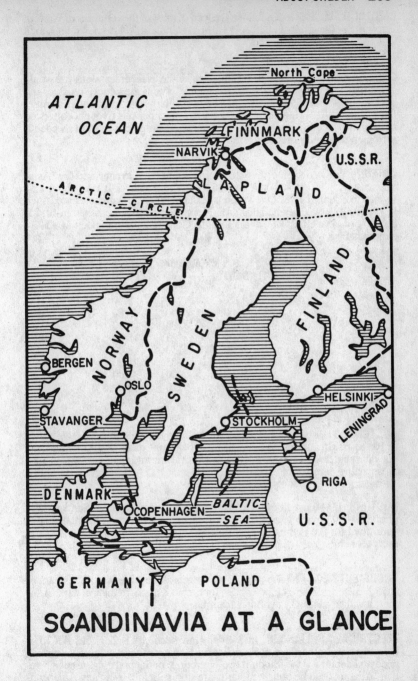

ATLANTIC
OCEAN

North Cape

FINNMARK

NARVIK

U.S.S.R.

ARCTIC CIRCLE

LAPLAND

NORWAY

SWEDEN

FINLAND

BERGEN

OSLO

STAVANGER

HELSINKI

STOCKHOLM

LENINGRAD

DENMARK

RIGA

COPENHAGEN

BALTIC
SEA

U.S.S.R.

GERMANY

POLAND

SCANDINAVIA AT A GLANCE

CLOTHING SIZES: Sweden follows the lead of most of the countries of Western Europe. See the listing under "A Preview of Denmark," Part 4, Chapter I, for a chart of both men and women.

CRIME: Don't worry about it. Of course, take the usual precautions you would when traveling anywhere. For the most part, Swedes are honest, reliable, and dependable. There have been reports, particularly during the busy summer months, of tourists ripping off fellow tourists. Pickpockets frequent congested areas in Stockholm, especially in the summer months. But most of Sweden is extremely safe and violence is rare.

CURRENCY: Sweden, too, has basic currency units of **kronor** and **öre.** As of this writing, 1 krona is worth about 12¢ in U.S. coinage. It take about 8.57 kronor to equal $1 U.S. One krona is equal to 100 öre. Banknotes are issued in 10, 50, 100, 1000, and 10,000 kronor, and silver coins are issued in 10, 25, and 50 öre, as well as 1, 2, and 5 kronor. Copper coins are issued in a 5-öre denomination.

Kronor	U.S.$	Kronor	U.S.$
0.25	$ .03	60	$ 7.20
0.50	.06	70	8.40
1	.12	80	9.60
5	.60	90	10.80
10	1.20	100	12.00
15	1.80	125	15.00
20	2.40	150	18.00
25	3.00	175	21.00
30	3.60	200	24.00
40	4.80	250	30.00
50	6.00	300	36.00

CUSTOMS: The government allows you to bring in—duty free—400 cigarettes or 100 cigars. In addition to that you are allowed one quart bottle of liquor and one quart bottle of wine or two quart bottles of wine and what the Swedes call a "reasonable" amount of film.

DOCTORS: If you are ill or have an aching tooth at night or on Sunday, telephone 90-000 anywhere in the country; otherwise, call upon the manager of your hotel for the name of a doctor, since an appointment will be necessary, except for emergency cases, of course.

DOCUMENTS FOR ENTRY: A valid passport is all an American, Canadian, or British citizen needs to enter Sweden for a visit of no more than 90 days. After that, it will be necessary to obtain a permit.

ELECTRICAL APPLIANCES: In Sweden, the electricity is 220 volts A.C. For hairdryers and other electrical appliances which you take with you, you will need an adapter for the standard two-pin round continental plugs used in Sweden. Adaptors can be bought at hardware stores. Before using any American-made appliance, always ask at your hotel desk.

EMBASSIES: Lost your passport? Go to the **American Embassy** in Stockholm at 101 Strandvägen (tel. 63-05-20). The **British Embassy** (tel. 67-01-40) is at 6-8 Skarpögatan, the **Canadian Embassy** at 4 Tegelbacken (tel. 23-79-20).

EMERGENCIES: If you need an ambulance, the police, or the fire department *(brandlarm),* telephone 90-000 wherever you are in Sweden.

FILM: The prices on cameras (especially the famed Hasselblad), film, projectors, and enlarging equipment are very good value in Sweden. Practically all the world's brands are represented in the stores of Sweden. Photographic shops give excellent service, often developing and printing in one day.

GAS: Many gasoline stations, usually self-service ones, pepper the south of Sweden. In the north they are less frequent, of course. Nearly every village and certainly every town or city in Sweden has a filling station that sells "petrol" 24 hours a day. That gas is expensive, too. For a super-grade gasoline, you'll pay, as of this writing, about 4.20 kronor (50¢) per liter. Gas is slightly cheaper in the self-service establishments mentioned, but you'll need some 100-krona ($12) notes.

GEOGRAPHY: Sweden is the fourth-largest nation in Europe, but it is sparsely inhabited. Moose-filled forests cover more than half the land, which is roughly the size of California.

It is a land of great contrasts: to go from the château area of Skåne in the south to Swedish Lapland, north of the Arctic Circle, is like crossing to a distant country.

Sweden has wheat plains, mansions and châteaux, thatched and half-timbered villages, sandy beaches, historic islands, bleak industrial towns, mountains and waterfalls, a rugged coastline studded with bays and islands . . . and much more.

It also has plenty of inland water, more than 95,000 lakes, including Vänern, the largest in Western Europe. From its manufacture of ball bearings to automatic beacons, it is a heavily industrialized nation; less than 10% of the land is used for agriculture.

The eastern half of the Scandinavian peninsula, Sweden shares more than 1000 miles of frontier with Norway, but less than 350 with Finland.

GOVERNMENT: A neutral country, Sweden carries a stick big enough to make Theodore Roosevelt proud. Caught in the conflicting pressures of East and West, the nation maintains one of the most powerful air forces in Europe, keynoted by its fearsome "Dragon" attack planes. It is perhaps the only country with enough subterranean passages to survive a nuclear attack.

Sweden is a constitutional monarchy. From the days of Queen Christina (which have been long remembered in Sweden), a law was in existence that only men could occupy the throne. However, the constitutional law was changed when the firstborn child of Queen Silvia and King Carl-Gustaf was a girl. The heir to the throne is now the child Crown Princess Victoria. A prime minister heads a cabinet appointed by the king, and the cabinet is in turn responsible to the single-chamber Riksdag, the Swedish parliament.

HAIRDRESSERS: There are women's hairdressers *(damfrisering)* in every city, town, and village. Tipping is not a must.

HOLIDAYS: Sweden celebrates the following public holidays: New Year's Day, January 6 (Twelfth Night), Good Friday, Easter Sunday, Easter Monday, May 1 (Labor Day), Ascension Day, Whitsunday, Whitmonday, Midsummer Day, All Saints' Day, plus Christmas and Boxing Day (December 25 and 26). Inquire at the tourist bureaus for the actual dates of most of these holidays which vary from year to year.

LANGUAGE: The common language is Swedish, one of the tongues of the Germanic group, and there are many regional dialects. Some minority groups speak Norwegian and Finnish. But none of this need be a problem for you, English is required in school and is commonly spoken, even in the hinterlands, especially among young people.

NEWSPAPERS: All of Stockholm's morning papers have daily summaries of the world news in English in the summer. Foreign papers, such as *The International Herald Tribune,* are available at the larger newsstands.

PETS: My advice is to leave Morris or Rover at home, even though they'll miss you. Sweden places nearly all animals, including cats and dogs, in quarantine before they're allowed inside the country.

PHARMACIES: A drugstore is called an *apotek* in Sweden. They are open from 9 a.m. to 6 p.m. weekdays, and until 1 p.m. on Saturday. In addition, there is one in every neighborhood open until 10 p.m., and one somewhere in the city of Stockholm open all night and on Sunday in case of emergency. All pharmacies have a list of names and addresses of these *Nattapotek,* as they are called, in their windows. For an around-the-clock drugstore in Stockholm, go to **C. W. Scheele,** 64 Klarabergsgatan (tel. 24-82-80).

POST OFFICE: Post offices in Stockholm are open from 9 a.m. to 6 p.m. Monday to Friday, on Saturday from 10 a.m. to 1 p.m. The Central Post Office on Vasagatan, near the Central Station, stays open Monday to Friday from 8 a.m. to 9 p.m., on Saturday from 9 a.m. to 3 p.m. The small postal station in the Central Station is open on weekdays from 7 a.m. to 9 p.m. for mailing letters and selling stamps only. To mail a picture postcard to North America costs 2.40 kronor (29¢). Letters not more than 20 grams are sent for 3.20 kronor (38¢). Post offices are easily recognizable by the sign of the yellow post horn on the blue background. You can also buy stamps in most tobacco shops and stationers. For information, phone 781-20-05.

RELIGIOUS SERVICES: Sweden is a Lutheran country, but its constitution guarantees freedom of religion. Statistics claim that 98% of the population belongs to the church, but that is a misleading figure, as a citizen more or less automatically becomes a member at birth.

Protestant services are at **St. Peter and St. Sigfrid Anglican Church,** 76 Strandvägen (tel. 67-01-40) (take bus 41, 54, or 69), and at **United Christian Congregation of Stockholm,** St. Eriks Kapell, Flemminggatan near St. Eriks

Hospital (tel. 21-01-88) (take bus 41 or 42). A Roman Catholic cathedral is at 46 Folkungagatan, and there's an Orthodox Jewish synagogue, **Adass Jeshurun,** at 12 Nybrogatan (tel. 61-82-82).

REST ROOMS: Sweden has good, clean rest rooms in all bus, air, and rail terminals. In an emergency you can also use the toilets in most hotels and restaurants, although in theory you're supposed to be a client.

SAUNAS: The Finns are not the only ones who love a dry bath hotter than anything this side of Hades. The Swedes, both men and women, are fond of roasting themselves on wooden platforms like chickens on a grill, then plunging under a shower of Arctic water. To top it off, an immersion into an icy pool is fashionable. Following the sauna, bathers emerge light-headed into the fresh air, raring for an evening of revelry. (Saunas are also recommended for those coming *from* a night of revelry.)

There is a combination sauna and outdoor heated pool, **Vanadisbadet,** at Vanadislunden, near Sveavägen (tel. 30-12-11), within easy walking distance of the Oden Hotel. It's the cheapest sauna in the city. You pay 12 kronor ($1.44) for admission to the pool, although the sauna is free. Bring your own towel or else rent one for 3 kronor (36¢). The Vanadisbadet, particularly popular with a younger crowd, remains open until 6:30 p.m., including weekends.

There are two more outdoor pools in Stockholm, **Eriksdalsbadet** and **Kampementsbadet.** Both are more modern than Vanadisbadet, which is still a fine bath. Kampementsbadet in Sandhamnsgatan features not only a large pool, but a paddling pool for children, as well as a sauna. Bus 41 to Östhammarsgatan or subway 13 and 14 go there. It's a five-minute walk from the Brantingsgatan exit.

Eriksdalsbadet in Eriksdalslunden offers a diving pool at controlled temperatures, plus a sauna and a children's paddling pool. Bathing facilities are available for 3000 persons. Take underground 17, 18, 19, 27, or 29, or else bus 48, or 54 to Skanstull.

SHOE REPAIRS: Shoe repair shops rarely do their work while you wait. In summer, especially in July, many shops close, but the larger stores in the center of Stockholm have their own repair departments. If all you want is a new heel, look for something called *klackbar* in the stores or shoe departments of the department stores. They repair while you wait.

SHOPPING HOURS: Most stores and shops are open between 9 a.m. and 6 p.m. on weekdays; on Saturday the closing time varies from 2 to 4 p.m. Once a week, usually on Monday or Friday, some of the larger stores are open from 9 a.m. to 8 p.m. (during July and August to 6 p.m.).

STUDENTS: Near Sweden House, at Sergels Torg in Stockholm, is the **Kulturhuset** (Culture House) (tel. 14-11-20). It is a favorite gathering place for young people. You can enjoy live performances by local talent and international entertainers, view exhibitions, look at theatrical activities, read books and newspapers in several languages, listen to records, watch TV, or eat at the snackbar. Just outside is a favorite place for Swedish protest movements.

Sweden has four major university centers—Stockholm, Gothenburg, Uppsala, and Lund, near Malmö—and each of these maintains a special Student

Reception Service for visiting foreign students. These local offices, staffed by students, are helpful and friendly places. Check them for information on student accommodations, restaurants, a schedule of current events, discos, or whatever you need to know.

The student travel service, **SFS Resor,** 89 Drottninggatan (tel. 34-01-80), books student flights and has information about low-cost youth fares on trains.

TAXES: Hold onto your wallet. As of this writing, Sweden imposes a "Value Added Tax" on most goods and services, currently 19%. Sweden, however, is not a member of the European Common Market. Serious shoppers can beat the tax by looking for "tax-free shopping" signs in store windows. Upon presentation of a passport and after obtaining the necessary forms, the foreign visitor can present the data to a Customs official at ferry and air terminals (or aboard the ships) and get a refund of the tax paid in cash. For tax-free shopping information in Sweden, call 0410/19-56-0.

TELEPHONE AND TELEGRAPH: To telephone or telegraph anywhere in the world, go to the "tele" office. The central office, open daily from 8 a.m. to midnight, is at 2 Skeppsbron, behind the Royal Palace in the Old Town in Stockholm. *Note:* Telegrams are sent at telephone offices, not at the post offices, as in some other countries.

In Stockholm, the telephone system is automatic (most numbers have six digits and you can dial direct). If you have questions, there are English-speaking operators willing to assist.

In Stockholm you'll find telephone boxes on the streets. Put your coins in the slot, lift the receiver, and wait for a dial tone. The dial your number. If the line's engaged, return the receiver and your coins will (or should) be returned in the flap at the bottom.

Try, if possible, to avoid placing long-distance calls from your hotel, where the charge may be doubled or tripled when you get your final bill.

TIME: When New Yorkers break for lunch at noon, Eastern Standard Time, it is cocktail time in Sweden—that is, 6 p.m.

TIPPING: Hotels include the service charge in the bill you will be given. Restaurants, depending on their class, add from 13% to 15% to your tab. Taxi drivers are entitled to about 10% to 15% of the fare, and cloakroom attendants usually expect 3 kronor (36¢). Porters usually get 4 kronor (48¢) for the first piece of luggage, 2 kronor (24¢) thereafter.

TOURIST SERVICES IN STOCKHOLM: The helpful **Stockholm Information Service** is at Sweden House (Sverigehuset), Kungsträdgårdgatan (tel. 789-20-00), at one end of the King's Park. Hours are from 9 a.m. to 7 p.m. daily from June 16 to August 31; 9 a.m. to 5 p.m. Monday through Friday and 9 a.m. to 2 p.m. Saturday and Sunday the rest of the year. Maps and other free material are available from the women in blue and yellow uniforms on the ground floor.

For more detailed information about study, cultural life, or whatever, apply at the informative **Swedish Institute Documentation Centre,** upstairs. Swedish librarians will show you the many pamphlets available on anything you need to know.

Another tourist service offered in Stockholm is the English-language news broadcast in summer from 8 a.m. to 7 p.m.

Phone the automatic answering service at 22-18-40 for details of the day's events.

WEIGHTS AND MEASURES: Like most countries of the world, Sweden follows the standard international metric system. For a chart of conversions, refer to the listing under "A Preview of Denmark," Part 4, Chapter I.

Chapter XI

SETTLING INTO STOCKHOLM

1. Getting Oriented
2. Where to Stay
3. Where to Dine

ONE SUMMER MORNING at three o'clock, you are jolted out of sleep by a rap on your bedroom door. You answer the door. It's your hostess, a charming Swedish woman, calling to invite you to join her and her family for coffee.

Coffee, at 3 a.m.? Too drowsy to refuse, you accept.

You dress and stumble down to the backyard terrace, where you find not only your hostess and her family, but the other guests as well. And now you know why you've been summoned—to watch the eerie blue sky, pure, crystal exquisite. You sit and sip, inhaling the damp, cleansing air and observing with fascination as the sky gradually is bathed in a peach color.

Stockholm . . . a city where you're glad to get up at 3 a.m. to watch the unveiling of a summer sky.

Summer is a novelty in Stockholm, but the true spirit of Stockholm appears in winter. The Stockholmers retreat behind closed doors, or venture out to dine intimately in candlelit cellar bistros. Leafless birches laden with icicles are silhouetted against the twilight.

A director of tourism one wintry evening sat in front of his television and watched Greta Garbo portray *Queen Christina* for the umpteenth time. After the screening, he tired of fish-market quotations and went for a walk—despite the snowflakes that eddied through the air.

At the Norrbro Bridge leading to the Royal Palace, he saw a lone, cape-clad figure plowing through the snow flurries in his direction. He came face to face with the stranger and gasped in astonishment. It was Greta herself. The legendary face gave him only a momentary glance, then disappeared into the night.

In Stockholm—a city in which the 16th century coexists with the 21st—anything can happen and everything does.

1. Getting Oriented

Stockholm is a city of bridges and islands, of towers and steeples, of cobbled squares and broad boulevards, of Renaissance splendor and glass-and-steel skyscrapers.

As would be imagined of a city built on 14 islands, Stockholm has water in every direction. On Lake Mälaren, the capital marks the beginning of an archi-

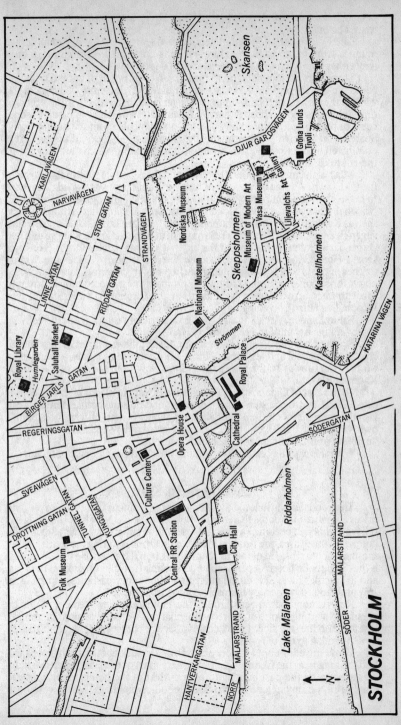

Skansen

DJUR GARDSVAGEN

Gröna Lunds
Tivoli

KARLAVÄGEN

NARVAVÄGEN

STOR GATAN

STRANDVÄGEN

Nordiska Museum

Vasa Museum

Museum of Modern Art

Liljevalchs Art Gallery

Skeppsholmen

Kastellholmen

LINNE GATAN

RIDDAR GATAN

National Museum

Strömmen

KATARINA VÄGEN

Royal Library

Humlegarden

Saluhall Market

BIRGER JARLS GATAN

REGERINGSGATAN

Royal Palace

Cathedral

SÖDERGATAN

SVEAVÄGEN

Opera House

DROTTNING GATAN

TUNNEL GATAN

KUNGSGATAN

Culture Center

Folk Museum

Central RR Station

City Hall

Riddarholmen

MALARSTRAND

HANTVERKARGATAN

MALARSTRAND

NORR

SÖDER

Lake Mälaren

N

STOCKHOLM

pelago that reaches all the way to the Baltic. Every Stockholmer has a boat—or wishes he or she had.

The Oslovians and Stockholmers share at least one thing in common: just minutes from either capital, nature abounds untouched. From Stockholm it may either be a birch forest or the garden of a skerrie.

Stockholm was founded more than seven centuries ago, but it did not become the official capital of Sweden until the mid-17th century. The medieval walls of the Old Town (**Gamla Stan**) no longer remain, but the twisting streets of the Middle Ages do. Through narrow lanes visitors wander in pursuit of some curio or other in an antique shop or a top-notch meal in some cellar hideaway. Spared from foreign bombardment, the island is a reminder of the past. It is dominated by the Royal Palace, where visitors gather to watch the changing-of-the-guard ceremony.

Most of the medium-priced hotels are on the islands of **Norrmalm,** north of the Old Town. A huge compound of junky old buildings was ripped down here to make way for a complex of small skyscrapers, the light and airy **Hötorget.** In Norrmalm are to be found Stockholm's major traffic and pedestrian arteries, such as **Kungsgatan** (the main shopping street), **Birger Jarls Gatan,** and **Strandvägen** (leading to the Deer Park). **Stureplan,** at the junction of Kungsgatan and Birger Jarls Gatan, is the hub of the city. At **Gustav Adolfs Torg** is the Royal Opera House, and the Royal Dramatic Theater is nearby. Near the flaming torches of the Opera is **Kungsträdgården,** a popular gathering place and resting perch for shoppers. Jutting out onto a promontory is the National Museum. Most tourists arrive first in Norrmalm, at the Central Railway Station (see "Room in a Hurry," coming up).

Kungsholmen, King's Island, is the western city island, visited chiefly by those seeking a tour of the elegant City Hall.

South of the Old Town is **Södermalm,** the southern quarter of Stockholm, chiefly commercial and residential. It need not concern us much—except when we take the subway to the Slussan stop for a view from the top of the nearby Katarina Elevator.

To the east of Gamla Stan is **Djurgården** (Deer Park), a lake-encircled forested island that is the summer pleasure ground of Stockholm. Here you can visit the open-air folk museums of Skansen, the *Wasa* man-of-war, Stockholm's own version of the Tivoli, the estate and gardens (Waldemarsudde) of the "painting prince" Eugen, and the Nordic Museum.

With this capsule orientation, we turn now to the major task of finding:

2. Where to Stay

The good news is that the Stockholm hotel picture is better than ever, and prices are more affordable than they have been in years. New hotel building has relieved what had become a very tight reservation situation. In fact, Stockholm hotels, in some cases, are actually lowering their prices during the tourist-heavy summer months instead of raising them, as is often the case. The reason for this is that Stockholm hotels depend on the commercial traveler for most of the year, and in summer most Scandinavians seem to find other pastimes, especially in July and August, to occupy themselves away from the city.

Reservations—arranged through the Hotellcentralen (see below) or by personally writing to one of my recommendations—are still advised in summer just to be on the safe side. In most cases a service charge, ranging from 10% to 15%, is added to the bill.

Those traveling about on foot and wanting to seek out their own hotels will find the area near the Central Station—where most of the least expensive lodgings are—to be the best hunting territory. Most of the hotels in this area are family run, occupying one or two floors of office buildings. Many were once impressive and exclusive private apartments that have now fallen upon less lavish days.

The hotels I'll lead off with lie in the center of the city. The next group will be those comparably priced accommodations within 10 to 20 minutes of the city, but easily reached by subway, streetcar, or bus. I'll have a few selections in the Old Town, but these choices are limited. To conclude, I'll preview the student-run hotels that are residence halls in winter. A final recommendation will be a selection of youth hostels.

But first, a—

ROOM IN A HURRY: The **Hotellcentralen** (tel. 24-08-80), on the lower level of the Central Station, is the official accommodation bureau of Stockholm—arranging rooms in hotels, pensions, hospices, and youth hostels. A 15-krona ($1.80) service fee is charged. In June, July, and August, the bureau is open Monday to Friday from 8 a.m. to 9 p.m.; Saturday from 8 a.m. to 5 p.m.; and Sunday from 1 a.m. to 5 p.m. September to April, it's open Monday to Friday from 8:30 to 11:30 a.m. and 12:30 to 4:45 p.m.

Here's how it works: a prospective guest states on a card the amount of money he or she wishes to pay, specifying the type of accommodation and location desired. One of the members of the English-speaking staff will consult a file, then make a telephone call (perhaps several telephone calls). If space is found, the visitor will be told the easiest and most convenient transportation. However, be warned that the bureau will not book a room in a private home, only in a hotel.

In addition, there are several private agencies that perform this service for a fee.

A private rental agency is **Hotelltjänst AB** (hotel service), at 38B Vasagatan (tel. 10-44-57), on the second floor of an office building. The English-speaking owner, Mr. Gustavsson, will locate and book a room for you in a private home or hotel, for which you will be charged about 150 kronor ($18) in a single and from 175 kronor ($21) up in a double room. Mr. Gustavsson never charges a booking fee. He is confident he can find you a room, but because he is only a one-man operation, he cannot attempt to answer your request for a reservation. Just show up on his doorstep and hope for the best.

If you want to rent a room by the week or month, providing you're going to be in Stockholm for such a long period, **Sommar Hyr** (Summer Rent) performs a unique service. It subleases rooms from students during their vacation break, then rents them to foreign visitors from May 15 to September 15. Open Monday to Friday from 1 to 4 p.m. the organization is at 4c Körsbärsvägen (tel. 16-61-09). Their postal address is Box 5654 114 89 Stockholm. They offer furnished student rooms for one person with a shower, toilet, and an opportunity to use a corridor kitchen. You bring your own bedding and take care of the cleaning yourself. The cost is 600 kronor ($72) for two weeks or less, and only 1000 kronor ($120) for a month. A deposit of 500 kronor ($60) is required when reserving a room.

HOTELS IN THE CENTER: Hotell Kom, 17–19 Döbelnsgatan (tel. 23-56-30), is one of the best hotel bargains in Stockholm. Built in 1980, the reddish-colored structure presents an angular façade to a section of town scattered with stores, apartments, and businesses. Because it's built on the slope of a hill, the reception area is easily accessible from the sidewalk, midway between the top and bottom floors. You'll be greeted by a friendly, English-speaking receptionist.

The efficiently comfortable bedrooms all contain kitchenettes, baths, color TV, and telephones. In summer and on winter weekends, the charge is 300 kronor ($36) in a single, 360 kronor ($43.20) in a double. In winter, singles rent for

450 kronor ($54), while doubles cost 540 kronor ($64.80). The place is ideal for extended stays in town, particularly since the decor and the setting are more like that of an apartment building than a hotel. There's a sauna on the premises, which you can use for a nominal fee. The in-house garage will shelter your car for an additional 25 kronor ($3) per night.

Hotell Sana, 6B Upplandsgatan (tel. 20-69-82). There's no telling what this hotel may look like when you arrive, since the owners, Per-ola Lindström and Roland Norling, plan to renovate each public area and each bedroom over an extended period of the next few years. The young partners purchased the hotel in 1984, and since then it has sheltered dozens of students, backpackers, and budgeteers from many countries. Don't expect the Ritz if you decide to ring the doorbell on the sidewalk level (someone will unlock the door from upstairs electronically). The decor is just a bit bleak at present, but the sincerity and charm of the owners make up for the paint buckets and spackle. The bedrooms are high-ceilinged and carpeted and represent bargains in a city whose hotels sometimes fill up quickly. Bathless units cost 240 kronor ($28.80) for a single and 360 kronor ($43.20) for a double. Rooms with bath cost 360 kronor ($43.20) for a single, 480 kronor ($57.60) for a double. There's a TV in each room, and you can be served breakfast there for an additional 20 kronor ($2.40) per person.

Wasa Park Hotell, 1 Sct. Eriksplan (tel. 34-02-85), was born when four different apartments were joined together to form a rambling collection of serpentine corridors and sitting rooms placed end to end like a series of railway cars. The format is about as unpretentious as anything you'll find in Stockholm, even though the building in which it is located is a solid and formally dignified construction of rhythmic windows and seemingly endless ocher walls.

You enter the hotel by taking a battered elevator, after going through an arched passage stretching the entire width of the ground floor. None of the 14 bedrooms contains a private bath, although many of them are freshly painted and were renovated as recently as 1984. The postwar baths are somewhat old-fashioned, but if you're looking for an inexpensive place to stay and if you don't mind meeting a sometimes gregarious crowd of students and even older people every time you head to and from your morning *toilette,* this might be an acceptable hotel for you. Single rooms cost 210 kronor ($25.20), with doubles renting for 330 kronor ($31.60). From June through August, breakfast is included in the room price, and the rest of the year, it costs an additional 30 kronor ($3.60) per person. There are three working TVs in three different sitting rooms.

Resman Hotel, 77 Drottninggatan (tel. 14-13-95), is a quietly elegant place which was completely renovated in 1983. It's owned by a Swedish lawyer, Fred Kristiansen, and his charming wife, Eva, whose abstract paintings hang near the palms of the tasteful gray sitting room. The hotel is in an old edifice with an ornate iron elevator which will creak you slowly to the third-floor reception area. The 18 comfortable rooms are scattered over two floors of the building, which is near Strindberg's birthplace. The in-house sauna is free. Each of the rooms has a digital alarm, a phone, and a price which, depending on the plumbing and the accommodation, ranges from 300 kronor ($36) to 550 kronor ($66) in a single, from 550 kronor ($66) to 660 ($79.20) in a double, all with breakfast included.

Hotel Karelia, 35 Birger Jarlsgatan (tel. 24-76-60), is an elegantly old-world kind of hostelry which sits behind an impressive turn-of-the-century façade graced with a copper-capped tower set into its corner. On a busy commercial street, it's owned by Finns who named the place after one of their homeland's provinces which was partially lost to Russia after World War II. In fact, many of the clients are Finnish visitors, who appreciate the small-stakes in-house casino, the sauna, the swimming pool, the 88 high-ceilinged, clean, and well-constructed rooms, each with a radio and TV, and the two restaurants, one of which has Finnish folkloric dancing nearly every night.

You enter the hotel from under a large Romanesque arch and climb one side of a decorative double staircase. You'll be quoted prices by the English-speaking receptionist of 265 kronor ($31.80) for a single, 480 kronor ($57.60) for a double in summer and on winter weekends. The rates are 620 kronor ($74.40) in a single, 800 kronor ($96) for a double in winter, spring, and on autumn weekdays. Breakfast is included in the prices.

A nearby restaurant under the same management, the Karelia, 4 Snickarbacken (tel. 20-01-05), offers a Finnish lunch board from 11 a.m. to 2 p.m. Monday through Friday for a reasonable 35 kronor ($4.20).

Hotell Bema, 13 Upplandsgatan (tel. 10-23-81). Many of the clients of this simple hotel are tourists, backpackers, and students. The blond partners who own the place, Anders Myrenberg and Tag Forssen (both of whom come from points on the Gulf of Finland north of Stockholm), maintain 12 clean rooms which were originally built in 1884 as apartments and which today contain sinks with running water and lots of simple charm. The showers and toilets for all the units are off the narrow central corridor. There's no elevator from the street two floors below the hotel, so patrons, after ringing a bell, climb a winding stone stairway to reach it. The price, however, is worth the inconvenience. Singles cost 180 kronor ($21.60), while doubles go for 275 kronor ($33). Breakfast, served in the rooms, costs an additional 25 kronor ($3) per person. Bus 59 comes from the railway station. Get off at the third stop after its departure from Tegnèrgatan.

Savoy, 12 Bryggargatan (tel. 22-12-80), is a typical business person's hotel in a noisy and busy section of Stockholm. However, most of its rooms are inside and therefore quieter. Facing the central post office, the hotel isn't very appealing, but many find it suitable for an overnight's stopover. Singles without bath cost from 170 kronor ($20.40) to 195 kronor ($23.40); bathless doubles, 280 kronor ($33.60). However, for a double room with private bath, expect to pay from 370 kronor ($44.40). These tariffs include breakfast.

It should be noted that Bryggargatan is one of the "hot" streets of Stockholm—that is, it contains a number of porno shops and is likely to be noisy late into the night. However, my hotel recommendations are perfectly respectable, although some families may object to staying on Bryggargatan.

Hotell Hospits Elim, 25 Gamla Brogatan (tel. 11-29-36), is a sinple second-floor pension in the center of Stockholm. Many economy-minded guests have found the rooms satisfactory. Certainly the price is right: 190 kronor ($22.80) in a single, 250 kronor ($30) to 275 kronor ($33) in a double. Although the rooms don't contain private showers, there is both a bath and shower available at no cost. Breakfast costs an extra 20 kronor ($2.40) per person.

Hotell Danielson, 31 Wallingatan (tel. 11-10-76), is a second-floor establishment, a short walk from Drottninggatan and Kungsgatan (bus 59 or 47 to Norra Bantorget). The building is ocher colored, almost art deco in style, with curved bay windows. The hotel is owned by Anssi Aro, who comes from Finland, as do many of his guests, some of whom are artists. The Danielson, furnished mostly with pieces of another day, has several big, comfortable rooms that lend themselves to all sort of doubling up possibilities. In the bathless doubles prices range from 230 kronor ($27.60). A bathless single is 175 kronor ($21). With a private bath, the cost goes up to 275 kronor ($33) in a single, rising even higher—to 350 kronor ($42)—in a double. All the rates quoted include service and taxes. Showers are free. A continental breakfast is available.

Sandströms Familyehotell, 75 Sct. Eriksgatan (tel. 30-83-32), is the smallest and one of the most intimate hotels in all of Stockholm. Since the rooms are literally within the living space of the humorous and English-speaking Bernt and Margit Eriksson, they tend to give the impression of being in a private home. The place is within the pink walls of a well-maintained building on a busy commercial street in the heart of town. It is almost essential that you phone the

Erikssons before arriving here, since the door will not open without the proper security code which they will give you if they have an available room. Although there's traffic in the street outside, all windows have triple glass for soundproofing, illuminating colorful and tasteful statements of Scandinavian modern design. Single rooms cost 400 kronor ($48), while doubles rent for 650 kronor ($78). Each unit contains a private bath, TV, wall-to-wall carpeting, and a clock radio. Breakfast, which is included in the price, is served in the rooms.

Hotel Residens, 50 Kungsgatan (tel. 23-35-40), is a completely renovated hotel facing the PUB Department Store in the heart of Stockholm. An elevator takes you directly up to the reception, breakfast, and TV room on the fifth floor. There are seven functionally furnished single rooms with hot and cold running water, plus 27 doubles with the same facilities. On each floor is a bath, shower, or sauna. However, many of the accommodations contain private toilets. A single without bath rents for 320 kronor ($38.40), going up to 420 kronor ($50.40) with private shower. The cheapest doubles—those without bath—cost 400 kronor ($48), rising to 550 kronor ($66) with private shower. Nearby is a garage with full service.

Marias Hotell AB, 38 Sct. Eriksgatan (tel. 54-18-85), is run by Paul Asmar and Gundel Löfgrim. They leased the fourth and fifth floor of this office building, which is, naturally, serviced by an elevator. Inside they have created a fresh, modern, friendly little hotel. Rooms are furnished in an up-to-date Nordic style, and on each floor are adequate bathroom facilities.

In spite of inflation, the management tries to keep the prices down. Tariffs depend entirely on how much plumbing youi require. The simplest single at 250 kronor ($30) has no bath. However, for a room with a "bath pantry," the cost goes up to 350 kronor ($42) in a single. A double without facilities is priced at 375 kronor ($45). However, doubles with either a shower and toilet or a "bath pantry" rent from 450 kronor ($54). To reach the hotel, take the subway to T-station at Fridhemsplan. Ring the bell of the first building to the left of the Fleminggatan exit.

Adlon Hotell, 42 Vasagatan (tel. 24-54-00), in an 1890s building, has adequately furnished rooms and offers personal service. The hotel has four floors, and the reception area is on the second. Singles, a total of 58 in all, come in a wide price range, depending on the plumbing. The most basic single units cost 250 kronor ($30), but that tariff rises to 350 kronor ($42) with complete bath. Bathless doubles go for 350 kronor ($42), peaking at 600 kronor ($72) with complete bath. A Swedish breakfast is included. All rooms contain telephones and radios, and a few are outfitted with TV. Beer, drinks, and sandwiches are sold at the reception area. A short walk takes you to the train station, air terminal, and underground.

Queen's Hotel, 71A Drottninggatan (tel. 20-08-89), is a small, fourth-floor establishment, ten minutes from the Central Station, that might do in an emergency. In an old film building, the hotel charges 360 kronor ($43.20) for bathless doubles, 250 kronor ($30) for singles (lots of them here). Baths and a buffet breakfast are included in the tariffs.

Hotel Regent, 10 Drottninggatan (tel. 20-90-04), is a family-run, third-floor hotel in a convenient area, a short walk from the sightseeing buses and boats at the habor and about a 10-minute walk from the main station. The hotel dates from around 1830 and is one of the oldest in Stockholm. Part of the old house in which the Regent is located dates from the 17th century. The 16 bedrooms, reached by elevator, have known greater splendor, but they have been redecorated with carpets and upholstered pieces. A bathless double rents for 225 kronor ($27) to 300 kronor ($36); a single, 175 kronor ($21) to 220 kronor ($26.40). All are clean and tidy. The prices include taxes and service, and baths are free.

Hotell & Pensionat Suta, 90 Odengatan (tel. 32-46-49), is centrally located, and its owners, Ferencz and Madga Suta, have offered many courtesies to readers. One couple wrote that they even gave them a small refrigerator in their room so they could keep milk and other food fresh for their baby. They also have a washer and dryer available for hotel guests. The small hotel overlooks the beautiful Vasa Park, and some of the units open onto that; others face a quiet side street. The accommodations have been redecorated, and all of them contain hot and cold running water (some also have private showers). The price in a double room is 300 kronor ($36) a night, a good bargain. A breakfast, described as "better than continental," is brought to your room each morning.

Hotel Ornsköld, 6 Nybrogatan (tel. 67-02-85), is easy to find, near the National Theater and the harbor. It's a one-floor establishment, reached through a narrow hidden-away entry, then up a winding staircase. The bathless doubles cost 450 kronor ($54), the price rising to 625 kronor ($75) with complete bath. Bathless singles begin at 350 kronor ($42), jumping to 400 kronor ($48) with complete bath. The generous size of the rooms makes this a bargain stopover, particularly for families traveling with children, since extra beds can be added. Breakfast is an extra 22 kronor ($2.64). The hotel, operated by Börje Ekstrand, offers 27 accommodations in all, each with private bath. Most of the rooms are large and well decorated. The hotel originally was built as a pension in 1910.

BRANCHING OUT: Gustav Vasa, 61 Västmannagatan (tel. 34-38-01), occupies three floors of a building which looks as if it were built at the turn of the century. The inside is very clean, although the hotel contains a minimum of plumbing and rather basic furnishings. The tropical murals in the breakfast room were done by a Portuguese male artist who lived at the hotel. Some clients move in for a week, appreciating the pinewood floors and the old furniture, including several antiques. One unit (no. 4) even has a 19th-century ceramic stove and brass headboards. Accommodations contain hot and cold running water, and corridor showers are available without charge. In all, there are 31 rooms, half of which are equipped with phones. Singles cost 220 kronor ($26.40); doubles go for 280 kronor ($33.60). Some three-bedded units are rented for 390 kronor ($46.80); a four-bedded room costs 500 kronor ($60). The Gustav Vasa lies within easy reach of the city center, bus and underground connections, and is within a 15-minute walk of the Central Station.

Anno 1647, 3 Mariagränd (tel. 44-04-80), opened in 1968, is suitable for those who don't mind being away from the center. It is easily reached, however, by taking the underground to the Slussen stop. One of the two buildings comprising the hotel dates from 1647, the other from 1776. The inside courtyard and entrance are of cobblestone. The hotel has been completely renovated, and the rooms, although a bit cramped for many tastes, are nevertheless pleasantly decorated and furnished in a Scandinavian modern motif. The location is on Södermalm, which lies south of the Old Town (you'll undoubtedly visit the location at least once when you come to the Katarina elevator—refer to sights).

Try to get a room overlooking Stockholm. A buffet breakfast is included. If you stay here on a weekend, the management usually grants considerable reductions (ask when you check in). Otherwise, singles with shower and toilet rent for 500 kronor ($60), doubles costing from 600 kronor ($72). The cheaper way to stay here is to ask for a single with only hot and cold running water, costing 325 kronor ($39) a night, a similar double going for 425 kronor ($51). If you'll settle for no plumbing facilities, you'll be given a single at 200 kronor ($24), a double at 275 kronor ($33).

SPLURGE HOTELS IN THE OLD TOWN: Frälsningsarméns Hotell Gamla Stan, 25 Lilla Nygatan (tel. 24-44-50), is a simple, clean, and friendly hotel, operated by the Salvation Army, 50 feet from the harbor in Gamla Stan. A little corner hotel in a building 300 years old, this hotel offers recently renovated rooms, some aspirin-box small but quite workable. A bathless single goes for 300 kronor ($36), rising to 540 kronor ($62.40). A bathless double rents for 450 kronor ($54), going up to 620 kronor ($74.40) with private shower and toilet, and peaking at 680 kronor ($81.60) with a complete private bath. If you're traveling with a child, the staff will put an extra bed into your room for 90 kronor ($10.80). The hotel is a short walk from some of the finest dining places and curio shops in the city. Take the subway to the Gamla Stan stop, or else bus 59 to Räntmästartrappan stop from Central Station.

Lady Hamilton Hotel, 5 Storkyrkobrinken (tel. 23-46-80), offers one of the most desirable locations in Stockholm, on a quiet street in the old town surrounded by antique shops and unusual restaurants. The theme inside is overwhelmingly—and charmingly—nautical, with dozens of antiques which even extend into the high-ceilinged and well-furnished bedrooms. You'll get an idea of the 16th-century origins of this hotel by reserving the luxurious sauna at 55 kronor ($6.60). It contains the stone-rimmed well which used to supply most of the household's drinking water. On the way either into the basement or toward your comfortable room, you'll pass a large 18th-century painting, an ivory model of a ship probably made by French prisoners in the 1700s, and several carved figureheads from the ancient sailing vessels. The ornate staircase even wraps itself around a large model of a clipper ship hanging in stately solitude from chains set into the ceiling. The rooms, each of which has the Latin name of a flower painted on its door, contain private baths. They rent for 800 kronor ($96) to 870 kronor ($104.40) in a single and for 900 kronor ($108) to 1000 kronor ($120) in a double, although the prices are reduced on some weekends and for most of the summer. There are 34 rooms in all.

Lord Nelson Hotel, 22 Västerlänggatan (tel. 23-23-90), is contained within a five-story, gracefully designed building whose enormous sheets of glass and decorative half-columns topped with expressionless sculptured heads look almost art nouveau, even though the foundation is said to date from 1690. Each floor is pierced with a full-length bay window filled with nautical memorabilia, including ships' helms, captains' chairs, military prints, navigational instruments, and a seaworthy reception desk crafted from teak and brass. Each of the comfortably efficient rooms is named after a type of ship and contains a private bath. The 31 rooms rent for between 600 kronor ($72) and 660 kronor ($79.20) in a single, from 760 kronor ($91.20) to 865 kronor ($103.80) in a double. Breakfast is included in the prices. An in-house sauna is available for a rental fee of 40 kronor ($4.80).

THREE STUDENT-RUN HOTELS: Stockholm has three principal student residential halls that were built to meet the needs of the Stockholm University students. In summer they are turned into some of the best living accommodations offered in the city. The hotels are well run, the English-speaking students manning the desks. These are hardly your basic back-home dormitories. Far from it. Most of the rooms have private showers and toilets. Struggling the student occupants may be, but they're struggling in style. Reservations for all three hotels should be made through SSRS Hotel Service, Box 5652, 11489 Stockholm, Sweden, which operates them.

Domus Hotel, 1 Körsbärsvägen (tel. 16-01-95), is open all year, attracting visitors of all ages. Completely renovated in 1984 it offers pleasant rooms with private showers, toilets, phones, TVs, and radio. The location is just five minutes by underground from the Central Station. Take the underground to the Techniska Högskolan station and walk one block. The location is just off a tree-lined boulevard, on a hillside with a good view. There's an outdoor terrace on which tables are set out under a pergola. The price of a single room is 300 kronor

($36), including a continental breakfast. Doubles cost 375 kronor ($45). Domus also lies within walking distance of the city air terminal and an open-air swimming pool. Meals at the restaurant, Babylon, are good and tasty, a lunch beginning at 35 kronor ($4.20), a dinner going for 50 kronor ($6).

Hotel Jerum, 21 Studentbacken (tel. 63-53-80), is a good tourist hotel standing virtually in its own park. It's in northeast Stockholm, but easily accessible. Take bus 62 from the heart of Stockholm, a 15-minute ride, or else use the much quicker underground. Get on at Gärdet, off at Furusundsgatan, and you'll be a short walk away. The hotel is a part of three buildings joined by courtyards and glassed-in passageways. The other two buildings are student apartments. Including service, doubles cost 110 kronor ($13.20) per person; singles, 190 kronor ($22.80). The steamlined Swedish-modern bedrooms contain desks, armchairs, private toilets, and showers. The lounges are also well designed, with walls of glass; one of them has a hooded fireplace. A complete breakfast is served in the cafeteria including well-brewed coffee. Guests of all ages and both sexes are received June 1 to August 31.

Hostel Frescati, 13–15 Proffessorslingan (tel. 15-79-96), is still another summer student hotel, under the same management as the Domus and Jerum. Ten minutes from the city center by underground, the hotel contains 170 rooms with a capacity of 400 beds, each unit with shower and toilet. The hostel is open to all ages and both sexes. A few singles are available, costing 110 kronor ($13.20) nightly. Twin-bedded rooms go for 55 kronor ($6.60) per person. The restaurant is self-service, and in fair weather you can sit out on the terrace. All accommodations contain private toilets and showers. The Frescati is open from June 1 to August 31. The nearest underground station to the Frescati is Universitetet.

THE SPLURGE HOTELS IN THE CENTER: Hotel City, 7 Slöjdgatan at Hötorget (tel. 22-22-40), is a first-class hotel owned by the Salvation Army. It stands only a five-minute walk from the Central Station and the bus from Arlanda International Airport. The hotel is in the middle of Stockholm, lying a block from the PUB Department Store and Åhléns Department Store. All the rooms have bath or shower, color TV, and radio, and the restaurant serves breakfast, lunch, and dinner. Singles cost 485 kronor ($58.20) to 540 kronor ($64.80) and twins are 550 kronor ($66) to 600 kronor ($72). The hotel opened in 1982. With a total of 300 rooms, it is one of the biggest hotels in Sweden.

Hotell Kung Carl, 23 Birger Jarlsgatan (tel. 22-12-40), was built as a turn-of-the-century hostelry on a main artery of Stockholm. The owners have followed a policy of alternating areas of old-fashioned charm with striking examples of modern design, the effect of which is an unusual—and sometimes confusing—mishmash of styles. Some of the hallways and many of the sitting areas are richly detailed, with an occasional antique. The lobby area, staffed by what may be the prettiest receptionists in town, contains a 12-foot mural of choppy seas below the Royal Palace and lots of streamlined modernism.

The conservatively comfortable bedrooms are usually well furnished. The 88 rooms rent for 600 kronor ($72) to 660 kronor ($79.20) in a single, for 800 kronor ($96) in a double, breakfast included. On winter, spring, and autumn weekends, the hotel lowers its rates to the same prices charged from June 20 to mid-August—420 kronor ($50.40) for a single, 460 kronor ($55.20) for a double. At that period, even a junior or a regular suite is more affordable, priced at 660 kronor ($79.20) and 900 kronor ($108). Motorists will appreciate the nearby car park, and everyone will be happy about the convenient location of the hotel in the commercial center of town.

Clas På Hörnet, 20 Surbrunnsgatan (tel. 16-51-30). Even if the prices are too much for your budget, you might enjoy dropping into the bar of this newly opened hotel, which is neatly contained within the walls of a 250-year-old aristocratic house. The hotel contains only 10 well-furnished and elegant rooms, each with a private bath, mini-bar, and breakfast included. The decor, and especially that of the restaurant and bar, is authentic, with charming wallpaper, wide floorboards, booths for intimate dining or drinking, lots of flickering candles, and waitresses wearing old-style dresses. Rooms are the least expensive on weekends, when they rent for 720 kronor ($86.40) in a single, 850 kronor ($102) in a double, and more for a suite. On weeknights, singles rent for 1300 kronor ($156), while doubles cost 1450 kronor ($174).

Castle Hotel, 14 Riddargatan (tel. 22-69-90). If a hotel can achieve star status in a country, this one undoubtedly has. To Swedish jazz lovers, it's famous as the home of theatrical and musical stars. It also gently surrounds the nonmusical guests with portraits, photos, and memorabilia of the greatest jazz musicians on earth. Many come for the legend of the hotel (it attracted Mary Pickford and Douglas Fairbanks in the 1930s) and for the magnetic appreciation of the musical artist demonstrated year after year by the owner, Lars Bjuhrs. In addition to being a jazz enthusiast (he picked it up, he says, nightcrawling after hours from a former job at the Waldorf Astoria in New York), he's a sophisticated hotelier, with experience in London and Hamburg as well.

Musicians and other artists who have stayed here (the list includes the Beatles, Maurice Chevalier, Count Basie's backup musicians, Josephine Baker, Chet Baker, and the divine Marlene Dietrich as well as an endless procession of modern stars) are offered practice rooms and publicity if they want it. A Swedish TV station filmed one of the dining room's jam sessions for which the Castle was host and later broadcast it nationwide.

If you don't want a room, or if the hotel is filled, you might enjoy a drink in the bar (see "Nightlife" below). The tastefully furnished bedrooms, costing far beyond the budget prescribed in this book, rent for between 690 kronor ($82.80) and 900 kronor ($108) for a single, between 840 kronor ($100.80) and 1150 kronor ($138) in a double, including breakfast.

Mälardrottningen, Riddarholmen (tel. 24-36-00). If you're checking into this hotel with 65 steamer trunks and a retinue of attendants, you may find the rooms somewhat cramped today. Lavishness like that, however, was *de rigueur* when American millionaire C. K. G. Billings had it built in 1924 as the world's largest power yacht. It was later owned by Woolworth heiress Barbara Hutton (1939–1940), who gave it to the British Navy when World War II made the oceans unsafe for pleasure yachting. In its heydey as the *Vanadis*, *Mälardrottningen* (Queen of Lake Mälaren) and its crew of 50 hosted passengers whose names (and relationships) would keep a gossip columnist busy for years.

Today, in a more democratized society, the yacht's two dining rooms, paneled library, and seven suites have been stripped and divided into porthole-size cabins which rent as hotel rooms. The decor is appropriately nautical (lots of hardwood and brass), with small baths which, although cramped, are a marvel of efficient engineering. Still, there's a warm nostalgia about a stay at this hotel, where the carpeting is royal blue and where sections of the powerful engines—considerably cleaned up—are visible through thick glass plates set into the floor of one of the sitting areas. Of course, there's a bar and a restaurant on the upper decks, covered separately in the "Where to Dine" section below, which may evoke memories of a society distinctly different from that of socialistic Sweden today.

Rooms come in a variety of combinations which include doubles with beds either bunk style or side by side. Singles range from 480 kronor ($57.60) to 840 kronor ($100.80), while doubles go from 625 kronor ($75) to 990 kronor ($118.80). Each room contains color TV, radio, phone, air conditioning, shower, and access to the ship's sauna. A discount of about 100 kronor ($12) is offered on all but the most expensive cabins every weekend. You'll find the yacht permanently moored at a satellite island of the old city.

HOSTEL LIVING: A/F Chapman (tel. 10-37-15), moored off Skeppsholmen (near the Museum of Modern Art), is an authentic oldtime three-masted schooner that no longer sails the high seas on training missions, but has been converted into a youth hostel. It has been well adapted to its role: the staterooms have two, four, six, and eight beds. One section is reserved for men, another for women. Each section has showers and washrooms, but there are no single cabins or family rooms. All the original fittings have been retained, and the shipshape illusion is maintained. The A/F *Chapman* is a budget oasis, costing only 43 kronor ($5.16). Without a youth hostel card, a guest has to pay an extra 15 kronor ($1.80). Sheets and pillowcases can either be brought by the guests or rented for 18 kronor ($2.16) for the entire stay. Personal lockers are available. The schooner has three drawbacks, none of them insurmountable: the gangplank goes up at midnight—no exceptions whatsoever; a five-day stay is maximum; and space is as difficult to come by as a suntan in Stockholm in winter. The schooner is open January 15 to December 15. In addition, it is forbidden to smoke in the cabins and below decks. No alcohol or other intoxicants can be brought into or consumed at the hostel. Hostelers have a healthy Swedish breakfast in the self-service coffee bar and dining room, which must have been the cabins of the officers. The cost is 22 kronor ($2.64) per person.

Guests are advised to join the International Youth Hostel Federation in their home country, although international guest cards can also be obtained at the A/F *Chapman*.

There is no bus service on the island.

Gustaf A/F Kling, Berth 153 Stadsgården (tel. 41-41-77), contains one of Stockholm's most unusual youth hostels, as well as a slightly more expensive and better appointed hotel. It was converted from a Swedish survey ship, which, after compiling data on the coastal waters for many years, was permanently moored in 1981 in an attempt to solve a shortage of inexpensive hotel accommodations. The hostel section contains about 16 cabins, most of which hold four beds stacked in bunk-style pairs. A few doubles are available as well as one triple.

Accommodations cost about 90 kronor ($10.80) for a bed in a double, about 75 kronor ($9) for a bed in a triple, and about 65 kronor ($7.80) for a bunk in a quad. It's required that if guests don't bring sheets, they must rent linen and towels for 25 kronor ($3). Unlike many other hostels in Europe, there is no curfew, and guests, who are given keys, can come in any time all night long. From the railway station, take the subway two stops to Slussen, then walk two minutes to reach the hotel at pier 153.

If rooms in the hostel are sold out, and/or if you prefer bigger, quieter, and more private accommodations, you can rent a room in the adjoining hotel section. There, singles cost 250 kronor ($30) and doubles go for 300 kronor ($36), although in summer prices are reduced to 240 kronor ($28.80) in a single, 250 kronor ($30) in a double. There's a café on the premises, and the friendly management says that they plan to install a bar soon. The establishment is closed two days in midsummer, a week at Easter, and over the Christmas holidays.

Skeppsholmen Youth Hostel, Skeppsholmen (tel. 20-25-06), is a 16th-century house which was converted in 1983 into a functional and unembellished youth hostel. It lies only about 100 yards from a neighboring youth hostel, the *A/F Chapman*, to which it frequently refers clients, and vice versa. Accommodations are simple and basic, in standard hostal format (either two, three, or four beds to a room). Per-person rates are 55 kronor ($6.60) for members of the International Youth Hostel Federation and 70 kronor ($8.40) for nonmembers. Sheets are required, and guests who do not bring their own must rent them at a cost of 30 kronor ($3.60) for cotton ones, 18 kronor ($2.16) for paper "linens." Towels rent for 8 kronor (96¢) each. Families are accepted if space is available. There's no nightly curfew, but guests are expected to vacate the premises between noon and 3 p.m., when the place is being cleaned. You can take bus 62 or 59 from the main railway station, getting off at Kungsträdgården. The establishment is closed from around mid-December to January 6.

Columbus, 11 Tjärhousgatan (tel. 44-17-17), is a privately run hostel that offers one of the lowest and most competively priced tariffs in Stockholm for a bed for the night. The English-speaking owners, Robert Carlsson and Helena Hyvärinen, welcome young people from all over the world, charging only 60 konor ($7.20) per person nightly for a bed. Showers and free facilities for cooking and washing clothes are also provided. There is no curfew, as in most hostels.

Zinken is a youth and student hostel at 2 Pipmakargränd (tel. 68-57-86). The accommodation is inexpensive—only 50 kronor ($6) for members of the Youth Hostel Organization or else 60 kronor ($7.20) for other guests. The location is equally as fine: in a green oasis in the middle of Stockholm. Offered are 100 twin-bedded rooms and some rooms with three or four beds for families. Showers are available, as are laundry and cooking facilities, and there is a cafeteria on the premises. A substantial breakast costs 22 kronor ($2.64). Sheets rent for 19 kronor ($2.28). The Zinken is near the underground (T) and buses. Sports available include badminton and croquet. They also have a Jacuzzi, sauna, and solarium.

Another boat-hostel is **Mälaren,** Söder Mälarstrand, Berth 6 (tel. 44-43-85). Members pay 60 kronor ($7.20) nightly, and nonmembers are charged 65 kronor ($7.80). The cabins sleep two persons, and sheets are extra. On the premises is a cafeteria serving light meals. A restaurant is licensed to sell beer and wine. At no extra charge you can drop in to hear Swedish folklore singing sessions nightly. Mälaren is open from 9 a.m. till 1 a.m.

GUESTHOUSE LIVING: An increasingly popular way of meeting the high cost of living in Stockholm, boarding houses operated by private citizens are often preferred over the second-class hotels.

One of my favorites is the **Egelstads Pensionat,** 23 Upplandsgatan (tel. 34-80-68), owned by Kristina Egelstad. Her rooms are freshly decorated and have color TV sets. Bus 59 goes right by the door, or else you can take the Metro to Odenplan, a five-minute walk away. A shower bath and toilet are found in the hall. Breakfast is served in the rooms which rent for 180 kronor ($21.60) in a single, 275 kronor ($33) in a double. The units are of good size, and all are well-kept and clean. Electric heat keeps you warm in winter. English is spoken here.

READER'S GUESTHOUSE SELECTION: "We had the good luck to stay in the private home of **Mr. Jonasson,** 78 Asogatan (84-70-08). His apartment is about ten minutes by subway from the center of the city. He is a warm, congenial host and gave us the full run of his apartment, including kitchen facilities and laundry hanger. His price is 120 kronor ($14.40) in a double, 90 kronor ($10.80) in a single, which is quite reasonable considering the savings in doing our own cooking and laundry. Above all we enjoyed Mr. Jonasson's hospitality. We watched TV together (he'd always tell us when something in English was on) and toasted each other with *akavit*. He made ou. visit to Stockholm quite special" (Lisa Irving Halprin, New York, N.Y.).

READER'S HOTEL SELECTION (NYNASHÄMN): "Readers who would like to stay at a very pleasant, super-quiet, spotlessly clean, hospitable hotel should try **Pensional Trehörningen,** 8 Oscarsgatan, 14900 Nynashämn (tel. 0752/120-24). Trehörningen is a turn-of-the-century mansion on the banks of a cove, with a huge shaded garden, free rowboats for guests, a TV room, kitchen facilities including a refrigerator, and very large rooms with lavatories. Most rooms have toilets. Singles are 185 kronor($22.20) to 220 kronor($26.40); doubles, 220 kronor($26.40) to 280 kronor($33.60). Showers are free. The hotel is a five-minute walk from the train station stop, Nynäs Havsbad. Trains run all day to Stockholm and back (about an hour's ride). No meals other than breakfast are available. No minimum stay is required" (Purvis J. Hebert, APO New York).

3. Where to Dine

Food is expensive in Stockholm, but there's no need to tighten your belt if you're planning a visit. Not when there are so many economy restaurants, some suitable for the gourmet, others for those who want to partake of simple home-style Swedish cooking.

The range of restaurants is varied: English-style pubs, old taverns and wine cellars, restaurants and cafés serving meals in the Parisian manner, rooftop snack spots, rustic dining places surrounded by gardens and parks, and grill rooms. There are several vegetarian restaurants for devotees of fresh salads.

The real money-savers are the self-service chain cafeterias. At all restaurants other than cafeterias, a 12½% to 15% service charge is added to the bill to cover tipping.

I've pointed this out before, but I'll warn you once again: don't rush into a bar in Stockholm for your pick-me-up martini. "Bars" in Stockholm are self-service cafeterias, and the strongest drink many of them offer is apple cider.

Budget-minded visitors should consider ordering a **dagens rätt** (daily special) in self-service restaurants, department store cafeterias, and other eating establishments.

A Preview of Swedish Food

The fame of the smörgåsbord is justly deserved. Utilizing a vast array of dishes—everything from Baltic herring to smoked reindeer—the smögåsbord may either be eaten as hors d'oeuvres, or as a meal in itself.

One cardinal rule of the smörgåsbord: Don't mix fish and meat dishes. It is customary to begin with herring (sill), prepared in many ways. Herring is usually followed by other treats from the sea (jellied eel, salmon); then diners proceed to the cold meat dishes, such as baked ham or liverpaste, which are accompanied by vegetable salads. Hot dishes, often Swedish meatballs, come next, and are backed up by cheese and crackers—perhaps a fresh-fruit salad for those who haven't been carted off to the emergency ward.

The smörgåsbord is not served as often in Sweden as many visitors seem to believe, as it is a difficult affair, requiring time-consuming preparation. Many Swedish families reserve it for special occasions. In lieu of the 40-dish smörgåsbord, some restaurants have taken to serving a plate of hors d'oeuvres (assietter).

One of the tricks for enjoying smörgåsbord is timing. It's best to go early, when fish dishes are fresh. Late arrivals may be more fashionable, but the food is often stale.

The average times for meals in Sweden are generally from 8 to 11 a.m. for the standard continental breakfast; noon to 2:30 p.m. for lunch; as early as 5:30 p.m. for dinner to around 8 or 8:30 p.m. (many restaurants in Stockholm are open to midnight—but don't count on this in the small villages).

Generally Swedish chefs tend to be far more expert with fish dishes (freshwater pike and salmon are star choices) than with meat courses. The Swedes go stark-raving mad at the sight of crayfish (kräftor), in season from mid-August to mid-September. This succulent, dill-flavored delicacy is eaten with the fingers, and much of the fun is the elaborate ritual surrounding its consumption.

A platter of thin pancakes, served with lingonberries (comparable to cranberries), is the traditional Thursday night dinner in Sweden. It is often preceded by yellow split-pea soup seasoned with pork. It's good any night of the week—but somehow better on Thursday.

The Swedish cuisine used to be deficient in fresh vegetables and fruits, relying heavily on the tin can, but this is no longer true of the Scandinavian countries. Potatoes are the staff of life, but fresh salad bars long ago peppered the landscape, especially in the big cities.

The calorie-laden Swedish pastry—the mainstay of the konditori—is tempting and fatal to weight-watchers.

Some Notes on Drinks

Coffee (kaffe) is the universal drink in Sweden, although tea (taken straight) and milk are also popular. The water is perfectly safe to drink all over Sweden. Those who want a reprieve from alcohol might find the fruit-flavored Pommac a good soft-drink beverage, although Coca-Cola is ubiquitous.

The state monopoly, Systembolaget, controls the sale of alcoholic beverages. Licensed restaurants may sell alcohol after noon only (1 p.m. on Sunday). Don't head into a bar and order a martini: "bar" is the Swedish term for cafeteria.

Snaps or aquavit—served icy cold—is a superb Swedish drink, often used to accompany smörgåsbord. The run-of-the-mill Swedish beer (pilsner) is only toe-high in alcoholic content. Those desiring a stronger beer should ask for either folköl, the people's beer (weak to medium strength), or export, as you do in Denmark. Most Swedes seem to drink their liquor straight; mixed drinks are uncommon. Either way the drink prices are sky-high.

In 1916, the government imposed liquor rationing, confining the consumption for an adult male ("of good social standing") to four liters a month and that of his female counterpart ("unwed but respectable") to four liters a year. Now the liquor monopoly is advertising that "hard liquor costs more than it tastes." Skol!

DINING IN THE CITY CENTER: For the first selection, we head for Hötorget City, which stretches from the Haymarket (PUB's Department Store) to the traffic circle at Sergels Torg. Hötorget City is the commercial complex—five 18-story skyscrapers—in the heart of Stockholm. The main (traffic-free) street is Sergelgatan, a shopper's promenade leading to Sergels Torg. The visitor to the city will probably want to spend a great deal of time here, walking up for the view on the multilevel terraces, inspecting the flowerbeds, checking out the merchandise.

If fast food is your thing, try, for a change of pace, the **Clock,** 22 Sergelgatan (tel. 21-40-44). You can eat well for about 50 kronor ($6) at this clone of McDonald's. Instead of the "Big Mac," they offer the "Big Clock." There are many other popular branches of this chain dining spot throughout Stockholm. As you go through the city, you can't miss them. At the most central branch, hours are Monday to Friday from 9 a.m. to 9 p.m.; Saturday, 9 a.m. to 7 p.m.; and Sunday, noon to 9 p.m.

Kungsträdgården, the Kings Garden, may no longer be the promenade of royalty, but it is the downtown resting spot for young people, old people, foreigners, and locals—sort of a Swedish Central Park. In summer there are free concerts at the bandshell, unguarded showcase window displays of Swedish arts and crafts, and refreshment stands and benchs galore. In the winter, you can rent skates cheaply.

The most popular budget dining spot here is the **SJU Sekel,**

Kungsträdgården, adjoining the tourist bureau. It offers self-service meals and snacks inside its glass dining room, or outside at the sidewalk tables. Open till 10 p.m., it's also one of the most popular spots for the early-risers, who come here for breakfast. The breakfast special, served between 8 and 9 a.m., goes for 25 kronor ($3) and includes eggs. You can sit at the outdoor tables and watch the Swedes go by. Open-face sandwiches, a favorite item anytime of the day, range in price from 15 kronor ($1.80). Other meals are in the 55-krona ($6.60) to 65-krona ($7.80) range. SJU Sekel is the gathering place for an international set.

City Lejon, 8 Holländergatan (tel. 20-76-35) (not far from the SAS office at Sveagägen), is one of the best moderately priced restaurants in town. In addition to the small but neat dining room, there are tables outdoors. Stained-glass and hanging lamps, along with paneled walls, create the aura of a Swedish bistro. In back is a standup bar. You get good, plain cookery here, including pork chops and flank steak with vegetables and potatoes. You'll find the portions hearty and filling, yet the tab will most likely be a reasonable 90 kronor ($10.80) for a meal. From Monday to Friday, hours are from 8:30 a.m. to 7:30 p.m.; on Saturday, from 11 a.m. to 4 p.m.

Timjan (Thyme), 8 Riddargatan (tel. 20-98-45), two blocks away from Stureplan, is a miniature one-room corner restaurant that would be equally at home in Greenwich Village or San Francisco. Huge windows, crystal chandeliers, lots of plants in the windows, and hanging baskets combine to create the ambience of this warm, friendly, inviting place. Especially popular among photographers, models, and the creative jeans set, this restaurant is usually packed at lunch, but is a pleasant place to take time off for a light lunch in midafternoon. Typical Swedish food is presented along with international dishes, and salad is a specialty. Try the fish soup with aïoli, served with garlic bread. On one occasion, I enjoyed a Russian main dish. There's always a surprise from the chef (a happy one, I mean). Meals cost from 160 kronor ($19.20), and are served from 11 a.m. to 10 p.m., Monday to Friday (on Saturday, only from 3 to 11 p.m.).

Nearby, **Smögåskringlan,** 14 Riddargatan (tel. 10-64-87), each day prepares a large choice of appetizing open-face sandwiches, costing from 28 kronor ($3.36). Each one, along with a beverage and dessert, can make a complete meal. Hours are Monday to Friday from 10 a.m. to 5:30 p.m. (on Saturday, from 11 a.m. to 4 p.m.).

Opera Pizzeria, 20 Gustav Adolfs Torg (tel. 11-51-13). It might seem strange to find an Italian restaurant with a view of the Swedish Royal Palace and the grandly symmetrical Gustav Adolfs Square, yet many readers have enjoyed this warmly decorated trattoria directed by Ivan di Valentino and Mario Billiotti. The façade is illuminated with the most grandly imaginative 19th-century wrought-iron lamps in Stockholm, but inside you'll find lots of plants, paneling, simple tables and chairs, and a long Italian menu where a noon meal costs from 65 kronor ($7.80) and a dinner goes for around 145 kronor ($17.40). These include a predictable assortment of standard Italian specialties. Pizzas cost from 30 kronor ($3.60) any time. The place is open from 11 a.m. till 1 a.m.

Albertina, 27 Drottinggatan (tel. 21-66-84), offers one of the best values in town: an inexpensive lunchtime buffet which costs only 32 kronor ($3.85) per person. Of course, drinks are extra, but if you're in this pedestrian-only shopping street in back of the Sergel Plaza Hotel any weekday between 10:30 a.m. and 3 p.m., you might take advantage of the street-level room, tastefully accented in black and green. If you're a vacationing Bavarian, or a North American with a taste for beer and alpine music, you might enjoy a drink in the basement Alpen Keller. It's open from 4 p.m. to 2:30 a.m. every Wednesday, Thursday, and Friday and from 1 p.m. to 2:30 a.m. on Saturday for an insight into how Scandinavia's Teutonic neighbors to the south live. You pass under a moosehead on your descent via a curved stairway and find yourself in a little corner of Austria, complete with alpine-style chairs, long wooden tables, and a live band which plays (after 8 p.m.) inside a re-creation of a mountain hut. Beer costs from 24 kronor ($2.88), and there's no cover charge.

Glada Laxen, Gallerian (tel. 21-12-90), is the main branch of a restaurant which is so popular that lines often form of loyal clients eager to eat some of the finest salmon dishes in town. Virtually everything here is made from the pinkish fish whose flavor has come to be associated so closely with Swedish cuisine. Examples include a wide range of soups (the shellfish bisque is superb), as well as salmon with orange sauce, with shrimp and mushrooms in cream sauce, in dill-flavored casseroles, smoked and cold served with melon and apple salad, lightly fried with creamed chanterelles and roe of bleak (a freshwater fish), or with gorgonzola sauce. If guests prefer, they can help themselves from the lengthy seafood buffet or order a salmon pudding (a real Scandinavian specialty), prawn, ham, or green salads either as an appetizer or as a main course. You'll find this place inside the biggest shopping center in the heart of town, nestled among dozens of other restaurants and shops, in the kind of all-weather arcade that the warmth-loving Swedes especially appreciated in the depths of winter. Full meals in this garden setting (the chairs are cast-iron ringed with plants) range upward from 180 kronor ($21.60), although less expensive luncheons are possible if you avoid an appetizer and a dessert.

Sturekatten, 4 Riddargatan (tel. 11-16-12). The gabled and appealingly crooked house which contains this landmark tea room dates from around 1750, a fact you'll appreciate as you navigate to the top of the winding staircase leading from a point near the building's central courtyard. If you show up at midmorning, you'll get a view of the kinds of elderly Swedish women, complete with an unusual array of rapidly vanishing hat styles) who might be cast as the mother of Mrs. Olsen on an American coffee commercial. Of course, the main focus of the place is the impeccably clean display case (one for each floor) of carefully prepared sandwiches and pastries from which you select what you want so that a pretty waitress can bring it to your Victorian-style settee or chair. If you decide on a seat on the upper level, you'll pass through a winding series of narrow hallways, past an unused fireplace, to one of several smallish rooms, one of which is lit with a spacious skylight. Sandwiches range in price from 8.50 kronor ($1.02) to 28 kronor ($3.36), while pastries and slices of luscious, calorie-laden cakes cost from 5.50 kronor (66¢) to 12 kronor ($1.44). A pot of coffee or tea is around 8.50 kronor ($1.02). The establishment is open from 7:30 a.m. to 6 p.m. every weekday, from 9 a.m. to 4 p.m. on Saturday, and from noon to 5 p.m. Sunday.

A LUNCHTIME RESTAURANT COMPLEX: Virtually every office worker in Stockholm (but few temporary visitors) knows about one of the commercial center's most popular (and best hidden) lunchtime restaurant centers. You'll find it in the subterranean world of the Kungshalle, whose entrance lies across the pedestrian walkway of the Sergels Torg, near the Swedish concert hall, the outdoor vegetable market, and the PUB department store of Hötorget Square.

There, set on two levels of ultramodern and ultra-clean tile, you'll find at least 20 different restaurants which sell everything from crisp vegetarian, meat, and fish salads to full dinners or simply a stand-up bowl of shrimp. You should feel free to explore, along with many of the neighborhood's lunch-goers. That would include restaurants selling everything from Mexican burritos to Swedish meatballs—the full range that's available—but two of the lower level's better choices include:

Harry's Krog and Butik, 44 Kungsgatan (tel. 11-52-44), which remains open for early dinners as well as for its extremely popular luncheons. A daily steak special is offered for either 55 kronor ($6.60) or 62 kronor ($7.44), depending on the size of the steak, and includes a walnut salad, herb butter, and potatoes. The soups (there's a rich chanterelle recipe every autumn) could constitute a full meal, while the chicken or California salads—around 36 kronor ($4.32) each—are all many Stockholmers seem to want. No one will mind if you order just a main platter, such as grilled chicken breast with shrimp in cream sauce, which, with rice, is superb. The restaurant is open from Monday to Friday from 11 a.m. to 8 p.m., Saturday from 11 a.m. to 3:30 p.m.

Another establishment a few shops away is the **Butik Glada Laxen** (tel. 11-70-13), which is an extension of a bigger branch of the same establishment visited above. Translated as "The Happy Salmon," it offers just about everything that can be made from the fish, including salmon with mussels and Swedish caviar, plus a platter of crabmeat, salmon, and shrimp or salmon with orange sauce. Main courses, which may be all you'll want, cost from 50 kronor ($6) and 60 kronor ($7.20) each, although a slightly cheaper fixed-price meal is offered after the lunchtime rush, between 2 and 6:30 p.m. The floor plan is fairly small, and the well-lit interior is more like a garden than an underground mall. The hours are the same as those at Harry's Krog and Butik.

VEGETARIAN AND SALAD RESTAURANTS: Örtagården, 31 Nybrogatan (tel. 67-17-00), is upstairs above the colorful indoor market, Östermalms Saluhall (see below), so you can be sure of fresh produce being used in the foods offered. Translated from the Swedish, the name of the restaurant means *Herb Garden,* and that's what adds to dining pleasure at this copious vegetarian buffet which draws sometimes as many as 600 people a day. You rarely get the impression of a large crowd, however, since the twin rooms containing the establishment are high-ceilinged, spacious, and filled with an appealingly formal combination of vertically striped wallpaper, fresh green paneling, and comfortably cushioned banquettes and chairs.

The entrance is on the right side of a large Romanesque arch whose left side leads into the busy market. The fresh vegetables and produce from the ground floor are served in many different concoctions on the buffet of the restaurant, which, while emphasizing vegetarian hot and cold dishes, also offers white meat specialties such as salmon or shrimp sandwiches for around 32 kronor ($3.84) each. A fixed-price luncheon buffet costs 45 kronor ($5.40), while a *middagsbuffé,* served after 5 p.m., goes for 55 kronor ($6.60). No eggs are used in the vegetarian buffet. The establishment is open Monday through Friday from 10:30 a.m. to 11 p.m. It's closed Saturday but opens again on Sunday from noon to 6 p.m.

Annorlunda, 50 Malmskillnadsgatan (tel. 21-95-69), is Stockholm's most popular salad restaurant, offering cafeteria-style specials which usually keep it filled during most of open hours. This is not just an ordinary cafeteria, however. It does everything it can to maintain a feeling of intimacy, with flickering candles at each table, even at lunchtime. The spotless dining room is filled with well-dressed, matronly shoppers, students, lovers, and office comrades who know well the location of this establishment (near a confusing series of multilevel street grids at the edge of the city's shopping district). A platter of French pâté with garnish costs 40 kronor ($4.80), and a full meal, which could be made up of just about anything you want, including excellent salads or roast beef with potato salad, could range upward from 70 kronor ($8.40). The Annorlunda welcomes clients weekdays from 10:30 a.m. till 10 p.m. and Saturday from noon till 6 p.m. It's closed Sunday.

Gröna Linjen, 10 Mäster Samuelsgatan (tel. 11-27-90), is a haven for lovers of spinach, carrots, parsnips, cauliflower, asparagus, beans, and peas. The second-floor self-service vegetarian restaurant occupies what must have been a very large private apartment (paneled walls, ornate ceiling trim, glazed-tile stove). Substantial garden delights, both raw and cooked, are offered. A "middag" is served until 4 p.m. at a cost of 45 kronor ($5.40). The restaurant is run by Sigyn Lindberg and Perola Brolin. They are open Monday to Friday from 10:45 a.m. to 7 p.m. and on Saturday from 11:30 a.m. to 3 p.m.

DEPARTMENT STORE FARE: Åhléns Cafeteria, 50 Klarabergsgatan (tel. 24-60-00), between the Central Station and Hötorget, dotes on Swedish specialties, served during the store's regular business hours (till 6 p.m.). In the modern second-floor cafeteria, shoppers can partake of such food as meatballs in a creamy sauce or fried liver with onions and mashed potatoes. For dessert, you might try the orange-flavored cream pie, or some such delicacy. For a complete lunch, expect to spend from 75 kronor ($9) up, depending on the main dish selected. If you come by subway, you'll exit near the store's basement food emporium. It's open daily and Sunday until 8 p.m. and sells just about everything, including ready-made snacks.

DINING IN GAMLA STAN (OLD TOWN): I'll lead off with some inexpensive dining selections, then follow with some super-splurge choices where, if you can afford it, you may want to have a major festive meal before departing from Stockholm.

Rodolfo i Gamla Stan, 16 Storkyrkobrinken (tel. 10-53-38), is the success story of the Old Town, and all because of lasagne verdi. Rodolfo, an enterprising Italian, brought his own special recipe to Stockholm, then found an enchanting little building in which to serve it. The specialty, the lasagne, goes for 38 kronor ($4.56), and there are at least 20 other items on the menu at equally reasonable prices. At least 18 different drinks are listed, including a Bloody Mary. Expect to spend from 75 kronor ($9) to 105 kronor ($12.60) for a complete meal.

Of course, you get far more than lasagne here. You may prefer the pasta carbonara, the antipasto misto, or the beefsteak parmigiana. For dessert, you can order the ice cream with Marsala, finishing with your choice of either Irish or Italian coffee. There is a green decor of brass hanging lamps and large gilt-framed portraits. The opulent detail of the place evokes the turn of the century, especially the crystal chandeliers and beveled glass dividers. A mirrored display wall holds racks of old patterned porcelain. The restaurant is open on weekdays from 11 a.m. to 10 p.m. and on weekends from noon to 10 p.m.

If you're into a red decor, instead of green, head across the street to **Rodolfino,** 1 Stora Nygatan (tel. 11-84-97), which is slightly less formal and, if possible, places more emphasis on pasta. It has a cozy trattoria appearance. The prices are the same.

Restaurant Cattelin, 9 Storkyrkobrinken (tel. 20-18-18), opened in 1897, a fish restaurant in Gamla Stan, serves some of the finest food in Stockholm. Excellent seafood, mouthwatering hors d'oeuvres and desserts, unusual and imaginative main dishes, polite old-world atmosphere—all these elements combine to make for a top restaurant. You can dine here inexpensively or otherwise, depending on your appetite and choices. The least expensive way is to order the 55-krona ($6.60) dinner: soup, a main dish, bread and butter. But the dessert is 14 kronor ($1.68) extra. This set meal is served until 7 p.m. After that, you must dine à la carte, which could easily cost from 180 kronor ($21.60). But the food is worth it. Look for the plat du jour, including, on my most recent visit, grilled filet of perch with a chive sauce. You might also try the grilled salmon with hollandaise, always a delight. Hot food is usually served until 11 p.m.

Bistro Cattelin, 8 Stora Gramunkegränd (tel. 20-65-71), is not to be confused with the major and more important Cattelin restaurant whose entrance lies just around the corner. This particular annex is across from a jazz club called Stampen and seems to attract a less formal clientele who might enjoy a rock concert or a soccer match more than an opera or a symphony. The walls are papered with posters from Stockholm's most recent art exhibitions. The wooden tables are placed in the big-windowed establishment's irregularly shaped floor space, surrounded by the warmly modern decor. Until 7 p.m., you can enjoy a fixed-price meal for 90 kronor ($10.80), although à la carte meals, priced at from around 215 kronor ($25.80), include all the well-prepared specialties as those served at the bistro's big sister nearby. Examples are fresh mushroom or tomato salad, lobster soup with sherry and plenty of cream, wienerschnitzel, entrecôte Café de Paris with béarnaise, and other continental dishes.

Caffegillet, 4 Trangsund (tel. 21-39-95), to the side of the cathedral in the Old Town, is straight out of the Middle Ages. In 13th-century cellar vaults, you are served tasty and well-prepared meals. Imbued with a coffeehouse atmosphere, the café offers simple hot soups, sandwiches, beverages, and desserts. Four kinds of homemade soups are featured daily. The open-face sandwiches not only are tempting, the are artistic achievements. A less glamorous, but quite American, offering would be a hot dog with potato salad. The cellar, once part of an old monastery, has several nooks, but my favorite is the one with its original open fireplace. Lunch is served Monday to Friday from 11 a.m. to 3 p.m. for 75 kronor ($9) and up.

Magnus Ladulas, 26 Österlånggatan (tel. 21-29-57), named after a Swedish king, is a pleasant restaurant converted from a vaulted inner room which, during the 12th century, served as a weaving factory for the canvas sails which propelled the ships that plied the waters around the old town. Today it's owned by members of the Christiernsen family. Visitors are greeted by the sight of an unused upper balcony and a long bar set up in an outer room near the front entrance. If you want to have a standup drink (illuminated with hanging lamps made from old gear mechanisms for some ancient machine), you might chat with a member of the friendly staff before heading into the inner room for your meal. There, you can help yourself from the big salad bar and enjoy full meals which begin at 180 kronor ($21.60). This could include a mixed seafood plate with lobster sauce, fresh salmon from Lapland, filet of beef in puff pastry with a deviled sauce, good lamb stew, and a different sorbet made fresh every day. The establishment is open Monday through Friday from 11 a.m. to 11 p.m. and is closed every weekend.

Kristina, 68 Västerlånggatan (tel. 20-05-29), might be the perfect destination after a walk through the antique shops and pubs of the old town. It sits on an important pedestrian walkway behind a stone façade graced with carved and helmeted heads, with two cannon trained vertically and set into the pavement as markers for the building imediately to Kristina's left. Once inside, past the display case with an array of pastries and Danish-style sandwiches (a few of which might make a meal in themselves), you'll pass down a few steps into a room with what may be the most beautiful ceiling in Stockholm. This, as well as the friendly waitresses who will bring your beverage and food if you want it, is illuminated with light from stained-glass windows and from rococo wall sconces set onto the paneled walls.

Menu items, if you're interested in more than a sandwich, include a platter of frikadeller with lingonberries and cream gravy, mussel or onion soup, chili con carne, croque monsieur, or a full selection of old-fashioned ice creams. There are even vegetarian menus for meatless dinners, if that's what you want. Full meals begin at 75 kronor ($9), although you can spend more if you're really hungry. Every Friday and Saturday between 8 p.m. and midnight, the establishment offers live music from such local groups as the Boogie Kings or Fred's Laundry. The rest of the week, when it isn't offering its special Friday and Saturday concerts, the place is open from 10 a.m. to 8 p.m. and on Sunday from 11 a.m. to 8 p.m.

Ashoka, 16 Stortorget (tel. 20-06-71), opens onto the old market square at Gamla Stan. It is one of the few Indian restaurants in the whole of Scandinavia. At lunch, 11 a.m. to 3 p.m., kebabs (chicken or pork) are served with bread and butter, plus a selection of three kinds of salad, along with coffee, including both vegetarian and curry platters. You'll spend around 75 kronor ($9) for lunch, perhaps 120 kronor ($14.40) for dinner. The Indian food is served in the evening. The quietly efficient service and the old-world politeness have earned it a loyal following. The decor is a blending of two worlds, Sweden and India. The building housing the restaurant has been restored under the watchful eye of a preservation-minded city. The 16th-century cellar has been converted into a café, where you can order coffee, chocolate, iced soft drinks, soft ice cream, and Swedish coffee breads from the restaurant's own bakery.

More Expensive Choices

Latona (Eklund's Kro in the Old Town), 79 Västerlanggatan (tel. 11-32-60), which opened in 1971, is an excellent example of the cellar restaurant tradition so popular in Stockholm's Gamla Stan. In a remodeled ancient building, Holger Eklund has installed comfortable private alcoves and larger dining areas. Weather permitting, you may dine on the patio. Carl Larsson paintings decorate the main dining room, which has vaulted ceilings of medieval origin. A marinated reindeer filet is a specialty, but less expensive dishes are available, such as lövbiff with onions and baked potato. All are served with bread and butter and potatoes. The chef is noted for his oyster menu. A favorite dish is crisply fried Baltic herring served with mustard sauce. A complete repast could easily reach 175 kronor per person at this super-splurge choice. Latona is open from 11:30 a.m. until 1 a.m. weekdays, and from 1 p.m. until 1 a.m. weekends. Some of the cellars are from the 13th century. The Latona is on four different levels, three of which are below street level. In summer, you can enjoy a drink in the courtyard. It is closed on Monday.

For a gastronomic adventure, head for **Källaren Diana,** 2 Brunnsgränd (tel. 10-73-10), which is rightly considered one of the 10 best restaurants in Stockholm. The building was originally owned by an ironmonger and merchant from Dalarna. His brother-in-law is credited with introducing the potato to Sweden, and in the brick cellar of this house, he stored the original potatoes which were to transform the eating habits of a country. When the cellar was dug out, the beautiful vaults were turned into a restaurant, which is one of the most charming and cozy—it's also expensive—in the Old Town. If you're on a tight budget, the best time to go is at lunch when good home-style Swedish cookery is featured, meals costing from 85 kronor ($10.20) and up. At night the extensive à la carte menu places its emphasis on fish and game, such as fresh salmon or reindeer steak in a creamy morel sauce with fried potatoes. At that time, count on spending around 225 kronor ($27) for not only a good meal but a unique one.

Stortorgskällaren, 7 Stortorget (tel. 10-55-33), is in many ways one of my favorite restaurants in Stockholm. The sight which greets visitors is a warmly decorated and very popular piano bar (see "Nightlife" section) on the street level off a charming square in the old town, just opposite the severely neoclassic Stock Exchange. If you go to the bottom of a flight of very old stone steps, you'll find yourself amid the living foundations of the oldest part of Stockholm, in cellars whose vaulted ceilings date from the 15th century.

Although the walls and the crudely elegant iron chandeliers are very old, the plush carpeting, the subtle lighting, and the sophisticated table settings have only been here since 1982, when the husband and wife team of Asa Deckeman and Lise Marcus improved standards dramatically in what had been a less desirable restaurant. Today, you're likely to find the best names in the capital dining here amid the fresh flowers and the antique pewter. In summer, diners can choose an outdoor table with a view of the square.

The menu changes often, but one of the most tempting ways to begin your meal is with an ice-filled wooden tray loaded with all the impeccably fresh fruits of the sea that the Baltic coast can provide, served with at least three sauces, a dollop of caviar, a slice of aromatic cheese, and all the toast you want. Your meal might also include saddle of veal with calvados, filet of reindeer with black-currant sauce, fried Norwegian salmon in cream sauce, house-style fish soup, hot scallop pâté with herb sauce, and chicken liver mousse with apples and wal-nuts. Expect to spend 300 kronor ($36) and up for a complete meal. If you pre-fer a solitary table for two, surrounded by the iron grates and vintage bottles of the well-stocked wine cellar (made more festive with candles and fresh flowers), you should request it when you phone for a reservation. It's open for lunch and dinner seven days a week.

If you prefer a less expensive restaurant, where both the setting and the crowd are less formal, you can try **Stortorgsfisken,** 7 Stortorget (tel. 20-63-60), next door the place just visited. Graced like its neighbor with summertime out-door tables which look over the colorful façades of the 14th-century houses around it, the fish restaurant is under the same management as the Stortorgskällaren, and it's attractive, trendy, intimate, and fun. Part of the decor includes illuminated plexiglass columns filled with bubbling water, unusu-al chandeliers, a long curved bar, and groupings of immaculate tables. Special-ties include a full array of broiled, steamed, or grilled fish, such as halibut and shellfish (including oysters and fresh lobster). Full meals cost around 145 kronor ($17.40). Like its neighbor, the Stortorgsfisken is open for lunch and dinner from 11:30 a.m. to 11 p.m. seven days a week.

Den Gyldene Freden, 51 Österlanggatan (tel. 10-12-59), dating from 1722 and owned by the Swedish Academy, is the oldest restaurant in Gamla Stan. Its interior looks as if a pleasantly tinted coat of brown gravy had been washed over the walls, the furniture, and the paintings. This produces a warmly textured in-terior lit up on dark nights by pools of light from the candles placed on each table. It's important to reserve ahead here, but even if you do, there's some-times no maître d'hôtel to guide newcomers to their tables. However, if you, like the Swedish troubadours who used to meet here, have chosen this place, you will enjoy meat and game dishes such as saddle of hare with pepper sauce, roast pheasant with cognac sauce, roast filet of reindeer with a morel-flavored cream sauce, and good fish dishes such as poached salmon trout with hollan-daise. Full meals range upward from 310 kronor ($37.20) and are served Mon-day through Friday from 11:30 till midnight and every Sunday from 1 p.m. till 10 p.m. This restaurant is dear to Scandinavian art lovers because it was restored in 1922 by one of Sweden's most famous artists, Anders Zorn.

Fem Små Hus, 10 Nygränd (tel. 10-87-75). If you happen to stand here on a busy night, you can see legions of taxis delivering parties of diners at what seem to be three-minute intervals. That's in keeping with the reputation of this histor-ic restaurant which is furnished like the interior of a private castle. Its floor plan is actually composed of the ground floors of five houses, each dating from the 16th or 17th century. There has been a tavern in one of the five—and, legend says, a notorious one—since 1694.

When the five houses were joined by ICA, a Swedish restaurant chain, they hired one of the foremost architects of Scandinavia. The antiques and paintings came from as far away as London and Amsterdam, with a few of the more valu-able ones dating from around the time the oldest of the five houses was con-structed. Today, owner Roland Person, a former manager who purchased the establishment from his employer, maintains high standards with the sophistica-tion of a professional, directing a trained staff in all the niceties worthy of the surroundings.

After being shown to a candlelit table somewhere in the nine rooms of the labyrinthine interior, you can order such specialties as coquilles St. Jacques, slices of fresh salmon in chablis, lobster-stuffed filet of sole in champagne sauce, braised scallops with saffron sauce, terrine of duckling with goose liver and truf-fles, filet of beef with herb sauce, and sorbets with seasonal fruits and berries. Expect to spend around 290 kronor ($34.80) for a full meal, which will be served between 11:30 a.m. and 11:45 p.m. weekdays, between 1 and 11:45 p.m. on Saturday, and between 1 and 10:45 p.m. on Sunday. Reservations are important.

BIG-SPLURGE RESTAURANTS IN THE CENTER: Caesar Restaurant, 4 Fredrikshovsgatan (tel. 60-15-99), a short walk from the Strandvägen, near the bridge to Djurgården, comes as close as one can get to a Left Bank French bistro in Stockholm. Its regular clientele includes writers, artists, and embassy personnel. The menu is posted on a blackboard hanging against a stone wall. The walls are a showcase for both struggling and well-known artists, and sales are made on the spot.

Caesar is an old restaurant specializing in Swedish home-cooking, such as elk steak with a chanterelle sauce, plus a few French specialties. A tiny kitchen, limited storage facilities, and an old-fashioned chef de cuisine have over the years formed a tradition for food made in time-honored ways from the best raw materials. Therefore the menu is changed daily and written up on a blackboard. Every Wednesday there is a special fish evening with a more ambitious menu. Prices are a little higher but the results are worth it. There is a 13% service charge, and tipping is not necessary.

All of the personnel speak English, and all are glad to help with translation or improvisation of the menu. A meal will cost from 175 kronor ($21). The kitchen is open from 11 a.m. until 9 p.m., but often guests are around until 10:30.

Prinsens, 4 Mäster Samuelsgatan (tel. 10-13-31), a two-minute walk from Stureplan, is a favorite haunt of artists and increasing loads of foreign visitors, who drift in for leisurely dining to the sounds of soft piano music. Later in the evening the restaurant takes on some of the quality of a drinking club. Not surprisingly, its dynamism and sense of style attract a lot of writers and theater people. The cookery is tasty and talented, notably the continental dishes such as spaghetti alla bolognese. You can order lunch as early as 11 a.m., dinner from 4 p.m. on. For the privilege, you'll pay from 180 kronor ($21.60).

Bakfickan, 12 Jakobs Torg (tel. 24-27-00) is tucked away like a hip pocket (that's what its name means) in the back of what is perhaps Stockholm's poshest restaurant, the Operakällaren, in the Royal Opera House at the harbor. For the visitors who want a chic place in which to dine for a moderate price, Bakfickan does very nicely. Everybody from fashion beauties to playwrights can be found here occupying the stools around the marble-topped, horseshoe-shaped counter. Although its food is from the same kitchen as the Operakällaren, its prices are bearable. This is a sophisticated version of home-cooking which the Swedes call *husmanskost.* The menu is in English, and every day of the week a different specialty is featured. Main dishes include such fare as boiled beef with horseradish sauce, potato pancakes with pork, and fresh grilled herring with juniperberry and a baked potato. A bowl of soup or a piece of pie is always the best choice to begin or end a meal here, which is likely to cost from 120 kronor ($14.40). The Bakfickan is open Monday through Friday from 11:30 a.m. till midnight; closed on Sunday. On Saturday it serves only till 8 p.m. However, from July 5 to August 5, it is closed.

The **Sturehof,** 2 Stureplan (tel. 14-27-50), in the heart of Stockholm, draws an attractive crowd of tourists during the summer and business people in winter and has done so since the turn of the century. In front is a Scottish-type pub especially crowded in the evening with eligible, beer-drinking Swedish bachelors; but in the rooms beyond, fish is the major attraction, including Swedish lobsters and oysters. Fried plaice is served along with grilled sole. Boiled salmon with hollandaise is a favorite dish, as is the fresh shrimp. Both courses might be preceded with assorted herring or else mussel soup. The Sturehof offers as well a daily menu consisting of genuine Swedish *husmanskost* (home-cooking) that is much cheaper. You can have a tray lunch in the pub for 90 kronor ($10.80) and up; otherwise, you will part with 230 kronor ($27.60) for a fish dinner. The restaurant is open between 11:30 a.m. and 11:30 p.m.

A warmly appealing restaurant which might be many things to many people is the **Brända Tomten,** 13 Stureplan (tel. 11-49-59). It contains two darkly paneled levels, both maintained by ICA-Restauranger, Sweden's largest privately owned restaurant chain. A receptionist near the entrance will guide you to the area best suited for your needs, which may be the basement bar area, illuminated with pierced tin hanging lamps, or the upstairs restaurant, where a drink order is usually accompanied by food.

The ambience is intimate, even in this spacious place and with a widely varying type of clientele showing up as the day progresses. The restaurant is open seven days a week, beginning the day with a complete breakfast that costs 30 kronor ($3.60) for an eye-opener. Menu specialties upstairs include something called a herring clover, which is four kinds of herring, sour cream, and garnishes, as well as mushroom soup, shrimp omelets, fish and meat dishes such as pork noisettes with pineapple and cherries, steak with béarnaise and french fries, and an alcohol-soused concoction, flavorfully known as drunken beef. Full meals cost around 200 kronor ($24), although a simple main course can begin for as little as 50 kronor ($6). The downstairs bar is closed Sunday and Monday but open every other day from 6 p.m. to midnight.

Djurgårdsbrunns Wärdshus, 68 Djurgårdsbrunnsvägen (tel. 67-90-95), is an inn in the Royal Deer Park dating from 1740 and catering to all tastes, from the elegant and aristocratic main dining room to the English-style pub to the outdoor Pavilion, which includes a garden grill in summer. Take a taxi or bus 69 past the U.S. Embassy and the Tower, and enjoy an inexpensive, Swedish home-style lunch in the self-service café at prices from 35 kronor ($4.20), or maybe have just a drink and snack in the pub. For a real splurge meal, the restaurant serves such dishes as grilled salmon with morel butter sauce or noisettes of deer with fresh vegetables. Dinners cost from 210 kronor ($25.20). The pub and restaurant are open Monday to Saturday from 11:30 a.m. to 11:30 p.m. and Sunday from 1 to 6:30 p.m. The café is open daily from 10 a.m. to 5 p.m. Watch out for the reindeer.

Restaurant Mälardrottningen, Riddarholmen (tel. 24-36-00). Even the menu's back cover carries a photo of a mink-swathed Barbara Hutton, heiress to the Woolworth fortune who once owned the vessel on which the restaurant lies. Built in 1924 and at the time the largest power-driven pleasure craft in the world, the yacht *Vanadis,* now the *Mälardrottningen* was donated by Miss Hutton to the British Navy in the early days of World War II. During her brief ownership, however, the heiress and guests bearing some of the most celebrated names of her time were taken by the yacht's crew of 50 to many of the world's ports.

Today, the glistening yacht is permanently moored at a pier off a satellite island off the old city, Gamla Stan. The bar with its richly oiled hardwood and gleaming brass fixtures (which in summer opens onto an exposed deck) and the ship-shape restaurant look just a bit more cramped than when Babs and her retinues used to party on the high seas, although the cuisine is considerably tastier than that usually enjoyed by Barbara (toward the end of her life, she subsisted mainly on Ry-Krisp and coffee).

To get to the upper deck—formerly the wheelhouse—you have to dodge waiters carrying platters of food on the narrow ladders (stairs to you landlubbers). Once you get there, export beer costs 20 kronor. A set menu in the softly lit restaurant below costs 400 kronor ($48). The cuisine is savory, well-prepared, and influenced strongly by nouvelle cuisine, Swedish-style. The staff is about as much fun and as lighthearted as the best of Barbara's guests during the yacht's heyday. For a description of the hotel also contained within this yacht, see the "Where to Stay" section above.

For less elaborate dining, take the double-decker bus 69 to the end of the line, **Blockhus Point,** at the end of the island, where there is a simple open-air cafeteria serving coffee and snacks from 45 kronor ($5.40). You can idle here and watch the many ships passing this point.

FOOD AT SKANSEN: The **Solliden Cafeteria** (tel. 60-10-55) at the open-air museum on Skansen on Djurgården (bus 47), is on the highest peak in the park, and thus offers one of the most panoramic views of any restaurant in the city. It is on two levels; the upper one for the haute cuisine is too haute in price, but the lower level shelters a gigantic self-service cafeteria. The most popular items on the menu are the selections of open-face sandwiches, averaging around 28 kronor ($3.36) per serving, but you can have hot main dishes for around 45 kronor ($5.40). Guests fill their trays and head outside to the terrace tables, where they take in the live entertainment from the bandstand, so good it's often televised. The cafeteria is open in summer from 11 a.m. to 8 p.m., in winter from 10 a.m. till 4 p.m.

At Solliden you can also patronize the **Café Jubilee,** where you are seated at a table and served by beautiful girls. You can order a hot meal for 45 kronor ($5.40) and up. The window tables, of course, have the best view over Stockholm. The café is also fully licensed and serves daily from 11:30 a.m. to 6 p.m.

ALL YOU WANT FOR BREAKFAST: You can eat as much as you want at the **Central Station Restaurant** (Centralens Restaurang) (tel. 24-44-65) in the heart of Stockholm. For about 45 kronor ($5.40) you can help yourself from the buffet from 6:30 to 9:30 a.m. daily (on Sunday from 8 to 10:30 a.m.). A breakfast here will fortify you until dinner. The new art nouveau interior has a touch of the *Orient Express,* suggesting luxury. You can also visit for lunch as well as dinner, as it stays open until midnight. The Central Cocktail Bar is an excellent meeting place, and you can have fun in the casino, enjoying roulette and the dice table.

LUNCHING AT "THE MODERN": **Modern Museum Cafeteria** (tel. 10-66-39), on the tiny island of Skeppsholmen, near the three-masted schooner A/F *Chapman,* is a luncheon and tea café in one corner of the main gallery. Weather permitting, the best way to dine here is to load up a tray at the counter, then take it out to the garden, with its sculpture, umbrella tables, and flower-bordered paths. The daily specials are the least expensive fare, going for 35 kronor ($4.20). Beer and wine are available. Art posters bedeck the walls, and outside is a garden. The café is open daily from noon to 9 p.m.

SPECIAL ATMOSPHERIC CHOICES: **Stadhuskållaren,** 105 Stadhuset (Town Hall) (tel. 50-54-54). Ragner Östberg, the architect who designed the renovations of the fortress-like city hall, also allowed provisions for the inclusion of a grandly dignified pair of restaurants in the building's basement. The entrance, which sits close to the edge of the water, is surrounded with the oversize handmade bricks that the monument is built of and set with a beautifully carved and geometrically patterned wooden door. The chefs who cook the food served in the magnificently paneled and vaulted interior also prepared the banquet for the annual Nobel prize winners, a fact which the savory courses make understandable.

The interior is divided into two sections, the Skänken, which serves only at lunchtime (from 11 a.m. to 2 p.m. weekdays except Saturday and Sunday), and the Stora Matsalen (open weekdays from 11:30 a.m. to 11:30 p.m. and Saturday from 2 to 11:30 p.m.; closed Sunday). A 140-krona ($16.80) fixed-price meal is served at lunchtime. Otherwise, more expensive fixed-price meals, priced at 200 kronor ($24) and 240 kronor ($28.80), are offered along with à la carte meals.

Coco and Carmen, 7 Banérgatan (tel. 60-11-05), is an immensely appealing restaurant which might best be enjoyed at lunchtime. It was set up about a decade ago by a husband and wife team fortuitously named Coco and Carmen Frisk. They mutually decided that the semiresidential neighborhood where they lived needed a stylish restaurant serving light lunches loaded with flavor. They transformed what had been a bakery (the cast-iron doors of the ovens are still visible against the tile walls leading to a back room) into a trendily minimalist decor loaded with palms and extraordinary paintings executed by Coco's mother. The façade is turn-of-the-century curved glass, although the interior might be called art deco, its effect heightened by the use of three or four chairs made around 1930 for the Stockholm World Exposition. Meals could include hot or cold avocado soup, vichyssoise, avocado with bacon salad, club sandwiches, cheese pie with parmesan, an assortment of frequently changing casserole dishes and beer or wine. You'll pay from 120 kronor ($14.40) up to eat here.

Garbo, 32 Blekingegatan (tel. 41-06-08). Movie lovers will appreciate the presence of this slickly decorated restaurant inside the ground floor of Greta Gustaffson's birthplace. That, perhaps, means little to most visitors until they realize that Greta Gustaffson was the original name of Greta Garbo, whose childhood home owners Mikael Sundberg and Kristina Söderlund (who work at the dinner and lunch hour, respectively) have practically made a tongue-in-cheek cult headquarters. Unfortunately, the reclusive Ms. Garbo has never made an appearance at the restaurant. (Letters of invitation have been returned unopened.) This does not prevent this place from doing a land-office business. This is especially true at lunch, when it's filled with polite businesspeople who gravitate to what might be the best restaurant in the neighborhood.

Many of the accoutrements in this establishment are said to have been connected with the legendary Swedish beauty. Her movie stills decorate the carefully groomed walls, designed by a top Scandinavian decorator. Even the plates have a silhouette of one of Greta's more dramatic profiles. A camera said to have filmed her is affixed above the bar, and one of her elegant dresses (from *The Legend of Gösta Berling)* covers the curves of a mannequin holding a lighted candle.

The menu here changes every month, although it is likely to include specialties such as tagliatelle à la Garbo (pasta with smoked salmon), pâté of venison, blackfish ragoût, shrimp with red sauce, and veal stuffed with exotic mushrooms (duxelles). Full meals cost from 180 kronor ($21.60) up and might be terminated with one of the ice-cream concoctions which are named after the reclusive star's most famous roles. Reservations are suggested for this popular place where the voice of Judy Garland provides much of the background music. The place is open daily except Sunday from 11:30 a.m. till 2 p.m. and from 7 p.m. till midnight.

OTHER DINING CHOICES: Hamlet, 8–10 Vasagatan (tel. 10-10-29), across the street from the central train station, offers quick lunches between 11 a.m. and 3 p.m. for less than 45 kronor ($5.40), including a hot meal, beer or milk, salad, coffee, bread, and butter. Hamlet's steak on oakboard is a popular choice from the à la carte menu. A complete meal here is likely to run from 50 kronor ($6) to 125 kronor ($15). The restaurant is decorated in a Swedish-English style with a big bar and pub for drinking guests.

KB Restaurant, 7 Smålandsgatan (tel. 11-02-32), is a traditional artists' hangout in the center of town. The mural is worth chuckling over, for those who like old-fashioned art. Good Swedish cookery, backed up by many continental dishes, is featured. The chef has a superb way of preparing fish. In addition, the best sourdough bread I've ever had in Stockholm is baked here. One reader went even further, declaring the bread "the best I have eaten in my life." A middag costs from 75 kronor ($9), and dinners go for 125 kronor ($15) and up. The restaurant is open Monday to Friday from noon to midnight. On Saturday, its hours are from 5 p.m. to midnight, and it is closed on Sunday, taking an annual vacation from mid-July to mid-August. There is also a relaxed and informal bar.

Tennstopet (The Pewter Tankard), 50 Dalagatan, at the corner of Odengatan (tel. 32-25-18), is an English pub in the northern quarter of town, just two blocks from the Hotel Oden. This is a favorite hangout of newspaper people, students, and assorted intelligentsia. There is a pub on one side, a restaurant on the other. The restaurant is decorated with hunting motifs, along with dark-grained wood and tartan carpeting. Main dishes are likely to include a ragoût of fish and shellfish, salmon schnitzel, plank steak, and the inevitable hamburger special. Full dinners go for 55 kronor ($6.60), including dessert. For lunch, you can have pork chops, vegetable, bread, butter, and coffee for 33 kronor ($3.96), or just order a draft beer for 15 kronor ($1.80), toss some darts, and admire the setting. From Monday to Friday, it is open from 11:30 a.m. to 12:30 a.m., on Saturday from 2 p.m. to 12:30 a.m., and on Sunday from 4 p.m. to 12:30 a.m.

For a firsthand view of all the fruits of a Baltic harvest, you can head for one of the most colorful indoor markets anywhere in Scandinavia. It's called the **Östermalms Saluhall,** and its entrance is at 31 Nybrogatan. Housed within an astonishingly clean, grangelike building whose neo-Romanesque brick façade is considered one of the architecturally noteworthy constructions of Stockholm, the market attracts scores of cheese, meat, vegetable, and fish merchants who combine efforts to supply the food for much of the area. After you walk around admiring the produce (and wishing a market like this could be found close to your home), you may want a Swedish snack or even a full meal at one of the restaurants set up under the soaring roof.

One of these, the Örtagarden, has already been reviewed under the heading "Salad and Vegetarian Restaurants," above. Others are:

Restaurant Tysta Mari, Östermalms Saluhall, 31 Nybrogatan (tel. 62-17-28). You select what you want from a glass counter and eat it under a canopy set out in the middle of one corner of the bustling marketplace. A meal costs from 90 kronor ($10.80) here and might include a range of open-face sandwiches, lobster soup, and salmon pudding.

Another establishment, this one with an oyster bar, is at the opposite corner of the market. **Lisa Elmquist,** 31 Nybrogatan (tel. 60-92-32), is slightly more elaborate, with a better defined seating area that looks like a pleasant bistro under a tent at some small town's country fair. Here, all sorts of shrimp dishes are sold, including with avocado or cocktail sauce, costing around 40 kronor ($4.80) for a dish of the freshly netted crustaceans which you'll peel and enjoy, perhaps with a cold beer. Full meals, whose specialties are written on a blackboard, cost from 90 kronor ($10.80). Both restaurants are open from 9 a.m. till 6 p.m. weekdays, from 9 a.m. till 3 p.m. Saturday. They're closed Sunday.

McDonald's has invaded, of course, and young Swedes seemed to like "Big Mac," at least to judge from the crowds. The capital offers seven branches —at 4 Kungsgatan, 71 Sveavägen, 32 Sct. Eriksgatan, 91 Götgatan, 13 Norrlandsgatan, 50 Folkungagatan, and 88 Hornsgatan. The chain sisters are open daily from 10 a.m. to midnight, charging around 90 kronor ($10.80) for a light meal. For families with children, the one at 88 Hornsgatan is especially recommended (take the subway to Mariatorget). Near the toy museum, it has a miniature fairground inside for children, and they dine sitting in a toy train. Parents can inspect them nearby. After a Big Mac, the children can be taken to the toy museum.

Chapter XII

STOCKHOLM: WHAT TO SEE AND DO

1. The Top Sights
2. Other Attractions
3. Stockholm After Dark
4. Shopping in Stockholm
5. Sigtuna
6. Skokloster Castle
7. Uppsala
8. Gamla Uppsala
9. Gripsholm Castle
10. Tullgarn Castle
11. Vaxholm

WHETHER IT'S DRINKING mead from a horn near the ancient Viking burial mounds in Old Uppsala, paying your respects to the Bernadottes at the Royal Palace, searching out the various shades of blond (or blonde) at the discos of Gröna Lund's Tivoli, grandly attending a chamber concert at an old manor house, sailing your own boat on the archipelago, or sharing in the histrionics at the most perfectly preserved 18th-century theater in the world, Stockholm is a smörgåsbord that has something for everybody.

KEY TO STOCKHOLM: The Key to Stockholm costs four different prices, from 50 kronor ($6) to 160 kronor ($19.20) and provides free entrance to most of Stockholm's major attractions. Its total worth is 500 kronor ($60) and up, depending on which card you buy. Among the many benefits of the card: free travel on Stockholm's public transportation system, free sightseeing by boat and by bus, free entrance and excursion to Drottningholm Castle. The card provides entrance to some 30 of the major museums and attractions. The three-day pass can be bought at the tourist office in Stockholm.

1. The Top Sights

Unless he or she is prepared to stick around till Lake Mälaren freezes over, the visitor to Stockholm—when faced with its number of sightseeing treasures—needs help in pruning. In museums, the city is as rich as the banking dynasty of Wallenberg, but its natural attractions—such as the archipelago—also are important. That's why I have compiled this personal list of the most important sights, but it will be followed by other attractions for those with extra days. I'll lead off with one of the newest sightseeing attractions, which you may want to visit first, not only for a thrill, but for orientation purposes.

The highest artificial structure in Scandinavia, the **Kaknäs Tower** (tel. 67-80-30) soars in the northern district of Djurgården, a ten-minute ride on bus 69 from Nybroplan. The radio and television tower stands 508 feet high. Two elevators that claim to be the fastest in Europe take visitors to an observation platform, where they can see everything from the cobblestone streets of the Old Town to the new concrete and glass structures, even the archipelago. Panoramic photographs help you to identify everything you see. The look-out floors at the very top are open from 9 a.m. to midnight during the summer season and for somewhat shorter periods during the rest of the year. Admission is 7 kronor (84¢) for adults, 3.50 kronor (42¢) for children.

The Kaknäs Tower isn't the only such in Stockholm—it's just the newest. (The Swedes seem to have a fetish for towers.) One of the longest established watchtowers is the **Katarina Elevator** (subway to Slussen). It costs 4 kronor (48¢) round trip. There's another tower at Gröna Lund's Tivoli amusement park on Djurgården (bus 47). More about this later.

Now, for the superstar sight, we head for the:

(1) ROYAL FLAGSHIP WASA: This 17th-century man-of-war is the Number 1 sight in all of Scandinavia and for good reason. Housed in a museum (tel. 22-39-80) specially constructed for it at Djurgården near Skansen (bus 47), the *Wasa* is considered the world's oldest identified salvaged Scandinavian ship.

On a bright sunny Sunday, August 10, 1628, the Royal Flagship *Wasa*—ordered built by Gustavus Adolphus II—set sail on her maiden voyage. But a gust of wind caused her to keel over, and she sank into the murky Stockholm harbor. Attempts by the experts of that day to salvage her failed, although more than 50 of her bronze cannons were saved, a miracle for those times.

The *Wasa*, famed in its day, faded from the public memory, until discovered in 1956 by Anders Franzén, an amateur marine archeologist, who deserves the credit—and subsequent fame. In one of the amazing salvage projects of our time, navy divers arranged to have the *Wasa* lifted from a depth of 110 feet and towed to shallower water. Six tunnels were pumped beneath her hull, and steel cables were fastened to lift her up.

On April 24, 1961, with a great deal of the world looking on, the *Wasa* was raised after having lain in clay deposits for more than three centuries. And to everyone's amazement, she was fantastically well preserved. But following her rise from the depths, the fight to keep her that way began with the spraying of polyglycol.

Attractive guides escort tourists around the ship every hour on the half hour, beginning at 10:30 a.m. The museum is open from mid-June to mid-August from 9:30 a.m. to 7 p.m. (10 a.m. to 5 p.m. otherwise), charging 15 kronor ($1.80) for adults, 7 kronor (63¢) for students, and 4 kronor (48¢) for children.

A recent film shot about the *Wasa* story lasts a half hour (English subtitles) and is shown every hour.

More than 4000 coins, carpenter's tools, "Lübeck gray" sailor pants, fishbones, and what have you were found aboard. All of the *Wasa* sculptures—97% of the 700 were found—are back on the ship, which looks stunning now that it is once again carrying grotesque faces, lion masks, fish-fashioned bodies, and other carvings, some still with the original paint and gilt left.

There is a new exhibition showing the results on ongoing research: 3000 fragments of textile show how coarse woolen cloth was sewn into Spanish-inspired sailors' clothing, while a bottle of rum, a clay pipe, and a backgammon board indicate that a seafaring life was not all drudgery. New light has also been shed on the most crucial of questions about the *Wasa:* Why did she capsize?

The great cabin of the ship has been rebuilt with the original oak panels decorated with elegant woodcarvings and ingenious fold-out beds. Visitors can walk right through the cabin. Also, a 16-foot-long interior cut-through model has been built. Ninety dolls representing soldiers and crew show life aboard.

The Swedish National Board of Public Planning held a competition among Nordic architects for a new and permanent *Wasa* Museum, which is planned to open during the 1988–1989 season.

(2) SKANSEN: Often called Old Sweden in a nutshell, this open-air museum is on Djurgården, near Gröna Lund's Tivoli. From Lapland to Skåne, more than 150 dwellings, primarily from the 18th and 19th centuries, have been brought here and reassembled on some 75 acres of parkland.

The exhibits range from a windmill to a manor house to a complete town quarter. Browsers can explore the old workshops and see where the early book publishers, silversmiths, and druggists plied their trade. Many handicrafts for which Swedes later became noted (glassblowing, for example) are demonstrated here, along with the traditional peasant specialties, such as weaving and churning. For a tour of the buildings, be at the park no later than 5 p.m. (3 p.m. off-season). Free guided tours are conducted daily in summer—every hour, beginning at 11 a.m. The admission fee to the park is 14 kronor ($1.68) for adults, 5 kronor (60¢) for children. But the fun doesn't stop here. Prim and proper chamber music recitals are given on Monday in July at the Skogaholm manor house; there's folk dancing to the fiddler's tune; and open-air symphonic concerts strike a cultural note. In summer, international stars perform at Skansen. Check the information office for these special events.

Skansen also has a zoo, home to everything from penguins to polar bears. It has as well a lot for children, including pony rides and a trip on a miniature train. There is also a baby zoo with small animals.

The park remains open in summer from 8 a.m. to 11:30 p.m. There's much to do at night here, and many places to eat—see the previous chapter for the latter, "Stockholm After Dark" in this chapter for the former.

To reach the park, take bus 47 from Nybroplan (or the ferry from Slussen, near the Katarina Elevator) to Gröna Lund, then walk up the hill.

(3) THE MILLES GARDEN: Carl Milles (1875–1955) was the most famous of Swedish sculptors (once a U.S. citizen, living in Michigan). On the island of Lidingö, northeast of Stockholm, is his former villa and sculpture garden beside the sea. Many of the best known works of Milles are displayed here (some are copies), as are works of other artists. Milles, who relied heavily on mythological themes, was a friend of Rodin.

His house and gardens are open daily from May 1 to October 15, 10 a.m. to 5 p.m. (in June and July also open on Tuesday and Thursday evenings, 7 to 9 p.m.). Admission is 12 kronor ($1.44). To reach the gardens, take the underground to Ropsten then board bus 221 (a bus every 15 minutes). Get off at the stop called Foresta. The Milles Garden is directly alongside the Foresta Hotel. This is a quiet residential area.

Most visitors are in the area for lunch. About half a mile away, the **Restaurant Fontana,** 4–6 Baggebytorg, Lidingö (tel. 765-91-98), prepares meals well with quality ingredients. The service, too, is friendly and polite. Including bread and a salad, the price of main dishes averages around 100 kronor ($12) and up. Reader Stanley Barkin, of Arlington, Virginia, found this to be a "bargain whether it be Sweden or the U.S.A."

(4) THE CITY HALL: Built in what is called the National Romantic Style, the Stockholm City Hall or **Stadshuset,** 1 Hantverkargatan (tel. 785-90-00), on the island of Kungsholmen, is considered one of the finest examples of modern architecture in Europe. It was designed by Ragnar Östberg, famed for his blending of innovative and traditional designs in architecture.

Completed in 1923, the red-brick structure is dominated by a lofty square tower 348 feet high, itself topped by three crowns, the symbol of Sweden and the national coat-of-ams. There are two courts, the open civic court and the interior covered court. The Blue Hall never got the bluish color tone on the brick walls as originally intended, as the architect was too entranced with the texture of the brick. This room is also used for banquets and other occasions. Following the awarding of the Nobel Prize, the banquet is given here. Best known is the Golden Hall, the most magnificent banquet room of the city hall. On its walls are about 18 million pieces of gold and colored mosaics made of special glass. The splendor of the Golden Hall was created by Prof. Einer Forseth, and the room can seat 700 persons. The southern gallery contains murals by Prince Eugen, the painter prince. The 101 City Council members meet in the council chamber with a predominant red tone, an old color tradition in Sweden.

Guided tours of the city hall are held at 10 a.m. daily; on Sunday both at 10 a.m. (free) and again at noon. The tower is open daily from 11 a.m. to 3 p.m., May 1 to September 30. Admission is 5 kronor (60¢) for adults (children under 12, free). To reach the city hall, on the shores of Lake Mälaren, take bus 48, 53, or 62, or the subway to Centralen.

(5) THE ROYAL PALACE: The pride of Gamla Stan, the Royal Palace (tel. 11-85-61) is one of the few in Europe still used as an abode for a monarch that may be visited by the general public. Built principally in the Italian baroque style between 1691 and 1754, the palace contains more than 600 rooms, 20 of which are occupied by the king.

Visitors may walk through the council chamber where the king and his ministers meet several times a year. The State Apartment with three magnificent baroque ceilings and fine tapestries, the Bernadotte Apartment, and the Guest Apartment are on view. They are beautifully furnished in Swedish rococo, Louis XVI, and Empire style.

Even the most hurried of visitors may want to see the changing of the guard ceremonies. From January through May, that is possible from 12:10 p.m. on Wednesday and Saturday. On Sunday, the guard is changed at 1:10 p.m. These same hours are also in effect from September through December. However, from June through August, it is possible to see the changing of the guard from Monday to Friday at 12:10 p.m. On Saturday, the guard is changed at 10 a.m. and again at 2 p.m. On Sunday, it is changed at 1:10 p.m.

The State Apartments, where the king swears in new governments, include the State, Bernadotte, and Guest apartments already referred to, along with ballrooms, banqueting halls, and parade bed-chambers. The apartments, charging 10 kronor ($1.20) for adults and 5 kronor (60¢) for children, are open from May to August daily except Monday from 10 a.m. to 3 p.m. On Sunday, hours are from noon to 3 p.m. In the off-season months, the apartments may be viewed daily except Monday from noon to 3 p.m.

The Treasury is also worth a visit, exhibiting one of the most celebrated collections of crown jewels in Europe. You will see a dozen crowns, sceptres, and orbs, along with stunningly beautiful pieces of antique jewelry. The display is in the cellar of the palace, which can be visited from May until mid-September from 10 a.m. to 4 p.m. including on Monday when the State Apartments are closed. Sunday hours are from noon to 4 p.m. Off-season hours are from 11 a.m. to 3 p.m. daily (on Sunday, from noon to 4 p.m.). Admission is 7 kronor (84¢) for adults and 5 kronor (60¢) for children.

Nearly all visitors want to head for the Royal Armoury, also housed in the cellars of the palace. In days when ostentation was in flower, kings rode around in these elegant, gilded coaches, which reached their zenith of finery at coronation time. You can be shown, as well, coronation costumes that date from the 16th century. Against a backdrop of a sound-and-light effect, you can also view weapons and armor. Guided tours are conducted weekdays except Saturday at 2 p.m. (there is also a Sunday tour for adults at 3 p.m., and a special tour for children at 2 p.m.) In summer, visits are possible weekdays from 10 a.m. to 4 p.m. (on weekends from 11 a.m. to 4 p.m.). Admission is 7 kronor (84¢) for adults and 5 kronor (60¢) for children. From September to April it is closed on Monday, but can be visited Tuesday to Friday from 10 a.m. to 4 p.m. (on weekends from 11 a.m. to 4 p.m.).

Since the present-day Royal Palace was built on the ruins of the old Three Crowns Castle, symbolizing the union of Sweden, Denmark, and Norway, there are many remains still left of this original structure which was founded in 1187. What's left over can be viewed in the Palace Museum, which is open daily from June to August, including Monday and Sunday, from noon to 3 p.m., charging an admission of 3 kronor (36¢) for adults and only 1 krona (12¢) for children.

One king, Gustav III, who ruled from 1746, was a devoted collector of sculpture from the days of the Roman Empire. He even went to Italy himself on what he termed a "shopping expedition." Many of the sculptures he purchased, apparently, were fakes, but others were genuine. You'll have to ask the guide, and you can do so daily, including Sunday, from noon to 3 p.m. for an admission of 3 kronor (36¢) for adults and 1 krona (12¢) for children. Visits are possible only from June to August.

Finally, the Hall of State, where the present king makes his "State of the Nation" addresses, is also on view from May to September from noon to 3 p.m. for an admission fee of 2 kronor (24¢) for adults and 1 krona (12¢) for children. In October, the hall is also open from noon to 3 p.m. on Saturday and Sunday.

(6) RIDDARHOLM CHURCH: On the tiny island of Riddarholmen, next to Gamla Stan, is this old church, founded in the 13th century as a Franciscan monastery, now the pantheon of Swedish kings and queens.

Almost all the royal heads of state are entombed here, with the exception of the elusive Christina, who is buried in Rome. But her father, Gustavus Adolphus II, who saw Swedish power reach its peak, is buried in a Dutch Renaissance chapel. Other notables include the soldier-warrior, Charles XII. Dag Hammarskjöld's father, a former Swedish prime minister, has a shield at Riddarholm Church, indicating that he was a Knight of the Seraphim Order.

There are three principal chapels of royalty, including one—the Bernadotte wing—that belongs to the present ruling family. Queen Desideria, the first queen of the Bernadotte dynasty, who hated the long Swedish winters and longed for the splendor of Paris, is buried here in a cold green marble sarcophagus.

Riddarholm—the second-oldest church in Stockholm—is open from May 2 to August 31, 10 a.m. to 3 p.m. (1 to 3 p.m. on Sunday). Admission is 3 kronor (36¢) for adults, 2 kronor (24¢) for children.

(7) THE NATIONAL MUSEUM OF ART: At the tip of a peninsula on Södra Blasieholmshamnen, a short walk from the Royal Opera House and the Grand Hotel, is the Swedish state's treasure house of paintings and sculpture—by both domestic and foreign artists.

The museum's former director, Carl Nordenfalk, was once quoted as saying: "Had she [Christina] retained the crown and continued building her collection, we would now have a Prado or a Louvre here." The Prado isn't—nor an Uffizi—but the Swedish collection includes a wide assortment of masterpieces by artists such as Rembrandt and Rubens *(Sacrifices to Venus)*.

The first floor is devoted to applied arts (silverware, handicrafts, porcelain, Empire furnishings, and the like), but the first-time visitor, if his or her time is limited, may want to head for the second floor to view Sweden's great collection of painting and sculpture.

Among the paintings from Northern Europe is Lucas Cranach's most amusing *Venus and Cupid.* Also displayed is a rare collection of Russian icons, most of them—such as *St. George and the Dragon*—from the Moscow School of the mid-16th century.

On view is an exceptional number of excellent paintings by such masters as Perugino *(St. Sebastian),* Ribera (his oft-rendered *Martyrdom of Bartolomé),* El Greco *(Peter and Paul),* Giovanni Bellini *(Portrait of Christ),* Lotto *(Portrait of a Man),* and Poussin *(Bacchus).* The gallery contains some outstanding Flemish works, notably Pieter Brueghel II's *Winter Landscape,* Pieter de Hooch's *Interior with Mother at Cradle,* and Jan Brueghel's *Jesus Preaching from the Boat.*

Room 45 is perhaps the most important in the entire gallery, with one whole wall featuring the works of Rembrandt *(Portrait of an Old Man* and *Portrait of an Old Woman),* along with his impressions of a maid (one of the more famous works in Stockholm). Here also is *The Oath of the Batavians.*

In yet another room Watteau teaches a *Lesson in Love,* and another salon is noted for its Venetian works by Guardi and Canaletto, as well as English portraits by Gainsborough and Reynolds.

Exhibited also are important modern works—Manet's *Parisienne,* Degas's dancers, Rodin's nude male *(Copper Age)* and his bust of Victor Hugo, Van Gogh's *Light Movements in Green,* landscapes by Cézanne, Gauguin, and Pissarro, paintings by Renoir, notably *La Grenouillère.*

The museum is open Tuesday through Sunday from 10 a.m. to 4 p.m., charging 12 kronor ($1.44) admission except on Tuesday, when it's free. It is also open Tuesday evening until 9.

(8) NORDIC MUSEUM: On the island of Djurgården (buses 44 and 47), the **Nordiska Museet** (tel. 22-41-20) contains an impressive collection of implements, costumes, and furnishings depicting life in Sweden from the 1500s to the present day. It is the most outstanding museum of national life in Scandinavia, perhaps in the world, and houses more than one million objects.

Highlights of the rich and varied collection include dining tables laid with food and all the implements, one from each century; period costumes ranging from matching garters and ties for men to the purple flowerpot hats of the strolling ladies of the 1890s. Anglers head for the basement, where there's an extensive exhibit of the tools of the Swedish fishing trade, plus relics once of use to nomadic Lapps. The museum, charging 10 kronor ($1.20) for adults, 5 kronor (60¢) for children, is open daily from June to August from 10 a.m. to 4 p.m. (on weekdays from noon to 5 p.m.). From September to May, it is closed Monday but open Tuesday to Friday to 10 a.m. to 4 p.m. It remains open on Thursday until 8 p.m. On off-season Saturdays and Sundays, hours are from noon to 5 p.m.

(9) DROTTNINGHOLM PALACE AND THEATER: On an island in Lake Mälaren, Drottningholm ("Queen's Island)—dubbed the Versailles of Sweden—lies about seven miles from Stockholm and is easily reached by boat, escorted motorcoach tour, bus, or subway.

Reflecting French baroque trends of the 18th century, Drottningholm, with its courtly art, royal furnishings, and Gobelin tapestries, is surrounded by fountains and parks. The palace is lived in by the royal family.

Nearby is the Drottningholm Court Theater (tel. 759-03-10), considered the best preserved 18th-century theater in the world, with the original stage machinery and settings still in use. Each summer, between May and September, operas and ballets are staged in full 18th-century regalia, complete with rococo costumes and powdered wigs. Write to the **Drottningholm Court Theater,** Box 27050, S-10251, Stockholm, for a schedule of performances. You may book tickets in advance. Generally, tickets range in price between 35 kronor ($4.20) and 190 kronor ($22.80).

Gustavus III loved this theater, and was himself an accomplished playwright and actor. Under his influence, Drottningholm became the center for the flowering of Swedish art during its "Renaissance" of the 18th century (being king, Gustavus could literally command a performance). In addititon to the stage, the auditorium, and the dressing rooms, the theater also offers to visitors a museum that charts the growth of the stage between the 1500s and 1700s.

During the rococo conquest of Europe, chinoiserie became the height of fashion, as arbiters of taste looked to the Orient for fresh inspiration. Drottningholm wasn't spared that invasion: witness the Chinese Pavilion on the grounds. Visitors wander through its red, yellow, green, and blue salons. Nearby is a place for refreshments (Swedish waffles).

Guided tours of the palace and theater are conducted every hour on the hour. The palace is open weekdays from 11 a.m. to 4:30 p.m.; the theater, from noon to 4:30 p.m. (Sunday, the palace opens at noon, the theater at 1 p.m., both closing at 4:30 p.m.), May through August. In September and October, the hours are 1 to 3 p.m. It costs 10 kronor ($1.20) for adults, 5 kronor (60¢) for children to enter the palace. The Theater Museum and the Chinese Pavilion each charge the same admission.

To reach Drottningholm on your own, take the subway to Brommaplan (18 minutes) and then a Mälaröbuss bus to Drottningholm (in all, about a one-hour ride). To attend performances at the theater, take one of the buses leaving from the Grand Hotel at 7:15 p.m. or from the Central Station at 7:20. But the most romantic way is to go by boat, leaving from the dock near the city hall and costing 32 kronor ($3.84) for adults, 16 kronor ($1.92) for children.

2. Other Attractions

THE ARCHIPELAGO: Stockholm is in what the Swedes call a garden of skerries, more than 24,000 islands (this figure includes some rocks jutting out of the water). In between admiring the fountains of the Milles garden and dancing at Gröna Lund's Tivoli, it is a good change-of-pace adventure to explore some of these islands on an organized tour. Parts of the archipelago—a mighty bulwark in the defense of Stockholm—are inhabited (particularly such resorts as

Vaxholm). Others you can discover in solitude and name after yourself. For any information about boat rentals or the possibility of tying in with another yachting group, go to Sweden House in Kungsträdgården.

GAMLA STAN: The Old Town of Stockholm contains two of our top sights: the Royal Palace and Riddarholm Church. But with its narrow lanes and medieval buildings, Gamla Stan is a major attraction in its own right. The old shops are well worth the trip, and they are backed up by a number of attractive, mainly expensive restaurants.

The **Stortorget,** the old marketplace, is the center of Gamla Stan. Dominated by a rococo palace, the square bears a resemblance to the Grand' Place in Brussels—minus the pure gold leaf. Most of its buildings date from the 16th and 18th centuries (the red building was constructed during the reign of the oft-mentioned Christina). The **Stock Exchange** (open weekdays—free) is housed in an 18th century building. The **Storkvran Church,** or **Great Church,** the oldest church in Stockholm (near the Royal Palace), was founded in the 13th century, but it has been rebuilt many times since. It is the scene of coronations and royal weddings. Kings are also christened here. The most celebrated piece of sculpture is *St. George and the Dragon,* a huge piece of artwork, dating from 1489. The royal pews have been in service for three centuries, and the altar, mainly in ebony and silver, is stunning, dating from 1652. You can also see the *Last Judgment,* a large painting (said to be one of the largest on earth) and the oldest preserved one in Stockholm. This is still a living church, and naturally you will want to confine your sightseeing to times when no services are being conducted. It's open from 9:30 a.m. to 7 p.m. weekdays, 12:30 to 5:30 p.m. on Sunday; admission is free.

PRINCE EUGEN'S WALDERMARSUDDE: This once-royal residence of the painting prince is an art gallery, surrounded by a sculpture garden and overlooking the water. Donated by the prince to the city, Waldermarsudde (tel. 62-18-33) is on Djurgården (bus 47, next to the last stop). The prince, who died in 1947, was considered one of Sweden's major landscape painters. He did the murals at City Hall. The visitor may also find his private collection—works by Edvard Munch, for one—rewarding. At one time, Prince Eugen possessed the largest collection in Sweden. The gardens and park are open from 8 a.m. to 10 p.m. every day. The gallery and house, furnished as he left it, are open every day except Monday from 11 a.m. to 4 p.m. (also from 7 to 9 p.m. on Tuesday and Thursday in summer). While at Waldermarsudde, see the Old Mill, built in 1784 and open only in the summer on Sunday from noon to 4 p.m. Admission is 8 kronor (96¢).

MUSEUM OF MODERN ART: On the tiny island of Skeppsholmen, a short walk from A/F *Chapman,* is this museum of contemporary works by both Swedish and international artists. In addition to changing exhibitions, the museum has a small, but good, collection of cubist art by Picasso, Braque, and Léger. It also contains Matisse's *Apollo* découpage, the famous *Enigma of William Tell* by Salvador Dali, and works by Brancusi, Max Ernst, Giacometti, and Arp, among others. There is, as well, a collection of pop art—from Rauschenberg's *Monogram,* via Oldenburg, to Segal and Rosenquist, to Andy Warhol. A $700,000 collection of the 1960s works of prominent New York artists was presented to the museum by a group of American and Swedish art patrons. Works include the 12-foot-high *Geometric Mouse* by Claes Oldenburg; *Fox Trot,* an early Warhol; and *Total Totality All,* a large sculpture by Louise Nevelson. Outdoors, in front of the museum, are *The Four Elements* by Alexander Calder, and behind and around the house a number of works by Nordic artists have been installed. Farther away, near the Skeppsholmen bridge, is *The Paradise,* a sculpture group by Niki de Saint Phalle and Jean Tinguely. The activities of the museum are wide ranging: a workshop for children, concerts, films, discussions, and theater, among other things. There is a bookshop with posters, cards, books, and reproductions, plus a restaurant with fresh salads and wine that you can also enjoy outdoors in the garden. The museum is open Tuesday through Friday from 11 a.m. to 9 p.m., Saturday and Sunday from 11 a.m. to 5 p.m.; closed Monday. Admission is 15 kronor ($1.80) for adults; children under 16, free. On Thursday, everybody gets in free.

THE THIEL GALLERY: Perhaps by now you've already visited the Painter-Prince Eugen's Waldermarsudde and admired the art there. Surpassing that royal gallery for many visitors is the **Thiel Gallery** (Thielska Galleriet) which stands at a tip of the royal Djurgården. Collected by a financier, banker, and patron of the arts (who subsequently went bankrupt), the gallery contains one of the major art collections of Sweden. Prince Eugen had nothing but loathing from Thiel, and succeeded in getting his gallery located far away from his own.

Once this gallery (tel. 62-58-84) was a meeting place of Swedish artists and poets until the lavish building was acquired by the state, following Thiel's bankruptcy in 1924. Charging 10 kronor ($1.20) admission, it is open year round from noon to 4 p.m., except on Sunday when hours are from 1 to 4 p.m. As you wander through the exhibition, you'll see some of the big names in Scandinavian art, including Norway's Edvard Munch and Sweden's Anders Zorn (see his nude, *In Dreams).* The furniture of Gustav Fjaestad is also displayed. You'll also see a portrait of Nietzsche, whom Thiel greatly admired. Thiel didn't confine his interest just to Scandinavian art, and in time he acquired works by Manet, Rodin, and Toulouse-Lautrec, among others. Thiel is buried on the grounds beneath a statue of Rodin's *Shadow.*

THE STOCKHOLM CITY MUSEUM: At Slussen, beside the Katarina elevator, is the **Stadsmuseet** (tel. 44-07-90), which charges no admission and is open Monday, Friday, Saturday, and Sunday from 11 a.m. to 5 p.m. from June to August. On Wednesday and Thursday, it remains open until 7 p.m. The best known exhibit is the rich Lohe treasure, but they also have a 600-year-old Viking ship, a simulated street from Old Town, an old-time schoolroom, and many relics relating to Stockholm in prehistoric times. If you're visiting out of season, the hours are different: from 11 a.m. to 5 p.m. on Monday, Friday, Saturday, and Sunday, and until 9 p.m. on Wednesday and Thursday.

THE TOY MUSEUM: Stockholms Leksaksmuseum, 1 Mariatorget (tel. 41-61-00). The most poignant part of this museum may be the rows and rows of children's studio portraits which stare out at the glass display cases containing old toys similar to the ones all of us discarded years ago. Today, many of little Olaf's and Elin's childhood toys of 50 years ago are displayed in a tall and narrow house whose floors are connected with steeply angled stairs guaranteed to tire an Olympic athlete but which don't prevent battalions of children from racing up and down at breakneck speed.

If you enter on a school holiday, you may have trouble reaching the unguarded cloakroom because of the dozens of baby carriages which park like badly positioned vehicles in the entryway. Your ticket will cost 10 kronor ($1.20) for adults and 5 kronor (60¢) for children. It will give you the right to examine case after case of old children's book covers, penny cars and trucks, porcelain dolls' heads, doll houses, and a small handful of vintage dolls. There are German-made Suzy miniature sewing machines from the 1920s, a scattering of idle toy steam engines, and model cars and planes patterned after originals, most of which reached the junk heap before World War I. The philosophy of the museum's founders was to create a dialogue between visiting parents, grandparents, and children through exposure to creative toys of another era. The museum is open from Tuesday through Friday from 10 a.m. to 4 p.m. and on weekends from noon to 4 p.m.

FARSTA: Drottningholm Palace and Riddarholm have their place—but the visitor doesn't get a complete picture of Stockholm without visiting one of the expanding satellite cities. Farsta, completed as late as 1960, is the most interesting. It is about six miles from the heart of the city, reached by subway, or else bus 18 to the end of the line. With its traffic-free shopping mall, its bright and airy ultramodern apartment houses, its stores and restaurants, it makes for a good afternoon's outing (also included on a motorcoach tour—see below).

MUSEUM OF FAR EASTERN ANTIQUITIES: This small, intimate museum (tel. 24-42-00), on Skeppsholmen, was opened in 1963 in an old building erected in 1699–1700 as stables for Karl XII's bodyguard. The permanent exhibition consists of archeological objects, fine arts, and handicrafts from China, Japan, Korea, and India. The museum's collection is considered one of the finest and most important of its kind outside the Orient. The exhibition includes an outstanding display of Chinese neolithic painted pottery, ritual bronze vessels, archaic jades, woodcarvings, ivory, lacquerwork, enamelware, Chinese glass, Buddhist sculpture, Chinese painting and calligraphy, T'ang tomb pottery figurines, Sung classical stoneware such as celadon and temmoku, Ming blue and white wares, and Ch'ing porcelain made both for the Chinese and the Western market. The museum is open daily except Monday from noon to 4 p.m. (Tuesday from noon to 9 p.m.). Adults pay 12 kronor ($1.44); students, 6 kronor (72¢); and youths under 16, free. Take bus 43, 46, 55, or 62 to Karl XII Square. The Museum of Far Eastern Antiquities is about a seven-minute walk from there and very near the Museum of Modern Art.

PRIPPORAMA: At Voltavägen, Bromma, this is an unusual museum. With advanced electronic equipment, TV, and films, Pripp's Brewery offers those interested in beer a glimpse into the history and traditions of brewing. Guided tours are by appointment. Telephone 98-15-00. Admission is free. It's closed from June through August.

FOR THE ECOLOGY-MINDED: You won't find the **Thé Hus** (Teahouse) on anyone's official list of Stockholm sights, but it's a fascinating place nonetheless. It is outdoors, around the corner from the Opera, at the foot of the Charles XII Statue. You can have tea here, but the major activity is meeting the people. For the Thé Hus is the gathering place of the ecology-minded Swedes who fought to save the giant elm trees hovering above your head here. It all started when the city fathers wanted to tear down these beautiful green elms to make a new subway station, and a number of concerned citizens got together to save them. If you see some people wearing "Grönere Stad" ("for a greener city") buttons, you'll know what's going on—that the ecology-consciousness of Sweden is swiftly being raised. You may notice, too, that above the rescued elms the air is much cleaner and fresher than it is back home. It is said that Sweden has the cleanest air in Europe.

ORGANIZED TOURS: The quickest and most convenient way to see the highlights of Stockholm is to take one of the motorcoach tours that leave from Karl XII Torg, near the Royal Opera House and the harbor. **Tourist Sightseeing AB,** 20 Skeppsbron (tel. 24-04-70), offers two "Grand City Tours," each lasting 2½ hours and costing 80 kronor ($9.60). The first (10 a.m. daily) is highlighted by a visit to the Royal Palace and a trip through Gamla Stan (Old Town), with a stop at the cathedral. The second tour, leaving at 2 p.m., goes to the *Wasa* museum and visits the city hall in the Old Town.

Other tours operated by Tourist Sightseeing AB include an all-day trip to Uppsala and Sigtuna, and an afternoon tour of Drottningholm Palace and the Royal Court Theater.

Tourist Sightseeing AB also takes to the water. A two-hour canal tour leaves Strömkajen, in front of the Grand Hotel. The cost is 45 kronor ($5.40). The tour passes under the bridges of Stockholm, through locks and canals, and by famous buildings and parks. It leaves three times daily.

By all means have a look at the archipelago that leads to the Baltic Sea. Tourist Sightseeing AB offers a daily tour, leaving Strömkajen at 10 a.m. and 2 p.m. and costing 60 kronor ($7.20).

The Tourist Sightseeing AB offers a 50% reduction to hostelers who can prove that they are residing in the A/F *Chapman*. This reduction is on all boat tours, including that of the archipelago.

Tickets and reservations for all tours may be obtained at all authorized travel agencies and tourist information centers.

WALKING TOUR OF THE OLD TOWN: A group of authorized Stockholm guides conduct walking tours of the medieval lanes of the Old Town of Stockholm. They are called "Evening Walk in the Old Town." In addition to the interest the Old Town has, these walks are one of the few evening programs in Stockholm appealing to the entire family.

Walks are conducted from the end of May until mid-September. Visitors can check the exact dates with the Tourist Center at Sweden House at Kungsträdgården (tel. 22-32-80). The tour starts daily at 6:30 p.m. from the Obelisk on Palace Hill (Slottsbacken in Swedish), lasting until about 8:30 p.m. The fee is 20 kronor ($2.40) for adults (free for children under 16 who are accompanied by their parents).

Reservations are not necessary, and the tours are never cancelled—rain, storm, or snow—as long as one single person wishes to take the walk.

In inflation-plagued Scandinavia, this tour is a remarkable bargain. Very often the evening ends with a cup of coffee and some sandwiches in an Old Town café, which is open as late as 10 p.m. Something unpretentious (and inexpensive) where everybody sits and talks under a romantic vault.

This tour carries my heartiest recommendation.

3. Stockholm After Dark

Time was, if you laughed too loud, drank too much, or whatever in a Stockholm club, someone at the next table would frown at you. That is, if the doorman would condescend to let you in in the first place. Now everything has changed. Pubs and discos, even nude shows long ago cropped up in the once-staid Swedish capital. Frank Ward appraised the situation this way: "It has finally dawned upon the proprietors that they are there to please and not *be* pleased. This transformation, as wonderful to behold as a drab caterpillar's metamorphosis into a gorgeous butterfly, has brought new customers by the thousands."

Nonetheless, **Djurgården** remains the favored spot for both indoor and outdoor spectacles on a summer evening. Although the more sophisticated may find it corny, it is the best bet in the early part of the evening. Then you can make the jazz den and disco circuit—some of the clubs don't close till 3 or 4 in the morning.

SKANSEN: This open-air museum, which closes at 11:30 p.m., has an outdoor dancing pavilion in the Grand Ole Opry style. Costumed musicians play, and the dances range from folk to *vals*. Weather permitting, post-30 couples flock here every night—except Monday and Tuesday—any time after 8:30.

After tiring, dancers can stoll over to the vicinity of the Solliden Restaurant, where there's a large bandstand with weekend performances—mostly vaudeville, operatic, and symphonic concerts, plus the Skansen Folk Dancers. Down the hill is:

GRÖNA LUND'S TIVOLI: Unlike its Copenhagen namesake, this is an amusement park—not a fantasy land. For those who like Coney Island-type amusements, it can be a nighttime adventure—costing 18 kronor ($2.16) admission for persons over 12. One of the big thrills of Tivoli is to go up on the revolving tower, with its after-dark look at Stockholm (it costs 7 kronor, or 63¢, which helps the owners realize a return on their half-million-dollar investment). Tivoli is open from April through September, from 2 p.m. to midnight (Sunday from noon to 10 p.m.). For information, telephone 67-01-85.

The amusement park has two choice nightspots, chief of which is:

Nightrock: This festooned second-floor nightclub features live music and dancing, reaching its zenith on Saturday night. It attracts the 20s and 30s set; the single men line up against one wall, and the unattached Swedish women occupy the tables. A mug of beer costs 22 kronor ($2.64) but it's not mandatory. Those who want to go out for a breath of fresh air can get stamped, then stick out a hand on their return for an ultraviolet check. The Nightrock is open from 8 p.m. to midnight.

Tyrol: Tyrol is a huge, crowded restaurant with German *Stimmung*. A genuine Bavarian orchestra entertains the happy crowd every night from 7:30 to midnight. Everybody sings the well-known German drinking songs and drinks Löwenbräu beer. The kitchen mixes the best Swedish and German cooking with meals costing from 125 kronor ($15). There is no cover charge.

To reach Tivoli, take either bus 47 or 44, or else the Djurgården ferry from Nybroplan.

DISCOS: **Alexandra's,** 1–3 Döbelnsgatan (tel. 10-46-46), is said by practically everyone in town to be the best and most sophisticated nightclub/disco in Sweden. It's named after its owner, Alexandra Charles. The strikingly modern interior is almost entirely black, with glass, crystal, and metal, all offset with mirrors. Well-focused spotlights illuminate one of the most attractive crowds in Scandinavia. You should be warned that entering this place requires all the political skill of garnering an invitation to the White House, although the concierges of the city's better hotels will usually be able to arrange it. You stand a better chance if you reserve for dinner instead of coming just to drink. The line outside will be rather long, especially on weekends, when drinks cost from 45 kronor ($5.40) up, and the cover charge will probably be from 60 kronor ($7.20). It is open from 9 p.m. to 3 a.m.

Embassy, 10 Sturegatan (tel. 61-60-07), is *le club chic* of Stockholm, attracting such personalities as Sammy Davis Jr., Eartha Kitt, and Shirley Bassey. It is an exclusive nightclub, restaurant, and piano bar, which is open between 8 p.m. and 3 a.m. every night except Sunday. Most of the well-dressed guests are from 25 and up. The restaurant has good food, service, and an attractive ambience, and the piano bar always has good entertainment. Drinks cost from 60 kronor ($7.20) and up.

The Daily News, Sverigehuset, at Kingsträdgården (tel. 21-56-55). It may seem strange to find so many Stockholm residents gravitating toward the ground floor of Sweden House, where the Swedish Tourist Office is located, but a quick look at the trendy bar will quickly tell you that the clientele is here for more than a list of the city sights. The entrance is a bit difficult to find, but once you're past the coat check area, you can go either upstairs into the spacious, angular bar or downstairs into one of the most popular and attractive discos in town.

A restaurant section serves meals in a separate upstairs dining area, full dinners costing from 145 kronor ($17.40), although the upstairs café is the real reason most people go to the upper floor. There you can enjoy a large export beer for 40 kronor ($4.80).

In the disco downstairs, you'll find intimate groupings of chairs not unlike someone's large private home, a long bar whose base is curved walls of illuminated glass blocks, a scattering of antiques, and a big dance floor. On Friday and Saturday, a cover charge of 40 kronor ($4.80) is required. A large glass of export beer costs the same as in the upstairs bar. The disco is open from 9 p.m. to 2:30 a.m. nightly except Sunday and Monday. The restaurant is usually from noon to 2 a.m. On winter weekends, however, hours are from 5 p.m. to 2 a.m.

READER'S DISCO SUGGESTION: Front Page Disco, 20 Kungsholmesgarten (tel. 51-43-16), is a swinging, crowded place frequented by locals. The minimum age is 25, with most people being around 30. The 45-krona ($5.40) cover charge is steep but common for Stockholm. The music is top 40, but a lot of it is from the '60s and '70s. The disco opens at 9 p.m., but get there early or plan to wait in line" (Johanna Ficaro, Cambridge, Mass.).

THE PUBS AND BARS OF STOCKHOLM: Although Stockholm can't boast London's numbers, pubs are on the upswing, enjoying a wave of new-found popularity. Most of them shut down around midnight. A favorite one is **Stampen,** 7 Stora Gråmunkegränd (tel. 20-57-93), a British-style pub which attracts a crowd in the 20s to 30s age bracket. From the high ceilings is suspended a menagerie of stuffed animals. It's owned by Mrs. Gun Holmquist. In the ground-floor pub, guests crowd in, listening to old tunes and drinking beer at 28 kronor ($3.36) for half a liter. And downstairs, a club operates in the speak-easy tradition, featuring Dixieland and swing. An entrance fee of 45 kronor ($5.40) is charged.

Tudor Arms, 31 Grevgatan (tel. 60-27-12). It's said off the record that this authentically decorated pub is the best ambassador of goodwill that Britain could possibly offer Sweden. The pub was established by Britisher Christopher Billowes. After work every day, beginning around 5:15 p.m., the place is likely to cram a standing-room-only crowd into its warmly paneled interior. Pitcher after pitcher of foaming beer is dispensed to crowds that don't disperse until closing time at 9:30 p.m. Monday to Saturday. The clientele is usually under 40, tends to be extroverted, is occasionally quite attractive.

At lunchtime, beginning at 11 a.m. weekdays and at 1 p.m. on Saturday, the pub does a brisk business, with typical pub specialties to eat, costing 130 kronor ($14.40) for a full meal. In the evening, a full range of beer and hard liquor from all over Europe is offered. The establishment closes Sunday and for part of July.

Victoria Café Matsalar, Kungsträdgården (tel. 10-10-85), advertises itself as "a vital part of your Stockholm education," and if you come here after the local business people leave at the end of the lunch hour, the claim may be true. The building, near the Sweden House opposite an outdoor skating rink, is graced with naked masonry nymphs in an 1890s-style garden forecourt. Equally naked bronze lighting fixtures illuminate the linden trees just outside the front door. Once inside, you'll find a long bar filled with members of all sexual persuasions amicably engaged in drinking. Export beer costs 30 kronor ($3.60), but pilsner is cheaper.

If you wish, you can try your luck at a small-stakes casino. The maximum bet is 2 kronor (24¢), and no doubling of a winning bet is permitted. You pick a color from the chips the articulate attendant will give you and stick with it until you decide to cash in (or out, as the case may be).

The place is most crowded after around 9 p.m., although you can have a well-prepared lunch or dinner served on immaculate tables in an inner section past the bar. Meals begin at 120 kronor ($14.40). Among the dishes offered, you may like reindeer or fried salmon trout with almonds.

Clipper Club, Hotel Heisen, 12–14 Skeppsbron (tel. 22-32-60). The leather upholstery and the rich paneling in this popular club would be the envy of any English library, while the brass tables, mirrors, attractive clients, soft lights, and live piano make it one of my favorite bars in Stockholm. The ceiling supports are designed to mimic the beams of a ship. The clientele often includes a friendly crowd of people relaxing after work; even something of a late shift made up of many who have worked until closing time at other bars and restaurants. The service is courteous. Drinks average from 40 kronor ($4.80) to 55 kronor ($6.60). The club is open until 2 a.m., with the piano music beginning at around 9 p.m.

Kurbits, 10 Trängsund (tel. 20-33-51), is a modern bar and pub beheath the ancient brick vaulting of a labyrinthine cellar in Gamla Stan, a few steps from the Stortorget. Customers, including many visiting Germans and Australians the last time I was there, descend a narrow brick and stone stairway into a series of rooms with intimate cubbyholes and zebra-skinned banquettes from which they can enjoy in comfort the live music emanating from the small stage. Much of the music heard here reflects the best traditions of the 1960s and 1970s in America. The place is open daily from 6 p.m. to 1 a.m. There's a 25-krona ($3) cover charge on Friday and Saturday after 9 p.m. Bavarian beer costs 19 kronor ($2.28) for a medium-size glass, 25 kronor ($3) for a large mug. During happy hour from 6 to 8 p.m., prices are lower.

The **Pub Engelen,** 59B Kornhamnstorg (tel. 10-07-22), offers entertainment nightly, featuring jazz bands and singers on Sunday. Go here only if you like lots of people. The atmosphere is enhanced by a gay '90s decor, as the pub is housed in a genuine old chemist's shop, said to be the oldest in Europe. The location is in Gamla Stan. Live performers appear nightly, the entrance fee beginning at 35 kronor ($4.20). It's free until 7 p.m. Beer costs from 30 kronor ($3.60). The pub opens at 5 p.m. daily and offers entertainment from 9 p.m. to midnight. It is connected to the Restaurant Engelen, at the same address, which offers some of the best steaks in town. Between 5 and 7 p.m., a Tourist Menu is served for 45 kronor ($5.40). Later, you can order tournedos with cognac for 85 kronor ($10.20).

Stortorgsbaren, 7 Stortorget (tel. 20-66-82), above one of the old town's most popular restaurants, Stortorgskällaren (see "Where to Dine" section), offers a spacious, warmly decorated, and amusing spot for a drink. The three comfortably appointed rooms are likely to be especially full during happy hour from

5 to 7 p.m., when drinks are reduced in price, and in the evening, when there's live piano music from the black lacquer and plexiglass instrument whose base is surrounded by bar stools. The music lasts from 9:30 p.m. until 1:30 a.m. Beer costs from 20 kronor ($2.40). The establishment is open from 11:30 a.m. till 1:30 a.m. Monday through Friday, from 1 p.m. till 1:30 a.m. Saturday, and from 1 till 11 p.m. Sunday. No one will object if you extend your drink into a full meal at the excellent restaurant in the cellar.

Castle Hotel Bar, 14 Riddargatan (tel. 22-69-90). The confines of this bar are closed to idle rubberneckers of the community, although it is, according to management, always open to visiting foreigners, especially those with a healthy appreciation of jazz and jazz musicians. It's at the end of a memorabilia-lined hallway of the well-known Castle Hotel (see "Where to Stay" section), which for years has housed virtually every jazz musician performing in Stockholm. The bar, with its colorfully primitive patterned carpeting, leather seats, brass-covered bar, antique airplane propellor, and oil portraits of former guests, seems like just the kind of place where the musical imagination of a jazz artist could run wild. Luckily, the staff and many of the other guests seem to appreciate the particular problems of a musician. If you hang out here, you might gain a few insights. Export beer costs from 20 kronor ($2.40).

NIGHTCLUBS: Café Opera, Operahuset, Karl's Torg (tel. 11-00-26). In many ways, the advertisement that touts this place as the "universal meeting place of Stockholm" is true, since it combines within its glass-studded walls a quadruple function of bistro, brasserie, and tea room during the day and one of the most crowded nightclubs in Stockholm in the evening. The entrance at the back of the building near the park is where both singers and patrons of the former Opera House used to come in for a quick glass of wine between acts.

Visitors have the best chance of getting in around noon when a "dagens lunch" is offered for 65 kronor ($7.80). If all you want is ice cream, tea, coffee, pastries, or between-meals sandwiches, you can be accommodated between Monday and Friday from 11:30 a.m. to 3 p.m., on weekends from 1 to 3 p.m.

Late at night, the three-deep crowd at the long, curving bar is one of the most animated in town. The entrance is below a life-size nude statue, where you may have to join a long waiting line, as no reservations are taken. You can stay in the ornate bar, in a garden-style extension of the main dining room, or else in a room with frescoes, coffered ceiling, and statues which were once considered provocative. Drinks cost around 35 kronor ($4.20) each.

This establishment is not to be confused with the opera's main and far more expensive dining room, the Operakällaren, whose entrance is through a different door. Near the entrance to the café is a stairway leading to one of the Opera House's most beautiful corners, the Operabaren (Opera Bar), which is likely to be as crowded as the café. It is a non-musical but historically charming place to have a drink.

Bacchi Wapen, 5 Järntorgsgatan (tel. 11-66-71). For the past 70 years, this place has provided distraction and amusement. Its multilevel decor looks a lot like San Francisco at the turn of the century, which seems appropriate to the building, which is about 150 years old. It is near the center of Gamla Stan. There's enough going on here to make an entire evening's entertainment for you. You pay a cover charge of 45 kronor ($5.40) to enter, but if you arrive before 9 p.m., one fee will cover two people. You can have dinner at tables set around the upper-level disco floor between 8 and 11 p.m., for 180 kronor ($21.60) and up.

Among the fun happenings here are the strip shows, which are popular, safe, tongue-in-cheek, and among the funniest in Stockholm, with men flocking in on Wednesday night to see the female strippers and women packing the house on Thursday when male ecdysiasts take it off. The place is closed on Sunday and

Monday, but the rest of the week a large export beer costs 32 kronor ($3.84), and the disco music goes on and on.

Also connected to the above-mentioned Engelen is a "cellar club," **Kolingen,** 59 Kornhamnstorg (tel. 10-07-22), that draws a nice crowd of people. Multicolored bulbs light your way through what one observer called a "fairy grotto effect." Old coach seats draped with fabric have been installed for that cozy tête-à-tête. Disco music is played. You're charged an entrance fee of from 40 kronor ($4.80).

THE CULTURAL SCENE: The theater and opera season begins in mid-August and lasts till mid-June. The **Royal Dramatic Theater** (*Dramaten*), where Greta Garbo got her start (Ingmar Bergman used to be the director), presents both the latest experimental play and the most classical one—but in Swedish only.

The **Royal Opera,** 2 Jakobstorg (tel. 29-82-40), on the other hand, is more universally appealing with its Royal Swedish Opera and Royal Swedish Ballet. Jenny Lind appeared here. The Opera dates from 1898 and can hold 1200 guests. Seats are reasonable in price, ranging from 10 kronor ($1.20) to 100 kronor ($12) in general. The opera is closed from mid-June to mid-August. Concerts (the **Stockholm Philharmonic** and the **Radio Orchestra**) are given at **Konserthuset** (tel. 20-83-00), at Hötorget, the scene of the awarding of the Nobel Prizes.

4. Shopping in Stockholm

In a country deservedly acclaimed for its functional design (Swedish modern has changed living rooms and bedrooms throughout Europe and North America), Stockholm has shop after shop of dazzling merchandise—often at dazzling prices. In the land of super-taxes and super-welfare, don't expect to buy merchandise made by slave labor. The Swedish craftsperson is noted for his or her high degree of skill and efficiency. That worker is also well paid, and the good wage is reflected in the high prices of the articles for sale.

It is recommended that bargain shoppers proceed with caution. There are good buys, admittedly, but it takes a lot of searching. If you're a casual shopper, you may want to confine your purchases to handsome souvenirs and gifts.

Swedish glass, of course, is world famous. Swedish wooden items are outstanding, and many prefer Sweden's functional furniture in blond pine or birch. Other items to look for include playsuits for children, silver necklaces, reindeer gloves, stainless-steel knives, hand-woven neckties and skirts, sweaters and mittens in Nordic patterns, Swedish clogs, and colorful handicrafts from the provinces. The most famous souvenir to buy is the Dala horse from Dalarna.

The Value Added Tax in Sweden is called "Moms," and it is imposed on all products and services. When buying larger and more expensive items, you can avoid Moms. Just give the firm your name, address, and passport number, and they will send your purchases home for you. Products purchased VAT-free may not be exported by the purchaser.

Most of the boutiques and department stores are right in the center of the city. The main shopping streets include **Biblioteksgatan, Gamla Brogatan,** and **Sergelgatan.**

DEPARTMENT STORES: Nordiska Kompanient (NK for short), 18 Hamngatan (tel. 762-84-70), is the largest department store in Scandinavia. It's a splendid emporium of Swedish design. At this queen of department stores, you'll find floor after floor of glittering merchandise. The store is so big that you can easily get lost.

Souvenir hunters traditionally buy one of the brightly colored wood-carved

Dala horses, as mentioned. They come in all different sizes, of course. NK also sells uniquely patterned wall plaques from the prestigious Arabia of Helsinki.

Most of the blockbuster names in Swedish glass are displayed at NK, chiefly Orrefors (see the Nordic Light collection) and Kosta, the two most famous houses. Look also for Argenta stemware in original, unusual designs. In the basement is an exciting collection of Swedish handicrafts, literally thousands of items. Stainless steel, as I've pointed out, is also a good buy in Sweden, and NK displays it profusely. For those who want to search out regional products, you'll find a Lapp cap or perhaps a pair of mittens from Iceland.

Åhléns, 50 Klarabergsgatan (tel. 24-60-00), is a modern, fully air-conditioned department store in the heart of Stockholm, with both a giftshop and a restaurant. Its food department is famous, and the store stays open in the evening until 9 p.m. (on Sunday from 11 a.m. to 9 p.m.). Seek out, in particular, their fine collection of home textiles and their exhibit of both Orrefors and Kosta crystal. Pewter with genuine Swedish ornaments makes a fine gift item. You'll also find a complete selection of cosmetics, including Pierre Robert from Sweden.

The other leading department store is **PUB,** at Hötorget (tel. 22-40-40). Greta Garbo got her start here in the millinery department. In general, the store offers less expensive merchandise than NK, but many fine, high-quality items in its own right. Connected by an escalator, PUB is housed in two buildings. In the PUB restaurant, you can enjoy a dish of the day for 28 kronor ($3.36).

SWEDISH GLASS AND CRYSTAL: Svenskt Glas, 8 Birger Jarlsgatan (tel. 21-04-70), is the pacesetter. Royal families patronize this establishment, but glass at most price levels is featured as well. The Orrefors glass displayed here is incomparable in its beauty, possessing its own special magic. A walk through the showrooms reveals a stunning array of glass that includes stemware in exciting, modern designs; beautiful candlesticks; flower-shaped bowls in full lead crystal; a masculine bar set, including an ice bucket; vases in solid, full lead crystal, classically cut in modern design; bowls with exquisite cut-glass finish; sparkling wine glasses with attractive visual effects; attractive pitchers of various types of drink; and perfume bottles for the dressing table. A selection of beautiful crystal animals sold exclusively by Svenskt Glas in cooperation with the World Wildlife Fund is another attractive feature of this beautiful store established in 1924. Worldwide shipping facilities are available. The shop is open from Monday to Friday from 9:30 a.m. to 6 p.m. (on Saturday from 10 a.m. to 2 p.m.).

Rosenthal Studio-Haus, 6 Birger Jarlsgatan (tel. 20-03-39), is one of the biggest repositories of modern crystal, porcelain, silverplate, and cookware in Stockholm.

Casselryds Glas & Porslin, in Skärholmen (tel. 08/710-5116), lies ten miles south of the center of Stockholm (take subway line 13 south to the Skärholmen Shopping Mall). The English-speaking owner, Peter Casselryd, suggests you purchase Swedish crystal where the Swedes buy it—that is, not in the high-priced center of the capital. He presents price lists for Orrefors crystal, detailing the advertised U.S. price, the advertised Swedish price, and *his* price, which allows you to do some comparative shopping. He'll show you how you can not only purchase glass and crystal "tax free," but how to arrange shipment back home.

HANDICRAFTS AND GIFTS: Svensk Hemslöjd (the Society for Swedish Handicrafts), 44 Sveavägen (tel. 23-21-15), has a wide selection of glass, pottery, gifts, and wooden and metal handicrafts, the work of some of Sweden's best artisans.

The shop celebrated its 80th anniversary in 1980. You'll also be shown a display of hand-woven carpets, upholstery fabrics, hand-painted materials, tapestries, lace, and embroidered items. You can also find many kinds of beautiful yarns for weaving and embroidery. The shop is open week-days from 9:30 a.m. to 6 p.m. (on Saturday from 9:30 a.m. to 1 p.m.).

Konsthantverkarna, 2 Mäster Samuelsgatan (tel. 11-03-60), has an unusual selection of some of the best Swedish handicrafts. A group of artisans started this shop back in 1951, collecting crafts from the whole country and exhibiting them under one roof. All the products must pass a strict jury test before they are offered for sale. Choose from glass, sculpture, ceramics, wall textiles, clothes, jewelry, silver, brass, and wood and leather work. Each item is handmade and original, coming from member workshops and studios from all over the country. Ask about the tax-free service.

Färöprodukter, 1 Tysta Gatan (tel. 67-22-02), offers high-quality exotic yarns, along with plant-dyed natural fibers, from the Faroe Islands. Many of the designs in knitting are quite modern. Unfortunately, the store is closed during the tourist-heavy weeks between June 15 and August 1.

Gunnarssons Träfigurer, 77 Drottninggatan (tel. 21-67-17), has one of the city's most interesting collections of Swedish carved wooden figures. You may become fascinated by pieces of sweet-smelling juniper or shiny beech.

De Pyras Bod, 12 Birger Jarlsgatan (tel. 20-30-24), has an array of well-made Swedish handicrafts, including embroidery, hand-woven goods of different kinds, as well as basket, wood, and metal work. The people here are very helpful and friendly, and visitors often pick up some fine bargains. All the work is done by handicapped artisans.

Tyger & Ting, 1 Köpmangatan (tel. 20-56-62), lies in the Old Town, across from St. George & the Dragon. In one of the most ancient business locations in Stockholm, Carin Scholander offers an assortment of unusual gift items, including cotton fabrics and interesting, well-made handicrafts. The shop is open daily, except Sunday, from 11 a.m. to 5:30 p.m. (till 2 p.m. on Saturday).

Brinken, 1 Storkyrkobrinken (tel. 11-59-54), offers a historic location in the lower floor of a corner building in the old town and a mail-order business that can send handcrafted brass, pewter, wrought-iron, or crystal to anywhere in the world. About 95% of the articles sold are made in Scandinavia and often show the marks of the laborious hand work it took to make them. The shop is open seven days a week, although hours are limited on weekends. Evy Norin is the hardworking owner, who has a thoughtful staff to help her.

Nordkalott Shopen, 48 Norrbackagatan (tel. 32-20-22), has the best selection of genuine handicrafts from Lapland. Many of the items are made from reindeer skin. The Lapps also make the most beautiful handicrafts by using simple materials such as roots, birch bark, and deer horn.

Duka, 41 Kungsgatan (tel. 20-60-41), offers a large selection of crystal, porcelain, and gifts in a shop near the Konserthuset (Concert Hall).

SWEDISH MODERN DESIGN: Svenskt Tenn, 5A Strandvägen (tel. 63-52-10), is considered one of the most exclusive shops for interior decoration and gifts in all of Scandinavia. For your convenience, they will pack, insure, and forward your purchase anywhere in the world. Store hours are weekdays from 10 a.m. to 6 p.m. (on Saturday from 10 a.m. to 2 p.m.). However, the store is closed on Saturday during July. The name, Svenskt Tenn, translates as Swedish pewter. But don't come here just for that. The showroom also includes furniture, lamps, textiles, cutlery, plated ware, crystal, china, and gifts, often in stunning, sophisticated designs. They carry an exclusive collection of Josef Frank's hand-printed designs on linen and cotton.

Josef Frank was a professor of architecture and a member of the Bauhaus group in Austria, but devoted most of his life to interior design for Svenskt Tenn. His fame rendered him two special exhibitions at the National Gallery. He is dead now, but all his masterpieces of design live on. Many of his handprinted textiles were made during Mr. Frank's stay in New York as visiting professor at the New School for Social Research.

PRINTS AND LITHOGRAPHS: Konst-Bibliofilen, 6 Västerlanggatan (tel. 21-27-68), has one of the best collections in Sweden. You're welcomed by the most hospitable Stefan Schueler, who speaks English, of course. He selected most of the merchandise, especially the limited editions. His shop is open Monday to Friday from 9:30 a.m. to 6 p.m. (on Saturday from 10 a.m. to 2 p.m.). The shop is closed in July for vacation.

TEXTILES: One of the oldest and most prestigious houses in this line is Handarbetets Vänner, 82–84 Djurgårdsslätten (tel. 67-10-26). Art weaving and embroidery are sold here, and you can wander at leisure through the textile gallery and shop any time between 11 a.m. and 3 p.m., Monday through Friday. The shop closes in July.

FURNITURE: Möbel-Shop Sven Larsson is at 94 Folkungagatan (tel. 44-40-00) and at 8 Roslagsgatan (tel. 11-67-17). They hand-fashion beautiful Swedish furniture in old pine. Write for a catalog.

KITCHENWARE: Cordon Bleu, 86 Drottninggatan (tel. 11-00-81), sells the most complete line of cookware in Stockholm, much of it imported from France. If you're looking for the oddly shaped saucepan you've needed since your last gourmet dinner party, this place probably has it. They also carry a line of small wood-burning stoves which, for a price, they'll ship back to America.

TOYS: If you have children, you'll find the biggest selection of wooden toys, handmade as well as mass-produced, at **Bulleribock,** 104 Sveavägen (tel. 31-61-21).

A BOUTIQUE FOR WOMEN: Amorina, 23 Västerlanggatan (tel. 21-96-86). English-speaking Monica Spångberg has assembled a tasteful, well-chosen collection of interesting and unusual clothing items for women. Her shop is fashionable and trendy.

DELI: Shopping for Swedish and international deli items? The **Metro Supermarket** at the T-Centralen subway station is open until 7 p.m weekdays and 11 a.m. to 4 p.m. on Sunday.

With Stockholm as our base, we turn now to the environs for some:

ONE-DAY TRIPS

Around Lake Mälaren are some of the best known attractions in Sweden— villages (Gamla Uppsala, for one) that go back centuries before Stockholm was a gleam in Birger Jarl's eye; castles (Uppsala and Gripsholm) that revive the pomp and glory of the 16th-century Vasa dynasty.

First, a day could be spent exploring Sigtuna Palace and Skokloster Castle; then Uppsala and Gamla Uppsala on the second day. Hotels offering good accommodations are available in both Sigtuna and Uppsala—so it isn't necessary to return to Stockholm. Finally, a day trip to either Gripsholm Castle in the town of Mariefred or Tullgarns Castle rounds out the itinerary.

A popular routing is to take the boat from Stockholm at 9:45 a.m., going along the beautiful waterway, Mälaren, and the Fyris River. Make a two-hour stop at Sigtuna and arrive at Uppsala at 5 p.m. There you can visit the magnificent cathedral and other interesting sights and have a meal in one of Uppsala's acclaimed restaurants (see below). Trains back to Stockholm, a 45-minute trip, run ever hour until 11 p.m.

Leading off the trip is:

5. Sigtuna

Founded at the dawn of the 11th century, Sigtuna, on the shores of Lake Mälaren, northwest of Stockholm, is Sweden's oldest town. Its High Street (**Stora Gatan**), with its low timbered buildings, is thought to be the oldest street in Sweden still following its original trail. Remnants of Sigtuna's Viking and early Christian heritage are to be found throughout the town.

Sigtuna was once the capital of Sweden. But it ran into trouble early, beginning with Estonian pirates, who once pillaged and destroyed the town near the end of the 12th century. Sigtuna was also a major missionary battleground in the effort to bring about the triumph of Christianity over the Viking gods. It abounds with church ruins—mostly from the 12th century. Chief among them is **St. Per's**, Sweden's first cathedral. The 13th-century **Monastery of St. Maria** is brick and step-gabled. It's open to the public daily.

The tourist bureau is on the old main street, near the well-preserved **Town Hall** that dates from the 18th century. It's a storybook place, much like the town hall in Ebeltoft, Denmark.

Walk down the narrow streets of Sigtuna, past its ancient ruins and old houses. And if time remains, pay a visit to the **Sigtuna Fornhem**, the archeological museum, housing artifacts found in and around Sigtuna, dating back to the early medieval period.

Founded near the turn of the century, the **Sigtuna Foundation** is a Lutheran retreat and cultural center. It is often frequented by writers. The foundation brought a resurgence to Sigtuna after the town had drifted into obscurity for centuries. It is open to the public from 1 to 3 p.m.

Do-it-yourselfers can make both bus and train connections daily between Stockholm and Sigtuna or between Sigtuna and Uppsala. From Stockholm take a train to Märsta, then a bus for the ten-minute ride to Sigtuna. In summer boats run from Klara Strand in Stockholm and from Uppsala to Sigtuna.

WHERE TO STAY: Mälarens Parla, Strandvägen 3 Stora Nygatan (tel. 501-00), was built in 1909. Also called the Stads, it has been modernized in a sedate manner (a few Gustavian antiques retained), becoming fit for a stopover here on the northern shores of Lake Mälaren. Most of its rooms—furnished in an odds-and-ends style—have a view of the lake. Singles with bath or shower rent for 350 kronor ($41) to 450 kronor ($54). Doubles with bath or shower cost from 600 kronor ($72), breakfast included.

Unknown to many visitors, **Sigtunastiftelsens Gästhem** (tel. 516-10), which is operated in conjunction with the already-mentioned Sigtuna Foundation, receives paying guests. Attracting only those interested in a spiritual and cultural retreat, the guesthouse is a gem. Most of its rooms face the Rose Garden, and many are named after such historical persons as St. Francis, St. Birgitta, Geijer, and Linné. With its canopied bed and beautiful white furniture, the Linné Room is a particular charmer. Other rooms are furnished in the style of the corresponding historical period. Two persons occupying a double are charged 410 kronor ($49.20).

6. Skokloster Castle

Skokloster, one of the most splendid 17th-century castles in Sweden and one of the most interesting baroque museums in Europe, is situated by Lake Mälaren, 40 miles from Stockholm and 31 miles from Uppsala. Still retaining its original interiors, Skokloster Castle is note for its rich collections of paintings, furniture, applied art, tapestries, arms, and books. A visit here is like a walk back in time to the days when Sweden was one of the great powers in Europe.

The state-owned castle may be seen daily from May 1 to September 30 on guided tours only, every hour on the hour from noon to 4 p.m. The cost is 12 kronor ($1.44) for adults, 6 kronor (72¢) for children.

Nearby is the **Skoloster Motor Museum,** right on the palace grounds, containing the largest collection of vintage automobiles and motorcycles in the country. One of the most notable cars is a 1905 De Dion Bouton with eight horsepowers. Unlike the castle, the museum is open all year. From May to September, its hours are from 10 a.m. to 5 p.m.; however, in the off-season it is open daily from 11 a.m. to 4 p.m. Admission is 15 kronor ($1.80) for adults, 10 kronor ($1.20) for children. For information, phone 24-11-00.

7. Uppsala

The major university city of Sweden, Uppsala is the most popular destination of day-trippers from Stockholm, and for good reason. Uppsala not only has a great university, but a celebrated 15th-century cathedral and a 16th-century castle. Uppsala once held sway as the center of royalty. Queen Christina occasionally held court here. The church is still the seat of the archbishop and the first Swedish university was founded here in 1477.

On the Fyris River, Uppsala lies 42 miles northwest of Stockholm. The city is reached in 45 minutes by train from the Central Station in Stockholm.

These days Uppsala is expanding rapidly and developing an industrial base. But the heart of the city is unmarred.

The best time to be in Uppsala is on April 30, Walpurgis Eve, when octogenarian alumni and the present student body in white caps celebrate the rebirth of spring and the death of winter with a torchlight parade and rollicking festivities lasting till dawn throughout the 13 student "nations" (residential halls).

The **Uppsala Student Reception Service** schedules frequent mixers and dances in the summer. Check with the tourist office for details.

THE SIGHTS: For those rushing through for the day, I'll quickly preview the chief sights. The longer you stay, the more you'll find to see.

Uppsala Cathedral

The largest cathedral in Scandinavia, the twin-spired Gothic structure, nearly 400 feet high, was founded in the 13th century, severely damaged in 1702 in a disastrous fire that swept over Uppsala, then restored to the very peaks of the spires near the turn of this century. Among the regal figures buried in the crypt is Gustavus Vasa. The remains of St. Erik, patron saint of Sweden, are entombed in a silver shrine. Botanist Linnaeus and philosopher-theologian

Swedenborg also are buried here. The cathedral is open from May 1 to August 31 daily from 8 a.m. to 8 p.m. Off-season it closes at 6 p.m. Admission is free.

Uppsala Castle

Protectively hovering over the city, this 16th-century castle—founded by Gustavus Vasa in 1540—was the setting for one of the most memorable moments in Scandinavian history: the abdication of Queen Christina in 1654. Along with the cathedral, it was badly damaged in the fire of 1702 and was partially restored in 1752 and 1816, but it never regained its original grandeur. The white-capped young greeters of spring have a Walpurgis songfest on this hill on April 30. The castle (tel. 14-48-10) may be visited daily from 11 a.m. to 4 p.m. from May to mid-September for 3 kronor (36¢). Off-season (August 20 to September 23) it is open daily only from 11 a.m. to 2 p.m. The castle is closed September 24 to May 1.

Linnaean Gardens and Museum

In Svartbäcksgatan, the gardens of Carolus Linnaeus (Carl von Linné) are open in summer (May 1 to August 15) from 9 a.m. to 9 p.m.; in winter, 9 a.m. to 4 p.m. The town house of Linnaeus may be visited May 1 to September 30 from 1 to 4 p.m. for 8 kronor (96¢); closed in winter.

Linnaeus, of course, was the Swedish botanist (the system of classifying plants and animals was named after him). Botanists of yesterday, today, and tomorrow come here and wander through the gardens where Linnaeus pondered stamens and pistils. He died in Uppsala in 1778, having held a chair of medicine and natural history at Uppsala University. A summer art gallery exhibiting works of contemporary Uppsala artists is also on the grounds.

The University Library

At the end of Drottninggatan is the **Carolina Rediviva** (tel. 18-39-00), with its more than three million volumes and 30,000 manuscripts, among them many rare works from the Middle Ages. But the one manuscript that draws the visitors is the *Codex Argenteus* (Silver Bible), translated into the Old Gothic language in the middle of the fourth century. The Silver Bible was written in about A.D. 525. It is the only book extant in the Old Gothic script. The Exhibition Room of the library, where the Silver Bible is kept, is open Monday to Friday from June 16 to August 15, 9 a.m. to 8 p.m.; Monday to Friday the rest of the year, 9 a.m. to 8:30 p.m., and Saturday all year, 9 a.m. to 5:30 p.m.; on Sunday from June 16 to August 15, 1 to 3:30 p.m.

ACCOMMODATIONS: To give Uppsala and its environs the attention they deserve, you'll have to spend the night. The hotels are limited but adequate. And in Uppsala, the hotel prices go *down* in summer. This is because Uppsala is primarily a university town and is more crowded when classes are in session.

Some visitors prefer to stay in Uppsala, and take the commuter train to Stockholm. If you have a Eurailpass, you ride free. Trains leave about every hour during the peak daylight hours. You can also get from Stockholm to Uppsala (or vice versa) by boat, the same vessel stopping at Skokloster and Sigtuna. For details, check with the tourist office in any of these towns.

Hotel Uplandia, 32 Dragarbrunnsgatan (tel. 10-21-60), is oriented to the future, even though it's in the heart of Sweden's oldest university town. It's large and of recent vintage, lying some 25 yards from the E4 highway. All 106 of its streamlined rooms come equipped with private baths or showers, plus radio and TV. For all this comfort and modernity, however, you must pay the price—

from 500 kronor ($60) in a single, from 700 kronor ($84) in a double. The hotel is superbly efficient, welcoming its visitors with flair and courtesy. Uplandia is often used by visiting business people who enjoy its ample facilities for conferences and congresses. All rooms contain mini-bars, trouser presses, and video films shown around the clock. The hotel also has a sauna and a Jacuzzi. There is, as well, a garage for parking. From many of its rooms, you'll have a view of Uppsala and such landmarks as the castle, the University Library, and the cathedral. The Uplandia also offers a modern restaurant.

Sara Hotel Gillet, 23 Dragarbrunnsgatan (tel. 15-53-60), has an attractive, sophisticated design, and, for those who can afford it, offers first-class comfort in well-furnished rooms. Colors are muted, and the comfort is first rate, including a phone, bath (with private shower), color TV, and radio. However, the least expensive single rents for 375 kronor ($45), going up to 630 kronor ($75.60) for the best unit. Doubles begin modestly at 450 kronor ($54), climbing all the way to 850 kronor ($102). "The Season" is a first-class restaurant serving fine food, everything from international dishes to Swedish country cookery. The breakfast room, handsomely furnished, is called the Benjamin Garden, and there is also a cozy cocktail bar and lounge, called Vivaldi's.

The above recommendations are really first-class hotels, with the amenities and prices that go with such establishments. However, to cut costs you may want to consider the following recommendations.

Samariterhemmets Gästhem, 16 Hamnesplanaden (tel. 17-71-80), is a surprisingly large guesthouse, offering a total of 40 bedrooms, 12 of which contain private basins and toilets. The charge in a double room is 220 kronor ($26.40) to 260 kronor ($31.20) per night, and the rooms are spotlessly maintained. Singles rent from 150 kronor ($18) to 190 kronor ($22.80) per night. You are allowed to use a kitchenette with a refrigerator, and, you can watch TV in the lounge. Breakfast is an additional 15 kronor ($1.80), and the guest home serves a good lunch for just 32 kronor ($3.84).

Hotell Svea, 59 Kungsgatan (tel. 13-00-30), stands in the old town of Uppsala, and it's good and clean, right across from the railroad station, convenient for touring. Wojtek Rybicki, the manager, speaks English. The hotel welcomes guests from many countries.

Rooms opening onto the inner court are preferred because they're quieter. A single without bath, but with breakfast included, rents for 190 kronor ($22.80), the price going up to 220 kronor ($26.40) for two persons. Guests can use the shower rooms free. If you prefer a private shower in your room, a single rents for 210 kronor ($25.20), the price going up to 280 kronor ($33.60) in a double.

The **Scandic,** 48 Gamla Uppsalagatan (tel. 10-02-80), is a good bargain at certain times, containing a total of 157 adequately furnished chambers, with radio, phone, and, in some cases, TV. There is also a restaurant, as well as a pool and solarium. A single room costs 400 kronor ($48), rising to 550 kronor ($66) in a double. There are also some cheaper rooms for families, with three to four beds. Rates quoted are for the weekdays. Should you arrive on a weekend, the double units, for example, are reduced to 320 kronor ($38.40), the single going for 260 kronor ($31.20).

Sankt Erik, 1 Bangårdsgatan (tel. 13-03-84), is a small, clean hotel with only 18 rooms. The welcome is polite, and it might be suitable for an overnight stopover. Singles are modest in price, beginning at 120 kronor ($14.40) and climbing to 220 kronor ($27.40). The double range is (bathless) at 150 kronor ($18), climbing to 230 kronor ($29.40). Some three-bedded units are also rented.

READER'S HOTEL SELECTION: "The **Hotell Linné,** 45 Skolgatan (tel. 13-92-60), is a recently renovated former student housing accommodation in the center of town. The hotel is beautifully furnished with fine examples of Scandinavian design, and all of its rooms look out onto the celebrated Linnaean Gardens. Breakfast (for non-smokers) is served on the patio overlooking the gardens. A small gate allows motel guests unobstructed access to them, allowing the peaceful appreciation of their beauty. Finally, hotel rates decrease in the summer in Uppsala, as noted in your guidebook. The tourist bureau in town secured a double room for me (rooms are segregated by smoker/non-smoker, which I truly appreciated). Upon arrival, I discovered that my room was really a suite. The price for it is 320 kronor ($38.40). However, in winter, the charge goes up to 550 kronor ($66). As the tourist bureau worker informed me, there are many first-class hotels in Sweden, but none is as distinctly (and beautifully, I may add) Scandinavian as the Hotell Linné" (Margaret Martin, Woodstock, Conn.).

WHERE TO DINE: The **Flustret,** on Munkegatan, is the rendezvous for university students and their professors. A dress-up place, it offers dining down by the riverside in a gingerbread building complete with peaked roof, gables, balconies, and terraces for dining. Here you can try reindeer steak with whortleberries and cream sauce. The hors d'oeuvres and desserts are hard on a tight budget—so order carefully. Four nights a week an orchestra plays for dancing. Good service and dignity prevail. Meals cost from 150 kronor ($18).

Italian food has also invaded Uppsala. Secondo Bertolino runs the **Restaurant Guldtuppen,** 31 Kungsgatan. It's popular with the student crowd which flocks here to order pizzas, in the 28-krona ($3.36) to 40-krona ($4.80) range.

The students' favorite medieval restaurant is **Domtrappkällaren,** a 13th-century cellar at Riddartorget, next to the cathedral. Meals are available for as little as 30 kronor ($3.60), and a special dish of the day costs from 28 kronor ($3.36).

Cheaper meals are available at the **Ubbo,** a student cafeteria at 7 Övre Slottsgatan, which is open Monday to Friday 8 a.m. till 5 p.m. In July hours are from 10 a.m. to 3 p.m. A simple meal here will cost from 25 kronor ($3) to 40 kronor ($4.80). (On the same floor is a student travel office, SFS, and a bank to exchange your money.)

FOR DANCING: **Baldakinen,** 35 Dragarbrunnsgatan, is where the slightly older crowd goes to dance. Entrance is 32 kronor ($3.84) to 50 kronor ($6.60), depending on the day of the week. The club features a live band and entertainment. On certain nights, the custom is for the women to ask the men to dance. Check the newspaper and if you see *Varannan dans damernas* along with Baldakinen's advertisement, you know you've got the right night (usually Tuesday).

8. Gamla Uppsala

About 15 centuries ago, this village was the capital of the Svea kingdom. In its midst was a sacred grove accustomed to the wail and cry of both animals and people sacrificed to ancient Nordic gods.

The Viking burial mounds date from the sixth century and are believed to have contained the pyres of three kings of the Ynglinga dynasty. These mounds —the most important ancient monuments in Sweden—are sometimes facetiously referred to as the "pyramids of Scandinavia." They were excavated in the 19th century but contained nothing of spectacular interest.

Nearby, on the site of the old pagan temple, is a 12th-century parish church, once badly damaged by fire and never properly restored. It has been described as a stave church turned into stone. Before Uppsala Cathedral was erected, Swedish kings were crowned here.

Across from the church is Disagården, an open-air museum with reassembled buildings depicting peasant life in Uppland (open from 9 a.m. to 5 p.m., June through August).

Gamla Uppsala lies about two miles north of Uppsala, from which there is frequent bus service (take bus 24).

No visit to the village is complete without a stopover at:

ODINSBORG: Within whispering distance of the three grave mounds is this old wooden inn, built like a chalet with an overhanging second story. Visitors come here to relive an ancient Viking custom: drinking mead from silver-tipped ornamental ox horns. A hornful of mead—plenty for three or four—costs 45 kronor ($5.40). Kings and presidents have lifted one of these eight horns to *skôl*. The inn's guestbooks date back to 1830. The waitresses wear Viking breastplates over their provincial dresses. The downstairs tavern has murals depicting the days when mead was the drink, a corner fireplace with copper kettles, and crude tables and chairs. Upstairs are ten rooms, furnished with country antiques, where guests have sandwiches, pastries, and tea. You may also have the gourmet plate for 60 kronor ($7.20) and a plate for children at 40 kronor ($4.80), if you order by phone before you arrive (tel. 32-80-88).

In the rooms upstairs you'll find a collection of old weapons, one of the most important of which is an iron shirt from the 12th century, considered the best preserved one of its time in Europe. There are, in addition, several old floor clocks, one of them made just of wood, including the wheels in its mechanism.

9. Gripsholm Castle

On an island in Lake Mälaren, Gripsholm Castle—the fortress built by Gustavus Vasa in the late 1530s—is one of the most history-rich castles in Sweden, certainly one of the best preserved. The castle is near **Mariefred,** one of the most idyllic little towns in Sweden.

During the reign of the actor-king Gustavus III (18th century), a theater was built at Gripsholm, but the outstanding feature of the castle is its collection of paintings of nearly 3000 stiff-necked aristocrats (and others), surely one of the world's largest such assemblages.

Gripsholm was last occupied by royalty in 1864 (Charles XV), and was formerly used as a prison. The castle is open from May 1 to August 31, 10 a.m. to 4 p.m. Admission is 12 kronor ($1.44).

10. Tullgarn Castle

The royal castle (tel. 720-11), on a bay of the Baltic Sea, is open to the public from May 15 to September 15. Guided tours leave the main entrance every full hour from 11 a.m. to 4 p.m. The palace was begun in 1719. It contains no world masterpieces, but is appreciated because of its beautiful setting. Admission is 12 kronor ($1.44).

AN INN WITH ROYAL CONNECTIONS: Tullgarns Värdshus (Tullgarn Inn), Vagnhärad (tel. 0755/720-26), is in one of the wings of the royal summer castle of Tullgarn, 37 miles south of Stockholm. By car it's easy to find: you just follow the European Highway 4 (E4) south. After 37 miles a sign to the right will direct you to Tullgarns slott. After another quarter of a mile, you are there. To go by public transport, take the Blue Train from the Central Station to Södertälje Södra, about 20 minutes. From there you can get a bus to Trosa.

At the inn you can order a full-course lunch or dinner, with three dishes, for 110 kronor ($13.20). Swedish specialties are featured. For example, you might enjoy the salted salmon with creamed potatoes. You can also eat in the beautiful royal park, ordering a picnic of cold chicken or roast beef. It is served with beer or coffee in a basket which you carry with you. Finally, if you'd just like to have a cup of coffee with a sandwich, you can in the old stable of Queen Viktoria. The basket and coffee service is open every day from 11 a.m. to 5 p.m.

The inn is kept by Gunilla and Bosse Lindahl, who have lived here all their lives. It is open May 15 to September 5, from noon to 2 p.m. and from 5 to 7 p.m. weekdays (on Saturday and Sunday from noon to 7 p.m.).

11. Vaxholm

Many Stockholmers buy weekend houses—red and yellow fishermen's cottages—at Vaxholm, a bathing resort on the island of Vaxö. Sometimes called the "gateway to the northern archipelago," Vaxholm, along with Saltsjöbaden, is the most popular resort in those myriad of islands that extend east of Stockholm.

A beautiful, unspoiled Swedish village, Vaxholm makes for a good day's outing from Stockholm. A bus (either 670, 671, or 672) will take you there in less than an hour. Or else you can board a ferry leaving from the heart of Stockholm, right in front of the Grand Hotel. In many ways, the boat ride is preferable, as you'll pass along some of the most attractive scenery in Sweden. The ferry ride takes slightly longer, although only an hour. Food is served aboard, although I recommend that you control your appetite until you arrive in Vaxholm, where you'll dine much better.

In the old fortress that used to protect Vaxholm, a museum has been established, with exhibits relating to the Swedish navy.

For a luncheon, I'd suggest the **Waxholms Hotel** (tel. 301-50), where you can enjoy a smörgåsbord on a terrace overlooking the water. However, the cost of a meal here is high. No one escapes for less than 110 kronor ($13.20). A sprawling post-World War I structure, the hotel charges about 550 kronor ($66) for a well-furnished double room with breakfast, should you wish to spend the night. Singles rent for 400 kronor ($48). Most of the rooms contain private baths or showers. The hotel is owned and managed by a television performer, Åke Söderqvist.

READERS' TRAVEL TIPS—FROM STOCKHOLM TO FINLAND: "It is very cheap to go from Stockholm to Finland nowadays, especially to **Aland,** the islands in the Baltic Sea. Swedes go there to buy cheap foods and other things of beautiful Finnish design. From Stockholm, you can go by bus and boat. Take SL-buses from Stockholm's Homelegarden and then the Viking Line. On the boat, it's inexpensive to eat smörgåsbord. It is possible to stay on the islands for some days. A room with a private family can be rented, but there are hotels, too. Prices might be slightly higher during July. By the Viking Line, you can go to Abo and even to Helsinki (Turku), too. From Abo it is possible to make pleasant trips in Finland" (Gunnar and Majken Juhlin, Danderyd, Sweden). . . . "If you want to see the Swedes let their hair down, and I do mean *down,* then by all means take the boat to the Finnish-owned islands of Aland. If you have never been on a boat before, the trip can be interesting just in itself. They have smörgåsbord and glasses of Finnish vodka. I enjoyed talking to many people who wanted to talk, once that so-called Swedish reserve broke down. But be careful—between the waves of the Baltic and those shots of vodka, oh, did I get a hangover!" (John G. Morris Jr., Baltimore, Md.).

Chapter XIII

DALARNA AND VÄRMLAND

1. Falun
2. Leksand
3. Tällberg
4. Rättvik
5. Mora
6. Karlstad
7. Skara
8. Vadstena

THESE TWO PROVINCES—long known in folklore and saga—represent the soul of Sweden.

Dalarna, in the Lake District, is the most tradition-laden of all the provinces of the country. Its splashes of local color would rival a Van Gogh painting —everything from maypole dancing, fiddlers' music, and folk costumes to handicrafts. The Dala horse is displayed in every souvenir shop in Sweden.

To the south lies Värmland, from which many Swedes emigrated to America in the 19th century. Today their descendants, now American citizens, are coming back to see where it all began. The land still retains much of its character, as depicted in the sagas of Selma Lagerlöf, the most famous daughter of the literary province.

Karlstad makes an ideal stopover for exploring Värmland. Dalarna, on the other hand, has five major bases: Falun, Leksand, Tällberg, Rättvik, and Mora.

The Leksand-Tällberg-Rättvik area draws a lot of people during summer with sports, folklore, and a music week. In winter, people come here for skiing. Autumn and spring are the inexpensive seasons, when prices are reduced.

DALARNA

Any time can be ripe for a visit to Dalarna. But midsummer (June 21) is a mellow moment to pay a call. It is then that the Dalecarlians—young and old— run around as if they've already popped open all the bottles of May wine. Every man is a Puck or Oberon, every woman a Tatiana, as they race through the forest gathering birch bows and nosegays of wildflowers, with which they cover the maypole. Then the pole is raised, and they dance around it—under the midsummer-lit sky—till dawn, a good old respectable pagan custom.

When a Dalecarlian isn't dancing or picking flowers, he or she might be up at an old mountain "saeter" blowing on a cowhorn.

The quickest and easiest way to reach this province is by train from the Central Station in Stockholm, the trip taking about 4½ hours. Motorists from Oslo can stop over in Dalarna before venturing on to the Swedish capital. Similarly, visitors to Gothenburg can head north to both Värmland and Dalarna before seeing Stockholm. Our first stopover could also be a day's excursion from Stockholm.

1. Falun

This town is noted for its copper mines, and, just 6½ miles to the northeast, one can visit the home of the famed Swedish painter Carl Larsson (1853–1919). The old capital of Dalarna, it lies on both sides of the Faluå River. The town itself merits a short visit. You might go first to the market square, Stora Torg, and view the Kristine Church, a copper-roofed structure dating from the mid-17th century (the tower dates from the close of 1865).

THE FALUN COPPER MINE: This mine traces its beginnings back to the days when the Vikings were the most important power on the northern seas. Even before the kingdom of Sweden was established, the mine was an important source of copper for the people of Scandinavia. During the 17th century, the mine was the world's largest producer of copper, and supplied the raw material for the roof of the palace at Versailles.

To reach the Falun Mine on the way to the Dalarna Lake District, visitors can detour at Borlänge to Falun, and after a tour of the mine, continue on to Rättvik.

The tour begins with an elevator trip 180 feet below the surface. Guides take you through old chambers and winding passages dating from the Middle Ages. In one section of the mine, you'll see a shaft divided by a timber wall more than 650 feet high, possibly the world's highest wooden structure. In an adjoining room, royal visitors have traditionally autographed the rock wall since the early 19th century.

The mine is open daily from May 1 to August 31, from 10 a.m. to 4:30 p.m. The tour costs 18 kronor ($2.16) for adults, 10 kronor ($1.20) for children and students.

CARL LARSSON'S HOME: A short trip from Falun will take you to **Sundborn,** a small village whose main claim to fame is **Lilla Hyttnas,** the quaint home where the celebrated artist Carl Larsson, who died in 1919, lived with his wife, Karin, and their children. Now known as **Carl Larsson-gården,** Lilla Hyttnas grew from a two-storied timber house built in 1837, being added to in various stages to suit the artist and his family. Through Larsson's watercolors, which almost photographically reproduce every corner of the house and the family's daily life, this house has become known throughout Sweden and the world. The house is open to visitors from May 1 to September 30 from 10 a.m. to 5 p.m. weekdays and Saturday and from 1 to 5 p.m. on Sunday and holidays. There are guided tours throughout the day, showing the rooms which were richly decorated by the artist. English-speakinig tours are sometimes available. The cost of the house tour is 20 kronor ($2.40). The house is only a 20-minute drive by car from Falun. Public buses leave from the Falun bus station several times a day dropping visitors in Sundborn, five minutes away from Carl Larsson-gården. The bus trip costs 12 kronor ($1.44) each way.

2. Leksand

Leksands Noret, as it is called, is a kind of doorway to **Lake Siljan,** and visitors knock on it year round to gain entrance to the province of Dalarna. No less an authority than Hans Christian Andersen found the setting idyllic. Leksand—in its present form—dates back to around the turn of the century, when it was reconstructed after a fire had razed the settlement. But a settlement of some sort of this site goes back to pagan times.

Many of the old traditions of the province still flourish here—and not just for the benefit of visitors. Many women still don traditional dress for church on Sunday. In June and July the long "churchboats," dating back to Viking times, may cross the lake carrying parish residents to church. These same boats on the first Sunday in July compete in a churchboat race, followed by fiddlers' music and folk dancing. Since World War II a miracle play—*The Road to Heaven*— has been presented in open-air performances, providing an insight into the customs and folklore of Dalarna. The play runs for ten days.

The parish church, founded in the 13th century but reconstructed in the 18th, was designed by a field priest who accompanied the Swedish armies to Russia. Perhaps that's why the church has an onion-shaped dome.

Near the lakeside church is an open-air museum, several buildings dating from the 18th and 19th centuries. At that time, during the flowering of peasant art in the province, troubadour-like painters went from farmhouse to farmhouse, painting the dining rooms. Examples of this art can be seen at the museum. The painters pictured Christ and his Apostles in Dalarna dress.

You can also visit a glass-blowing factory and several handicraft shops.

At Hjortnäs, near Leksand, is the **Tennfigur Museum,** housing 20,000 tin figures, the collection of a former advertising man from Stockholm. The museum is open from 10 a.m. to 5 p.m. (tel. 611-13).

Sports is a major pursuit in Leksand, with several prepared tracks for walking and skiing starting from here. Skiers will find this a good center for using the ski tow at Käringberget and both the lift and tow at Åsleden, less than four miles away. Other skiing facilities include electrically lit cross-country tracks. A sports center has a swimming pool, sauna, skating rink, and curling hall, and tennis and miniature golf are available when the weather is right for them.

Visitors who want to hook up with one of the boat trips around **Lake Siljan** or go on a tour of the province should stop at the tourist bureau for information.

WHERE TO STAY: Those who wish to base in Leksand will find a suitable range of accommodations. In the summer, you might find it fun to rent yourself a stuga (log cabin) with four beds for 150 kronor ($18) per night. The Leksand tourist office (tel. 104-11) will book you into one. Rooms in private homes average around 60 kronor ($7.20) to 75 kronor ($9) per night for a single.

The **Youth Hostel** is just a short distance from the center of Leksand, and it charges 40 kronor ($4.80) to 50 kronor ($6) per night.

Then there's **Tre Kullor,** Rättviksvagen (tel. 113-50), a guest home (circa 1908) that looks like a New England farmhouse. It was the dream of three girls (hence the name) who wanted to create a warm and friendly place, exemplifying the old-fashioned hospitality of Dalarna. The "girls" have died, and the management is in the capable hands of Ruth Samuelson. ("Help yourself to the cherries on that tree," she says to guests. "That's what they're there for.")

In her year-round guest home (three buildings, actually) are 40 homey and comfortably furnished bedrooms, each with toilet and water basin. Full board, including service, ranges from 320 kronor ($38.40) to 350 kronor ($42) per person, the higher price for a room with private bath.

Over the years, this retreat has been popular with a number of regulars, drawn here by the good hearty meals that emerge from the tremendous old kitchen ("eat all you want"), the impromptu folk singing (Mrs. Samuelson alternates between the accordion and the piano), the chats around the corner brick fireplace, the sauna in the basement, and the personally escorted sightseeing trips around Lake Siljan.

Hotel Furuliden, 17 Hjortnäsvägen (tel. 114-05), is set on secluded grounds, about a ten-minute walk from the center. The sleeping rooms are large and decorated in the modern style. Considering the quality of the service and the welcome, prices are reasonable: bed-and-breakfast at a cost of 225 kronor ($27) per person. The food is some of the best I've had in the whole province. A lunch or dinner if ordered separately costs about 75 kronor ($9). The U-shaped dining room has two aisles with large windows opening onto the garden. The decorations are Empire, as is the furniture.

Finally, **Holiday Village** at Orsandbaden, on the lake about one mile from Leksand, is a government-run camping ground where you can stay for 50 kronor ($6). You can also rent a summer cottage (five of these are specially designed for handicapped persons). The cost of a stuga here is 800 kronor ($96) to 1700 kronor ($204) per week. A cabin with four beds rents for one night for 150 kronor ($18). There is a heated open-air swimming pool (free) and a water slide near the lake. Contact the Leksand tourist office (tel. 104-11).

READERS' MOTEL SELECTION: "A real find we made in Dalarna was the **Moskogen Motel** (tel. 111-01), just south of Leksand. It is an excellent place for making excursions in the beautiful surroundings—Lake Siljan, Rättvik, Mora, Orsa. In the motel, you may have every kind of accommodation. A little cottage with TV, shower, toilet, telephone, and some even with pantries, costs 275 kronor ($33). The smörgåsbord includes everything, and costs 55 kronor ($6.60)" (Gunnar and Majken Juhlin, Danderyd, Sweden).

3. Tällberg

This lakeside village, eight miles north of Leksand, is charmingly in tune with the spirit and tradition of Dalarna. It's the most favored spot in the whole province—and a choice oasis for thousands of nature-lovers in both summer and winter. Skiing, curling, skating, and sleigh rides are popular sports, and swimming and boating lure summer visitors.

The mass discovery of Tällberg's beauty came in the the wake of its recognition and adoption as a haven by artists and other cultural celebrities, who built summer houses in the village. Gustaf Ankarcrona, one of the artists, created **Holens Gammelgård** (farmstead), which later became the center of the Dalarna folklore movement. The old farmhouse of Ankarcrona is now a museum, at the highest point of Tällberg, providing a superb view over Lake Siljan.

WHERE TO STAY: Långbers (tel. 502-90) is a compound of the cranberry-red buildings typical of Dalarna, and it offers a restful interlude for 310 kronor ($37.20) to 350 per day for full board, 270 kronor ($32.40) to 290 kronor ($34.80) per day for half board. The hotel is about 1000 feet above sea level, and offers a fine view of Lake Siljan and its surroundings. It's a mile from the bus and railway station. All the bedrooms have private baths or showers and are furnished informally, with a workable blend of Nordic modern and traditional pieces. Most rooms have phones.

Åkerblads i Tällberg (tel. 508-00), 1¼ miles from Tällberg station, is an old-fashioned family hotel, under the guidance of Christina and Arne Åkerblad. The land has been in the same family for 15 generations, dating back to the early 17th century, and the place has operated as an inn since 1910. Between Leksand and Rättvik, this traditional compound stands on land sloping down toward Lake Siljan. The core of the house is still the wooden storehouse in the courtyard, although there has been much rebuilding over the years. The fully licensed hotel is known for its buffets, priding itself on "grandmother's good cooking." The homemade bread along with many other Swedish specialties are a feature.

The rooms are done in an attractive Dala style and they are most comfortable. A double room with shower and toilet costs 280 kronor ($33.60) to 360 kronor ($43.20) per person for full board. Some of the rooms don't have private plumbing, and if you're booked in one of these you get a reduction.

Recently, six new rooms have been added and two more honeymoon suites. The most interesting addition, however, is the pub, developed by moving one of the oldest cottages into the dining room, taking care of every detail to make it into a replica of an old pub. Here you can get a glass of beer or a drink and a cheap pub lunch. The hotel offers use of a massage pool, a sauna, and a solarium.

It's ideal to be here in winter when guests, wrapped in large wolfskin furs, are taken on sleigh rides to the sound of snorting horses and jingling bells. On their return, a log fire and hot mulled and spiced wine await them.

4. Rättvik

Thirteen miles from Leksand, Rättvik is one of the most popular resorts bordering Lake Siljan. It has some of the best hotels in the district. In summer, there are conducted tours from here around Lake Siljan (inquire at the tourist bureau).

For a view over the area, go to the top of the old wooden tower at **Vidablick,** about three miles from town on the road to Falun.

On the outskirts of the village is **Gammelgården** (tel. 114-45), an old farmstead of Dalarna through which guides conduct tourists. It is open from mid-June to mid-August, weekdays from 11 a.m. to 6 p.m. (On Sunday from 1 to 6 p.m.). Guided tours are conducted at 1 p.m. and 3 p.m. Admission is 6 kronor (72¢).

If you're interested in art, you can visit the artists' village at **Slöjdtuppen,** established by the Swedish artist, Sören Erikson. Children can take a ride on a miniature train.

WHERE TO STAY: Hotel Siljanshill (tel. 133-50), just under a mile from the center of Rättvik, sits high above Lake Siljan with a wonderful view of the lake. A small, cozy hotel with a continental atmosphere, the Siljanshill has just 12 bedrooms, all with showers, phones, color TV, and radios. Bed-and-breakfast costs from 220 kronor ($26.40). The slalom slope is a stone's throw from the hotel, and the summer alpine slide and ski and walking tracks are just around the center.

Sätergården (tel. 200-57) is a boarding house about 4½ miles northwest of Rättvik along road 70. It has 18 rooms with 50 beds. Some of the rooms have toilets *en suite.* Housekeeping apartments are available, although you can take full board if you choose. The cost of bed-and-breakfast is from 190 kronor ($22.80) per person per night.

OK Motorhotell, Storgatan (tel. 110-70), is a small, 32-room, red-brick structure, attracting a lot of Dalarna-bound motorists in the summer months. Rooms are plain, but adequately equipped and very clean. Singles cost 300 kronor ($36), with doubles going fro 340 kronor ($40.80). On the grounds is a cafeteria, and in the warmer months tables and chairs are placed outside in the continental fashion. There's also space to park your car, and you can even obtain auto service if you need it. Other facilities of the motel include a sauna and a giftshop.

A Christian Retreat

Stiftsgården (tel. 110-20) is a pilgrimage place attracting mainly Christians who come from all over Europe and America to live comfortably in an authentically Dalecarlian lakeside retreat where one can make a connection with the spirit of Old Sweden. This diocesan center began modestly in 1942, and the original three-story building was a 100-year-old *Klockargård* or bell-keeper's house.

The staff who run the place is likely to include everybody. Many activities are planned for summer residents, including folk dances. A short walk, enjoying a midsummer sunset, will take you to **St. Davidsgården,** a house for directed retreats and a center for Zen meditation, lying in a forest of birch and pine trees. The director of this international community is Dr. Jonas Jonson, who has worked in Geneva, specializing in the Lutheran mission in China.

In a single room, the center charges 250 kronor ($30), the cost dropping to 200 kronor ($24) per person in a double. These tariffs include not only breakfast, but lunch, dinner, and a welcome cup of tea at night. The units have toilets, but no private baths. Always write well in advance for a reservation, because of the popularity of the place.

5. Mora

In Upper Dalarna, between Lake Orsa and Lake Siljan, the provincial town of Mora is our final stopover in the province. Summer travelers find this business and residential center a good base for exploring the district. See the tourist bureau, Mora Turistbyrå, Ångbåtskajen, about organized tours. Telephone 0250/265-50 for information.

In Swedish history, Mora played an important role as the village where Gustavus Vasa—after an unsuccessful first attempt—finally rallied the peasants in Sweden's 16th-century war to free itself from the Danish yoke. In March of every year, the 50-mile Vasa Race—commemorating a chase after Gustavus to inform him that the reluctant peasants had agreed to fight—is one of the major ski events.

Mora has also opened a **Santa complex,** inaugurated for the Christmas of 1984. But it has year-round appeal, featuring Santa's house and his factory. Visitors can meet "Santa," and see his favorite helpers making and gift-wrapping presents for children all over the world.

Mora was also the hometown of Anders Zorn, perhaps Sweden's most famous painter—more about him below. But first, a look at Mora's two hotels.

WHERE TO STAY: Mora Hotel, 12 Standsgatan (tel. 117-50), is a well-groomed modern hotel in the center of the village, just a minute's walk from the tourist bureau. Used mostly by commercial travelers who know where to find substantial bargains, the Mora charges 650 kronor ($78) to 820 kronor ($98.40) for its doubles with bath. Bathless singles cost 450 kronor ($54), and singles with bath go for 600 kronor ($72) to 700 kronor ($84). Bathless rooms have private toilets and water basins. Breakfast is included. In July, rates are lowered, doubles costing 500 kronor ($60), singles 375 kronor ($45). The dining room opens onto a terrace with flowers, and the patio overlooks the water. For a change of cuisine, try the Chinese restaurant at the hotel.

Siljan Hotel, 6 Moragatan (tel. 130-00), is the most contemporary in design of the hotels in this area. Sleekly commercial, it is right in the center of the village, only a block from the tourist bureau. Doubles with water basins cost 425 kronor ($51) nightly. Bathless singles are priced at 330 kronor ($39.60), and a few singles with shower cost 400 kronor ($48). Breakfast is an extra 35 kronor ($4.20). Either lunch or dinner is available, costing from 75 kronor ($9). The rooms are up-to-date, with compact, built-in furniture relying on teak and Formica.

THE TOP SIGHTS: Mora has three top sights—all associated with the life and times of painter Anders Zorn (1860–1920). Although by today's standards, he would be considered traditional, he was quite a shocker in his time—I suspect because he painted a lot of nudes.

The first attraction is the **Zorn Museum** (*Zornmuseet*), containing not only a wide collection of the artist's own works (among them, *Cowgirl*), but paintings from his private collection—including works by Prince Eugen and Carl Larsson, also of Dalarna. Major foreign artists (sculpture by Kai Nielsen of Denmark and Auguste Rodin) are also presented, along with rural art and handicrafts of Dalarna. In summer hours are Monday to Saturday from 9 a.m. to 5 p.m. (on Sunday from 11 a.m. to 5 p.m.). In winter, it is open Monday to Saturday from 10 a.m. to 5 p.m. (on Sunday, from 1 to 5 p.m.). Admission is 10 kronor ($1.20).

The **Zorn Gardens** contain the former home of the artist and his wife Emma. It has been left just as it was when Mrs. Zorn died in 1942. Its chief attraction, aside from the paintings displayed, is Zorn's personally designed studio on the top floor, with its sloping ceiling and clerestory windows. In summer, the gardens are open Monday to Saturday from 10 a.m. to 5 p.m. (on Sunday, from 11 a.m. to 5 p.m.). Admission is 10 kronor ($1.20) for adults, 2 kronor (24¢) for children.

READER'S SHOPPING SELECTION: "An interesting place to visit in Dalarna is the little workshop where the traditional Swedish Dala horse is made. You are free to walk around watching the craftsmen as they work, and the finished product can be bought in the tourist shop on the premises at quite a substantial savings over what you would pay elsewhere. They also sell wooden shoes and other craft items. The workshop is a **Nusnäs,** a small village east of Mora. From the main road, turn off to the right at Farnäs. When coming from Rättvik, turn left at the village of Fu. Both the workshop and the tourist shop are open Monday to Friday from 7 a.m. to 5 p.m. The tourist shop is also open on Saturday" (May-Britt Richardson, Seattle, Wash.).

From Mora the road leads south to:

VÄRMLAND

In one of her most famous works, *The Saga of Gösta Berling,* Nobel Prize winner Selma Lagerlöf eerily and lyrically described Värmland life in the early 19th century.

Despite the encroachments of industry, tradition-rich Värmland remains much as Lagerlöf saw it. Both her former mansions—Mårbacka, now a museum, and Rottneros Manor, the Ekeby of her saga—may be visited.

The literary province was also the birthplace of John Ericsson (later he became a naturalized U.S. citizen), the inventor of the screw propeller. He built the first armored turret ship, the Union's *Monitor,* which defeated the Confederate ram, *Merrimack,* in the most famous naval clash of the American Civil War. His body, returned to Sweden by the U.S. Navy in 1890, was entombed in a mausoleum in Filipstad, 40 miles northeast of Karlstad.

The best center for exploring the province is:

6. Karlstad

The capital of Värmland, this port city lies on the Klarälven River, which flows south to Lake Vänern, one of the largest in Europe. Chiefly a commercial center, the headquarters of a booming wood pulp and timber industry, Karlstad also has many moderately priced restaurants and comfortable hotels. They tend to be overcrowded in summer—so reservations are important.

The tourist bureau is in the Municipal Library (Bibliotekshuset) at 26 V. Torggatan, one kilometer north of the railroad station. It provides information and arranges accommodation in both hotels and private homes.

Karlstad is reached quickly by air, about a one-hour trip, from either Stockholm or Gothenburg. The train from Gothenburg takes about three hours; from either Oslo or Stockholm, about four.

For a good preview of the local culture—arts and handicrafts—visit the **Värmlands Museum** in a park on Sandgrund, within walking distance of the Stads and Ritz Hotels and the town center. The museum is open daily from noon to 4 p.m. Admission is free.

The town also has an open-air park in **Marieberg Forest,** with a summer theater, an animal park, dance pavilions, and a restaurant.

One of the best ways to acquire a quick orientation of Karlstad is to take a guided tour on a **Sola** sightseeing boat, moored at Residenstorg. A boat leaves about every 1½ hours daily from 11 a.m. to 7 p.m., until 8 p.m. in June, July, and August.

Another excursion possibility is to visit the town of **Arvika,** which in the summer months has an artists' village. From all over Värmland, artists come here to work and display their creations.

HOTELS OF KARLSTAD: Carlstad Hotel, 2 V. Torggatan (tel. 10-02-00), is a new hotel, opened in 1984, near the Central Station. You can rent a double with shower for 550 kronor ($66), a single with the same facilities for 400 kronor ($48). The hotel restaurant, Artisten, serves dishes à la carte and is open for lunch as well as dinner.

Stadshotellet, 22 Kungsgatan (tel. 11-52-20), is in the center of town on the Klarälven River, with almost a century of tradition behind it in providing for the needs of travelers. A single with bath costs 500 kronor ($60); with shower, 425 kronor ($51); and with only a toilet and a wash basin, 280 kronor ($33.60). For a double with bath, you'll pay 600 kronor ($72); with shower, 550 kronor ($66); and with toilet and wash basin, 400 kronor ($48). Some of the doubles are big enough for hockey matches—well, almost.

The Stadshotellet is one of the most imposing and impressive of Stads hotels in Sweden. There are so many public rooms that you can visit a different one every night of the week. The main dining room is decorated in a folkloric theme. The hotel's Monk's Cellar, Vinkällaren Munken (see below), was created out of a 1654 church vault.

Gösta Berling, 1 Drottninggatan (tel. 15-01-90), stands at the beginning of the biggest shopping street in Karlstad. The recently renovated hotel is popular with traveling salespeople. Singles with shower cost 400 kronor ($48) and doubles with the same plumbing go for 500 kronor ($60). The hotel was named for the Selma Lagerlöf novel which was made into a Greta Garbo film, *The Legend of Gösta Berling.*

KARLSTAD'S RESTAURANTS: Vinkällaren Munken, on Västra Torggatan, around the corner from the entrance to the Stadshotellet (see above), is tucked away in the crypt and cellar of an old church. Wrought-iron lanterns and candles provide a touch of glamour, lighting the simple dinners available from 60 kronor ($7.20). For 85 kronor ($10.20), you can order an entrecôte smothered in mushrooms, with a big plate of french fries. The liveliest restaurant in town, the Monk's Cellar is at its best by night. The Selma Lagerlöfs of tomorrow come here with their boyfriends to listen to singers lament. There's a honeycomb of rooms—all with thick arches and wood paneling. Around the walls are artifacts of copper, brass, and wood. It isn't necessary to order dinner; many of the young men and women come here for the entertainment and the draft beer. The place is open from 11 a.m. to 11:30 p.m. weekdays, from 6 to 11 p.m. Saturday. It is closed Sunday.

Värdshuset Alstern, 4 Morgonvägen (tel. 13-49-00), lies between Filipstad and Karlstad on route 63, in a quiet spot near Lake Alstern. But this restaurant doesn't need the beautiful surroundings to make it popular with locals and visitors alike, because the food is outstanding in its own right. Although the chefs are of German origin, they blend nouvelle cuisine with Swedish culinary arts to produce dishes using local foods insofar as possible: game from the forest, fish from the lakes, mushrooms and vegetables grown in the area. You can enjoy complete meals here for from 175 kronor ($21) up. It's open from 11:30 a.m. to 2:30 p.m. Monday to Friday, reopening at 6 p.m. on Wednesday and closing at 11 p.m. You can reach the restaurant by car or bus.

Oasen, 1 Järnvägsgatan, is a salad restaurant near the Central Station. At this popular place, you can sample varying dishes, costing from about 45 kronor ($5.40). They also have excellent ice cream here.

If you're driving on route E18 from Karlstad to Oslo, turn right in Grums (road sign: Borgvik 14), take former E18, and you will pass right by **Borgviks Bruk.** There, about 20 miles west of Karlstad, you can order a hearty Swedish luncheon for around 75 kronor ($9). The rock house on the water is like a picture-postcard scene. Nearby is an old stone bridge.

ROTTNEROS MANOR: The Ekeby in the saga of Selma Lagerlöf, Rottneros Manor is one of Sweden's major attractions. Although the manor cannot be visited by the public, its park and sculpture garden can.

On the western shores of the Fryken Lakes, Rottneros Manor lies 40 miles north of Karlstad. From the Central Station of Karlstad, it is reached by train via Kil.

In all, the park has more than 100 pieces of sculpture, including works by Carl Milles. The foremost sculptors of each of the neighboring Scandinavian countries are also represented: Kai Nielsen of Denmark, Gustav Vigeland of Norway, and Wäinö Aaltonen of Finland.

In a strange twist—reality imitating art—Rottneros was reshaped to fit more accurately its description by Miss Lagerlöf. The park, charging 12 kronor ($1.44) admission, is open from 10 a.m. to 6 p.m. from mid-May to the end of September (open 9 a.m. to 7 p.m. in July). On the grounds is a cafeteria.

MÅRBACKA: On the other side of the water is the former home of Selma Lagerlöf, safely secured with the money she won when she received the 1909 Nobel Prize for literature. The building is kept much as she left it at her death in 1940 (she was born here in 1858). The estate, filled with her furnishings and mementos, is open from mid-May to September 20 daily from 10 a.m. to 7 p.m., at 8 kronor (96¢) admission. Her pillared home is 6 miles from Sunne and 36 miles north of Karlstad. (There is a good youth hostel at Sunne, just north of Rottneros.)

JOSSEFORS: On route E61, three miles west of Arvika, is this arts and crafts center well worth a side trip from Karlstad. Among the many sights here is a replica of a Viking shop—also the local people, who sometimes dress like Vikings. It is open to view seven days a week.

For our next exploration, we head south from Karlstad to:

7. Skara

Between Karlstad and Gothenburg lies this highly recommended stopover in the province of Västergötland, the ancient western country of the once-dreaded Goth. In the heart of the province, Skara, reached by Europe Highway 3, makes a good center for exploring some of the district's major sights, such as Läckö Castle and Varnhem Abbey.

Both an educational center and a cathedral town, Skara was an ancient Episcopal see with a colorful history. With its wooden buildings and green squares, it remains unspoiled.

There is an excellent outdoor swimming pool here, plus a small one for children.

The tourist information office (tel. 144-70) is just across from the main square.

THE TOP SIGHTS: For those passing through for the day, I'll quickly highlight the top three sights, beginning with the:

Cathedral

Classical in its purity of line, **Sancta Maria,** in the center of town, was founded in 1150, although it was extensively restored in the 19th century. The twin-spired building is open from 9 a.m. to 5 p.m. from May 1 to August 31 and 10 a.m. to 4 p.m. from September 1 to April 30 (9:30 a.m. to 1:30 p.m. on Sunday). Inside, look for the magnificent stained-glass windows by Bo Beskow. Excavations beneath the cathedral have revealed remains of the only known Swedish medieval crypt. One of the cathedral's treasures is a funeral chalice, the property of a bishop dating from 1065.

Library

North of the cathedral is a diocesan and regional library, founded in the 12th century. Considered to be the most ancient library in Sweden, it houses a prized treasure, *Skara Missal,* dating from about 1150 and believed to be one of the oldest books written in Scandinavia. The library also contains a collection of other manuscripts from the Middle Ages. It may be visited during the summer from 8 a.m. till 7 p.m. weekdays and from 9 a.m. till 1 p.m. on Saturday.

Västergötland Museum/Skaraborgs Länsmuseum

In the Town Park of Skara lies one of Sweden's most impressive provincial museums, rich in artifacts—such as ecclesiastical woodcarvings and medieval stone art—from the surrounding district. The museum also houses the "Ancient Village," old wooden buildings torn down in the province and reassembled on this site. An Agricultural Museum is housed in an old barn. Here, too, is Kråks Manor, a fully furnished 18th-century manor house. The museum is open weekdays from 10 a.m. to 4 p.m. (on Saturday and Sunday from noon to 4 p.m.). For information, phone 133-25.

WHERE TO STAY IN SKARA: Stadshotellet, 5 Järnvägsgatan (tel. 130-00), in the heart of town, a block from the cathedral, is built like a small French château. It is one of the best of the Stads hotels architecturally. Its ballroom and dining room reflect the social events that take place here. Its large bedrooms are equally impressive and are decorated in a contemporary style. Each double has a private bath, equipped with a heated pole for speedy drip-drying, and rents for 450 kronor ($57.60). Singles with bath go from 330 kronor ($39.60). Breakfast is included, and a lunch costs from 60 kronor ($7.20).

Skara Motell, 74 Skaraborgsgatan (tel. 131-10), is small, containing only 35 rooms, each furnished in a simplistic Nordic fashion and each containing a private shower, toilet, phone, radio, and color TV. A single rents for 275 kronor ($33), a double going for 380 kronor ($45.60), with breakfast included. Some good regional dishes, along with standard fare, are available in the self-service cafeteria n the premises. Outside your room you'll find a covered parking space for your vehicle.

Hotell Anglé, 15 Skaraborgsgatan (tel. 134-10), is an unassuming 42-room hotel which has 20 baths and showers. English is spoken, and the reception is warm. Simple and modest, the hotel is adequately comfortable. Depending on the plumbing, singles range in price from 200 kronor ($24) to 320 kronor ($38.40), and doubles are priced from 240 kronor ($28.80) to 420 kronor ($50.40), these tariffs including breakfast.

EXCURSIONS: There are several popular day trips from Skara:

Läckö Castle

On an island in Lake Vänern, 14 miles north of the old town of Lidköping (see below), Läckö is a rustic, towered castle, founded in the 13th century. It has 250 rooms—barren and bleak. See the painted ceiling and walls and the banqueting hall. The castle flowered under Count Magnus Gabriel de la Gardie, a contemporary of Queen Christina.

There are guided tours every day from May through August at 9:30, 10:15, and 11:30 a.m., and 1, 2:15, 3:30, and 4:40 p.m. In September, hours are 11 a.m. to 1 p.m. daily. Admission is 10 kronor ($1.20). Popular exhibitions, which can be viewed from 10 a.m. to 6 p.m., are held each summer from mid-June to mid-August. There is also an excellent restaurant in the castle.

Lidköping

This is a small town and market center (pop. 35,000) not to be confused with the largest Swedish town of Linköping. The tourist information office (tel. 605-05), in the main square (colorful market day every Saturday), is actually an old hunting lodge transported here from Läckö Castle.

Gamla Lidköping (Old Lidköping) is an open-air museum. Here, you can wander around the well-preserved 17th-, 18th-, and 19th-century heritage, seeing that the small town is alive and well in the 20th century. Flowers bloom in windowboxes, the gardens are well kept, and in several places you can watch artisans working in wood, clay, and various metals. These products are for sale in the shops of the people making them. There's a sweet shop in the marketplace, and a spice garden, with about 200 spices and medicinal plants, is well worth a visit.

The **Maritime and Craft Museum,** 9 Mellbygatan (tel. 830-65), a working-life museum, traces the history of Lidköping. It has a section devoted to local crafts and another to various marine activities, such as sailmaking and boat building. An excellent collection of model boats is displayed. Entrance is free.

The **Rörstrand Museum and Factory Shop** at Fabriksgatan (tel. 220-30) displays three centuries of the work of this company. Rörstrand is Sweden's oldest and most prestigious ceramics works. Founded in 1726, it is known for its beautiful china and stoneware. It's open Monday to Friday from 10 a.m. to 5 p.m. (on Saturday from 9 a.m. to 1 p.m.).

Besides Rörstrand, visitors are welcome at the **Design-House at Tofta,** where the Stålhane Group makes, exhibits, and sells its works, and at the **Pomona House,** another center for artists and craftspeople.

In summer you can take boat excursions, experiencing the unique **Eken Archipelago.** Excursions leave from the Läckö landing-stage (tel. 103-28 for more information).

Varnhem Abbey

Nine miles east of Skara, this former Cistercian monastery was completed in 1260, after the previous abbey had burned. Angry Danes razed it again in the mid-16th century, but it was restored by Christina's friend, Count Magnus Gabriel de la Gardie, who is buried here. Designed as a cross-vaulted, three-aisled basilica, the medieval abbey also contains the grave of Birger Jarl, founder of Stockholm. Varnhem is open from mid-April till the end of September, 9 a.m. to 7 p.m. for 3 kronor (36¢).

Habo Church

This church stands outside the village of Habo, 12 miles north of Jönköping, near lake Vättern. (It's close enough to Varnhem to be visited on the same day.) Habo Kyrka is an old barn-red frame church. During 1721–1723 it was enlarged to its present structure. The sandstone altar was consecrated about 1347, and the baptismal font is from the 13th century.

READER'S SIGHTSEEING TIP: "You should not miss the beautiful little town of **Hjo** on **Lake Vättern.** It is becoming increasingly popular as a vacation spot for Swedes and foreigners alike. Its access to Lake Vättern and nearby forests and fishing waters makes it a tempting refuge from the big city. Just outside Hjo, there is a church you should not miss. It is called the **North Fågels Church,** and once you get a glimpse of the building through the trees, it is hard to resist a closer inspection. The church structure goes back to the 12th century, and the church as it stands today is a result of extensive renovation and rebuilding that took place during the 17th century. During this period, the ceiling was fitted with wooden arches, the arms hall painted with pictures depicting the Creation and Judgment Day. Elegant standards and carved family crests, statuary, and the beautiful altar relics, including the casing from the organ used in 1775, are now part of he church inventory" (George D. Rehnquist, Knoxville, Tenn.).

GRÄNNA: An idyllic little town founded in 1652, Gränna was built on the slopes of Grännaberget (hill) in the form of steps leading down to a centuries-old church and village on Lake Vättern. There are still a lot of the old wooden buildings which have been preserved since the town's origin, and the original town plan is still followed.

Grännaberget can be reached either by car from the road between Gränna and Tranås or by steps up to the top, found in a couple of places in the town. Here, you'll find a splendid view and a fine area for walking. A small **open-air museum** has been created by grouping together a few buildings from the 17th century. If you're energetic, you can walk along a trail to **Skogstornet** (the Forest Tower) from which the view of the area around Lake Vättern is breathtaking.

The Gränna area is a rich repository of Iron Age weapons, tools, menhirs, and burial grounds, some 4000 years old. Many such relics are on display in the **Vättern Museum** in the center of the town.

Gränna was the birthplace of North Pole balloonist-explorer Salomon August Andrée, whose ill-fated attempt to reach and cross the Pole in the balloon, *Ornen* (The Eagle), was the subject of an award-winning movie, *The Flight of the Eagle.* Andrée and his crew of three left from Spitzbergen in the *Ornen* in 1897 but were forced down, and all died in a desperate effort to reach civilization. The remains of the expedition were found in 1930 and may be seen in the **Andrée Museum** here. It contains a collection of his belongings, diaries, and relics of the fatal ordeal, giving a rare insight into a bold pioneering voyage. Museigården, a part of the museum, houses exhibits illustrating the history of the area.

WHERE TO STAY: The **Scandic Hotel Gyllene Uttern** (tel. 108-00), halfway between Stockholm and Copenhagen, a mile from Gränna, is the honeymoon Shangri-la of Sweden, complete with a baroque wedding chapel in the basement. A step-gabled imitation castle overlooking Lake Vättern, Gyllene Uttern offers the best in food and lodgings.

Doubles with bath go for 500 kronor ($60). Singles with bath cost 400 kronor ($48), including service and breakfast. Open all year, the inn also offers multilevel cottages on its grounds.

The public rooms are furnished with antiques. The main dining room, its deeply set windows overlooking the lake, is highlighted by 17th- and 18th-century gilt-framed paintings, medieval suits of armor, and a bas relief fireplace.

8. Vadstena

The most important stopover on the Göta Canal trip is in this medieval-looking town on the eastern shores of Lake Vättern. Famed for its Renaissance Vasa castle and an abbey founded by Saint Briget, Vadstena has lots of narrow streets and old frame buildings. It is known all over Sweden for the lace made by hand here. To see samples of this delicate product, walk along High Street.

VADSTENA CASTLE: Founded by Gustavus Vasa, king of Sweden, in 1545 but not completed until 1620, this is one of the most splendid of the Renaissance Vasa castles, erected during a period of national expansion. It dominates the town from its moated position on the lake. Restored in the 19th century after having fallen into disrepair (once used as a granary), Vadstena was last inhabited by royalty in 1715. Since 1899, the greater part of the castle has been used by the provincial archives. Tours are conducted weekdays from May to September for 7 kronor (84¢).

VADSTENA ABBEY CHURCH: Built between the mid-14th century and the 15th, to specifications set out by its founder, Saint Biraitta (Bridget) of Sweden, this Gothic-style church is rich in medieval art. The abbey, parts of which date from 1250, housed the nuns of Saint Birgitta's order until their expulsion in 1595.

The **New Monastery and Church,** built in 1973 to celebrate the 600th anniversary of the founder, show the same traditional simplicity of style Saint Birgitta prescribed for her order. The domed ceiling in the church has aroused much interest, and the combination of stone and timber adds to the impression of strength and humility which marks the character of the saint. The view through the huge windows is the only decoration in this otherwise stark and exciting church. The structure is open daily all year. The nuns, who returned to Sweden in 1963, will show the church and their guesthouse to interested visitors at times convenient to themselves.

ACCOMMODATIONS IN VADSTENA: **Vadstena Turistbyrå,** the tourist bureau, at Rådhustorget (tel. 102-50), dispenses information about tours and private homes that accept paying guests. It's an excellent way to economize while experiencing life in a Vadstena home. Vadstena also has three highly recommended and unique accommodations.

Kungs Starby Inn, Route 50 (tel. 114-20), on the southern outskirts of the town, is an old manor house that has been converted into a licensed restaurant and inn. There is also a 1984-built hotel part with modern and suitable rooms.

Accommodations, including a buffet breakfast and service, cost 140 kronor ($16.40) per person. Rooms with private bath/shower are priced from 225 kronor ($27) per person. As an estate, Starby dates back to the 13th century, owned by the Vasa dynasty.

Vadstena Klosters Gästhem, Lasarettsgatan (tel. 115-30), is an old convent and royal summer castle from in the early part of the 13th century. Completely modernized by the St. Birgitta Society, it offers 25 well-appointed rooms with private baths for 450 kronor ($54) in a double, breakfast and service included. On the lake, the cloisters guest home adjoines the historic abbey church. There are three lounges, all fresh and light.

Birgittasystrarnas Gästhem, Myntbacken (tel. 109-43), is the guest home of the modern cloister. Some 25 well-appointed rooms are rented out by the nuns, providing a convenient and quiet accommodation in a friendly atmosphere. Rooms with private baths/showers cost from 200 kronor ($24) per person for full board, based on double occupancy.

Chapter XIV

KALMAR AND THE BALTIC ISLANDS

1. Gotland (Visby)
2. Kalmar
3. Växjö (The Glassworks District)
4. Öland

IN 1556, WHEN GUSTAVUS VASA invited a Venetian glassblower to Sweden, the king launched a booming business that one day would make his nation known all over the world for its achievements in the art. Breaking from Venetian tradition, Swedish glass won its reputation for purity and simplicity of line.

In the forests of the province of Småland lie some of the most famous glass factories in the world (Orrefors, for example), all heavily visited by those flocking to see the highly skilled artisans at their work.

But we'll not confine ourselves to glassworks on this expedition. Kalmar, while a good base for exploring the district, is well worth an exploration in itself. It was here that the Agreement of Kalmar was signed in 1397, wedding Denmark, Norway, and Sweden in an ill-fated union. Across the water from Kalmar is the Baltic island of Öland, settled in prehistoric times.

Before journeying on to Kalmar or Öland, we'll hop over to Sweden's most popular tourist island, Gotland, nestling in the Baltic.

1. Gotland (Visby)

In the middle of the Baltic sits the ancient home of the Goths, the island of Gotland, about 75 miles by 35 miles in its longest and widest spans. The Swedes go to Gotland for sunny holidays by the sea; North Americans are more interested in the old walled city of Visby. But an investment of a little extra time will prove that Gotland, with its cliffs, odd rock formations, bathing beaches, and rolling countryside, is rich territory. Buses operated by the Swedish Railways traverse the island, as do organized tours out of Visby.

GETTING THERE: Gotland is easily reached on a 35-minute flight from Stockholm to Visby. But it also has good sea and train connections. From the Central Station in Stockholm, take the train south to the port of **Nynäshamn**, a ride of about an hour. From there, take the car ferry to Visby. It leaves at midnight and takes about five hours.

The bus service between Visby and the airport is run by Gosta Westberg, 363 Tradgardsgat, who is a charming, friendly, and informative man. The fare is about 10 kronor ($1.20) each way. Mr. Westberg also conducts tours of Visby.

After exploring Gotland, take a ferry from Visby to **Oskarshamn.** From Oskarshamn, train connections can be made to the next recommended stop-over, Kalmar and the glassworks district.

ABOUT VISBY: At the end of the 12th century and during the 13th, the walled city of Visby rose to its zenith of power as the seat of the powerful Hanse-atic merchants and as the trade center of Northern Europe. Seventeen churches sprouted up during its heyday. Step-gabled houses were built of stone, and the townspeople lived in splendor behind their all-protective walls.

But Visby flourished only a short time as a great Baltic power. Sacking Danes, led by King Valdemar, penetrated the walls in 1316 and demanded a crippling ransom. The city subsequently declined, drifting into decay and pover-ty. Its emergence as a tourist center, once it was recognized as a virtual treasure house of art of the Middle Ages, has been in recent times.

It is amazing that so much of Visby remains in recognizable shape, consid-ering the looting, burning hordes who have passed through it. But today it is the only city in Northern Europe, the Number One spot in all of Scandinavia, for those seeking medieval charm.

ACCOMMODATIONS: Visby, for all its lures, lacks hotels, particularly for the budgeteer. Accommodations are sardine-packed in summer—so *reserve in advance.*

But if you haven't, head for the **Accommodation Center** of the tourist bu-reau (tel. 190-10). The charge is 30 kronor ($3.60) for booking a room. The English-speaking personnel here will arrange rooms in hotels or private homes in or near Visby. The average rate for an accommodation in a private home is 65 kronor ($7.80) per person per night. The tourist bureau is near the harbor, 3 Färjeleden, but it's better to telephone for reservations from Stockholm. The office is open Monday through Friday from 9 a.m. to 5 p.m. (in high season, also Saturday from 9 a.m. to 1 p.m. and 4 to 5 p.m.; Sunday 9 to 11 a.m. and 4 to 5 p.m.).

Here follow the limited budget choices Visby proper:

NYA Hotel Solhem, 3 Solhemsgatan (tel. 790-70), is on a hilly slope over-looking the harbor. It's about the best low-cost hotel in Visby, all considered. In a modernized wing out back, the tiniest double rooms this side of Lilliput rent for 310 kronor ($37.20) nightly. Singles rent for 200 kronor ($24). From June 1 to August 31, guests are booked in here on the half-board plan, costing 280 kronor ($33.60) in a single, from 420 kronor ($50.40) for two persons in a double. Children up to 12 years of age get a 25% reduction. Otherwise, you can rent one of the family rooms, ranging in price from 640 kronor ($76.80) for half board for parties of three, going up to 890 kronor ($106.80) for half board for four. The Solhem is a gabled building with a small garden. On the ground floor is a bar that gets a little rowdy on Friday and Saturday nights—so don't count on turning in early.

Donnersplats Hotel, in the center of town at 6 Donnersplats (tel. 149-45), is actually a rooming house (enter with your own key), run by the local Reso travel agency. A single room goes for 180 kronor ($21.60); a double, 280 kronor ($33.60)—plus another 40 kronor ($4.80) for breakfast. It's nothing special but will do in a pinch. A kitchenette in the hall may be used by patrons.

Living on the Outskirts

Vacation-wise Swedes have long known they can have an idyllic holiday in one of the moderately priced guesthouses and hotels on the outskirts of Visby. The setting is rustic, and Visby is within easy reach. Below are previewed just a few of these heretofore secret places.

Toftgårdens Guest House, 11 miles south of Visby (tel. 654-00), is a cottage colony, quite near the sandy beach of Tofta. It consists of a 14-room main building and a dozen cottages, offering a total of 53 rooms. Set in a wooded garden, it is run by the Göransson family. A double without bath costs 200 kronor ($24); a double with bath, 300 kronor ($36). Half board, depending on the room, goes for 200 kronor ($24) to 340 kronor ($40.80) per person. There are several comfortable lounges, plus a sauna. Licensed for beer and wine, the guesthouse occasionally offers dancing. English is spoken.

Tofta Strandpensionat, 11 miles south of Visby (tel. 650-09), is a low frame bungalow right on the sea, in a beach setting with pines as a backdrop. Open from May through September, it is run by Mia and Erik Jacobson, who offer more than 80 bedrooms in their main building. Each unit has a toilet and a shower. You may, however, prefer the more rustic living in one of the cottages. For a high-season rate of from 200 kronor ($24) to 340 kronor ($40.80) per person daily, you receive a room and two meals. Reductions for children are granted. The proprietors often provide dancing and entertainment, and arrange fishing trips as well. English is spoken.

WHERE TO EAT: Burmeister Garden, on Strandgatan, next to the tourist office, is a deceptively large restaurant—part of it indoors, but most of it under shady fruit trees. From many of the tables, diners look out on the surrounding medieval buildings. Lunch averages around 50 kronor ($6) to 100 kronor ($12), and dinner plates are served for 55 kronor ($6.60) to 110 kronor ($13.20). The food is well prepared and presented with style. At night a more festive beer-garden atmosphere prevails as diners are serenaded by an orchestral trio.

Jacob Dubbe, 16 Strandgatan, offers you a cozy sidewalk café, a pizza parlor, or a captain's table embracing an exotic aquarium. In the background stereo music is played. The tasty pizzas cost from 50 kronor ($6), and the specialty is Dubbe's pizza delight. Complete dinners cost from 65 kronor ($7.80) to 100 kronor ($12), and you can eat as much salad as you want. The restaurant, run by Roger Svensson, is open weekdays from 11 a.m. (Sunday from 1 p.m.).

Monk's Café, on Munktorget, in the center of a little shopping arcade opening off Stora Torget, is a charming place for snacks and coffee (best coffee in town). Beer and pizza are also served. Snacks begin at 35 kronor ($4.20). The little shops along the arcade have many good handicraft buys. It's open daily from 9 a.m. to 6 p.m. Closed Sunday.

Värdhuset (Guesthouse), 26 Strandgatan, offers pleasant garden dining for decent prices. A hot lunch can be had for 45 kronor ($5.40) and up. It is open from 8:30 a.m. until 10:30 p.m.

Faventia, 20 Hästgatan (near Österport gate), is a popular restaurant featuring Italian pizza for 30 kronor ($3.60) and up. Lunch is served from 11 a.m. to 3 p.m. and dinner from 3 until 11 p.m.

Domus Department Store has a cafeteria that serves hot meals in the 25-krona ($3) to 75-krona ($9) range, but they're nothing special.

TOURS OF THE TOP SIGHTS: Visby is a town meant for walkers. It can easily be explored on foot, but you may want to take an organized tour leaving three times daily in season. Since so many of the sights, particularly the ruins of the 13th- and 14th-century churches, may not easily be appreciated without knowing their background, the tour is recommended.

The two-hour tour—combined coach and walking—leaves daily from near the tourist bureau at the 17th-century Lübeck merchant's house, **Burmeister.** It operates from mid-June to mid-September, always at 11 a.m. The cost is 40 kronor ($4.80), including entrance fees.

The tour takes guests to the old **Hanseatic harbor** (not the same harbor used today) and includes a walk through the beautiful **Botanical Gardens** (you'll know why Visby is called the city of roses), and passes two of the most famous towers in the old wall—the **Maiden's Tower** (a peasant girl was buried alive here for helping a Danish king) and the **Powder Tower** (the most ancient fortification in Visby). Later the bus passes **Gallow Hill,** a medieval hanging station in use till the mid-19th century.

Later still, visitors leave the bus and take a walk to the old ruins of the former Dominican **Monastery of St. Nicholas,** built in the early 13th century. A mystical opera pageant is staged here annually during the Visby Festival in July and August (see below). Finally, the tour goes to the Gothic and Romanesque **Cathedral of St. Mary,** dating back to the 13th century.

A final sightseeing recommendation—to be done on your own—is the **Gotlands Historical Museum** opposite the Burmeister House on Strandgatan, a medieval street noted for its step-gabled houses. The museum contains some of the most interesting artifacts discovered on Gotland, including carved stones dating back to A.D. 400, works of art from medieval and later periods, plus furniture and household items. It is open weekdays from 11 a.m. to 5 p.m. (Sunday from 1 to 5 p.m.), costing 12 kronor ($1.44).

A tour of the island—different every day—leaves from the tourist bureau. The price may be as low as 100 kronor ($12) or as high as 130 kronor ($15.60). But each day the tour visits the **Lummellunda Caves,** north of Visby, with their stalactite and stalagmite formations, fossil remains, and subterranean waters.

VISBY FESTIVAL: Since 1929, an annual festival, featuring a mystical opera pageant (often with top stars) by Friedrich Mehler, is performed in the ruins of St. Nicholas, the 13th-century Dominican monastery. The pageant, *Petrus de Dacia,* is named after a prior of the monastery, a leading figure in Visby in the Middle Ages. He is known as "the first author of Sweden." His body, it is said, is buried somewhere in the ruins, where the drama immortalizes him. All the mystery of the Middle Ages comes alive as the moonlight streams through the outlines of the Gothic windows, eerily illuminating the actors portraying the harassed spiritualist, the robed friars, the medieval soldiers. The festival is held in July and August, beginning at 9 nightly. The opera alone is worth the trip to Visby. Tickets range from 38 kronor ($4.56) to 70 kronor ($8.40). For specific dates and reservations, write to the Visby Festival, 47 Tranhusgatan, S-62155, Visby, Sweden.

With Visby behind us, we ply across 60 miles of water on a car ferry back to the mainland, then head south by train for:

2. Kalmar

Strategically situated **Kalmar Castle,** founded in the 12th century, was once called the key to Sweden, meaning that the person who held Kalmar could unlock the country. As a gateway city, Kalmar has seen a lot of cannon blasting in its day.

Today a thriving commercial center, Kalmar still retains many of its 17th-century buildings and homes of sea captians, clustered in particular around Stortorget. From the marketplace, you can wander over to inspect **Kalmar Cathedral**—also from the 17th century (open from 8 a.m. to 7 p.m.; no charge).

The first Swedish emigration to America, more than three centuries ago, originated from Kalmar, ending in Wilmington, Delaware. In Kalmar, Wilmington is referred to as a sister city.

Kalmar boasts good **swimming** right in town, including one nude bathing area. Other things to do: Every Saturday from 8 a.m. to 3 p.m., a big outdoor market is held in front of the cathedral.

The **Folkets Park,** a short distance from the center of town (south side), has discos and concerts on summer evenings.

The largest and oldest handicrafts shop in Sweden, **Hemslöjden,** 26 Larmgatan (tel. 209-01), invites browsers or shoppers. It has an export department.

KALMAR ACCOMMODATIONS: Go to the Kalmar tourist office, **Kalmarbygdens Turisttrafikförening** (tel. 153-50), near the railway station, right in the center of town, where Wiola Hägglöf and the efficient English-speaking staff will be delighted to help you. Good rooms in private homes are available here at 65 kronor ($7.80) for a single, 100 kronor ($12) for a double, plus a booking fee of 20 kronor ($2.40). The office is open from 9 a.m. to 9 p.m. weekdays, 9 a.m. to 6 p.m. on Saturday, noon to 7 p.m. on Sunday.

In addition, Kalmar and its vicinity offer an adequate range of accommodations, although many visitors prefer to stay on the island of Öland.

Ritz Hotel, 6 Larmgatan (tel. 155-40), is a third-floor private hotel reached by an elevator in an older building, near the railway station. Remodeled, it offers doubles with bath for 500 kronor ($60) with breakfast. Singles with breakfast range from 330 kronor ($39.60) to 360 kronor ($43.20). Even more economical are the family rooms. Thought and care have gone into the planning of the bedrooms. Many have good original oil paintings, beds with modern rattan headboards, televisions, and telephones.

For a splurge in Kalmar, try the **Stadshotellet,** 14 Stortorget (tel. 151-80). The best bargain is a family room (sleeping four). Singles range in price from 250 kronor ($30) to 425 kronor ($51), with doubles going for 350 kronor ($42) to 550 kronor ($66), including breakfast. Low-cost meals are available in the cafeteria here, 45 kronor ($5.40) to 85 kronor ($10.20).

Hotel Villa Ängö, 20 Baggensgatan (tel. 854-15), is another good possibility for motorists who prefer a location ten minutes from the center of town. The villa is a stately Swedish house, almost like a manor house. The English-speaking owner will welcome you and see that you are provided with much comfort. Her expertise makes this a fine place for a holiday. Rooms are immaculately kept and come in a variety of sizes. A single rents for 145 kronor ($17.40) to 180 kronor ($21.60), depending on the plumbing. A double goes for 200 kronor ($24). However, some of the more spacious rooms are ideal for families, housing from three to five guests. Breakfast is the only meal served, although you can order sandwiches in the evening. Facilities include a TV room, a sauna, a solarium, and billiards.

Villa Lindö, 18 Lindölundsgatan (tel. 142-80), is the home of Monica and Torsten Everbrand, an English-speaking couple. Their hotel is an old wooden house set in a nice big garden. Most of their visitors seem to like this place very much. There is little traffic around the villa, yet it lies just a ten-minute walk from town. In rooms with hot and cold running water, the charge is just 125 kronor ($15) in a single, rising to 180 kronor ($21.60) in a double. In the corridor is a bath and toilet. They don't serve meals, but offer coffee or tea along with fresh bread and country butter.

WHERE TO EAT: Theater Grill, Larmtorget, is one of several restaurants owned by the Frimurarehotellet. The attractive grill—oil paintings adorn the walls—offers self-service meals, such as a simple fried fish. For a tasty dinner, try the wienerschnitzel with peas and potatoes. Meals cost around 100 kronor ($12). Around the corner from the hotel, the grill is open from 7 a.m. to 10 p.m. weekdays (Sunday from 9 a.m. to 8 p.m.), and is a large corner room with six huge arched picture windows opening onto the square.

Piazza di Spagna, 4 Södra Långgatan (tel. 865-25), is a pizzeria with many wooden tables set under a low-beamed ceiling. Pizzas cost from 45 kronor ($5.40). If you'd prefer the other more succulent Italian specialties, a complete meal is likely to run in the 75-krona ($9) to 100-krona ($12) range.

Witten's Vardshus, 42 Södra Långgatan, serves meals in a tavern-like atmosphere. A light club luncheon, such as fish fillet with dill, costs 45 kronor ($5.40). Tasty dinner plates, preceded by soup, are served for 50 kronor ($6). The tavern is open from 11 a.m. to 11 p.m. weekdays (Sunday from 1 p.m. to 11 p.m.).

"Byttan" Restaurant in the City Park is a terraced pavilion overlooking the water, one of the best spots for dining in Kalmar. Guests may dine in the pavilion or in the vine-covered courtyard. The food is attractively prepared, but the restaurant makes a good stopover only for afternoon tea or lunch (dinner could be budget breaking). The best buy is the 75-krona ($9) lunch.

Low-cost meals can be had at **Tempo Department Store.** Its self-service cafeteria is open till 7 p.m., dinner costing 55 kronor ($6.60).

Domus Department Store, 21 Storgatan, also offers inexpensive self-service meals. A complete meal costs 55 kronor ($6.60).

KALMAR CASTLE: This, of course, is the chief sight. In the 16th century, under orders of Gustavus Vasa and two of his sons, Erik XIV and Johan III, this moated medieval fortress was transformed into a Renaissance palace. The Kalmar Läns Museum, or County Museum, is housed in the castle, containing archeological finds, royal furnishings, military artifacts, and objects connected with shipping. Be sure to see the prison for women from the 18th and 19th centuries and the restored castle chapel. An interesting exhibit is the one concerning the royal ship *Kronan,* which sank outside the island of Öland in the Baltic during a sea battle against the Danes in 1676, with only 42 of the 840 persons on board surviving. The county museum is responsible for excavations taking place at the wreck site, and the objects found by the marine archeologists are on exhibit at the castle. These include such things as glass bottles, tin plates, nautical instruments, a seaman's chest, and a great many gold coins.

The castle is open May through September, weekdays 10 a.m. to 4 p.m. (Sunday from 1 to 4 p.m.); June 15 to August 15, weekdays, 10 a.m. to 6 p.m. Tours are conducted every hour. Off-season, the castle is open from 1 to 3 p.m. except from December to February when it is open only on Sunday. The admission is 8 kronor (96¢); children 7 to 15, 3 kronor (36¢); under 6, free.

3. Växjö (The Glassworks District)

Sweden's celebrated Kingdom of Glass starts in Växjö, the central community for all of Småland, the province encompassing the glass district, plus lakes, forests, and the old family homes, many of them traditional red-timbered cottages, of emigrants to the United States. From about 20 factories in Småland emerges the world-renowned Swedish glass.

The name Växjö comes from *Vägsjön,* the lake where the ways meet, and many ways today lead here. You can come by car on the good national highways, fly in from Stockholm or Copenhagen, or come by train from Kalmar/Kariskrona, Gothenburg, or Stockholm.

However you come to this 14th-century city (its cathedral has parts dating from the 12th century), a visit to **Smålands Museum** (tel. 451-45), Sweden's oldest provincial museum, will give you a preview of the area as well as a look at history of Swedish glass. Here you'll see hand tools and archives from the very early times of this craft, with a special collection of more than 25,000 articles from this unique hand work. In a separate exhibit are displays of the finest artistic examples of Swedish glass produced over the centuries.

In other areas of the museum, you can see one of Sweden's largest coin collections, collections of art and religious objects and of weapons, and a special room housing an ethnological collection. Forestry and agriculture exhibits are included. The museum is open Monday to Friday from 9 a.m. to 4 p.m., Saturday from 11 a.m. to 3 p.m., and Sunday from 1 to 5 p.m.

Many Americans who have tried to seek their roots in other countries may be envious of Swedish-American people, after a visit to the **House of Emigrants** (tel. 201-20). This institution, founded in 1968, preserves the memories of the Swedish emigrant epoch and of the 1.3 million persons who left their homeland and moved to America. The house contains different exhibits on interesting parts of emigrant history as well as archives and a research library. In a premanent exhibition, The Dream of America, views and insights into the background of the emigration and its consequences can be seen. One-fourth of Sweden's population left their homeland in the "American Fever" years between the 1850s and the 1920s. The house is open Monday to Friday from 9 a.m. to 4 p.m., Saturday from 11 a.m. to 3 p.m., and Sunday from 1 to 5 p.m. A Minnesota Day is a folk festival held the second Sunday in August each year, drawing thousands of Swedes and Swedish-Americans.

In Växjö, there are numerous sports facilities, including one of Europe's most modern indoor swimming halls.

In summer, tours on Helgasjön are arranged on the 90-year-old steamer *Thor.* For information on this and other activities, see the Växjö Tourist Information Office, 8 Kronobergsgatan (tel. 223-25).

THE GLASS FACTORIES: Lying to the east of Växjö, within less than an hour's drive, are several glassworks, including Orrefors, Boda, and Kosta, where you can see the master glassblowers at work.

Orrefors Glasbruk (tel. 303-00), at Orrefors, is the best-known name in Swedish glass. Guided tours are conducted Monday through Friday at fixed hours during the tourist season and on request during the rest of the year. The factory is open from 8 a.m. to 3:30 p.m. Exhibition halls and shops are open until 5:30 p.m. The factory shuts down for annual vacations in July, but glassblowers demonstrate their work during this period. It is possible to purchase seconds (in most cases hardly distinguishable from perfect pieces), and gift shipments can be arranged. Tax-free shopping can also be arranged in the factory's shop.

Kosta Glassworks (tel. 503-00) and **Boda Glassworks** (tel. 240-00) are open Monday through Friday from 6 a.m. till 3 p.m. They are closed in July, but one workshop in each factory remains open all summer. The tourist shops and exhibition rooms are open Monday to Friday from 8:30 a.m. to 5:30 p.m., Saturday from 8:30 a.m. to 3 p.m., and Sunday from noon to 4 p.m.

WHERE TO STAY: Sara Hotell Statt, 6 Kungsgatan (tel 134-00), is a venerable old hostelry which, after several restorations, has become a choice place to stay, successfully combining the old and the new. The well-equipped bedrooms go for 450 kronor ($54) in a single, 600 kronor ($72) in a double, all rates including breakfast. The hotel dining room, serving excellent meals, is open seven days a week. If you're looking for relaxation, try the Golden Grace and The Gyllene Oxen pub. The hotel also has a sauna and swimming pool, with a whirlpool bath and solarium. The Sara Hotell Statt is conveniently located right in the center of Växjö.

One of the best bargain hotels in Växjö is the **Scandic Hotel,** 15 Hejareg (tel. 220-70), which has 106 adequately furnished bedrooms, including four family rooms. Each of the units has a private bath or shower. The price is the same in a single or double: 320 kronor ($38.40) per night.

Out in the District

The hostel **Backabyggningen** (tel. 300-20), at Orrefors, is clean and comfortable, with some family rooms costing from 85 kronor ($10.20) per person.

The **Turistgården,** 22 Vasagatan (tel. 109-32), in Nybro, less than 10 miles from Orrefors, is quite a modern hostel, with kitchen and showers available. Singles without bath cost 110 kronor ($13.20), while bathless doubles go for 180 kronor ($21.60).

READER'S ACCOMMODATION SELECTION: "The tourist information office at Växjö directed us to the **Bergdala Glass Factory,** where five former workers' cabins have been remodeled recently and turned into tourist rooms. For 75 kronor ($9) per person, we got lovely rooms, disposable sheets for each bed, a light breakfast, and the use of a kitchen and lounging area, all clean and newly decorated. The couple in residence speaks no English, but we got along fine. They even gave us a blue glass flower or heart as a souvenir of the place" (Mrs. Robert Pedersen, St. Paul, Minn.).

READER'S SIGHTSEEING TIP: "In the heart of the Glassworks District is the small town of **Lessebo,** which also has its own glass factory, where you can see hand-blown glass being made. I found that the factory store sold its glass products for less than the more touristy places of Boda and Kosta. Of course, the glass factories owned by one conglomerate sell each other's products. However, the great attraction at Lessebo is the famous **Lessebo Papermill** (tel. 106-00), the world's oldest working producer of handmade paper, in existence since 1693. The mill is open to the public so that you can see paper being made through its various stages, from cotton pulp to individual sheets which are pressed and hung up to dry. There is a giftshop where you can purchase the handmade products. Lessebo Papermill is open June through August, with free tours given in English at 9:30 and 10:45 a.m. and 1 and 2 p.m." (Johanna Ficaro, Cambridge, Mass.).

4. Öland

More Swedes emigrated from Öland to the United States during the 19th century than from any other province in Sweden. The Baltic island—shaped like a giant salmon—across the Kalmar Sound lost a quarter of its population. Surely every Ölander has at least three or four cousins in the United States.

But in one of the twists in emigration sagas, large numbers of Ölanders returned to retire on the island of their birth. Little wonder, considering how beautiful it is, with its sandy beaches, its treeless steppe (**Alvaret**) with wildflowers galore (enough to earn the praise of Linnaeus), its birdlife, and its profusion of windmills silhouetted against the summer sky.

Europe's longest bridge, nearly four miles long, connects Kalmar with Öland, a popular summer beach resort.

The island is 87½ miles long (10 miles wide at the widest point). Beaches run along both coasts, and there is only one town, **Borgholm**, a quiet summer retreat. The royal summer residence is **Solliden.** To rent a summer house on the beach, get in touch with the Öland Tourist Association, Box 115, 38700 Borgholm.

FOOD AND LODGING: **Skansen Hotel & Restaurant,** Färjestaden (tel. 305-30), is just across the bridge. If you're here for a meal, try stekta kroppkakor, an Öland specialty (spicy meat inside a cooked potato), 35 kronor ($4.20) for lunch. Another specialty of the house is smoked eel. At this comfortable inn, you can get a room for 175 kronor ($21) single, 330 kronor ($39.60) double. Service is an extra 10%.

At Boda in northern Öland is the **Bödabaden Hotel** (tel. 220-12), with a good beach nearby. The rooms are simply furnished, but adequately equipped. Half board ranges in price from 275 kronor ($33) per person. A smörgåsbord is served in the main dining room.

Halltorps Gästgiveri (tel. 552-50) at Borgholm is one of the oldest manors of Öland. A charming oasis, it lies in a tranquil setting, with a view across the Kalmarsund and the Halltorp Wood. Once it was a royal farming estate, and later it was a home for the elderly before it was transformed into an inn of good food and personalized accommodations. Rooms are cozy and intimate, often with beamed ceilings. A bathless single rents for 250 kronor ($30), increasing to 300 kronor ($36) in a single with shower. A bathless double is rented for 400 kronor ($48), the tariff jumping to 420 kronor ($50.40) in the most expensive rooms in the house, doubles with shower. The hostelry has only ten rooms, six of which have a lounge and loft. Color TV, radio, and phone are practical considerations in each room.

The inn prides itself on its food, the best in the area. Guests help themselves from a buffet mounted on an old wagon. The glow of candlelight adds to the mellow ambience. Ingredients used here come from local suppliers insofar as possible. The Baltic salmon comes directly from the fishermen in Boda. Fresh vegetables and mushrooms picked in the woods are brought to the chefs from neighboring farms, and the inn's home-spiced schnapps are flavored with herbs picked in the meadows roundabout. A hostelry lunch is presented for 40 kronor ($4.80), a three-course menu of the week going for 110 kronor ($13.20). There is an à la carte menu as well. Dishes are carefully and well prepared, and the staff is always friendly and eager to please.

Hotell Borgholm (tel. 110-60) at Borgholm is for those who want to be where the action is. Both foreigners and locals visit the place at night, because of its big dance hall with restaurant. You can eat and drink here seven nights a week. There's also a smaller restaurant for those who want to order their viands in calmer surroundings. The hotel has been considerably modernized. Only five rooms are bathless; the other 24 units contain bath, toilet, and TV. The price for a room ranges from 400 kronor ($48) to 450 kronor ($54) in a double, from 340 kronor ($40.80) to 380 kronor ($45.60) in a single, plus another 35 kronor ($4.20) for breakfast.

READER'S TOURING TIP: "Öland is difficult to explore. Bus service is poor, and visitors should count on renting a car to really see the island. Bike rental is another alternative. Visitors coming on the weekend of midsummer's eve in late June should be aware that everything, including bike and car rental agencies, is closed for the weekend" (Peter H. Guldberg, Bedford, Mass.).

Chapter XV

GOTHENBURG AND THE CHÂTEAU COUNTRY

1. Gothenburg (Göteborg)
2. Båstad
3. Helsingborg
4. Malmö
5. Lund
6. Ystad
7. Simrishamn
8. The Sights of Skåne

THOSE STRIKING OUT from Denmark to Sweden have a choice of three coastal gateway cities: Gothenburg, Helsingborg, and Malmö. There are about 60 ferry trips daily connecting Malmö with Copenhagen. Gothenburg, the terminus of the Swedish American Line, is across the water from Frederikshavn on the peninsula of Jutland on the mainland of Europe.

None of these three cities, despite their attractions, is among the finalists in European tourism. But as a stopover en route to other parts of Sweden, each of them can occupy a day or two of time. All three offer a profusion of moderately priced hotels and restaurants.

If a visitor has at least a week, he or she could spend it exploring the rolling countryside of Skåne, Sweden's southernmost province, filled with moated castles, manor houses, holiday resorts, and towns such as Ystad that date from the Middle Ages. The sights range from the oldest medieval fortress still preserved in its original state, Glimmingehus, to something of more recent times, Dag Hammerskjöld's Backåkra.

1. Gothenburg (Göteborg)

Called the gateway to Northern Europe, Gothenburg (Göteborg in Swedish) is the country's chief port and second-largest city. Swedes say that Gothenburg is a friendlier town than Stockholm. Canals, parks, and flower gardens rescue it from drabness.

The city has a large number of museums and an amusement park that is the largest in Northern Europe. It makes a good center for excursions to the fishing

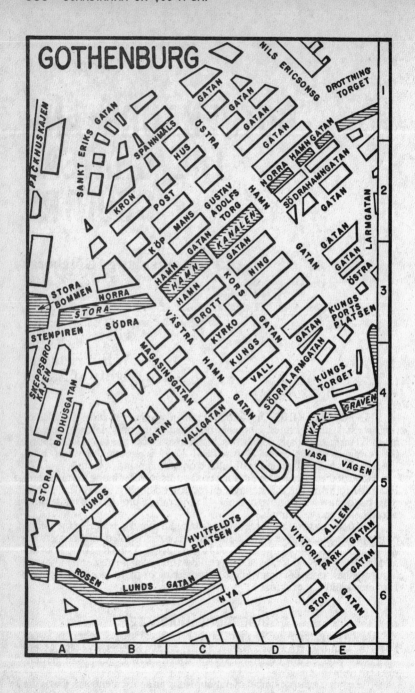

villages and holiday resorts north of the city. Gothenburg's pedestrain street is heated by underground pipes in the winter so that the snow melts.

Gothenburg received its city charter from King Gustavus Adolphus II in 1621 ("here the city shall stand"). The port contains a shipyard for repairs, City-varvet, and a manufacturer of platforms, Gotaverken/Arendal. The city is also the home of the Swedish passenger car, Volvo (the plant is about 15 minutes by car from the heart of the city), and of the Hasselblad space camera. Spanning the Göta River, Alvsborg Bridge is almost 3000 feet long and built high enough to allow ocean-going liners to pass underneath. The longest suspension bridge in Sweden, it attracts lively interest.

Travel in Gothenburg is moderate in expense, a single tram ticket costing 6 kronor (72¢). There is a 24-hour travel pass costing 15 kronor ($1.80). If you don't have a ticket, you have to board the first car of the tram and buy one from the driver. When you finally have purchased that 6-krona (72¢) ticket, you have to get the time of entry stamped in the automat and the ticket then becomes valid for one hour.

ACCOMMODATIONS: Reservations are important, but those who want to play cavalier can skip over to the **Gothenburg Tourist Office** at 2 Kungsportsplatsen (tel. 10-07-40), and throw themselves upon the mercy of the English-speaking staff.

The office has a list that covers the city's hotels and pensions and also reserves rooms in private homes. Reservations can be made in advance, by letter or phone. The tourist board charges a reservation fee of 15 kronor ($1.80) (for advance reservations, add another 6 kronor, (72¢). Single rooms in private homes range from 80 kronor ($9.60), doubles from 130 kronor ($15.60).

In summer, the best lodgings for the money are:

Hotell Liseberg Heden, Sten Sturegatan (tel. 20-02-80), is a subsidiary of the amusement park, Liseberg. A hotel of 147 rooms, it stands in a park in the center of Gothenburg, quiet and withdrawn from the noise of traffic. The units are modern Scandinavian design, and can easily be converted into a single or a double, all with TV, radio, and shower. A single rents for 425 kronor ($51), a double going for 580 kronor ($69.60), breakfast included. The hotel has a cocktail bar and a restaurant which is a little bit exclusive, although meals begin at 55 kronor ($6.60) and can take off from there.

Hotel Orgryte, 68–70 Danska Vägen (tel. 19-76-20), has a polish and expertise that makes it one of the more appealing choices. That is true, in spite of the fact that style and flair have been sacrificed to an extreme modern. The interior is a blend of light wood paneling and deep carpeting, with much lounging room. The exterior is solid, but impersonal. The bedrooms are furnished with built-in furniture in the contemporary idiom. The most expensive rooms, those with private showers and toilets, cost 375 kronor ($45) in a single, 500 kronor ($60) in a double. Breakfast is an extra 35 kronor ($4.20). During the day sandwiches, coffee, tea, cakes, beer, lemonade, and wine are offered, but not hot meals.

Hotel Kung Karl, 23 Nils Ericsongatan (tel. 17-28-35), is an old and established hotel in the heart of Gothenburg which was recently renovated. It is close to the air bus terminal and the railway station. The hotel appears to be better than ever, with new furniture, carpeting, and textiles. Each well-furnished accommodation now has a private shower or bath, along with comfortable beds, color TV, in-house video, and phone. The most expensive rates are quoted on weekdays, ranging from 400 kronor in a single ($48) to 550 kronor ($66) in a double. However, in summer, from June 20 to August 19 and on winter weekends, tariffs are lowered to only 285 kronor ($34.20) in a single and about 350 kronor ($42) in a double. Guests have free access to the sauna.

Hotel Onyxen, 23 Sten Sturegatan (tel. 16-01-36), is yet another candidate if your needs are simple. Rooms are modestly furnished and rent for 175 kronor

($21) in a single, rising to 275 kronor ($33) in a double. Some four-bedded rooms are available as well, and these are the best bargains, costing only 115 kronor ($13.80) per bed. Breakfast at 25 kronor ($3) is the only meal served.

Pensionat Kungsport, 21 Karl Gustavsgatan (tel. 13-52-36), is one of the best of the small, family-operated boarding houses of the city. It contains only six rooms, however, two of which have private showers. Singles, depending on the room assignment, range from 140 kronor ($16.80) to 180 kronor ($21.60), with doubles going for 200 kronor ($24) to 240 kronor ($28.80). An extra bed can be placed in a room for another 100 kronor ($12).

Upper Bracket Living

Those who want more comfort—and can afford to pay more—should consider the **Sara Hotell Scandinavia,** 10 Kustgatan (tel. 42-70-00), in the heart of the Port of Gothenburg, where you can have a sweeping view from your window of the harbor traffic and the magnificent Älvsborgs Bridge to the islands beyond. The 323 rooms include accommodation for disabled persons. Each room has a complete bath, color TV, radio, and phone. Rates range from 450 kronor ($54) to 550 kronor ($66) in a single, from 650 kronor ($78) to 720 kronor ($86.40) in a double. Guests have the use of a sauna, pool, solarium, and pool bar. A section of the restaurant, Oscar IV, is a library café, where you can peruse a book from the selection on a shelf while you enjoy your lunch or dinner in light, airy surroundings. A piano and cocktail bar, Musslan, is an inviting place to relax over a drink, play roulette, or order a simple platter from the bar. There's free indoor parking.

Youth Hostel

The Gothenburg youth hostel, **Ostkupan,** 2 Mejerigatan (tel. 40-10-50), lies in the southern sector of the city. It is well run, although the accommodations, as to be expected, are basic. The hostel rents out about 196 beds, charging about 45 kronor ($5.40) for members, 60 kronor ($7.20) for nonmembers. The hostel has two- and three-bed rooms, a members' kitchen, and each guest is given his or her own key. The reception desk is open from 7:30 a.m. to 10:30 p.m.

READERS' GUESTHOUSE SELECTION: "Our discovery was **Mrs. Elsa Otterdahl,** 5 Carlandersplatsen (tel. 20-29-14). Her home is a convenient location, within walking distance of downtown. She lives in a charming old building, an apartment house, and rents out three bedrooms. Her charge for a double room with breakfast is 175 kronor ($21). Mrs. Otterdahl is a pleasant, friendly woman, who speaks a moderate amount of English" (Ken and Jane Olson, Boulder, Colo.).

RESTAURANTS: Gothenburg is a merry-go-round of restaurants—many of them attractively priced. Being a seaport, the city is noted for its variety of fish dishes, such as fresh salmon, pike, and the inevitable herring.

The Hunter's Pub, 30–34 Östra Hamngatan (tel. 11-85-05), remains a time-tested favorite. Opening onto Gustav Adolfs Torg, it stands beside the Stora Hamn Canal. It's a suitable choice for breakfast, lunch, or dinner, as it's open from 8 a.m. to midnight, with music featured in the evening. The cooking is good and tasty, including such offerings as grilled pork chops served with plenty of mashed potatoes and gravy. Meals cost from 85 kronor ($10.20).

The ÄttaGlas restaurant (tel. 13-60-15), on the Göta Canal at Kungsportsbron (bridge), is an old ship from the Sessan line. This stationary vessel serves good food; the service is fast, the atmosphere elegant. Each day fresh fish plates are offered, and the meat dishes, including the peppersteak, are also good. Expect to pay from 110 kronor ($13.20) for a meal here.

Restaurant Tidblom, 23 Olskroksgatan (tel. 19-20-70), will give you a "Taste of Sweden." The chef specializes in very fresh fish, and, in season, game dishes. The reindeer steak here is excellent. A menu of the day is offered for around 55 kronor ($6.60) at lunch; however, you'll spend from 110 kronor ($13.20) or more for dinner. It is open weekdays from 11 a.m. to 2:30 p.m. and from 6 to 11:30 p.m. On Saturday, it serves only from 5 p.m. to 11:30 p.m., and on Sunday from 2 to 10 p.m.

The **Åhléns** or **Tempo** department store restaurants are also suitable for low budgets, offering a meal of bread and butter, a hot dish, and a cup of coffee for 30 kronor ($3.60). Meals cost from 85 kronor ($10.20).

Walking and Eating Along "The Avenue"

To see Gothenburg, a walk down "The Avenue" is a tradition. This is **Kungsportavenyn,** called "Avenyn" (The Avenue) by Gothenburgers. Sit at one of the many outdoor cafés and watch the passing parade. Start at Park-gatan, at the foot of The Avenue.

On your left is the **Gondoliere,** 2 Kungsportsavenyn (tel. 11-16-93), a restaurant/pizzeria which has an outdoor Italian-style café in good weather. It is much frequented by local Swedes. A luncheon with a different specialty is served here every day from 11 a.m. to 4 p.m. at a cost of 38 kronor ($4.56). You can also enjoy a lunch pizza for the same price, the flavors ranging from capricciosa to cacciatora. At dinner you can order from an expensive menu that begins with spaghetti bolognese and goes on to include more expensive main dishes such as Tuscan-style chicken. Desserts include a banana Africana. Dinners cost from 100 kronor ($12).

A few steps farther up the street is its sister restaurant and pizzeria, **La Gondola,** 4 Kungsportsavenyn (tel. 11-68-28). In summer this restaurant also has an outdoor café. It, too, does a lively pizza trade. I recently enjoyed the pizza Margherita. However, it has a more elaborate menu, with many of the classic dishes of the Italian kitchen. It does a very good ravioli alla carbonara and a tasty saltimbocca ("jump in your mouth") alla romana. The minestrone is good and filling, and some velvety-smooth ice cream is served. It, too, offers a 45-krona ($5.40) lunch served between 11 a.m. and 4 p.m. with a different specialty every day of the week. However, an à la carte dinner will cost from 110 kronor ($13.20).

Both restaurants are open until midnight.

A big restaurant, **White Corner,** 43B Vasagatan (tel. 81-28-11), contains three dining places. One is a first-class American steakhouse, among the best known in Scandinavia; the other is a pub where you can have your buffet lunch with bread and butter, three kinds of salads, and your choice of two hot dishes, all for about 45 kronor ($5.40). The third is a Japanese restaurant, Mikado, where meals cost from 120 kronor ($14.40).

Elegant buildings line The Avenue. Farther up on your left is the Windsor Hotel. On your right as you continue is the **Lilla London** (tel. 18-40-62), a pub and restaurant owned by Sven and Greta Lindstrand. Meals here run from 45 kronor ($5.40) to 125 kronor ($15), and there's a daily special offered for 45 kronor ($5.40). In the same building, the Lindstrands also own the nightclub, **Valand** (tel. 18-30-93), where midnight snacks are available. To go to the night-club, men must wear ties and jackets.

At the corner of Fredsgatan and Drottninggatan, the Chinese restaurant **Peking,** 50 Drottninggatan, will serve you a fair and abundant meal for from 25 kronor ($3) to 75 kronor ($9).

As we approach the end of this fine street, the public library, **Stads-**

biblioteket (tel. 81-04-80), is on the left at Götaplatsen. This is the main library of Gothenburg, the home of some 400,000 volumes in 40 languages—and a café. The library also contains a listening room with recorded music, as well as a reading room with more than a hundred foreign daily newspapers. In one hall exhibitions are continuously replacing each other. From Monday to Thursday, hours are from 10 a.m. to 9 p.m., on Friday and Saturday from 10 a.m. to 6 p.m., and on Sunday from noon to 6 p.m. While here, I might as well mention that across the street is a grocery store, Gunnarslivs, which stays open Sunday in summer from 5 to 10 p.m. (in winter between 1 and 7 p.m.).

At the top of the street, the broad avenue flows into Götaplatsen, the cultural heart of Gothenburg. Here, three buildings are grouped around the Poseidon Fountain (by Carl Milles)—the concert hall, the city art museum, and the city theater. In summer, young people congregate at this end of The Avenue.

Entertainment in Liseberg Park

Liseberg Park is the number one tourist attraction in Sweden. It is the largest amusement park in Scandinavia.

For dining, nightlife, and entertainment in general, Gothenburgers head for this pleasure garden of fountains, pavilions, and flowers. Open from mid-April to September, the festively lit park comes alive with music, artists, dances, 21 rides, and open-air vaudeville shows on seven stages. To reach the park, take streetcar 4 or 5 from the city. The admission price is 15 kronor ($1.80) for adults, free for children under 7. Admission is free from 10 a.m. to one hour before the rides start, Monday through Friday.

Värdhus Restaurant (tel. 83-62-83), a pocket-size manor house, has verandas opening onto the plaza. In its rooms—decorated with a liberal sprinkling of antiques and crystal chandeliers—you can dine inexpensively if you're careful of the extras. There are several hot main dishes offered daily. It is open weekdays from 5 to 11 p.m. (on Saturday and Sunday from 3 p.m. to 11 p.m.). Meals begin at 85 kronor ($10.20).

Rondo (tel. 83-62-75), a large, splendidly modish dance place in the middle of the park, offers summa dancing to an orchestra till 3 a.m. The Rondo has become a fully licensed restaurant, but you can drink and dance without dining. Menus range from 35 kronor ($4.20) to 80 kronor ($9.60).

There are many kiosks in Liseberg Park, offering hot dogs and pizzas from 22 kronor ($2.64). They open at noon.

THE MAJOR SIGHTS: For a quick orientation in Gothenburg, visit the **Guldhedens Vattentorn** (Water Tower), 400 feet high. Take streetcar 7 from the center of the city, about a ten-minute ride. The streetcar is in two parts, and the rear car is the one going to Guldhedens (the front part is detached at one point and heads for a different section of the city). The elevator ride up the tower is free, and there's a cafeteria-snackbar on top.

For a look at Gothenburg, the traditional starting point is the cultural center of **Götaplatsen,** with its Poseidon Fountain, the work of Carl Milles, Sweden's most important sculptor. The big triumvirate of buildings here is the **Concert Hall,** the municipally owned theater, and the—

Göteborgs Konstmuseum on Götaplatsen is the leading art museum of Gothenburg. The museum has a good collection of modern artists, notably French impressionists. Bonnard, Cézanne, Van Gogh—even Picasso—are represented, along with sculptures by Milles and Rodin. The gallery is noted for its collection of the works of 19th- and 20th-century Scandinavian artists (Zorn and Larsson of Dalarna, Edvard Munch and Christian Krohg of Norway). Also old masters are to be found including Rembrandt and Rubens. There's a 5-krona (60¢) admission charge. The museum is open Tuesday to Saturday from noon to

4 p.m., Sunday from 11 a.m. to 5 p.m. On Wednesday off-season, it is also open from 6 to 9 p.m. It's closed Sunday.

A short walk north leads to the **Röhss Museum of Arts and Crafts,** 37 Vasagatan, housing a large collection of European furnishings, china, glass, pottery, and Oriental artifacts plus permanent and temporary exhibitions of modern handicraft and industrial design. It is open Tuesday to Saturday from noon to 4 p.m., Sunday from 11 a.m. to 5 p.m. May through August. Admission is 5 kronor (60¢).

Continuing north along Kungsportsavenyn, we reach the **Stora Teatern,** Kungsparken (tel. 13-13-00), the 19th-century opera house. The opera season lasts from mid-August to mid-June. If you're in Gothenburg then, by all means attend a performance. Eleonora Duse and Sarah Bernhardt have appeared in front of the footlights. The theater presents not only operas, but operettas and ballets. Tickets range in price from 5 krona (60¢) all the way up to 60 kronor ($7.20).

On a fair day, another beauty oasis in the center of the city is **Trädårdsföreningen,** across the canal from the Central Station. The park is open till 9 p.m. in summer, and costs only 2 krona (24¢) to enter. In the center is a Palm House, a large hothouse.

In south Gothenburg is the admission-free botanical garden, **Botaniska Trädgården,** opposite Slottsskogen Park, with Asiatic trees and shrubs, rock gardens, orchid plants, and greenhouses. It's open daily from 9 a.m. until sunset. The greenhouses are open Monday to Friday from 10 a.m. to 3 p.m. and on Saturday and Sunday from noon to 3 p.m. Take streetcar 1 or 2 to the Änggårdsplatsen stop.

Early risers can take in the daily **Fish Auction** at the harbor, the largest fishing port in Scandinavia. The amusing auction begins at 7 a.m. sharp.

Finally, take a boat trip along the canals and out into the harbor. **Paddan** sightseeing boats show you the old parts of central Gothenburg from the canals, going under 20 bridges and taking you out into the harbor, where the guide will tell about the technical innovations implemented. The 55-minute tour leaves daily from May to September several times a day between 10 a.m. and 4 p.m. from the terminal at Kungsportsplatsen in the city center. Adults pay 26 kronor ($3.12), children 15 kronor ($1.80), and families (two adults and two children), 65 kronor ($7.80). For information and reservations, call 13-30-00.

You can also go to **NYA Elfsborg,** in the 17th-century fortress at the harbor's mouth. The boat takes you from Stenpiren on a 20-minute tour through the harbor to the fortress. A guide will be waiting for you at the cafeteria, museum, and souvenir shop. Departures are seven times a day from May to September. Adults pay 25 kronor ($3), children 15 kronor ($1.80), and families 60 kronor ($7.20).

SHOPPING TIPS: It's cheaper to shop in Sweden than it has been in more than a decade. Many Danes come over just for the day to buy Swedish merchandise. Sweden has a unique system for foreign visitors. Keep your eyes open for the tax-free sticker which is displayed in many of the shops in Gothenburg. Shop owners or clerks will explain the red tape involved.

Most purchasers or browsers in this city head first for the **Nordiska Kompaniet** (NK for short), the leading department store recommended previously in the Stockholm shopping section. The Gothenburg branch is at 42 Östra Hamngatan (tel. 17-33-00). The store is open every day, except Sunday, in summer from 9:30 a.m. to 6 p.m. (on Saturday to 2 p.m.). The store's packing specialists take care to see that your merchandise arrives safely. Typically Swedish and other Scandinavian articles are offered, with special concern provided for the overseas visitors. NK carries more than 200,000 items, ranging from Kosta "sculpture" crystal, Orrefors crystal in all types and shapes, Rörstrand high-fired earthenware and fine porcelain, stainless steel, pewter items, dolls in national costume, leather purses, Dalecarlian horses, Finnish carpeting, books about Sweden, Swedish records, and much, much more.

For Swedish glass, I'd recommend **C. J. Josephssons Glas Porslin,** 12 Korsgatan and 34 Kyrkogatan (tel. 17-56-15), which has been doing business since 1866, and has established an enviable reputation. The selection of Orrefors crystal and porcelain is stunning. Even more intriguing are the "ice blocks" of Vicke Lindstrand of Kosta. There is a tourist tax-free shopping service plus full shipping service.

B. W. Berry, 16 Geijersgatan (tel. 16-77-48), is run by Johan Zetterberg, who speaks English and will be only too happy to show you his collection of antique glass and china. His shop is usually closed in July.

Hemslöjd i Göteborgs och Bohus Län, 13 Drottninggatan, exhibits and sells handicraft from West Sweden. It's open weekdays from 10 a.m. to 6 p.m., Saturday from 10 a.m. to 2 p.m., and Sunday from noon to 4 p.m.

Bohusslöjd, 25 Kungsportsavenyn, also exhibits and sells handicraft products.

Kronhusbodarna, Kronhusgatan, was originally used as shops for the artillery of the city and now contains shops in turn-of-the-century style. One of them offers candy and snuff, and you'll also find a goldsmith, a coppersmith, a lithographer, and shops selling watches, ceramics, and coffee. The attractive complex is open all year.

MEETING THE SWEDES: At the tourist bureau, visitors to Gothenburg can apply to meet a local family ("of similar background and interests"). Sometimes it takes at least two days to arrange a visit—so make sure you'll be in Gothenburg that long. No cost is involved.

SWIMMING POOL: Valhalla Bad, across the parking lot from the Liseberg amusement park, has both outdoor and indoor pools, as well as three steamrooms. For 10 kronor ($1.20) you get a locker, a steambath, and a swim in either pool. It is open weekdays from 7 a.m. to 7 p.m., on Saturday from 7 a.m. to 3 p.m.

FERRIES TO DENMARK: Stena Line has five crossings a day in summer to North Jutland. The ferries take about three hours to cross. The one-way fare for passengers is 85 kronor ($10.20) in high season. For information about specific hours of crossing (which vary seasonally), telephone 42-09-40. The boats have excellent dining rooms.

ONE-DAY TRIPS FROM GOTHENBURG: Several days could be spent exploring the west coast north of Gothenburg, centering at such coastal towns and fishing villages as **Lysekil, Smögen,** and **Strömstad** near the Norwegian border. Bikini-clad Swedes lie on the rocks along this shore—lounging in the sun against a backdrop of yachts and fishing craft. If pressed for time, do at least see:

Kungälv

On E6 Highway, 11 miles north of Gothenburg, lie the ruins of the 14th-century **Bohus Fortress,** a bastion that played a leading role in the centuries when Sweden, Norway, and Denmark were engaged in periodic strife to establish supremacy. In fact, when Bohus Castle and Fortress *(Bohus Fästning)* was built it was by order of Norway's King Haakon on Norwegian territory. Through wars and marriages, the three Nordic kingdoms were united not long after the construction of this fortress in the early 1300s and remained so until 1512. Bohus Fortress was often besieged but never fell into the hands of the enemy—although the identity of enemy and friend changed frequently. It was later used as a prison, after it was ceded to Sweden in 1658, and the governor of the province called *Göteborg och Bohus Län* even made his headquarters there until Gothenburg brought pressure to bear to have the seat of government placed in the city. Since the late 1780s, the fortress has been allowed to fell into disuse and consequent dilapidation. Kungälv is easily reached by bus in less than half an hour from Gothenburg. Climb the tower—"Father's Hat"—for a splendid view. Bohus is open from 10 a.m. to 8 p.m. May 1 to August 15, noon to 6 p.m. August 16 to September 15, charging 5 kronor (60¢) for admission. Kungälv, known by the Vikings as Kongahälla, has traditions going back 1000 years.

Marstrand

This once-royal resort, frequented by the former Swedish king Oscar II, lies on a secluded island. Its little shops, art galleries, and pleasant walks are reminiscent of Nantucket, Massachusetts. Part of the fun of Marstrand is the trip to it—particularly if you go by coach or private car, a one-hour ride from Gothenburg.

Young people from Gothenburg and the surrounding district flock to Marstrand on weekends, filling up the clapboard hotels. The resort, quiet all week, comes alive with the rocking sounds of folk singers and the twang of guitars. But the big event on Marstrand's calendar is the international regatta, held annually—usually the first two weeks in July.

While exploring the island, don't miss the 17th-century **Carlstens Fortress,** towering over the island. After a climb up the hill, pay a visit to the chapel, then walk through the secret tunnel to the fortress, paying 7 kronor (84¢) for adults, 3 kronor (36¢) for children. In 1658, King Charles X Gustaf arrived at Marstrand and decided that a fortress should be built to protect the Swedish west coast fleet. In the years 1680–1689 the redoubt was rebuilt and two floors were added. The tower was also rebuilt. The bastions around the lower castle courtyard were constructed in 1689–1705, and were completed during the first half of the 19th century. The vaults were used for offices and barracks rooms for soldiers and prisoners.

The star restaurant choice is at the **Grand** (tel. 60-322), once the grand lady of the Victorian gingerbread hotel circuit, receiving fashion-conscious guests drawn here by King Oscar II. It is now only an excellent restaurant, **Lustgården.** This is a good spot for lunch, costing 45 kronor ($5.40); dinner averages around 85 kronor ($10.20).

For accommodations, the **Båtellet** (tel. 600-10), a former bathing house, has been converted into a hotel with four to five beds per room, 103 beds in all. The cost is 75 kronor ($9) per bed, not including linen. Sheets can be rented for an additional 18 kronor ($2.16).

Trollhättan

In Västergötland, Trollhättan is an important river town of 50,000 on the Göta Canal and one of the largest power stations in Europe. The canal and lock area is an imposing sight with the new and old locks, power stations, rocky outcrops, and islands. To see the river rush forth into the old river bed is a dramatic experience you can enjoy at 2 p.m. on Saturday and Sunday in May and June and on Wednesday and Sunday in July and August.

Just south of Lake Vänern, the town has one of the finest youth hostels in Scandinavia, on a hill overlooking Trollhättan. This hostel, **Strömsberg**, is an old wooden manor, with an outdoor cafeteria where you can enjoy typically Swedish meals costing from 25 kronor ($3) to 55 kronor ($6.60).

From Trollhättan, we head back to Gothenburg, then strike out for the province of Skåne, visiting first the resort of:

2. Båstad

Jutting out on a peninsula, surrounded by hills and a beautiful landscape, Båstad is the fashionable international seaside resort in Sweden. Accessible by rail on the run to Malmö, it lies approximately 125 miles south of Gothenburg.

The scene of international tennis matches in summer, Båstad is also noted for one of the principal attractions of southern Sweden—the **Norrviken Gardens** *(Norrvikens Trädgårdar)* (tel. 710-70), lying 1½ miles from the center of the resort. These gardens, founded in 1906 by Rudolf Abelin, have been expanded and maintained according to his plans. They embrace a number of styles, and you may find it difficult to settle on which is your favorite, so beautiful is each one. One is in Italian baroque style, with a pond framed in pyramid-shape boxwood hedges, complemented by triads of tall cypresses. The Rhododendron Dell, seen at its peak, is breathtakingly beautiful, with huge clumps of flowering rhododendrons and azaleas, most of the plants being gifts to the gardens from King Gustav Adolf VI. A Renaissance Garden reminds you of the tapestry art of 15th-century Italy, with its boxwood patterns, and the flower garden, with bulb flowers competing with colorful annuals, is a delight to the eye. The mystic Orient is evoked by the Japanese Garden, with its elements of religion, culture, and feeling for nature, and the Oriental Terrace, with a little Persian temple and sedum-planted section, inspired by the art of Persian carpet-weavers. A Romantic Garden, following the 18th-century back-to-nature style, and the Water Garden, inspired by those at the Villa d'Este and Villa Aldobrandino near Rome, are sure to please visitors. At Villa Abelin, designed by the gardens' founder, wisteria climbs on the wall and is in bloom twice a year. The villa houses shops, exhibits, and facilities for providing information. There is also a restaurant in the grounds. The gardens may be viewed daily from the first of May until the end of September from 10 a.m. to 6 p.m.

ACCOMMODATIONS: Båstad has several rooming houses where single rooms cost from 85 kronor ($10.20) up, doubles from 180 kronor ($21.60). Consult the tourist office for information.

I prefer **Grand Hotel Skansen,** 2 Kyrkogatan (tel. 720-50), a former grain warehouse which has been transformed into a handsome and comfortable hotel. Guests can relax on the terrace of this sturdy stone building, or have lunch or drinks served at the little tables in the courtyard under awnings or basking in the sun. Well-appointed bedrooms rent for from 200 kronor ($24) to 260 kronor ($31.20) in a single, from 250 kronor ($30) to 400 kronor ($48) in a double.

Hotel Båstad, 29 Köpmansgatan (tel. 720-90), is open year round, even in winter when its nearby fair-weather sisters close. In the center of the resort, the Båstad is like an old new England coaching inn, with tiny dormer windows, dark wood paneling, and walls covered with ivy. It's large enough to have a headwaiter, but still small enough to have a housekeeper for all jobs. Well-furnished bathless doubles are rented out. Half-board terms range from 425 kronor ($51) to 550 kronor ($66) per person daily. On the ground floor is a miniature bar and a dining room, with windows overlooking the water.

Hotel-Pension Enehall, 26900 Båstad (tel. 702-12), stands on the slope of a forested mountain chain, Hallandsåsen. Set in the midst of such greenery, it is still only a few minutes' walk from the sea. Catering mainly to Swedish families, and some occasional Danes and Germans, it is run by Margaretha and B. A. Skogh. The place is cozy and intimate, with many personal touches, and the rooms, although small, are adequately equipped. Depending on the plumbing in your room, the half-board rate ranges from 150 kronor ($18) to 225 kronor ($27) per person daily. Add 15% for service to all accounts. The food is tasty, the service polite and efficient. Guests are accepted from May to September.

Nybo Pensionat, 81 Köpmansgatan (tel. 701-92), is one of the most alluringly priced places at the resort, but its 16 rooms fill up quickly. The boarding house is pleasantly and attractively furnished, and accommodations are cozy and comfortable. For a single room, the charge is 150 kronor ($18), rising to 225 kronor ($27) in a double, these tariffs including service and taxes. Breakfast, at 30 kronor ($3.60), is served in Nybo's cafeteria; otherwise, the staff will direct you to moderately priced restaurants nearby for other hot meals.

Continuing south along the coast, we come to:

3. Helsingborg

At the narrowest point of Öresund, separating Sweden and Denmark, three miles across the water, lies the industrial city and major port of Helsingborg. Many people rushing up from Copenhagen to visit Kronborg Castle at Elsinore take a 25-minute ferry ride across the sound—leaving every few minutes—for a look at Sweden.

Of course, what they see isn't Sweden, but a modern city with an ancient history. Because of its strategic location, Helsingborg jointly controlled shipping along the sound with Elsinore in the Middle Ages.

WHAT TO SEE: For a quick view of Helsingborg, take the elevator at Stortorget up to the thick-walled medieval keep, **Kärnan,** completed in the beginning of the 19th century. From the tower 225 feet above sea level, there's an excellent panorama of the sound and both the Swedish and Danish coasts. The tower, one of the most important medieval monoments in Sweden, represents the remains of Helsingborg Castle, which was torn down in the 17th century. The keep is open from 9 a.m. to 8 p.m.; admission is 4 kronor (48¢).

Kärnan, incidentally, is just one of the attractions administered by the **Helsingborgs Museum,** 31 Södra Storgatan (tel. 10-59-50). Others include the **Stadsmuseet,** the town museum; the **Vikingsbergs Konstmuseum** (an art museum, and **Pålsjö Kvarn,** a small watermill. Besides Fredriksdal (coming up), the museum also has exhibitions at **Sofiero,** the summer residence of the late King Gustav Adolf VI, which is open May to August from 10 a.m. to 6 p.m.

The second monument of the Middle Ages is the step-gabled **Church of St. Mary** (tel. 18-02-35) on Södra Storgatan, a short walk from the harbor. Built in the 13th century, but substantially rebuilt in the 15th century, it is noted for its medieval altarpiece and its intricately carved Renaissance pulpit. It is open from 8 a.m. to dusk.

One of the most interesting outings on a fair day is to the **Fredriksdal Open-Air Museum and Botanical Gardens.** Farmhouses, a windmill, barns, even a malt drier, have been reassembled on the grounds of an 18th-century mansion donated to the Helsingborg Museum. The Botanical Garden contains chiefly the vegetation of Scania. The grounds are open daily from 10 a.m. to 7 p.m., costing 4 kronor (48¢). Take bus 19.

Tours

The easiest way to see Helsingborg is to take a walk through the center of town. The tourist bureau in the town hall will supply you with pamphlets and maps. You might also check with the tourist bureau about coach tours in the surrounding area.

READER'S TOUR SUGGESTION: "To capture the essence of the southern Swedish countryside, take a drive out from Helsingborg on route 22 to the harbor village of **Mölle**. There is a nature reserve on the point of land—a lighthouse, many walking trails, and a golf course. The highlight of our afternoon's outing was a stop at the thatched cottage tea house of the three charming Lundgren sisters. Travel east from Mölle on secondary route 112 toward Arild. About 1¼ miles beyond Arild, watch for the sign, **Flickorna Lundgren** (only open from May through August). Choose from an array of home-baked Swedish cakes and cookies served with an abundant supply of coffee, tea, or rich, hot chocolate. You may eat in the cottage, whose decor is from the 1800s, or one of two beautiful gardens. This is truly a treat fit for a king—as the two framed presentation scrolls from Sweden's monarch testify" (Jean White, Belleville, Ont., Canada).

ACCOMMODATIONS: Helsingborg hostelries, for the most part, have been spruced up with a bit of modernization. In the Rådhuset, the town hall, there is an accommodation bureau, **Turistföreningen I Helsingborg,** open in May and September from 9 a.m. to 5 p.m. Monday to Friday and 9 a.m. to noon on Saturday. In June and August, hours are from 9 a.m. to 7 p.m. Monday to Saturday and 3 to 7 p.m. on Sunday. In July, it is open from 9 a.m. to 8 p.m. Monday to Saturday and 3 to 8 p.m. on Sunday.

    Magnus Steubock, 5 Lilla Strandgatan (tel. 12-62-50), is a small, 30-room hotel, a short walk from the ferryboats and Central Station. It's one of the accommodations in the moderate range—500 kronor ($60) for bathless doubles, 360 kronor ($43.20) for singles, with service included. Some family rooms are also available. The Magnus Steubock is housed in a four-story French-style building with mansard roof. Breakfast is served.

    Hotel Anglais, 14–16 Gustaf Adolfsgatan (tel. 12-61-20), is polished modernity, enjoying a central location. The bedrooms are small, but restful, and furnishings are contemporary. A bathless single costs 265 kronor ($31.80), going up to 360 kronor ($43.20) with shower. A double is rented for 450 kronor ($54) with shower. The director has a capable staff, and sees that everything is run expertly.

    Hotel Hälsingborg, 14 Stortorget (tel. 12-09-45), sits in a premium position, in the center of the city at the foot of the stairway leading to the medieval keep (Helsingborg's answer to Rome's Spanish Steps). Its four-domed corner towers link it architecturally to the past. A cage elevator takes guests up to rooms with a view. Bathless doubles rent for 400 kronor ($48) to 600 kronor ($72); bathless singles go for 400 kronor ($48), peaking at 450 kronor ($54). These rates include service and breakfast. The bedrooms aren't memorable, but they are clean and adequate.

    Grand Hotel, 8–12 Stortorget (tel. 12-01-70), is old-fashioned in a grand manner. With antiques, fine reproductions, many chandeliers, old paintings, and bowls of fresh flowers everywhere, the hotel makes its guests feel well cared for. A single costs 600 kronor ($72) to 750 kronor ($90) with bath. Depending on the plumbing, doubles cost from 780 kronor ($93.60) with shower, peaking at 900 kronor ($108) with complete bath. Breakfast is included. Altogether there are 80 bedrooms in the hotel.

    Hotel Mollberg, 18 Stortorget (tel. 12-02-70), is a comfortable hotel, providing good service and excellent food. The 80 recently restored bedrooms all have private baths, plus other amenities to contribute to the well-being of guests. Singles rent for 500 kronor ($60), doubles going for 625 kronor ($75). Besides the hotel restaurant and a continental café, there's a lounge which is reminiscent of an English gentlemen's club library. Here you can enjoy an apéritif or have your coffee served after breakfast. The Mollberg is within walking distance of air and bus terminals, ferries, and the railway station.

A Youth Hostel

Villa Thalassa, Dag-Hammarskjöldsvägen (tel. 11-03-84), is one of the finest hotels in Scandinavia. It's an impressive villa surrounded by gardens, terraces, and Tudor-style cottages (there is even a pond with swans). The hostel is four miles outside Helsingborg, but well worth the inconvenience to reach it. Inquire at the tourist bureau for directions and transportation. The cost is low. A bed costs 38 kronor ($4.56), plus another 27 kronor ($3.24) for breakfast. Four persons are accommodated in rooms with bunk beds. There are plenty of clean shower rooms as well. The dining room is large, and the sounds of the many languages spoken at mealtime are almost intoxicating. Mrs. Gudmundson is a mother to everyone. She accommodates as many as 200 guests on some occasions. You must have a youth hostel membership to stay here, but that's easily arranged. Take bus 4 from town, get off at the final stop, and walk along a marked path to the villa.

WHERE TO EAT: In the dining room of the **Grand Hotel,** Stortorget (tel. 12-01-70), you can partake of a noonday smörgåsbord (till 4 p.m.) for 55 kronor ($6.60). You help yourself from a central table, taking first some of a dozen cold dishes, then returning for the hot entrees. It's like dining in a private club, with well-appointed booths, walnut paneling, and sparkling brass lights.

Night and Day is a restaurant and café, one of the most popular in town, lying at the Parapeten immediately south of Pålsjöbadet. Even though it opened only in the summer of 1984, it already has an enviable reputation among foreign visitors as a rendezvous point for all ages. In fair weather, there are outside tables with a view over the sound. The place is somewhat French in style and rather unsophisticated. Meals cost from 75 kronor ($9) and up.

For your really festive meal in Helsingborg, head for the first-class **Restaurant Oscar** at the Sundstorget, which also opened in 1984 but has quickly become known as one of the finest dining rooms in town. Of course, the fresh fish platters will cost you a lot more here, but they are prepared superbly and served with fresh vegetables and salads. You get a good range of food, from soups to desserts. Meals are priced from 150 kronor ($18).

4. Malmö

Sweden's third-largest city, an hour's train ride from Helsingborg, is the capital of Skåne and makes a good base for exploring the ancient castles and manors on its periphery. This busy port lies across the sound from Copenhagen, reached in 35 minutes by hydrofoil, 1½ hours by ferry boat. Both an old city, dating back to the 13th century, and a modern one, it has many attractions.

Once a shining gem in the 16th-century Danish crown, Malmö's **Town Hall** still retains its look of Renaissance splendor. But, in contrast to this, its **City Theater** at Fersens Väg, completed near the end of World War II, is considered one of the most modern and best equipped in Europe.

ACCOMMODATIONS: Can't find a room? Head directly for the **Malmö Tourist Office,** 1 Hamngatan, across the canal from the Central Station. The English-speaking staff here will help you out free of charge. If the hotels are booked solidly, and if you prefer, the staff will ring up a private home, which charges about 65 kronor ($7.80) per person. In summer, June 25 to August 5, the tourist office is open daily from 9 a.m. to 8 p.m. Saturday and from 9 a.m. to 3. To get the office to reserve a room in advance, specify requirements and price. Telephone 34-12-68 or 34-12-70.

Sara Hotel Winn, 3 Jörgen Kocksgatan (tel. 10-19-00), is a quiet and calm place to stay, despite being in the very heart of Malmö, only a couple of minutes from the hydrofoils to Denmark and a short distance from the railway station and buses to the airports. The 101 rooms are large, with comfortable chairs and beds and generously sized shower/bathrooms. Each has a radio and automatic alarm clock and color TV, with an in-house video channel. A lavish buffet breakfast is served, with hostesses on hand to help you fill up your plate with cheese, sausages, liverpaste, jam, egg, and a variety of breads. The hotel has a sauna and a recreation room for the enjoyment of guests. Singles rent for 400 kronor ($48), doubles 580 kronor ($69.60).

Hotel Hembygden, 7 Isak Slaktargatan (tel. 10-49-50), has a small entrance and reception office, but its rooms are good, and the location ideal—a two-minute walk from Stortorget, and a five-minute walk from Central Station and the ferries from Copenhagen. The rooms are clean and fresh, with bathless doubles renting for 210 kronor ($25.20). For a bathless single, a guest pays 150 kronor ($18). Some of the rooms open onto the street, others onto a courtyard where breakfast is served on warm summer days. Use of the corridor bath is free.

Adlon, 13 Mäster Johansgatan (tel. 715-60), a hidden street a short walk west of Stortorget, is a star among less-recommended hotels in this area. It's a quiet little haven for a night's sleep. Doubles cost 520 kronor ($62.40), and singles go for 400 kronor ($48). There's a lounge with a marble floor and fireplace. A continental breakfast, included in the rates, is served in your own room or the breakfast salon. Parking facilities are available.

Atlas Hotell, 2 Hospitalsgatan (tel. 12-19-77), stands in the center of town near Stortorget. The rooms are adequately furnished and kept clean. The 50 units, with 100 beds, have been recently renovated. Bathless singles cost 240 kronor ($28.80), 290 kronor ($34.80) with shower. A bathless double goes for 310 kronor ($37.20) and a double with shower for 375 kronor ($45). Family rooms with four beds rent for 400 kronor ($48) to 450 kronor ($5.40). Breakfast is included in the rates.

Frälsingarmens Hotel Anglais, 15 Stortorget (tel. 714-50), on the main square facing the town hall, is one of the Salvation Army's best old-world showcases. Efficiently run, it has few frills but plenty of comfort—and is kept as immaculate as if the Old Dutch Cleanser scrubwoman had just passed by. The rooms are cavernous enough to offer bed-sitting areas. All units have showers or complete baths. A double with bath is 520 kronor ($62.40), a single with shower going for 400 kronor ($48) and with bath for 425 kronor ($51). Price reductions are granted during the summer season. The hotel has a tea room but no restaurant. However, many low-cost cafés are within easy walking distance.

Familje-Hotellet, 17 Engelbrektsgatan (tel. 12-84-85), doesn't waste time on sentimental frills, but is a winning choice for guests who want reasonable comfort, a smooth, well-functioning, older hotel, and service that is unobtrusive. Spacious rooms are modestly furnished and well kept, costing 175 kronor ($21) in a single, from 300 kronor ($36) in a double. To honor its namesake, the hotel also rents out some family rooms as well, a three-bedded unit going for 285 kronor ($34.20), a four-bedded unit costing 340 kronor ($40.80). Breakfast, at 23 kronor ($2.76), is the only meal served.

A Youth Hostel

Södergårdens Youth Hostel, 18 Backavägen (tel. 822-20), stands in a setting of leafy greenery, and receives guests from February 1 to November 30. One of the better run youth hostels in southern Sweden, it offers 174 beds distributed in two-, four-, and six-bedded rooms, each with private toilet and hot and cold running water. The charge is 45 kronor ($5.40) per person nightly. If they wish, guests can prepare their own meals in a kitchen. Dinner is only provided for groups of 20 or more. In addition to the kitchen, guests may also use the washing machine, drying room, and ironing room. Outdoor courts are provided for badminton and volleyball, and in the cellar is a sauna bath. Margith and Frank Tjellander, the managers, look after their guests very well. Take bus 36 from the Central Railway Station, right near the Malmö tourist office.

WHERE TO DINE: Did you know that Malmö has more restaurants per head than any other Swedish city, even more than Stockholm? Most of them are in the central part of town. **Saluhallen** by Lilla Torg is an indoor food market with several small restaurants.

Rådhuskällaren, in the town hall, on Stortorget, entrance at 6 Kyrkogatan (tel. 790-20), should at least be visited for lunch. In the ancient vaults and halls under this 16th-century Renaissance building, atmosphere joins hands with attractively prepared food. Don't be scared off by the witches' cellar. For the most part, the fare is typically Swedish, including veal with mushrooms and wienerschnitzel with potatoes and peas. Each candlelit table is well appointed, and the well-groomed waiters are efficient and polite.

For a restaurant with a view of Malmö, Lund, and Copenhagen (on clear days), go to the 26th floor at **Översten,** which serves a 60-krona ($7.20) tourist lunch, including beer or mineral water, coffee, and service charge, from noon to 5 p.m.

Or, to save money, eat at the **EPA Cafeteria** down the street where hot dishes are priced from 22 kronor ($2.64), and then go to the Översten just for the view.

Just across from the oldest house in town, the **Restaurang Gourmet Crêperi** is at 2 Lilla Torg (tel. 12-08-35). Here you can order crêpes, of course. A lunch costs from 55 kronor ($6.60), including a typical French main course, salad, and bread, or a dinner from 80 kronor ($9.60).

A fine restaurant in Malmö, although somewhat expensive for those on a tight budget, is **Kockska Krogen.** A cozy cellar restaurant is 3 Frans Suellsgatan (tel. 703-20) on the Stortorget (main square), it is in what used to be the old brick-lined mint named for Jörgen Kock, 16th-century mayor of Malmö. A Swedish lunch is served here, costing from 55 kronor ($6.60). Classical music is played in the background. It is open every day from noon until 1 a.m. Late eaters can get wine, beer, liquors, and cheese from 1 to 3 a.m. in the bar. If you like the Swedish-made utensils you eat with, you're in luck: they can be bought. Check with the waiter.

For dining in the park in Malmö, **Chez Olga,** Pildammsparken (tel. 12-55-26), offers fine meals. You can dine indoors, or out, by the lake. It is open weekdays from 11 a.m. till midnight, Saturday and Sunday from 1 p.m. until the witching hour. Meals cost around 125 kronor ($15).

THE TOP SIGHTS: Malmöhus Castle, founded in the 15th century by Eric of Pomerania and rebuilt by Christian III in the 16th century, was once a prison but has now joined forces with the City Museum. Instead of prisoners, it houses an art gallery, a handicrafts exhibit, and a natural history and a history museum and an aquarium. The greatest treasure of the brick castle is the **Malmö Museum** (tel. 34-10-00), containing a collection of old Scandinavian masters, especially those from southern Sweden, such as Carl Fredrik Hill (1849–1911), who is now reckoned as one of Sweden's best landscape painters and one of the forerunners of European modernism. Most interesting is the large collection of Russian oil paintings from around 1900. In fact, it is the largest collection outside the Soviet Union. But it also keeps abreast of new developments in modern art, and has good samples of Swedish furniture and textiles as well. The lyrical sketches in the foyer are by Carl Larsson, one of Sweden's best known artists. The museum is open Tuesday to Saturday from noon to 4 p.m., on Sunday from 10 a.m. to 4 p.m., charging 5 kronor (60¢) for adults, free for children 15 and under. West of Stortorget, the castle can easily be reached on a pleasant stroll.

A stone's throw away from the castle lies the **Technical/Maritime Museum** with the submarine *U-3*. Technical history can be followed from the steam engine to the jet. The history of aviation in south Sweden is the subject of displays, as is that of navigation in the Sound, from Viking ships to paddle streamers to hydrofoils. The children's department even has a pirate ship.

The **House of the Commandant,** between the castle and the Technical Museum, contains military history and an exhibit on "How we have lived since the turn of the century."

At Drottningtorget (The Queen's Square) lies the **Transport Museum,** with coaches, carriages, and cycles.

Another major sight is the Gothic-style **Malmö S:t Petri** or St. Peter's Church, a copper-roofed brick church dating from the 14th century. Off Stortorget, it is noted for its Renaissance altar, baptismal font, and elegantly carved pulpit. It is open from 8 a.m. to 4 p.m.

SHOPPING TIPS: If you're visiting Malmö just for the day from Copenhagen, you might want to take in some shopping.

In glassware and crystal, **Silverbergs Möbler,** 31 Baltazarsgatan (tel. 740-80), makes a big claim, "There is nowhere in Scandinavia a store comparable to this one." That is a matter of dispute; however, Silverbergs is quite famous, and it does ship stunning collection of glassware, crystal, furniture, and gifts all over the world, doing so competently and reliably. The establishment is open in summer, Monday to Friday, from 9:30 a.m. to 6 p.m. (on Saturday from 9:30 a.m. to 2 p.m.). After September 6, it is open till 6:30 p.m., Monday to Friday, and until 3 p.m. on Saturday.

For children, **Charlotte Weibull Dockcenter,** 45 Gustav Adolfs Torg (tel. 11-32-34), is like a dollhouse, filled with toys and gifts to delight children. The shop is also for adults, selling traditional Swedish folk costumes. Dockcenter is open Monday to Friday from 10 a.m. to 5 p.m. (on Saturday from 10 a.m. to 2 p.m.).

In handicrafts, **Panduro Hobby,** 17 Järnysegatan (tel. 94-65-00), offers raw materials which can be shaped into Nordic crafts.

Mattssons Päls, 98 Norra Vallgatan (tel. 12-55-33), is one of Sweden's leading furriers. Saga mink coats and jackets are the best buy, but Mattssons has a full range of fine furs. In the boutique, there are fur-lined poplins and accessories, all tax free for tourists.

In department stores, **Nordiska Kompaniet** (NK for short) has a branch in Malmö at 50 S:t Nygatan (tel. 770-00). Mattssons also now has a shop here. It was previously recommended in Stockholm and Gothenburg sections.

NIGHTLIFE: Since Copenhagen is nearby, Malmö does not have much nightlife, but there are a few spots.

From May to September, the citizens of Malmö head for **Folkets Park** (The People's Park), 35 Amiralsgatan (tel. 709-90), a sprawling amusement grounds and pleasure gardens, with dancing pavilions, vaudeville performances, open-air concerts, and restaurants. There are also a reptile center and a glass factory. Children will find a whole house to play in, plus a small zoo and a puppet theater. Admission is free on weekdays, but on Saturday and Sunday the fee is 18 kronor ($2.16) for adults. Children under 12 are always admitted free, however. Take bus 32, 36, 37, or 38 from Gustav Adolfs Torg.

Hotel Kramer, Stortorget (tel. 701-20), has the most action in town. At its Kramer Salong Night Club, you can listen to live music, and have a drink or dine in its casino. The entrance fee is about 55 kronor ($6.60). Kramer Pub, a popular place for a rendezvous, is said to be one of the most attractive restaurants in Sweden. In R's Café, it's easy to have a quick lunch (you can also drop in for afternoon tea). Another nightclub, the After Nine, offers two dance floors with disco music. Life in the After Nine is less formal than in Kramer's other nightspots.

The **Golden Days,** 59 S:t Nygatan (tel. 10-31-20), is English through and through. It's decorated in the Ye Olde English Music Hall motif, with playbills on the walls, and old records playing all the time. It's definitely nostalgia time. You can get main dishes such as marinated salmon and stewed potatoes with dill, 12 kronor ($1.44), a special on Monday night. It's open from 11:30 a.m. to 1 a.m. (from 1 p.m. on Sunday). A lunch costs from 25 kronor ($3) to 30 kronor ($3.60). There's no dancing but there's entertainment nightly. This chain has proved so popular that two more restaurants have opened, the **Golden Days** at 29 Kungsgatan (tel. 23-20-15) in Stockholm, and the **Golden Days,** 31 Södra Hamngatan (tel. 13-209-22), in Gothenburg. The same prices are charged at all three restaurants.

In Malmö, there are also several movie houses showing English and American films.

5. Lund

Frequent train services from Malmö takes passengers in just 15 minutes to this great old university and cathedral city. Here is the charm of yesteryear, with cobbled streets and medieval buildings. Launched in the early 11th century by Canute the Great, Lund rose, with the founding of its cathedral in the 12th century, to become the ecclesiastical and cultural center of all of Scandinavia. Lund University was opened in 1668.

The most exciting time to be in Lund, as in Uppsala, is on Walpurgis Eve, April 30, when the rollicking revelry of the student body signals the advent of spring. But a visit to Lund at any time is a pleasure.

Lunds Turisttrafikförening, the tourist information office, 4 S:t Petri Kyrikogata (tel. 12-45-90), is open from September 1 to May 31, 9 a.m. to 5 p.m. weekdays. From June 1 to August 31, 9 a.m. to 6 p.m. weekdays, to 1 p.m. on Saturday. During July and August also on Sunday from 11 a.m. to 1 p.m. At the office you can obtain accommodations in private homes for as little as 80 kronor ($9.60) per person, plus the booking fee of 15 kronor ($1.80) when reserved in the office and 25 kronor ($3) when booked in advance.

WHAT TO SEE: For those on a quick tour, the top sights are:

The Cathedral of Lund

In this ancient cathedral, **Lunds Domkyrokoförsamling,** 4 Tegnérplatsen (tel. 15-95-00), the flowering of Romanesque architecture in Scandinavia reached its fullest bloom. During a major restoration in the 19th century, the towers were rebuilt, but the exterior of the east part of the church displays one of the finest expressions of Romanesque architecture in Northern Europe. The interiors, in sandstone, have sculptural details of quality and character similar to that in Lombardy and other parts of Italy. There is also a crypt with a high altar dedicated in 1123. A major restoration was carried out in the early 16th century by Adam van Düren. A drawing card inside is a partly reconstructed 14th-century astronomical clock that not only tells the time and the date, but stages a splashy tournament from the Middle Ages—complete with clashing knights and the blare of trumpets. That's not all: the three Wise Men come out to pay homage to the Virgin and Child. To see all this, time your visit to the cathedral for when the clock strikes noon (1 p.m. on Sunday) and 3 p.m. Other highlights of the interior include intricately carved choir stalls from about 1375. The cathedral charges no admission and is open from 8 a.m. to 6 p.m., on Sunday from 9:30 a.m. to 6 p.m.

The Museum of Cultural History

After leaving the cathedral, walk across the university grounds to **Adelgatan,** which the local citizens consider their most charming street. Here you'll find **Kulturen,** another of the open-air museums of Sweden—this one containing reassembled, sod-roofed farms and manor houses, a carriage museum, ceramics, peasant costumes, Viking artifacts, and old handicrafts, even a wooden church moved to this site from the Glassworks District. Admission is 10 kronor ($1.20). The hours, May to September, are daily from 11 a.m. to 5 p.m. From October to April, hours are daily from noon to 4 p.m.

WHERE TO STAY IN LUND: Universitetshotellet Sparta, 39 Tunavägen (tel. 12-40-80), is open all year, with 150 rooms, 75 designated as youth hostel units, but the other 75 now being full-fledged hotel accommodations. These have been redecorated and equipped with color TV and phones. These rooms rent for 200 kronor ($24) to 275 kronor ($33) for a single, for 300 kronor ($36) to 375 kronor ($45) in a twin. The more expensive rooms come with a complimentary breakfast. The youth hostel units, also with toilets and showers, cost 55 kronor ($6.60) per bed or 110 kronor ($13.30) in a twin. The student center in which the hotel is located also houses a post office, bank, large food market, a self-service restaurant, a pub, and a cinema. Free parking is provided for guests.

Hotell Temperance, 7 S:t Petri Kyrkogata (tel. 11-34-40), is only a small hotel, with just ten rooms. But it is one of the cheapest accommodations to be found in Lund, and it's centrally situated. The friendly, English-speaking owner is Karl-Erik Slättberg, who will welcome you, charging you 160 kronor ($19.20) in a single, 210 kronor ($25.20) in a double. He also offers some family rooms, accommodating as many as four or five guests, at tariffs to be negotiated. Units contain wash basins with hot and cold running water, and showers and toilets are found in the corridor. The rooms are cleaned daily, and a change of towels is provided.

Park Hotel, 8 Bantorget (tel. 11-54-53). The friendly and helpful Mia Andersson, who speaks English, welcomes you to this modest eight-room hotel. The place is kept clean, and guests must share the one bathroom. A single costs 160 kronor ($19.20), a double rising to 220 kronor ($26.40), plus another 22 kronor ($2.64) charged for a Swedish breakfast.

READER'S GUESTHOUSE SELECTION: "I recommend the **Albrechtsson** home, 6 Karl XI Gatan (third floor) (tel. 11-37-75), about a ten-minute walk from the train station, as being a good value for the krona. For 80 kronor ($9.60) per person nightly, you're given a bed, a real bargain. Mrs. Albrechtsson rents only one large room with three beds. For an additional 35 kroner ($3), you can have a big breakfast. The Albrechtssons speak English, and they radiate Swedish charm. I was treated to coffee and sweets on the house" (Barry Isaac, Chicago, Ill.).

WHERE TO EAT: Stäket Taverna, 6 Stora Södergatan, is a reward for those seeking old taverns that serve good food in an unspoiled atmosphere. A 15th-century cellar in a narrow, step-gabled, brick building in the heart of Lund, this is one of the city's finest restaurants—well known, smart, exciting, and reliable,

Stäket caters to hearty appetites. Its 55-krona ($6.60) lunches draw the locals. Pizzas range from 28 kronor ($3.36).

One of the best spots for dining is the **Domus Department Store,** at 13 Mårtenstorget, which operates what it terms Tre Kök, or Three Kitchens. The place is self-service, but you get good food, ranging from typically Swedish fare (that is, home cooking) to pizzas and salads. There is always a "dish of the day" offered. Meals cost from 55 kronor ($6.60).

The **Tempo Department Store** on Södergatan offers a newly redecorated self-service cafeteria, where a plat du jour is a regular feature. On the whole, the prices here are less expensive than those encountered in Malmö. Popular with both shoppers and students, the Tempo offers meals from 55 kronor ($6.60).

Carlssons Trädgård, 6 Mårtenstorget (tel. 13-81-20), is a British pub-like place, and it offers entertainment in the evening in the pub part. Its prices are reasonable, around 75 kronor ($9) for a meal, and the food is fairly good. During the day it's strictly self-service, but in the evening there is table service. It is open Monday to Saturday from 11 a.m. to midnight.

A DETOUR TO DALBY: From Lund, those with their own transportation may want to make an important side trip to:

Dalby Church. In Dalby, eight miles east of Lund, lies this former bishop's church. The oldest in Scandinavia, it was built in the mid-11th-century. The church, open daily, is starkly beautiful and well preserved. Be sure to visit its crypt.

Another base for exploring the castles and manors of Skåne is:

6. Ystad

Once an important port during the Middle Ages, Ystad has preserved its ancient look, with about 300 half-timbered houses, mazes of narrow lanes—even a watchman who sounds the hours of the night in the tower of St. Mary's Church. For a capsule preview of medieval Sweden, head for **Per Hälsas Gaard,** in the center of town, a courtyard encircled by brick-and-timbered houses.

For the most part, you may prefer to stroll about and not to dwell particularly on specific buildings. However, St. Mary's Church at Stortorget, dating back to the early 1200s, shouldn't be overlooked. It is noted for its white and gilt baroque interior. It is open from 9 a.m. to 6 p.m. from mid-May to mid-September charging no admission.

The **Town Hall,** also at Stortorget, was built on the site of a burned medieval municipal center. It still has the original vaulted cellar.

North of Stortorget lies the **Grey Friars' Monastery,** the country's best preserved monastery after Vadstena. It was consecrated in 1267. The east wing with its built-in cloister houses the collections of the Society of Ancient Monuments as well as St. Peter's Church, which after a restoration celebrated its 700th jubilee in 1967. The **Art Museum and Dragoon Museum** lies on S:t Knuts Torg (tel. 770-00), in the same building as the tourist office and the town library. It can be visited from June 1 to August 31 Monday to Friday from 11 a.m. to 5 p.m., on Saturday from 11 a.m. to 3 p.m., and on Sunday from 1 to 5 p.m. From September 1 to May 31, it is open Monday to Friday from noon to 5 p.m., Sunday from 1 to 5 p.m.

Boats from Ystad go to Poland and Bornholm. From nearby Trelleborg there is regular boat service to East Germany and West Germany.

The tourist bureau, at the bus station in the same building as the art museum (Kunstmuseum), is open June 15 to August 15, 9 a.m. to 8 p.m. Monday through Friday, 8 a.m. to 6 p.m. Saturday, 4 to 7 p.m. Sunday. From August 15 to June 15, it is open 9 a.m. to noon and 1 to 5 p.m. Monday through Friday.

FOOD AND LODGING: If you'd like to stay near the ferry boats, try **Hotel Continental du Syd,** 13 Hamngatan (tel. 137-00). Singles rent from 325 kronor ($39) on Friday and Saturday, rising to 475 kronor ($57) on weekdays. Doubles go from 400 kronor ($48) Friday and Saturday, 600 kronor ($72) on weekdays. All rooms have showers or baths and color TV. Breakfast is included in the tariffs.

Bäckagård Gästrum, 36 Dammgatan (tel. 195-08), is a very small hotel, with just seven rooms, five of which are doubles. The furnishings are adequate, and each unit is equipped with hot and cold running water. In the corridor is a shower and a toilet. Rates are 140 kronor ($16.80) in a double room, dropping to 100 kronor ($12) in a single.

Another good possibility for lodgings is the **Hotell Tornväktaren,** 33 S:t Ostergatan (tel. 129-54), where the welcome is friendly and English spoken. You should book well in advance, because the little hotel is popular with the Swedes. A few of the rooms contain private showers, and you must pay more for these—from 180 kronor ($21.60) in a single, from 230 kronor ($27.60) in a double. Other doubles with less plumbing rent for 175 kronor ($21). Breakfast is an extra 25 kronor ($3). Guests in one of the bathless rooms will find a shower and toilet in the corridor.

Rådhuskällaren Ystad (tel. 185-10) is in a vaulted cell with small tables and a romantic atmosphere enhanced by candlelight. The choice of meals is wide. The cooking is fine. I suggest the specialty, flounder in a sauce with vegetables. Meals cost from 75 kronor ($9), and a glass of beer is 12 kronor ($1.44).

For an alternate center along the southern coast, continue east on Highway 10 to:

7. Simrishamn

One of the most idyllic towns along the Skåne coastline, Simrishamn also appears medieval, with half-timbered buildings, courtyards, and gardens. This old seaport is the jumping-off point to the Danish island of Bornholm.

While here, be sure to see the 12th-century, step-gabled **St. Nicholai Church,** built of sandstone and containing a baroque altar. Ship models are suspended from the ceiling (open 10 a.m. to 4 p.m.). Also, a visit to the park, **Bergengrenska Trädgården,** off Stortorget, reveals one of the most charming aspects of the town.

If you want any information about hotels, boarding houses, summer cottages, and apartments, check with the tourist bureau, **Simrishamns Kommun Turistbyrån,** 2 Tullhusgatan, 27200 Simrishamn (tel. 106-66).

Hotel Kockska Gården (tel. 117-55) is like an unspoiled black-and-white timbered coaching inn, built around a large medieval courtyard. But its lounge inside combines both old and new, a stone fireplace contrasting with balloon lamps. The bedrooms have been modernized, and the furnishings are up-to-date with tastefully coordinated colors. Doubles with private bath cost 320 kronor ($38.40). Doubles without bath cost 280 kronor ($33.60). Bathless singles rent for 200 kronor ($24), increasing to 255 kronor ($30.60) with bath. The only meal served here is breakfast, which is included in the tariffs.

8. The Sights of Skåne

BOSJÖKLOSTER: On Lake Ringsjön, about a 30-minute drive northeast of Lund (off Route 23), lie the step-gabled, white buildings of Bosjökloster, a former Benedictine nunnery that is believed to have been founded in the 11th century. It flourished until shut down in the Reformation of the 16th century. Now restored, after years of decay, Bosjökloster is one of the most popular stopovers for motorists on the Malmö-Stockholm run. The present resident, Count Thord Bonde, opens part of the estate to the public daily from May 1 to October 1, 9 a.m. to 5:30 p.m., charging 12 kronor ($1.44) for admission. Be sure to visit the old vaults (once a refectory for the nuns), the Stone Hall (the most ancient room in the château), and walk through the gardens. In one chamber is a gallery of handicrafts, as well as an exhibit from the factories of the Glassworks District (purchases may be made). In the garden is a self-service cafeteria, offering lunches for around 45 kronor ($5.40).

SVANEHOLM: Between Malmö and Ystad is Svaneholm, once a fortress founded in 1530 and later partially converted into an Italian-style palace. Today it houses a museum of paintings, furnishings, and tools of life dating primarily from the 18th and 19th centuries. In a rural lakeside setting, Svaneholm is built around a central courtyard. In the skillfully converted cellar rooms, guests can order snacks. Hot main dishes, costing from 32 kronor ($3.84), are served in the elegant dining room from noon till 8 p.m.

BACKAKRA: On the coastal road between Ystad and Simrishamn sits the farm that Dag Hammarskjöld, the late United Nations secretary-general, purchased in 1957 and intended to make his home. His death in a plane crash cut short that ambition. However, the old farm—almost monastic looking—was restored according to his instructions. He last saw it in 1959, and in his will left it to the Swedish Touring Club. It is open May 1 to September 1, 1 to 5 p.m., charging 6 kronor (72¢) for admission. The rooms are filled with many gifts presented to Mr. Hammarskjöld—everything from a Nepalese dagger to a lithograph by Picasso.

GLIMMINGEHUS: Also lying between Ystad and Simrishamn is the bleak castle of Glimmingehus, a fortress dating back to the 15th century. A somewhat Gothic, step-gabled building, it is unfurnished, and its interior looks like a dungeon. From April 1 to September 30 it is open from 9 a.m. to 5 p.m., charging 8 kronor (96¢) for admission. The castle is also open from October 1 to March 31 from 9 a.m. to 3 p.m. (closed Monday, however, in the off-season). At a café on the premises, guests can order snacks or afternoon tea.

CHRISTINEHOF: Owned by the Count Carl Piper, Christinehof Castle, built in the 18th century, lies on the Ystad-Kristianstad road, northwest of Eljaröd. The château is preserved essentially as it was when it was first built. The fully furnished castle is open from June to August, weekdays from 11 a.m. to 6 p.m. (till 8 p.m. on Sunday). Admission is 8 kronor (96¢).

THE KIVIK TOMB AT BREDAROR: North of Simrishman along the coast of Kivik is this remarkable prehistoric tomb discovered in 1748. In a 1931 excavation, the tomb furniture, fragments of bronze, and some grave carvings were uncovered. Experts have stated that Kivik is one of the "most remarkable monuments of the Bronze Age" and that it has "played a part in the history of European archeological research." The tomb is open from 10 a.m. to 6 p.m., May 1 to August 31, charging 4 kronor (48¢).

SILVER HILL AT KLIPPAN: A fine place for excursions for you and whoever you're traveling with is at Klippan, the most beautiful part of Skåne, next-door to the beech woods of Söderåsen and the Rönneås Rapids. Here in a billowing landscape of hills and valleys is Silver Hill, which has a collection of attractions which it bills as "Wheels, Wings, and Horses."

The wheels part is found at the **Car Museum,** which has the world's largest Rolls Royce exhibition, including the entire range from the Silver Ghost to the Silver Shadow, plus one which once belonged to Queen Elizabeth II. Other classical and historic cars are also on exhibit in a hall with street lamps and pillars, looking like a castle avenue.

An **Aircraft Museum** and a **flight show** fulfill the wings part of the billing. The museum is fairly modest in its collection of planes and aircraft motors, but the flight show is a breathtaking air performance using such planes as the legendary Tiger Moth, the Chipmunk, the Saab Safir, the Bellanca Decathlon, and the Pitts Special. You'll see balloon-chasing with the old flying machines, among other fascinating aerial ventures. The air show takes place every Sunday at 1 p.m. from May 1 to September 25.

Performances by **Lipizzaner horses** with all the classical movements of that superb equine troop evokes memories of the Vienna Spanish Riding School, and here, too, there is a performance for children before the regular show. When Silver Hill is open, the Lipizzaners go through their paces every day at 3 p.m., with the children's show being given at 1 p.m.

Silver Hill also has a zoo, a restaurant, a cafeteria, and shops, with an Indian Village where children can ride on mini-Lipizzaners or Indian ponies. There are also mini-cars which can be driven by persons the right size for them. The whole thing is open from April 15 to May 31 and September 1 to October 15 on Saturday and Sunday; from June 1 to August 31 daily. Hours are 11 a.m. to 5 p.m. You only need one ticket, which costs from 35 kronor ($4.20) to 45 kronor ($5.40) per person.

SWEDISH LAPLAND

OFTEN CALLED "God's country," Swedish Lapland is the last wilderness of Europe. Here during sunlit nights you can commune with nature. This vast northern wonderland is characterized by glaciers, roaring-white waterfalls, rushing rivers, crystal-blue lakes, forests, and majestic mountains.

In this land of the Midnight Sun, the sun never sets for six weeks in June and July. It just dips close to the horizon. The sky is illuminated with brilliant colors. In spring and autumn many visitors come here to see the Aurora Borealis as well.

The Swedes call this vast northern tract of their country **Norrland.** Roughly, Norrland covers half of the area of Sweden. One-quarter of the country lies north of the Arctic Circle.

About 10,000 Lapps inhabit Europe's last frontier. Frankly, most of them have been assimilated into Swedish society, but some 3000 still lead the nomadic life of their ancestors, herding reindeer. With their whirling hooves and antlers, the migrating reindeer often confer movement on an otherwise dead landscape. These Lapps, of course, are Swedish citizens, although their origins are unknown. Many of them still wear their multicolored costumes.

GETTING THERE: On a latitude with Alaska, the territory can be easily reached. Fast electric trains take you from Stockholm to Narvik in Norway, with stops at Kiruna and Abisko. The express train, *Nordpilen,* takes one day and a night to travel from Stockholm to far north of the Arctic Circle. Once there you'll find mail-coach buses connecting the other villages and settlements in the north.

It's much quicker to fly, of course, and there are airports at Umea, Lulea, and Kiruna. The last, for example, is reached by air in four hours from Stockholm. Those with more time may want to drive there. From Stockholm, just stay on the E4, the longest road in the world. From Stockholm to the Finnish border town of Haparanda, you'll ride along about 700 miles of good surface.

NOTES FOR EXPLORERS: In all of Europe, no one has as much free land to ramble over as in Swedish Lapland. If you don't mind the mosquitoes in summer, and they are legion, it's a paradise for hikers and campers. As you push northward, the forests thin out, becoming wind-dwarfed scrub. An occasional bear or wolf can be seen.

If you're planning to do much trail blazing, you should get in touch with the **Swedish Touring Club** (Svenska Turistföreningen) before you go. This outfit maintains mountain hotels, and it has built bridges and marked hiking routes. It's even made it possible to cross waterways by introducing regular boat services on some lakes.

Out in the wilderness you'll find hundreds of miles of marked hiking and skiing tracks. (For skiing, March and April, even May, are recommended.) Some 80 mountain hotels or Lapp-type huts (called *fjällstugor* and *kåtor*) are offered, with beds and bedding, cooking utensils, and firewood. Huts can be used for one or two nights only. The club also sponsors mountain stations (*fjällstationer*), some of which are large and comfortable, others "sporty."

You must be in good physical condition and have suitable equipment before setting out, as most of the area is uninhabited. Neophytes should join one of the hiking or conducted tours offered by the STF. For more details, write the Swedish Touring Club, P.O. Box 25, S-10120, Stockholm (tel. 22-72-00). Membership costs about 115 kronor ($13.80) per person per year. An overnight accommodation and the use of facilities in a mountain hut go for 55 kronor ($6.60) for members, 65 kronor ($7.80) for nonmembers if room is available. Use of these huts during the day is another 18 kronor ($2.16).

In **Padjelanta National Park,** with its mountain flora and Virihaure and Vastenhaure lake districts, the National Swedish Environment Protection Board owns several huts. Overnight accommodations cost 32 kronor ($5.76).

The Royal Trail

The greatest trail blazing is on the Kungsleden or Royal Trail, running from Abisko to Hemaven for a total length of about 210 miles. This is considered one of the most fascinating trails in Europe. It's marked, of course, and mountain huts are spaced a day's hike apart if you can maintain the pace. Most of the stops are at what Swedes call *kåtors.* Here you cook your own food and clean up before leaving. At points the trail crosses lakes and rivers where boats will be found. The trail actually follows the old nomadic paths of the Lapps. Those with less time or energy will find the trail broken up into several smaller routings.

SOUTHERN LAPLAND

South of the Arctic Circle, Lapland is less forbidding. The mountains are easier to scale. If you hike to Rissjöen, you'll find one of the most attractive mountain lakes in Scandinavia. The two best centers of Southern Lapland are Kittelfjäll and Tärnaby, previewed below.

1. Kittelfjäll (Dikanäs)

In a massif of sculptured peaks, Kittelfjäll is surrounded by lake-studded valleys.

WHERE TO STAY: Hotel Kittelfjäll, Dikanäs (tel. 810-20). Set in a birch forest, this hotel is open only from February 15 to May and June 15 to October 30. The establishment is comfortable and contemporary, in a simple way. In the lounges are fireplaces, and the windows open onto the surrounding landscape. The accommodations are not large, but they are decorated with a cheerful mountain-chalet touch. A single without bath goes for 185 kronor ($22.20); a double without bath, 280 kronor ($33.60). It's best to take the half-board rate of 185 kronor ($22.20) to 330 kronor ($39.60) per person daily. The food isn't fancy, but the portions are large. Often you serve yourself from an open table. The hotel has a mountain guide who'll arrange treks for you. Anglers will find good fishing in several nearby lakes and in a river. In winter and early spring the hotel fills up with skiers.

2. Tärnaby and Hemavan

In a companion valley to Kittelfjäll, Tärnaby offers beautiful mountains and a chain of lakes. From there, you can make excursions to the Norwegian frontier. The village lies on the Blå Vägen (European Road 79), and is considered the center of Sweden's grandest and most accessible alpine region. Known for its Stenmark slopes, Tärnaby is a good center for excursions. Hikers can strike out for Artfjället, Norra Storfjället, Mortsfjället, and Atoklinton. Guides can be hired to accompany one on these hikes. Of course, there is Laxfjället with its fine ski hills and gentle slopes.

Hemavan is the largest tourist resort in the area and the starting point for the renowned hiking path, Kungsleden (King's Way). Many paths lead toward Norra Storfjället. A delta by Ahasjön and the River Ume is particularly rich in birdlife. In the center of the village of Hemavan in the brook are some restored water-driven grindstones.

WHERE TO STAY: Laisalidens Fjällhotell (tel. 210-63). This 23-room mountain hotel is traditionally decorated, its windows opening onto views of the lakes. The rooms are pleasant, but undistinguished. They are kept immaculate. It's preferable to take the half-board rate ranging from 250 kronor ($30) to 300 kronor ($36) per person daily. The hotel will arrange fishing trips as well as motorboat excursions on the nearby lakes. It's open from February 25 to May 16 and from June 15 to August 26.

Tärnaby Fjällhotell, 16 Östra Strandvägen (tel. 104-20), is modern, its main building dating from 1966. Offered are comfortable rooms, each with shower, phone, and toilet. In the main building, doubles are rented, costing 300 kronor ($36) per night. If you rent a single room in the main building, you'll have to pay

240 kronor ($28.80). Breakfast is another 30 kronor ($3.60). The hotel contains a sauna, table tennis, a ski room, and a "drying off" room as well as several lounges.

Near the main building is the Sportgården, where rooms open onto views of Lake Gäutan and the mountain ranges beyond. This is an annex of the hotel, and a form of self-service applies, as guests clean their own room. For their trouble, they are quoted a good price—125 kronor ($15) per person nightly. The rooms are bathless, although there are showers and pleasant lounges.

Sånninggården, Klippen (tel. 330-38), is a warm, inviting place set against the backdrop of a wilderness. The cranberry-red building traces its origins back to 1800, although it has been modernized and made up-to-date. Barbro Ottosson will greet you and see to your needs. The rooms are pleasantly furnished, costing 180 kronor ($21.60) per person in a double, 225 kronor ($27) in a single. Breakfast is an additional 25 kronor ($3) per person. The food is good, the portions generous, and the service friendly. If you stay at least three days, you can apply for the half-board rate of 280 kronor ($33.60) per person. The little hotel is both a winner and a summer treat.

3. Ammarnäs

Ammarnäs, in the Swedish Highlands, is a holiday paradise near the source of the River Vindel, in the center of one of Europe's largest nature reserves, the Vindel Mountains. Leisure activities abound, although some of them may not strike a leisurely pace. You can fish, ski, hike, whatever, depending on the time of year you come here. The area is rich in varieties of birdlife.

Craftsmen who live hereabouts specialize in the traditional handicrafts of the *Same,* a semi-Nomadic tribe of reindeer herders living in the north of Sweden. Each year, visitors here at the summer solstice, around June 21, can take part in the **Same Festival.** The best time to be here for an unforgettable experience, however, is in September, when you can watch the yearly reindeer roundup.

Don't miss seeing the **Potato Hill.** It's called one of nature's mysteries—a place where tasty *Mandel* potatoes grow even though it's been called a natural impossibility.

Ammarnäs has air taxis in summer and snow-scooter taxis in winter, to take you to the mountain and rivers. The village has such facilities as a filling station, post office, library, church, and store, and a skiing and leisure center at Näsberget (Näs mountain) nearby. Slalom skiing, ski lifts, and ski schools are all provided.

The famous Kungsleden (King's Way) hiking trail goes near here, leading down to Hemavan, visited above.

WHERE TO STAY: The **Ammarnäsgården Hotel** (tel. 600-03) is a focal point in Ammarnäs village, which has been extensively rebuilt to make a stay here comfortable. Of the hotel's 30 rooms, 26 have showers and four have wash basins and showers. It is open only from around New Year's until the end of September, but during that time, rates are 200 kronor ($48) to 250 kronor ($30) in a single, depending on the plumbing. In a double, you pay from 280 kronor ($33.60) to 350 kronor ($42). Most guests stay here on the full-board plan, which costs 280 kronor ($33.60) per person per day. There is a swimming pool, with a children's pool, and the hotel has two saunas for use of its guests. In the licensed restaurant, you can feast on freshly caught fish or reindeer meat. Once or twice a week, there are dances in the Gobbakällar, an intimate disco.

NORTHERN LAPLAND

This is true Lapp country, and most visitors with limited time will want to explore it at the expense of the southern sector. A wide range of centers, from Lapp settlements to mining towns to lakeside Arctic Circle resorts, are previewed below.

4. Arvidsjaur

A modern community, Arvidsjaur has an old Lappish center with well-preserved, cone-shaped huts. Reindeer are rounded up and marked here in June and July. The Norrbottens forests around this inland borough merit a visit. Arvidsjaur lies in a belt of coniferous forests bordering on the highland region. It's on the inland railway, a line which stretches for nearly 800 miles, running between Kristinehamn in Värmland to Gällivare in Lapland. Arvidsjaur also has rail connections with the Northern Mainline from Stockholm up to the Finnish border.

You can take a road up to a skiing hut from which a lift will take you to excellent terrain. In the district is a reserve, an untouched wilderness with an abundance of wildlife. Anglers go to the Pite and Skellefte Rivers, where the fishing is good. There are also many lakes in the vicinity.

The old homestead museum at **Glommersträsk** is the largest farmers' village in Sweden.

WHERE TO STAY: If you have a little time to spend in the area, you can ask at the tourist office about renting one of any number of restored farms in the vicinity.

Those passing through for the day will find accommodations at **Hotel Laponia** (tel. 108-80), which has its own lake just across the road for the fishing fraternity. Well-furnished and suitably maintained singles rent for 430 kronor ($51.60); doubles, 550 kronor ($66). An extra bed costs 115 kronor ($13.80).

Less preferred, but better for the budget, is the basic **Edström** (tel. 107-08), charging 300 kronor ($36) to 375 kronor ($45) in a bathless single, 400 kronor ($48) to 500 kronor ($60) in a bathless double. If the manager takes a liking to you, he might bake you some of his flat bread.

Centralhotellet, 63 Järvägsgatan (tel. 100-98), is yet another selection for overnighting. Right at the station, this simple little hotel offers only 10 rooms, a total of 17 beds. Each of the adequately furnished units is bathless, a single renting for 130 kronor ($15.60), a double going for 180 kronor ($21.60). The hotel also has TV in the rooms, and a shower in the hall. Breakfast, at 28 kronor ($3.36), is the only meal served, and English is spoken.

5. Arjeplog

This settlement is reached by mail-coach service from Arvidsjaur. There is no rail connection, even though Arjeplog has a rail station. In the middle of lake landscape, Arjeplog sits on the edge of high mountain country. It's on a peninsula between the great lakes of Uddjaur and Hornavan.

Arjeplog was colonized in the 16th century when silver mining started in Nasafjäll on the Norwegian border. Reindeer at that time carried the silver to Piteå for shipment. In **Aldolfström,** the silver village, you can still see some of the buildings from the old purifying plant. Today lead ore is mined in the "underwater mine" at **Laisvall.**

The church at Arjeplog was built 1767, and it contains a bridal crown. Legend says it was once stolen by the Lapps but was found again up in the mountains.

In and around the settlement, the highlands are studded with excellent fishing waters. You can catch whitefish almost from the roadside.

WHERE TO STAY: The main hotel at Arjeplog is expensive. It's the **Nya Silverhatten Hotell** (tel. 107-70), offering 36 well-scrubbed and functional rooms. Singles go for 325 kronor ($39) with shower. Doubles contain private baths or showers and rent for 450 kronor ($54). All the prices include breakfast. It's possible to stay here and take all your meals for 320 kronor ($38.40) to 420 kronor ($50.40) per person daily. On the premises is a sauna, a heated swimming pool, a special children's pool, a tennis court, and mini-golf.

6. Jokkmokk

On the Luleå River, this Lappish center of Norrbotten is a modern community of charm. Since the 17th century it's been a Lapp trading and cultural center. The Lapps have an annual market here the first week of February, when they sell their local handicrafts.

WHERE TO STAY: Hotell Gästis (tel. 100-12) has all the qualities of a frontier country hotel. Everything's uncomplicated, and the situation calls for self-reliance. If you need help with anything, the limited staff is most cooperative. The 25 rooms are decidedly old-fashioned. Bathless singles cost 225 kronor ($27); bathless doubles, 280 kronor ($33.60). With bath, the cost in a single is 300 kronor ($36), 350 kronor ($42) in a double. The hotel is open year round.

From Jokkmokk a 75-mile road has been constructed along the lakes of the Little Lula River to reach the mountain village of—

7. Kvikkjokk

One of the most beautiful resorts of Lapland, Kvikkjokk is the gateway to **Sarek National Park.** The largest wild area in Europe, this park is considered one of the most representative of the highland regions. It's virtually inaccessible, almost entirely without tracks, huts, or bridges. Nevertheless, the most adventurous plunge into it, as it contains widely fascinating flora and fauna.

WHERE TO STAY: Kvikkjokk Fjällstation (tel. 210-22) is run by the Swedish Touring Club, and it's open only from June 22 to September 2. A 19-room mountain chalet, it offers views over river and lake to the peaks of Sarek National Park. Fishing and hiking trails fan out in all directions. Furnishings are traditional—in all, a no-nonsense atmosphere. Bathless doubles cost 150 kronor ($18) to 225 kronor ($27). You can stay here and take full board at rates from 200 kronor ($24) to 240 kronor ($28.80), depending on the room. On the premises is a sauna.

8. Saltoluokta

This village merits attention, even though it's hard to reach and the accommodations are basic. From Luspebryggan, eight miles from Porjus, a journey takes nearly six hours by boat (in two stages) to reach the mountain station of Saltoluokta.

Here you can spend the night, then continue the route through mountain scenery to the **Stora Sjöfallet** waterfall. This extensive mountain region embraces the lakes of the Stora–Lule river system, from the coniferous forests in the east to the Norwegian frontier. Huts for overnight accommodations are available.

WHERE TO STAY: Saltoluokta Fjällstation (tel. 410-10) is a mountain chalet belonging to the Swedish Touring Club. Open from June 18 to September 7, it offers 30 bedrooms (92 beds) with uncluttered furnishings and open, friendly atmosphere. Bathless doubles cost from 110 kronor ($13.20). The half-board rate ranges from 165 kronor ($19.80) to 180 kronor ($21.60) per person daily, depending on the room. If you go for a walk, you'll feel alone in the wilderness.

9. Gällivare

A shining silver river was discovered here, and the town grew up around it. **Mount Dundret** (Thunder Mountain), with an aerial ropeway, attracts visitors in both winter and summer. From its 2500-foot peak, you can look over the Sarek and Kebnekaise areas.

At the end of March, Gällivare hosts a **Lapland Fair** and Sweden's foremost alpine competition, the **Lapland Cup.** The **Ettöre Church,** built in 1742, was financed by a nationwide collection.

WHERE TO STAY: Gällivare Hotell, 1 Lasarettsgatan (tel. 110-20), is a fairly commercial establishment. Faintly clinical rooms in summer cost from 385 kronor ($46.20) in a single with bath. Doubles with private baths or showers go for 500 kronor ($60), breakfast included. The hotel is open all year, except Christmas.

Hotell Dundret, 1 Per Högströmsgatan (tel. 110-40), is a small hotel with six double rooms, one three-bedded chamber, and one with four beds. These modestly furnished units are equipped with hot and cold running water, TV, and phone. A bath with a shower is found in the hall. A short walk from the railway station, the hotel is often fully booked for parts of the summer, so he or she who writes in advance gets the room. The price in a single is 175 kronor ($21), going up to 250 kronor ($30) in a double. Rooms for three to four guests are rented at a rate of 115 kronor ($13.80) per bed. No meals are served.

10. Kiruna

Kiruna is the largest city in the world, embracing more than 3000 square miles. This town has such extensive boundaries it incorporates both **Kebnekaise Mountain** and **Lake Torneträsk.** Kebnekaise, 50 miles from Kiruna, rises 6965 feet above sea level, the highest mountain in Sweden. A regular bus goes to **Aroksjokk** village, where you can get a motorboat to the Lapp village of **Nikkaluokta.** Here Lapp families can put you up overnight and arrange hikes or boating trips for you. From their settlement it is 13 miles by foot to Kebnekaise, including a short boat trip. The Swedish Touring Club has a mountain station at Kebnekaise. The station guide there arranges mountaineering parties to the summit. It takes about four hours to reach the peak.

WHERE TO STAY: Hotell Ferrum, 1 Köpmangatan (tel. 186-00), is the best place to stay in town. It's run by the Reso chain. All of its rooms contain private baths or showers. The hotel is of functional and uniform design and could use a touch of human warmth. However, in this part of the world, a warm haven takes on more imposing and inviting qualities. Singles cost from 500 kronor ($60), doubles going for a peak 610 kronor ($73.20). An extra bed in the room costs an additional 115 kronor ($13.80), and all these tariffs include breakfast. Prices are sometimes lowered in summer.

11. Karesuando

From Kiruna, a bus goes to the most atmospheric Lapp center at Karesuando, Sweden's most northerly village, near the Finnish border. Fare is 136 kronor ($24.48). This excursion, and certainly Karesuando, is decidedly offbeat.

Some adventurous motorists drive to Karesuando, 120 miles north of the Arctic Circle. For seven midwinter weeks, the sun disappears. To compensate, it never sets at all between May 26 and July 17.

Once at Karesuando, you can make car-ferry connections to Finland, where the road continues north through tundra regions to the most northerly part of Scandinavia. The Finnish tourist resort of Kilpisjärvi lies 72 miles northwest of Karesuando.

WHERE TO STAY: The **Grapes Hotell** (tel. 200-22) is open year round. A simple inn, it charges 400 kronor ($48) in a double room with shower or bath. A single without shower goes for only 285 kronor ($34.20), both tariffs including breakfast. You can ask also for a three-bedded room with shower, at a cost of 425 kronor ($51) nightly. A sauna is on the premises.

12. Abisko

A resort north of the Arctic Circle is a curiosity. But Abisko, on the southern shore of Lake Torneträsk, is such a place.

On the Narvik railway, a 22-hour run from Stockholm, Abisko offers superb views over the lake. The resort comprises the valley of Abiskojokk and contains part of the lake and the island of Abiskosuolo. A lift takes passengers to **Mount Nuolja.**

Nearby is the protected **Abisko National Park,** containing remarkable flora, including orchids.

Abisko is one of the best centers for watching the Midnight Sun. Also, it's the start of the longest marked trail in the world, the already-mentioned Kungsleden. You'll also see a reconstruction of a Lapp encampment at the resort.

WHERE TO STAY: The **Abisko Turistation** (tel. 400-00) is big and modern, 160 antiseptic rooms in all, 52 in cottages. Owned by the Swedish Touring Club, it offers a choice of accommodations in the main building, as well as some basic chambers in the annex and bungalows. From the hotel you look out onto the lake and backdrop of mountains. The staff is helpful about providing information about excursions. Rooms are comfortable, and some have exceptional views. Bathless singles go for 140 kronor ($16.80) to 180 kronor ($21.60), bathless doubles for 180 kronor ($21.60) to 260 kronor ($31.20). No singles contain a private bath, but doubles with shower range in price from 270 kronor ($32.40) to 310 kronor ($37.20). You can stay here and take full board for 210 kronor ($25.20) to 310 kronor ($37.20) per person per day. The hotel is open from February 25 to May 13 and from June 9 to September 16.

Hotel Gästgården, Abisko Östra (tel. 40-100), stands 50 yards from the railway station. A simple place, Gästgården has 25 rooms to rent, making for a total of 65 beds. Twelve rooms are strictly self-catered. The price of this hostel-like place is 65 kronor ($7.80) in a bed without sheets, 70 kronor ($8.40) with sheets. Thirteen bedrooms, a shop, and a small restaurant are found in the main build-

Chapter XVII

A PREVIEW OF FINLAND

1. Flying To and Around Finland
2. The ABCs of Life

FINLAND IS THE LAST frontier country of Western Europe, and it is one of the northernmost countries in the world, with nearly a third of its land, Lapland, north of the Arctic Circle.

Despite the confiscation of nearly a tenth of its territory following the Winter War with Russia, Suomi (its Finnish name) is still one of the largest countries of Europe, about the size of Italy. But it is also one of the least populated, having only a little less than five million people.

Geographically remote (although easily accessible from a transportation point of view), Finland does not attract the visitors that Denmark, Norway, and Sweden do. And that is a shame, for Finland has much to offer the visitor in both summer and winter. It remains little known to most Americans, some of whom remember it only as a country that paid its World War II debts through great sacrifice. There are several misconceptions about Finland, including the popular one that alleges that polar bears wander the streets of Helsinki.

The worst of the misconceptions is that Finland is a satellite of the Soviet Union. While the Kremlin dallies with Finnish politics, Suomi is far from being a satellite. It is a brave, staunchly independent country that has felt the grisly arms of the Russian bear—even its bite—too many times.

But regardless of the political character of Finland, regardless of how much it may lean toward the West, the people of Suomi are forced to walk a tightrope between East and West. That they haven't fallen from the tightrope into the waiting arms of the Russians is one of the miracles of 20th-century European history. If the Finns seek any reminder of the danger (after World War II, they surely don't), they need only look across the Baltic to their southern neighbors, Estonia, Latvia, and Lithuania—three countries far less skilled as trapeze artists.

But Finland has survived, admittedly at a cruel and painful price. Why? It has something to do with *sisu*. Sisu is one of two Finnish words (the other is sauna) that has infiltrated the English language. Books have been written explaining the meaning of the word, but there is no English equivalent—although the most colorful definition is "guts." It was guts that led Finland to fight 42 wars with Russia—despite the fact that it lost them all.

Technically, Finland is not a Scandinavian country. But in spirit it is, a spirit reflected in a style of living (dazzling modern architecture, such as Tapiola Garden City), its standard of living (one of the highest in the world), its avant-garde ing. The price for these rooms is 75 kronor ($9) for a bed without sheets, 80 kronor ($9.60) with sheets. Boats and canoes are available for rent, and a small swimming pool lies 50 yards from the hotel. You can ski, fish, take walks in the mountains, look at the Midnight Sun in summer or the Northern Lights in winter in a fantastically clean and natural atmosphere.

13. Björkliden

Close to Abisko this competitive resort north of the Arctic Circle also opens onto Lake Torneträsk. From here you can see the Lapp Gate, a saddle mountain through which the souls of the Lapps are supposed to pass into eternity. You'll also find a ski lift up to the mountains and the world's most notherly golf course.

Björkliden lies 155 miles north of the Arctic Circle and south of the mountain lake Tornesträsk, which has a length of 43 miles.

High mountains at the very doorstep make for excellent skiing country.

WHERE TO STAY: Turiststationen Björkliden (tel. 410-50) is a pleasant stopover. From its precincts views open onto Lake Torneträsk and the Lapp Gate. Rooms are comfortably furnished, but simple. It's customary to stay here on partial partial- or full-board terms. Half board ranges in price from 230 kronor ($27.60) to 330 kronor ($39.60) per person daily. The hotel is open from February 15 to May 22 and from June 12 to September 18.

The Swedish Railroads, which owns this facility as well as two others nearby, has added 80 modern cottages which sleep five in real comfort (bring your own linen or pay a small charge). The cottages are rented by the week, costing from 1300 kronor ($156) to 3500 kronor ($420). Each has two bedrooms, a living room, and a kitchenette with an electric stove and refrigerator, along with a shower, toilet, and drying cabinet. There's also radio and TV. A food shop is found in the station house.

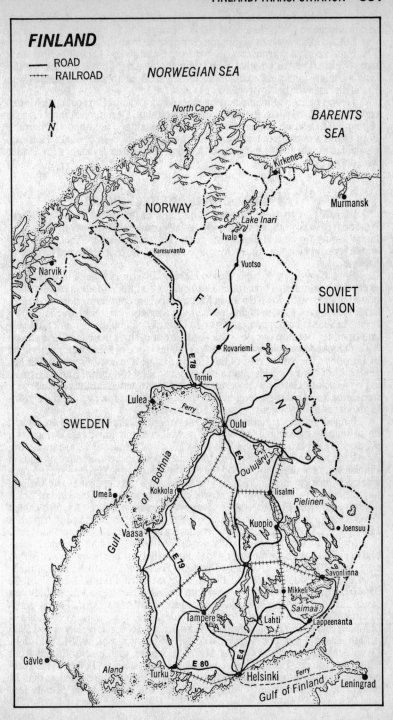

FINLAND

— ROAD
····· RAILROAD

NORWEGIAN SEA

North Cape

BARENTS
SEA

N

Kirkenes

NORWAY

Murmansk

Lake Inari

Ivalo

Karesuvanto

Vuotso

Narvik

F
I
N
L
A
N
D

SOVIET
UNION

Rovariemi

E78

Tornio

Lulea

Ferry

SWEDEN

Oulu

Oulujärvi

E4

Umeå

Kokkola

Iisalmi

Pielinen

Gulf

of

Bothnia

Kuopio

Joensuu

Vaasa

E79

Savonlinna

Mikkeli

Saimaa

Tampere

Lahti

Lappeenanta

Gävle

Aland

E80

E4

Turku

Helsinki

Ferry

Leningrad

Gulf of Finland

designs (a leader in textiles, furniture, ceramics, among other achievements), and in education (it claims almost 100% literacy).

Still, in many ways the Finns are far removed from their Nordic neighbors. The Finns speak a language as distinct from Swedish and Danish as Spanish is from Welsh. The truly native Finn is not a Norseman, but a member of the Finno-Ugrian family of man, more closely related to the Hungarians and Estonians than to the Norwegians.

Geographically, Finland may be the cold shoulder of Europe, but no inference should be drawn from this about its hospitality. Despite the Finn's fanciful reputation as a stubborn, hard-drinking, knife-wielding, tight-lipped loner, the Finn offers a boundless welcome. However, outside cosmopolitan Helsinki, particularly in the towns and villages, foreigners are often as rare as a Laplander who doesn't ski.

1. Flying To and Around Finland

Finnair flies to Helsinki from more parts of the world (including North America) than any other airline, and it usually proves the best way to go. It is, in fact, the only airline that flies nonstop from North America to Finland, doing it with a style and comfort that have made it one of the best-respected airlines of Europe.

From New York, Finnair flies to Helsinki five times a week in winter and every day in summer. Three times a week in both winter and summer, Helsinki-bound planes touch down briefly in Montréal before continuing nonstop to Finland. In summer, Finnair flights leave Los Angeles once a week, touching down briefly in Seattle before continuing on to Helsinki, although in summer, the airline operates nonstop once-a-week flights from each of the cities. In case you haven't looked at a polar map recently, Finland is one of the closest points in all of Europe to the West Coast of the United States. Because of this, Finnair has geared itself to making Helsinki a major entry point to Central Europe, stressing a "Helsinki Gateway" program that offers attractive incentives, such as a free sauna for ongoing passengers with more than a four-hour wait at the Helsinki airport or a free overnight stay at a deluxe hotel.

Finnair's cheapest ticket from North America is the Weekend Fare which, unfortunately for summer jet-setters, is available only in winter. It permits a Wednesday departure from JFK in New York and requires a return to the Big Apple the following Monday. With this ticket, you can cross-country ski and sip Finnish vodka beside a larchwood fire for $495 round trip. Tickets require a two-week advance payment, although you can change the departure date with no payment of any cancellation fee if you change your plans. This kind of ticket doesn't exist from Finnair's other gateways. However, there is a senior citizen fare with no restrictions (also available only in winter) for $695 round trip from Los Angeles, $595 round trip from Seattle, and $495 round trip from New York.

Most travelers, however, will want to spend more than an extended weekend in Finland, perhaps moving on to explore other parts of Scandinavia. In that case, an APEX ticket (Advance Purchase Excursion) might be appropriate. This kind of ticket requires selection of a departure and return date at least 21 days in advance, as well as full payment, and also requires a wait of between seven days and one year before use of the return half of the ticket. For purposes of fares, each year is divided into low, shoulder, and high season. With this kind of ticket, round-trip passage from New York costs $690 in low season and $985 in high season. From Los Angeles, it costs $966 in low season and $1238 in high. From Seattle, you pay $925 and $1176, according to the season, and from Montréal, you pay $926 in Canadian dollars in low season, $1186 in high. Travelers should know that if they decide to change their departure date less than 21 days prior to leaving North America, Finnair will impose a $75 penalty fee.

Also, if they decide to change their return date once they are in Europe, a $100 rerouting fee will be charged.

For customers wanting better service and meals, Finnair offers executive class seating at higher fares. This kind of service provides larger seats, upgraded meal service, and electronic headsets at no charge.

Flying Around Finland

In a country as vast as Finland, travel by air offers the quickest and most convenient way of lifting yourself, say, from Helsinki to Rovaniemi, capital of Finnish Lapland. Finnair offers the lowest domestic airfares in Europe and has one of the densest routings, covering towns and cities with about 100 inland flights daily.

Finnair also offers an unlimited-mileage "holiday ticket," entitling a passenger to travel on all Finnair (also Kar-Air) domestic routes for a 15-day period. Total cost: around $240 (U.S.). This special ticket is sold in the offices of travel agents and major airlines in North America. The ticket can also be purchased in Finland, provided it is paid for in dollars and you can prove with your passport that you're not a permanent resident of Scandinavia. You can also purchase it in other Scandinavian countries, provided you show proof of non-Scandinavian residency. It can't be transferred, but it is available all year. This bargain gives North Americans a chance to see Lapland and the Finnish lake district and to travel north of the Arctic Circle. Regular flights to such points would cost far more.

A Preview of Tours

Finnair, of course, is more than just an airline. For travelers wanting the best of the North Country's tours (the most unusual of which occur in winter), a reservations agent will offer some of what might be the most memorable expeditions in Europe. Among the many offerings are a ski trekking venture into some of Lapland's wildest country with an experienced guide, or cross-country ski weekends in the country around Kuusamo, where Finland's Olympic teams have trained for many years and where the trails are said to be among the best in Europe. Finnair also offers a reindeer safari, where teams of sleds (one person and one reindeer per sled) make expeditions into Lapp communities far north of the Arctic Circle. Finally, for travelers who want to get to know the sailing patterns of the Baltic, there's a summer sailing safari, where each member sails his or her own boat among a flotilla of other vessels, meeting each evening for communal meals and activities at the islets scattered along the south of Finland.

Finnair can also arrange tours of the Soviet Union, although visa arrangements for entry there are cumbersome and lengthy. The shortest and least expensive tour lasts 15 days and costs around $988.

For information about fares to Finland from North America, as well as the increasingly popular tours, you can call toll-free from throughout the United States to 1/800/223-5700. In New York City, call 889-7070.

If you really want to take another airline flying into Helsinki, you might try SAS, KLM, British Airways, Air France, Austrian Airways, or Swissair. All of them make connections—sometimes lengthy ones—at other cities throughout Europe.

2. The ABCs of Life

To help you settle into this strange land, I've compiled an alphabetized listing of miscellany. All this is done to ease your adjustment into Helsinki, the capital, and Finnish life in general. You'll be advised about what to do in an emergency, such as locating a doctor when you need one.

AIRPORT: Helsinki-Vantaa Airport (tel 8251) lies 12½ miles from the center of Helsinki. It takes about 30 minutes by motor coach. Buses to the airport leave from the Air Terminal at the Hotel Inter-Continental in Helsinki, 21 Töölönkatu, one to five times an hour between 5:50 a.m. and 10:10 p.m. The ticket price is 10 markkaa ($1.60). The coach also departs from the Hotel Presidentti, 4 Eteläinen Rautatiekatu, once an hour Monday to Friday from 6:05 a.m. to 8:20 p.m., Saturday from 8:20 a.m. to 5:20 p.m., and Sunday from 10:55 a.m. to 7:20 p.m., a ticket costing 7.20 markkaa ($1.15). From the Railway Square (platform 26), bus 615 leaves one to three times an hour from 5:25 a.m. to 11:50 p.m., the ticket also costing 7.20 markkaa ($1.15).

For a domestic flight, you must check in 20 minutes before departure, 30 minutes for a European flight, 40 minutes for a flight to the Soviet Union, and 45 minutes for a flight to the United States.

ALCOHOLIC BEVERAGES: Alcohol is retailed only from **Alko,** the state liquor monopoly shops. These are open on weekdays from 10 a.m. to 5 p.m. (on Friday from 10 a.m. to 6 p.m.), Saturday from 9 a.m. to 2 p.m., closed Sunday, May 1 and September 30. Liquor by the drink can also be purchased in hotels, restaurants, and nightclubs. Some establishments, incidentally, are licensed only for beer or beer and wine. Before noon only beer can be served, and that is only if it accompanies food. From then on, alcoholic drinks can be sold with or without food. The exception is schnapps and vodka, both of which must be sold with food. In Helsinki most licensed establishments often stay open until midnight (until 11 p.m. in some of the other cities).

AMERICAN EXPRESS: The agent of American Express in Helsinki is at 16 Eteläranta (tel. 171-900).

BABYSITTERS: Try the university students at **Ylioppilasvälitys** at 649-001. All of these young women invariably speak English. Otherwise, check with your hotel or the local city tourist office.

BANKS: Most banks are open Monday to Friday from 9:15 a.m. to 4:15 p.m. Banks are closed on Saturday. Outside banking hours, you can exchange money at the railway station in Helsinki Monday to Saturday from 8:30 a.m. to 8 p.m., Sunday, 12:30 to 7 p.m. You can also exchange money at the airport from 7 a.m. to 11 p.m. daily.

BICYCLES: Bicycles can be rented at the **Youth Hostel Stadionin Maja,** 3B Pohjoinen Stadionintie, at the Olympic Stadium (tel. 496-071). The fee is 25 markkaa ($4) a day, plus a deposit of 50 markkaa ($8). However, the deposit is not required if you have an international youth hostel card.

BUSES, TRAMS, METRO: City transport in Helsinki is most efficient. For information about it, telephone 4722-252 Monday to Friday from 7 a.m. to 7 p.m., Saturday and Sunday from 9 a.m. to 5 p.m. A single ticket costs 4.60 markkaa (74¢) for adults, 1.70 markkaa (27¢) for children. It's cheaper to purchase **a**

multitrip ticket, allowing ten individual journeys for 41 markkaa ($6.56) for adults, 9 markkaa ($1.44) for children. Transfers are allowed for single and multitrip tickets within one hour of the time stamped on the ticket.

You can also purchase **a tourist ticket** for 24 markkaa ($3.84), allowing unlimited travel on city transport lines within 24 hours. This ticket is sold in the City Transport Office, the City Tourist Office, and the Hotel Booking Centre.

For an orientation sightseeing trip without a guide, catch tram 3T which takes you by 35 major buildings and monuments of the city, with a four-language commentary, including English. The trip is conducted only in summer, lasting 45 minutes. Tram 3T may be boarded in front of the railway station or at the Market Square Monday to Friday from 10 a.m. to 3 p.m. and 6 to 8 p.m.; Saturday and Sunday from 9 a.m. to 8 p.m. It leaves regularly every 4 to 15 minutes from about 6 a.m. to 12:30 a.m., costing 4.60 markkaa (74¢), for adults, 1.70 markkaa (27¢) for children.

Helsinki Card: This card entitles you, among other things, to unlimited travel on the city's public buses, trams, and metro and to a free guided sightseeing tour by bus (in summer daily, in winter on Saturday), as well as to free entry to about 40 museums and other sights in Helsinki. It also includes attractive hotel packages in several hotels in the capital. The Helsinki Card is available for one-, two-, or three-day periods. The price of the card for adults is 45 markkaa ($7.20) for one day, 60 markkaa ($9.60) for two days, and 75 markkaa ($12) for three days. Children pay 20 markkaa ($3.20) for one day, 25 markkaa ($4) for two days, and 30 markkaa ($4.80) for three days. The cards can be bought at 35 sales points in the Helsinki area, including the Helsinki City Tourist Office, the Hotel Booking Center, travel agencies, and hotels. For further information, check with the Finnish Tourist Board, 655 Third Ave., New York, NY 10017 (tel. 1/212/949-2333), or the Helsinki Tourist Association, 7 Lönnrotinkatu (tel. 645-225).

The **City Transport Office** is at Rautatientori metro station (tel. 4723-231).

BUS TRAVEL: Where the rail leaves off, the sturdy bus takes over. Finland has an extensive network of private motorcoach companies. It is a comfortable, convenient means of exploring the country. In some parts of Finland, passengers are carried on mail-carrying buses painted a bright yellow. If you'd like to find out about bus travel, telephone 602-122 in Helsinki, Monday to Friday from 7:30 a.m. to 7 p.m., Saturday from 7:30 a.m. to 5:30 p.m., and Sunday from 8 a.m. to 5:30 p.m. Tickets can be purchased on board or at the bus station Monday to Wednesday from 7:30 a.m. to 6 p.m., Thursday and Friday from 7:30 a.m. to 7 p.m., Saturday from 7:30 a.m. to 5 p.m., and Sunday from 8 a.m. to 5 p.m.

CAR RENTALS: You can tour Finland in a car if you wish. The motorist need only show proof of ownership if bringing a car into the country. If you rent in Finland, a U.S., British, or Canadian driving license is acceptable.

The roads in the south generally are fair (some newer ones are excellent), but in some places I've driven in the north I would have been better advised to stick to reindeer. All the major cities and tourist sights, however, have suitable arteries leading to them.

Many car-rental firms in Helsinki offer weekly rates with unlimited mileage. If you're planning to do much touring, this is the cheapest method, of course.

Among the more popular firms, **Avis Rent-a-Car** is at 36 Fredrikinkatu (tel. 6944-400), and **Hertz** operates out of the Hotel Inter-Continental at 46

Mannerheimintie (tel. 446-910). To make reservations in Finland for a **Budget Rent-a-Car,** telephone 176-644.

CIGARETTES: American and British brands are available in all Finnish cities and towns—and they're expensive, about 10 markkaa ($1.60) for a package of 20. Most Finns buy their tobacco in Helsinki at one of the R-kiosks which are all over the city.

CLIMATE: The joke is that summer in Helsinki lasts from Tuesday to Thursday. In Lapland the Midnight Sun and the mosquitoes offer the visitor an unforgettable experience. The Midnight Sun is visible in the north from June 1 to July 31. Spring arrives in May, and the summers are short (but not as short as in the joke). July is the warmest month, with temperatures averaging around 59 degrees Fahrenheit. The coldest months are January and February, when the Finnish climate has been compared to that of New England.

CLOTHING SIZES: Finland, like all the Scandinavian countries, follows the same clothing sizes as the countries of Europe. See Chapter I, "A Preview of Denmark," for a chart.

CRIME: There's relatively little. Helsinki is the most dangerous city in Finland, and it's one of the safest places in Western Europe.

CURRENCY: The Finnish unit of currency is the mark—**markka** in Finnish—which is divided into 100 **penniä** (abbreviated "p"). As of this writing, one Finnish markka is equal to about $.16 in U.S. coinage. It takes about 6.253 markkaa to make $1 U.S. Coins are issued in denominations of 5, 10, 20, and 50p, and 1 and 5 markkaa. Notes are issued at 5, 10, 50, 100, and 500 markkaa.

Markkaa	U.S.$	Markkaa	U.S.$
0.25	$ .04	60	$ 9.60
0.50	.08	70	11.20
1	.16	80	12.80
5	.80	90	14.40
10	1.60	100	16.00
15	2.40	125	20.00
20	3.20	150	24.00
25	4.00	175	28.00
30	4.80	200	32.00
40	6.40	250	40.00
50	8.00	300	48.00

CUSTOMS: All personal effects, including cameras and a reasonable amount of film, bedding, and other such articles for personal use, are duty free. Gifts to the value of 500 markkaa ($80) may be brought in duty free. You can bring in 400 cigarettes or one pound of other manufactured tobacco. You can also bring in either two liters of beer, one liter of wine, and one liter of spirits or two liters of beer and two liters of wine, if you are over 20. Only the beer and wine can be brought in by persons 18 to 20. There are no restrictions on the amount of Finnish or foreign currency you can bring in, but you can only take it out if you can prove you brought it with you. Import or export of 500-markkaa ($80) notes is forbidden without permission of the Bank of Finland.

DOCUMENTS FOR ENTRY: American, British, and Canadian citizens entering Finland as visitors do not need a visa. A valid passport, however, is required.

DRINK: Milk (sometimes curdled) is the national drink of Finland, and it can be drunk safely by North Americans. Similarly, water throughout Finland is safe to drink. Two famous Finnish liqueurs should be imbibed: **lakka,** made from the saffron-colored wild cloudberry, and **mesimarja,** made from the Arctic brambleberry.

The Finns are heavy drinkers (schnapps is their favorite for an all-around tipple). A federal monopoly regulates the sale of alcohol, as Finland's attempt at prohibition didn't work out. But hard liquor, often imported, is expensive—and the person on a budget had better stick to a domestic beer (*Lahti* is a good local brand).

DRY CLEANING AND LAUNDRY: Lindstrom Ltd., doing one-day dry cleaning on the premises, has a shop in the City Passage opposite the railway station (tel. 657-251) in Helsinki; in the shopping center in Tapiola (tel. 463-633); and at 10 Aleksis Kivenkatu (tel. 149-409) in Tampere. For further addresses and telephone numbers of shops, please refer to the telephone directory.

Reader Edward Karpoff writes: "I couldn't find a laundromat in Helsinki, but the laundry **Exprès Pikapesula,** 2 Laivurininne (tel. 639-524), is the next best thing. Clothes brought in early in the morning can be ready by the 5:30 closing time. A week's shirts, socks, underwear, and p.j.s cost me about 35 markkaa ($5.60), washed, dried, and neatly folded, including touching up of the tumble-dried shirts with an iron. The downtown location is accessible by two tram lines."

ELECTRIC CURRENT: Finland operates on 220 volts A.C. Plugs in general are the two-pin continental size. Always ask at your hotel desk before plugging in any electrical appliance.

EMBASSIES: In case you've lost your passport or whatever, you may need to know the address of your embassy. The **U.S. Embassy** is at 14A Itäinen Puistotie (tel. 171-931), the **British Embassy** at 16–20 Uudenmaankatu (tel. 647-922), and the **Canadian Embassy** at 25B Pohjoisesplanadi (tel. 171-141).

If you're going to the Soviet Union from Finland, you should have arranged for your visa in your home country. There could be considerable delays if you apply in Finland, and you might lose the chance. Sometimes it takes three weeks to get a visa. Take your problems to the embassy of the **Union of Soviet Socialist Republics,** 1B Tehtaankatu (tel. 661-876).

EMERGENCIES: From any telephone you can call for help free. Dial 000 or 181-000 in Helsinki for medical help, police, or for a fire alarm. To call for an ambulance, dial 006.

FARM HOLIDAYS: More than 30 English-speaking Finnish farm families have opened their homes for farm holidays, arranged through **Suomen 4H-litto,** 28 Bulevardi, 7th floor, SF-00120, Helsinki 12 (tel. 646-833). The farms, including one in Lapland, offer varying accommodations but have one thing in common: an opportunity to meet with Finnish people at home and join in their farming activities, or just relax. You can reach your holiday destination most easily in your own car, but if you travel by train or bus, you can arrange to be met.

Full board, which includes your room, meals, bed linen, sauna twice a week, and the use of a rowboat, costs from 113 markkaa ($18.08) to 128 markkaa ($20.48) per person per day for an adult, from 56.50 markkaa ($9.04) to 64 markkaa ($10.24) per person per day for a child. The prices depend on the category in which a house has been placed by 4H-litto, the Finnish 4H federation, based on its facilities and amenities. A minimum of six days is required for a farm holiday.

FINNRAIL PASS: Finland has its own Finnrail Pass for use on the country's elaborate network of railroads. You can travel comfortably and at low cost; the fares are among the lowest in Europe. Intended for foreign tourists only, the pass entitles a person to unlimited travel on all passenger trains of the Finnish State Railways. An eight-day ticket costs 370 markkaa ($59.20), a 15-day for 540 markkaa ($86.40), and a 22-day for 720 markkaa ($115.20). All the above quotations are for second-class travel only. Second-class trains in Finland are equivalent in quality to first-class trains in many other countries. The Finnrail Pass can be purchased both in Finland and the U.S. As trains tend to be crowded, it's recommended that you book a seat in advance; the reservation fee is 8 markkaa ($1.28) on ordinary express trains, 12 markkaa ($1.92) on all express trains marked EP on the timetable.

For more information, get in touch with **Finnish State Railways,** 13 Vilhonkatu (tel. 707-2592) in Helsinki.

GASOLINE: Petrol stations are plentiful enough in Helsinki and for most of the south of Finland. In the north they can be few and far between in certain areas. Petrol prices as of this writing are as follows: 92 octane, 3.59 markkaa (57¢) per liter; 96 octane, 3.66 markkaa (59¢) per liter; and 98 octane, 3.73 markkaa (60¢) per liter. Petrol vending machines at service stations accept 10-markka notes (the old type).

In Helsinki, the following filling station is open 24 hours a day: **Esso,** 27 Pohjoinen Rautatiekatu (tel. 440-611).

GEOGRAPHY: Finland has a common western border with Norway and Sweden, plus an 800-mile eastern border with the Soviet Union. The Gulf of Bothnia and the Gulf of Finland wash up on its shores. An unspoiled virginal country, Finland is characterized chiefly by its lakes (about a tenth of the land area is water) and by its forests (nearly 40% of the land is timber).

GOVERNMENT: Finland, except for Iceland, is the only Scandinavian country without royalty. It is a parliamentary republic, with power vested in a president (six-year term) and a one-chamber parliament.

HITCHHIKING: This is not necessarily commonplace, but not frowned upon either. Most Finns you'll encounter on the roads speak English, and that helps matters a bit. Trouble is, there are often long, lonely, vast stretches of highway with not a car in sight. And when one comes along, it's likely to be full. Because of the weather, you should dress well in case of waits for a ride. If you hitchhike off-season, you might freeze while waiting for someone to come along. Often fellow tourists, especially Swedes, will pick up passengers along the road.

HOLIDAYS: The following holidays are observed in Finland: New Year, Epiphany, Good Friday, Easter Monday, Labor Day (May 1), Ascension Day,

Whitmonday, the Friday before Midsummer Day, Midsummer Day (a Saturday), All Saints Day, Independence Day (December 6), Christmas, and Boxing Day.

HOLIDAY VILLAGES AND COTTAGES: There are more than 200 holiday villages in Finland, many in the luxury class. The villages consist of self-contained bungalows by lakes and offer varied leisure activities, such as fishing, rowing, hiking and swimming. Some are open all year. Some villages have hotels and restaurants for those who don't want to do their own cooking. Prices range from 1200 markkaa ($192) to 2500 markkaa ($400) per week in the best villages, with some luxury bungalows costing up to 4500 markkaa ($720) per week. The cottages consist of two to five beds each.

There are also individually owned holiday cottages ranging from fishing huts on the coast to luxury villas on the inland lakes. These are furnished with all needed equipment except bed linen and towels. Rates can range from 500 markkaa ($80) to 2500 markkaa ($400) per week, depending on location, size, and equipment.

For information and reservations, get in touch with **Lomarengas ry-Holiday Chain,** 3 Museokatu, 00100 Helsinki 10 (tel. 441-346), or a local tourist office.

LANGUAGE: Few foreigners ever master Finnish, and I'm amazed that the Finns learn to speak it themselves. It's as difficult as Chinese. More than 90% of the population speak Finnish, while the remaining citizens, for the most part, speak Swedish. Finland is officially a bilingual country, with street signs, directions, whatever, appearing in both languages in cities and bilingual areas. And unless you're an explorer who ventures very far from the beaten path, you'll find English commonly spoken, too, especially among young people. In all major hotels, restaurants, and nightclubs, English is spoken almost without exception.

MEDICAL: An emergency hospital for foreigners is the **Helsinki University Central Hospital,** Meilahti Hospital (for both medical and surgical care), at 4 Haartmaninkatu (tel. 4711). To summon a physician for emergency calls, telephone 008. For private medical service, the **Aleksi Medical Station** in the City Passage, 21A Aleksanterinkatu, fifth floor (tel. 176-199 for an appointment), is available. It is open only Monday to Friday from 8 a.m. to 6 p.m.

MOTORISTS: Finland observes right-hand traffic and speed limits of 60, 80, 100, or 120 kilometers per hour are strictly enforced. Many streets in Helsinki are one-way. It is illegal to drive a motor vehicle under the influence of alcohol, and this law is enforced with a tight fist. The penalties are severe. The alcoholic content of one's blood may not exceed 0.5%.

NEWSPAPERS: English-language newspapers, including *The International Herald Tribune,* are available at the larger bookstores, at the railway station, and at many kiosks in central Helsinki.

PHARMACIES: Pharmacies here are known as *apteekki.* Service 24 hours in Helsinki is available at the **Yliopiston apteekki,** 96 Mannerheimintie (tel. 415-788), and from 7 a.m. to midnight at 5 Mannerheimintie (tel. 660-294).

POST OFFICE: For information, telephone 1955-117. The main post office in Helsinki is at 11 Mannerheimintie, open Monday to Friday from 9 a.m. to 5 p.m. (closed on Saturday and Sunday). If you don't know your address in Helsinki, have your mail sent *Poste Restante* (general delivery) in care of the main post office in Helsinki. Telephone 1955-123 for information about general delivery. At this Poste Restante, you can pick up mail (upon presentation of your passport) Monday to Saturday from 8 a.m. to 10 p.m. and on Sunday from 9 a.m. to 10 p.m.

You can purchase stamps at the railway station post office Monday to Friday from 7:15 a.m. to 8 p.m. and on Saturday and Sunday from 10 a.m. to 8 p.m. Yellow stamp machines outside post offices function with 1- or 5-markka coins.

An airmail letter sent to North America costs 2.50 markkaa (40¢), providing it doesn't exceed a maximum of 20 grams. A postcard to North America costs 2 markkaa (32¢).

If you're a stamp collector, as many are these days, you'll find a philatelic section on the fourth floor at 3 Paasivuorenkatu (tel. 1954-731), which is open Monday to Friday from 8 a.m. to 3 p.m.

RADIO: In Helsinki a program in English is broadcast on 254, 558, and 963 kHz on the AM dial daily at 10:30 p.m., and on 963 kHz daily at 11:30 p.m.

RAILWAYS: For information, telephone 659-411, Monday to Friday from 7 a.m. to 9 p.m., on Saturday to 6 p.m., and on Sunday from 9 a.m. to 6 p.m. Tickets are sold at the main railway station in Helsinki Monday to Saturday from 4:30 a.m. to 1:30 a.m., Sunday from 5:30 a.m. to 1:30 a.m. See "Finnrail Pass."

RELIGIOUS SERVICES: Lutheranism is the major religion, claiming about 90% of the population. Smaller groups—Catholics, Jews, Greek Orthodox—are also represented, and there is religious freedom for all. **Christian church** services information is available at 22 Kolmas Linja (tel. 70-921).

Roman Catholic services are conducted at St. Henrik's Church, 1 Puistokatu (tel. 637-853). The **Anglican** church, Cathedral Chapel, Senate Square (tel. 538-648), has services in English on Sunday at 10:30 a.m. There's a **synagogue** at 26 Malminkatu (tel. 6941-302 or 6941-297 for information).

REST ROOMS: Most public rest rooms are in terminals (air, bus, and rail). Hotels usually have very clean toilets, as do the better restaurants and clubs. Don't be surprised when you enter public toilets to discover a burly woman who'll give you your "quota" of toilet paper before you enter a stall. Most toilets are designated by appropriate symbols to distinguish between facilities for men or women. Otherwise, know that *naissile* is for women and *miehille* is for men.

SAUNA: Regardless of where you've bathed, you really haven't been cleaned to the core till you've participated in the local ritual—a Finnish sauna.

Whether for giving birth to babies or entertaining Russian ambassadors, the Finns regard the sauna as a national institution. It is estimated that there is one sauna in Finland to about every six citizens.

The most authentic ones are log cabins beside a lake. Families and friends strip and head inside the chamber to take their places on slats. Later, someone throws water on heated rocks that give off hissing sounds like a snake, and the temperature reaches the point reserved for hangmen in Hades. As is the custom, well-meaning friends pick up water-soaked birch bows and switch the backs of fellow saunatics—great for the circulation, Finns claim.

When the heat becomes unbearable—usually after 10 or 15 minutes for neophytes unaccustomed to 140-degree Fahrenheit temperatures—the bathers sprint out of the sauna and outdistance Paavo Nurmi to the icy-cold blue waters of a Finnish lake. In winter, rolling in the snow serves the same purpose.

Public saunas—contrary to popular foreign belief—are not mixed. Attending a mixed sauna would invariably be a private affair, depending upon invitation. To be invited to a sauna by a Finn is the epitome of hospitality. To turn down the offer would be as gauche as burning the Stars and Stripes at an American Legion meeting.

Today in Finland, as in North America, most hotel saunas are heated by electricity. But unlike a Turkish bath, the air in a sauna is dry. Some saunas have women attendants who soap, scrub, scour, and rinse the men. But never are these women bare-chested vampirettes. Most of them look like Brünnhilde's great aunt and seem generations removed from desires of the flesh. But if you're dainty and coy, then go to a do-it-yourself sauna and scrub your own back.

After emerging parboiled from the sauna—at a shade of shocking pink—a good rest is in order.

Most of the student hotels recommended have public saunas, which guests rent individually or with others to share the expense. The least expensive sauna in Helsinki (but not the most authentic) is the one at the **Olympic Swimming Stadium** at Eläintarha (streetcar 3). It costs 6 markkaa (96¢) for adults, 3 markkaa (48¢) for children. On the grounds is a swimming pool.

For a more typical sauna, head for **Marttahotelli**, 24 Uudenmaankatu (tel. 646-211), where everyone is welcomed. The cost is 30 markkaa ($4.80) for two persons, 5 markkaa (80¢) for every additional adult. Take bus 17 from the Central Station. This sauna is open every Wednesday, Thursday, Friday, and Saturday.

SENIOR CITIZEN DISCOUNTS: North Americans more than 65 years of age, who vacation in Finland, can save considerable dollars on transportation costs inside the country, through the courtesy discounts extended to senior citizens. All modes of travel offer these savings. They include:

Buses: "65 Tickets" are sold in bus stations, travel agencies, and on buses to those who have a special "65 Card." This is available to persons aged 65 or over. The price of the card is 5 markkaa (80¢), and it entitles the holder to a reduction of 30%. A photograph and passport are necessary when the card is bought.

Airplanes: Finnair, the country's national airline, allows a 50% discount to passengers 65 years and older on domestic flights, except on Friday from noon till midnight and on Monday from 12:01 a.m. till noon.

SHOPPING HOURS: The hours of stores or snops can vary. Most of them open at 9 a.m., closing at 5 p.m., Monday to Friday. Saturday hours are from 9 a.m. to 2 p.m. Nearly everything shuts down on Sunday. Many shops in the center of Helsinki are open until 8 p.m. on certain nights, particularly Monday and Friday. Shops in the Station Tunnel in Helsinki are generally open Monday to Saturday from 10 a.m. to 10 p.m. and on Sunday from noon to 10 p.m.

Gift and souvenir shops on the fourth floor of the Finnjet terminal in Katajanokka are open on days of arrival and departure of Finnjet.

There are R-kiosks all over Helsinki which are open from Monday to Saturday from 8 a.m. to 9 p.m. (on Sunday from either 9 or 10 a.m. until 9 p.m.). In addition to confectionery and tobacco, these kiosks sell toiletries, cosmetics, and souvenirs.

TAXES: A 6% tax is added to most retail purchases in Finland. However, department stores and several other shops have an export service by which the goods you have bought can be mailed abroad direct. This entitles you to a 5% reduction (on foodstuffs, only 5%) of the sales tax.

TAXIS: There are a number of taxi stations around Helsinki, but taxis can also be hailed in the street or by phone. A taxi is free if the yellow *taksi* dome is lit. Taxis are metered, a basic fare costing 9.40 markkaa ($1.50) in Helsinki. An extra charge of 3 markkaa (48¢) is imposed at night and on weekends from 2 p.m. Saturday until 6 a.m. on Monday. Tipping has become fairly common.

TELEGRAPH AND TELEX: Tele-Service, 11B Mannerheimintie, is open daily from 7 a.m. to 11 p.m. But it offers 24-hour service by phone (tel. 021).

TELEPHONES: For information and number inquiries, call 92020 in Helsinki. If you're thinking about calling home (providing you're not calling collect) and want to know how much it'll cost, dial 92023. Call boxes throughout the city take 1-markka (16¢) and 5-markka (80¢) coins. Automatic intercity calls can be made from these call boxes. The routing numbers and rates are listed in the phone directory. Other long-distance calls can be made at the Tele-Service office, 11B Mannerheimintie. Automatic calls to other countries can also be made from these call boxes, or else from the Tele-Service office. If you call from your hotel, the bill might be doubled or tripled.

TIME: Finland has "summer time" from March 28 (3 a.m.) to September 26 (4 a.m.). In summer, it is three hours ahead of Greenwich Mean Time (GMT), in winter two hours ahead of GMT.

TIPPING: Hotels add a service charge of 15%, and usually no further tipping is necessary. Restaurants add 14% to the check, 15% on Saturday, Sunday, and holidays. It's customary to leave just the small change. Taxi drivers, as mentioned, do not expect a tip. However, it's proper to offer from 2.50 markkaa (40¢) to 3 markkaa (48¢) to cloakroom personnel and doormen. Bellhops usually get 2 markkaa (32¢) per bag, but most often in Finnish hotels you carry your own luggage up. At railway stations, porters get 2 markkaa (32¢) a bag, a fixed charge. But I dare you to find one when you need him. Surprisingly, hairdressers and barbers do not expect to be tipped.

TOURIST INFORMATION: The **Helsinki City Tourist Office,** 19 Pohjoisesplanadi (tel. 174-088 or 1693-757), is open Monday to Friday from 8:30 a.m. to 6 p.m., and on Saturday from 8:30 a.m. to 1 p.m. For recorded information on what's happening in Helsinki, telephone 058.

TRIPS TO RUSSIA: Increasingly, Finland is emerging as a gateway to the Soviet Union.

Since Finland and Russia have the small rail gauge, there are train connections from Turku and Helsinki to Leningrad and Moscow. The 19-hour Helsinki to Moscow trip costs 309.90 markkaa ($49.58) in second class (four berths), and 437.80 markkaa ($70.05) in first class (two berths). The shorter trip from Helsinki to Leningrad (less than 12 hours) costs 149.10 markkaa ($23.86) in second class, 298.30 markkaa ($47.73) in first.

Warning: These jaunts tend to be booked solidly—so reservations are imperative. Travel agents in North America can arrange the tour. Or write the **Finland Travel Bureau Ltd.,** Finland Tours Department, 10A Kaivokatu, Helsinki 10 (tel. 18-261). Prospective visitors to the Soviet Union should obtain a visa in their home country.

From June to August, **Blue White Tours** operates a Leningrad-by-motorcoach tour. The round trip is first class, costing 1400 markkaa ($224) in low season, 1600 markkaa ($256) in high season, and includes not only transportation, but room and meals en route, plus visits to such places as the Hermitage Art Museum and the summer residence of Peter the Great. The trip lasts four days.

WEIGHTS AND MEASURES: Like the rest of Scandinavia, Finland follows the international metric system. Refer to the listing in Chapter I, "A Preview of Denmark."

YOUTH HOSTELS: There are about 150 youth hostels in Finland, many open only from June 10 to August, but about 50 open also in winter. A lot of them offer family rooms, accommodating two to four persons. In general, the hostels do not serve food, but coffee and refreshments are available at most of them, and some have self-service kitchens. There are no age restrictions on hostel use. If a visitor does not have sheets, they can be rented from the hostel. The overnight charges vary between 25 markkaa ($4) and 55 markkaa ($8.80). In all of the establishments, at least some of the beds are available in the lowest price. For more information about staying in a hostel, get in touch with the **Finnish Youth Hostel Association,** 38 B Yrjönkatu, 00100 Helsinki 10 (tel. 6940-377).

Chapter XVIII

DISCOVERING HELSINKI

1. Where to Stay
2. Where to Dine
3. The Major Attractions
4. Other Attractions
5. Shopping in Helsinki
6. Helsinki After Dark

AT THE CROSSROADS of East and West, Helsinki is a uniquely Finnish creation totally distinct from the other capitals of Europe. Her temples are not ancient like those of Greece. Rather they are granite—neoclassical Empire—very formal.

Unlike Vienna, Helsinki is not full of unicorns, gargoyles, palaces, and tombs that testify to architectural splendor and the glory of empire. Finland is a modern nation. Any king who has ruled has been a foreigner. Instead of glorifying monarchy, the Finns are more likely to honor an athlete or a worker in their sculpture. For proof just take a look at the figures standing proudly, even defiantly, in front of Stockmann's Department Store: three nude blacksmiths à la WPA.

ORIENTATION: Helsinki (Helsingfors in Swedish) is a peninsula city, skirted by islands and skerries. The main artery of life is the wide and handsome **Mannerheimintie,** named in honor of the former field marshal. East of Mannerheimintie, opening onto Kaivokatu, is the **Central Station.** Toward the harbor is **Senaatintori,** crowned by the landmark cathedral. This Senate Square, designed by Engel, also includes the government and university buildings.

Continuing east, we approach a bridge crossing over to a tiny island—**Katajanokka**—dominated by the Eastern Orthodox Cathedral. Walking back across the bridge and sticking close to the harbor, we pass the President's Palace and then come to the most colorful square in Helsinki, the **Marketplace** (see it early in the morning). From the pier there, it's possible to catch boats for **Suomenlinna,** fortified islands that guard the entrance to Helsinki.

The great promenade street of Helsinki—**The Esplanade**—begins west of

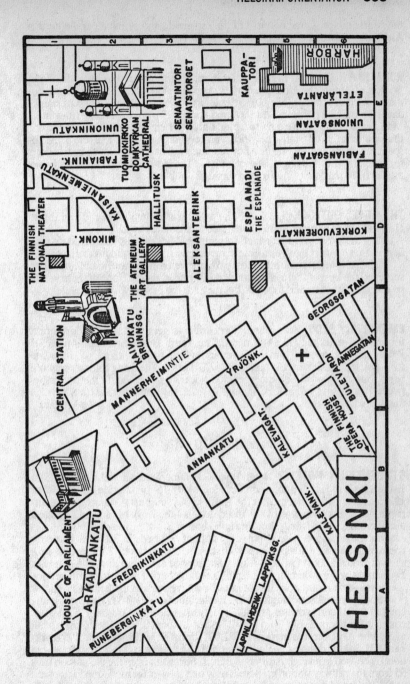

the Marketplace. Directly north of the esplanade and running parallel to it is **Aleksanterinkatu,** the principal shopping street.

ROOM IN A HURRY: At the railroad station, in the heart of the city, is the Hotel Booking Center, the **Hotellikeskus,** 3 Asema-aukio (tel. 171-133), which remains open in summer (May 16 to September 15) from 9 a.m. to 9 p.m. weekdays, 9 a.m. to 7 p.m. on Saturday, and noon to 7 p.m. on Sunday (in winter, Monday to Friday from 9 a.m. to 6 p.m. only), to help late-arriving visitors from the continent. You state the price you're willing to pay, and the English-speaking attendant will ring up a hotel. A map will be provided with instructions for reaching your lodgings. The secretary at the Hotellikeskus charges a booking fee of 10 markkaa ($1.60) for a single or double room.

THE HOTEL OUTLOOK: Let's face the awful truth, then proceed from there. Helsinki hotels in summer often are filled to absolute capacity.

Yet the situation isn't dismal. In summer, Helsinki has many student residences that convert into good hotels, modern and run by student managers.

The private hotels, for the most part, are well run and well maintained. I've surveyed the best of them in the moderately priced range. None of them would be considered a bargain stopover, but they are the best of what is available.

EMERGENCY BEDS: Year round, it's possible to get a bed, mainly dormitory, for only 24 markkaa ($3.84) a night. The **Youth Hostel Stadionin Maja,** 3B Pohjoinen Stadionintie, is in the Olympic Stadium with rooms to accommodate from two to four. Linen is 14 markkaa ($2.24) extra. The living couldn't be more basic, but it's handy in an emergency. Lodgers must evacuate the rooms between 10 a.m. and 4 p.m. for cleaning. To reach the stadium, take tram 3T. Call first: 496-071.

1. Where to Stay

STUDENT-RUN HOTELS: Hotel Dipoli, 1 Jämeräntaival (tel. 460-811), at Espoo, is six miles from the center of Helsinki (a 15-minute ride on bus 102 or 192, leaving from platform 51 at the Helsinki bus station). A suburban student-run hotel, it is a showcase of advanced design—the work of Finland's greatest architect, the late Alvar Aalto. The hotel buildings are surrounded by pine forests on the seashore. The Dipoli offers about 600 beds in 300 neat and cozy rooms at reasonable rates: a single with shower, 200 markkaa ($32); double with shower, 260 markkaa ($41.60)—including service and breakfast. The hotel has two saunas and a swimming pool, plus a tennis court. Four restaurants service the hotel—one is outdoors. There are a beer tavern and a nightclub as well.

Summerhotel Satakuntatalo, 1A Lapinrinne (tel. 6940-311), was originally created for undergraduates attending Helsinki University from the west coast county of Satakunta. But from May 20 to September 10, it accepts tourists of all ages, who pay from 135 markkaa ($21.60) for bathless singles, from 195 markkaa ($31.20) for doubles, including service and breakfast. On a tiny street, the hotel is housed in an eight-story building, a short walk from the bus station (bus 55 from the railway station). There is only one shower for men, one for women —but the hotel has other services to compensate for this, including a handy laundry with a washing machine for the use of guests. On the premises is a licensed restaurant. Lunch here goes for 55 markkaa ($8.80). However, a self-service lunch ranges in price from 25 markkaa ($4) to 35 markkaa ($5.60), a better bargain, of course. Dinner costs 55 markkaa ($8.80). Two saunas are available.

Academica Hotel, 14 Hietaniemenkatu (tel. 440-171), provides super-modern accommodations in a Helsinki student hotel, only a ten-minute walk from the center of the city. A wing was built onto the original structure, putting the Academica in the foreground of the student-run summer hotels (open from June 1 to September 1). The hotel contains 216 rooms—a grand total of 420 beds. In the newer house, all the rooms have a private toilet and bath, as well as a refrigerator. The bedrooms are sleekly designed as well. In the older wing are a few rooms with private bath, and all have hot and cold running water. The furnishings are compact, with built-in pieces, fine woods, and all kinds of gadgets. Both houses are joined by a common entrance and a lobby reception desk, and they share a souvenir shop, dining room—even an authentic sauna and a large swimming pool. A double costs 260 markkaa ($41.60). Singles range from 220 markkaa ($35.20). Continental breakfast and a service charge are included in the prices quoted. In addition, you can order your main meals in the fully licensed restaurant; dinner here comes to 65 markkaa ($10.40).

Now on to the all-year-round hotels.

HOTELS IN THE CENTER: Lähetys-Hospiz, 1 Annankatu (tel. 648-011), occupying five floors of an elevator brick building, is about a three-minute walk from the junction of two major streets, Mannerheimintie and Esplanadi. A single room, bathless, rents for 155 markkaa ($24.80), increasing to 215 markkaa ($34.40) in a bathless twin-bedded room. However, for a single with shower or bath, expect to pay from 200 markkaa ($32) to 230 markkaa ($36.80), 280 markkaa ($44.80) to 285 markkaa ($45.60) in a similar twin-bedded room. The service charge and breakfast are included.

Hotel Finn, 3B Kalevankatu (tel. 64-09-04), is a clean and functional hotel whose clients ride an elevator from the street level to the sixth-floor reception area. The establishment's 28 rooms are scattered over two floors of the centrally located office building which contains it. Staying here are likely to be dockworkers residing temporarily away from their homes in Western and Northern Finland, a scattering of tourists, and a handful of Moscow diplomats in Helsinki on official or unofficial business. There is no bar, no restaurant, and no sauna, since the hotel's only real public room is a large, starkly furnished area with a scattering of unpretentious furniture. The owner, Mr. Mäkinen, is often on the premises, charging around 200 markkaa ($32) for a bathless single, 280 markkaa ($44.80) for a bathless double. A single with shower costs 245 markkaa ($39.20), while a double with bath goes for between 340 markkaa ($54.40) and 395 markkaa ($63.20). Breakfast can be served in your room for an additional 26 markkaa ($4.16).

Ursula, 1 Paasivuorenkatu (tel. 750-311), puts its money into furnishing its bedrooms properly, not into a fancy lobby or an impressive interior. It's one of the finest of the small hotels of Helsinki, and just a bit sedate. The rooms have wall-to-wall desks, bed sofas, and large picture windows. A handful of double rooms with private toilet go for 310 markkaa ($49.60), and the more expensive ones, with private shower, rent for 340 markkaa ($54.40). But the real value is in one of a trio of three-bedded rooms, all with private bath, renting for 430 markkaa ($68.80). Singles range from 185 markkaa ($29.60) to 135 markkaa ($21.60), depending on the plumbing. All these rates include service. The Ursula is across the water from the Botanical Gardens, right near a small park, and off a busy boulevard (take streetcar 7 or 10 from the Central Station).

Kaukokiito Motel, 11 Metsäläntie (tel. 799-055), is a modern, brick accommodation, also housing a bank and a 24-hour-a-day cafeteria. It's recommended mainly to motorists, as there is ample parking outside, as well as a service station nearby. If you're not driving, bus 62 passes by the door, taking you into town. Rooms are comfortably and agreeably furnished, along sleek design lines. The hotel's 76 doubles are furnished with good pieces, as well as phones, radios, showers, and toilets. The cost is 290 markkaa ($46.40) for two, plus an extra 35 markkaa ($5.60) for breakfast. The motel also serves reasonably priced meals until 6:30 p.m., but no alcohol. You can go jogging in the woodland adjoining the motel, and later relax in the sauna.

Marttahotelli, 24 Uudenmaankatu (tel. 646-211), is a cozy, friendly little hotel in the center of Helsinki where English is spoken. Both the passing tourist and visiting business person use it because of its central position and its no-nonsense decor. Everything is pristine, built around a streamlined, Finnish design—certainly not luxurious, but peaceful and comfortable, nonetheless. The Martta offers 45 rooms, a total of nearly 100 beds, although it seems smaller. A single with toilet rents for 170 markkaa ($27.20), going up to 220 markkaa ($35.20) with a complete private bath. A double without bath costs 280 markkaa ($44.80), rising to 330 markkaa ($52.80) with complete facilities. Ask about the triple rooms with shower, costing from 420 markkaa ($67.20). These tariffs aren't as high as they seem at first when you consider that they include breakfast, taxes, and service. The hotel has a lunch restaurant on its roof terrace, and it's also got one of the best saunas in the city (see my recommendations coming up).

Hotel Hospiz, 17 Vuorikatu (tel. 170-481), is a large and well-maintained hotel whose turn-of-the-century core was expanded with a new wing in 1956. Today, the establishment is owned and operated by the YMCA, which accepts both male and female business persons, tourists, and a handful of semi-permanent shipbuilders who return to their northern homes on weekends. The neighborhood is residential and quiet even though its location is only about four pedestrian minutes from the main train station. Of the 170 impressively clean and comfortable bedrooms, only a handful (about 33) are without private baths. The better rooms contain TVs and mini-bars, and all the ones in the newer wing have unusually large windows. There's an inexpensive restaurant on the premises serving full meals for around 35 markkaa ($5.60) for a luncheon buffet, 60 markkaa ($9.60) for a full dinner. Single rooms cost 270 markkaa ($43.20), while doubles go for 390 markkaa ($62.40). Trams 3, 6, and 10 run nearby.

Hotel Metrocity, 7 Kaisaniemenkatu (tel. 171-146). Even though the curved and blackened brick façade of this central hotel sits only a few feet from one of the busiest streets in town, the comfortable bedrooms are fairly quiet because of their height and their double windows. Even so, you might prefer one of the rooms looking over an inner courtyard, directly into the offices of a rival hotel chain. After registering at the ground-floor reception desk, you take an elevator to the sixth or seventh floor, where thickly carpeted hallways will lead you to your room. Extra features include two-station radio, TV, and a private bath in each room. The hotel is only a two-minute walk from the railway station, which may account for its popularity with tour groups from the north of Finland. If you are lucky enough to get a room, singles cost around 325 markkaa ($52), while doubles rent for 430 markkaa ($68.80), with breakfast included. An extra bed can be set up in any room for an additional 95 markkaa ($15.20).

Helsinki Hotel, 12 Hallituskatu (tel. 171-401). Because the owners realized that there was cash value in the nostalgia evoked by this comfortable hotel, they renovated it in 1983 in the same decor and colors that were a part of it when it first opened in 1930. It's in a commercial part of the city center in what looks like a modern building whose lobby has been stripped bare of almost everything except a glistening layer of white marble. The wide and carpeted upstairs hallways lead to plushly decorated rooms, where the colors were shades of gray, maroon, and peach at the time of my last visit. The modern baths contain heated towel racks and tiled walls. There's an art deco restaurant, a ninth-floor sauna, and a sophisticated disco, covered separately in the section of this guide on

"Helsinki After Dark." The hotel maintains two rooms for use of allergic persons. They will rent these only to nonsmokers. In them, practically everything that could make a susceptible individual sneeze has been replaced with an attractive substitute. With breakfast included, single rooms cost around 410 markkaa ($65.60), while doubles go for 530 markkaa ($84.80).

Hotel Vaakuna, 2 Asema-aukio (tel. 171-811). Although you might not realize it while looking at this massive hotel from the railway station across the street, the form of the building is actually an irregularly shaped quadrangle whose sides correspond to the streets of one of the most central locations in Helsinki. The severely modern façade opens into one of the most dramatic lobbies in Finland, which will probably become more and more architecturally noteworthy as time goes by. In a high-ceilinged and dramatically stark entranceway, there's a porphyry statue of what may be a satyr struggling with a dolphin, which is spraying water at the birds and clouds curved into the illuminated dome above it. The hotel shares its premises with one of Helsinki's major department stores.

The bedrooms are on floors five through nine, as are the two saunas and all of the public rooms except for the reception area and its mezzanine bar. The grill, restaurant, disco, and roof terrace are frequented by well-dressed business people, many of whom are staying at the hotel. The 290 rooms rent for between 480 markkaa ($76.80) and 550 markkaa ($88) in a single, for 635 markkaa ($101.60) and up in a double. A continental breakfast is included. Weekend prices go down considerably (Friday, Saturday, and Sunday), to 300 markkaa ($48) in a single, 385 markkaa ($61.60) in a double.

Torni Hotel, 26 Yrjönkatu (tel. 644-611). The tower of this downtown hotel looks like a modern version of a crenellated fortress in Italy. When it was built, architectural purists wanted it torn down, but the hotel's role as a meeting place of diplomats and spies during the turbulent years before World War II almost guaranteed that it would become an important hostelry. A view of both the entrance lobby and the beautifully paneled dining room makes the hotel seem older than it really is, although most of the recently renovated bedrooms are as comfortably contemporary as anything in town.

Each contains a private bath, big windows, and thick carpeting. They cost 475 markka ($76) in a single, 625 markkaa ($100) in a double, with a continental breakfast included. On the premises are four saunas, a semicircular American-style bar with a skylit ceiling, and a dining room, the Balkan, done in a kind of modernized medieval style which is augmented by the large coats of arms crafted into the enormous stained-glass windows. There are an Atelier Bar with art exhibits that change every month and what is said to be the only Irish pub in Helsinki. The Parilla Españolade Torni, the finest Spanish restaurant in the capital, is also in this hotel.

Hotel Rivoli Jardin, 40 Kasarminkatu (tel. 177-880). At press time, this sophisticated hotel offered the newest accommodations in Helsinki. It opened in June of 1984 with a slickly designed format of thick carpets, pink and black Finnish marble, unusual murals composed of mirrors and textiles, and shiny lacquer. Guests have full use of the garden-style bar and breakfast room, whose plants and white tiles are illuminated with a skylight and lots of windows, and of the hotel sauna. The 54 rooms are filled with blond built-in furniture, wall-to-wall carpeting, and the latest in attractively simple yet rich-looking design. The manager, Heidi Lindfors, is connected to the family whose company owns seven restaurants in Helsinki. In this, their first hotel venture, they charge around 520 markkaa ($83.20) for a single and 600 markka ($96) for a double, breakfast included. Each room has a private bath, TV, hairdryer, refrigerator, radio, and telephone. Every window in the hotel contains sashes, which I was told have four separate layers of glass, and therefore may make this the best insulated building in Helsinki.

You reach the hotel by passing beneath a covered passage leading into an open courtyard, at the far end of which is the pink and white modern building which is the Rivoli Jardin.

BRANCHING OUT: Hotel Olympia, 2 Läntinen Brahenkatu (tel. 750-801). This hotel is more famous for the dining and drinking operations contained within than for its bedrooms, although few overnight guests are disappointed with the comfortably modern and colorful accommodations which await them. It's near the main Sports Hall of Helsinki, slightly more than a mile from the central train station. There's a shower or bath in each of the 100 rooms, as well as an eighth-floor sauna and swimming pool, tennis courts, and a bowling alley. Single rooms cost 380 markkaa ($60.80), while doubles go for 500 markkaa ($80), with a continental breakfast included. The restaurants on the premises include the Kazbek (see "Where to Dine" section below) and a cocktail/disco bar, Josafat.

Hotel Haaga, 10 Nuijamiestentie (tel. 579-311), is a small hotel in one of the northern suburbs, a location that is easily reached by bus 42, 46, or 47. You'll find it a pleasant albeit remote place to stay. It has a sauna and an indoor swimming pool on the premises. Comfortably simple rooms all contain private baths, phones, and radios. Dinners in the hotel restaurant, which is licensed to sell drinks, cost from 75 markkaa ($12) up. Single rooms go for 285 markkaa ($45.60) and doubles for 355 markkaa ($56.80).

CAMPING: Your best bet is the **Rastila Camping Site** in Helsinki (tel. 316-551), which is open from mid-May to mid-September (a bit chilly then). The cost is 50 markkaa ($8) per day, including the cost of parking your car, tent, or caravan, as well as persons staying in that tent or caravan. The fee for one person is 30 markkaa ($4.80). In addition, there are 16 simply furnished cottages, suitable for four persons, costing 120 markkaa ($19.20) daily, and four cottages for two persons going for 150 markkaa ($24) per day. The site provides electric contacts for 52 caravans, and on the premises are enough showers, washing, and cooking facilities. Take the Metro from the railway station, and bus 96 from Itäkeskus Metro station.

There's also a camping site in the cityof Espoo. This **Oittaa Camping Site** (tel. 862-585) accepts guests from May 30 until around the end of August, charging a camping fee of 50 markkaa ($8). It also rents out 15 cottages, suitable for two to four guests, at a rate of 140 markkaa ($22.40) per day. There's electric connections for some 20 caravans, and in the service buildings are showers and cooking facilities. If you're driving, go north from Helsinki for about two kilometers to the Bemböle crossing at Turunväylä, taking the Kehätie III motor road.

READER'S HOTEL SELECTION: "The **Private Hotel Borg,** a pension at 16 Cygnaeuksenk, Apartment A-1 (tel. 499-990), has five large double rooms in which the rate for single occupancy is 125 markkaa ($20) per night, with a higher charge for two people. The bath is down the hall. Breakfast, at an extra charge, is optional. Mrs. Borg, who lived in London for 10 years, speaks English well. This hotel is two blocks south of the in-town Finnair bus terminal at the Intercontinental and Hesperia hotels and 150 meters from a street car stop on Mannerheimintie. Parking is available on streets in the neighborhood. I stayed at Mrs. Borg's private hotel for a week during an international conference in Helsinki. After the conference, some of my colleagues gave up their expensive downtown hotel accommodations and transferred to Mrs. Borg's for the duration of their sightseeing" (Edward Karpoff, Kensington, Md.).

2. Where to Dine

Someone once wrote that in Finland the architecture or setting of the restaurant is almost as important as the food served. That is true to some extent.

Restaurants are often found in dramatic locations, perhaps by a lake. Food isn't neglected, however.

Every Finn looks forward to the crayfish season between July 20 and September. Some 225,000 pounds of this delicacy are caught yearly in inland waters. Finns approach the eating of crayfish like an art, sucking out every morsel of flavor. After devouring half a dozen, they down a glass of schnapps. Called *rapu,* the crayfish is usually boiled in salt water and seasoned with dill. Of course, with all this slurping and shelling, you'll need a baby's bib. Unless you're accustomed to schnapps, I suggest you break with local custom and order a beer or glass of white wine instead.

The icy-cold waters of Finland produce some very fine fish, some of which are unknown elsewhere in the world. A cousin to the salmon, the two-inch-long *muikku fritti* is found in inland waters of Finland. The fish is highly praised by gastronomes, and its roe is considered a delicacy.

The most common fish, however, is *silakka* (Baltic herring), which is consumed in vast quantities. Rarely larger than sardines, the herring is not only pickled, but fried and grilled as well. Sometimes it's baked between layers of potato, the sauce made with milk, cheese, and egg. The fish is usually spiced with dill. In fact, dill seems the most popular herb in the country, enjoying many uses.

Finland has its own version of the Swedish smörgåsbord. It's called *voileipäpöytä,* which means "bread and butter table." That definition is too literal. Expect not only bread and butter, but an array of dishes, including many varieties of fish, such as pickled salt herring, fresh salted salmon, along with several cold meat dishes, including smoked reindeer.

Along with their elk, bear, or reindeer tongue, Finns like the sharp taste of *puolukka,* a lingonberry. Hopefully, you'll also have a chance to enjoy the Arctic cloudberry as well.

With any array of dishes, you can expect the two most popular salads of Finland: beet and cucumber.

Bread is invariably served as well, including brown, white, black, and rye versions. The most typical is called *ruislëipa,* a dark, sour rye.

Those open-face sandwiches, so familiar in all Scandinavian countries, are called *voileivat* here.

Fresh vegetables are plentiful in the summer, appearing less frequently during the long winter months. Boiled new potatoes are the most common vegetable, and are served with sprays of fresh dill. Only in the most elegant places will you be served a convoluted morel known as "the black truffle of the north." It's the prize of all the mushrooms which grow in the vast forests of Finland.

Some Finnish hors d'oeuvres are especially good, especially *vorschmack,* a favorite of Marshal Mannerheim. Herring is ground finely, then mixed with garlic, onions, and lamb, which is then cooked in butter over a low flame for a long time, often several hours.

This dish may have been introduced by Russian officers from St. Petersburg in the mid-19th century. The Russians have introduced a lot of dishes to Finland, and beef Stroganoff invariably appears on many menus, especially in Helsinki. Borscht, a beet soup with sour cream, is another ubiquitous item.

One of the best known regional specialties is from the province of Savo. *Kalakukko* is a mixture of a whitefish (known only in Finland) and pork baked in rye dough. I'm not especially fond of it, and I doubt if you will be either, unless you were born in Finland. Then it will bring a nostalgic joy to your heart.

Another typical dish—this one from Karelia—is *karjalanpaisti,* a hotpot made with a combination of different meats. Another entry from Karelia is *karjalan piirakka,* oval-shaped rye pasties made with either rice or potatoes.

Boiled or broiled pike-perch and smoked whitefish are some of my favorite dishes, and perhaps you'll like them, too.

The Finns are hearty eaters, so portions are usually generous.

Food is expensive in Helsinki, with many fat-cat tabs resembling the war indemnity slapped on Finland by Russia. But don't retreat.

Because the cost of living is so high, consumers have banded together, as in Sweden, to form cooperative movements. These co-ops virtually dominate the distribution of food—and they've gone into the restaurant business, too, specializing in reasonably priced meals.

Frequenting the chain restaurants, usually self-service cafeterias, is still another means the budgeteer has of protecting his or her wallet.

I recommend that these co-ops or chain self-service cafeterias be patronized almost exclusively, although there are many other privately owned establishments that are moderate in cost. I'll conclude with a varied assortment of dining spots for those who can afford to spend more.

THE CHAINS—THE BEST BARGAINS: Colombia, 3 Keskuskatu (tel. 177-710), is a favored member of this popular chain during the day. Opposite Stockmann's Department Store, it sits in an enclosed courtyard on the second floor next to the most centrally located of the Marimekko shops. It prepares and serves good and wholesome meals from 8 a.m. till 6 p.m. weekdays. A quite filling meal here is a large order of wienerschnitzel, served with boiled potatoes, for 50 markkaa ($8). You might also have breakfast, an order of bacon and eggs costing 21 markkaa ($3.36). The salads here are fresh and crisp.

Café de Colombia, 12 Siltasaarenkatu (tel. 7532-800), is an all-modern self-service cafeteria, opening onto a large plaza in a completely different part of the city (reached by streetcar 3B or 10 from the Central Station). Behind picture windows, diners make their selections from a limited choice of dishes. A big bowl of minestrone, with lots of vegetables, is practically a lunch in itself. Or you may want to try an order of the stuffed cabbage, served in sauce with boiled potatoes and spaghetti. Meals cost from 75 markkaa ($12). The cafeteria is open weekdays from 7 a.m. till 10 p.m. (on Sunday from 2 to 10 p.m.).

Marian Restaurants has four establishments—each detailed below—in different parts of Helsinki. All are quality restaurants where careful attention is paid to comfort and good food. Reasonable prices, combined with a peaceful, smoke-free atmosphere, add to the enjoyment. With your entree you'll receive a salad, vegetables, and coffee at no extra charge. And one of the nicest features of the chain is that tipping is not permitted.

The **Marian Helmi** (Pearl), 17 Snellmanninkatu (tel. 179-651), just a short walk from the cathedral, is a cozy place with good food. The Pearl is a popular midday restaurant, so it's wise to avoid the 11 a.m. to 3:30 p.m. lunch hour. Here you may choose dishes which change daily. If you want something special, try the Chinese roast beef or the chicken à la maison. Meals cost from 75 markkaa ($12). The Marian Helmi is open from Monday to Friday from 8 a.m. to 5:30, Saturday from 10:30 a.m. to 4:30 p.m., and Sunday from noon to 5 p.m.

The **Marian Grilli** (Grill), at 26 Kapteeninkatu (tel. 636-373), is another popular lunchtime restaurant, this one away from the city center in the southern part of Helsinki. The waiters here are attentive, and the headwaiter speaks English and will even provide an English menu if needed. A good choice here is the escalope of veal. The Marian Grilli also serves excellent ice cream. For a complete lunch, expect to spend from 65 markkaa ($10.40).

The **Marian Kammari** (Chamber), at 19 Munkkiniemenpuistotie (tel. 481-437), is well worth a visit just for its tasty desserts. Specialties are the "Green Meadows" (Vihreät Niityt) dessert and the ohukaisia (small pancakes). Lunch or dinner costs about 65 markkaa ($10.40).

The **Marian Kulma** (Corner), at 104 Mannerheimintie (tel. 418-528), is at a busy location, but inside the restaurant you'll find a peaceful atmosphere in which to enjoy an array of spicy foods. Entrees include a fine chateaubriand, or try the chicken à la maison. Home-brewed ale or mild beer are the perfect accompaniments. Lunch or dinner costs about 70 markkaa ($11.20).

OTHER RESTAURANTS: Happy Days, 2 Pohjoisesplanadi (tel. 624-023), looks something like a summertime garden pavilion, especially since its façade fronts onto a long, flower-filled downtown park. The interior contains four different eating and drinking establishments, which vary in price, in food specialties, and in the clientele they attract. The least expensive division is a self-service pizza restaurant near the plant-filled front entrance, where you can get a meal for 40 markkaa ($6.40). You'll dine better, however, at the adjoining Café Royale, where a full array of salads, meat, and fish dishes is offered in an attractive setting not unlike someone's Victorian garden. Before you select from the menu, be sure to glance at the salad table for anything that may particularly catch your eye. Otherwise, you can have shrimp casserole, Baltic herring, or any of the eight kinds of salad not displayed on the buffet table. Salads and casseroles cost around 32 markkaa ($5.12), and no one will mind if that's all you order.

Also on the premises is the Sitting Bull steak house, a sort of mixture of an American ranch and an English pub. Juicy steaks are available, as well as full meals costing around 145 markkaa ($23.20). Finally, there's a drinking pub called the Trattoria, which might wisely be avoided late at night, especially on weekends. By many accounts (including those of the harried roulette attendants), this is the only one of the four "Happy Days" which can become more than acceptably rowdy. Keep in mind that since all the establishments are owned by the same company, it's possible sometimes to get the specialties of one area served in another. In summer, the operations expand onto several outdoor terraces.

Fazer Café, 3 Kluuvijatu (tel. 666-597), has a conservatively decorated dining room on the left side as you enter, which may be Helsinki's closest rival to New York's Schrafft's. Lunches here cost from 38 markkaa ($6.08) and can include spaghetti carbonara, vol-au-vent, steak, tournedos Rossini, grilled veal schnitzel, and salmon soup. The spacious café on the right, however, is the really popular section of this place. It contains a bistro-style, summery decor of ice-cream wagons, red-and-white tablecloths, lots of framed artworks, a deli case loaded with salads and cakes, and dozens upon dozens of pastries and chocolates. You can also select from the racks of deli and konditorei shelves in another part of the store. The establishment is open from 9 a.m. to 10 p.m. The history of Fazers began in 1891, when Karl Fazer founded a pastry and chocolate shop which quickly became a popular tea house. Today, many incarnations later, the pastries are still delicious, although the place is considerably more modern.

Chez Marius, 1 Mikonkatu (tel. 669-697), is named for its founder. It was started more than 25 years ago by a husband-and-wife team, a Frenchman named Marius, who has since returned to his homeland, and his Finnish wife, Henie Raichi. The absence of Marius has neither changed the restaurant's name nor the loyalty of the many devoted customers, some of whom have come here for lunch nearly every day for years. The French ambience makes this one of the most charming bistros in Helsinki. The walls are covered with hand-painted murals of tongue-in-cheek scenes of life in Paris, as well as a picture of a beaming Henie greeting former French President Giscard d'Estaing during one of his trips to Finland.

The floor space is usually crowded,with many neighborhood office workers, including the crews from a nearby television station, jostling for space at the tables, covered in red-checked cloths, or at the bar. Open from 11 a.m. to 7 p.m. weekdays (it closes Saturday and Sunday), the restaurant offers a daily special, which, with a drink, is all many clients seem to need at lunchtime. When I was last there, the special was sailors' roast of beef with vegetables. The à la carte items looked equally tempting, including onion soup, medallions of veal house-style, steak au poivre, and veal Oscar. Full meals range from around 190 markkaa ($28.80) à la carte, although a simple plat du jour usually costs from 40 markkaa ($6.40).

Kasvisravintola, 3 Korkeavuorenkatu (tel. 179-212), is a vegetarian restaurant whose simple interior contains naturally finished wood planking, hand-made weavings, and lots of original chalk drawings. A uniformed and attractive staff works at a glassed-in cafeteria counter which features salads, soups, wholewheat grains, and many of the standard vegetarian specialties. Set-price meals cost between 24 markkaa ($3.84) and 33 markkaa ($5.28), depending on how many courses you take.

Restaurant El Greco, 22 Eteläesplanadi (tel. 607-565). The array of Greek food served here is extensive and seems to be appreciated by many lunchtime regulars. The decor is almost like something you'd find in the Aegean, with a blue-and-white color scheme as vivid as that of the Greek flag, plus remnants of antique busts in the window. The restaurant contains additional tables on an upper floor, where the view is of the park just outside. Menu specialties are stuffed grape leaves, moussaka, veal schnitzel Thessalia, feta cheese soup, Greek salads, and entrecôte. The restaurant serves three fixed-price menus for from 69 markkaa ($10.88) to 95 markkaa ($15.20), depending on what you order. The establishment is open Monday through Friday from 11:30 a.m. to half past midnight, Saturday from noon to half past midnight, and Sunday from 1 to 8 p.m.

Vanhan Kellari, 3 Mannerheimintie (tel. 654-646), across from Stockmann's Department Store, serves a dual function: it makes a choice spot for lunch, offering both self-service and waitress service; and in the evening it becomes an atmospheric beer cellar. It's a popular place with Helsinki residents, who gravitate to good food in a warm and friendly atmosphere. The attractive dining rooms are divided by walls of natural stone with thick arches (some tables on the lower levels are lit by spots). You dine while seated in soft leather armchairs. From 11 a.m. till 3 p.m. you can order lunch dishes: meat, fish, or chicken, and coffee to finish. Meals cost from 100 markkaa ($16). On the à la carte menu are such selections as Russian borscht; marinated Baltic herring; and rump roast à la maison. The self-service cafeteria offers more moderate prices: around 60 markkaa ($9.60) and up for a light meal.

Bellevue, 3 Rahapajankatu (tel. 17-95-60), has been a favorite of mine ever since I came in one day for lunch long ago, escaping the Baltic cold by ordering the borscht. Sill (herring) is served Russian style here, and it's always a good beginning. Some Helsinki diners tend to overlook the Bellevue these days, particularly in the wake of the current sprouting of several other Russian restaurants in the capital, but it's been long enduring because of its good cuisine and moderate prices, with meals beginning at 110 markkaa ($17.60) and going up. The chicken Kiev is one of the most recommendable of the main dishes. You can dine in a long corridor-like main dining room or else select one of the cozier and tinier chambers off to the side. Hours are from 11 a.m. to 1 a.m.

Kellarikrouvi, 6 Pohjoinen Makasiinikatu (tel. 17-90-21), in the center of town, is a cellar restaurant with a long series of vaults. Drawing a devoted following, it is usually crowded with a lively clientele who like to eat and drink with gusto. Each day different specialties are offered, including, for example, lamb chops with garlic potatoes, or chicken in a pot with rice. Sandwiches are also offered, including one I recently sampled made with the roe of whitefish. Count on spending from 100 markkaa ($16) and up for a meal here. The cellar is open daily from 9 a.m. to midnight.

Ravintola Solna Restaurant, 26 Solnantie (tel. 48-31-61), has steadily improved since I first found it some 20 years ago. It lies only a five-minute walk from the popular Kalastajatorppa Hotel, and many guests from that establishment frequent the place. A staff which includes the helpful English-speaking

Laura Kivikoski has made an effort to offer better and better Finnish dishes, and has succeeded. Lunches range from 50 markkaa ($8) to 75 markkaa ($12), and à la carte meals are priced from 45 markkaa ($7.20) to 100 markkaa ($16). The setting is immaculate, and the restaurant has a certain charm. You can reach it by taking tram 4 heading northbound, getting off at the next to the last stop. Better yet, take the tram to the North Terminus. After leaving the station, get off at the first stop. From there, head southeast for about a block. You'll see the recently enlarged restaurant around the corner on the right.

Perho, 7 Mechelininkatu (tel. 49-34-81), is the showcase restaurant of Finland's training school for future restaurateurs. Have no fear: It's far from an amateur chef contest. All the cooking is professionally supervised and served efficiently and politely in attractive modern surroundings. The price for a full dinner is from 100 markkaa ($16), and it's most often well worth the price. The food is not only prepared with enthusiasm but served with a certain flair. A recent meal began with a succulent oyster and crabmeat cocktail, which was followed with tender veal cutlets with sautéed mushrooms and fluffy rice, then dessert. Hours are from 11 a.m. to midnight weekdays and from noon to 11 p.m. Saturday and Sunday.

Restaurant Walhalla, Suomenlinna (tel. 668-552). You have to arrive here by boat, which many visitors claim is half the fun. This collection of brick-and-granite vaults is right in the center of the Viapori fortress. Several eating places are on the premises, including a self-service restaurant, a panoramic terrace with waiter service, and a café. Meals in the cafeteria range from 60 markkaa ($9.60) up, while a lunch in the restaurant usually begins at 100 markkaa ($16). Partially because of the difficulty of heating the 18th-century brick casemates, the restaurant is open only from June 1 till the end of August, Monday through Saturday from 11:30 a.m. to 12:30 p.m., Sunday from 11:30 a.m. to 6 p.m.

Pam Pam, 15 Hallituskatu (tel. 65-39-36), is one of the more attractive and trendy of the newer restaurants of Helsinki. It has a romantic, sophisticated ambience in spite of its modern location, across from the Helsinki Hotel, recommended previously. You take an escalator to the second floor. It's next door to an Alko wine and liquor retail outlet. In summer, tables are placed in the rather small area outside. Inside, the decorators have given the place a continental bistro charm, and the candlelight on the tables helps. Sometimes diners come in here as early as 3:30 in the afternoon to order dinner. You can actually dine throughout the day, as hours are from 10:30 a.m. to 1 p.m. Monday through Saturday. The main-dish specials change daily. At lunch the buffet selection begins at 35 markkaa ($5.60), but count on spending from 100 markkaa ($16) and up for a meal here. Italian espresso is featured, along with several coffee drinks made from liqueur. One is a café banana with rum from Martinique.

Mestarikrouvi, 7 Töölöntorinkatu (tel. 496-386). Although at first glance you'd think this was nothing more than a cozy neighborhood restaurant, the service and the Finnish specialties give it an added dimension. Sometimes the place serves as a pleasant oasis for clients of the nearby Intercontinental Hoetl, although they are sure to be outnumbered by the loyal residents of the area, who appreciate the paneled bar and the numerous framed pictures, the homey checked curtains, and the friendly service. Finnish cuisine, such as elk filet with juniper berries and a selection of fish dishes, are the featured items, although usually you'll find a staff member who will translate from the menu, so you can make your own selection. Full meals range from 140 markkaa ($22.40), with service added. There's an upper level as well to absorb the overflow from downstairs.

Kosmos Restaurant, 3 Kalevankatu (tel. 607-717), is on a cobblestone street behind the severe stone façade of the building whose upper floors contain the Hotel Finn. The restaurant is known throughout Finland as a gathering place for artists, writers, and television personalities. The menu specialties, all served on tablecloths embroidered with the name of the restaurant, include chicken Cassandra, served with sweet peppers, peaches, onion, and soy sauce. You can also order sweetbreads with curry, boiled tongue in roquefort sauce, caviar, grilled rainbow trout, fried Baltic herring, and roquefort soup for two. Light meals, such as club sandwiches and borscht, are also available. Full meals range upward from 110 markkaa ($17.60), although a 38-markka ($6.08) lunch is served daily from 11 a.m. to 3 p.m. A smooth dessert might be pears drenched with a chocolate cream sauce.

Restaurant Kazbek, 2 Läntinen Brahenkatu (tel. 763-848), is considered one of Helsinki's better Russian restaurants. It's on the ground floor of the Hotel Olympia, behind imposing, tall, stained-glass windows whose designs, like the cuisine, carry modernized Georgian themes. As you sit on the peasant-style carved chairs with the rounded tops, you'll enjoy specialties which include several varieties of skewered meat called shashlik (your choices are chicken, lamb, or beef), borscht, a collection of fiery Georgian appetizers, and a juicily tender rib roast of lamb. Full meals here cost from 180 markkaa ($28.80), to which you must add the service charge.

Richard's Pub, 4 Rikhardinkatu (tel. 179-281), is an old-fashioned establishment containing both a high-ceilinged restaurant with red-velvet wall coverings and one of the most popular pubs in town. The entrance is at the corner of an ocher 19th-century building with Italianate window frames. Someone will undoubtedly be enjoying a beer hours before lunch here, so if you're a drinker, you'll never want for company. The spacious dining room serves specialties such as entrecôte Richard, Caucasian shashlik, fish and chips, Russian herring, and salmon sandwiches. Full meals will cost from 180 markkaa ($28.80), although a simple meal will go for less. A liter of beer in the pub costs 12 markkaa ($1.92). This is said to be the oldest pub in town. It's open weekdays from 9 a.m. to 11:45 p.m. and weekends from 10 a.m. to 11:45 p.m.

A HAMBURGER BREAK: Regardless of how good Finnish cuisine is, there comes a time when an American visitor will want a hamburger. The craving for that type of food is satisfied by **Carrols.** The most central location is near the railway station (tel. 611-632), in the City Passage, opposite the famed Stockmann Department Store. If you're staying close to the Olympic Stadium, you'll find another Carrols at 19 Mannerheimintie (tel. 490-469). Instead of the Big Mac, you get the Big Carrolina at a cost of 18 markkaa ($2.88). Other fast-food is also featured.

CAFÉS AND TEA ROOMS: Café Paulig, 19 Aleksanterinkatu (tel. 629-401). Many customers coming into this shop will want to buy pastries to take home and enjoy later, but if you have the time, you may want to relax with a cup of tea or coffee at one of the pleasant tables. A cup of coffee with a light snack costs around 35 markkaa ($5.60).

Market Square coffee house. In some ways, this place is almost a temporary building, set up during good weather on the market square. Open-air drinks cost from 12 markkaa ($1.92) up. What better place from which to watch the city walk by? It's open daily except Sunday from 6 a.m. to 1 p.m.

Agora Tea Room, 30 Unioninkatu (tel. 607-092). The big bay window of this pleasant, high-ceilinged gathering place is the proper illumination for the frequently changing art exhibits which cover the gray walls. There are more than 30 kinds of tea offered here, as well as pastries from the on-the-premises bakery. Tea with a snack costs from 35 markkaa ($5.60) up. It's open from 9 a.m. to 7 p.m. daily except Sunday. Saturday closing is at 6 p.m.

Bulevardin Kahvisalonki, 1 Bulevardi (tel. 604-685), is a simple and well-directed café in the center of town. Its interior contains many rather small tables, which cluster around a self-service buffet in the center of the room. This contains a coffee stand and fresh pastries and sandwiches. These sell for from 13 markkaa ($2.08) to 29 markkaa ($4.64). No alcohol is served. Coffee costs around 4 markkaa (64¢).

READER'S RESTAURANT SELECTION: "For the vegetarians, I discovered a real treat in the second-floor restaurant of the **Hotel Olympia**, 2 Läntinen Brehenkatu (tel. 750-801)—a *seisovapoyta* (standing table) of more than two dozen tasty items of vegetarian fare (meat eaters will love this, as well). It is a truly outstanding salad bar that you will have to go a long way to beat. Some of the fare: Brussels sprouts, cheeses, three different styles of turnips, alfalfa and fenugreek sprouts, different kinds of rye and wheat bread, and dessert of granola and fruits. The pot of coffee is included in the price of 45 markkaa ($7.20). You will waddle back to your hotel. Beware: They have a 7 p.m. closing" (Matti Anttila, Duncan, B.C., Canada).

3. The Major Attractions

MANNERHEIM MUSEUM: At 14 Kallionlinnantie (tel. 635-443), you can visit the home of Baron Gustaf Mannerheim, Finland's former field marshal and president—a sort of George Washington to his countrymen. Now a museum, his former residence houses his collection of European furniture, Asian art and rugs, and personal items (uniforms, swords, decorations, gifts from admirers) that he acquired during his long career as a military man and statesman. The house remains the same as it was when he died in 1951. It is open from 11 a.m. to 3 p.m. on Friday and Saturday (Sunday until 4 p.m.), charging an admission of 10 markkaa ($1.60).

THE HOME OF SIBELIUS: Ainola, in Järvenpää (tel. 287-322). Few countries seem as proud of one of their native composers as the Finns are of Jean Sibelius. In 1904, while he was skiing with his brother-in-law, Sibelius discovered a forested hill, which inspired him to commission construction of what would eventually become his family home. When it was fully completed in 1911, he named it after his wife, Aino, and maintained a residence there with his children for many years. Today, he and his wife are buried on the property which has become a shrine to music lovers. Some claim that they can hear the beginning of his violin concerto as they approach the house on a still day.

The house was designed in a steep-roofed, comfortably proportioned format by Lars Sonck, who also designed the summer residence of the president of Finland. The wooden interior of Ainola is lined with books and surprisingly modern-looking furniture. It is open from May till September from 10 a.m. to 6 p.m. On Wednesday, the hours are from noon till 8 p.m. It's closed Monday. Admission costs 10 markkaa ($1.60). Järvenpää is not quite 24 miles from Helsinki. To get there, take a bus from platform 1 of the Helsinki bus station, following the Helsinki–Hyryla–Järvenpää route and getting out where the road forks at a sign saying "Ainola," about a four-minute walk from the home. Trains also go from Helsinki to Järvenpää station.

SEURASAARI OPEN-AIR MUSEUM: In a national park on the island of Seurassaari (tel. 488-712) is clustered a miniature preview of Old Finland—about 100 homesteads (authentically furnished), a 17th-century church, and a gentleman's manor dating from the 18th century and containing period furnishings. In addition, visitors can see one of the "aboriginal" saunas, which resemble a smokehouse. In summer, a restaurant operates and on most evenings from June to August (usually on Monday, Tuesday, Thursday, and Sunday nights), there's folk dancing to the tunes of a fiddler: 15 markkaa ($2.40) admission. From

Erottaja, take bus 24 to the island, about a 15-minute ride, a distance of nearly three miles. The museum is open daily from May to September. Admission is 3 markkaa (48¢) for adults, 1.50 markkaa (24¢) for children.

SUOMENLINNA FORTRESS: Known as the Gibraltar of the North, this 18th-century fortress (tel. 66-81-54) lies in the archipelago, guarding the approach to Helsinki. With its walks and gardens, cafés, restaurants, and old frame buildings, the island makes for one of the most interesting outings from Helsinki. There is frequent ferry service from the Marketplace until September 15, a one-way ticket costing 7 markaa ($1.12) for adults, 4 markkaa (64¢) for children. There is a guided tour daily at 12:30 p.m. which costs 14 markkaa ($2.24). The museums on Suomenlinna are open daily from 11 a.m. until 5 p.m. Entrance fee is 3 markkaa (48¢) for adults, 1.50 markkaa (24¢) for children.

TAPIOLA GARDEN CITY: Perhaps the most model of the model communities of Scandinavia is Tapiola, a self-contained city-within-a-city six miles west of Helsinki in the capital's neighbor, Espoo. Buses leave about every ten minutes from the bus station. You may catch any bus that pulls into platform 52 or 53 at the station. All are marked Tapiola. This garden city is filled with parks, splashing fountains, handsomely designed homes and apartments, shopping centers, playgrounds, schools, and churches—an idealistic look at the world of tomorrow. In the center of Tapiola is a large office building with a self-service cafeteria on top (a good choice for lunch).

GALLEN-KALLELA MUSEUM: This museum at Tarvaspää, 27 Gallen-Kallelantie, in Espoo (tel. 513-388), is dedicated to the great Finnish artist, Akseli Gallen-Kallela (1865–1931), who built the studio between 1911 and 1913, according to his own plans. It contains a large collection of his paintings, graphics, posters, and industrial design products. A wooden villa from the 1850s, beside the museum, is occupied by a café. The museum is open in summer, Tuesday through Thursday from 10 a.m. to 8 p.m. and Friday through Sunday from 10 a.m. to 5 p.m. In winter, hours are 10 a.m. to 4 p.m. Tuesday through saturday, 10 a.m. to 5 p.m. on Sunday. Closed Monday all year. The entrance fee is 8 markkaa ($1.28) for adults and 6 markkaa (96¢) for students and children. To reach the museum, take tram 4 to Munkkiniemi. From Munkkiniemi, you can take bus 33 to Tarvo or walk about 1¼ miles along the seaside. Bus 33 runs on weekdays from 9:20 a.m. to 11 a.m. and 1 to 3 p.m.

4. Other Attractions

THE PARLIAMENT: On Mannerheimintie Boulevard this building of red Finnish granite, built in 1931, shelters all the political parties. Although austere on the outside, it warms up considerably inside, especially in the gallery of nudes. The Parliament can only be visited by appointment.

THE CATHEDRAL: Dominating the city's skyline on Senate Square is this green-domed 19th-century cathedral, designed by Carl Ludvig Engel. It is open daily (free) from 9 a.m. to 7 p.m.

OLYMPIC STADIUM: Way back in 1952 Helsinki was host to the Olympic Games. At its impressive sports stadium from that time is a tower; an elevator whisks up passengers for an exciting view of the city as well as the archipelago. It costs 4 markkaa (64¢) for adults and 2 markkaa (32¢) for children to take the ride. The tower is open daily from 9 a.m. to 6 p.m. Take streetcar 3, 4, or 10. The tower is closed to tours during competitions.

THE SIBELIUS MONUMENT: A magnificent monument created by sculptor Eila Hiltunen in honor of the celebrated Finnish composer Jean Sibelius (1865–1957) stands in the Sibelius Park on Mechelininkatu. The monument is welded into an impressive whole out of hundreds of steel pipes. Take bus 18, which leaves from the railroad station every 10 minutes.

TEMPPELIAUKIO CHURCH: This church (tel. 494-698), built into solid rock and consecrated in 1969, has inner walls with unfinished surface. The wall surrounding it is of rock quarried on the site. The inner and outer surfaces of the dome are of copper. It is open Monday to Saturday from 10 a.m. to 9 p.m., Sunday from noon to 3 p.m. and 4 to 9 p.m. It is about two blocks west of the National Museum. Only the roof is visible from outside.

HELSINKI CITY MUSEUM: At Villa Hakasalmi, 2 Karamzininkatu (tel. 1693-444), the museum presents the history of Helsinki from its founding up to modern times. A small-scale model of the town in the 1870s is on display, together with a variety of artifacts illustrating the handicrafts and trade guilds at that time. There is also an exhibit of art with a Helsinki theme, home decorations from the 18th and 19th centuries, glass, jewelry, porcelain, costumes, and toys. The museum is open Sunday to Friday from noon to 4 p.m., to 8 p.m. on Thursday. It's closed Saturday. Admission is 4 markkaa (64¢) for adults, 1.50 markkaa (24¢) for children.

NATIONAL MUSEUM OF FINLAND: The museum, 34 Mannerheimintie (tel. 4025-229), was designed in the style called National Romantic. Opened in 1916, it contains three major sections—prehistoric, historic, and ethnographic. The country's prehistory in the light of archeological finds may be seen, revealing that after the Ice Age and at the dawn of the Stone Age humans made their homes in Finland. Of particular interest are the Finno-Ugric collections tracing the heritage of present-day Finland to the coming of tribes from somewhere in the Ural mountains some 2000 years ago. Church art of the Medieval and Lutheran periods, folk culture artifacts, folk costumes and textiles, furniture, and an important coin collection are exhibited. The museum is open in summer daily from 11 a.m. to 4 p.m., reopening from 6 to 9 p.m. on Thursday. Otherwise, it closes daily at 3 p.m. Admission is 4 markkaa (64¢) for adults, 1.50 markkaa (24¢) for children.

HVITTRÄSK: The studio home of architects Eliel Saarinen, Armas Lindgren, and Herman Gesellius, Luoma, Kirkkonummi (tel. 2975-779), was built of logs and natural stone and stands in a forest. It ranks among the most remarkable architectural creations of its time. Its artistic unity with its surroundings is a distinguished achievement. Today, it is also a center for exhibits of Finnish art and handicraft. Hvitträsk is open to visitors from 11 a.m. to 7 p.m., 11 a.m. to 6 p.m. on weekends. A restaurant is open from noon to 6 p.m. on weekends, noon to 10 p.m. other days. You can take buses from the central bus station, platform 62, or a train to Luoma, then walk about 1¼ miles. To drive here, follow the Jorvas motorway about 12¼ miles, turn off at Kivenlahti exit, and drive 3 miles in the direction of Kauklahti and follow the Hvitträsk signs.

KORKEASAARI ZOO: Helsinki's zoo (tel. 761-672) on Korkeasaari Island in the archipelago has an important collection of northern European animals, including a herd of reindeer who enjoy posing for cameras. Take the waterbus from Hakaniemenranta in front of the Merihotelli (hotel) every hour on the half hour and return from Suomenlinna on the hour. It stops at Korkeasaari on request. The Helsinki Card does not cover admission to the zoo. Entrance is 10 markkaa ($1.60) for adults, 5 markkaa (80¢) for children 7 to 16. From June 25 to September 19, the zoo is open daily from 10:30 a.m. to 5:30 p.m., to 6:30 p.m. on Sunday.

TOURS: **Suomen Turistianto Oy,** 97 Mannerheimintie (tel. 58-51-66), offers a city tour departing at 1 p.m. and lasting 1½ hours. It costs 45 markkaa ($7.20) for adults and 20 markkaa ($2.40) for children. The tour takes in the most important city sights, including the Sibelius Monument.

You can also see Helsinki by boat. Departures are from the front of the Market Hall (terminal B) at Market Square (Kauppatori). The cost ranges from 35 markkaa ($5.60) to 45 markkaa ($7.20) for adults; children are free. Check with the head office about departure times.

5. Shopping in Helsinki

Finland has boldly taken a creative lead in many forms of design in Scandinavia, being among the first to throw off the routinely conservative if it lacked flair and functionalism. In particular, search out ceramics and glassware (Arabia is famous), hand-woven articles, hand-carved wood, jaunty fashions such as Marimekko, and rugs (don't walk on a *ryijy*—hang it on the wall).

Textiles and jewelry also bear the distinctive stamp of Finland, and toy stores brim with educational toys for all stages of a child's development. Among souvenirs, the range includes decorations of reindeer skin, costume dolls, baskets, and unusual and interesting-tasting berry liqueurs made from the yellow cloudberry and the Arctic brambleberry. Of course, you'll find all your sauna needs here as well.

FINNISH DESIGN: To begin your shopping adventure, I'd suggest you pay a call at the **Finnish Design Center,** 19 Kasarmikatu (tel. 626-388), where some handmade articles can be purchased. In addition, English-speaking attendants will supply the names of retailers who carry the works of Finland's leading industrial designers and handicrafts artisans. In some cases you'll be directed to a studio or atelier. The nonprofit design center is open weekdays from 10 a.m. to 5 p.m., on Saturday from 10 a.m. to 3 p.m., and on Sunday from noon to 4 p.m. The managing director is the most helpful Anu Hynynen.

DEPARTMENT STORE: **Stockmann,** 52 Aleksanterinkatu (tel. 176-181), with the main entrance opening onto that street and other entrances onto Keskuskatu and Mannerheimintie, is the leading department store in Helsinki, and in the whole country. It is also the oldest department store in Finland. If you are seeking Finnish design or the best imported products, Stockmann has a little bit of everything, the most diversified sampling of Finnish and imported merchandise of any store: glassware, stoneware, ceramics, lamps, furniture, luxurious furs, beautiful contemporary jewelry, clothes and textiles by Marimekko and Vuokko, handmade candles, reindeer hides—everything.

The Export Service on the fifth floor will send your purchases to your address back home. The price of the purchases with the sales tax of 16% (5.5% on food) deducted and the delivery cost are tallied up for you. The delivery cost is based on the wrapping and weight of the purchases and on the means of delivery. This includes the cost of insurance.

In addition to the department store in the center of the city, there are small shops at the airport, the Hotel Kalastajatorppa, and the Hotel Intercontinental. In 1981, a new Stockmann department store was opened in Tapiola.

JEWELRY: Kalevala Koru, 25 Unioninkatu (tel. 662-408), presents both traditional and modern jewelry in Finnish design. Shoppers here are "patrons," since the profits go to aid orphans and the poor, as well as to promote Finnish arts. For nearly half a century, Kalevala Koru has manufactured traditional Finnish jewelry in bronze, silver, and gold. These pieces of jewelry are based on originals uncovered in archeological excavations. The modern jewelry for sale is designed by some of Finland's foremost artisans in the field. Some motifs date back to the 11th century. Belt buckles are often stunning, one depicting two serpents facing each other (based on an eighth-century design). The store works in close cooperation with the Finnish National Museum. The shop is open Monday and Friday from 8:30 a.m. to 6 p.m.; Tuesday, Wednesday, and Thursday from 8:30 a.m. to 5:30 p.m.; on Saturday from 8:30 a.m. to 1 p.m.

Excelling in Lapponia jewelry, as well as sculpture and glass, **Galerie Björn Weckström,** 30 Unioninkatu (tel. 656-529), has won Grand Prix prizes in international jewelry competitions. Björn Weckström has earned a reputation for making shapes that seem a part of nature. The jewelry sold here has been called miniature sculptures. In addition, acrylic sculptures have subdued lighting, yet manage to be radiant. The glass collection of bowls, bottles, and dishes sometimes comes in lovely, mysterious colors. The gallery is open in summer, Monday to Friday, from 9:30 a.m. to 5:30 p.m. (on Saturday from 9:30 a.m. to 2 p.m.). Direct your inquiries to the secretary, Mrs. Anne-Marie Westerling.

GLASS, PORCELAIN, CERAMICS: Arabia Nuutajärvi, 25 Pohjoisesplanadi (tel. 170-055), is one of the world's most prestigious manufacturers of household porcelain, glass, and enamelware, and art ceramics. It combines both a flair for utility and artistic quality. Its shop is open from 9 a.m. to 5:30 p.m. Monday to Friday, to 2 p.m. Saturday; closed Sunday. It is also possible to visit its factory anytime but from June 30 to August 1. If you're in Helsinki at some other period than that, get in touch with Mrs. Kira Reuter at **Oy Arabia Ab,** 135 Hämeentie (tel. 790-211).

Juliana, 21 Aleksanterinkatu (tel. 177-611), in the heart of Helsinki, is the place for that special glass, china, gift, or kitchenware. The collection is stunning.

HANDICRAFTS: One of the best collections is at the previously recommended **Kalevala Koru,** 25 Unioninkatu (tel. 171-520). The giftshop here is known as Lahjavakka. The knitwear collection comes in both traditional Finnish motifs and modern design. On sale are dresses, coats, handmade pullovers, knitted caps and mittens, both for women and men. Seek out, in particular, the Lapland counterpanes in the colors of nature. In contrast, the traditional provincial counterpanes have colorful stripes and designs. Hanging ceramic ornaments represent skillfully finished handwork, and each piece is unique. Many other typically Finnish artisan products are offered for sale as well. (For shopping hours, refer to the description of Kalevala Koru under "Jewelry.")

Poppana, 19 Liisankatu (tel. 627-889), features typically Finnish handicrafts. Displays include various kinds of arts and crafts in ceramics, wood, and textiles. The shop is open from 10 a.m. to 4:30 p.m.

Artisaani, 28 Unioninkatu (tel. 665-225), is a cooperative of artisans who sell their own arts and crafts fresh from their country workshops. Ceramic sculptures, pottery, glassware, gold, silver, and bronze jewelry, leather goods, printed fabrics, and other textiles are displayed. Weekday hours are from 10 a.m. to 5 p.m.

Suomen Käsityön Ystävät (Friends of Finnish Handicraft), 7 Meilahti (tel. 418-530), was founded in 1879 to maintain and develop the traditions of Finnish handicraft. The center of activity is in an old villa about three miles from the city center. Here you can see a permanent exhibition of ryijy tapestries and also visit the weaving studios. Textiles, table linens, towels, and gift items such as shawls and embroidered work can be purchased here. Export service is available. Take bus 24 leaving in front of the Swedish Theatre at Erottaja. Across the road from the second stop on Seurasaarentie, you'll see the signs to the studio and exhibits. It's open weekdays from 9 a.m. to 5 p.m., to 3 p.m. on Saturday.

FASHION: **Arola Oy,** 4 Kalevankatu (tel. 605-700), traces its origins back to 1948 when it was founded in the heart of the Finnish countryside about 100 miles north of Helsinki. The aim was to manufacture high-quality original fashions, using fabrics designed and woven by Arola itself. The production includes knitted tops in matching colors and various styles. Arola has shops at 36 Aleksanterinkatu (tel. 652-522) and at City Center, 6 Keskuskatu (tel. 656-987).

Marimekko Oy, 31 Pohjoisesplanadi (tel. 177-944), has spread its fashions far and wide. Using printed cottons and woolens, "the Marimekko look" is often based on a simple country frock that has been given flair and originality. Dresses, jerseys, fabrics, even wallpapers, are often radiantly colored. In addition, Marimekko also offers beachwear, children's clothes, and accessories.

Lena Rewell Shops, Hotel Intercontinental (tel. 409-494) and 15B Mariankatu (tel. 628-843), come up with handmade textiles. The capes and ponchos have distinctive flair and styling. The mohair blankets are luxurious and subtly colored, and each is designed by Lena Rewell. The shop is open weekdays from 9 a.m. to 5 p.m. (on Saturday from 9 a.m. to 1 p.m.).

WEAVING: One of the leaders is **Metsovaara/Peltola,** 23 Pohjoisesplanadi (tel. 662-525), which has one of the best collections of interior decoration fabrics in Helsinki—upholstery fabrics, cotton prints, curtains, travel rugs, and bedspreads.

LEATHER: **Pentik,** 27C Pohjoisesplanadi (tel. 625-558), is a retail shop carrying exclusive leather outfits. It also runs a wholesale office. The store is open all summer.

STAMPS: **Suomen Postimerkkeily Oy,** 51–53 Fredrikinkatu (tel. 642-501), has a good offering of stamps for collectors, either professional or amateur. It's open Monday to Friday from 8 a.m. to 5 p.m., to 2 p.m. on Saturday.

FURNITURE: **Sokeain Myymälä** (The Blinds Shop) owned by Helsingin Näkövammaisetry, 16 Annankatu (tel. 604-893), has an impressive collection of unusual and well-designed furniture in rattan and bamboo. Furnishings have style and flair, and are suited to both indoor and outdoor living.

Artek, 3 Keskuskatu (tel. 177-533), offers furniture based on designs of the late, great architect Alvar Aalto. His first models were designed in the late '20s and early '30s, but today they are considered classic pieces. They continue to live regardless of changing styles and the whims of fashion. In addition to furnishings, the store sells lamps, ceramics, glassware, and textiles.

SAUNA: Sauna Soppi-Shop, 22–24 Mannerheimintie (tel. 602-536), gets a lot of foreign visitors, because of the increasing popularity of the Finnish sauna. Here you'll find all the articles related to the sauna, ranging from brushes to birch slippers. If you're ordering by mail, write Marketta Neuvonen.

6. Helsinki After Dark

Nightlife is not the reason to visit Suomi, although there are the usual restaurants with three- or four-piece bands. Finland has few nightclubs with shows.

For an all-around good time, do as the Finn does and head for **Linnanmäki,** a fun fair full of splashing fountains, merry-go-rounds, ferris wheels, restaurants, cafés, theaters, and discos. Founded in 1950 by the Children's Foundation to raise funds to care for the thousands of war orphans, Linnanmäki continues today to raise money to aid a new generation of children.

One of the main attractions on the grounds of the park is the **Peacock** (tel. 7012-155), a variety theater with 90 minutes of nonstop entertainment in July and August. Performances are Tuesday to Friday at 7 p.m., on Saturday and Sunday at 4 p.m and again at 7 p.m. Tickets sell for 30 markkaa ($4.80) for adults, 15 markkaa ($2.40) for children. The amusement park has a total of 25 different rides, including Europe's highest "big dipper," a fun house, and a railway for the kids.

To reach the park, take either streetcar 3B or 3T. The entrance fee is 4 markkaa (64¢) for adults, 2 markkaa (32¢) for children, but during the first three hours on Sunday and holidays children are allowed in free. The amusement park is open from Tuesday to Friday from 5 to 10 p.m., on Saturday and Sunday from 1 to 10 p.m. For more information, telephone 750-391.

Baker's Pub, 2 Kalevankatu (tel. 605-607), in many ways may have Helsinki's most complete nightclub entertainment. Part of the show includes watching what may be the biggest collection in town of apparently unattached people rubbing elbows with each other. After checking your coat near the entrance (and being checked out by the resident bouncer), you climb a staircase to an upper floor. This contains a restaurant, two bars, a small-stakes casino, a disco, and lots of space for milling around with the energetic crowd.

The decor is filled with Scottish red and black plaid carpeting whose pattern almost matches the vests worn by the staff, which works energetically to keep everyone's glasses filled. Entrance is free except for the cost of the coat check. Beer costs from 18 markkaa ($2.88). Dinner is served in one of three or four different rooms, some of them more intimately secluded than the others. It's available either à la carte or by ordering a set dinner costing from 100 markkaa ($16). Menu specialties include fish salad, shrimp in a pot with herbs and garlic, consommé of smoked meat, many beef dishes, several kinds of fresh fish, and potatoes prepared seven different ways. Although the place caters to a crowd aged roughly between 25 and 35, no blue jeans are permitted. The establishment is open daily except Sunday.

Helsinki Club 12 Hallituskatu (tel. 171-401), is one of the most sophisticated discos in town. Although the establishment is inside the Hotel Helsinki (see "Where to Stay" section), most guests enter from under a canopy over the sidewalk outside the club entrance. Inside, there's a circular series of glass or mirrored bars, a collection of small tables, a dance floor with a centerpiece of potted palms, and lots and lots of peach-color and black glass. Perhaps best of all, the sound here is focused onto the dance floor, so you are able to hear conversation if you're not totally absorbed by the ebb and flow of the crowd. The minimum age here is 24 for men and 22 for women, but many of the patrons are a few years older than that. There's never a cover charge for guests of the hotel, although for everybody else, there's a 35-markkaa ($5.60) entrance fee which is collected every night except Sunday and Monday. The club serves as the bar for the hotel beginning at 4 p.m. daily, turning into a disco after 8 p.m. Export beer costs 15 markkaa ($2.40), while Irish coffee goes for 35 markkaa ($5.60).

Gambrini, 3 Iso Roobertinkatu (tel. 644-391). It's only been in the last few years that gay people in Finland began to be allowed to congregate in public homosexual enclaves. Gambrini is the result of a changing sociology in which this country seems to have lagged several years behind Denmark and Sweden. There's a restaurant on the premises, but the real reason most of the male and female clients come here is to see, be seen, and perhaps to figure out their role in a changing society. A visiting English-speaking person won't have any problem striking up a conversation with someone, especially since the place seems almost charmingly innocent and usually just as friendly as the rest of Finland. There's disco dancing in a small room to the side, but most of the guests gather near the long bar. All the staff speak English. Beer costs 18 markkaa ($2.88), and entrance, other than checking your coat, is free. The establishment is open daily from 7 p.m. to 1 a.m.

Club Tropical, 4 Kivelänkatu (tel. 441-311). South Americans may argue that any rhythm taken out of the tropics loses energy, but the aficionados of this vibrantly decorated restaurant and nightspot can claim otherwise. There's usually a lively crowd and Latin-American music to warm up a cold Helsinki night. There's no cover charge, and drinks cost around 18 markkaa ($2.88) for a beer. It's open Tuesday through Saturday from 7 p.m. till 2 a.m.

Groovy, 4 Ruoholahdenkatu (tel. 6945-118). As in many jazz spots, no one really comes for the food, which is nonetheless adequate and inexpensive. The real thing here is the jazz which is produced enthusiastically by the leading artists of Helsinki. Admission is free, although once you get inside, a drink will cost between 18 markkaa ($2.88) and 30 markkaa ($4.80), depending on your choice. The establishment serves lunch, with recorded jazz playing softly in the background. The real energy, however, is at night when the live music begins. The place is open weekdays from 9 a.m. to 1 a.m., Saturday from 11 a.m. to 1 a.m., and Sunday from 2 to 11 p.m.

The **Red Room,** in the Hotel Kalastajatorppa, 1 Kalastajatorpantie (tel. 488-011), is considered the most inexpensive nightclub in Helsinki. It doesn't even charge an entrance fee like most other places. There is mostly live music. Many of the guests will be staying at the hotel, but a lot of young professional people from Helsinki are also attracted to the place. Beer begins at 18 markkaa ($2.88). To reach the hotel, you can board tram 4 which you take to its terminus. Then you head a block up Uimarinpolku to the hotel.

Foreign students visiting Helsinki might consider the **Foreign Students Club,** which plans evenings for foreign students. For information, call 335-412. The club sponsors dances and various festive student activities.

The best way to meet Finnish students is to go to the **Student Houses,** 5A and 5C Mannerheimintie (tel. 176-616). The place where students have discussions and hold open meetings is Kirjakahvilla. There are also club evenings Wednesday, Friday, and Saturday in Old Students House in which you'll meet students dancing and talking.

Helsinki has a number of motion-picture theaters showing English-language films. The booking office for films is **Lippupalvelu,** 23

Aleksanterinkatu. Most films are shown twice nightly, at 7 and again at 9, with tickets averaging 20 markkaa ($2.40) to 30 markkaa ($4.80).

CULTURAL: The Finnish National Opera (**Finnische Nationaloper**), 23–25 Bulevardi (tel. 642-60l), might interest those visiting Helsinki at times other than summer. Its ballet and opera presentations enjoy fame internationally. The box office opens 1½ hours before performances.

The Finnish National Theater (**Finnisches Nationaltheater**), 11 Vilhonkatu (tel. 171-826), also enjoys world renown, but its performances, naturally, are in Finnish. The theater was established in 1872, and usually presents 15 to 20 plays a year.

The Swedish Theater (**Svenska Teatern**), Erottaja (tel. 170-438), might be visited if you speak Swedish. It has been presenting plays since 1866.

But the language of **Philharmonie Helsinki** (Helsinki Philharmonic Orchestra) is universal. The oldest symphony orchestra in the Scandinavian countries performs at the beautiful Finlandia Hall, 4 Karamzininkatu (tel. 40-241), which was designed by Alvar Aalto. The box office at the hall opens one hour before concerts. For information about tickets at other times, telephone 643-043.

HELSINKI FESTIVAL: This is a highlight of the Finnish summer and a prelude to the capital city's generous autumn arts program. Attracting international artists, the festival is held at the end of August and the beginning of September. The nearly three-week-long program offers concerts, opera, ballet, theater, exhibitions, jazz, and pop music. The main stage is the **Finlandia Hall,** Helsinki's concert and congress center opened in 1971. The Helsinki Festival, a member of the European Association of Music Festivals, is preceded by the Helsinki Summer Concerts in June and August, and in November there is a special festival for children. Further details may be obtained from Helsinki Festival, 28 Unioninkatu, 00100 Helsinki 10 (tel. 659-688). The hotel situation is rather difficult in Helsinki during the festival season, so travelers should make their reservations well in advance.

EXCURSION TO PORVOO: The second oldest town in Finland, Porvoo, 30 miles northeast of Helsinki, provides visitors with a look at what a small town in this area was like a century or so ago. Simply strolling in the Old Quarter with its narrow winding streets is a pleasant experience, but this colorful little town, closely linked with Finland's history, has a number of worthwhile sights to see.

Founded as a Swedish town, Borgå, in 1346 at the mouth of a river, this was already an important trading center in the Middle Ages. Even before the town was given its charter, the Swedes had a wooden fortress on a hill to the north, which permitted control of river and sea trade for several centuries when Finland was a Swedish province. The town, whose houses were mostly of wood, suffered over the years from fire and conflict. After Sweden finally relinquished Finland to the Russians, Porvoo was the scene of the first Finnish Diet in the early 19th century, when Czar Alexander I made the little country a Grand Duchy. Despite this break with Sweden, many of the citizens of Porvoo still consider themselves Swedes, almost half of the town's residents speaking Swedish and clinging to the old name of the town, Borgå.

The 15th-century **cathedral,** where the first Diet of the duchy was held, is a stone house of worship which has been much restored. The belfry is a mixture of materials, part of it dating from medieval times, although actual construction of the one you see took place in the 18th century. The cathedral is open May to September weekdays from 10 a.m. to 6 p.m., Sunday from 2 to 5 p.m.; October to April Tuesday to Saturday from noon to 4 p.m., Sunday from 2 to 4 p.m. (closed Monday).

The **Old Town Hall** and **Historical Museum** stands on the Museum Square of the Old Town. The stone building contains artifacts of the town, dating mostly from the 1800s, probably because fires which destroyed the town hadn't left much else. The museum is open May to August from 11 a.m. to 4 p.m.; September to April from noon to 3 p.m. It's open Sunday from noon to 4 p.m.; closed Monday.

Porvoo is particularly proud of its association with the Finnish national poet, **John Ludvig Runeberg,** who spent the last 25 years of his life here. His home is now a museum, at 3 Alekstanterkatu. It's open May to August weekdays from 9:30 a.m. to 4 p.m., Sunday from 10:30 a.m. to 5 p.m. September to April hours are 11 a.m. to 3 p.m. weekdays, from noon to 4 p.m. Sunday. Admission is free. Runeberg's tomb is also in Porvoo, in the old cemetery west of the river.

Works of the poet's son, sculptor Walter Runeberg, can be seen here, especially interesting is a statue of his father.

If you come to Porvoo by the most interesting transportation, by boat from Helsinki, you will get a good view of the old merchants' houses and warehouses along the water. Most of these are from the 18th century, others having gone up in flames earlier.

The town's most important industry today is the publishing firm of Werner Söderström, established in 1853, one of the largest in Scandinavia.

The most interesting way to come to Porvoo, mentioned above, is by M/S *J. L. Runeberg,* which sails in summer from the Market Square in Helsinki on Wednesday, Friday, and Sunday. A one-way ticket costs 30 markkaa ($4.80) for adults, 15 markkaa ($2.40) for children. For a round-trip ticket, adults pay 40 markkaa ($6.40), children 20 markkaa ($3.20).

You can also come by bus from the capital, or you can fly.

For further information, get in touch with the **City Tourist Office,** 20 Rauhankatu in Porvoo (tel. 140-145).

Chapter XIX

ALL AROUND FINLAND

1. Turku
2. Tampere
3. Saimaa Lakeland
4. Finnish Lapland

NO VISIT TO FINLAND would be complete without a trip to its azure lakes, its virgin forests, its modern cities—and its past.

Because the country is so vast, yet underpopulated, much of the landscape emerges as a wilderness. Every boy of Suomi is a Huck Finn for at least a part of his adolescence.

For the time-pressed traveler, I've narrowed our look at the rest of Finland to only the major centers: These include Turku, the cradle of Finnish civilization; Tampere, a modern industrial city with unexpected charm; Lappeenranta, in East Finland, the gateway to the lake district; Savonlinna, the oldest town in East Finland and site of the country's best preserved medieval castle; Kuopio, the tourist capital of the Eastern Lake District of Central Finland; and of course, Rovaniemi, the gateway to Finnish Lapland.

1. Turku

On the western coast lies the seaport of Turku (Abo in Swedish). The oldest city of Finland, it was an ecclesiastical center as early as the 13th century. It also was the capital until the early 19th century, when the Russians decided the government should be closer to what is now Leningrad than to Stockholm. Turku suffered still another loss—most of the city burned in 1827 in one of the worst fires in the history of Scandinavia.

But Turku has bounced back admirably, developing not only into an important port and industrial city, but as a university town as well, with both a Swedish and a Finnish Academy. Turku is 102 miles from Helsinki, easily reached by train or plane. Ferries ply daily between Turku and Stockholm.

WHERE TO STAY: Turku offers a number of moderately priced lodgings, the star choices of which are:

The Summer Hotels

Domus Aboensis, 10 Biskopsgatan (tel. 921-29-470), is a student hotel opened by the Abo Academy—the best in Turku. The spacious bedrooms are the most winning feature here: many look like living Mondrian paintings, with large blocks of color. Each room has a private shower bath. Doubles rent for 220 markkaa ($35.20), singles for 160 markkaa ($25.60), service and breakfast included. The hotel is open from June 1 to August 31. Three meals a day are available in the Restaurant Kåren. Lunches are 35 markkaa ($5.60); dinners, 45 markkaa ($7.20).

Summerhotel Ikituuri, 7 Pispalantie (tel. 376-111), is an inviting choice, housing an international clientele in its 576 comfortable rooms, each of which comes equipped with shower and toilet. A single rents for 190 markkaa ($30.40) a day, a double going for 230 markkaa ($36.80), breakfast included. You can enjoy all the same facilities the students do in the winter: swimming, playing games, going bicycle riding. Naturally, there are saunas on the premises. Bus 50 goes four times an hour to the marketplace about 1½ miles away, and there's also a taxi station in front of the hotel. In a separate building you'll find a disco and pub. Meals are served in the hotel's restaurant until 12:30 a.m. The hotel is open from June 1 to August 31.

Hostel Kåren, 22 Hämeenkatu (tel. 921-20420), is a student-run hotel open to guests of all ages between June 1 and August 31. During the school year, it is a residence hall for Swedish students. It's near a canal, a swimming pool, and the university. Tariffs are 220 markkaa ($35.20) for a double, 85 markkaa ($19.38) for a single, including service and breakfast. Each room has all the necessities—sink, armchair, and comfortable bed—but no frills. There are adequate showers on each floor, all free. On the premises is a restaurant serving lunch for 35 markkaa ($5.60), dinner for 50 markkaa ($8).

Year-Round Hotels

Turun Keskushotelli Oy, 12A Yliopistonkatu (tel. 337-333), takes Finnish modern to a rather alarming degree. Immaculate in line and concept, the hotel makes full use of such Finnish materials as marble and birch. Finnish design reigns rampant in this well-run hotel which was built in 1974 and has already been expanded twice because of its increasing popularity. If available, you're given a choice of colors such as orange, green, and yellow in various shades. Units are equipped with one to three beds, and all of them have contemporary Finnish furniture, along with private baths or showers, phones, and radios. A single rents for 260 markkaa ($41.60) to 320 markkaa ($51.20); a double goes for anywhere from 320 markkaa ($51.20) to 400 markkaa ($64). The three-bedded room mentioned costs 500 markkaa ($80). After a day of touring, you can relax in the hot steam of the sauna. On the ground floor is the reception and TV corner. This is also the place where you can order breakfast, perhaps tea or coffee in the evening.

Hotelli Henrik, 29A Yliopistonkatu (tel. 20-921), is one of the best hotels in the moderately priced range. In the heart of old Turku, near many of the town's most interesting sights, it offers smallish but reasonably comfortable rooms that are neat and well maintained. Restored in 1984, it rents 87 rooms in all, 56 of which are doubles. Singles begin at 250 markkaa ($40), with doubles climbing to 380 markkaa ($60.80). There is an attractive luncheon restaurant on the premises which is licensed for light beer.

Hotelli Maakunta, 7 Humalistonkatu (tel. 337-337), is a newly renovated hotel in the town center. A blockbuster corner building, it rents out a total of 166 rooms, making it one of the biggest in town, with a bed capacity of 310. I've been able to find a room here when the other, smaller hotels were packed to the rafters. With breakfast included, a single rents for 325 markkaa ($52), a double costing 450 markkaa ($72). If you stay for lunch, expect to pay from 75 markkaa

($12), slightly more for dinner. There are two dance restaurants at this big hotel.

A Youth Hostel

Turku Youth Hostel, 39 Linnankatu (tel. 16-578), the rock-bottom dormitory accommodation in the center of Turku, is graced by architectural beauty. The building is entered through a well-planted courtyard. There are no private rooms—generally 10 to 20 persons are housed in a dormitory. Each bed rents for 20 markkaa ($3.20). Sheets can also be rented. The use of sheets is obligatory, by the way. No meals are served, but there is a self-service kitchen. The hostel is closed between 9 a.m. and 1 p.m. *Warning:* There is a midnight curfew.

WHERE TO EAT: Pinella, Porthaninpuisto (tel. 11-102), in a park in the old center of Turku, has attracted artists and intellectuals for more than a century with its joie de vivre and attractively served meals. Swedish graduate students create a cheerful hubbub. Open till 11 p.m., Pinella serves good lunches and dinners for around 40 markkaa ($6.40) to 50 markkaa ($8). A lunch here can easily be tied in with a visit to Turku Cathedral. The upper part of this venerated old restaurant is now a pizzeria.

Café and Restaurant Lyra, 4 Humalistonkatu (tel. 23-255), has been likened to a doll's house. Its location is in one of the old timbered structures along this colorful street. The most expensive dining is on the ground floor, where there is a restaurant serving good food, with meals beginning at 85 markkaa ($13.60) and going up. Upstairs is a café where you can enjoy not only coffee and a piece of moist cake, but light snacks as well.

Le Pirate, Bore Square (tel. 511-443), once sailed the Baltic, but now this barge has been turned into a restaurant. Naturally, its past history has been respected, and it's been decorated in a nautical style. On a summer day, if the weather's right, you can dine out on the deck in the open air. In the restaurant, you can order excellent fish dishes, including an array of Baltic herring. Meals begin at 100 markkaa ($16).

Brahenkellari, 1 Puolalankatu (tel. 25-400), is Turku's best known wine restaurant. In a setting of ancient stone walls, diners can enjoy not only the atmosphere but some of the best dishes—both meat and fish—in town. The service is polite and attentive, and the wine list is excellent, but expensive, with meals costing from 100 markkaa ($16).

WHAT TO SEE: The seaport presents some interesting sights, among them—

Turku Castle

Finland's largest castle was constructed in the 13th century, but its main building was renovated after World War II. At the mouth of the Aura River, the outer castle houses the **Turku Museum,** where military relics and antique furnishings are displayed. The castle is open from May 1 to September 30 from 10 a.m. to 6 p.m. Off season, the hours are 10 a.m. to 3 p.m. Admission is 4 markkaa (64¢). Refreshments and light snacks are offered in the self-service cafeteria in the southern wing. From the center of the city, take bus 1.

Turku Cathedral

The foundation of this brick cathedral also goes back to the 13th century, but in its present form it represents the architectural styles of many centuries.

One of the most important medieval monuments in Finland, the cathedral contains the tombs of many famous men of Scandinavia—bishops and military heroes—but of only one crowned head, Karin Månsdotter, the wife of Erik XIV of Sweden. The admission-free cathedral is open October 1 to April 30 from 10 a.m. to 4 p.m. Monday to Friday, 10 a.m. to 3 p.m. Saturday, and 2:30 to 4:30 p.m. Sunday. The hours May 2 to September 30 are 9 a.m. to 5 p.m. Monday to Friday, 9 a.m. to 3 p.m. Saturday, and 2:30 to 4:30 p.m. Sunday. The Cathedral Museum is open the same hours, for 3 markkaa (48¢) admission. The collection consists of relics and liturgical artifacts from the Middle Ages on.

Handicraft Museum

This outdoor compound, **Turun Maakuntamuseo**, 4 Kalastajankatu, the only part of old Turku that escaped the fire of 1827, lies a five-minute walk from the city center on Luostarinmäki (Cloister Hill). Unlike most Scandinavian open-air museums, this one is preserved intact from the 18th century; the buildings were not moved to the site and reassembled. Following the fire, the houses were taken over by craftspeople, and a museum today preserves their handicrafts. From May 2 to September 30, it is open from 10 a.m. to 6 p.m.; October 1 to April 30 from 10 a.m. to 3 p.m. The admission is 3 markkaa (48¢).

Sibelius Museum

Although Finland's beloved composer neither lived nor worked in Turku, there is nevertheless a fine collection of Sibeliana here. The museum, 17 Piispankatu (tel. 13-728), is an oasis for visiting music lovers, who can sit in a small concert hall and listen to the works of the master once a day or at concerts held on Wednesday. The museum is open May 2 to September 30 from 11 a.m. to 3 p.m., October 1 to April 30, from noon to 3 p.m. It's closed Monday. Admission is 4 markkaa (64¢) for adults, 1.50 markkaa (24¢) for children. If you wish to attend a Wednesday concert, it's best to stop by in the morning to book your ticket, as early sell-outs are usual.

Market Hall

A visit to Turku's cobblestone marketplace and the market hall is the best way to experience the life rhythms of the city at no cost. At the market hall, 16 Eerikinkatu and 15 Linnankatu, stalls in long corridors are filled with fresh vegetables, the best of Finnish cheeses, meat, fish, bread, cakes, health foods, and souvenirs. There's a café and a bank handy if you want to sip coffee or change travelers checks in this pleasing ambience. Other stalls in the market square offer such produce as lingonberries, cloudberries, salmon, and other typical Scandinavian foods brought here for sale Monday through Saturday from 8 a.m. to 1 p.m. The covered market hall stays open until 5 p.m. Monday to Friday, closing at 1 p.m. on Saturday.

SHOPPING NOTES: Stockmann Department Store, 22 Yliopistonkatu (tel. 337-344), is called the Harrod's of Turku. Here you can find Finnish and international fashions, textiles, jewelry, and cosmetics. You'll pay only about half as much (or less) for Finnish goods such as Arabia pottery and china, Marimekko fabrics, and Iittala crystal, and Stockmann will ship your purchases home for you. The store is open Monday to Thursday from 9 a.m. to 7 p.m., Friday from 9 a.m. to 8 p.m., and Saturday from 9 a.m. to 4 p.m. You can have coffee and cake in the Stockmann cafeteria while you're shopping.

Neoviska, 8 Kuninkaankartanonkatu (tel. 351-435), is the studio and shop of textile designer Pia Neovius. Here, you'll find unique, hand-woven wall carpets at special prices. There is also a continuous exhibition to be seen. Hours are Monday to Friday from 11 a.m. to 5 p.m.; closed Saturday and Sunday. Take bus 2A, 2B, 3A, or 3B.

Sylvi Salonen, 10 Kauppiaskatu (tel. 334-100), offers hand-sewn screens, linen towels, and tablecloths, and many other kinds of handicrafts are to be found here also. You can find both decorative articles and those for everyday use, handmade from natural materials. The establishment is open from 9 a.m. to 6 p.m. Monday, 9 a.m. to 5 p.m. Tuesday to Friday, and 9 a.m. to 2 p.m. Saturday.

TURKU MISCELLANY: From June 1 till August 31, a guided bus tour (in English) leaves daily at 1 p.m. from the **Turku City Tourist Office,** 3 Käsityöläiskatu (tel. 336-366). Each tour lasts 2½ hours. . . . The tourist office not only dispenses information, but will help visitors secure accommodations. . . . Students visiting Turku can have fun at the **Turku International Student Clubdisco,** 5 Rehtorinpellontie (tel. 21-120). It is open on Friday and Saturday from 8 p.m. to 1 a.m. Popular sauna nights and excursions are also organized by the club, and they are cheap for foreigners.

2. Tampere

On a narrow isthmus between two lakes, Finland's second-largest city (pop. 170,000) is primarily an industrial center—cottons and cobblers. But where's all the smog, grit, and grime? Tampere is one of the cleanest, brightest cities in Scandinavia, filled with parks, water, museums, art galleries, theaters, and statues (works by Wäinö Aaltonen, for example—a nude virgin I understand, but a nude tax collector?).

A frisky young city with a university life, Tampere is host to one of Scandinavia's major attractions: the outdoor theater on Pyynikki with a revolving auditorium.

The terminus of a number of lake excursions (Silver Line, Poet's Way), Tampere is easily reached by rail or air from Helsinki (108 miles away) and Turku (100 miles away). Incidentally, Tampere's Swedish name is Tammerfors.

WHERE TO STAY: Tampere has a number of comfortable hotels, beginning with:

Uimahallinmaja, 10–12 Pirkankatu (tel. 29-460), is a modern hostel near a park and an art museum in the western section of the city (bus 25). In the Swimming Hall House, Uimahallinmaja offers lodgings, meals, swimming pools, saunas, and even art (the Art Gallery of Tampere is beside the hostel). Bathless doubles, starkly modern but comfortable, range from 150 markkaa ($24) to 200 markkaa ($32). A few six-bedded rooms with basins and individual lockers offer the cheapest living yet; 65 markkaa ($10.40) per person. The public rooms are light and sun-filled, and in the self-service cafeteria dinners average around 50 markkaa ($8). In the adjoining wing is the city's swimming pool and sauna.

Domus, 9 Pellervonkatu (tel. 50-000), is one of Finland's finest student-run hotels, offering moderately priced accommodations from June 1 to September 1. It's a compound of modern buildings (200 rooms), with grassy courtyards. The bedrooms are compact and decorated in Finnish-modern style. A single without bath costs 115 markkaa ($18.40), going up to 130 markkaa ($20.80) with bath. Doubles without bath go for 155 markkaa ($24.80), rising to 200 markkaa ($32). An extra bed costs 60 markkaa ($9.60), and breakfast is an additional 20 markkaa ($3.20). Most of the bedrooms have wall-to-wall desks, birch armchairs, wall shelves, built-in wardrobes, and sofa beds. There's a liberal use of brightly colored fabrics. In the self-service restaurant, a lunch averages around 28 markkaa ($6.38), a three-course dinner for around 35 markkaa ($7.41). The use of the sauna is 30 markkaa ($6.84) for two persons; extra persons pay 10 markkaa ($2.28) each. There's a swimming pool also. To reach the Domus, take bus 25 from the railway station.

Kesähotelli Rasti, 1 Itsenäisyydenkatu (tel. 30-640), hugs up to its bigger sister, the jointly managed Victoria. Right in the center of town, Rasti is a summer hotel, known for its economy rates. It offers a total of 94 rooms with 200 beds, and in each unit there is hot and cold running water. Showers and toilets are found on every floor. Including service, a single rents for 115 markkaa ($18.40), a double for 180 markkaa ($28.80), and a triple room for 220 markkaa ($35.20). For vacationers who'd like to do their own cooking, facilities are provided on every floor. The meals provided in the compound cost 100 markkaa ($16) for either a lunch or dinner. All of the facilities of the Victoria, including a swimming pool and sauna, are available to Hotel Rasti guests. There is also a private car park and a garage. Visitors are received only from May 1 to August 31.

Hotelli Tampere, 1 Hämeenkatu (tel. 21-980), is one of the largest hotels in Finland—a total of 260 rooms, with 115 singles and 112 doubles (the rest are suites and exhibition rooms). Right in the swirl of Tampere life, the hotel stands opposite the railway station. Rooms are equipped with private baths or showers as well as toilets, radios, and telephones. Singles cost 280 markkaa ($44.80) to 320 markkaa ($51.20); doubles, 350 markkaa ($56) to 380 markkaa ($60.80). Breakfast, swimming, and service are included. Its drawing rooms are large, and the restaurant seats 150. In addition, there are six saunas and two swimming pools in the complex, as well as a travel agency and garage.

Victoria, 1 Itsenäisyydenkatu (tel. 30-640), in the center of Tampere, adjoining the Rasti student summer hotel, is a superbly modern, 100-room hotel. All its attractively appointed doubles have private baths, and they rent for 310 markkaa ($49.60). A single room without bath rents for 175 markkaa ($28), the price going up to 250 markkaa ($40) with a private bath or shower. All rates include service, tax, a morning swim, and breakfast. The quietly reserved and efficient managers are both helpful and courteous. The Victoria offers you a refrigerator for on-the-spot ice, a well-upholstered bar, two modern saunas, and a swimming pool. Its restaurant, open from 11 a.m. to 2 a.m. and specializing in fresh fish dishes, serves some of the finest food in Tampere. In the evening, a band plays for dancing and the Victoria brings a cosmopolitan air to a provincial city.

Kaupunginhotelli, 11 Hämeenkatu (tel. 21-380), renovated in 1984, is bright, airy, and modern, also a bit expensive. However, its rooms are well conceived and designed, most comfortable, costing 280 markkaa ($44.80) in a single with shower, and 350 markkaa ($56) in a double with private bath. These tariffs include breakfast, a sauna in the morning, and service. The location is in the center of town. On the premises is an attractive bar as well as a first-class restaurant serving good meals, a lunch or dinner costing around 65 markkaa ($10.40). The restaurant stays open until midnight.

Hotel Cumulus, 5 Koskikatu (tel. 35-500), which opened its doors in 1979, is a major hotel on the Tampere scene today, with 230 rooms, a main restaurant, the Café Claudia and lobby bar, and the Finnair Terminal next to the reception area. Singles cost 290 markkaa ($46.40), with doubles priced at 360 markkaa ($57.60). However, on weekends, singles are reduced to 200 markkaa ($32), and doubles go for 275 markkaa ($44). Lunch or dinner is another 65 markkaa ($10.40) or more. The hotel, built in the park overlooking the

Tammerkoski Canal, offers guests absolute peace five miles from the city center.

On the Outskirts

Härmälä Motel, 50 Nuolialantie (tel. 650-400). You really don't have to be driving a car to stay at this 85-room countryside hotel, about three miles from the center of Tampere. Bus 1 takes you to this spot in just ten minutes. The motel is tranquil, built in the woodland beside Lake Phyäjärvi, where you can swim, boat, or take water-bus trips. Doubles cost 160 markkaa ($25.60); singles 115 markkaa ($18.40). Each bedroom is tastefully furnished in contemporary style, and is equipped with telephone, private toilet, shower, refrigerator, and simple cooking facilities. You can make breakfast in your room (or a noon snack), but you'll be tempted to order lunch for 45 markkaa ($7.20) or dinner for 55 markkaa ($8.80) in the restaurant, which has a lake view. There are living-room lounges on each floor, plus separate rooms for washing and ironing. Best of all is a pine-paneled Finnish sauna, where you can relieve your travel aches. The friendly staff speaks English.

Camping

Tampere Härmälä (tel. 651-250) lies three miles to the south of the center of Tampere. Bus 1 from the heart of the city stops about 200 yards from the campsite. All the necessary equipment and buildings for modern camping are provided. Here you'll find a TV room, a self-service food store, log cabins, two lakeside saunas, and a special area for caravans. Boats can be rented, and outdoor games are provided free. Stoves and showers are included in the overnight charge of 45 markkaa ($7.20) per person. Electricity is provided for caravan dwellers at a cost of 12 markkaa ($1.92) per night. The site, guarded around the clock, is open from June 1 to the end of August.

WHERE TO EAT: Tikankolo, 18 Rautatienkatu, opposite the railway station and open daily till 11 p.m., is right for our taste and purse. Bypass the simple snackbar upstairs and head for the cellar, where there's a Karelian log cabin peppered with gas masks and helmets related to the play *The Unknown Soldier.* If a grisly war atmosphere doesn't intrigue you, then you may prefer the "New Mexican Renaissance" section, where wagon-wheel chandeliers set the mood. Hot meals are served throughout the day. One of the most popular listings is a big plate of wienerschnitzel with potatoes. A set lunch costs 35 markkaa ($5.60), and dinner is from 75 markkaa ($12). Licensed for pilsner, the café is frequented predominantly by young people.

Siilinkari, 9 Hämeenkatu. Owned by the same management as the Tikankolo, it, too, is popular with young people, some of whom dine outside in summer (next door to a cinema). Both table and self-service are offered. A beef steak with onions and potatoes is always featured. Dinners go for 75 markkaa ($12) and up. Sometimes there's entertainment, such as folk singing or guitar playing.

Tüliholvi, 10 Kauppakatu (tel. 21-220), offers an international menu, featuring the specialties of the Finnish cuisine. The atmosphere is cozy and intimate: red brick walls, wooden tables, and candlelight. The restaurant is in the very heart of Tampere, down in the cellar vaults of the old Jugend-style bank building. A complete lunch goes for 55 markkaa ($8.80), and a table d'hôte dinner runs to 75 markkaa ($12). Also many tempting à la carte dishes are offered. Lunch is served between 11 a.m. and 2 p.m., dinner between 5 and 8 p.m.

Sorsapuiston Grilli, 1 Sorsapuisto (tel. 556-550), is a festive al fresco place at which to dine. The restaurant is surrounded by a park, and its interior is spacious, with an entire wall of glass opening onto the woodland. Tables are set on the lower level, but traditionalists prefer the tavern-style mezzanine. Tubes of copper lights hang over tables, creating an intimate atmosphere. A 50 markkaa ($8) to 95 markkaa ($15.20) lunch or dinner is featured every day. The food is well prepared, and the portions are generous. From the beginning of May until the end of August, Sorsapuiston Grilli also has an outdoor restaurant, with 100 seats, near a beautiful park and impressive aviary. Both food and drinks are served here.

Rustholli, Aitolahti (tel. 620-111), is a fun restaurant near the lake, where you can dine in the midst of wandering animals. You can even swim and then have a sauna before dinner. All dishes on the menu are à la carte, ranging in price from 60 markkaa ($9.60) to 85 markkaa ($13.60). The restaurant is fully licensed and open from noon to 1 a.m. daily.

AFTER DARK: At the **Ohranjyvä,** 15 Näsilinnankatu, is a cozy, L-shaped beer hall. The local habitues, a crowd of bright young people, gather here in the evening for gabfests and many rounds of beer from ceramic steins. A motto over the door, roughly translated, reads: "Water is the oldest cure—but the weakest."

TAMPERE MUSEUMS: The **Art Museum of Tampere** (the District Art Museum of Pirkanmaa), at 34 Puutarhakatu (tel. 931-110), has a collection of paintings, sculptures, drawings, and graphics, as well as exhibits of native art since the early 19th century and the Tampere art collection. The museum has changing art exhibits. It is open from 11 a.m. to 7 p.m. daily. Admission is 5 markkaa (80¢) for adults, 1 markkaa (16¢) for children.

The city museum at Hatanpaan Kartano, **Tampereen Kaupungin Museolautakunnan Toimisto** (tel. 20-535), presents the history of Tampere. Room interiors range in styles from neoclassic to functionalism. The museum is open daily, Tuesday to Sunday, from noon to 6 p.m., charging adults 5 markkaa (80¢) for admission, 1 markkaa (16¢) for children.

Just outside the city of Tampere is one of the most unusual museums in the world. The **Haihara Doll Museum,** Haihara Manor, Kaukajarvi (tel. 630-350), houses a collection of nearly 2100 dolls, in every material imaginable, from soap to fine china. The oldest doll in the collection, 3000 years old, was found in an Egyptian tomb, and another, 1000 years old, was taken from the grave of an Inca child. In all, more than 80 countries are represented in the museum. Besides the doll exhibits, the museum organizes various displays of the history of costume. Costumes from 1920 to 1950 will be shown during 1985. The collection of costumes at the museum totals more than 200 historical exhibits. To reach the Haihara Doll Museum, take bus 24 from Tampere. Admission is only 8 markkaa ($1.28) for adults, 2.50 markkaa (40¢) for children.

Sara Hildén Art Museum (tel. 113-134) at Särkänniemi, opened in 1979, presents changing exhibitions of modern art. Quite close to the center of Tampere, the location is at the foot of the Näsinneula Observation Tower. You can get there by taking bus 16 from the railway station. In summer, you can also take bus Y4. The museum is open daily from 11 a.m. to 7 p.m. (from May 1 to September 30, to 8 p.m.). Admission is 5 markkaa (80¢) for adults, 1 markkaa (16¢) for children and students.

The Sara Hildén Foundation was founded in 1962 by Sara Hildén who donated the works of art in her possession. Since then, the collection has been greatly expanded, concentrating mainly on postwar art, including sculptures by Henry Moore and a painting by Francis Bacon. The location of the museum in beautiful natural lakeside surroundings was used to good advantage in the layout and design of the building. Some of the sculptures are displayed on the shores of Lake Näsijärvi next to the museum.

Politically oriented visitors may want to go to the **Lenin Museum,** 19 Hallituskatu (tel. 127-313), which presents material dealing with Lenin and the history of the Russian Revolution. In addition, material is exhibited which illustrates Lenin's connection with Finland. The museum is open Tuesday to Saturday from 11 a.m. to 3 p.m., on Sunday from 11 a.m. to 4 p.m. Adults are charged 5 markkaa (80¢) and children pay 1 markkaa (16¢).

FUN FOR THE FAMILY: About a mile from the center of Tampere, the 25-acre **Särkänniemi Leisure Center** (tel. 31-333), stands on the shores of Lake Näsijärvi.

Towering over the grounds, the **Näsinneula** is an observation tower, the highest in Finland, rising 560 feet. The tower has a café and an open observation platform. The observation levels are open May through August from 10 a.m. to 8 p.m., September to April from 10 a.m. to 5:30 p.m. To take the elevator up costs 6 markkaa (96¢) for adults, 4 markkaa (64¢) for children.

Extending over two floors, the **Aquarium** has on display 2000 specimens representing nearly 200 different species. It also has a seal pool (feeding times at 11 a.m. and 4 p.m.). The Aquarium is open May to August from 10 a.m. to 8 p.m., September to April from 10 a.m. to 5:30 p.m. Admission is 10 markkaa ($1.60) for adults, 8 markkaa ($1.28) for children under 12 years of age.

In the **Planetarium,** open throughout the year, you can lean back in an armchair and follow the movements of the firmament to an expert commentary. During the show you can see the movements of 6000 stars through the skies. From May through August, performances are from 10 a.m. to 7 p.m. on the hour. From September to April, performances take place between noon and 5 p.m. Adults pay 10 markkaa ($1.60) and children are charged 8 markkaa ($1.28).

In summer only, a **Funfair** provides such entertainment as ferris wheels and merry-go-rounds. Children enjoy the rides. The amusement park charges only 4 markkaa (64¢). It is open from noon to 8 p.m. on Saturday and Sunday from April 30 to May 8. After that, until August 14, it is open daily. For the rest of August, it is open only on Saturday and Sunday.

Finally, the **Children's Zoo,** just west of the Näsinneula Tower, provides a common playground for children and animals. It is open from May 12 to August 19 daily from 11 a.m. to 7 p.m., charging 7 markkaa ($1.12) for adults, 5 markkaa (80¢) for children. No wild animals, such as tigers or lions, live in the children's zoo. There are only domestic animals, most of which are familiar to children. A pony ride or a ride in a donkey-pulled carriage is also available. Also on the grounds is the **Sara Hildén Art Museum** (see above). You can easily get to Särkänniemi by city bus 4.

In the **Delfinarium,** open daily in summer, there are five dolphins giving seven performances daily. This is the only delfinarium in Finland.

SAUNA: At the **Swimming Hall House**, 12 Pirkankatu, is an elaborate sauna and an indoor swimming pool professional enough for aquatic events. The sauna and swimming cost 24 markkaa ($3.84) for two persons, plus another 8 markkaa ($1.28) for the additional person in the private sauna. You pay extra for a scrubdown by an attendant. Every hotel in Tampere also has a sauna.

Organized Tours

From June 1 to August 31, a daily guided tour leaves at 2 p.m. in front of the City Tourist and Congress Service, Aleksis Kiven Katu 14-B (tel. 26-652), costing 25 markkaa ($4) for adults, 10 markkaa ($1.60) for children under 16. The trip lasts an hour and 15 minutes, and the commentary is given in English. As to boat tours, the two water trips, "The Poet's Way" and "The Finnish Silver Line," both start from Tampere.

THE OUTDOOR THEATER: At the **Pyynikki Summer Theater**, 11 Verkatehtaank on the edge of Lake Pyhäjärvi, about a mile from the center of Tampere (bus 12), is the first outdoor theater in the world built with a revolving auditorium. The audience of 1000 whirls around to follow the action of summer plays presented from mid-June to mid-August every night at 7 except Monday; two performances are given on weekends. Although the plays are in Finnish, a synopsis of the action is outlined in English. And for most of these action-packed plays, you don't need to know the subtleties of dialogue.

Tickets must be reserved in advance (imperative!). The cost is 55 markkaa ($8.80) per seat. For reservations, telephone 126-792.

3. Saimaa Lakeland

Saimaa, an extensive lake district in East Finland, has thousands of islands, straits, and blue water. It's a land of sunshine, small villages, holiday centers, and pleasant people, wrapped in the peace and quiet of the wilderness.

From Lappeenranta, the center of Finnish lake tourism, action-filled cruises lasting two hours or two days in the southern waters of Lake Saimaa can be booked, or you can take a cruise to the Saimaa Canal and experience the special atmosphere of the Russian border. In this region, you can swim in clean, clear water, fish with a seine, eat fish cooked on a campfire, enjoy saunas, sail, windsurf, paddle a boat, and dance.

LAPPEENRANTA: Lying 137 miles northeast of Helsinki and some ten miles from the Soviet border, Lappeenranta is one of the most important summer resort and excursion centers in East Finland. A bright, modern town, it nestles at the southern edge of large Lake Saimaa.

Once ruled by the Russians, Lappeenranta has assumed increasing importance since World War II, following the loss of great hunks of Karelia. For more than century and a half, the town has been a spa.

This historic town was founded in 1649 by Queen Christina of Sweden, a border town between two different cultures. It was fortified first by the Swedes who governed Finland as a province, then by the Russians. You meet the history of Lappeenranta in the fortress, the oldest part of the town. Here you'll find fortified walls from the 18th century, the oldest orthodox church in Finland, the South Karelian Museum, and the Cavalry Museum. There are pottery and other handicraft shops in the fortress area.

Linnoitus, the fortress of Lappeenranta, was begun by the Swedes and continued by the Russians as a link in the chain of defenses they erected. The entire chain fell into disuse after the Peace of Turku in 1812, when the part of the country known as Old Finland, including Lappeenranta, was reunited with the rest with other Finnish territory. The fortress was turned over to the town in 1835, and the defenses slowly deteriorated. However, restoration was started in 1976 and is an ongoing program.

The old orthodox church was completed as, of course, a new house of orthodox worship in 1785, but only the high and narrow nave belonged to the original building. One of the most valuable icons here is the *Communion of the Holy,* more than 200 years old. The Orthodox Church of Finland owes allegiance to the Ecumenical Patriarch of Constantinople.

The **South Karelian Museum** (Etelä Karjalan Museo) (tel. 953-518), is situated at the northern end of the fortress in the former military storehouse built early in the 19th century. The museum, founded in 1962, serves also as the town museum for Lappeenranta, which now owns it. Life in the present and the ceded (to Russia) areas of South Karelia is shown through museum displays. The textile department of this museum is worth looking at, as there are examples of traditional Karelian clothes here. The art museum connected with the South Karelian museum, occupying one of the two granite buildings joined together by a glass-covered passageway, has changing exhibits.

In summer, the museum is open from Tuesday to Friday from 10 a.m. to 6 p.m., Saturday and Sunday from 11 a.m. to 7 p.m., and it's closed Monday. In winter, hours are from 11 a.m. to 3 p.m. Tuesday to Sunday (Wednesday also from 6 to 8 p.m.) and closed Monday.

The **Cavalry Museum** is in the oldest building in Lappeenranta, the former guardhouse of Linnoitus by the town gates, built in 1772. The history of the Finnish cavalry from the *hakkapeliitat* (the cavalry in the 1618–1648 war) until modern times is followed through uniforms, guns, and objects related to horse care. The museum is open the same hours as the South Karelian Museum (above).

As noted, Lappeenranta is a lake town, the heart of Lake Saimaa and the eastern lake district. Both passenger ships and private boats sail from the harbor of Lappeenranta to the lake and down the Saimaa Canal, through which vessels pass for 26 miles to the Gulf of Finland. For a good view of the town, the lake, and surrounding islands, take the elevator to the top of the pillar-supported water tower. It's open from 9 a.m. to 9 p.m. and charges 4 markkaa (64¢) for adults, 2 markkaa (32¢) for children.

This is also a cultural town, with summer concerts held in the parks and summer theater on the fortified walls.

Don't miss the **marketplace** (see it in the morning) in the center of town. Here you can flirt with gypsies and eat boat-shaped Karelian pies.

Where to Stay

Hotel Patria, 21 Kauppakatu (tel. 11-940), is one of the leading hostelries in town, a 65-room establishment accommodating 115 guests. Opposite a well-maintained public park, the main building is a typical Scandinavian timbered structure. It has been renovated to offer solid, serviceable lodgings. The rooms in the modern motel-type wing have private baths and are particularly attractive and up-to-date. The rate in a double ranges from 350 markkaa ($56); singles go for 275 markkaa ($44). The multilevel dining room offers three square meals a day, with lunch or dinner ranging from 75 markkaa ($12). Breakfast, included in the price of the room, brings together an assemblage of international guests, many from the hammer-and-sickle countries.

Karelia Park, 1 Korpraalinkuja (tel. 15-620), is a summer hotel outside the town, near Lake Saimaa. You can take a bus from Lappeenranta. Open from

June 1 to August 31, the hotel offers 73 modern, well-equipped rooms for 150 markkaa ($24) in a single, 210 markkaa ($33.60) in a double, breakfast included. You dine in a large restaurant decorated with Finnish dragon symbols. (Lappeenranta is the home of old military traditions in Finland). The hotel has four saunas, color TV, a souvenir shop, and bicycles for hire, and there are good swimming beaches and walking paths in the neighborhood. Half and full board are available.

Hotel Lappeenranta (tel. 14-940) is a 40-room hotel built in the Holiday Inn fashion. Every one of its rooms has a private bath with shower, radio, telephone, and a splendid view over Lake Saimaa, where guest spend their leisure time—swimming, waterskiing, boating, or learning the art of windsurfing under the guidance of a competent instructor. All rooms have a view over Saimaa, and half of the units have a door leading directly out on the lawn sloping down to the shore. The rooms are pleasant, with modern furniture. A restaurant, bar, cafeteria, and saunas are on the premises. At night you can dance in the restaurant in a cheerful South Karelian spirit. In addition, the Beat Club Disco friends of music à la mode from autumn till the summer. In summer, an outdoor restaurant serves good food. Motor and rowboats are for hire. Singles rent for 255 markkaa ($40.80) to 285 markkaa ($45.60), doubles for 310 markkaa ($49.60) to 340 markkaa ($54.40). Breakfast and service are included in the tariffs.

Hotelli Hospiz, 40 Valtakatu (tel. 13-430), caters efficiently for the traveler who is here today, but gone tomorrow heading north on a Midnight Sun tour. In a commercial section of town, the hotel has no frills, but is clean and comfortable. This hotel, which welcomes summer guests from abroad, although remaining open all year, charges 280 markkaa ($44.80) in a single, the cost rising to 360 markkaa ($57.60) in a double. Breakfast is included. The hotel also serves other meals, simple fare, but good, and I've found the staff helpful, willing, and polite.

Rotelli, 23 Huhtiniemi (tel. 15-555), is one of the better youth hostels in Finland. Most of the accommodations are in four-person units; however, there are some single and double rooms available as well. The big attraction of the Rotelli is its large indoor swimming pool. Later you can enjoy the hot air of its two saunas. Guests are allowed cooking privileges in the hostel's special kitchens, and there are a number of lounges for guests. The rooms may remind you of your university lounges. Some of the furnishings are painted in a dramatic red. All is functional and uncluttered. A single person pays 125 markkaa ($20), and two persons are lodged for 160 markkaa ($25.60), breakfast included. You can also take your meals here, paying from 50 markkaa ($8) for either a lunch or dinner. The hostel lies 1½ kilometers from the town center (take bus route 22 from Market Square).

Where to Dine

Lappeenranta is known for its excellent restaurants, which range from quiet dining spots to those where you can dance. Traditional South Karelian dishes or international cuisine will be found in most eating places.

Adriano Bar, 27 Kauppakatu (tel. 13-454), rather exotic for East Finland, combines both Italian and Finnish cooking. Created by a native of Milan, Adriano Vinciguerra, and his Finnish wife, the "Bar" consists of four dining rooms, each decorated in a different theme, but all done with flair. A modern dining room contrasts sharply with the old. The street floor looks like a bodega, while a primitive Finnish log-hut theme predominates downstairs. You might try a large order of veal steak, with french fries and an Italian salad, or a plate-size authentic pizza with lots of cheese. Still cheaper is the spaghetti, a long way from Italy but you can't tell it by the taste. Meals cost from 75 markkaa ($12). The restaurant usually stays open till midnight.

Sirmakka, 36 Valtakatu (tel. 12-410). The name of this intimate dining place, on the first floor of the Lappeenranta Matkatalo, means "accordion" in Karelian dialect. It's decorated in Karelian textiles and with old musical instruments. Sirmakka specializes in Karelian cooking, such as Karjalan paisti (Karelian steak) with onions and rich sauce and Karjalan piirakat (Karelian stuffed pastries) with scrambled eggs and butter. On sunny summer days, you can watch the busy traffic in the center from the open-air balcony under tall, old oaks.

IMATRA: Already an attraction in the days of the Russian czars, Imatra is today a lively industrial and tourist city. The **Imatra Rapids,** a mighty torrent rushing through a cleft in the rock cut by the Vuoski River, became Finland's most celebrated tourist attraction in the 18th century, when Catherine the Great ruled Russia and came to see them. Foreigners thronged to the rapids, many from around St. Petersburg, and accommodations were in short supply. But a group of titled Englishmen, looking after themselves, founded a private fishing club on the Vuoski in the 19th century, on present-day Varpasaari Island in Mansikkala.

The rapids were harnessed at Imatrankoski, the power being used for a hydroelectric plant, but they are released as a tourist attraction on selected Sundays in summer.

Imatra's beautiful natural surroundings provide excellent opportunities for sports and recreation in both summer and winter. The **Imatra Leisure Centre** at Ukonniemi on Lake Saimaa offers a wide range of activities all year.

Cooperation between Finland and the Soviet Union strongly influences Imatra's economy. This city is, after all, on Finland's southeastern edge and shares a border with Russia along about a 12-mile stretch.

Besides the rapids in spate, the **Church of the Three Crosses,** designed by Alvar Aalso, is worth seeing. It was the architect's first "multipurpose church."

The **Industrial Workers House Museum** shows how living conditions have changed for Finnish workers since the turn of the century. The museum is open May 1 to August 31 from 10 a.m. to 6 p.m.; closed Monday. Admission is 3 markkaa (48¢) for adults, 1 markkaa (16¢) for children.

In **Niskalampi,** you can see restored turn-of-the-century houses of the working-class quarter.

The **Karelian Farmhouse Open-Air Museum** takes you back to a 19th-century South Karelian farm setting. It comprises 11 different buildings. Hours are 10 a.m. to 6 p.m. daily except Monday May 1 to September 15. Admission is 3 markkaa (48¢) for adults, 1 markkaa (16¢) for children.

Imatra's summer markets offer special South Karelian delights, and you'll also find interesting items for souvenirs and gifts in the city's cottage industry shops.

The **City Tourist Office,** Keskusasema (tel. 23-333), will provide you with information, arrange guides, and help you with sightseeing tours.

Where to Stay

Valtionhotelli (The Imatra State Hotel) (tel. 63-244) is an art nouveau château by the Imatra Rapids, happily combining the traditional and the modern. Guests have the use of a swimming pool and three saunas. There is dancing to live music in the large restaurant every evening. Roulette and the latest music provide entertainment in the Kosken-kellari Disco into the wee hours. The hotel is in the midst of a verdant landscape, which you can view from the window of your room or stroll through. Units rent for 280 markkaa ($44.80) in a single, 380 markkaa ($60.80) in a double.

The hotel, ordered built by the Finnish Senate at the beginning of this century, is proud of its reputation as a custodian of Finnish and Karelian gastronomic tradition. Guests can order foods whose roots can be traced back to the St. Petersburg gentry, serving such viands as *kurniekka* (whitefish baked inside rye dough), salmon prepared by a special "ice cellar" method, and meat simmered in sour cream.

The **Ukonsalem Kartanohotelli** (Ukonsalmi Manor House) (tel. 41-811) lies on the shores of Lake Saimaa with a view of the beautiful Ruokolahti Church Hill. In summer, guests can swim in the lake, go boating, or enjoy surfing, or, for the less energetic, admiring the scenery from the open terrace may be sufficient. The hotel has 22 double rooms, renting for 100 markkaa ($16) to 220 markkaa ($35.20) for single occupancy, 160 markkaa ($25.60) to 260 markkaa ($41.60) for two persons. A fully licensed restaurant offers a choice of international cuisine and traditional Karelian dishes. A specialty is a "bandit's lamb evening," when a whole lamb is slowly cooked buried under a fire. This can be enjoyed in the open-air restaurant in summer. The hotel also has a bar, two saunas, a gymnasium, tennis courts, a physiotherapy clinic, and a solarium.

Kesähotelli Mansikkala (Summer Hotel Mansikkala), 3 Rastaankatu (tel. 23-333), in the center of Imatra, has 52 double rooms which can also be used as singles or have an extra bed added to accommodate three persons. Groups of four units share a shower, toilet, and kitchenette. Singles pay 230 markkaa ($36.80), doubles 300 markkaa ($48). The hotel, open June 1 to August 15, also offers hostel accommodations, although guests must bring their own bed linen and the prices do not include breakfast. Otherwise, a light breakfast served in Restaurant Kuusenkorva next door (see below) is included in the tariffs. The restaurant also provides meals if you choose to stay here on a half- or full-board plan. The young, helpful hotel staff will act as guides if you wish. The hotel has two saunas, a café, and ample parking space.

Where to Dine

The **Restaurant Kuusenkorva,** 6 Asomäenti (tel. 21-215), offers Karelian dishes at its luncheon table daily, including jellied meat, fish prepared in a variety of ways, mushroom salad, and beet salad with herring. Fish dishes include the chef's special salmon and *rantakala* (fish stew). Meals cost from 60 markkaa ($9.60). Sample the Karelian pasties and the casseroles. The fully-licensed restaurant has dancing five nights a week.

The **Buttenhoff Café-Restaurant,** 4 Lapeentie (tel. 11-316), is a cozy place to have lunch, and the menu offers such dishes as borscht made according to grandmother's own recipe. Try also the mutton pot roast. Meals cost from 50 markkaa ($8).

SAVONLINNA: Founded in 1639 and built on islands, Savonlinna is the oldest town in East Finland. Its major attraction, the Castle of Olavinlinna (see below), dates back even before that—to 1475 when it was founded to protect what was then the eastern border of Sweden. The town slowly grew up on the islands around the castle.

The area around the town, forming part of the Saimaa waterway, has more lakes than anywhere else in Finland. Because of that stragegic location, Savonlinna has been the scene of many a battle. In fact, it once belonged to Russia, a period of captivity that lasted 70 years, until Savonlinna was returned to the Grand Duchy of Finland in 1812. In its heyday, wealthy families of what was then St. Petersburg used to come up to Savonlinna, using it as a holiday and health resort.

And so it is today, with the relatively new **Spa Hotel Casino** (tel. 22-864) attracting more tourist traffic to the area. The old spa, the one that was known to czarist Russia, was burned to the ground in 1964. Only a few czarist villas and the Wanha Kasino summer restaurant were spared. Opened in 1969, the Spa Hotel Casino (see "Where to Stay" section) offers completely modern facilities, including not only the baths but clay treatment, massage, a swimming pool, and the inevitable saunas. All in all, the "islands of the Casino" form a quiet, relaxing natural park—yet they are right in the center of Savonlinna. In good weather you can jog along the tracks, in winter ski across frozen Lake Haapavesi.

Savonlinna is about 225 miles from Helsinki.

The **Olavinlinna Castle,** a three-towered medieval fortress founded in 1475, is the major attraction, on a small island in the middle of Kyrönsalmi Straits. In 1975 Savonlinna celebrated its 500th jubilee. The castle is reached by a rotating bridge and it is open all year. Guided tours, with a commentary in English, are available.

The **Opera Festival,** traditionally held in July in Olavinlinna Castle, is an international event. The festival first took place in 1912 within the castle walls. The performers include artists of international repute, and a Finnish opera is always presented. To learn more about the festivals, including specific dates, write to the Savonlinna Opera Festival Office, 35 Olavinkatu, SF-57130 Savonlinna, Finland (tel. 22-648). Ticket prices range from 120 markkaa ($19.20) to 250 markkaa ($40).

Suruton Villa in Savonlinna, previously the summer residence of Aino Ackté, Mika Waltari, and Eino Leino, is on the Kasinonsaari island. Since its restoration, an exhibition presenting the history of the Opera Festivals is displayed there.

In addition to local concerts which are arranged in conjunction with the festivals, there are numerous other musical events here.

Two art galleries are open to the public throughout the year, the **Bellarte** and the **Ars Nova.** Also there are many summer art exhibits, including Retretti in Punkaharju.

The sculptor Niilo Lehikoinen can be seen at work in his studio at Punkaharju railway station. He produces wooden sculptures based on characters and themes from the *Kalevala*, the Finnish national epic.

In Savonlinna, you can visit the S/S *Salama* **museum ship.** Built in Vyborg in 1874, this is the only steam schooner in Finland and perhaps in the world.

The oldest house of worship is the **Little Church,** designed by Visconti in 1846. It was previously an orthodox church named St. Zachariah's and St. Elizabeth's.

You can also visit the 1851 **Riihisaari grain warehouse,** which is now used for museum displays and exhibitions.

The **marketplace** in Savonlinna is one of the most interesting in Scandinavia. It's the town's focal point in summer.

As in Venice, sightseeing in Savonlinna is done by boat. Many around-the-town cruises depart from the harbor every day. In addition to the local tours, there are cruises to Punkaharju, Puumala, Rantasalmi, Kuopio, Mikkeli, and Lappeenranta (see below).

Where to Stay

Spa Hotel Casino, Kasino Islands (tel. 22-864), described above, is accessible by walking across a bridge about 220 yards from the central railway station or driving just over half a mile. The hotel has a first-class restaurant, a spa department, saunas, a swimming pool, and 79 bedrooms, all with phones, radios, and complete baths. A double, with breakfast included, rents for 400 markkaa ($64) to 485 markkaa ($77.60).

In the town, you can stay at the **Hotel Seurahuone,** 4 Kauppatori (tel. 22-267), a 76-bed establishment which has the aura of a commercial hotel. Try to get a room overlooking the marketplace. The furnishings are modern but simple; everything is clean and fresh. Expect to pay 300 markkaa ($48) to 400 markkaa ($64) in a double room, breakfast included.

Summerhotel Malakias, 6 Pihlajavedenkuja (tel. 23-283), is the newest of the summer hotels to be built in Savonlinna. Lying less than a mile from the center of town, along Highway 14, it is perfectly suitable for a Finnish holiday. The double rooms are comfortably furnished, containing not only a shower but a small kitchenette as well. You can stock up on supplies at the marketplace, and do some of your own cooking, cutting down on food costs. They rent out 220 double rooms, going for 225 markkaa ($36) to 285 markkaa ($45.60) nightly, breakfast included. The hotel has a breakfast room, and guests often take their meals at the far more luxurious Spa Hotel Casino, which is run by the same management. It's open from June 1 to August 30.

Summerhotel Vuorilinna, Kasinonsaari (tel. 22-864), is situated in the courtyard square of the Spa Hotel Casino. You can stay right on Casino Island, within walking distance over a footbridge to the center of town, enjoying all the facilities of the larger hotel. Built in 1972, the hotel rents out 51 comfortable double rooms, at a cost of 300 markkaa ($48) to 345 markkaa ($55.20) nightly, breakfast included. All units are equipped with shower, kitchenette, phone, and wall-to-wall carpeting. The island is situated in the midst of beautiful lakeland scenery. The Wanha Kasino, next to the hotel, is a rendezvous on summer evenings.

Summerhotel Mertamalakias, 8 Otavankatu (tel. 20-685), is less than two miles from the center of town in the direction of Punkaharju. The rooms are comfortable and have small kitchenettes, which will help your food budget. Doubles—28 of them—rent for 225 markkaa ($36) to 280 markkaa ($44.80), while the 12 single rooms go for 175 markkaa ($28) to 215 markkaa ($34.40). Breakfast is included in the tariffs. The hotel is open from June 1 to August 30.

Hotel Tott, 1 Satamakatu (tel. 22-925), offers comfortable and well-furnished rooms with 102 beds. Singles are priced at 300 markkaa ($48), while doubles go for 400 markkaa ($64) to 480 markkaa ($76.80).

Another possibility worth considering is the **Hotel Kyrönsalmi,** 15 Olavinkatu (tel. 22-901), where they charge you 200 markkaa ($32) to 230 markkaa ($36.80) for a single, 230 markkaa ($36.80) to 300 markkaa ($48) for a double. All rooms have a telephone, shower, and toilet and are comfortable, the staff friendly and helpful.

Savonlinna Hospits, 20 Linnankatu (tel. 22-443). It is a clean and pleasant place, with single rooms at 185 markkaa ($29.60) to 210 markkaa ($33.60), doubles from 215 markkaa ($34.40) to 240 markkaa ($38.40), breakfast and service included. Its main attraction is a dining room overlooking the lake; when the weather is good you can dine on the balcony. The food is simple but tasty, a meal going for 45 markkaa ($7.20). After dinner you can stroll through an orchard to a nearby lake, with a swimming area. In the same building, you can stay overnight cheaply in the **Youth Hostel Hospits,** where a bed for the night costs 45 markkaa ($7.20), with linen setting you back 18 markkaa ($2.88) and breakfast going for 20 markkaa ($3.20).

Hostel Otava, 27 Talvisalonkatu (tel. 22481), is near the bus station. There are seven rooms, with a shower and toilet on each floor. Expect to pay 140 markkaa ($22.40) to 180 markkaa ($28.80) for a double room.

On the Outskirts

About 10 miles west of Savonlinna at Lehtiniemi is the **Hotel Rauhalinna** (tel. 253-119), which was built as the holiday castle villa of a czar's general toward the end of the 19th century. Now both a sightseeing attraction and a hotel, it is characterized by its lace-like carvings. Its tower commands a view over the hotel's own park grounds to the open waters of Lake Haapavesi and beyond toward Savonlinna. An avenue of linden trees, where General Nils Weckman and his wife, Alma, used to stroll, leads down to the shore. After it was restored, Rauhalinna was opened as a hotel in 1973. It can be reached by road, and sightseeing boats make the 40-minute trip here, also.

The hotel has only eight double bedrooms, renting for from 300 markkaa ($48) to 360 markkaa ($57.60), with breakfast included. For single occupancy, you'll pay from 225 markkaa ($36) to 280 markkaa ($44.80). Rooms are handsomely furnished.

Even if you don't stay here, you may want to come to dine in the first-class restaurant, which is open daily from 10 a.m. to 8 p.m.; from 11 a.m. to 6 p.m. on Sunday and Monday, serving an excellent cuisine, with an emphasis on Finnish dishes. In season, game is featured.

Where to Eat

The **Puna-Apila** (The Red Clover), 2 Tullinportinkatu (the street is a continuation of Olavinkatu, the main street; tel. 22-228), is recommended. The cafeteria is near the bus station and open from 7 a.m. to 10 p.m. Expect to spend from 25 markkaa ($4) to 50 markkaa ($8) for a meal here.

Restaurant Majakka, 11 Satamakatu (tel. 21-456), is a pleasant place near the passenger harbor. You can eat well here at moderate prices—40 markkaa ($6.40) to 50 markkaa ($8).

Steak House San Martin, 46 Olavinkatu (tel. 13-004), in the center of town, is a convenient place to lunch or dine, which you can do for 30 markkaa ($4.80) to 40 markkaa ($6.40).

You'll find good food and polite service at **Restaurant Musta Pässi,** 2 Tulliportinkatu (tel. 22-228), near the bus station. You'll pay from 30 markkaa ($4.80) to 40 markkaa ($6.40) for a meal.

Café Terezza, 44 Olavinkatu (tel. 22-941), is upstairs in the Possentornit building. You can get excellent pizza here, paying only 20 markkaa ($3.20) to 40 markkaa ($6.40).

In the front of the Norppa department store is **Café Kondik,** 19 Tulliportinkatu (tel. 24-145). It's popular with shoppers, who like to drop in for coffee or for a lunch, costing from 20 markkaa ($3.20) to 35 markkaa ($5.60).

A favorite with visitors and locals is **Restaurant Ship** *Hopeasalmi* (tel. 21-701), in front of the marketplace. Meals cost a reasonable 35 markkaa ($5.60) to 60 markkaa ($9.60).

Excursions from Savonlinna

The boats for 1½-hour cruises around the Savonlinna isles via Rauhalinna leave twice within 2 hours from 10 a.m. to 4 p.m. daily. The cruise rates are 30 markkaa ($4.80) to 40 markkaa ($6.40) for adults, 20 markkaa ($3.20) to 25 markkaa ($4) for children. It is possible to make fishing cruises at 10 a.m. and 6 p.m., as well as night-fishing cruises at midnight. The cost is 60 markkaa ($9.60) to 120 markkaa ($19.20).

There is regular boat traffic to **Punkaharju** by S/S *Heinävesi* and local cruises in Punkaharju by S/S *Punkaharju* every day.

Punkaharju is 15½ miles from Savonlinna. At this point, Lake Puruvesi is divided by a long Ice Age ridge stretching for 4½ miles. It forms a causeway between the Puruvesi and Pihlajavesi Lakes. This "thread" has been turned into a national park, one of the most famous and photographed beauty spots of Finland. You can also reach Punkaharju by bus, or by train, but the preferred method is by boat.

Passengers disembark at Punkaharju and continue by bus for local sightseeing, which includes a visit to a summer art exhibit and a look at a typical holiday village. A leisurely lunch can be taken at a restaurant in the holiday village or at Valtionhotelli, an old and historic hotel. The return trip is by train, drawn by an old steam locomotive, TK 3, formerly used to transport freight. Coach seats are typical of the era, built on wooden frames and upholstered. Carrying only 72 passengers, the train leaves Savonlinna daily at 2 p.m., arriving at Punkaharju at 4:50 p.m. The day trip operates from July 1 to August 3.

Kerimäki, 14½ miles from Savonlinna, has the biggest wooden church in the world. Built more than a century ago, and large enough to accommodate 3300 parishioners, the church is open to visitors from sunup to sundown, May to September. In addition, you can visit the **Hytermä nature reserve and museum islands,** where you'll see a large folkloric collection. The reserve is reached by boat, and Kerimäki is connected with frequent bus service to Savonlinna.

Nearby is **Putkinotko,** the setting for Joel Lehtonen's novel of the same name.

If you want to spend a leisurely day on board and see the beautiful archipelago, make a cruise to Kuopio by M/S *Heino* or M/S *Kuopio* or to Lappeenranta aboard M/S *Kristina Brahe.*

MIKKELI: The city of Mikkeli was founded in 1838. It is the capital of Mikkeli county and diocese and the main center of the southern part of the Savo province. It lies on the shore of Lake Saimaa. The surroundings of Mikkeli have seen many wars, placed as it is in the borderland between east and west, beginning with prehistoric feuding between tribes. During World War II, the headquarters of the Finnish Defense Forces were loated in Mikkeli.

The cultural history is represented by the many public sculptures of the city, old wooden houses, and a complete section of such houses, Emola, as well as the neoclassical and art nouveau buildings in the center of the city, the churches, and the collections of museums. A unique place to visit is the Visulahti Tourist Center with its three main attractions: the Wax Museum, Miniland, and the Museum Automobile Exhibition (see below).

To get a view of the city and its surroundings, go to **Naisvuori** (Women's Mountain), where a former water tower is now used as a viewing tower. It opens May 1 and closes August 31. You can get your daily exercise by climbing the 142 steps leading up to the lookout platforms and afterward reward yourself with a cup of coffee with cake or waffles at the café downstairs.

Jalkaväkimuseo (the Infantry Museum), 6–8 Jääkärinkatu (tel. 369-666), presents the development, equipment, and activities of the main branch of service of the Finnish Defense Forces, the Infantry, from 1881 until the present. In the old main guardhouse, there is a café. The museum has a postal mark of its own. It's open from May to September Tuesday to Sunday from 11 a.m. to 6 p.m.; October to April Wednesday, Saturday, and Sunday from noon to 5 p.m. Admission is 7 markkaa ($1.12) for adults, 3 markkaa (48¢) for children.

Päämajamuseo (the Headquarters Museum), 1–3 Päämajankuja (tel. 369-666), shows the Staff Common Room of the Finnish Defense Forces headquarters during the years 1939–1944. This was the office of the Marshal of Finland, C. G. E. Mannerheim, now restored to its wartime order. It is in the present Central School. It is open daily in summer. Admission is free.

Kivisakasti (the Stone Sacristy), 32a Porrassalmenkatu (tel. 366-161), is the sacristy of a wooden church of the old Mikkeli parish, probably the oldest preserved building from the Middle Ages in the entire province. The church itself was pulled down in the 18th century. In the sacristy, you can see old church artifacts, such as stocks for four offenders, the stool of repentance, a churching bench, and a beadle's stick. The sacristy is open daily May 15 to August 31 from 11 a.m. to 5 p.m. No admission is charged.

The **Suur-Savon Museum,** 11 Otavankatu (tel. 13-606), is the cultural history museum of the province of Savo, telling through its collections about the life of the gentlefolk, the bourgeoisie, and the common people of Mikkeli and Savo. It is open April to September Tuesday to Sunday from 11 a.m. to 3 p.m., and in other months from 11 a.m. to 3 p.m. Sunday and 6 to 8 p.m. Wednesday.

A cultural center for the district is the **Mikkeli Art Museum,** 5 Ristimäenkatu (tel. 366-161), which has three sections: the Martti Airio collection of works of well-known artists, bequeathed to the city; the sculpture collection of Professor Johannes Haapasalo; and exhibits which are usually changed monthly. The gallery is open Tuesday to Sunday from noon to 6 p.m., to 3 p.m. on Saturday. Entrance is free.

Visulahti Tourist Center (tel. 362). The **Wax Museum,** open daily from 9 a.m. to 9 p.m., has a gallery of Finnish personalities, as well as some foreign celebrities. Admission is 22 markkaa ($3.52) for adults, 12 markkaa ($1.92) for children. **Miniland,** open daily from 9 a.m. to 9 p.m. May to September, has small-scale models of famous buildings of Finland. Admission charges are the same as for the Wax Museum. The **Museum Automobile Exhibition** follows the history of the auto from its beginnings to the present, with actual cars, plus photos and slide shows. It's open in May daily from 11 a.m. to 6 p.m.; June to August daily from 11 a.m. to 9 p.m.; and September Saturday and Sunday from 11 a.m. to 6 p.m. Adults pay 10 markkaa ($1.60) to enter, children 5 markkaa (80¢).

Where to Stay

Hotel Cumulus, 9 Mikonkatu (tel. 369-222), part of a chain, is in the center of Mikkeli. Of its 115 rooms, doubles rent for 400 markkaa ($64) and singles for 330 markkaa ($52.80). The Cumulus has a restaurant and bar, and there is dancing on occasion.

Hotel Kaleva, 5 Hallituskatu (tel. 12-041), is a pleasant hostelry with 34 comfortable rooms, a restaurant, and a bar. A single accommodation rents for 240 markkaa ($38.40), while a double goes for 320 markkaa ($51.20).

Summerhotel Tekuila, 1 Raviradantie (tel. 366-542), is open only from May to August, but if you're in the area at that time, you'll enjoy a stay in one of the 69 pleasant rooms. It is a little over half a mile from the center of Mikkeli. Singles cost 155 markkaa ($24.80) per night, and doubles rent for 200 markkaa ($32).

Excursions

You can take cruises on Lake Saimaa on M/S *Jaarli,* lasting 2 hours, from June 16 to August 18 daily at 1 and 6 p.m., with an additional Sunday cruise at 3:30 p.m. The charge for adults is 30 markkaa ($4.80), for children 15 markkaa ($2.40). A whole-day cruise to **Anttolanhovi** takes place Monday, Wednesday, Friday, and Sunday leaving at 10 a.m. and returning at 7:30 p.m. Adults pay 95 markkaa ($15.20), children 50 markkaa ($8). A special family rate, two adults and two children, is 250 markkaa ($40). Fares include lunch in Anttolanhovi.

KUOPIO: The tourist capital of the Eastern Lake District of central Finland, Kuopio is the cultural and economic center of Savo province, the capital of old Karelia, one of Finland's most beautiful areas. Tourists flock to this old lakeside garrison town in summer to take cruises on the Saimaa steamers, some of which are rather antiquated. Overlooking beautiful Lake Kallavesi, the town is a good starting point for excursions to Savonlinna, previously recommended. There is daily service, the trip taking about 12 hours. Kuopio, incidentally, is the northernmost point served by the Saimaa lake steamers.

Dominating Kuopio is **Puijo Hill,** a wooded area lying about 1½ miles northwest of the town. In summer it is reached by a good road and in winter it is crisscrossed by ski trails. At the top of this 770-foot hill is a tower with a revolving restaurant (see below); it's best to go here just for a drink. The hill is the site of the international Puijo Winter Games.

The town center is the lively **Market Square,** called **Kauppatori** in Finnish. It contains colorful displays of fruit and vegetables. The town hall standing there dates from 1882. In the southeast sector of town, you can visit the **Orthodox Church Museum,** 1 Karjalankatu, with its collections from old Karelian churches and monasteries, unique in the west.

If you're visiting in summer, you can explore the narrow peninsula of Väinölänniemi, with its bathing beach, a summer restaurant, and playgrounds.

Where to Stay

The newly expanded **Hotel Cumulus,** 32 Asemakatu (tel. 123-555), is a handsome modern building with clean, simple, but well-furnished bedrooms. Singles rent for 300 markkaa ($48), while doubles cost 400 markkaa ($64). You'll find good food in the grill and main restaurant, and a friendly mood in the lobby bar with its late-night disco. You'll be greeted with typical Savo hospitality.

Savonia, 2 Sammakkolammentie (tel. 225-333), is a student-run hotel that offers one of the best bargains in this tourist center. Its rooms are furnished in a modern, functional style, costing from 235 markkaa ($37.60) in a single and from 300 markkaa ($48) in a double. The **Summerhotel Savonia,** open from June 1 to August 15, has cheaper prices, a single room costing 140 markkaa ($22.40), a double 180 markkaa ($28.80). Your morning swim is free. The hotel also operates a fine restaurant run by the students, who are learning the hotel trade. A recently sampled mushroom omelet was well prepared. For dinner, expect to pay around 50 markkaa ($8) to 65 markkaa ($10.40). The staff is polite and friendly, most helpful, and will give you good advice about touring in the area.

Kalla, 17 Tulliportinkatu (tel. 123-522), is adequate, right in the heart of town, just off the principal shopping street of Kuopio. Owned by a cooperative chain, it's more suited for overnight stopovers than for longer stays. Its rooms were recently renovated. The hotel has expanded in recent years, now offering 14 singles and 23 doubles. The singles rent for 200 markkaa ($32) to 235 markkaa ($37.60), the doubles for 300 markkaa ($48) to 330 markkaa ($52.80). The tariffs include a Finnish breakfast and service. The higher room rates are for units with private baths and showers, and there's a sauna on the premises.

Hospitsi NNKY, 4 Myllykatu (tel. 114-501), stands next to an old-fashioned wood-framed building, although it is built in a severe boxy modern. If you're seeking a reasonable lodging for the night, you should find it useful. Comforts are rather utilitarian ones, with singles costing 110 markkaa ($17.60), doubles going for 200 markkaa ($32). For 60 markkaa ($9.60), an extra bed will be placed in your room. The cookery is good and honest, without scaling any heights in brilliance. A Finnish breakfast costs 25 markkaa ($4), the price increasing to anywhere from 35 markkaa ($5.60) to 50 markkaa ($8) for either lunch or dinner. Incidentally, dine early, as the kitchen closes at 7 p.m.

Where to Eat

If you want to enjoy good food and an excellent view, go to **Puijon Torni** (tel. 14-841). The restaurant specializes in provincial dishes. The food is straightforward and quite adequate. The panoramic view is extraordinary, as you look out upon woodlands and a myriad of lakeland scenery. The highest platform is almost 750 feet above Lake Kallavesi. Meals here cost from 60 markkaa ($9.60) up. Torni is open from 11 a.m. to 10 p.m.

Back in town, the **Taverna,** 40–42 Kauppakatu (tel. 127-646), is much more suited to the budget. It stands on the mall, a block west of the marketplace. Sinikka Erjavaara welcomes you, presenting a menu in Finnish which will probably baffle you. If available, request an order of *kalakukko,* Kuopio's local food dish. From the province of Savo, this is a pie made from pork and a small whitefish native to Finland. Main dishes average 40 markkaa ($6.40). The helpings are extremely large, so take that into consideration when ordering.

READER'S CAMPING SELECTION: "About five kilometers south of Kuopio at **Rauhalahti** (tel. 312-244), there's a campground where cabins are also available at 180 markkaa ($28.80). These cabins sleep four, and the setting is truly beautiful" (Matti Anttila, Duncan, British Columbia, Canada).

IISALMI: This town lies in the middle of Finland, in the northern part of the Lake Saimaa system. It is the same distance, 298 miles, from Helsinki along trunk road 5 and the Arctic Circle. The railway came to Iisalmi in 1902. Many Stone Age remains have been found in this area. The name of the town is derived from the Lapp word for night, and it means "night straits," because hunters in the old days used to bed down here during their long journeys. Iisalmi received its town charter in 1891.

Runni is Iisalmi's oldest tourist attraction. A mineral spring was discovered here in the 1700s, and today in addition to the spring, there is a health spa, youth hostel, holiday home, and the special Neulatammi, a dam across the river under which one can take showers.

There are three renovated hotels in the center of Iisalmi, and in summer there is a youth hostel and a large, first-class campsite with many facilities.

Iisalmi lies at the junction of four waterways. Canoes or small motorboats can be hired at the campsite, and there are waterbus cruises from the harbor in summer, daily except Monday.

The area of Upper Savo around the town is unpolluted, and there are large wilderness areas. Even in the town, there are no large factories. There is, however, a pottery, and you'll find handicraft studios.

The **Lutheran New Church** (1934) is at the western end of the Church Park in the center of Iisalmi, and the **Orthodox Church of St. Elijah** is at the eastern end. St. Elijah's, built in 1779, is 1¼ miles north of the town center and is open to visitors on summer afternoons.

The museum of the writer **Juhani Aho** is at Mansikkaniemi in Koljonvirta (see below) and is open in summer from 11 a.m. to 3 p.m. and 4 to 8 p.m. It's open in winter from 9 a.m. to 1 p.m. and 2 to 6 p.m. except Saturday and Monday.

The **Upper Savo local museum** is on the south side of the marketplace. It has a large collection of objects connected with the area's traditions and is open all year from noon to 8 p.m.

An Upper Savo delicacy you should sample while you're here is a griddle cake cooked on the bottom of an iron pot. These crispy, lacy cakes are available at the local museum on weekends. It is also worth asking about them at the **City Tourist Office** (tel. 22-346).

The **Koljonvirta** tourist center is 2½ miles north of the center of Iisalmi. Here you'll find a large campsite with many facilities, the Juhani Aho museum with its windmill, and two monuments to the War of 1808–1809.

A traditional provincial festival is held annually at the amphitheater-like Mansikkaniemi festival ground at the beginning of August. The area also has a parish education center, a jogging track, riding stables, two nature trails, and two excellent bathing beaches.

Where to Stay

Hotel Seurahuone, 24 Savonkatu (tel. 23-501), is a hotel with 47 comfortable bedrooms. It also has three restaurants, one of which is Russian-style. For a single accommodation, you'll pay 250 markkaa ($40), 350 markkaa ($56) in a double. Breakfast is included in the rates, but if you'd like to take half board, you must add 35 markkaa ($5.60) per person to the prices quoted.

Hotel Kaupunginhotelli, 20 Savonkatu (tel. 21-831), is an inviting hostelry, with its dance restaurant, lunch restaurant, and pub. Its 28 rooms rent for 200 markkaa ($32) in a single and 290 markkaa ($46.40) in a double, with breakfast included. For an additional 30 markkaa ($4.80) per day per person, you can take half board.

Hotel Koljonvirta, 18 Savonkatu (tel. 23-511), has a pizzeria in addition to a dance restaurant and pub. It charges from 185 markkaa ($29.60) to 220 markkaa ($35.20) for a single room, 320 markkaa ($51.20) for a double, including breakfast. Half board will cost you 35 markkaa ($5.60) per person extra per day.

Health Spa Runni (tel. 48-201). Runni is Iisalmi's oldest tourist attraction, as mentioned above, and the spa hotel rents rooms for 200 markkaa ($32) in a single and 350 markkaa ($56) in a double, with breakfast included. If you wish to take half board, it will cost an extra 30 markkaa ($4.80) per person. Alcohol is not served in the restaurant of the health spa.

4. Finnish Lapland

Finnish Lapland is often called "The Last Wilderness in Europe." This is true. Above the Arctic Circle, you will experience a spacious land of unspoiled nature and scenic grandeur. One-third of Finland is Lapland, the country's northernmost as well as its largest and most sparsely populated province—one of the most diverse in all Finland.

Lapland puts on a new face four times a year, although the people sometimes talk about eight seasons a year. In the summer, the vegetation sprouts, flowers, and bears fruit all within three months. This is possible because the sun does not set for weeks on end. In Utsjoki, in the northernmost part of Lapland, starting in the middle of May, the sun does not set for nearly 70 days. If summer with its "Midnight Sun" is an extraordinary experience for the traveler, then so is the polar night, the twilight time of the year, when darkness is never really total, the sun glowing softly on the horizon. Starlight and moonlight reflect on freshly fallen snow, and an occasional dash of color is added by the Northern Lights.

Before winter, there is autumn when Lapland is painted in brilliant colors from nature's spectacular palette. All vegetation from the largest deciduous trees to the low-lying heather on the fells changes color before winter comes. Winter is the longest time of the year, but with it is the grand light show of the night, the Northern Lights. After the polar night come the dazzling spring snows, which can be used for skiing until May. The sun now gives twice as much light as it so grudgingly bestowed in the dead of winter.

Lapland is a country of great forests, making their management and agriculture the most important sources of income. Running through it is Finland's longest river, the Kemijoki, whose lower reaches are terraced with seven hydroelectric plants. Lapland also has western Europe's largest man-made lakes—Lokka and Porttipahta.

Despite man's intrusion, this is still a land of bears, wolves, eagles, and wolverines. The true natural wilderness has been preserved untouched in many nature reserves. But the animal that symbolizes this land is the reindeer, with more than 300,000 and nearly 1000 families making their living from reindeer husbandry.

It is easy to travel to the far reaches of Lapland. Regular flights go to the province's capital, Rovaniemi, and beyond the Arctic Circle to Ivalo. By bus, one can travel comfortably to every corner of the province. Lapland also offers the traveler a kaleidoscopic array of events. These include the midsummer celebrations on Ounasvaara, Asvasaksa fells, and in Posio; the Whitefish Festival in Kukkolankoski; the Cloudberry Fair and Market in Ranua; Hetta's music festival; and the increasingly popular Arctic Canoe Race from Kilpisjärvi to Tornio.

To add to the pleasure of the visitor in the north is the "Lapland à la carte" menu, which consists of all the delicacies of the province, such as grouse, reindeer, salmon, and berries.

There is a great variety of hotels, summer hotels, motels, hostels, and cabins in Lapland, the cheapest being the youth hostels. There are 22 of them in the province, with prices from 35 markkaa ($5.60) to 65 markkaa ($10.40) a night if you have your own sheets, only 30 markkaa ($4.80) to 55 markkaa ($8.80) if you have a youth hosteling organization membership card. Many youth hostels have family rooms and even single rooms. For further information, get in touch with the Finnish Youth Hostel Assocation, 39B Yrjönkatu, 00100 Helsinki (tel. 6940-377). The summer hotels have somewhat higher standards. The lodging houses *(matkustajakoti)* also have moderate prices—from 100 markkaa ($16) to 200 markkaa ($32) for a single room. There are many varieties of cabins, from high-level ones with their own saunas and kitchens to cheaper ones with just beds.

Note that the Arctic hill hotels have high- and low-season prices, the high being for March and April. Breakfast is normally included in the prices. Nearly all hotels and motels have saunas.

There is a wide range of restaurants, too, from first class to small cozy coffee bars. From 11 a.m. to 1 p.m., many restaurants serve solid lunches at low prices on weekdays. Costing from 30 markkaa ($4.80), these are usually from a buffet that consists of salads, soups, and main courses, plus desserts. In the evening, you can order from an à la carte list or ask for a set dinner—but don't forget the Lapland à la carte menu.

ROVANIEMI: When the Nazis began their infamous retreat from Lapland in 1944, they burned Rovaniemi to the ground. The gateway to Lapland and a prime rail and communications center, it was a tempting target for their scorched earth policy. But with characteristic Finnish sisu, Rovaniemi bounced back, becoming a completely modern town in the wilderness—this time to the specifications of Finland's greatest architect, Alvar Aalto.

When your plane—after a three-hour flight from Helsinki—lands in Rovaniemi, you may feel that you've been exiled to the not-so-distant wastelands of Siberia. But the illusion is quickly dispelled as the unique character of the region begins to take form.

Man and nature meet head-on in Lapland. The starkly modern contrasts dramatically with the primitive. Some see it as a romantic wilderness—land of the Midnight Sun, of the mysterious Northern Lights, of reindeer herds and Lapps—a place to find the peace and serenity lost on the main pathways of civilization. Still others view it—in the words of one American woman returning south from Ivalo—as "a place to send your enemies to." She saw only the severity and bleakness of the Arctic world. But many of Finland's best known designers and craftsmen retreat to Lapland, where they find that the isolation, especially during the exceptionally long winter, affords them an opportunity to create some of their finest work.

Chances are you'll take a bus into Rovaniemi, although a reindeer-drawn *pulkka* would be a more colorful vehicle. Lumberjacks and an occasional Lapp may be seen, but they are not typical of the thousands of progressive Finns who inhabit Rovaniemi. In the town, the Rivers Kemijoki and Ounasjoki meet. The Arctic Circle is only five miles to the north.

Regardless of the time of your arrival, you'll surely escape the heat. In July, the "hot" month, the temperature remains coolly under the 60-degree Fahrenheit mark, although you'd never know it to judge from the number of Finns jumping into the lake. But what you won't escape are the mosquitoes. From the swampy wastelands, these summer pests are a constant reminder that you're in a wilderness.

Before seeing the sights, such as the castration of a reindeer herd, we'll survey the hotel situation.

Where to Stay

Rovaniemi has a few expensive hotels and a fledgling group of less costly lodging houses. During the peak migration period in summer, reservations are strongly recommended.

Rovaniemen Ammattikoulun Kesähotelli, 73–75 Kairatie (tel. 192-651), becomes a summer hotel after its vocational students leave on vacation. The simple but comfortable rooms rent for 120 markkaa ($19.20), going up to 180 markkaa ($28.80) in a double. The place is open as a hotel from June 8 to August 5.

Rantasipi Pohjanhovi, 2 Pohjanpuistikko (tel. 313-731), is the biggest hotel in Rovaniemi (214 rooms), in the town center on the bank of the River Kemijoki. It offers a popular restaurant where you can have superb meals, saunas, swimming pool, nightly entertainment with an orchestra for dancing, and squash. The Café Ritz has a terrace facing the river. There's a hairdresser on the premises. A single room costs 370 markkaa ($59.20), with a double going for 475 markkaa ($96). All rates include a large breakfast plus a morning swim and use of the sauna.

Hotel Polar, 23 Valtakatu (tel. 23-751), lies in the town center. It has 53 cozy, nicely decorated rooms with private bathrooms. A single is priced at 330 markkaa ($52.80) and a double at 400 markkaa ($64). The hotel has a restaurant, two bars, and the only nightclub in town, the Lapponia.

City-Hotel, 9 Pekankatu (tel. 314-501), is also in the center of town. It's new with comfortable rooms and a sauna at the top of the house. A single room rents for 300 markkaa ($52.80) and a double for 400 markkaa ($64). A wine restaurant is downstairs, serving good food at low prices. Beer and wine here are probably the cheapest in town.

Hotel Ounasvaara (tel. 23-371) stands right at the top of the hill Ounasvaara. From the big windows of the hotel bedrooms, guests have a magnificent view down the hill. There are possibilities for downhill and cross-country skiing here, as well as hiking in summer. All the ski tracks are lit in winter. A single room here costs from 250 markkaa ($40) to 350 markkaa ($56), a double going for 300 markkaa ($48) to 350 markkaa ($56).

Houses that receive paying guests are the best bargains in fat-tab Rovaniemi. For the most part, these are simple buildings, sprinkled throughout the town, and, although they aren't bleak, they are lacking in luxuries and frills. Generally, they are run by a small staff (usually a family), and the rooms are neat and modern (at least post-World War II). But don't expect a private bath; most of the accommodations have water basins with hot and cold running water.

Perhaps the best of the lot is **Aakenus,** 47 Koskikatu (tel. 22-051). You can choose between two different types of rooms: bathless or with complete baths.

Singles range from 80 markkaa ($12.80) to 175 markkaa ($28), depending on the plumbing. Doubles, with the same difference, cost from 180 markkaa ($28.80) to 225 markkaa ($36). An extra bed placed in a room goes for 50 markkaa ($8). All rates include breakfast, but a sauna costs 10 markkaa ($1.60) per person.

Matkustajakoti Rovaniemi, 27 Koskikatu (tel. 22-066), is one of the finest of the private lodgings and it has been improved, with better decoration and furnishings. English-speaking Helena Kenttälä and Raija Lokio are your hostesses. Only one single is offered, costing 110 markkaa ($17.60). There are, however, five doubles ranging from 120 markkaa ($19.20) to 140 markkaa ($22.40). A continental breakfast is 20 markkaa ($3.20).

READER'S GUESTHOUSE SELECTION: "I was tired and my backpack was heavy when I was offered a room at the home of **Peter Zinke,** 21 Konkelotie (tel. 193-315). He and his wife Sara are helpful about the area and are warm, friendly people who are eager to make contact with people traveling. I felt I couldn't have done better. They rent a single with sheets for 65 markkaa ($10.40). A double with sheets goes for 125 markkaa ($20). Breakfast costs another 20 markkaa ($3.20), and lunch and a sauna are available" (Jancy Kopp, Lausanne, Switzerland).

Where to Eat

Most hotels have a lunchtime buffet from 11 a.m. to 1 p.m., which normally includes salad or soup, three main courses from which to choose, dessert, bread and butter, plus milk, buttermilk, or homemade malt drinks. The prices vary from 25 markkaa ($4) to 45 markkaa ($7.20) in smaller hotels and restaurants. You can eat as much as you wish.

Such buffets are found in Rovaniemi at the **Hotel Pohjanhovi,** the **Hotel Polar,** and the **Lapinportti.** Restaurants offering buffet lunch are **Restaurant Pinja,** 19 Valtakatu (tel. 10-272), and **Restaurant Sampo,** 32 Korkalonkatu (tel. 12-574).

Exploring

Before striking out on an expedition from Rovaniemi, visit the **Rovaniemen Seurakunta,** 1 Kirkkotie, the Evangelical Lutheran parish of Rovaniemi, which was built in 1950 to replace the church destroyed during the war. Architect Bertel Liljequist designed the church on the same spot where three other churches had stood. The interior is quite beautiful, noted for its decorations by Antti Salmenlinna (walls and ceiling), the woodcarvings by Gunnar Uotila, and, the best yet, the altar fresco *Source of Life* by Lennart Segerstrale. This fresco portrays the struggle of the conflicting powers in the hearts of people, the motifs taken from Lapland's everyday life. The church is open daily from June 1 until the end of August from 9 a.m. to 8 p.m.

In the center of town, you can visit **Lauri-Tuotteet Oy,** 25 Pohjolankatu (tel. 22-501), a log cabin built in the typical architectural style of the Peräpohjola region. Inside it shelters workshops where craftspeople turn out both modern and traditional designs in decorative articles, using as their raw materials such elements as reindeer antlers or the gnarled roots of pussy willows. In the café, decorated in a traditional farmhouse style, is a permanent sales exhibition, selling such items as curly birch products, wool and leather goods, jewelry, and Puukko knives.

Alvar Aalto designed the **Library House,** 9 Hallituskatu (tel. 2991), which has a valuable Lapland collection and may be visited from September 1 to May 31, Monday to Friday, from 11 a.m. to 8 p.m. (on Saturday from 10 a.m. to 4 p.m.) and from June 1 through August from 11 a.m. to 7 p.m., Monday to Friday (10 a.m. to 4 p.m. on Saturday).

Aalta also designed **Lappia-House,** 11 Hallituskatu (tel. 299-497), which is the theater, congress, and concert hall building of Rovaniemi. Visiting hours are June 1 to August 15, Monday to Friday, 10 a.m., 1 p.m., and 4 p.m.

In the same building is the **Lapland Provincial Museum** (tel. 299-483), which has some Lapland exhibits. It is open daily June 1 to August 31 from 10 a.m. to 7 p.m., from 3 to 7 p.m. Monday. In May, it is open daily except Monday from 10 a.m. to 6 p.m. September 1 to April 30, it is open daily except Monday from noon to 4 p.m. Admission is 2 markkaa (32¢).

At the city tourist office, 2 Aallonkatu (tel. 16-270), you can book **river cruises,** at a cost of 30 markkaa ($4.80). Lasting 1½ hours, the tour leaves from City Pier from mid-June to mid-August at 4 p.m. and 6 p.m. daily. On Saturday and Sunday, departures are at noon and again at 8 p.m.

On the outskirts, **Raanupirtti** (tel. 88-014) lies 12 miles from Rovaniemi. It exhibits and sells hand-woven textiles in a restored log house, hewn with an ax at the beginning of the 18th century. The location is in the village of Oikarainen, to the esat of Ravaniemi on the Kemi River and the road to Kuusamo. It is open from June through August, Monday to Friday, from 9 a.m. to 6 p.m. (on Saturday and Sunday from 10 a.m. to 6 p.m.). Admission is 4 markkaa (64¢).

Tours to the Arctic Circle

If you don't have a car, the easiest way to go to the **Arctic Circle** is to take one of the sightseeing buses that depart from near the Lapland Travel Bureau, 2 Pohjanpuistikko. Tours cost 45 markkaa ($7.20) per person, and they leave daily except Monday at 1 p.m. from June 17 to August 19.

You can ask about arranged sightseeing tours of the area at the City Tourist Office, 2 Aallonkatu (tel. 16-270), open in summer from 8 a.m. to 7 p.m.

On the Arctic Circle, you can buy a certificate to prove that you have been there. The county's most noteworthy site is the Arctic Circle Lodge, where almost all visitors stop. If you mail your postcards there, they'll have a special Arctic Circle postmark on them. There is also a workshop and café. In summer, behind the cabin, a reindeer family grazes.

KEMI: The mouth of the Kemijoki River is one of the oldest areas of habitation in Finland. The people harvested such a great stock of fish from the mouth of the river that by the 1300s, the fish catch was already attracting far-off merchants. Kemi, with a population of about 28,000, is the center of the province's wood-processing industry. Its two harbors function as Lapland's ports to the rest of the world. The city has substantial plans for the harbor expansion.

The finest view of Kemi is from the roof of the city hall. In the same building, there is also an art museum. Near here, Finland's largest river was blocked off in 1947 by the Isohaara hydro-electric plant.

Where to Stay

Kemi has a few expensive hotels and many less costly small hotels, lodging houses, and a summer hotel.

Hotel Cumulus, 3 Hahtisaarenkatu (tel. 20-931), is a new, modern hostelry with a popular dance restaurant. Single rooms rent for 330 markkaa ($52.80) and doubles for 420 markkaa ($67.20).

Hotel Palomies, 12 Valtakatu (tel. 23-322), is a family-run small hotel with good, clean rooms. They charge 220 markkaa ($35.20) in a single unit, 275 markkaa ($44) in a double accommodation.

Matkustajakoti Turisti, 39 Valtakatu (tel. 21-410). Recently renovated, this is one of the best of the lodging houses. Rentals are 120 markkaa ($19.20) in a single, going up to 175 markkaa ($28) in a double room.

Kesähotelli Relletti, 1 Miilukatu (tel. 20-941), is a student hotel operating from June 6 to August 15 as a summer hotel. The basic but adequate rooms rent for 130 markkaa ($20.80) in a single, 180 markkaa ($28.20) in a double.

Where to Eat

Restaurant Samaani, 6 Nahkurinkatu (tel. 15421), serves Lapland delicacies at moderate prices. A meal will cost you from 50 markkaa ($8). The restaurant is open weekdays from 10 a.m. to 8 p.m.

Täti Emilia, 7–9 Valtakatu (tel. 15-192), is a fully licensed restaurant where you can enjoy such specialties as reindeer chops. Expect to pay from 50 markkaa ($8) for a complete meal. It's open from 10:30 a.m. to midnight.

Don't miss Finnish pastry shops where you can have a cup of good coffee and a luscious pastry. The shop in Kemi is **Konditoria Miorita,** 3 Valtakatu (tel. 16-811). Light fare will cost you from 35 markkaa ($5.60). The establishment is open from 9 a.m. to 6 p.m. on weekdays, from 9 a.m. to 4 p.m. Saturday and Sunday.

TORNIO: Founded in 1621 on Suensaari Island, Tornio was Swedish Finland's most northern town at that time. It was an important seaport 200 years ago, and its main industry was shipbuilding. The town's industries today include a steel refinery, textile plants, and the province's oldest enterprise, a brewery.

The most noteworthy sight is the wooden church built in the 1600s. It is one of the country's oldest ornamentally carved wooden houses of worship. A short distance away are the rapids of Kukkolankoski and Matkakoski, which have been preserved from being used for power generation.

The Finnish–Swedish border is known as the world's most peaceful boundary line. It's crossed by millions of people annually.

Where to Stay

There are two hotels in Tornio. One is the **Kaupunginhotelli,** celebrated for its splendid collection of famous Finnish artists which it allows visitors to admire from everywhere in the hotel. Its address is 4 Itaranta (tel. 42-921). Single rooms are priced at 200 markkaa ($32) to 375 markkaa ($52), while doubles rent for 220 markkaa ($35.20) to 360 markkaa ($57.60).

The other hotel, the **Tornio,** 11 Keskikatu (tel. 42-401), is a small, cozy, new hostelry with a pleasant dance restaurant. It charges the same prices as the Kaupunginhotelli.

Matkakoti Heta, 39 Saarenpäänkatu, is the best of the lodging houses in Tornio. You can occupy a single room for 95 markkaa ($15.20). Doubles cost 150 markkaa ($24).

Where to Eat

Kahvila Siltapuisto, 15 Hallituskatu, is a convenient café where they serve simple lunches costing from 45 markkaa ($7.20).

Lämpimäinen Coffee Bar and Grill, 6 Hallituskatu, serves good food at low prices, meals costing from 35 markkaa ($5.60) up.

Exploring

You can visit a pottery workshop, **Iso-Pahkala,** 1¼ miles from Tornio toward Kemi. It has a café and a display room. Hours are from 10 a.m. to 8 p.m. June 1 to September 16 daily. From September 16 to May 31, it's open from 10 a.m. to 6 p.m. Monday to Saturday. The water tower café is open from 9 a.m. to 9 p.m. June 1 to August 15.

Lapland Shop, 2½ miles toward Kemi, sells Lappish souvenirs. There's a café here also.

YLITORNIO: This town is best known for the Aavasaksa fell, on whose slopes the midsummer festivals have been held for decades. Fast-flowing rivers and broad lakes enliven the district. Aavasaksa is a large tourist center with lit ski trails, skiing-instruction schools, and downhill slopes. Alexander II, czar of Russia, built a log hunting lodge, complete with priceless paintings, on the slopes of Aavasaksa in 1882.

Where to Stay

Ylitornio is a large district with two centers: Ulitornio village and Aavasaksa village. In Ylitornio, there is the **Hotel Kievari** (tel. 31-201), which rents out 36 good beds in a total of 14 rooms. This small hotel charges 180 markkaa ($28.80) in a single, 200 markkaa ($32) in a double, with breakfast included. Lunch or dinner is from 45 markkaa ($7.20).

In Aavasaksa, there is the **Hotel Rajahovi** (tel. 38-171), which is slightly larger, with 22 comfortable bedrooms that rent for 220 markkaa ($35.20) in a single and 400 markkaa ($48) in a double, breakfast included. Meals here cost from 45 markkaa ($7.20) up.

Heikki Niemi, 95610 Kainuunkylä (tel. 34-146), is a typical farmhouse with moderate prices, a few miles south of Ylitornio. They charge from 135 markkaa ($21.60) per person per night. You can stay here longer, have full board, and take part in the working life of the farm if you're interested in how farm life is carried on in Finnish Lapland.

ENONTEKIÖ: The grouse pictured on the coat-of-arms of Enontekiö country symbolizes not only the nature of Lapland but the trapping industry. Grouse is caught here and sold all over the country. The Kilpisjärvi area has the highest point in Finland, the Halti fell, which is 4356 feet. More than 40 peaks are more than 3000 feet high. The county's main sources of income are natural, such as reindeer husbandry, fishing, hunting, and berry gathering.

For the visitor, there are backpacking and ski trails, the Hetta music festival at Easter, and the Laplanders' colorful church festival, Lady Day (March 24), complete with reindeer competitions.

A point where the borders of Finland, Sweden, and Norway meet is the Malla nature reserve near Kilpisjärvi.

Where to Stay

Enontekiö is a large district with three villages, the most northern of which is Kilpisjärvi in the foot of Saana Arctic hill. The hotel there is called **Kilpisjärvi Tourist Hotel** (tel. 77-761). Singles cost 220 markkaa ($35.20), doubles 330 markkaa ($52.80) at the high season.

Kilpisjärvi Tourist Center (tel. 77-771), rents bathless rooms for from 95 markkaa ($15.20). This is basic living.

There is another village, Karesuvanto, where the **Hotel Ratkin** (tel. 52-101) rents 26 simple rooms, costing 200 markkaa ($32) in a single, 285 markkaa ($45.60) in a double. Breakfast is included, and other meals cost from 65 markkaa ($10.40).

At the village of Hetta, the new **Hotel Hetta** (tel. 51-361) welcomes you. Singles are priced at from 220 markkaa ($35.20) and doubles go for 300 markkaa ($48). It attracts adventurous types.

RANUA: This is a thriving county of agricultural and forest production and service industries. The county has many beautiful rivers and lakes. The Simojoki River is presently being stocked for salmon fishing. In August, Ranua holds the Lapland golden berry festival, the Cloudberry Fair and Market.

A popular tourist attraction is the **Ranua Wildlife Park,** open from 10 a.m. to 4 p.m.; in September and May from 8 a.m. to 6 p.m.; and in June, July, and August from 8 a.m. to 8 p.m. Admission is 20 markkaa ($3.20) for adults, 10 markkaa ($1.60) for children.

SODANKYLÄ: Many say that the *real* Lapland begins at Sodankylä. Rovaniemi, they aver, is only the gateway. On highway 4 going north, the fell country begins here. Toward the south rises the Luosto fell, and in the north behind the manmade lakes of Lokka and Porttipahta is the well-known Saariselkä area with its grand fell district.

The best sights are the Tankavaara gold washings (see below) and museum and the Finnish and World Goldpanning Championships in summer. The wooden church, built in 1689, is the oldest in Lapland. Porttikoski's logging games are an important summer event. The winter sports center on Luosto fell is one of Santa Claus's workshops in Lapland.

Where to Stay

In the village of Sodankylä, **Hotel Kantakievari** (tel. 11-926) rents single rooms for 270 markkaa ($43.20) to 290 markkaa ($46.40) and doubles for 380 markkaa ($60.80) to 400 markkaa ($64). Lunches here cost 65 markkaa ($10.40).

Pohjan Iirtti, 19 Ojennusti (tel. 11-216), and **Komulainen,** 6 Sompiontie (tel. 11-030) are lodging houses with the same low prices: 100 markkaa ($16) in a single, 140 markkaa ($22.40) in a double.

In the Luosto hill area, there is a hotel, **Kanatakievari Luosto** (tel. 44-214), which is a big pinetree building, the biggest such structure in Scandinavia. It's decorated in a personal Lappish style. A double room costs 330 ($52.80). Special Lapp delicacies are served in the dining room, where a dinner will cost you 65 markkaa ($10.40).

Where to Eat

Restaurant Revontuli (Northern Lights) serves a lunch buffet for 30 markkaa ($4.80).

Restaurant Poronsarvi (Reindeer Antler) also lets you select your lunch from a buffet spread. It costs 30 markkaa ($4.80).

Can you imagine a pizza with smoked reindeer meat on it? That taste treat is yours if you try the **Pizzeria Porosso** in the Sokos department store building.

Excursion to Tankavaara

About 62 miles from the village of Sodankyla to the north is **Tankavaara Gold Village** (tel. 46-158), where you can try your luck at finding the precious metal. For 100 markkaa ($16), you can wash gold for a whole day, getting an introduction to gold panning and a pan for your own use. The price includes a place for a tent at the camping site. If you just want to try gold washing for a little while, you can take a course and get a pan for 25 markkaa ($4). Here the gold museum portrays the life of gold panners in Finnish Lapland. Admission to the museum is 8 markkaa ($1.28).

Don't miss the **Old Gold-Diggers Café,** where you can have Prospector's Steak served from a gold pan for 50 markkaa ($8). The meal includes a giant reindeer steak, pea stew, and mashed potatoes, plus a salad.

Cabins here cost 150 markkaa ($24) to 240 markkaa ($38.40). They can accommodate two to four persons. Cabins with private baths cost 240 markkaa ($38.40) to 340 markkaa ($54.40).

INARI: Finland's largest county in area is Inari, whose most remarkable feature is the large, clear lake which is about 50 miles long. More than 3000 islands dot the lake. You can take a waterbus to the ancient sacrificial island of Ukko, among others.

The Saariselkä resort area, Finland's largest, has seven downhill ski runs, three lifts, marked ski trails, and hiking paths complete with wilderness huts.

Some sights to see are the Ivalo River gold fields with buildings and equipment. This was the site of Finland's first gold strike. You can also see the wilderness church of Pielpajärvi, built in the 1700s, and the Lapp museum. In March, Reindeer King Races are held in Inari.

Where to Stay

Inari district is known among Finnish holiday-makers. Here you can find accommodations ranging from new, modern hotels to remote cabins.

In the village of Ivalo, **Hotel Ivalo** (tel. 11-911) is the newest in the area. It charges 330 markkaa ($52.80) in a single, 400 markkaa ($64) in a double.

Matkakoti Juiri (tel. 11-106) is a lodging house which rents single rooms for 180 markkaa ($28.80) and doubles for 220 markkaa ($35.20).

In Saariselkä hill area, there are hotels and holiday villages. **Hotel Riekonkieppi** offers a single room for 260 markkaa ($41.60) to 300 markkaa ($48), doubles for 330 markkaa ($52.80) to 500 markkaa ($80).

Where to Eat

All the hotels mentioned above have restaurants where special Lappish food is served.

Restaurant Kultahippu, 2 Rantatie (tel. 11-312), serves excellent food at moderate prices. Braised reindeer meat with lingonberries and mashed potatoes, a typical Lappish meal, costs 55 markkaa ($8.80). Morel soup with toast is offered for 35 markkaa ($5.60).

UTSJOKI: The lifeblood of this area is the Tenojoki Valley, said to be Finland's most beautiful. Through the fell highlands from the south, the motorist drops suddenly into the valley where the fells are massive and vegetation scarce. The repaved road from Kargasniemi to Utsjoki makes travel easier.

This is Finland's northernmost county and the only one whose population has a majority of Lapps, 70%.

Don't fail to see the Kevo canyon, and the Teno Valley rapids. Becoming more popular each year is the Finland Runs, an international jogging event which begins in Utsjoki and ends a week later in Helsinki.

Where to Stay

Utsjoki Tourist Hotel (tel. 71-121), rents singles for 165 markkaa ($26.40) to 185 markkaa ($29.60), doubles for 185 markkaa ($29.60) to 230 markkaa ($36.80). You'll find good, basic living here.

POSIO: Posio is Lapland's richest waterways county. The Kitka has the clearest water of all the large lakes in Europe. Livojarvi Lake has a "tropical" sandy beach, and Hietajarvi Lake, with its beaches, has been called one of the wonders of Lapland. The county's best known and internationally acclaimed business is Pentik, which makes ceramics and leathergoods.

SALLA: Salla was razed to the ground, much like Rovaniemi, during World War II. Of historical significance are a large line of tank traps built from blocks of stone, called the Salpa Front, which goes right through this parish village. The tourist trade is increasing rapidly in Salla.

Where to Stay

Motel Takka-Valkea (tel. 31-801) provides comfort in a forlorn world. A double room costs 280 markkaa ($44.80) to 340 markkaa ($54.40).

About six miles from Salla in the direction of the Russian border is hill area Sallatunturi. Here you'll find a hotel and two holiday villages. **Hotel Revontuli** (tel. 31-161) has a special front wall that reminds you of the Northern Lights, especially after dark when the lights move along the wall. A single costs 160 markkaa ($25.60) to 280 markkaa ($44.80), a double going for 220 markkaa ($35.20) to 330 markkaa ($52.80).

KEMIJÄRVI: This is Finland's largest city in the area. It is also the country's northernmost city. The Suomu fell tourist center here is open all year, and it's claimed to have the best downhill slopes in the country. Pelkosenniemi's Pyhätunturi tourist center is also within driving distance.

Where to Stay

In the town center is **Hotel Mestarin Kievari,** a family-run hostelry, where a single room costs 110 markkaa ($17.60) to 180 markkaa ($28.80) and a double 220 markkaa ($35.20) to 300 markkaa ($48).

Hotel Koilliskunta (tel. 11-841), charges 320 markkaa ($51.20) for a single, 380 markkaa ($60.80) for a double.

In the Suomutunturi hill area is **Hotel Suommu** (tel. 12-951). The Arctic Circle crosses the hotel just in the middle of the dining room. A single here costs 220 markkaa ($35.20) to 280 markkaa ($44.80), a double going for 280 markkaa ($44.80) to 360 markkaa ($57.60).

Chapter XX

ICELAND

THIS SAGA ISLAND in the middle of the North Atlantic is the western-most outpost of Europe.

The country is exotic, having the fascination of the strangely beautiful and unfamiliar. Iceland is a land of stark beauty and amazing contrasts. Primeval earth-mother fire and the red lava of brooding black volcanoes contrast with the freezing white ice-glare of Europe's greatest glaciers.

The untamed forces of nature overwhelm you in Iceland. Scenic waterfalls, the greatest in Europe, create gossamer rainbows. The ground is often riddled with boiling, seething mud holes, occasionally bursting into a sprouting spring. It's "moon country" as well. U.S. astronauts, including Neil Armstrong, have trained here.

Lava cliffs, fertile valleys, rustic farms, coastal fishing villages, lakes, streams, and crystal-clear rivers—ecology is balanced here. Factories operate on abundant hydro-electric power. There is no air pollution.

The country is not covered with ice or snow, as its name suggests. (Iceland would have better described Greenland.) Although located just below the Arctic Circle, it is bathed by the Gulf Stream.

Settled by Norwegians and some Celts from the British Isles in the ninth and tenth centuries, Iceland today is inhabited by more than 225,000 people. The sheep outnumber the people almost five to one. The flocks roam the grasslands freely and are rounded up twice yearly for culling and shearing.

The people are poetic and cultured. "Better shoeless than bookless" is a national motto. More books are published and read, and there are more book-stores per capita than in any other country on earth.

In this Ohio-size island of some 40,000 square miles, everybody is equal, whether fisher folk or president. It is one of the most democratic countries in the world.

The Icelandic language is the oldest unchanged spoken language. Ice-landers today can read the Sagas and Eddas written 800 or 900 years ago. These saga writers told dark and dramatic tales of the early days of Ice-

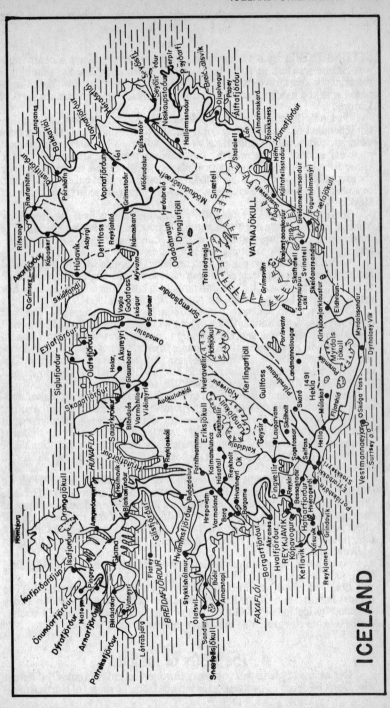

land–grim epics of a grim people in a grim world where to be weak was to be dead.

GETTING THERE: By air is the quickest, easiest way. Iceland is nearly midway on the shortest air route between New York and Moscow, requiring a refreshingly short, five-hour flight from JFK airport in New York, compared with the much longer time required for reaching more distant parts of Europe.

Iceland's international airline is **Icelandair,** which is the only airline offering scheduled service into the country from North America. It also operates domestic routes within Iceland, as well as routings to Luxembourg (the most popular), London, Glasgow, five other Scandinavian cities, Greenland, and the Faroe Islands. From North America, passage to all of these destinations, with the exception of some of the flights to Luxembourg, requires either a touchdown or a change of planes at Keflavík airport, a 45-minute drive from the center of Reykjavík.

Icelandair operates stretch DC-8s and some 727s on its flights from New York, Chicago, Baltimore/Washington, Detroit, and Orlando, Florida. The most popular departure point is New York, from which flights leave every evening in summer and four times a week in winter.

Icelandair has always prided itself on being the airline with the highest load factor of any transatlantic carrier, filling more seats in its single-class planes than almost any other airline. It has been a pioneer in low-budget flights since the first crush of tourists began crossing the Atlantic in the early 1960s.

Today, fares to Iceland are divided into high and low seasons. The least expensive fare is the Super APEX, which requires a stay abroad of between 7 and 60 days, with an advance reservation and payment of between 7 and 14 days, depending on the season. In summer, this fare (as of this writing and subject to change) is $575 round trip from New York to Iceland and $629 from Chicago. In winter, round-trip fares cost $379 and $419 from New York to Iceland (depending on the day of the week) and $529 from Chicago.

Even if your final destination is mainland Europe, Icelandair makes stopovers in its own country easy and inexpensive. If you decide to add another country to your list of the places you've visited, the airline will arrange several drastically discounted rates on hotels, transfers from the airport, sightseeing tours, rental cars, and shopping purchases. A stopover, including all of the extra listed above, costs $37 for 24 hours, $62 for 48 hours, and $87 for 72 hours.

In addition, the airline offers a variety of tours through the richly scenic countryside, ranging in length from five days to three or more weeks. (In fact, the most popular tour sold is one of the most expensive, encompassing most of the rugged southwest section of Iceland in 15 days.) An experienced guide will direct you to many of the island's fjords, waterfalls, geysers, and bubbling mud pits, taking in the unusual scenery in amounts that will satisfy even the most addicted outdoors person.

For toll-free reservations and information throughout the United States, call 1/800/223-5500. New York City residents call 757-8585.

Once in Iceland, the airplane is still the best method of transportation. The country has no railway lines. Rather, there is an extensive domestic air network operated by Icelandair to all the main centers of the population. Of course, motor coaches run to all inhabited areas in summer as well.

1. The ABCs of Iceland

Regardless of where you've been in Europe, Iceland is an entirely different trip. Don't be deceived by the short plane ride from the shores of North America or Europe. You've entered an entirely different world when you step onto the soil of Iceland.

AIRPORT: You'll arrive at **Keflavík International Airport** outside Reykjavík. A section at this airport is unique, with a tax- and duty-free shop which is open to *arriving* passengers, who may buy liquor, tobacco, and chocolates. The airport has a large and well-stocked tax- and duty-free shop open to both in-transit and departing passengers. The bus ride into town takes about 45 minutes and costs 90 krónur ($2.70).

ALCOHOLIC BEVERAGES: The sale of alcohol is a state monopoly, and you can purchase liquor only in specially designated state stores. Surprisingly, when you venture outside the main towns of Akureyri and Reykjavík, you'll find few hotels licensed to sell alcoholic beverages.

Drinks are moderately priced in Iceland. A shot of whisky is likely to begin at 65 krónur ($1.95) and go up.

Around the time of American Prohibition, Icelandic legislators prohibited the sale of beer containing alcohol because, in theory, the country's productivity was suffering from the effects of daytime beer consumption. Since then, the inventive Icelanders have taken the case to court several times, always to no avail. However, since most other kinds of alcoholic beverages are permitted, someone invented the method of adding the clear tasteless liquid which is distilled from Icelandic berries to the alcohol-free beer, giving it a potency unmatched by the original brew. The additive is called *Klára vin,* and occasionally, just to give the new "cocktail" an added boost, a bartender will add a splash of Glenfiddich scotch. The process, in effect, is one whereby beer is first de-alcoholized and then re-alcoholized in a legal attempt to bypass an existing law. Take note that the process is legal unless you're drunk while driving. Both the percentage of alcohol that determines drunkenness and the penalties are strict.

If you want "real" unadulterated beer, several flavorful varieties are made in Iceland, although they're sold only in duty-free shops to passengers exiting from aircraft, before they pass through Customs. They may buy an absolute maximum of 12 bottles.

AMERICAN EXPRESS: You'll find an office at Keflavík International Airport (tel. 24323). In Reykjavík, the representative is Útsýn travel agency, 17 Austurstraeti (tel. 20100).

BANKS: For exchanging money, I'd recommend the **Landsbanki Islands,** the national bank of Iceland, at 11 Austurstraeti (tel. 17780) in Reykjavík. Most banks are open Monday to Friday from 9:15 a.m. to 4 p.m. (also on Thursday from 5 to 6 p.m.).

BUSES: The Bus Lines Association of Iceland issues an **Omnibus Passport** and a **Circle Passport,** offering foreign visitors expanded motorcoach travel at a savings. The tickets are valid for use all year.

The Omnibus Passport, or ticket, gives visitors unlimited travel by coach on any and all bus lines in Iceland, within a specified time limit. The tickets are sold in four categories—one week duration at $112 (U.S.), two weeks at $150, three weeks at $180, and four weeks at $208.

It's so easy to use. Just buy your "passport" at most major travel bureaus or

BSI Travel, Umferdarmidstödinni in Reykjavík (tel. 22300). Then board a coach, present the passport to your driver, and sign. You can get off wherever you like, and whenever you like. You can start or stop whenever your fancy chooses. Icelandic coach drivers stop anywhere by request, and they'll give you all the advice you want about local conditions and other scheduled services.

The Full-Circle Passport allows the holder of the ticket to take a circular route around all of Iceland—either clockwise or counterclockwise, with no restrictions as to time for use. Travelers can make unlimited stops en route and stopovers can be for any length of time. Detours, however, off the main route will cost extra. The price for the Full-Circle route ticket is only $102 (U.S.). Children aged 4 to 8 pay half of the normal fare for these passes, and children 9 to 12 are charged three-quarters of the regular fare.

For further information, get in touch with the **Iceland Tourist Board,** 655 Third Ave., New York, NY 10017 (tel. 1/212/949-2333).

If you're touring the country, most buses depart from the main bus station near the airport outside Reykjavík. It's called **Hringbraut** (tel. 22300), and once there, you'll find an English-speaking staff who can provide data about tours available and give you times and schedules.

For information about the municipal bus service inside Reykjavík, call 22180.

BUSINESS HOURS: Shops are open weekdays from 9 a.m. to 6 p.m., on Saturday from 9 or 10 a.m. to noon. Many shops, however, close completely on the weekends. Most business offices are open only from 9 a.m. to 5 p.m. Monday to Friday, shutting down completely for the weekend.

CAR RENTALS: This is an expensive method of transport, especially for readers of this budget guide. It's best to shop around as prices fluctuate widely, and will probably change several times during the lifetime of this edition. To make matters worse, a 23.5% sales tax is added, not to mention the cost of your fuel.

A reliable agency in Reykjavík is **Inter-Rent,** 9 Skeifan (tel. 86915). Their cars, at least as of this writing, begin at $29 per day for a V.W., plus 29¢ per kilometer. Four-wheel-drive vehicles are also rented.

CHURCHES: The state church of Iceland is the Evangelical Lutheran church. Its main church in Reykjavík is **Dómkirkjan** at Austurvöllur Square, near the Alt-hing. Roman Catholics worship at **Krists Konungs Kirkja,** at Landakot in Túngata, near the heart of town (dial 13042 for information about services).

CLIMATE: Iceland's climate is very much affected by the Gulf Stream. The climate is mild, often rainy. Iceland's midwinter temperatures average higher than Boston, New York, or Chicago. January, the coldest month, averages 30 degrees Fahrenheit. Summer tends to be short, however, and that season usually isn't hot, the temperature rarely going beyond the 65 degree Fahrenheit mark. If you, like most visitors, come during midsummer, expect temperatures of 50 to 54 degrees Fahrenheit in the populated lowlands, and dress accordingly.

The best time of the year for touring Iceland is from mid-June until early

September. But a visit in spring or autumn can be rewarding for the hearty and adventurous. From the end of May until the beginning of August, there is perpetual daylight for 24 hours. In Reykjavík only two hours separate sunset from sunrise, and in the northern part of the country the sun hardly sets at all.

CLOTHING: Your clothing for touring Iceland by coach or car in summer should include lightweight woolens, a sweater or cardigan, rainproof coat, and sturdy shoes. As there are ample opportunities for swimming in water from the warm springs, bathing attire should be brought along at any time of the year.

CURRENCY: The Icelandic monetary unit is the króna, equal to 100 aurar. Coins are 5 krónur, 1 króna, and 50, 10, and 5 aurar. Banknotes are 10, 50, 100, and 500 krónur.

On January 1, 1981, the Icelandic currency was changed. Under new regulations, 1 new króna equals 100 old krónur. New banknotes and coins were introduced at that time. Old banknotes and coins were exchanged only until the end of 1982.

As of this writing, $1 U.S. is exchanged for 32.57 krónur.

Krónur	U.S.$	Krónur	U.S.$
0.25	$.01	60	$1.80
0.50	.02	70	2.10
1	.03	80	2.40
5	.15	90	2.70
10	.30	100	3.00
15	.45	125	3.75
20	.60	150	4.50
25	.75	175	5.25
30	.90	200	6.00
35	1.05	250	7.50
40	1.20	300	9.00
45	1.35	400	12.00
50	1.50	500	15.00
55	1.65	750	22.50

CUSTOMS: Tourists can bring into Iceland tax and duty free one liter of wine or other drinks (up to 21% alcohol), or 12 bottles of beer, plus one liter of liquor (up to 45% alcohol), and 200 cigarettes or the equivalent of other tobacco products.

It is permitted to bring up to 700 krónur into the country in banknotes of no higher denomination than 100 krónur. Travelers, however, are allowed to bring in any amount of foreign currency, which is easily cashed into krónur in Icelandic banks.

DOCTORS: In case of an emergency, such as first aid, go to **Borgarspítalinn** (tel. 81200), the city hospital in the suburb of Fossvogur in Reykjavík. The emergency room is open 24 hours a day, and doctors are always on duty there.

DOCUMENTS FOR ENTRY: A valid passport is all an American, French, Canadian, or British citizen needs to enter Iceland.

ELECTRICAL APPLIANCES: Like most European countries, the voltage is 220, the current alternating (A.C.) at 50 cycles. Adapters are needed to fit sockets. It's best to ask at your hotel before plugging in any electrical appliances.

EMBASSIES: Hopefully, you'll not need such services. But in case of a lost passport or some such emergency, the following addresses, all in Reykjavík, may prove useful. The **U.S. Embassy** is at 21 Laufásvegur (tel. 29100), and the **British Embassy** is at 49 Laufásvegur (tel. 15883). There is no Canadian embassy, but the Canadian Consulate General is at 20 Skulagata (tel. 25355).

EMERGENCY: To call an ambulance or report a fire, dial 11100. Summon the police at 11166; first aid, 81212.

FILM: It's lethal in price. Bring in what you think you'll need. Otherwise, the biggest photo store in the center of Reykjavík is **Hans Petersen,** 4 Bankastraeti (tel. 20313), which sells film and accessories (many well-known brands such as Kodak). Photo processing is very slow, I've found, so it's best to wait until you return home. In general, it's wise to use slow films in the summer months.

GAS: "Petrol" is sold by the liter in Iceland. Gasoline prices fluctuate, and are always expensive if you're driving around the country in the usual vehicle, say, a Land Rover or minibus, make sure you always inquire as to how far the next gasoline filling station is. In general, they are fairly close to one another in the inhabited areas. Shell, BP, and Exxon seem to have a monopoly. But, remember, there are vast *uninhabited* areas in Iceland.

GOVERNMENT: Although the nation has Europe's oldest parliament, founded in A.D. 930, it is Europe's youngest republic, established on June 17, 1944, in the final months of World War II. Iceland broke from its long domination by Denmark, then under Nazi rule.

HOLIDAYS: The main holidays are January 1 (New Year's Day), Maundy Thursday (Thursday before Easter), Good Friday, Easter Sunday, Easter Monday, first day of summer (date varies), May 1 (Labor Day), Ascension Day (date varies), Whitsunday (date varies), June 17 (National Day), Bank Holiday (first Monday in August), Christmas Eve (from midday on December 24), Christmas (December 25), and Boxing Day (December 26). Everything closes at midday on December 31 to begin the New Year's Eve celebration.

INFORMATION: Before you go, call on the **Iceland Tourist Board,** 655 Third Ave., New York, NY 10017 (tel. 1/212/582-2802). The **Iceland Tourist Board** in Reykjavík is at 3 Laugavegur (tel. 27488).

LANGUAGE: Everybody, seemingly, speaks English. Of course, as mentioned, the native tongue is Icelandic, which is one of the Germanic tongues. Foreigners rarely learn to pronounce Icelandic properly, and fortunately they don't have to learn. If you can't make yourself understood, know that an interpreter is always near at hand.

NEWSPAPERS: English-language papers are on sale at nearly all newsstands and in kiosks at the major hotels.

PETS: Forget it. In fact, Iceland forbids the keeping of dogs with some exceptions. Permission to bring in a pet has to be obtained from the Ministry of Agriculture, and it's virtually impossible to get their okay.

PHARMACY: In Reykhavík one drugstore is open day and night seven days a week. It's **Noeturvarzla Lyfjabúoa,** 1 Stórholt (tel. 23245).

POST OFFICE: The central post office in Reykjavík, **Posthusid,** is open on Monday from 8 a.m. to 5 p.m., Tuesday through Friday from 9 a.m. to 5 p.m., and on Saturday from 9 a.m. to noon. The post office at the Central Bus Station is open Monday through Saturday from 2 to 7:30 p.m.

Main post offices are at 5 Pósthússtraeti and 15 Austurstaeti. If you want to send your mail in care of general delivery, mark it *Poste Restante.*

RADIO: The U.S. armed forces at Keflavík International Airport broadcasts programs in English in the Reykjavík area. From May to October, you can hear news broadcast in English at 6 p.m. Otherwise, all broadcasting in Iceland is done by the Iceland State Broadcast Service.

SWIMMING: Outdoor swimming is possible in Iceland, even in the dead of winter. Pools are heated from the hot springs near Reykajvík. They are especially crowded on Sunday mornings, when it's popular to go there to cure a hangover. The outdoor pool, **Sundlaugur Reykjavíkur** in Sundlaugavegur in the eastern part of town, is the largest of its kind in Iceland. Saunas are available for men and women, and a special pool is reserved for children. Open daily, it charges an entrance fee of $2 (U.S.).

TAXES: Watch it: you could get burned. Iceland imposes a sales tax of 23.5% on most goods and services. In addition, an airport tax is levied on all domestic flights. Currently, it is 18 krónur (54¢).

TAXIS: A typical taxi ride in Reykjavík—say, a distance of three kilometers—is likely to cost from 200 krónur ($6). Taxi stations include **Hreyfill** (tel. 85522) and **Steindor** (tel. 11580). Sometimes you can hail a cab on the street.

TELEGRAMS: (See "Telephones.") Cables and telegrams are accepted at the central telephone and telegraph office day and night. During the day, dial 06. After 9 p.m., call either 16411 or 06.

TELEPHONE: Phone calls can be made and telegrams can be sent at **Simstödin,** the main telephone and telegraph office in Reykjavík on Austurvöllur Square in the heart of town, near the post office. It is open weekdays from 9 a.m. to 7 p.m., on Sunday from 11 a.m. to 6 p.m. You can make overseas calls day or night by telephoning either 08 or 09. There is direct dialing to most European countries and to the U.S.

TIPPING: There is *no* tipping in Iceland, and that applies even to taxi drivers and washroom attendants. In hotels and restaurants (and almost everything else), the service charge is automatically included in the bill, along with the tax.

2. Reykjavík

On a broad, sweeping bay in the southwest corner of the country, Reykjavík is the northern most capital in the world. Its cosmopolitan inhabitants enjoy one of the highest per capita living standards in the world. The international airport at Keflavík is about a 45-minute coach ride from the center of Reykjavík. When you finally reach the city, you'll notice rooftops in Christmas green and red.

But you won't see any pollution, even though Reykjavík means Smoky Bay. This is a misnomer, like the name of the country itself. Reykjavík is practically a smokeless city, heated for the most part by hot water from geo-thermal underground springs. The air is clear and invigorating.

The first Viking settler in Iceland made his home here about 11 centuries ago. He was Ingólfur Arnarson.

Reykjavík is nearly encircled by a ring of mountains, extending far out to sea in Faxa Bay and capped by a glacier-topped extinct volcano, the **Snaefellsjökull,** which was immortalized by the Jules Verne story *Journey to the Center of the Earth.*

The Icelandic capital was the scene of the Fischer-Spassky World Chess Championships in 1972, and it is also the site of the international arts festival in June, featuring well-known performers in drama and music.

ACCOMMODATIONS: Prices are paralyzing. The only compensation is that there is no tipping, and the service charge and state purchase tax are included. The cheapest way to obtain accommodations is by booking a room in a private home. Because Iceland has such a high standard of living, rooms of this nature are usually of good quality. As a rule, however, they do not contain private baths. Generally, the family bath has to be shared. Daily rates average $28 (U.S.) in a single, $38 in a double, plus $12 for an extra bed. Breakfast is from $6. (At these prices for private homes, you can well imagine what the hotel rates are.) Reservations are recommended in high season.

The Best for Value

Óðinsvé Hotel, 1 Þorsgata (tel. 25224). Because the decor is so imaginative and because it's the newest hotel in Reykjavík, this is my favorite hotel in the entire city. Although there was a good-value restaurant on the site for 20 years, the hotel opened with very little fanfare in mid-1984. Designed from three older houses joined together, the hotel has a white-stucco façade, peach-color trim, and a relatively central location. Part of the decor includes racks of stuffed Icelandic birds, many of them rare, which could inspire either a love or hatred of ornithology, but which will nonetheless prove endlessly interesting for anyone who ever wondered how a bird can fly. Included among the dozens of specimens are snow owls, ptarmigans, and falcons, all assembled over many years by hotel owner Bjarni (Bernie or B.J.) Arnason.

In one of the tastefully lighthearted sitting rooms, a cast-iron, wood-burning stove has been converted into a steam radiator, providing heat and an antique touch at the same time. Many of the framed artworks scattered throughout the hotel are hand-printed woodcuts of figures representing characters from the ancient Nordic sagas, with English translations at the bottom. Most of the rooms contain private baths, but the few which do not have access to clean, tiled facilities in the hallways. In summer, bathless doubles cost $59 (U.S.), while doubles with bath go for $70. Bathless singles are $40. In winter, prices go down to around $37 for a bathless double, $48 for a double with bath, and $30 for a bathless single.

Hotel Stadur, 27 Skipholt (tel. 26210), is a recently constructed hotel scattered over two floors of a rectangular structure built in 1984. It contains 24 simple rooms where, in the words of the partial owner, Erlingur Thorodsen, services are at a minimum. Rooms here are clean, functional, and attractive, lying within a 20-minute walk of the center of town. You have to ring the bell and be buzzed in before walking up to the second-floor reception area. During summer, with breakfast included, singles cost between $38 (U.S.) and $48, while doubles range from $50 to $60, depending on the plumbing. Winter prices average about 20% less.

Hotel Loftleidir, Keflavík Airport (tel. 22322), was opened in 1966 as the northernmost first-class hotel in the world. The hotel is at the air terminal, and you can see domestic planes land and take off. The largest hotel in Iceland, it is owned and operated by the airline. This is likely to be your base of operations if you're on the stopover plan. If you're not, you'll pay $67 (U.S.) in a single, $91 in a double. All rooms have twin beds and a tasteful decor, with private baths or showers, even soundproofing. It's the only hotel in Iceland offering guests an indoor swimming pool. The water is drawn directly from hot springs nearby. A Finnish sauna bath is also available. The Floral Restaurant serves Icelandic specialties, and a simple meal is offered in the cafeteria for about $14.

Hotel Esja, 2 Sudurlandsbraut (tel. 82200), is one of the two major hotels in Reykjavík owned by Icelandair. It opened in 1971 in an undistinguished yet functional format of exposed masonry and glass. It's considered one of the best hotels in town, containing 134 comfortable rooms, each of which has big windows, a modern tiled bath, and a phone. You'll find a nightclub/disco on the top floor (see "Nightlife" section), a ground-floor cafeteria, an in-house souvenir shop, and easy connections through Icelandair's bus to either of the city's airports. Single rooms cost around $55 (U.S.), while doubles go for $67. An extra bed can be set up in any room for an additional $14. Prices here are frequently reduced for passengers arranging their stay with Icelandair from North America. The hotel was named after a mountain peak visible across the bay.

Hotel Borg, 11 Posthusstraeti (tel. 11440), is a venerable hotel which opened in 1930 in the center of town. It contains a lobby filled with an unusual set of oak settees and chairs made especially for the hotel before its opening, a marble-trimmed foyer and a spacious restaurant where, every Sunday at 9 p.m. the management holds old-fashioned Icelandic dances. There are 44 rooms, most of which contain private baths. The fourth floor has been rented on an almost permanent basis to a local bank. The most charming and biggest rooms, all bathless, are on the fifth floor. Depending on the plumbing and the season, single rooms rent for between $30 (U.S.) and $55, while doubles cost between $41 and $82.

Hotel Holt, 37 Bergstadastraeti (tel. 25700). Moderately sized, it is on a quiet street in the old part of town, a few minutes' walk from the center. All accommodations have baths or showers. Rates are from $47 (U.S.) in a single, from $67 in a double. The dining room serves both international and local specialties. The atmosphere throughout is enhanced by works of local artists.

Hotel Hof, 18 Rauoarárstigur (tel. 28866), is one of the newer hotels of the capital, a boxy modern structure right in the center. Basic as in the style of the far north, it is nevertheless an appealing choice for many. Streamlined bedrooms, 31 in all, are spread across three floors, and each is fairly large, containing twin beds, private baths (plus showers), carpeting, and radio. The cost in a single is about $42 (U.S.) daily, rising to nearly $60 in a twin, with breakfast an extra $6. The English-speaking staff, I have found, is most helpful, directing one to the local attractions such as a heated swimming pool. Sightseeing tours begin right at the entrance to the hotel. A restaurant in the hotel is open all day, serving meals and a large selection of homemade cakes. On the premises you'll find a hairdresser and a beauty salon.

City Hotel, 4A Ránargata (tel. 18650), stands in a quiet location, right in the heart of Reykjavík, offering comfortable rooms, 54 beds in all, at prices that go from $44 (U.S.) in a single and from $63 in a double, both with bath. The staff is courteous and attentive, giving an individual welcome to each guest. Some rooms contain complete private baths. Breakfast is an extra $7.

A Summer Hotel

Hotel Gardur, on Hringbraut, at the University of Iceland (tel. 15918), is a summer hotel close to downtown Reykjavík, renting out 90 rooms in two university dormitories. In addition, it also offers ten units in a modern housing project for married students. The walking time to the center of town is about five or ten minutes, depending on your speed.

As befits a college dormitory, rooms are simply, but comfortably, furnished, each with hot and cold running water. On each level is a bathroom. A single room rents for $34 (U.S.), a double for $47. If you're traveling with a child, the management will put in an extra cot for $13.

Also available are some studio apartments, costing $84 a night. These units are pleasantly furnished, containing kitchens, living rooms, bedrooms, baths, and balconies. Guests in the suites have a common lounge with TV. Another advantage for families is that children can use the playground, and the staff can arrange for child-care as well, while you're out touring.

Food is available in two places in the Student Center. Both breakfast, costing $5.50, and dinner at $15 are served in the first-floor restaurant. However, serious budgeteers will patronize the basement coffeeshop (open until 11:30 p.m.), serving open-face sandwiches and pastries. Both places are self-service.

Guesthouses

Gistiheimilid, 52 Snorrabraut (tel. 16522), is one of the better guesthouses of Reykjavík. The location is central, and the manager, Gudmundur J. Árnason, gives each guest personal attention and is known for his hospitality. The guesthouse has been in business for nearly a quarter of a century, offering 19 single and double rooms, as well as suites, all of which are comfortably furnished. Both singles and doubles consist of a living room, plus a separate bed-room, with a wash basin and closet. Showers are located outside the rooms. The single rate is $25 (U.S.) nightly, going up to $35 in a twin, $41 in a triple, and $47 in a family room, with breakfast costing yet another $5.50 per person. On each floor guests can use kitchen facilities, and there is, as well, a refrigerator and radio in each room. The house is modern, in good condition, and Mr. Árnason takes care of painting and other repairs when required. Open all year, the guest-house also has fine parking facilities.

Guesthouse, 22 Brautarholt (tel. 20986), is in the downtown section of the capital, near the Hlemmur bus terminal. The friendly owner there offers clean and simply furnished rooms, at prices that range from $29 (U.S.) in a double, from $21.50 in a single. A typically Icelandic breakfast costs an additional $6.

The **Viking Guest House,** 12 Ránargata (tel. 19367), has good, basic rooms, charges moderate prices, and is situated right in the center of the capital. In addition to that, I've found the reception friendly, the small staff helpful and coop-erative. Single rooms rent for $24 (U.S.) nightly, doubles going for $34. An extra bed in the room will cost yet another $11, and a continental breakfast, $6.50.

The Edda Hotels

The Iceland Tourist Bureau, 6 Skógarhlíd (tel. 25855), operates 19 summer hotels in public boarding schools. All are at or near beauty spots in various parts of the country, and are suitable for nature lovers. The hotels are neat, clean, and comfortable, but certainly not luxurious. All rooms have hot and cold running water. Swimming pools and saunas are often available. Trout fishing and horse-back riding are usually available, too. The hotels are run by competent staffs, and the quality of the food is supervised by professional chefs. Public transpor-tation is available to and from all these hotels, which are open from mid-June to the end of August. Those in the south of Iceland include two at **Laugarvatn,** one at **Skógar,** and another at **Kirkjubaejarklaustur.** Edda Hotels without private baths accompanying the bedrooms, and that's most of them, charge $28 (U.S.) in a single, $36 in a double, plus $7 for breakfast. Sleeping bag accommodations (bring your own bag) cost $11. In the few Edda Hotels where private showers and toilets are available, the prices are $38 in a single and $43 in a double.

Farmhouse Accommodations

If you have a car, you might want to branch out from Reykjavík and get closer to the spirit of the island. Families with children often enjoy farmhouse holidays. A few farms in Iceland accept paying guests, and they provide full or half board. At some, you can have a bed-and-breakfast. On some of the farms you can hire Viking horses, even arrange for trout fishing, paying from $7 (U.S.) per day for the privilege. The average cost of full board is $35 per person in a double, $42 in a single. If a child shares a room with parents, the charge is an additional $17.50 per day. Prices for bed-and-breakfast are $18 per person in a double, $26 in a single. The farms display a sign on the roadside, so you can drop in and find out about vacancies when you spot one you like.

Youth Hostels

Salvation Army Hostel, 2 Kirkjustraeti (tel. 13203), should not put you off by the pristine sound of its name. It is, in fact, the best youth hostel in the capi-tal, offering singles for $26 (U.S.) with breakfast, $21 without breakfast, dou-bles for $37 with breakfast, $27 without. Some rooms shelter three at a cost of $47 with breakfast, $32 without breakfast. They also have sleeping bag spaces for $13.50 per person with breakfast, $7.50 without. You're not charged extra for taking a hot sulfurous shower. The hostel's dining room is in the communal style, and the portions are most generous. Incidentally, if you're going on a tour of Iceland, ask the manager if you can store your luggage in a room set aside for that purpose. The hostel is only closed between 1 and 7 a.m., except Saturday night when closing is between 3 and 7 a.m.

One of the lowest cost accommodations in Reykjavík is **Farfuglaheimilid,** 41 Laufásvegur (tel. 24950), offering 70 beds in basic surroundings for $9 (U.S.) to $10 nightly. Members share the kitchen. It is open from June 1 to October 1.

WHERE TO EAT: Low-fat skyr is the national dish of Iceland. This very perishable concoction belongs to the soft cheese group. Made from skim milk, it is pasteurized. A fermenting agent curdles the milk, and the curds are separated from the whey. The curds form skyr. The dish is sprinkled with granulated sugar before it is eaten.

Fish, however, is the chief source of food. Salmon and herring are delectable. An acquired taste is hakarl or cured shark meat. Along with fish, sheep is the next major food. A specialty is hangikjöt or smoked lamb. Another popular dish is svid, made from singed sheep heads.

Blodmör once took the place of bread in the nation's diet. It's made from sheep's blood which has been salted and thinned out with equal amounts of water. A thick mixture is made with rye or barley flour, plus suet from the innards of the sheep. This mixture is put in small bags fashioned from the largest intestines of the sheep and boiled for several hours.

Of course, you can get "regular" food as well.

The least expensive eating places in Iceland charge a minimum of $6 (U.S.) for a plain breakfast or a sandwich and a glass of milk for lunch or supper. Even food you prepare yourself is quite expensive to buy in Iceland. Prices are at least double in Iceland as against, say, New York. Practically everything, except fish, butter, cheese, milk, and some vegetables, is imported and carries an import tax.

Hressingarskálinn, 20 Austurstraeti (tel. 15292), is a café-konditori in the center of town on a traffic-free mall, just off Laekjartorg Square. Original paintings decorate the walls, and young people frequent the premises at night, although shoppers are attracted at midday. The fried fish filet is the most popular item on the menu, although you can also order more expensive meat dishes, such as a pretty good veal steak. For lunch, you can dine lighter and less expensively if you stick to such fare as a grilled cheese sandwich. Depending on your selection, count on spending from 300 krónur ($9) for a meal here. Hours are from 8 a.m. to 9 p.m. weekdays, from 9 a.m. to 9 p.m. on Saturday and Sunday. Many guests, both foreign and domestic, like to drop in for breakfast.

Braudbaer, 1 Thórsgata on Ódinstorg (tel. 25090), is a friendly little place, quite near Laugavegur, the eastern continuation of the main street. The cookery here is satisfying and consistent, and makes no aspiration to brilliance, although the chefs pride themselves on serving the best smørgaas and herring in Reykjavík. Other specialties are steaks of lamb and beef steaks. You'll spend about 500 krónur ($15) and up here. Of course, by sticking to herring (of which I'm so fond) and smørgaas, you can eat for less. Hours are from 9 a.m. (drop in for breakfast) to 11:30 p.m. on weekdays and from 10 a.m. to 11:30 p.m. on Sunday.

Askur, 14 Sudurlandsbraut (tel. 81344), is near the Sports Center of Reykjavík, with its football field, swimming pool, and stadium. Their featured dish is also grilled leg of lamb. Here it's served with a béarnaise sauce and other accompaniments, and the price of the main dish also includes a hearty bowl of soup. Expect to spend from 500 krónur ($15) for a simple meal. Askur is open from 11 a.m. to 11:30 p.m. daily. It's licensed after 6 p.m. on weekdays and all day Sunday.

Esjuberg, 2 Sudurlandsbraut (tel. 82200), in the Hotel Esja, is a fully licensed cafeteria-style restaurant. The food is pleasant, hot, and appetizing, and the service is quick. Again, as in my above recommendations, the specialty is lamb. Here you can not only order a grilled leg of lamb but also tender lamb chops. Deep-fried fish is featured on the menu daily, as is a grilled sandwich with ham and cheese. A fresh salad bar is arranged every day, and if you wish just soup and a selection from the salad bar, you'll pay from 220 krónur ($6.60). However, if you order a main dish and one or two other courses, your tab can quickly climb to 500 krónur ($15). The well-decorated cafeteria, one of the best in town, has picture windows opening onto views of the water in the distance.

Kokk Húsid, 8 Laekjargötú (tel. 10340). Don't be fooled into thinking this is anything but a diner, but if what you want is a light American-style meal, you can safely head here. It's on a main street in the center of town and usually does a land office business from the neighborhood office workers at lunchtime. You can order fish and chips (french fries), five different versions of hamburger, three kinds of pizza, four daily soups, and several curry dishes. Meals range from 350 krónur ($10.50) up.

Chinese fare above the Arctic Circle? Such cuisine is possible at **Drekinn,** 22 Laugavegur (tel. 13628), which is open daily from 11 a.m. to 10 p.m. Your favorite Oriental dish may lose something in translation all the way up here, but the restaurant is a welcome change of pace. Prices are reasonable, too: from 400 krónur ($12) for a pretty fair meal.

More Expensive Choices

Restaurant Laekjarbrekka, 2 Bankastraeti (tel. 14430), is included in a complex of four buildings whose existence a few years ago engendered a raging debate between preservation groups and real estate developers. Today, the darkly stained, wood-sided building is safely preserved as one of the capital's best-known restaurants. Although it's set near a busy street corner, you'll never notice this as you dine because of the double-paned, lacquered windows shutting out the noise. The simple decor extends over two floors of well-maintained, modernized simplicity, much of it reminiscent of the year it was built, 1834. Specialties include smoked raw lamb with horseradish, Icelandic caviar, pan-fried ocean perch with raisins and almonds in cognac cream sauce, three different varieties of herring, broiled lamb chops, and pan-fried lamb's liver. Lunches cost between $16 (U.S.) and $22, while dinners cost from $26 to $32. Breakfast is available every day at 8:30 a.m.

Torfan Restaurant, 1 Amtmannsstígur (tel. 13303). This building is honored by its location among four other ancient buildings, all of which came close to being replaced with modern concrete structures a few years ago but were eventually saved and restored. Today, this building and its neighbors are cited as examples of vintage Icelandic architecture. It attracts almost as many visitors who are interested in the history as it does diners who are seeking good food. This last can be found in plentiful quantities. The chef specializes in shellfish on ice, grilled lobster tails, lamb filet in cognac, pâté maison, and dessert of deep-fried camembert. There is also a full range of cocktails and wines. The dining room is pleasantly pastel, with wide planked flooring, unusual paintings and graphics, and immaculate napery. Full meals range upward from 1050 krónur ($31.50) and are served daily from 9 a.m. to 11:30 p.m.

Restaurant Naust, 6–8 Vesturgötu (tel. 17758). When the wood-frame building which houses this restaurant was built in 1898, it sheltered a netmaker and his business. Today, it's one of the most glamorous restaurants in Iceland, with a special corner reserved for any visiting monarch who may happen to have reserved a table for that particular evening. The establishment has seen its share of royalty: four Scandinavian kings and their spouses and two Scandinavian presidents have dined on the Icelandic specialties offered by the affable owner, Omar Hallsson, and his wife, Ruth Ragnarsdóttir. In a decor of dark, vertical paneling and perhaps to the strains of a dance band (which plays on weekends after 8 p.m.), you can enjoy such viands as mixed seafood platter, lobster tails, smoked salmon, oven-baked red salmon, filet of lamb with tarragon, lamb pepper steak, and many other fine dishes. Dessert could be Icelandic crêpes with ice cream and fruit. Lunch costs from $13 (U.S.) to $21, while dinner ranges from $28 to $32. Nordic sailors will appreciate the way each of the tables is named after a type of sailing vessel from days of yore. The establishment, which also contains a cozy bar upstairs, is open daily except Sunday.

Restaurant Ódinsvé, 1 Porsgata (tel. 25224), is a restaurant on the ground floor of the Hotel Ódinsvé, containing a garden addition on one side surrounded by windows and a scattering of plants for customers who want an open view of the neighborhood. Fish and lamb are the specialties, which are posted every day on an artist's palette that serves as a bulletin board. Other items on any given day might include fish soup of the day, pâté maison, fresh oven-baked mushrooms, fresh shrimp Chinese style, filet of plaice Colbert, lamb goulash, and a salad bar, included with each main course. Full meals cost from 1100 krónur ($33) up. A fish buffet is offered every Friday night for 350 krónur ($10.50) per person. The establishment is open every day for lunch and dinner.

EXPLORING THE TOWN: The city is divided into two sectors, east and west. The oldest part is near the harbor and **Tjörnin Lake.** Arctic terns nest by this lake in the center of town. Ducks and swans drift by. The nearby park, **Tjarnargardar,** contains trees, rare in Reykjavík, and a statue of Thorfinn Karlsefni, the Icelander who was the first European to attempt a permanent colonization of North America in the early 11th century.

The main square, **Austurvöllur,** contains a monument to Jón Sigurdsson, the Icelandic national hero who led the nation in its fight against the Danes. Across the square stands the **Reykjavík Lutheran Church,** the oldest in the city, built in 1790. Bertel Thorvaldsen made the baptismal font. Also on the square is **Althing,** the Parliament Building, built in 1881.

Laekjartorg Square is in the center of Reykjavík. You can catch all buses there headed for the western part of the city or take any east-bound bus for the main terminal at Hlemmur to connect with buses heading for the outlying sectors in the eastern part of the city. It's dominated by a two-story stone structure, the residence of the prime minister. Overlooking the square is a grassy knoll with a statute of the first settler.

At some point you might want to walk down the busy **fish harbor,** at the far western end where small boats and trawlers come in to land their catches.

The largest church in Reykjavík is **Hallgrímskirkja,** in the process of being built. From its tower a panoramic view unfolds. Calder made the monument in front; it honors Leif Eriksson and was a gift from the American people.

Near this church is the **National Einar Jónsson Gallery,** at Eiríksgata. This art museum contains the works of Iceland's best known sculptor. His mystical art can be viewed in summer daily from 1:30 to 4 p.m. Off-season hours are the same, but days of opening are Sunday and Wednesday.

The **Ring Road (Hringbraut)** sweeps out to the mushrooming New Town in the east. On this road is the **National Museum** (tel. 13264), close to the university. On the ground floor is a historical museum, depicting Icelandic history and culture from its earliest days. On the second floor is the **National Art Gallery** (tel. 10665). It's open daily in summer from 1:30 to 4 p.m. In winter it keeps the same hours, but is open only on Sunday, Tuesday, Thursday, and Saturday.

The **Nordic House** (tel. 17030), across from the main entrance to the university, is a center for Nordic culture. It was built jointly by all Scandinavian nations and designed by the well-known Finnish architect, Alvar Aalto. It contains a cafeteria open from 9 a.m. to 7 p.m., a Nordic library, and exhibition rooms.

The **Icelandic Handicrafts Centre** is at 3 Hafnarstraeti (tel. 11748). In its showrooms and workshop you'll find a wide variety of handicrafts, including hand-knitted sweaters, mittens, hats, scarves, and shawls, plus hand-knitted children's woolen articles. In addition, a selection of woodcarvings and ceramics made of lava is exhibited.

The **Asmundur Sveinsson Museum** is at Sigtún. His garden is full of statues, and you can view them, and if you're on the Reykjavík Excursions city sightseeing tour, you'll be able to tour his studio here as well. Born in 1893, the sculptor became one of Iceland's best known artists.

The works of yet another artist, this one a painter, can be viewed at 74 Bergstadastraeti (tel. 13644). The **Ásgrímur Jónsson Museum** is open daily June through August from 1:30 to 4 p.m., except Saturday (open Sunday, Tuesday, and Thursday in winter). Admission is free. A bachelor who died in 1958, Jónsson was born in 1876, the son of a farmer. He was the first Icelander to make painting a full-time profession.

Finally, the **Árbaejarsafn Reykjavík Museum** (Arbaer Folk Museum) is an open-air museum founded in 1957. The center of the museum is Arbaer farm. The buildings date from 1890 to 1920 but have retained traditional features from the Icelandic turf farm. At Arbaer there is also a turf church from the north of Iceland. Several buildings have been moved to the museum from the center of Reykjavík. On display also is a steam locomotive used in the building of Reykjavík harbor. The museum is open June through August daily except Monday. From September to May it is open only on request. Telephone 84412 between 9 and 10 a.m. Take bus 10 from Hlemmur.

NIGHTLIFE: There is some. Nighttime festivities reach their peak on Saturday night when every club in town is filled to overflowing. Eager lines form at the doors, waiting to get in.

Hollywood, 5 Ármúli (tel. 81585), is unchallenged in its ability to draw thousands of Icelandic disco lovers during the average winter weekend. Although there's a minimum age limit of 18 on weekdays and 20 on weekends, most of the guests don't reach much above those figures, making up a younger crowd than that which goes to Broadway (see below). The decor here is lighthearted and fun, filled with pictures of once-great Hollywood stars, seven bars, and many kilometers of flashing marquee-style lights. The establishment is spread over two floors of a building about a block from Icelandair's Esja Hotel. The cover charge varies according to the day of the week, going from 145 krónur ($4.35) to 200 krónur ($6). The average drink once you enter costs 75 krónur ($2.25). Unlike Broadway, Hollywood is open seven nights a week. It opens at 10 p.m. On popular nights, there's often a long line waiting to enter.

Broadway, 8 Álfabakki (tel. 77500), is almost certainly the premier nightspot for the over-30 crowd in all of Iceland. It's owned by the same entrepreneur who directs the Hollywood and who selects the yearly contestant from Iceland for the Miss Universe contest. There's a live, two-hour cabaret show presented here every night the place is open. If you decide to include dinner with the show, the combined price is around 1100 krónur ($33) per person. Dinner begins at around 7 p.m. If you don't want to dine but wish to see the show, the doors open for non-dinner guests at around 9 p.m. Then customers pay a cover charge of 200 krónur ($6), plus 75 krónur ($2.25) per drink. All of this takes place in a single enormous room whose stage is visible from almost every section. Broadway is open only on Friday and Saturday, unless there's a special event, when it might be open on Thursday and Sunday as well. Broadway lies within a five-minute drive of the center of Reykjavík and contains no less than eight bars.

Esja Bar, Hotel Esja, 2 Sudurlandsbraut (tel. 82200), is the plush modern bar on the top floor of one of Icelandair's hotels, the Esja. Take the elevator and then a flight of stairs as high as you can go, pass the coat check area, and you'll find yourself amid a sea of coffee-colored velvet couches, black walls, and panoramic windows. Disco music plays softly during the cocktail hour and increases in volume as the evening progresses until the dance floor is filled. There's an 85-króna ($2.55) entrance fee for everyone except residents of the hotel. Non-alcoholic beer costs 70 krónur ($2.10), while a scotch-and-soda will cost you 130 krónur ($3.60). The establishment opens at 7 every night of the week. It becomes very crowded on weekends.

EXCURSIONS FROM REYKJAVÍK: Although you can explore Iceland on your own by bus, it's better to take one of the organized tours. Dozens, widely varying in price and length, are offered in summer.

Geysir

The most important tours include a trip to this thermal area where you can see the namesake of spouting springs throughout the world. The Great Geysir spots a column of boiling water to a height of more than 150 feet. However, it's temperamental and irregular in performance. (Don't despair: its smaller neighbor, **Strokkur,** "The Churn," makes up for Geysir's lethargy with an eruption every eight minutes.) Geysir, reached via Hveragerdi, lies 74 miles from Reykjavík.

Gullfoss

Four miles away from Geysir is Gullfoss, that beautiful "golden waterfall," with its ever-present rainbow. Thousands of tons of icy water thunder majestically down the double falls into a deep gorge.

Thingvellir or Parliament Plains

Thingvellir, 31 miles east of Reykjavík, is considered one of the most hallowed places in Iceland. Here in a great amphitheater of lava, and high, jagged rocky ramparts that overlook a beautiful lake and tranquil river favored by canoeists, the Icelandic nation was founded in 930. Icelanders of yore congregated every summer to pass laws, mete out justice, and celebrate. The Republic lasted until 1262, when Iceland came under Norwegian rule.

Hveragerdi

Twenty-five miles from Reykjavík is a hot-springs town heated by natural thermal water. Hot springs can be seen erupting all over the place. Flowers and vegetables, even such showplace crops as "Arctic bananas," are grown here.

You can visit Hveragerdi, Gullfoss, Geysir, and Thingvellir on a ten-hour bus tour, leaving Reykjavík at 9 a.m. June through September, and costing approximately $30. Lunch is not included.

Selfoss

This is a business center for the farming district in the south. However, tourists sometimes use it as a base for tours to such places as Gullfoss, the Hekla volcano, and the Laugarvatn-Geysir district. The Ölfusá, a salmon river, runs right through the village of Selfoss.

In the town, 38 miles from Reykjavík, there is a bed-and-breakfast accommodation, **Hotel Thoristun,** 1 Póristún (tel. 99-1633), run by Mrs. Steinunn Hafstad. She has a large, adequately furnished house, renting out 17 comfortable rooms. A bathless single costs $29 (U.S.); a single with shower, $39. A bathless double goes for $39; a double with bath, $50. An extra bed will be placed in a room for about $10, and breakfast costs another $7. Advance reservations are recommended. Mrs. Hafstad will direct you to a restaurant in the village.

EN ROUTE TO AKUREYRI: If you're driving from Reykjavík to Akureyri, you may find the following recommendation useful. The **Staðarskáli** (tel. 95-1150) is called a Skáli for short. This one is really in the wilderness, a frontier outpost lying between Reykjavík and Akureyri in Hrutafiroi, a very busy place in summer, as most of the traffic to the north stops off here. It's not really a hotel, more of a wayside inn. Most tourists stop just to patronize the gift shop, fill up their car with gasoline, or have a meal in the cafeteria. The menu consists mainly of grills, although typical Icelandic specialties are prepared as well. The service is excellent, and the young waitresses are among the friendliest and kindest I've encountered in any country. The place is very popular, so reservations are imperative if you're considering an overnight stopover. There are only four bedrooms, with three beds in each room, and across from these units you'll find a shower and a toilet. A single pays $34 (U.S.) nightly, and two persons sharing the same room are charged $40.

3. Heimaey and Surtsey

Two geographic oddities form the basis of this excursion.

Part of the chain of Westman Islands, Surtsey on the south coast is one of the newest entries on world maps. It was formed during a spectacular submarine volcanic eruption, lasting from November 1963 till June 1966. It is forbidden to land on the island, although boats encircle it and planes fly over it Surtsey is visited in conjunction with Heimaey on some tours.

Another one of the Westman Islands, Heimaey is a new Pompeii. On the night of January 22, 1973, Iceland's largest fishing village was split open. Red lava soared into the sky. More than 5000 inhabitants were evacuated, as the eruption destroyed a third of the homes and covered the rest with a 20-foot layer of pumice. Most residents have returned to restore homes that are salvageable. The fishing fleet's busy once again.

Long before the eruption Heimaey was known for its puffins. Islanders descend cliffs by rope to rob puffin nests of their eggs. If caught, the birds are not only eaten, but considered a delicacy.

Visitors can fly here from Reykjavík on daily scheduled flights by Icelandair.

Another two-hour air tour leaves daily, weather permitting, all year round. It costs about $70.50 (U.S.). Volcanoes and glaciers are viewed from the air. One of the most spectacular sights of this tour is a look at the **Hekla Volcano.** The ancients once thought this was one of the gateways to hell. In 1947 its eruption lasted more than a year, in 1970, and again in 1981, two eruptions occurred.

4. Höfn in Hornafjördur

This small township of about 1000 people is on the southeastern coast of Iceland, about an hour's flying time from Reykjavík. Its main attraction is its splendid and unusual scenery.

The biggest glacier in Europe is at its doorstep; **Vatnajökull,** called the glacier of lakes. In places its ice is more than half a mile thick, and it covers an area of 3240 square miles.

From Höfn you can set out on a trip of 87 miles to explore **Skaftafell National Park** and the **Fláajökull Glacier.**

On an independent excursion of this southeastern corner of Iceland, you can find food and lodging at **Hotel Höfn** (tel. 97-8240), a large, modern building in the Hornafjörour district. The manager here offers 40 comfortable rooms, with and without shower or bath. The hotel lies 4½ miles from the airport in the town of Höfn (pop. 1600) which is very near the largest glacier in Europe, Vatnajökull. Singles range in price from $31 (U.S.) to $46, with doubles going for $44 to $60. Breakfast costs $6. The hotel has a sauna bath, as well as a TV and bar, plus a good restaurant serving typically Icelandic dishes. Nearby is a nine-hole golf course, one of the best in Iceland. Sightseeing tours to well-known local sights can be arranged, and English is spoken.

On the second day a motorcoach crosses glacial sands past Skaftafell National Park, an oasis sheltered by Vatnajökull. Departures are Tuesday, Wednesday, Friday, Saturday, and Sunday in July and August.

5. Akureyri

Iceland's second most important town lies in a sheltered position at the head of Iceland's longest fjord, Eyjafjördur. Flanked by high mountains, it is a trim little town of parks and gardens, with a fishing harbor.

You can fly here from Reykjavík, explore the town, and return to the capital on the same day. However, it's best to settle in and go exploring the next day to Lake Mývatn (see below).

If the wind is blowing from the north, it can be quite cold at Akureyri, even in summer. In June and July, the Midnight Sun glows over the ocean to the north.

Many visitors who stay over fly the next day to **Grímsey,** the Arctic Island where you're presented with a diploma, proving your membership in the Arctic Viking Order. The island is bisected by the Arctic Circle, and it lies 25 miles off the coast. It's possible in summer to take a Midnight Sun flight direct from Reykjavík, although the usual air connections are via Akureyri.

MAIN ATTRACTIONS: At the top of 112 steps towers **Akureyri Church,** completed in 1940. Reached from the church steps is the **Matthías Jochumsson Memorial Museum,** 3 Eyrarlandsvegur, open daily in summer from 3 to 5 p.m. The house, known as Sigurhaedir, was the home of Matthías Jochumsson, the clergyman-poet (1835–1920) who wrote the words of the national anthem, among other works (including translations of Shakespeare). Personal mementos are exhibited.

The **Akureyri Museum (Minjasafnid),** 58 Adalstraeti (tel. 24162), at the south side of Hafnarstraeti, contains historical exhibitions of North Iceland. It is, in essence, a folk museum, open daily from 1:30 to 5 p.m. Admission is 10 krónur (30¢).

Davídshús, the home of yet another poet, David Stefánsson (1895–1964), can be visited at 6 Bjarkarstig. His personal mementos are exhibited. In summer, it is open daily from 4 to 6 p.m.

Still another literary figure is honored at Nonnahús, the **Nonni Memorial Museum,** dedicated to Jón Sveinsson, the Jesuit author (1857–1944). His former home dates from the mid-19th century. His Nonni stories, based on his childhood adventures in North Iceland, were translated into more than two dozen languages. The museum, owned and operated by the Akureyri Zonta Club, is at 54B Adalstraeti, and it's open daily in summer from 2 to 4:30 p.m. Admission is $1 (U.S.) for adults; children free.

Try to stroll around the harbor, close to Hafnarstraeti. The **Höfnin,** as it's called, is filled with freighters, trawlers, and fishing boats.

Near the church is the **Andapollur** or duck pond at Thingvallastraeti, where species of Icelandic ducks and other birdlife may be seen.

WHERE TO STAY IN AKUREYRI: It's possible to obtain rooms in private homes on a bed-and-breakfast basis. Daily rates average $38 (U.S.) in a double, $28 in a single. Inquire at the tourist office.

K.E.A. Hotel, 89 Hafnarstraeti (tel. 22200), is one of the biggest and best hotels in north Iceland. It's owned by the largest enterprise in town, a cooperative society founded by farmers in 1886. Right in the center of town, it offers spacious and comfortably furnished rooms which are decorated in light, cheerful colors. Some units have their own private balcony and bath, and each one is provided with a phone and radio. Bathless singles rent for $31 (U.S.), going up to $56 with bath or shower. Bathless doubles or twins are priced at $42, rising to $70 with complete bath or shower. An extra bed can be placed in a room for $16. Before dinner you can order a drink in the cozy and intimate bar. The second-floor restaurant serves the best food in town, a lunch costing from $14.50, a dinner going from $22. Breakfast is from a buffet table, costing $6.50. In addition, the recently renovated cafeteria on the ground floor is open all day.

Hotel Vardborg, 7 Geislagata (tel. 22600), is bandboxy modern, but centrally located. Built in a severe architectural style, it is neat and pleasant. The staff is friendly and helpful. A single with shower rents for $32 (U.S.), going up to $42 with shower. A twin-bedded room without bath costs $50, the tariff rising to $57 with bath or shower. A cold-table breakfast is served for $7.

Hotel Edda, Menntaskóli (tel. 24055), is a hotel in summer, a student residence in winter. Rates are $28 (U.S.) in a single, $36 in a double, with an extra $6.50 charged for breakfast. The hotel, standing on the grounds of the Akureyri Junior College, has a peaceful setting, near the town's botanical gardens. The hotel staff can arrange a flight to Grimsey Island on the Arctic Circle.

The youth hostel, **Farfuglaheimilid,** 1 Storholti (tel. 23657), is open year round, offering dormitory accommodations for about $8 per person nightly.

A camping site, **Tajaldstaedi Akureyrarbaejar,** Thórunnarstraeti, is near the center of town, adjacent to an open-air swimming pool. For a fee of $3.50 (U.S.) it offers space for 100 tents. A warden is on duty from 8 a.m. to 11 p.m. The site is open from June 5 to August 31.

WHERE TO EAT: You can obtain morning coffee or breakfast in summer at the already-mentioned **Hotel Edda.** This is the least expensive place to eat in town.

For some of the best seafood caught off the coast of Iceland, head for **Sjallinn,** 14 Geislagata (tel. 22-770), which is fully licensed. The chef shines brightly at his seafood buffet which is offered both at lunch and again in the evening. Lunch is likely to cost from $8 (U.S.) to $15, with dinner priced at between $18 and $24.

6. Lake Mývatn

Sixty miles from Akureyri is one of the most beautiful districts of Iceland. About a two-hour drive delivers you to Lake Mývatn, with its hot spring caves and volcanic landscape.

This northern lake, the fourth biggest in the country, is said to be the largest gathering place of summer water fowl in the world. You can spot sawbills, the red-breasted merganser, and the goosander. The horned (Slavonian) grebe, the only Icelandic grebe, reaches its greatest breeding density on Mývatn, where several hundred pairs nest. Nearby are steaming Dante-like sulfur fields and cliffs inhabited by the rare Icelandic falcon.

WHERE TO STAY: **Hotel Reynihlíd** (tel. 44170) is a modern and comfortable tourist hotel on the northern shore of Lake Mývatn. It offers a total of 44 stream-lined, functional rooms, 26 of which have private showers and toilets. A single without bath rents for $26.50 (U.S.), increasing to $45 with shower and toilet. Bathless doubles go for $40, rising to $57 with shower and toilet. An extra bed costs $11. Breakfast is an additional $5.30, and lunches and dinners begin at $12. Count yourself lucky if you're presented with a fresh trout from the lake. The staff at the hotel will provide car-rental services, fishing rights, and sightseeing and scheduled excursions.

EXCURSIONS FROM LAKE MÝVATN: Once at the lake, you'll find travel agents offering all sorts of full-day or half-day excursions, even longer ones if you have the time. Some of these are assembled more or less casually, depending on the number of visitors in the area on any given day.

If possible, try to go to **Dettifoss,** the highest waterfall in Europe. The trip is rough, however. You pass over pothole-studded gravel roads and seemingly endless miles of black lava fields. Another magnificent waterfall, **Godafoss,** a twin falls, is also reached by a jolting bus ride.